Tony White

Statistics for Engineers

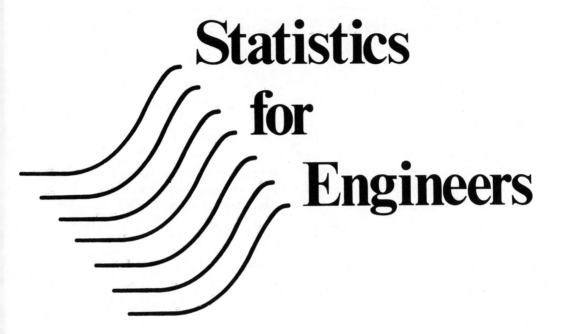

Richard L. Scheaffer
James T. McClave
University of Florida

 Duxbury Press **Boston**

PWS PUBLISHERS

Prindle, Weber & Schmidt · ✿ · Duxbury Press · ♠ · PWS Engineering · 𝅘
Statler Office Building · 20 Park Plaza · Boston, Massachusetts 02116

PWS Publishers is a division of Wadsworth, Inc.
Printed in the United States of America

85 — 10   9   8   7   6   5   4   3

Library of Congress Cataloging in Publication Data

Scheaffer, Richard L.
    Statistics for engineers.

    Includes index.
    1. Statistics. 2. Probabilities. I. McClave,
James T. II. Title.
TA340.S33   519.5'02462   81-19436
ISBN 0-87872-298-X   AACR2

ISBN 0-87872-298-X

Text designed and edited by Helen Walden. Artwork by J&R Services. Composition by Syntax International. Text printed and bound by Maple-Vail. Covers designed by Helen Walden. Covers printed by Maple-Vail.

Preface

This textbook is an introduction to probability and statistics with emphasis on techniques and applications that are useful in engineering and the physical and biological sciences.

Although many of the examples and exercises deal with problems related to engineering, the book is suitable for students in many other areas of science. Problems dealing with energy, pollution, weather, chemical processes, size and abundance of animals, and earthquakes show the breadth of statistical applications in the sciences and provide interesting examples for students from a wide variety of sciences. These examples tend to be based upon real problems.

The notion of *probabilistic models* for real phenomena is emphasized throughout the text. This idea contains two key components, as the two words suggest. First, probability is used in model building since many, if not most, experiments do not produce outcomes that can be precisely predetermined. When that is the case, one should look at the probability, or relative frequency, distribution of the possible outcomes. Second, the word model is used to suggest that what we finally achieve is only an approximate, and usually oversimplified, description of the real phenomenon.

After a brief introductory chapter, Chapters 2 through 4 develop the basic ideas of probability and probability distributions for random variables. These probability distributions are, in fact, used as models for outcomes of experiments. Chapter 5 presents a transition between probability and statistics, as it deals with the probability distributions of certain common statistics. Chapters 6 through 11 develop the basic ideas of statistics, which is, in one sense, the process of fitting models to data and then using the models in making inferences. Chapter 12 is concerned with special applications to quality control.

The book is fairly compact in style, but contains many motivational examples and worked examples. Random variables are introduced early in Chapter 2 since physical scientists commonly deal with numerical outcomes of experiments. Multiple regression is presented with both quantitative and qualitative independent variables so that analysis of variance models can be easily embedded into the discussion.

The entire textbook can be covered in a two-quarter (6 quarter hour) sequence. For a one-semester (3 hour) or a one-quarter (4 hour) course, a good outline would be to cover chapters one through seven, possibly skipping section 5.6, and then merely introduce regression techniques by covering sections 8.1 through 8.5. An adequate presentation of introductory concepts plus multiple regression and analysis of variance will necessitate more than three semester hours of instruction. In any case, Chapter 12 may be omitted if students are not interested in quality control.

The authors thank Jerry Lyons and Pat Fitzgerald of Duxbury Press for their excellent guidance during the writing and production of this text, and for their patience. We also thank numerous colleagues for their encouragement and helpful suggestions. Lastly, we thank the reviewers for their constructive criticisms.

The writing of this textbook has been an enjoyable task, and we hope that students in engineering and the physical and biological sciences find the book both enjoyable and informative as they seek to learn statistics.

Contents

1

Statistics in Engineering

2

Probability

Common Discrete Probability Distributions

Common Continuous Probability Distributions

Statistics and Sampling Distributions

Estimation

Hypothesis Testing

Simple Regression

Multiple Regression Analysis

The Analysis of Variance

11

Nonparametric Statistics

12

Applications to Quality Control

Appendix

References

1

Statistics in Engineering

About This Chapter

What impression does the term "statistics" bring to mind? Is it merely a list of facts and figures on sporting events, the national economy, or a group of diseases? Certainly facts and figures (or data) will be used in subsequent chapters. However, our basic concern is not the sets of data themselves, but rather the use of these sets of data to make intelligent and rigorous decisions. In this chapter we introduce the fundamental idea of using sample data to infer some property of the larger set of data from which the sample was drawn.

Contents

1.1   *What Is Statistics?*

We live in an age in which we are deluged by facts and figures, or "statistics," on almost every subject imaginable. We hear or read government reports on the number of people on welfare and the number of armaments that the U.S. has available, business reports on quarterly earnings, and sports reports on batting averages and yards gained. In the midst of all of these facts and figures, most of them of little interest to us, why would anyone want to study a discipline called statistics? What is statistics, anyway?

Quantitative facts such as those indicated above will form the basis of our study, but we are about to study more than just lists of data. In this text, we present an introduction to "inferential statistics," as opposed to the layman's view of statistics as merely observable facts. By the term "inferential statistics" we mean that we want to use the data to make intelligent, rigorous, statements (inferences) about a much larger phenomenon from which the data were selected.

Let's take a look at a few examples of how inferential statistics might aid an engineer. Suppose a civil engineer wants to study the traffic intensity at a certain intersection. He might observe the traffic flow at some representative times, including mornings, evenings, weekdays, and weekends, and then come up with an estimate of the average number of vehicles passing through the intersection per hour. The actual observations are important to him, but only as they help him form his estimate of the intensity over a wide time span.

We might wish to compare various combinations of drying times and amount of aggregate as to their effect on the strength of concrete. Certain test samples will have to be formed and their strengths measured. The measurements are listed, but they are only important as they relate to the inferential process of determining which combination of drying time and amount of aggregate produces the best product.

Computer components might be tested until they fail, with their lifelengths being recorded. This set of measurements might then be applied to the inferential problem of estimating the reliability of the entire computer system.

A quality control engineer might periodically sample a few manufactured items coming off an assembly line and count the number of defectives. This number is important to him only as it helps him to decide whether or not the line is operating within nominal standards.

So, you see, the figures, or measurements, are important, but they are being collected for a well-defined inferential purpose. It is this inferential procedure that is the subject of modern statistics, and the main theme of this text.

1.2   *Elements of Inferential Statistics*

The ideas in Section 1.1 form a general notion of inferential statistics, but we now make these ideas more specific. Any problem in statistics has as its starting point a *population* of interest.

A **population** is the complete set of measurements of interest in a particular problem.

In a reliability study, the population may consist of the lifelengths of all the components of a certain type produced by Factory A. In a quality control study, the population may consist of a status report (which could be numerical) on the quality of each item contained in a large shipment.

Of course, the population measurements are unknown at the outset, and we will assume that they can never be completely determined. We cannot, for example, test all of Factory A's components in order to get a complete list of lifelengths, for this would be too time consuming and leave the factory with nothing to sell. We can, however, obtain a representative set of measurements from the population by performing an *experiment*.

For example, we could obtain a measurement from a population of component lifelengths by performing an experiment that consists of testing a component from Factory A until it fails and recording its lifelength. Or, we could examine a set of four manufactured items and record whether or not each is defective. This experiment would yield four measurements from the population of defective/nondefective classifications of all the manufactured items. The set of measurements yielded by an experiment is called the *sample*.

A **sample** is a subset of the population containing those measurements actually obtained by experiment.

The sample might consist of a number of lifelength measurements or recorded observations on frequency of defectives. Our objective is to use these sample data for purposes of making inferences about the population from which the sample was obtained. We might estimate the average lifelength of all components in the population, or estimate the reliability of a system made up of such components. We might estimate the proportion of defective items in a population, or decide whether to accept the lot from which the sample was drawn as meeting the standards of our factory.

1.3   *Deterministic and Probabilistic Models*

In order to formally develop the methodology for inference-making we must start with a *model* for the phenomenon under study. A model, as we use the term, may be thought of as a theoretical, and usually oversimplified, explanation of a complex system. In the sciences, these models usually take the form of a mathematical equation, such as the equations for heat transfer in physics or the equations for various chemical reactions. It is important to discuss the concept of models in some detail, as we will be referring to specific models throughout the remainder of this text.

The models most commonly seen in the physical sciences and engineering are called *deterministic models*. These models have the distinguishing feature that specific outcomes of experiments can be accurately predicted in advance. One such model, for example, is Ohm's Law, $I = E/R$. The law states that electric current, I, is directly proportional to the voltage E, and inversely proportional to the resistance, R, in a circuit. Once the voltage and resistance are known, the current is determined. If many circuits with identical voltages and resistances are studied, the current measurements may differ by small amounts from circuit to circuit, owing to inaccuracies in the measuring equipment or other uncontrollable influences. Nevertheless, the discrepancies will be negligible, and for all practical purposes Ohm's Law provides a useful deterministic model of reality.

The amounts of certain chemicals to be produced in a controlled experiment can likewise be fairly accurately predicted, given the initial conditions, although again there is almost always some slight variation among observed results.

On the other hand, the models that arise from statistical investigations are called *probabilistic models*. These models are characterized by the fact that although specific outcomes of an experiment cannot be predicted with certainty, *relative frequencies* for various possible outcomes are predictable. Suppose that ten items are drawn from a large lot and examined for defects. We cannot say specifically how many defective items we will see, but given an appropriate model and some assumptions on the nature of the lot, we can give figures for the *chance* (or probability) that we will see, say, more than 8 or fewer than 3 defectives. The formal definition of probability will be given in Chapter 2.

Deterministic models leave no room for statistical inference; probabilistic models are the building blocks upon which a rigorous theory for inference-making is based.

It is not always clear which type of model is best for certain situations, and deterministic models are sometimes used for situations in which probabilistic models might have been more appropriate. Consider a traffic flow problem again. Suppose that, over a long period of time, the number of automobiles entering a certain intersection averages ten per minute. A deterministic model might interpret this figure as a constant, and predict that exactly ten automobiles enter the intersection during every minute. A probabilistic models would treat the arrivals as random events with some minutes having perhaps no arrivals and some perhaps 25 arrivals, but with 10 arrivals per minute as the average. Which model is appropriate? The answer, no doubt, depends on the use to which the model is to be put. If one only wants to assess a rough figure for total arrivals over a month, then the deterministic model might be good enough. If, however, one wants to study peak loads and answer questions related to how often the arrivals exceed 20 per minute, then the deterministic model is of absolutely no value. Our philosophy is to employ a probabilistic model whenever there is more than negligible variation among outcomes of an experiment. Thus, probabilistic models will be used throughout this text.

To review, our study of statistical inference will depend on a clear definition of the population under investigation, on the availability of an experimental method to produce sample measurements, and on the postulating of a probabilistic model to allow us to use the sample measurements for inference-making.

This book emphasizes probabilistic models, and discusses how appropriate models can be chosen from a combination of theoretical factors and empirical evidence.

2
Probability

About This Chapter

What is it that allows us to make inferences from a sample to a population, and then measure the degree of accuracy in that inference? The answer is the theory of *probability*. Outcomes of most experiments cannot be predetermined, but certain outcomes may be more likely than others. This leads us to the notion of probability distributions, which are fundamental to our development of statistical inference.

Contents

In Chapter 1 we saw that any statistical problem begins with a clear definition of the population of interest, follows with an experimental mechanism to generate a sample set of measurements, and then, with the aid of a probabilistic model, uses these measurements for inference-making. We illustrate these steps in a simple example.

Suppose the population consists of individual quality assessments on a carload of component parts being supplied to a production process. The inference will ultimately involve our deciding whether to accept or reject the lot. The experiment consists of inspecting each of ten sampled components, and recording whether or not it is defective. The sample is the defective/nondefective classification of each of the ten items. Suppose that, after examination, no defectives are observed among the ten. What does this information tell us? The answer is "not much" unless we associate this number with a certain probabilistic model. One such model often appropriate for this type problem (the binomial of Chapter 3) will allow us to calculate the probability of the observed outcome, if we make an assumption about the fraction of defectives in the entire lot. Certainly, if there are no defectives in this lot, then the chance, or probability, of observing zero defectives is unity. If the true fraction of defectives in the lot is 5%, the chance of observing no defectives, under the binomial model, is 0.599. Assuming the true fraction of defectives to be 20%, the probability of observing no defectives is 0.107, and if the true fraction of defectives rises to 30%, this probability drops to 0.028.

Now, we see that we have observed an outcome (zero defectives) that has a very small chance of occurring if the true fraction is very large (say greater than 20%). Therefore, we might be willing to conclude that the true fraction of defectives is quite small, and accept the lot. These notions will be made more formal, and more rigorous, as we go along, but this illustrates one common type of inference problem. Note that the probabilities assigned to observable outcomes depend on the model, and so it is of the utmost importance to select a model that truly reflects the nature of the process generating the data.

After giving a brief review of set notation, we will formally develop the basic ideas of probability.

2.2   *A Review of Set Notation*

Before going into a formal discussion of probability it is necessary to outline the set notation we will use. Suppose we have a set S consisting of points labeled 1, 2, 3, and 4. We denote this by $S = \{1, 2, 3, 4\}$. If $A = \{1, 2\}$ and $B = \{2, 3, 4\}$, then A and B are subsets of S, denoted by $A \subset S$ and $B \subset S$ (B is "contained in" S). We denote the fact that "2" is an element of A by $2 \in A$. The **union** of A and B is the set consisting of all points that are either in A or in B or in both. This is denoted by $A \cup B = \{1, 2, 3, 4\}$. If $C = \{4\}$, then $A \cup C = \{1, 2, 4\}$. The **intersection** of two sets, A and B, is the set consisting of all points that are in both A and B, and is denoted by $A \cap B$, or merely AB. For the above example, $A \cap B = AB = \{2\}$ and $AC = \Phi$, where Φ denotes the **null** set, or the set consisting of no points.

The **complement** of A, with respect to S, is the set of all points in S that are not in A and is denoted by $\bar{A}$. For the specific sets given above, $\bar{A} = \{3, 4\}$. Two sets are said to be **mutually exclusive**, or **disjoint**, if they have no points in common, as in A and C above.

Venn diagrams can be used to effectively portray the concepts of union, intersection, complement, and disjoint sets, as in Figure 2.1.

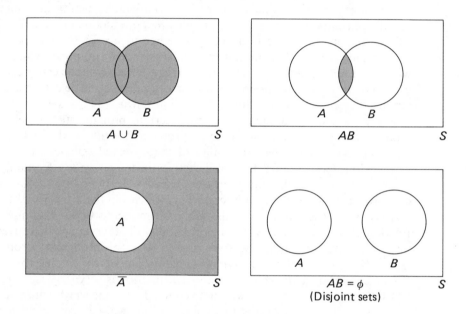

Figure 2.1   Venn Diagrams of Set Relations

2.3   *Probability*

As stated in Chapter 1 and in Section 2.1, an *experiment* is a mechanism by which we generate an observation or measurement. We use the term experiment to refer to both controlled laboratory measurements, such as measuring the tensile strength of a copper wire produced by a certain annealing process, and casual observations made in uncontrolled situations, such as recording the lifelength of a transistor or measuring daily rainfall. We have, then, the following definition.

DEFINITION 2.1   An **experiment** is the process of making an observation.

We can see that an experiment such as measuring the lifelength of a transistor has infinitely many possible outcomes associated with it. In fact, it is conceivable that any positive real number is a possible outcome for a lifelength measurement. On the other hand, an experiment such as inspecting a manufactured item to determine whether or not it is defective has only two possible outcomes: the item is a defective or a nondefective. In this section, we concentrate on experiments that produce only a finite number of outcomes. The ideas will be generalized to the infinite case in later sections.

The ideas presented next will be more easily seen if we develop a simple example to carry along for illustrative purposes. Suppose a supply room has five electric motors in stock, numbered 1 through 5, all of which seem to be identical. Motors 1 and 2 come from supplier I and motors 3, 4, and 5 come from supplier II. Unknown to the potential user of these motors, motor 2 is defective while the others work properly. The experiment consists of selecting a single motor, from among the five, to be used for a certain job.

This experiment has five possible basic outcomes since motor numbered 1, 2, 3, 4, or 5 must be selected. We can display these five separate outcomes as sets E_1, E_2, E_3, E_4, and E_5, where $E_1 = \{1\}$, $E_2 = \{2\}$, $E_3 = \{3\}$, $E_4 = \{4\}$ and $E_5 = \{5\}$. These sets will be referred to as the *simple events* for the experiment.

DEFINITION 2.2   A **simple event** is a set consisting of a single possible outcome.

The complete collection of simple events will be called the *sample space*.

DEFINITION 2.3   A **sample space** for an experiment is the union of all simple events.

For the motor selection problem, the union of the simple events is the set $S = \{1, 2, 3, 4, 5\}$, which consists of all five motors available for selection.

There are, in addition to the simple events, certain composite outcomes that are of interest for this experiment. Certainly, we would be interested in the event that a "nondefective motor is selected." We might also be interested in the event that "a motor from supplier I is selected." If we refer to these events as A and B, respectively, then A occurs if motor 1, 3, 4, or 5 is selected and B occurs if motor 1 or 2 is selected. Thus,

$$A = E_1 \cup E_3 \cup E_4 \cup E_5 = \{1, 3, 4, 5\}$$

and

$$B = E_1 \cup E_2 = \{1, 2\}.$$

We can see that any event that is likely to be of interest can be written as a union of simple events, and turns out to be a subset of the sample space. The events E_i, A, and B are shown diagramatically in Figure 2.2.

DEFINITION 2.4   An **event** is a union of simple events or, equivalently, a subset of the sample space.

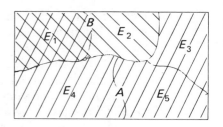

Figure 2.2   Events for the Motor
Selection Problem

The notions of event and sample space give us a set structure for an experiment. It is now possible to define probability in terms of these sets.

The definition of probability is motivated by relative frequency considerations and usually can be interpreted in a relative frequency context. Referring to the motor selection problem, suppose the motors are in no particular arrangement and one is selected "at random." What is the probability of E_1, the event that motor 1 is selected? We would be inclined to assign a probability of 1/5 to E_1 since, if we repeated the experiment over and over again with the same pool of five motors, we would anticipate that motor 1 should be selected 1/5 of the time. Likewise, we would assign a probability of 1/5 to each of E_2, E_3, E_4 and E_5.

Suppose we want to assign a probability to event $B = E_1 \cup E_2$. It seems intuitively reasonable that the relative frequencies for E_1 and E_2 should be added together, so that the probability of B, the event that a motor from supplier I is selected, turns out to be $1/5 + 1/5 = 2/5$.

We formalize these ideas in the following definition.

DEFINITION 2.5   Suppose that an experiment has associated with it a sample space S. A **probability** is a numerically valued function that assigns to every event A in S a real number, $P(A)$, so that the following axioms hold:
  (1) $P(A) \geq 0$.
  (2) $P(S) = 1$.
  (3)   If A and B are mutually exclusive events in S, then $P(A \cup B) = P(A) + P(B)$.

The third axiom tells us that we can complete a probabilistic model for any experiment with a finite number of outcomes by assigning a probability to each simple event. Since any event, A, is a union of simple events, we can find the probability of A by adding up the probabilities of the simple events in A. Symbolically, if

$$A = E_1 \cup E_2 \cup \cdots \cup E_n$$

then

$$P(A) = \sum_{i=1}^{n} P(E_i).$$

We now illustrate these concepts with other examples.

EXAMPLE 2.1

A purchasing clerk wants to order supplies from one of three possible vendors, which are numbered 1, 2, and 3. All vendors are equal with respect to quality and price, and so the clerk writes each number on a piece of paper, mixes the papers, and blindly selects one number. The order is placed with the vendor whose number is selected. Let E_i denote the event that vendor i is selected ($i = 1, 2, 3$), B the event that vendor 1 or 3 is selected, and C the event that vendor 1 is *not* selected. Find the probabilities of the events E_i, B, and C.

Solution

The events E_1, E_2, and E_3 constitute the simple events for this experiment. Thus, if we assign appropriate probabilities to these events, the probability of any other event is easily found.

Since one number is picked "at random" from the three available, it should seem intuitively reasonable to assign a probability of 1/3 to each E_i. That is,

$$P(E_1) = P(E_2) = P(E_3) = \frac{1}{3}.$$

In other words, there is no reason to suspect that one number has a higher chance of being selected than any of the others.

Now,

$$B = E_1 \cup E_3$$

and by Axiom (3) of Definition 2.5,

$$P(B) = P(E_1 \cup E_3) = P(E_1) + P(E_3)$$
$$= \frac{1}{3} + \frac{1}{3} = \frac{2}{3}.$$

Similarly,

$$C = E_2 \cup E_3$$

and thus

$$P(C) = P(E_2) + P(E_3) = \frac{2}{3}.$$

Note that different probability models could have been selected for the sample space connected with this experiment, but only this one model is reasonable under the assumption that the vendors are all equally likely to be selected. □

Suppose an experiment involves a sequence of two trials, with n_1 possible outcomes on the first trial and n_2 possible outcomes on the second trial. For example, a quality control inspector may inspect two items, each of which may be defective or nondefective. In that case, $n_1 = n_2 = 2$. Similarly, a firm may be deciding where to build two new plants, having listed four eastern cities as possible choices for the first plant and two western cities as possible choices for the second.

To find the total number of outcomes for the two trials of the experiment, we can use the following rule.

MULTIPLICATION RULE   If the first trial of an experiment can result in n_1 possible outcomes and the second trial can result in n_2 possible outcomes, then there are $n_1 n_2$ possible outcomes for the two trials together.

We can verify that this rule works by listing the outcomes on a two-way table, as in Figure 2.3. Returning to the example of an inspector examining two items, each of which can be defective or nondefective, Figure 2.3 shows that there are $n_1 n_2 = 2(2) = 4$ possible outcomes for the experiment.

Figure 2.3   Possible Outcomes for Inspecting Two Items (D_i denotes that the ith item is defective.) (N_i denotes that the ith item is nondefective.)

| | 2nd Item | |
	D_2	N_2
D_1	$D_1 D_2$	$D_1 N_2$
N_1	$N_1 D_2$	$N_1 N_2$

1st Item

Tree diagrams are also helpful for verifying the multiplication rule. Returning to the example of the firm that is building two new plants, we can see that there are $n_1 n_2 = 4(2) = 8$ possible choices by looking at Figure 2.4.

The multiplication rule only helps us to find the number of outcomes, or simple events, for an experiment. We must still assign probabilities to these simple events in order to complete our probabilistic model.

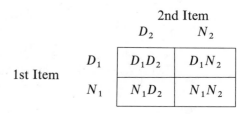

First plant (eastern city)   Second plant (western city)

Figure 2.4   Possible Outcomes for Locating Two Plants (A, B, C, D denote eastern cities.) (E, F denote western cities.)

EXAMPLE 2.2

Referring to the firm that plans to build two new plants, the eight possible simple events are shown in Figure 2.4. If all eight choices are equally likely (i.e., one of the pairs of cities is selected at random), find the probability that city E gets selected.

Solution   City E can get selected in four different ways, since there are four possible eastern cities to pair with it. Thus,

$$\{E \text{ gets selected}\} = \{AE\} \cup \{BE\} \cup \{CE\} \cup \{DE\}$$

and, since the simple events $\{AE\}$, $\{BE\}$, and so on are mutually exclusive,

$$P\{E \text{ gets selected}\} = P\{AE\} + P\{BE\} + P\{CE\} + P\{DE\}$$

$$= \frac{1}{8} + \frac{1}{8} + \frac{1}{8} + \frac{1}{8}$$

$$= \frac{1}{2}.$$

Each simple event has probability 1/8, since the eight events are assumed to be equally likely.   □

EXAMPLE 2.3

Refer to the example on page 7 in which five motors are available for use, and motor number 2 is defective. Motors 1 and 2 come from supplier I and motors 3, 4, and 5 come from supplier II. Suppose two motors are randomly selected for use on a particular day. Let A denote the event that the defective motor is selected and B the event that at least one motor comes from supplier I. Find $P(A)$ and $P(B)$.

Solution   We can see on the tree diagram in Figure 2.5 that there are $5(4) = 20$ possible outcomes for this experiment. That is, there are twenty simple events of the form $\{1,2\}$, $\{1,3\}$, etc. Since the motors are randomly selected, each simple event has probability 1/20. Thus,

$$P(A) = P(\{1,2\} \cup \{2,1\} \cup \{2,3\} \cup \{2,4\} \cup \{2,5\} \cup \{3,2\} \cup \{4,2\} \cup \{5,2\})$$

$$= \frac{8}{20} = 0.4,$$

since the probability of the union is the sum of the probabilities of the simple events in the union.

The reader can show that B contains 14 simple events and, hence, that

$$P(B) = \frac{14}{20} = 0.7.   \square$$

In Section 2.4 we will look at two more basic concepts in probability theory.

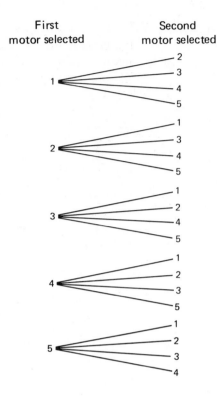

First
motor selected

Second
motor selected

Figure 2.5 Outcomes for
Experiment of Example 2.3

Exercises

2.1   A vehicle arriving at an intersection can turn left, turn right, or continue
straight ahead. If an experiment consists of observing the movement of
one vehicle at this intersection, do the following.
(a) List the simple events.
(b) Attach probabilities to the simple events if all possible outcomes are
equally likely.
(c) Find the probability that the vehicle turns, under the probabilistic
model of part (b).

2.2   Refer to Exercise 2.1. Suppose an experiment consists of observing the
movements of two vehicles at this intersection.
(a) List the simple events.
(b) Assuming the outcomes to be equally likely, find the probability that
at least one vehicle turns left.
(c) Assuming the outcomes to be equally likely, find the probability
that at most one vehicle makes a turn.

2.3   A commercial building is designed with two entrances, say I and II. Two
customers arrive and enter the building.
(a) List the simple events for this observational experiment.
(b) If all simple events in (a) are equally likely, find the probability that
both customers use door I; that both customers use the same door.

2.4 A corporation has two construction contracts that are going to be assigned to one or more of three firms bidding for these contracts. (One firm could receive both contracts.)
(a) List the possible outcomes for the assignment of contracts to the firms.
(b) If all outcomes are equally likely, find the probability that both contracts go to the same firm.
(c) Under the assumptions of (b), find the probability that one specific firm, say firm I, gets at least one contract.

2.5 Among five portable generators produced by an assembly line in one day, there are two defectives. If two generators are selected for sale, find the probability that both will be nondefective. (Assume the two selected for sale are chosen so that every possible sample of size two has the same probability of being selected.)

2.6 A manufacturing company has two retail outlets. It is known that 30% of the potential customers buy products from outlet I alone, 50% buy from outlet II alone, 10% buy from both I and II, and 10% of the potential customers buy from neither. Let A denote the event that a potential customer, randomly chosen, buys from I and B the event that the customer buys from II. Find the following probabilities:
(a) $P(A)$ (b) $P(A \cup B)$
(c) $P(\bar{B})$ (d) $P(AB)$
(e) $P(A \cup \bar{B})$ (f) $P(\bar{A}\bar{B})$
(g) $P(\overline{A \cup B})$

2.4   *Conditional Probability and Independence*

Refer once more to the example in which five motors are available for use, and one is to be selected. Motor 2 is defective, motors 1 and 2 come from supplier I and motors 3, 4, 5 come from supplier II. Suppose that the motors are marked so that the supplier can be identified.

    A randomly selected motor has probability 1/5 of being defective. However, if a motor is selected and then observed to have come from supplier I, the probability that it is defective will change. Of the two motors from supplier I, one is defective. Thus, the probability of observing a defective motor *given that it is from supplier I* should be 1/2. This is an example of a *conditional* probability, with general definition as follows:

DEFINITION 2.6   If A and B are any two events, then the **conditional probability** of A given B, denoted by $P(A|B)$, is

$$P(A|B) = \frac{P(AB)}{P(B)}$$

provided $P(B) \neq 0$.

In the motor selection example define A to be "the selected motor is defective" and B to be "the selected motor comes from supplier I." Then,

$$P(A|B) = \frac{P(AB)}{P(B)} = \frac{1/5}{2/5} = \frac{1}{2}.$$

Note that, in this case, the event AB ("the motor is defective and comes from supplier I") is the same as event A since there are no defectives from supplier II.

EXAMPLE 2.4

Refer to Example 2.3. Find the probability that the second motor selected is nondefective, given that the first was nondefective.

Solution   Let N_i denote that the ith motor selected is nondefective. We want $P(N_2|N_1)$. From Definition 2.6:

$$P(N_2|N_1) = \frac{P(N_1N_2)}{P(N_1)}.$$

Looking at the twenty simple events given in Figure 2.5, we can see that the event N_1 contains 16 of these simple events and N_1N_2 contains 12. Thus, since the simple events are equally likely,

$$P(N_2|N_1) = \frac{P(N_1N_2)}{P(N_1)} = \frac{12/20}{16/20} = \frac{12}{16} = \frac{3}{4}.$$

Does this answer seem intuitively reasonable?   □

If the extra information in an event B does not change the probability of A, that is, if $P(A|B) = P(A)$, then the events A and B are said to be independent. Since

$$P(A|B) = \frac{P(AB)}{P(B)},$$

the condition $P(A|B) = P(A)$ is equivalent to

$$\frac{P(AB)}{P(B)} = P(A)$$

or

$$P(AB) = P(A)P(B).$$

DEFINITION 2.7   Two events, A and B, are said to be **independent** if

$$P(A|B) = P(A)$$

or

$$P(B|A) = P(B).$$

This is equivalent to stating that

$$P(AB) = P(A)P(B).$$

EXAMPLE 2.5

Suppose that a foreman must select one worker, for a special job, from a pool of four available workers, numbered 1, 2, 3, and 4. He selects the worker by mixing the four names and randomly selecting one. Let A denote the event that worker 1 or 2 is selected, B the event that worker 1 or 3 is selected, and C the event that worker 1 is selected. Are A and B independent? Are A and C independent?

Solution

Since the name is selected at random, a reasonable assumption for the probabilistic model is to assign a probability of 1/4 to each individual worker. Then, $P(A) = 1/2$, $P(B) = 1/2$, and $P(C) = 1/4$. Since AB contains only worker 1, $P(AB) = 1/4$. Now, $P(AB) = 1/4 = P(A)P(B)$ and so A and B *are* independent. Since AC also contains only worker 1, $P(AC) = 1/4$. But, $P(AC) = 1/4 \neq P(A)P(C)$ and so A and C *are not* independent. A and C are said to be *dependent*.   □

Now we will show how these definitions aid us in establishing rules for computing probabilities of composite events.

2.5   *Rules of Probability*

We now establish four rules that will help us in calculating probabilities of events. First, recall that the complement, $\bar{A}$, of an event A is the set of all outcomes in a sample space, S, that are not in A. Thus, $\bar{A}$ and A are mutually exclusive and their union is S. That is,

$$\bar{A} \cup A = S.$$

It follows that

$$P(\bar{A} \cup A) = P(\bar{A}) + P(A) = P(S) = 1$$

or

$$P(\bar{A}) = 1 - P(A).$$

RULE 1   Complements   If $\bar{A}$ is the complement of an event A in a sample space, S, then

$$P(\bar{A}) = 1 - P(A).$$

We will subsequently see that it is often easier to find the probability of the complement of A than to find the probability of A, and Rule 1 is very useful in that case.

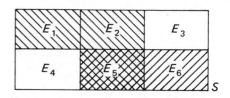

Figure 2.6 $A \cup B$

The diagram of Figure 2.6 illustrates the event $A \cup B$ for a sample space containing six simple events, E_1 through E_6. $A = E_1 \cup E_2 \cup E_5$ and $B = E_5 \cup E_6$. To find the probability of $A \cup B$ we must find

$$P(A) = P(E_1) + P(E_2) + P(E_5)$$

and add to it

$$P(B) = P(E_5) + P(E_6).$$

But, $P(AB) = P(E_5)$ has been added in twice, and should be subtracted out once in order to make

$$P(A \cup B) = P(E_1) + P(E_2) + P(E_5) + P(E_6).$$

We have, then, that

$$P(A \cup B) = P(A) + P(B) - P(AB).$$

RULE 2 Unions   If A and B are any two events, then

$$P(A \cup B) = P(A) + P(B) - P(AB).$$

If A and B are mutually exclusive, then

$$P(A \cup B) = P(A) + P(B).$$

The next rule is actually just a rearrangement of the definition of conditional probability, for the case in which a conditional probability may be known and we want to find the probability of an intersection.

RULE 3 Intersections   If A and B are any two events, then

$$P(AB) = P(A)P(B \mid A)$$
$$= P(B)P(A \mid B)$$

If A and B are independent, then

$$P(AB) = P(A)P(B).$$

We illustrate the use of these three rules in the following examples.

EXAMPLE 2.6

Records indicate that for the units coming out of a hydraulic repair shop at an airplane rework facility, 20% will have a type I defect, 10% will have a type II defect, and 75% will be defect free. For an item chosen at random from this output, find the probability of

A: the item has at least one type of defect.

B: the item has only a type I defect.

Solution   The percentages given imply that 5% of the items have both a type I and a type II defect. Let D_1 denote the event that an item has a defect of type I, and D_2 the event that it has a defect of type II. Then

$$A = D_1 \cup D_2$$

and

$$
\begin{aligned}
P(A) &= P(D_1 \cup D_2) \\
&= P(D_1) + P(D_2) - P(D_1 D_2) \\
&= 0.20 + 0.10 - 0.05 \\
&= 0.25.
\end{aligned}
$$

Another possible solution is to observe that the complement of A is the event that an item has no defects. Thus,

$$
\begin{aligned}
P(A) &= 1 - P(\bar{A}) \\
&= 1 - 0.75 = 0.25.
\end{aligned}
$$

To find $P(B)$ note that

$$D_1 = B \cup D_1 D_2$$

and observe that B and $D_1 D_2$ are mutually exclusive. Therefore,

$$P(D_1) = P(B) + P(D_1 D_2)$$

or

$$
\begin{aligned}
P(B) &= P(D_1) - P(D_1 D_2) \\
&= 0.20 - 0.05 = 0.15.
\end{aligned}
$$

You might try to sketch these events on a Venn diagram and verify the results derived above.   □

EXAMPLE 2.7

A section of an electrical circuit has two relays in parallel, as shown in Figure 2.7. The relays operate independently, and when a switch is thrown, each will close properly with probability only 0.8. If the relays are both open, find the probability that current will flow from s to t when the switch is thrown.

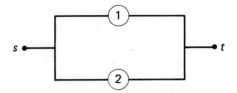

Figure 2.7 Two Relays in Parallel

Solution Let O denote an open relay and C a closed relay. The four sample events for this experiment are given by

$$
\begin{array}{ccc}
 & \text{Relay} & \text{Relay} \\
 & 1 & 2 \\
E_1 = \{ O & , & O \} \\
E_2 = \{ O & , & C \} \\
E_3 = \{ C & , & O \} \\
E_4 = \{ C & , & C \}
\end{array}
$$

Since the relays operate independently, we can find the probabilities for these simple events as follows.

$$P(E_1) = P(O)P(O) = (0.2)(0.2) = 0.04$$

$$P(E_2) = P(O)P(C) = (0.2)(0.8) = 0.16$$

$$P(E_3) = P(C)P(O) = (0.8)(0.2) = 0.16$$

$$P(E_4) = P(C)P(C) = (0.8)(0.8) = 0.64$$

If A denotes the event that current will flow from s to t, then

$$A = E_2 \cup E_3 \cup E_4$$

or

$$\bar{A} = E_1.$$

(At least one of the relays must close for current to flow.) Thus,

$$
\begin{aligned}
P(A) &= 1 - P(\bar{A}) \\
&= 1 - P(E_1) \\
&= 1 - 0.04 = 0.96,
\end{aligned}
$$

which is the same as $P(E_2) + P(E_3) + P(E_4)$. □

The fourth rule we present in this section is based on the notion of a *partition* of a sample space. Events $B_1, B_2, \ldots, B_k$ are said to partition a sample space, S, if

(1) $B_i B_j = \Phi$ for any pair i and j
(2) $B_1 \cup B_2 \cdots \cup B_k = S$.

For example, the set of tires in an auto assembly warehouse may be partitioned according to suppliers, or employees of a firm may be partitioned according to level of education. For the case $k = 2$, we illustrate a partition in Figure 2.8.

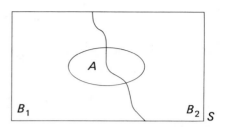

Figure 2.8   A partition of S, into B_1 and B_2

The key idea involving a partition is to observe that an event A (see Figure 2.8) can be written as the union of mutually exclusive events AB_1 and AB_2. That is,

$$A = AB_1 \cup AB_2$$

and thus

$$P(A) = P(AB_1) + P(AB_2).$$

If conditional probabilities $P(A|B_1)$ and $P(A|B_2)$ are known, then $P(A)$ can be found by writing

$$P(A) = P(B_1)P(A|B_1) + P(B_2)P(A|B_2).$$

In problems dealing with partitions, it is frequently of interest to find probabilities of the form $P(B_1|A_1)$, which can be written

$$P(B_1|A) = \frac{P(B_1A)}{P(A)}$$

$$= \frac{P(B_1)P(A|B_1)}{P(B_1)P(A|B_1) + P(B_2)P(A|B_2)}.$$

This result is a special case of Bayes' Rule.

RULE 4   Bayes' Rule   If $B_1, B_2, \ldots, B_k$ forms a partition of S and A is any event in S, then

$$P(B_j|A) = \frac{P(B_j)P(A|B_j)}{\displaystyle\sum_{i=1}^{k} P(B_i)P(A|B_i)}.$$

EXAMPLE 2.8

A company buys tires from two suppliers, supplier 1 and supplier 2. Supplier 1 has a record of delivering tires containing 10% defectives, whereas supplier 2 has a defective rate of only 5%. Suppose 40% of the current supply came from supplier 1. If a tire is taken from this supply and observed to be defective, find the probability that it came from supplier 1.

Solution   Let B_i denote the event that a tire comes from supplier i, $i = 1, 2$, and note that B_1 and B_2 form a partition of the sample space for the experiment of selecting one tire. Let A denote the event that the selected tire is defective. Then,

$$P(B_1|A) = \frac{P(B_1)P(A|B_1)}{P(B_1)P(A|B_1) + P(B_2)P(A|B_2)}$$

$$= \frac{0.40(0.10)}{0.40(0.10) + (0.60)(0.05)}$$

$$= \frac{0.04}{0.04 + 0.03} = \frac{4}{7}.$$

Supplier 1 has a higher chance of being the party supplying the defective than does supplier 2.   □

In Section 2.6 we discuss the fact that we are frequently interested in *numerical* outcomes associated with experiments.

Exercises

2.7   Refer to Exercise 2.2. Find the probability that at least one of the two vehicles turns *left*, given that at least one of the two vehicles turns.

2.8   Refer to Exercise 2.4. Find the conditional probability that firm I gets a contract, given that both contracts do not go to the same firm.

2.9   Refer to Exercise 2.6. Find the answers to (b) through (g) by using the rules of probability given in Section 2.5.

2.10 Resistors are produced by a certain firm and marketed as 10-ohm resistors. However, the actual ohms of resistance produced by the resistors may vary. It is observed that 5% of the values are below 9.5 ohms and 10% are above 10.5 ohms. If two of these resistors, randomly selected, are used in a system, find the probability that:
(a) Both have actual values between 9.5 and 10.5.
(b) At least one has an actual value in excess of 10.5.

2.11 Consider the following segment of an electric circuit, with three relays. Current will flow from a to b if there is at least one closed path when the relays are switched to "closed." However, the relays may malfunction. Suppose they only close properly with probability 0.9 when the switch is thrown, and suppose they operate independently of one another. Let A denote the event that current will flow from a to b when the relays are switched to "closed."

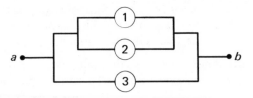

(a) Find $P(A)$.

(b) Find the probability that relay 1 is closed properly, given that current is known to be flowing from a to b.

2.12   Electric motors coming off two assembly lines are pooled for storage in a common stockroom, and the room contains an equal number of motors from each line. Motors are periodically sampled from that room and tested. It is known that 0.10% of the motors from Line I are defective and 0.15% of the motors from Line II are defective. If a motor is randomly selected from the stockroom and found to be defective, find the probability that it came from Line I.

2.13   Two methods, A and B, are available for teaching a certain industrial skill. The failure rate is 20% for A and 10% for B. However, B is more expensive and hence is only used 30% of the time. (A is used the other 70%). A worker is taught the skill by one of the methods, but fails to learn it correctly. What is the probability that he was taught by Method A?

2.14   A diagnostic test for a certain disease is said to be 90% accurate in that, if a person has the disease, the test will detect it with probability 0.9. Also, if a person does not have the disease, the test will report that he doesn't have it with probability 0.9. Only 1% of the population has the disease in question. If a person is chosen at random from the population and the diagnostic test reports him to have the disease, what is the conditional probability that he does, in fact, have the disease? Are you surprised by the size of the answer? Would you call this diagnostic test reliable?

2.15   A proficiency examination for a certain skill was given to 100 employees of a firm. Forty of the employees were male. Sixty of the employees passed the examination, in that they scored above a preset level for satisfactory performance. The breakdown among males and females was as follows.

	Male (M)	Female (F)	
Pass (P)	24	36	
Fail (F)	16	24	
			100

Suppose an employee is randomly selected from the 100 who took the examination.

(a) Find the probability that the employee passed, given that he was male.

(b) Find the probability that the employee was male, given that he passed.

(c) Are the events P and M independent?

(d) Are the events P and F independent?

2.16   By using Venn diagrams or similar arguments, show that, for events A, B, and C

$$P(A \cup B \cup C) = P(A) + P(B) + P(C) - P(AB) - P(AC) - P(BC) + P(ABC).$$

2.17   By using the definition of conditional probability, show that

$$P(ABC) = P(A)P(B \mid A)P(C \mid AB).$$

2.6   *Random Variables*

Almost all of the experiments that we will encounter will generate outcomes that can be interpreted in terms of real numbers, such as lifelengths, numbers of defectives, and strength measurements. For example, refer to Example 2.7 in which two relays are operating in parallel. When the switch that supposedly closes the relays is thrown, the *numerical* event of interest is the number of relays that close properly. If we denote the number of relays that close by Y, then Y can take on three possible values, 0, 1, or 2. We can, in fact, assign probabilities to these values as follows:

$$P(Y = 0) = P(E_1) = 0.04$$
$$P(Y = 1) = P(E_2 \cup E_3) = P(E_2) + P(E_3) = 0.32$$
$$P(Y = 2) = P(E_4) = 0.64.$$

Thus, we have mapped the sample space of four simple events into a set of three meaningful real numbers, and attached a probability to each. The quantity Y is called a *random variable*.

DEFINITION 2.8   A **random variable** is a function that maps a sample space onto a set of real numbers.

Random variables will be denoted by uppercase letter such as X, Y, and Z. The actual numerical values that a random variable can assume will be denoted by lowercase letters, such as x, y, and z. We can then talk about "the probability that X takes on the value x," denoted by $P(X = x) = p(x)$.

In the relay example on p. 17, the random variable, Y, has only three possible values and it is a relatively simple matter to assign probabilities to these values. Such a random variable is called *discrete*.

DEFINITION 2.9   A random variable, X, is said to be **discrete** if it can take on only a finite number, or a countable infinity, of possible values, x. In this case

(1) $P(X = x) \geq 0$
(2) $\sum_x P(X = x) = 1$, where the sum is over all possible values, x.

The "countable infinity" case comes about, for example, in an experiment like counting the number of flaws, per bolt, in the manufacture of a textile. The number of flaws could be 0, 1, 2, ..., but there is no upper bound to the possible number that could be seen. We will come back to this type of problem in Chapter 3.

A second type of random variable comes about in an experiment like measuring the lifelength, X, of a transistor. In this case, there is an infinite number of possible values that X can assume. We cannot assign a positive probability to each possible outcome of the experiment because, no matter how small we might make the individual probabilities, they would sum to a value greater than one when accumulated over the entire sample space. We can, however, assign positive probabilities to *intervals* of real numbers in a manner consistent with the axioms of probability. To introduce the basic ideas involved here, let us consider a specific example in some detail.

Suppose that we have conducted an experiment designed to measure the lifelengths of 50 batteries of a certain type, selected from a large population of such batteries. The experiment is completed, and the observed lifelengths are as given in Table 2.1.

0.406	0.685	4.778	1.725	8.223
2.343	1.401	1.507	0.294	2.130
0.538	0.234	4.025	3.323	2.920
5.088	1.458	1.064	0.774	0.761
5.587	0.517	3.246	2.330	1.064
2.563	0.511	2.782	6.426	0.836
0.023	0.225	1.514	3.214	3.810
3.334	2.325	0.333	7.541	0.968
3.491	2.921	1.624	0.334	4.490
1.267	1.702	2.634	1.849	0.186

Table 2.1   Lifelengths of Batteries (in Hundreds of Hours)

How can these numbers help us to establish a probabilistic model for X, the lifelength of an arbitrary battery of this type? Perhaps the first thing that comes to mind is that it would be nice to obtain some relative frequency information on these lifelengths. In what intervals do most of the observations lie? A relative frequency histogram (or graph) constructed from these data is given in Figure 2.9. The histogram is constructed by dividing the interval (approximately 0 to 9) in which the lifelengths fall into a convenient number of subintervals. In this case, we choose to use nine subintervals, each one unit in length. Then we record the fraction of observations that fall into each subinterval. The height of the bar over any one subinterval is equal to the fraction of observations that fall into that

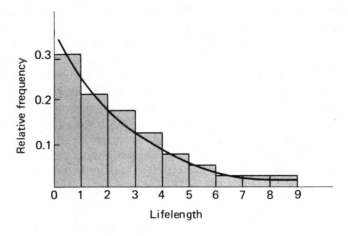

Figure 2.9   Relative Frequency Histogram

particular subinterval. For example, 16 of the 50 observations (32%) fall into the first subinterval (0 to 1) and 11 of the 50 (22%) fall into the second (1 to 2).

By looking at Figure 2.9, we see that most of the observations lie between 0 and 1, and that there is an almost regular decline in frequency.

This sample relative frequency histogram not only allows us to picture how the sample behaves, but it also gives us some insight into a possible probabilistic model for the random variable X. This histogram of Figure 2.9 looks like it could be approximated quite closely by a negative exponential curve. The particular function

$$f(x) = \frac{1}{2} e^{-x/2}, \qquad x > 0,$$

is sketched through the histogram in Figure 2.9, and seems to fit reasonably well. Thus, we could take this function as a mathematical model for the behavior of the random variable, X. If we want to use a battery of this type in the future, we might want to know the probability that it will last longer than four hundred hours. This probability can be approximated by the area under the curve to the right of the value 4. That is, by

$$\int_4^\infty \frac{1}{2} e^{-x/2} \, dx = 0.135.$$

Note that this figure is quite close to the observed sample fraction of lifetimes that exceed 4, namely, $(8/50) = 0.16$. One might suggest that, since the sample fraction 0.16 is available, we do not really need the model. But, there are other questions for which the model would give more satisfactory answers than could otherwise be obtained. For example, suppose we are interested in the probability that X is greater that 8. Then the model suggests the answer

$$\int_8^\infty \frac{1}{2} e^{-x/2} \, dx = 0.018,$$

whereas the sample shows no observations in excess of 8. These are, in fact, quite simple examples, and we will see many examples of more involved inferences for which a model is quite essential.

Why did we choose the exponential function as a model here? Wouldn't some others do just as well? The choice of a model is a fundamental problem and we will spend considerable time in later chapters delving into theoretical and practical reasons for these choices. We will also talk about methods of statistically assessing whether or not a model fits the data. For this early discussion we will merely suggest some models that look like they might do the job.

A random variable, X, that is associated with a continuum of values, such as in the lifelength example, is called *continuous*. The function $f(x)$, which models the relative frequency behavior of X, is called the *probability density function*.

DEFINITION 2.10   A random variable, X, is said to be **continuous** if it can take on the infinite number of possible values associated with intervals of real numbers, and there is a function $f(x)$, called the **probability density**

function, such that

(1) $f(x) \geq 0$, for all x
(2) $\int_{-\infty}^{\infty} f(x) \, dx = 1$
(3) $P(a \leq X \leq b) = \int_a^b f(x) \, dx$.

Note that for a continuous random variable X,

$$P(X = a) = \int_a^a f(x) \, dx = 0$$

for any specific value, a. The fact that we must assign zero probability to any specific value should not disturb us, since there is an infinite number of possible values that X can assume. For example, out of all the possible values that the lifelength of a transistor can take on, what is the probability that the transistor we are using will last exactly 497.392 hours? Assigning probability zero to this event does not rule out 497.392 as a possible lifelength, but it does say that the chance of observing this particular lifelength is extremely small.

EXAMPLE 2.9

Refer to the random variable X of the lifelength example, which has associated with it a probability density function of the form

$$f(x) = \begin{cases} \frac{1}{2} e^{-x/2}, & x > 0 \\ 0, & \text{elsewhere.} \end{cases}$$

Find the probability that the lifelength of a particular battery of this type is less than 200 or greater than 400 hours.

Solution   Let A denote the event that X is less than 2 and B the event that X is greater than 4. Then, since A and B are mutually exclusive,

$$P(A \cup B) = P(A) + P(B)$$

$$= \int_0^2 \frac{1}{2} e^{-x/2} \, dx + \int_4^\infty \frac{1}{2} e^{-x/2} \, dx$$

$$= (1 - e^{-1}) + (e^{-2})$$

$$= 1 - 0.368 + 0.135$$

$$= 0.767. \quad \square$$

EXAMPLE 2.10

Refer to Example 2.9. Find the probability that a battery of this type lasts more than 300 hours, given that it has already been in use for more than 200 hours.

Solution   We are interested in $P(X > 3 \mid X > 2)$ and, by the definition of conditional probability, we have

$$P(X > 3 \mid X > 2) = \frac{P(X > 3)}{P(X > 2)},$$

since the intersection of the events $(X > 3)$ and $(X > 2)$ is the event $(X > 3)$. Now,

$$\frac{P(X > 3)}{P(X > 2)} = \frac{\int_3^\infty \frac{1}{2}e^{-x/2}\,dx}{\int_2^\infty \frac{1}{2}e^{-x/2}\,dx} = \frac{e^{-3/2}}{e^{-1}} = e^{-1/2} = 0.606. \quad \square$$

We sometimes study the behavior of random variables by looking at their *cumulative* probabilities. That is, for any random variable X we may look at $P(X \le b)$ for any real number b. This is the cumulative probability for X evaluated at b. Thus, we can define a function $F(b)$ as

$$F(b) = P(X \le b).$$

DEFINITION 2.11   The **distribution function**, $F(b)$, for a random variable X is defined as

$$F(b) = P(X \le b).$$

If X is discrete,

$$F(b) = \sum_{x = -\infty}^{b} p(x).$$

If X is continuous,

$$F(b) = \int_{-\infty}^{b} f(x)\,dx,$$

for some function $f(x)$, called the **probability density function**.

The random variable, Y, denoting the number of relays closing properly (defined at the beginning of this section), has probability distribution given by

$$P(Y = 0) = 0.04$$
$$P(Y = 1) = 0.32$$

and

$$P(Y = 2) = 0.64.$$

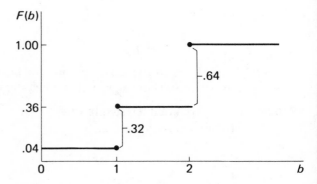

Figure 2.10   A Distribution Function for a Discrete Random Variable

The distribution function for this random variable then has the form

$$F(b) = \begin{cases} 0 & b < 0 \\ 0.04 & 0 \le b < 1 \\ 0.36 & 1 \le b < 2 \\ 1.00 & 2 \le b. \end{cases}$$

This function is graphed in Figure 2.10.

In the lifelength of batteries examples, X has a probability density function given by

$$f(x) = \begin{cases} \frac{1}{2}e^{-x/2}, & x > 0 \\ 0, & \text{elsewhere.} \end{cases}$$

Thus,

$$F(b) = P(X \le b) = \int_{-\infty}^{b} f(x)\,dx$$

$$= \int_{0}^{b} \frac{1}{2} e^{-x/2}\,dx$$

$$= -e^{-x/2}\Big]_{0}^{b} = 1 - e^{-b/2}, \qquad b > 0.$$

This function is shown graphically in Figure 2.11.

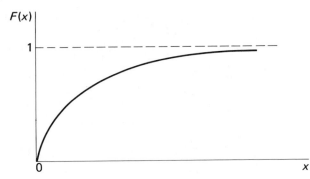

Figure 2.11   A distribution function for a continuous random variable.

We close this section with one more example.

EXAMPLE 2.11

A supplier of kerosene has a 200 gallon tank filled at the beginning of each week. His weekly demands show a relative frequency behavior that increases steadily up to 100 gallons, and then levels off between 100 and 200 gallons. Letting X denote weekly demand in hundreds of gallons, suppose the relative frequencies for demand are adequately modeled by

$$f(x) \begin{cases} = 0, & x < 0, \\ = x, & 0 \le x \le 1, \\ = 1/2, & 1 < x \le 2 \\ = 0, & x > 2. \end{cases}$$

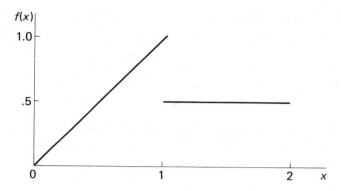

Figure 2.12 $f(x)$ for Example 2.11

This function has the graphical form shown in Figure 2.12. Find $F(b)$ for this random variable.

Solution   From the definition

$$F(b) = \int_{-\infty}^{b} f(x)\,dx$$

$$= 0, \quad b < 0$$

$$= \int_{0}^{b} x\,dx = \frac{b^2}{2}, \qquad 0 \le b \le 1$$

$$= \frac{1}{2} + \int_{1}^{b} \frac{1}{2}\,dx = \frac{1}{2} + \frac{b-1}{2} = \frac{b}{2}, \qquad 1 < b \le 2$$

$$= 1, \qquad b > 2.$$

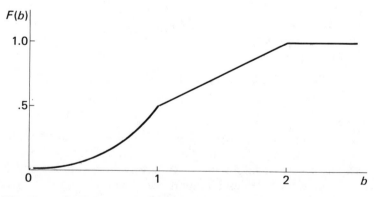

Figure 2.13 $F(b)$ for Example 2.11

This function is graphed in Figure 2.13. Note that $F(b)$ is continuous over the whole real line, even though $f(b)$ has two discontinuities.   □

___

Exercises

___

2.18   For each of the following situations, define an appropriate random variable and state whether it is continuous or discrete.
(a) An environmental engineer is looking at ten field plots to determine whether or not they contain a certain type of insect.
(b) A quality control technician samples a continuously produced fabric in square yard sections, and counts the number of defects he observes for each sampled section.
(c) A metallurgist counts the number of grains seen in a cross-sectional sample of aluminum.
(d) The metallurgist of (c) measures the area proportion covered by grains of a certain size, rather than simply counting them.

2.19   Suppose a random variable X has a probability density function given by

$$f(x) = \begin{cases} kx(1-x), & 0 \le x \le 1 \\ 0, & \text{elsewhere.} \end{cases}$$

(a) Find the value of k that makes this a probability density function.
(b) Find $P(0.4 \le X \le 1)$.
(c) Find $P(X \le 0.4 \,|\, X \le 0.8)$.
(d) Find $F(b) = P(X \le b)$, and sketch the graph of this function.

2.20   Refer to Exercise 2.3. Define X to be the number of times entrance I is used, as the two customers enter the building. Find the probability distribution for X.

2.21   The "on" temperature of a thermostatically controlled switch is set at $60°$, but the actual temperature, X, at which the switch turns on is a random variable having probability density function

$$f(x) = \begin{cases} \frac{1}{2}, & 59 \le x \le 61 \\ 0, & \text{elsewhere.} \end{cases}$$

(a) Find the probability that it takes a temperature in excess of $60°$ to turn the switch on.
(b) If two such switches are used independently, find the probability that they both require a temperature in excess of $60°$ in order to turn on.

2.22   Refer to Exercise 2.21. Suppose three switches of the type discussed operate independently in the system diagrammed as follows:

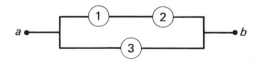

When the switches are turned on, it is possible for electric current to pass through them. Let X denote the number of closed paths from a to b when the temperature reaches $59.5°$. Find the probability distribution for X.

2.23 The proportion of time, during a forty-hour work week, that a certain machine was in operation was measured for a large number of weeks, and the measurements can be modeled by the probability density function

$$f(x) = \begin{cases} 2x, & 0 \le x \le 1, \\ 0, & \text{elsewhere.} \end{cases}$$

If X denotes the proportion of time this machine will be in operation during a coming week, find the following:
(a) $P(X > 1/2)$ (b) $P(X > 1/2 \,|\, X > 1/4)$
(c) $P(X > 1/4 \,|\, X > 1/2)$
Find $F(x)$ and graph this function. Is $F(x)$ continuous?

2.24 For many situations, histograms of lifelength measurements do not have the exponential shape shown in Figure 2.9. They are frequently characterized by a probability density function similar to

$$f(x) = \begin{cases} xe^{-x}, & x > 0, \\ 0, & \text{elsewhere.} \end{cases}$$

Sketch this curve and comment upon its reasonableness as a model for lifelengths. (This type of function will be discussed in Chapter 4.)

2.7 *Joint Distributions*

In previous sections we considered experiments that generate one particular kind of response, or random variable. Actually, it is most common for an experiment to simultaneously generate a number of types of responses, or random variables. For example, inspection of a manufactured item may result in a weight measurement, a number of size measurements, and a number of performance measurements. We would then be interested in the joint behavior of all of these measurements. This behavior is modeled by a *joint probability distribution*.

To simplify the basic ideas of joint distributions, we will consider a bivariate example in some detail. Suppose two light bulbs are to be drawn sequentially from a box containing four good and one defective bulb. The drawings are made without replacement, that is, the first one is *not* put back into the box before the second one is drawn. Let X_1 denote the number of defectives observed on the first draw and X_2 the number of defectives observed on the second draw. Note that X_1 and X_2 can take on only the values zero and one. How might we calculate the probability of the event ($X_1 = 0$ and $X_2 = 0$)? There are five choices for the bulb drawn first, and then only four choices for the bulb drawn second. Thus, there are $5 \cdot 4 = 20$ possible ordered outcomes for the drawing of two bulbs. Since the draws were supposedly made at random, a reasonable probabilistic model for this experiment would be one that assigns equal probability of 1/20 to each of the twenty possible outcomes. Now, how many of these 20 outcomes are in the event $X_1 = 0$, $X_2 = 0$? There are four good bulbs in the box, any one of which could occur on the first draw. After that one good bulb is removed, three are left for the second draw. Thus, there are $4 \cdot 3 = 12$ outcomes which result in no defectives on either draw. The probability of the event in question is now apparent:

$$P(X_1 = 0, X_2 = 0) = \frac{12}{20} = 0.6.$$

After similar calculations for the other possible values of X_1 and X_2, we can arrange the probabilities as in Table 2.2.

Table 2.2   Joint Distribution of X_1 and X_2

X_2 \ X_1	0	1	Row Totals (Marginal Probabilities for X_2)
0	0.6	0.2	0.8
1	0.2	0	0.2
Column Totals (Marginal Probabilities for X_1)	0.8	0.2	1.0

The entries in Table 2.2 represent the *joint probability distribution* of X_1 and X_2. From these probabilities we can extract the probabilities that represent the behavior of X_1, or X_2, by itself. Note that

$$P(X_1 = 0) = P(X_1 = 0, X_2 = 0) + P(X_1 = 0, X_2 = 1)$$
$$= 0.6 + 0.2 = 0.8.$$

This entry (0.8) is found on Table 2.2 as the total of the entries in the first column (under $X_1 = 0$). In similar fashion one finds $P(X_1 = 1) = 0.2$, the total of the second column entries. These values 0.8 and 0.2 occur on the margin of the table and hence are termed the *marginal* probabilities of X_1. The marginal probability distribution for X_2 is found by looking at the row totals, which show $P(X_2=0)=0.8$ and $P(X_2 = 1) = 0.2$. The distributions considered in previous sections were, in fact, marginal probability distributions.

In addition to joint and marginal probabilities we may be interested in conditional probabilities, such as the probability that the second bulb turns out to be good given that we have found the first one to be good, or $P(X_2 = 0 | X_1 = 0)$. Looking back at our probabilistic model for this experiment, we see that, after it is known that the first bulb is good, there are only three good bulbs among the four remaining. Thus, we should have

$$P(X_2 = 0 | X_1 = 0) = \frac{3}{4}.$$

The definition of conditional probability gives

$$P(X_2 = 0 \mid X_1 = 0) = \frac{P(X_1 = 0, X_2 = 0)}{P(X_1 = 0)}$$

$$= \frac{0.6}{0.8} = \frac{3}{4},$$

and so the result agrees with our intuitive assessment above.

EXAMPLE 2.12

There are three checkout counters in operation at a local supermarket. Two customers arrive at the counters at different times, when the counters are serving no other customers. It is assumed that the customers then choose a checkout station at random, and independent of one another. Let X_1 denote the number of times Counter A is selected and X_2 the number of times Counter B is selected by the two customers. Find the joint probability distribution of X_1 and X_2. Find the probability that one of the customers visits Counter B, given that one of the customers is known to have visited Counter A.

Solution

For convenience let us introduce X_3, defined as the number of customers visiting Counter C. Now, the event $(X_1 = 0$ and $X_2 = 0)$ is equivalent to the event $(X_1 = 0, X_2 = 0$ and $X_3 = 2)$. It follows that

$$\begin{aligned}
P(X_1 = 0, X_2 = 0) &= P(X_1 = 0, X_2 = 0, X_3 = 2) \\
&= P(\text{Customer I selects Counter C and} \\
&\quad\ \text{Customer II selects Counter C}) \\
&= P(\text{Customer I selects Counter C}) \\
&\quad\ P(\text{Customer II selects Counter C}) \\
&= \frac{1}{3} \cdot \frac{1}{3} = \frac{1}{9},
\end{aligned}$$

since customer choices are independent and each customer makes a random selection from among the three available counters.

It is slightly more complicated to calculate $P(X_1 = 1, X_2 = 0) = P(X_1 = 1, X_2 = 0, X_3 = 1)$. In this event Customer I could select Counter A and Customer II

Table 2.3   Joint Distribution of X_1 and X_2 for Example 2.9

X_2 \ X_1	0	1	2	Marginal Probabilities for X_2
0	1/9	2/9	1/9	4/9
1	2/9	2/9	0	4/9
2	1/9	0	0	1/9
Marginal Probabilities for X_1	4/9	4/9	1/9	1

Counter C, or I could select C and II could select A. Thus,

$$P(X_1 = 1, X_2 = 0) = P(\text{I selects A})P(\text{II selects C})$$
$$+ P(\text{I selects C})P(\text{II selects A})$$

$$= \frac{1}{3} \cdot \frac{1}{3} + \frac{1}{3} \cdot \frac{1}{3} = \frac{2}{9}.$$

Similar arguments will allow one to derive the results in Table 2.3. The second statement asks for

$$P(X_2 = 1 \,|\, X_1 = 1) = \frac{P(X_1 = 1, X_2 = 1)}{P(X_1 = 1)}$$

$$= \frac{2/9}{4/9} = \frac{1}{2}.$$

Does this answer of 1/2 agree with your intuition?   □

As we move to the continuous case, let us first quickly review the situation in one dimension. If $f(x)$ denotes the probability density function of a random variable X, then $f(x)$ represents a relative frequency curve and probabilities, such as $P(a \leq X \leq b)$, are represented as areas under this curve. That is,

$$P(a \leq X \leq b) = \int_a^b f(x)\,dx.$$

Now, suppose we are interested in the joint behavior of two continuous random variables, say X_1 and X_2, where X_1 and X_2 might, for example, represent the amounts of two different hydrocarbons found in an air sample taken for a pollution study. The relative frequency behavior of these two random variables can be modeled by a bivariate function, $f(x_1, x_2)$, which forms a probability, or relative frequency, surface in three dimensions. Figure 2.14 shows such a surface.

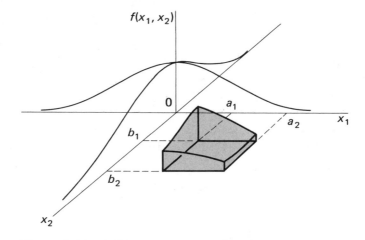

Figure 2.14   A Bivariate Density Function

The probability that X_1 lies in some interval and X_2 lies in another interval is then represented as a volume under this surface. Thus,

$$P(a_1 \leq X_1 \leq a_2, b_1 \leq X_2 \leq b_2) = \int_{b_1}^{b_2} \int_{a_1}^{a_2} f(x_1, x_2)\, dx_1\, dx_2.$$

Note that the above integral simply gives the volume under the surface and over the shaded region in Figure 2.14.

We will illustrate the actual computations involved in such a bivariate problem with a very simple example.

EXAMPLE 2.13

A certain process for producing an industrial chemical yields a product containing two predominant types of impurities. For a certain volume of sample from this process, let X_1 denote the proportion of impurities in the sample and let X_2 denote the proportion of type I impurity among all impurities found. Suppose the joint distribution of X_1 and X_2, after investigation of many such samples, can be adequately modeled by the following function:

$$f(x_1, x_2) = \begin{cases} 2(1 - x_1), & 0 \leq x_1 \leq 1, 0 \leq x_2 \leq 1 \\ 0, & \text{elsewhere.} \end{cases}$$

This function graphs as the surface given in Figure 2.15. Calculate the probability that X_1 is less than 0.5 and that X_2 is between 0.4 and 0.7.

Solution   From the preceding discussion, we see that

$$P(0 \leq x_1 \leq 0.5, 0.4 \leq x_2 \leq 0.7) = \int_{0.4}^{0.7} \int_{0}^{0.5} 2(1 - x_1)\, dx_1\, dx_2$$

$$= \int_{0.4}^{0.7} \left[-(1 - x_1)^2\right]_{0}^{0.5} dx_2$$

$$= \int_{0.4}^{0.7} (0.75)\, dx_2$$

$$= 0.75(0.7 - 0.4) = 0.75(0.3) = 0.225$$

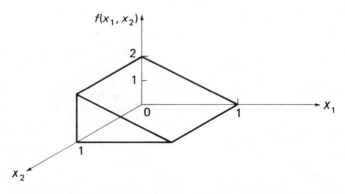

Figure 2.15   Probability Density Function for Example 2.13

Thus, the fraction of such samples having less than 50% impurities and a relative proportion of type I impurities between 40% and 70% is 0.225.   ☐

Just as the univariate, or marginal, probabilities were computed by summing over rows or columns in the discrete case, the univariate density function for X_1 in the continuous case can be found by integrating ("summing") over values of X_2. Thus, the *marginal density function* of X_1, $f_1(x_1)$, is given by

$$f_1(x_1) = \int_{-\infty}^{\infty} f(x_1, x_2)\, dx_2.$$

Similarly, the marginal density function of X_2, $f_2(x_2)$, is given by

$$f_2(x_2) = \int_{-\infty}^{\infty} f(x_1, x_2)\, dx_1.$$

EXAMPLE 2.14

For Example 2.13, find the marginal probability density functions for X_1 and X_2.

Solution   Let's first try to visualize what the answers should look like, before going through the integration. To find $f_1(x_1)$ we are to accumulate all probabilities in the x_2 direction. Look at Figure 2.15 and think of forcing the wedge-shaped figure back onto the $(x_1, f(x_1, x_2))$ plane. Then, much more probability mass will build up toward the zero point of the x_1-axis than toward the unity point. In other words, the function $f_1(x_1)$ should be high at zero and low at one. Formally,

$$\begin{aligned}
f_1(x_1) &= \int_{-\infty}^{\infty} f(x_1, x_2)\, dx_2 \\
&= \int_{0}^{1} 2(1 - x_1)\, dx_2 \\
&= 2(1 - x_1), \qquad 0 \le x_1 \le 1.
\end{aligned}$$

This function graphs as in Figure 2.16. Note that our conjecture is, indeed, true. Thinking of how $f_2(x_2)$ should look geometrically, suppose the wedge of Figure 2.15 is forced back onto the $(x_2, f(x_1, x_2))$ plane. Then, the probability mass should

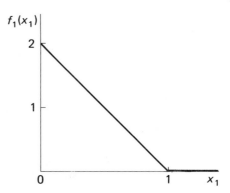

Figure 2.16   Probability Density
Function $f_1(x_1)$ for Example 2.14

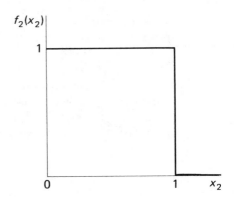

Figure 2.17 Probability Density
Function $f_2(x_2)$ for Example 2.14.

accumulate equally all along the $(0, 1)$ interval on the x_2-axis. Mathematically,

$$f_2(x_2) = \int_{-\infty}^{\infty} f(x_1, x_2)\, dx_1$$

$$= \int_0^1 2(1 - x_1)\, dx_1$$

$$= \left[-(1 - x_1)^2\right]_0^1 = 1, \qquad 0 \le x_2 \le 1$$

and again our conjecture is verified, as seen in Figure 2.17. □

As another (and somewhat more complicated) example, consider the following.

EXAMPLE 2.15

Gasoline is to be stocked in a bulk tank once each week and then sold to customers. Let X_1 denote the proportion of the tank that is stocked on a particular week and let X_2 denote the proportion of the tank that is sold in that same week. Due to limited supplies, X_1 is not fixed in advance, but varies from week to week. Suppose a study of many weeks shows the joint relative frequency behavior of

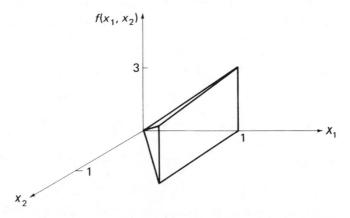

Figure 2.18   The Joint Density Function for Example 2.15.

X_1 and X_2 to be such that the following density function provides an adequate model:

$$f(x_1, x_2) = 3x_1, \qquad 0 \le x_2 \le x_1 \le 1,$$
$$= 0, \qquad \text{elsewhere.}$$

Note that X_2 must always be less than or equal to X_1. This density function is graphed in Figure 2.18. Find the probability that X_2 will be between 0.2 and 0.4 for a given week.

Solution   The question refers to the marginal behavior of X_2. Thus, it is necessary to find

$$f_2(x_2) = \int_{-\infty}^{\infty} f(x_1, x_2)\, dx_1$$

$$= \int_{x_2}^{1} 3x_1\, dx_1 = \left. \frac{3}{2} x_1^2 \right]_{x_2}^{1}$$

$$= \frac{3}{2}(1 - x_2^2), \qquad 0 \le x_2 \le 1.$$

It follows directly that

$$P(0.2 \le X_2 \le 0.4) = \int_{0.2}^{0.4} \frac{3}{2}(1 - x_2^2)\, dx_2$$

$$= \left. \frac{3}{2}\left(x_2 - \frac{x_2^3}{3} \right) \right]_{0.2}^{0.4}$$

$$= \frac{3}{2}\left\{ \left[0.4 - \frac{(0.4)^3}{3} \right] - \left[0.2 - \frac{(0.2)^3}{3} \right] \right\}$$

$$= 0.272$$

Note that the marginal density of X_2 graphs as a function that is high at $x_2 = 0$ and then tends to zero as x_2 tends to one. Does this agree with your intuition after looking at Figure 2.18?   □

Recall that in the bivariate discrete case, the conditional probabilities for X_1 for a given X_2 were found by fixing attention on the particular row in which $X_2 = x_2$, and then looking at the relative probabilities within that row. That is, the individual cell probabilities were divided by the marginal total for that row in order to obtain conditional probabilities.

In the bivariate continuous case, the form of the probability density function representing the conditional behavior of X_1 for a given value of X_2 is found by slicing through the joint density in the x_1 direction at the particular value of X_2. This function then has to be weighted by the marginal density function for X_2 at that point. We will look at a specific example before giving the general definition of conditional density functions.

EXAMPLE 2.16

Refer to the joint density function of Example 2.15. Find the conditional probability that X_2 is less than .2 given that X_1 was known to be 0.5.

Solution

Slicing through $f(x_1, x_2)$ in the x_2 direction at $x_1 = 0.5$ yields

$$f(0.5, x_2) = 3(0.5) = 1.5, \qquad 0 \le x_2 \le 0.5.$$

Thus, the conditional behavior of X_2 for a given X_1 of 0.5 is constant over the interval $(0, 0.5)$. The marginal value of $f(x_1)$ at $x_1 = 0.5$ is obtained as follows:

$$f(x_1) = \int_{-\infty}^{\infty} f(x_1, x_2)\, dx_2$$

$$= \int_0^{x_1} 3x_1\, dx_2$$

$$= 3x_1^2, \qquad 0 \le x_1 \le 1,$$

$$f_1(0.5) = 3(0.5)^2 = 0.75.$$

Upon dividing, we see that the conditional behavior of X_2 for a given X_1 of 0.5 is represented by the function

$$f(x_2 | x_1 = 0.5) = \frac{f(0.5, x_2)}{f_1(0.5)}$$

$$= \frac{1.5}{0.75} = 2, \qquad 0 < x_2 < 0.5.$$

This function has all the properties of a probability density function, and can be used to evaluate

$$P(X_2 < 0.2 | X_1 = 0.5) = \int_0^{0.2} f(x_2 | x_1 = 0.5)\, dx_2$$

$$= \int_0^{0.2} 2\, dx_2 = 0.2(2) = 0.4.$$

That is, among all weeks in which the tank was half full immediately after stocking, sales amounted to less than 20% of the tank 40% of the time. □

We see that the above manipulations used to obtain conditional density functions in the continuous case are analogous to those used to obtain conditional probabilities in the discrete case, except that integrals are used in place of sums. In general, the conditional probability density function for X_1 given X_2 is

$$f(x_1 | x_2) = \frac{f(x_1, x_2)}{f_2(x_2)}, \qquad \text{provided } f_2(x_2) > 0,$$

and for X_2 given X_1 is

$$f(x_2 | x_1) = \frac{f(x_1, x_2)}{f_1(x_1)}, \qquad \text{provided } f_1(x_1) > 0.$$

Before defining independent random variables, we will recall once again that two events, A and B, are independent if $P(AB) = P(A)P(B)$. Somewhat analogously, two discrete random variables are *independent* if

$$P(X_1 = x_1, X_2 = x_2) = P(X_1 = x_1)P(X_2 = x_2)$$

for all real numbers x_1 and x_2. A similar idea carries over to the continuous case.

DEFINITION 2.12   Discrete random variables X_1 and X_2 are said to be **independent** if

$$P(X_1 = x_1, X_2 = x_2) = P(X_1 = x_1)P(X_2 = x_2)$$

for all real numbers x_1 and x_2.

Continuous random variables X_1 and X_2 are said to be **independent** if

$$f(x_1, x_2) = f_1(x_1)f_2(x_2)$$

for all real numbers x_1 and x_2.

The concepts of joint probability density functions and independence extend immediately to n random variables, where n is any finite positive integer. The n random variables $X_1, X_2, \ldots, X_n$ are said to be independent if their joint density function, $f(x_1, \ldots, x_n)$ is given by

$$f(x_1, \ldots, x_n) = f_1(x_1)f_2(x_2) \cdots f_n(x_n)$$

for all real numbers $x_1, x_2, \ldots, x_n$.

EXAMPLE 2.17

Show that the random variables having the joint distribution of Table 2.2 are not independent.

Solution   It is only necessary to check one entry in the table. We see that $P(X_1 = 0, X_2 = 0) = 0.6$, whereas $P(X_1 = 0) = 0.8$ and $P(X_2 = 0) = 0.8$. Since

$$P(X_1 = 0, X_2 = 0) \neq P(X_1 = 0)P(X_2 = 0)$$

the random variables cannot be independent.   □

EXAMPLE 2.18

Show that the random variables in Example 2.13 are independent.

Solution   Here

$$f(x_1, x_2) = 2(1 - x_1), \qquad 0 \le x_1 \le 1, 0 \le x_2 \le 1,$$
$$= 0, \qquad \text{elsewhere.}$$

We saw in Example 2.14 that

$$f_1(x_1) = 2(1 - x_1), \qquad 0 \le x_1 \le 1$$

and

$$f_2(x_2) = 1, \qquad 0 \le x_2 \le 1.$$

Thus, $f(x_1, x_2) = f_1(x_1)f_2(x_2)$, for all real numbers x_1 and x_2, and X_1 and X_2 are independent random variables.   □

Exercises

2.25   Refer to Exercise 2.4, in which two construction contracts are to be assigned to one or more of three firms. Numbering the firms I, II, and III, let X_1 be the number of contracts assigned to firm I and X_2 the number assigned to firm II.
(a) Find the joint probability distribution for X_1 and X_2.
(b) Find the marginal probability distribution for X_1.
(c) Find $P(X_1 = 1 | X_2 = 1)$.

2.26   A radioactive particle is randomly located in a square area with sides one unit in length. Let X_1 and X_2 denote the coordinates of the particle. Since the particle is equally likely to fall in any subarea of a fixed size, a reasonable model for (X_1, X_2) is given by

$$f(x_1, x_2) = \begin{cases} 1, & 0 \le x_1 \le 1, 0 \le x_2 \le 1, \\ 0, & \text{elsewhere.} \end{cases}$$

(a) Sketch the probability density surface.
(b) Find $P(X_1 \le 0.2, X_2 \le 0.4)$.
(c) Find $P(0.1 \le X_1 \le 0.3, X_2 > 0.4)$.

2.27   A group of 9 executives of a certain firm contain 4 who are married, 3 who are single, and 2 who are divorced. Three of the executives are to be selected for promotion. Let X_1 denote the number of married executives and X_2 the number of single executives among the three selected for promotion. Assuming that the three are randomly selected from the nine available, find the joint probability distribution for X_1 and X_2.

2.28   An environmental engineer measures the amount (by weight) of particulate pollution in air samples (of a certain volume) collected over the smoke-stack of a coal-operated power plant. Let X_1 denote the amount of pollutant per sample when a certain cleaning device on the stack is *not* operating, and X_2 the amount of pollutant per sample when the cleaning device is operating, under similar environmental conditions. It is observed that X_1 is always greater than $2X_2$, and the relative frequency behavior of (X_1, X_2)

can be modeled by

$$f(x_1, x_2) = \begin{cases} k, & 0 \leq x_1 \leq 2, 0 \leq x_2 \leq 1, 2x_2 \leq x_1, \\ 0, & \text{elsewhere.} \end{cases}$$

(That is, X_1 and X_2 are randomly distributed over the region inside the triangle bounded by $x_1 = 2$, $x_2 = 0$ and $2x_2 = x_1$.)
(a) Find the value of k that makes this a probability density function.
(b) Find $P(X_1 \geq 3X_2)$. (That is, find the probability that the cleaning device will reduce the amount of pollutant by one third or more.)

2.29   Refer to Exercise 2.26.
(a) Find the marginal density function for X_1.
(b) Find $P(X_1 \leq 0.5)$.
(c) Are X_1 and X_2 independent?

2.30   Refer to Exercise 2.28.
(a) Find the marginal density function for X_2.
(b) Find $P(X_2 \leq 0.4)$.
(c) Are X_1 and X_2 independent?

2.31   Let X_1 and X_2 denote the proportion of two different chemicals found in a sample mixture of chemicals used as an insecticide. Suppose X_1 and X_2 have joint probability density given by

$$f(x_1, x_2) = \begin{cases} 2, & 0 \leq x_1 \leq 1, 0 \leq x_2 \leq 1, 0 \leq x_1 + x_2 \leq 1. \\ 0, & \text{elsewhere.} \end{cases}$$

(Note that $X_1 + X_2$ must be less than unity since the random variables denote proportions within the same sample.)
(a) Find $P(X_1 \leq 3/4, X_2 \leq 3/4)$.
(b) Find $P(X_1 \leq 1/2, X_2 \leq 1/2)$.
(c) Find $P(X_1 \leq 1/2 | X_2 \leq 1/2)$.

2.32   Refer to Exercise 2.31.
(a) Find the marginal density functions for X_1 and X_2.
(b) Are X_1 and X_2 independent?

2.33   Let X_1 and X_2 denote the proportions of time, out of one work week, that employees I and II, respectively, actually spend on performing their assigned tasks. The joint relative frequency behavior of X_1 and X_2 is modeled by the probability density function

$$f(x_1, x_2) = \begin{cases} x_1 + x_2, & 0 \leq x_1 \leq 1, 0 \leq x_2 \leq 1 \\ 0, & \text{elsewhere.} \end{cases}$$

(a) Find $P(X_1 < 1/2, X_2 > 1/4)$.
(b) Find $P(X_1 + X_2 \leq 1)$.
(c) Are X_1 and X_2 independent.

2.34   An electronic surveillance system has one of each of two different types of components in joint operations. Letting X_1 and X_2 denote the random lifelengths of the components of type I and type II, respectively, the joint probability density function is given by

$$f(x_1, x_2) = \begin{cases} (1/8)x_1 e^{-(x_1+x_2)/2}, & x_1 > 0, x_2 > 0, \\ 0, & \text{elsewhere.} \end{cases}$$

(Measurements are in hundreds of hours.)
(a) Are X_1 and X_2 independent?
(b) Find $P(X_1 > 1, X_2 > 1)$.

2.35   Refer to Exercise 2.28.
(a) Find the conditional density function for X_2 for an arbitrary given value of X_1.
(b) Find $P(X_2 \leq 1/4 \mid X_1 = 1)$.

2.36   Refer to Exercise 2.31.
(a) Find the conditional density function for X_1 if X_2 is fixed at x_2.
(b) Find $P(X_1 > 1/2 \mid X_2 = 1/4)$.

2.37   Refer to Exercise 2.33. Find the probability that employee I spends more than 75% of the week on his assigned task, given that employee II spends exactly 50% of the work week on his assigned task.

2.8   *Mathematical Expectation*

It is sometimes cumbersome or inconvenient to deal with an entire probability distribution for a random variable, and hence, we would like to be able to condense some of the key information on this distribution into a few constants. One such constant is the mean, or *expected value*, of the random variable in question. We will illustrate how to obtain an expected value before giving a formal definition.

Suppose that the probability of a certain machine breaking down on any one day is 0.1. Assume that it takes longer than a day to repair a breakdown, so that no more than one breakdown can occur per day. Let X denote the number of breakdowns per day. Then the probability distribution for X is

$$P(X = 0) = p(0) = 0.9, \qquad P(X = 1) = p(1) = 0.1.$$

If this machine is viewed over a large number of days, what is the mean value (or average value) of X? Since probability has a relative frequency interpretation, we know that X should be 0 on 90% of the days and 1 on the other 10%. Thus, the mean value of X is given by

$$0p(0) + 1p(1) = 0(0.9) + 1(0.1) = 0.1.$$

The machine averages 0.1 of a breakdown per day. Certainly, on any given day there are either 0 or 1 breakdowns, but over a ten-day period we would expect to see exactly one breakdown. We refer to the mean value of X as the *expected value*, and are led to the following definition.

DEFINITION 2.13   The **expected value** of a discrete random variable
X having probability distribution $p(x)$ is given by

$$E(X) = \sum_x xp(x).$$

(The sum is over all values of x for which $p(x) > 0$.)
We sometimes use the notation

$$E(X) = \mu.$$

Occasionally we will be interested in expected values for functions of
random variables. For example, suppose it costs \$50 to repair a breakdown for
the machine under discussion. Then, $50X$ represents the daily repair cost. The
expected daily repair cost is given by

$$50(0)p(0) + 50(1)p(1) = 50(0)(0.9) + 50(1)(0.1) = 5.$$

Thus, \$5 per day should be budgeted to meet éxpected repair costs, although on any
one day the cost is going to be either zero or fifty dollars.
   Again, this idea generalizes to the following definition.

DEFINITION 2.14   If X is a discrete random variable with probability
distribution $p(x)$ and if $g(x)$ is any real-valued function of X, then

$$E[g(X)] = \sum_x g(x)p(x).$$

The expected value, or mean, of a random variable measures, in some
sense, the "center" of the probability distribution. Another constant that is very
useful in assessing the behavior of a random variable is the *variance*, which measures
the spread of the probability mass to either side of the mean.

DEFINITION 2.15   The **variance** of a random variable X with expected
value μ is given by

$$V(X) = E(X - \mu)^2.$$

We sometimes use the notation

$$E(X - \mu)^2 = \sigma^2.$$

The smallest value σ^2 can assume is zero, and that would occur if all the
probability was at a single point (that is, X takes on a constant value with probability one). The variance will become larger as the points with positive probability
spread out more. We will see numerous statistical uses of the variance in later
chapters.

Observe that the variance squares the units in which we are measuring. A measure of variation that maintains the original units is the *standard deviation*.

DEFINITION 2.16   The **standard deviation** of a random variable X is the square root of the variance, given by

$$\sigma = \sqrt{\sigma^2} = \sqrt{E(X - \mu)^2}.$$

We illustrate the calculation of expected values in the following examples.

EXAMPLE 2.19

The manager of a stockroom in a factory knows from his study of records that the daily demand (number of times used) for a certain tool has the following probability distribution:

Demand	0	1	2
Probability	0.1	0.5	0.4

(That is, 50% of the daily records show that the tool was used one time.) If X denotes the daily demand, find $E(X)$ and $V(X)$.

Solution   From Definition 2.13, we see that

$$E(X) = \sum_x xp(x)$$

$$= 0(0.1) + 1(0.5) + 2(0.4) = 1.3,$$

that is, the tool is used an average of 1.3 times per day.
From Definition 2.15 we see that

$$V(X) = E(X - \mu)^2$$
$$= \sum_x (x - \mu)^2 p(x)$$
$$= (0 - 1.3)^2(0.1) + (1 - 1.3)^2(0.5) + (2 - 1.3)^2(0.4)$$
$$= (1.69)(0.1) + (0.09)(0.5) + (0.49)(0.4)$$
$$= 0.410. \quad \square$$

Our work in manipulating expected values is greatly facilitated by making use of the two results of Theorem 2.1.

THEOREM 2.1

For any random variable X and constants a and b,

(i) $E(aX + b) = aE(X) + b$

and

(ii) $V(aX + b) = a^2 V(X).$

We sketch a proof of this theorem for a discrete random variable X having probability distribution given by $p(x)$. By Definition 2.13,

$$E(aX + b) = \sum_x (ax + b)p(x)$$
$$= \sum_x [(ax)p(x) + bp(x)]$$
$$= \sum_x axp(x) + \sum_x bp(x)$$
$$= a \sum_x xp(x) + b \sum_x p(x)$$
$$= aE(X) + b.$$

(Note that $\sum_x p(x)$ must equal unity.) Also, by Definition 2.15,

$$V(aX + b) = E[(aX + b) - E(aX + b)]^2$$
$$= E[aX + b - (aE(X) + b)]^2$$
$$= E[aX - aE(X)]^2$$
$$= E[a^2(X - E(X))^2]$$
$$= a^2 E[X - E(X)]^2$$
$$= a^2 V(X).$$

We illustrate the use of these results in the following example.

EXAMPLE 2.20

Refer to Example 2.19. Suppose it costs the factory $10 each time the tool is used. Find the mean and variance of the daily costs for use of this tool.

Solution   Recall that the X of Example 2.19 is the daily demand. The daily cost of using this tool is then $10X$. We have, by Theorem 2.1,

$$E(10X) = 10E(X) = 10(1.3)$$
$$= 13.$$

The factory should budget $13 per day to cover the cost of using the tool.
Also, by Theorem 2.1,

$$V(10X) = (10)^2 V(X) = 100(0.410)$$
$$= 41.$$

(We will make use of this value in a later example.)   ☐

Theorem 2.1 leads us to a more efficient computational formula for a variance, as given in Theorem 2.2.

THEOREM 2.2

If X is a random variable with mean μ, then

$$V(X) = E(X^2) - \mu^2.$$

The proof is as follows. Starting with the definition of variance, we have

$$
\begin{aligned}
V(X) = E(X - \mu)^2 &= E(X^2 - 2X\mu + \mu^2) \\
&= E(X^2) - E(2X\mu) + E(\mu^2) \\
&= E(X^2) - 2\mu E(X) + \mu^2 \\
&= E(X^2) - 2\mu^2 + \mu^2 \\
&= E(X^2) - \mu^2.
\end{aligned}
$$

EXAMPLE 2.21

Use the result of Theorem 2.2 to compute the variance of X as given in Example 2.19.

Solution   In Example 2.19, X has probability distribution given by

x	0	1	2
$p(x)$	0.1	0.5	0.4

and we saw that $E(X) = 1.3$.
   Now,

$$
\begin{aligned}
E(X^2) = \sum_x x^2 p(x) &\\
&= (0)^2(0.1) + (1)^2(0.5) + (2)^2(0.4) \\
&= 0 + 0.5 + 1.6 \\
&= 2.1.
\end{aligned}
$$

By Theorem 2.2,

$$
\begin{aligned}
V(X) = E(X^2) - \mu^2 &\\
&= 2.1 - (1.3)^2 = 0.41. \quad \square
\end{aligned}
$$

For a continuous random variable X with probability density function $f(x)$, the expected value can be computed in a manner analogous to the discrete case, except that the summation is replaced by an integral. We summarize in Definition 2.17.

DEFINITION 2.17   The **expected value** of a continuous random variable X having probability density function $f(x)$ is given by

$$E(X) = \int_{-\infty}^{\infty} xf(x)\,dx.$$

If $g(X)$ is any real-valued function of X, then

$$E[g(X)] = \int_{-\infty}^{\infty} g(x)f(x)\,dx.$$

The definitions of variance and standard deviation and the properties given in Theorems 2.1 and 2.2 hold for the continuous case as stated above.

We illustrate the expectations of continuous random variables in the following examples.

EXAMPLE 2.22

For a certain industrial machine, let X denote the percentage of time out of a forty-hour work week that the machine is actually in use. Suppose X has a probability density function given by

$$f(x) = \begin{cases} 3x^2, & 0 \le x \le 1, \\ 0, & \text{elsewhere.} \end{cases}$$

Find the mean and variance of X.

Solution   From Definition 2.17 we have

$$\begin{aligned}
E(X) &= \int_{-\infty}^{\infty} xf(x)\,dx \\
&= \int_0^1 x(3x^2)\,dx \\
&= \int_0^1 3x^3\,dx \\
&= 3\left[\frac{x^4}{4}\right]_0^1 = \frac{3}{4} = 0.75.
\end{aligned}$$

Thus, on the average, the machine is in use 75% of the time.

To compute $V(X)$, we first find $E(X^2)$ by

$$\begin{aligned}
E(X^2) &= \int_{-\infty}^{\infty} x^2 f(x)\,dx \\
&= \int_0^1 x^2(3x^2)\,dx \\
&= \int_0^1 3x^4\,dx \\
&= 3\left[\frac{x^5}{5}\right]_0^1 = \frac{3}{5} = 0.60.
\end{aligned}$$

By the result of Theorem 2.2,

$$V(X) = E(X^2) - \mu^2$$
$$= 0.60 - (0.75)^2$$
$$= 0.60 - 0.5625 = 0.0375. \quad \square$$

EXAMPLE 2.23
　　　　Refer to Example 2.11. The weekly demand, X, for kerosene has a density function given by

$$f(x) = \begin{cases} x, & 0 \le x \le 1 \\ 1/2, & 1 < x \le 2 \\ 0, & \text{elsewhere.} \end{cases}$$

Find the expected weekly demand.

Solution　　　　Using Definition 2.17 to find $E(X)$, we must now carefully observe that $f(x)$ has two different nonzero forms over two disjoint regions. Thus,

$$E(X) = \int_{-\infty}^{\infty} xf(x)\, dx$$
$$= \int_{0}^{1} x(x)\, dx + \int_{1}^{2} x(1/2)\, dx$$
$$= \int_{0}^{1} x^2\, dx + \frac{1}{2} \int_{1}^{2} x\, dx$$
$$= \frac{x^3}{3}\bigg]_{0}^{1} + \frac{1}{2}\left[\frac{x^2}{2}\right]_{1}^{2}$$
$$= 1/3 + 1/2[2 - 1/2]$$
$$= \frac{1}{3} + \frac{3}{4} = \frac{13}{12} = 1.08.$$

That is, the expected weekly demand is for 108 gallons.　　$\square$

　　　　As we have seen in Section 2.6, we often encounter problems that involve more than one random variable. We may be interested in the lifelengths of five different electronic components within the same system or three different strength test measurements on the same section of cable.
　　　　Given that we have n random variables, $X_1, \ldots, X_n$, of interest in a particular problem, we may frequently form linear combinations of the form $\sum_{i=1}^{n} a_i X_i$ for constants a_i. For example, the average of n lifelength measurements would be one such linear combination. The following theorem, which we state without proof, shows us how to find means and variances of linear functions under certain conditions.

THEOREM 2.3

Let $X_1, \ldots, X_n$ denote random variables and let

$$Y = \sum_{i=1}^{n} a_i X_i$$

for known constants $a_1, \ldots, a_n$. Then

$$E(Y) = \sum_{i=1}^{n} a_i E(X_i)$$

and, if $X_1, \ldots, X_n$ are independent,

$$V(Y) = \sum_{i=1}^{n} a_i^2 V(X_i).$$

The next example illustrates the use of this result.

EXAMPLE 2.24

A firm purchases two types of industrial chemicals. The amount of type I chemical purchased per week, X_1, has $E(X_1) = 40$ gallons with $V(X_1) = 4$. The amount of type II chemical purchased, X_2, has $E(X_2) = 65$ gallons with $V(X_2) = 8$. Type I chemical costs \$3 per gallon while type II chemical costs \$5 per gallon. Find the mean and variance of the total weekly amount spent for these types of chemicals, assuming X_1 and X_2 are independent.

Solution   The dollar amount spent per week is given by

$$Y = 3X_1 + 5X_2.$$

From Theorem 2.3,

$$\begin{aligned} E(Y) &= 3E(X_1) + 5E(X_2) \\ &= 3(40) + 5(65) \\ &= 445, \end{aligned}$$

and

$$\begin{aligned} V(Y) &= (3)^2 V(X_1) + (5)^2 V(X_2) \\ &= 9(4) + 25(8) \\ &= 236. \end{aligned}$$

The firm can expect to spend \$445 per week on chemicals.   □

EXAMPLE 2.25

Refer to Example 2.15. With X_1 denoting the amount of gasoline stocked in a week and X_2 the amount sold, $X_1 - X_2$ will represent the amount left over at the end of the week. Find $E(X_1 - X_2)$.

Solution   The joint density function of X_1 and X_2 was given to be

$$f(x_1, x_2) = \begin{cases} 3x_1, & 0 \le x_2 \le x_1 \le 1 \\ 0, & \text{elsewhere.} \end{cases}$$

The marginal density of X_1 is found to be

$$f_1(x_1) = \begin{cases} 3x_1^2, & 0 \le x_1 \le 1 \\ 0, & \text{elsewhere.} \end{cases}$$

Thus,

$$E(X_1) = \int_0^1 x_1(3x_1^2)\,dx,$$

$$= 3\left[\frac{x_1^4}{4}\right]_0^1 = \frac{3}{4}.$$

In Example 2.12, the marginal density of X_2 is found to be

$$f_2(x_2) = \begin{cases} 3/2(1 - x_2^2), & 0 \le x_2 \le 1. \\ 0, & \text{elsewhere.} \end{cases}$$

Thus,

$$E(X_2) = \int_0^1 (x_2)\frac{3}{2}(1 - x_2^2)\,dx_2$$

$$= \frac{3}{2}\int_0^1 (x_2 - x_2^3)\,dx_2$$

$$= \frac{3}{2}\left\{\left[\frac{x_2^2}{2}\right]_0^1 - \left[\frac{x_2^4}{4}\right]_0^1\right\}$$

$$= \frac{3}{2}\left\{\frac{1}{2} - \frac{1}{4}\right\} = \frac{3}{8}.$$

It then follows from Theorem 2.3 that

$$E(X_1 - X_2) = E(X_1) - E(X_2)$$

$$= \frac{3}{4} - \frac{3}{8} = \frac{3}{8}.$$

That is, the amount left at the end of a week will be 3/8ths of a tank, on the average. □

One other type of function comes up repeatedly in applications: namely, the product. Theorem 2.4 gives a result in finding expectations of products of *independent* random variables.

THEOREM 2.4

Let X_1 and X_2 be independent random variables. If $g(X_1)$ is a function of X_1 alone and $h(X_2)$ is a function of X_2 alone, then

$$E[g(X_1)h(X_2)] = E[g(X_1)]E[h(X_2)].$$

We relegate the proof of this result to an exercise.

EXAMPLE 2.26

Refer to Example 2.13. In that example, X_1 is the proportion of impurities in chemical samples and X_2 is the proportion of type I impurities among all impurities found. The joint density for X_1 and X_2 is

$$f(x_1, x_2) = \begin{cases} 2(1 - x_1), & 0 \le x_1 \le 1, 0 \le x_2 \le 1 \\ 0, & \text{elsewhere.} \end{cases}$$

The random variable $X_1 X_2$ represents the proportion of type I impurities in the samples. Find $E(X_1 X_2)$.

Solution   For this joint density function

$$f_1(x_1) = \begin{cases} 2(1 - x_1), & 0 \le x_1 \le 1 \\ 0, & \text{elsewhere} \end{cases}$$

and

$$f_2(x_2) = \begin{cases} 1, & 0 \le x_2 \le 1 \\ 0, & \text{elsewhere.} \end{cases}$$

It follows that X_1 and X_2 are independent, since

$$f(x_1, x_2) = f_1(x_1)f_2(x_2).$$

Also,

$$
\begin{aligned}
E(X_1) &= \int_0^1 x_1 2(1 - x_1)\, dx_1 \\
&= 2 \int_0^1 (x_1 - x_1^2)\, dx_1 \\
&= 2 \left\{ \left[\frac{x_1^2}{2} \right]_0^1 - \left[\frac{x_1^3}{3} \right]_0^1 \right\} \\
&= 2 \left\{ \frac{1}{2} - \frac{1}{3} \right\} = \frac{1}{3}
\end{aligned}
$$

and

$$E(X_2) = \int_0^1 x_2\, dx_2 = \frac{1}{2}.$$

From Theorem 2.4, with $g(X_1) = X_1$ and $h(X_2) = X_2$, it follows that

$$E(X_1X_2) = E(X_1)E(X_2)$$

$$= \frac{1}{3}\left(\frac{1}{2}\right) = \frac{1}{6},$$

and 1/6 of the sample value should be due to impurities of type I, on the average. □

Exercises

2.38 Refer to Exercise 2.19.
    (a) Find $E(X)$.   (b) Find $V(X)$.

2.39 Refer to Exercise 2.20. Find the expected number of times entrance I is used.

2.40 Refer to Exercise 2.21. Find the expected temperature at which the switch turns on.

2.41 Refer to Exercise 2.22. Find the expected number of closed paths from a to b when the temperature reaches $59.5°$.

2.42 Refer to Exercise 2.23.
    (a) Find $E(X)$ and $V(X)$.
    (b) For the machine under consideration, the profit, Y, for a week is given by $Y = 200X - 60$. Find $E(Y)$ and $V(Y)$.

2.43 Refer to Exercise 2.25. If each contract has a potential profit of $90,000, find the expected potential profit for firm I.

2.44 Refer to Exercise 2.28. The random variable $X_1 - X_2$ represents the amount by which the weight of pollutant can be reduced by using the cleaning device.
    (a) Find $E(X_1 - X_2)$.   (b) Find $V(X_1 - X_2)$.

2.45 Refer to Exercise 2.31. Suppose that the market value of a sample of the insecticide is given by

$$Y = 3X_1 + 2X_2.$$

(a) Find $E(Y)$.   (b) Find $V(Y)$.

2.46 Refer to Exercise 2.33. Employee I has a higher productivity rating than Employee II, and a measure of the total productivity of the two employees is $30X_1 + 25X_2$. Find the expected value and variance of this measure of productivity.

2.47 Refer to Exercise 2.34. The cost, C, of replacing the two components depends upon their lifelengths at failure, and is given by

$$C = 50 + 2X_1 + 4X_2.$$

(a) Find $E(C)$.   (b) Find $V(C)$.

2.48   Prove Theorem 2.4 if X_1 and X_2 are continuous random variables with joint density function $f(x_1, x_2)$.

2.9 *Tchebysheff's Theorem*

We have computed means and variances for a number of probability distributions, and argued that these two quantities give us some useful information on the center and spread of the probability mass. Now, suppose we know only the mean and variance for a probability distribution. Can we say anything specific about probabilities for certain intervals? The answer is "yes" and one useful theorem on the relationship between mean, standard deviation, and relative frequency is due to Tchebysheff.

THEOREM 2.5   *Tchebysheff's Theorem*
Let X be a random variable with mean μ and variance σ^2. Then, for any positive k,

$$P(|X - \mu| \le k\sigma) \ge 1 - \frac{1}{k^2}.$$

The inequality in the statement of the theorem is equivalent to

$$P(\mu - k\sigma \le X \le \mu + k\sigma) \ge 1 - \frac{1}{k^2}.$$

To interpret this result let $k = 2$, for example. Then, the interval $\mu - 2\sigma$ to $\mu + 2\sigma$ must contain at least $1 - 1/k^2 = 1 - 1/4 = 3/4$ of the probability mass for this random variable. We give more specific illustrations in the following two examples.

EXAMPLE 2.27
The daily production of electric motors at a certain factory averaged 120 with a standard deviation of 10.
(a) What fraction of days will have a production level between 100 and 140?
(b) Find the shortest interval certain to contain at least 90% of the daily production levels.

Solution   (a) The interval 100 to 140 is $\mu - 2\sigma$ to $\mu + 2\sigma$, with $\mu = 120$ and $\sigma = 10$. Thus, $k = 2$,

$$1 - \frac{1}{k^2} = 1 - \frac{1}{4} = \frac{3}{4},$$

and at least 75% of the days will have total production in this interval.

(b) To find k we must set $(1 - 1/k^2)$ equal to 0.9 and solve for k. That is,

$$1 - \frac{1}{k^2} = 0.9,$$

$$\frac{1}{k^2} = 0.1,$$

$$k^2 = 10,$$

or

$$k = \sqrt{10} = 3.16.$$

The interval

$$\mu - 3.16\sigma \quad \text{to} \quad \mu + 3.16\sigma$$

or

$$120 - 3.16(10) \quad \text{to} \quad 120 + 3.16(10)$$

or

$$88.4 \text{ to } 151.6$$

will then contain at least 90% of the daily production levels.   □

EXAMPLE 2.28

Refer to Example 2.20. The daily cost for use of a certain tool had a mean of $13 and a variance of 41. How often will this cost exceed $30?

Solution   First we must find the distance between the mean and 30, in terms of the standard deviation of the distribution of costs. We have

$$\frac{30 - \mu}{\sqrt{\sigma^2}} = \frac{30 - 13}{\sqrt{41}} = \frac{17}{6.4} = 2.66,$$

or 30 is 2.66 standard deviations above the mean. Letting $k = 2.66$ in Theorem 2.5, we have that the interval

$$\mu - 2.66\sigma \quad \text{to} \quad \mu + 2.66\sigma$$

or

$$13 - 2.66(6.4) \quad \text{to} \quad 13 + 2.66(6.4),$$

or

$$-4 \quad \text{to} \quad 30$$

must contain at least

$$1 - \frac{1}{k^2} = 1 - \frac{1}{(2.66)^2} = 1 - 0.14 = 0.86$$

of the probability. Since the daily cost cannot be negative, at most 0.14 of the probability mass can exceed 30. Thus, the cost cannot exceed $30 more than 14% of the time.   □

EXAMPLE 2.29

Refer to Example 2.24. The weekly amount, Y, spent for chemicals has a mean of $445 and a variance of 236. Within what interval would these weekly costs for chemicals be expected to lie at least 75% of the time?

Solution   To find the shortest interval containing at least 75% of the probability mass for Y, we get

$$1 - \frac{1}{k^2} = 0.75,$$

which gives

$$\frac{1}{k^2} = 0.25,$$

$$k^2 = \frac{1}{0.25} = 4$$

or

$$k = 2.$$

Thus, the interval $\mu - 2\sigma$ to $\mu + 2\sigma$ will contain at least 75% of the probability. This interval is given by

$$445 - 2\sqrt{236}, \qquad 445 + 2\sqrt{236},$$
$$445 - 30.72, \qquad 445 + 30.72,$$

or

$$414.28, \qquad 475.72.   □$$

Exercises

2.49   Refer to Exercises 2.23 and 2.42. Find an interval in which the true profit figure will lie for at least 75% of the weeks under study.

2.50   Refer to Exercises 2.28 and 2.44. Find an interval in which $X_1 - X_2$ will lie with probability at least 0.90.

2.51   Refer to Exercises 2.33 and 2.46. Find an interval that will contain the productivity measurements for the two employees on at least 95% of the weeks observed.

2.52   Refer to Exercises 2.34 and 2.47. Would you expect the cost of replacement to exceed 100 very often? Why?

2.10   *Conclusion*

Probability theory is the basic building block in constructing models for outcomes of experiments when these outcomes vary from trial to trial. Most experiments result in outcomes that are given in terms of real numbers. Hence, we are most interested in random variables, which map experimental outcomes into real numbers. Almost all examples in future chapters are given in terms of random variables.

Both discrete and continuous random variables are widely used in practice. Some common discrete distributions are discussed in Chapter 3 and common continuous distributions are the subject of Chapter 4.

Throughout the remainder of this text, most of the discussions that involve joint distributions assume the random variables in question to be independent. This allows almost all of our probability work to be done in the univariate case. The most notable exception is the multinomial distribution of Chapter 3.

Supplementary Exercises

2.53   Of the persons arriving at a small airport, 60% fly on major airlines, 30% fly on privately owned airplanes and 10% fly on commercially owned airplanes not belonging to an airline. Of the persons arriving on major airlines, 50% are traveling for business reasons, while this figure is 60% for those arriving on private planes and 90% for those arriving on other commercially owned planes. For a person randomly selected from a group of arrivals, find the probability that
(a) the person is traveling on business.
(b) the person is traveling on business and on a private airplane.
(c) the person is traveling on business given that he arrived on a commercial airliner.
(d) the person arrived on a private plane given that he is traveling on business.

2.54   In testing private wells in a county for two kinds of impurities commonly found in drinking water, it was found that 20% of the wells had neither impurity, 40% had impurity A and 50% had impurity B. (Obviously, some wells had both impurities.) If a well is randomly chosen from those in the county, find the probability distribution for X, the number of impurities in the well.

2.55   Consider the system of water shown on p. 57, flowing through values from a to b. Valves 1, 2, 3, and 4 operate independently and each correctly opens on signal with probability 0.8. Find the probability distribution for Y, the number of paths open from a to b after the signal is given.

2.56   A merchant stocks a certain perishable item. He knows that on any given day he will have a demand for either 2, 3, or 4 of these items with prob-

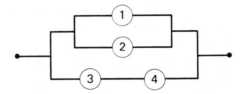

abilities $0.1, 0.4$, and 0.5 respectively. He buys the items for $1.00 each and sells them for $1.20 each. If any are left at the end of the day, they represent a total loss. How many items should the merchant stock so as to maximize his expected daily profit?

2.57   A retail grocer has a daily demand, X, for a certain food sold by the pound, such that X (measured in hundreds of pounds) has probability density function

$$f(x) = \begin{cases} 3x^2, & 0 \le x \le 1 \\ 0, & \text{elsewhere.} \end{cases}$$

(He cannot stock over 100 pounds.) The grocer wants to order $100k$ pounds of food on a certain day. He buys the food at 6 cents per pound and sells it at 10 cents per pound. What value of k will maximize his expected daily profit?

2.58   A coffee machine has a random amount X_2 in supply at the beginning of a day and dispenses a random amount X_1 during the day (measurements in gallons). It is not resupplied during the day. It has been observed that X_1 and X_2 can be modeled by the joint density function

$$f(x_1, x_2) = \begin{cases} \frac{1}{2}, & 0 \le x_1 \le x_2, 0 \le x_2 \le 2 \\ 0, & \text{elsewhere.} \end{cases}$$

Find the probability that less than 1/2 gallon is sold given that the machine contains more than 1 gallon at the start of the day.

2.59   A particular fast-food outlet is interested in the joint behavior of the random variables Y_1, defined as the total time between a customer's arrival at the store and his leaving the service window, and Y_2, the time that a customer waits in line before reaching the service window. Since Y_1 contains the time a customer waits in line, we must have $Y_1 \ge Y_2$. The relative frequency distribution of observed values of Y_1 and Y_2 can be modeled by the probability density function

$$f(y_1, y_2) = \begin{cases} e^{-y_1}, & 0 \le y_2 \le y_1 < \infty \\ 0, & \text{elsewhere.} \end{cases}$$

(a) Find $P(Y_1 < 2, Y_2 > 1)$
(b) Find $P(Y_1 \ge 2Y_2)$.
(c) Find $P(Y_1 - Y_2 \ge 1)$. (Note that $Y_1 - Y_2$ denotes the time spent at the service window.)
(d) Find the marginal density functions for Y_1 and Y_2.

2.60   Refer to Exercise 2.59. If a customer's total waiting time for service is known to be more than two minutes, find the probability that he waited less than one minute to be served.

2.61   Refer to Exercise 2.59. The random variable $Y_1 - Y_2$ represents the time spent at the service window.
(a) Find $E(Y_1 - Y_2)$.
(b) Find $V(Y_1 - Y_2)$.
(c) Is it highly likely that a customer would spend more than two minutes at the service window?

2.62   The lifelength, Y, for fuses of a certain type is modeled by the exponential distribution with

$$f(y) = \begin{cases} \frac{1}{3}e^{-y/3}, & y > 0, \\ 0, & \text{elsewhere.} \end{cases}$$

The measurements are in hundreds of hours.
(a) If two such fuses have independent lifelengths, Y_1 and Y_2, find their joint probability density function.
(b) One fuse in (a) is in a primary system and the other is in a backup system, which only comes into use if the primary system fails. The total effective lifelength of the two fuses is then $Y_1 + Y_2$. Find $P(Y_1 + Y_2 \le 1)$.

2.63   Refer to Exercise 2.62. Suppose three such fuses are operating independently in a system.
(a) Find the probability that exactly two of the three last longer than 500 hours.
(b) Find the probability that at least one of the three fails before 500 hours.

2.64   Refer to Exercise 2.58.
(a) Find the conditional density function for X_1 given a fixed value of X_2.
(b) Find the probability that less than 1/2 gallon is dispensed, given that the machine contained exactly one gallon at the start of the day.

2.65   Refer to Exercise 2.59. Suppose a customer spends a length of time y_1 at the store. Find the probability that this customer spends less than half of that time at the service window.

2.11   *Appendix: Combinatorial Rules Useful in Probability (Optional)*

The multiplication rule of Section 2.3 is basic to solving many probability problems involving experiments with more than one trial. Many other counting, or combinatorial, rules can be developed from the multiplication rule. Knowledge of these rules is helpful in solving some probability problems but is *not* necessary for completing the remaining chapters in this book.

We now outline the formulas for counting permutations, combinations, and partitions.

THEOREM 2.6

The number of ordered arrangements, or **permutations**, of r objects selected from n distinct objects is given by ($r \le n$):

$$P_r^n = n(n-1) \cdots (n-r+1) = \frac{n!}{(n-r)!}.$$

Proof

The basic idea of a permutation can be thought of as filling r slots, with one object in each slot, by drawing these objects one at a time from a pool of n distinct objects. The first slot can be filled in n ways, but the second in only $(n-1)$ ways after the first is filled. Thus, by the multiplication rule, the first two slots can be filled in $n(n-1)$ ways. Extending this reasoning to r slots, we have that the number of ways of filling all r slots is

$$n(n-1) \cdots (n-r+1) = \frac{n!}{(n-r)!} = P_r^n.$$

Hence, the theorem is proved.

We illustrate the use of Theorem 2.6 with two examples.

EXAMPLE 2.30

From among 10 employees three are to be selected for travel to three out-of-town plants, A, B, and C, one to each plant. Since the plants are in different cities, the order of assigning the employees to the plants is an important consideration. How many ways can the assignments be made?

Solution

Since order is important, the number of possible distinct assignments is

$$P_3^{10} = \frac{10!}{7!} = 10(9)(8) = 720.$$

In other words, there are 10 choices for plant A, but then only 9 for plant B and 8 for plant C. This gives a total of 10(9)(8) ways of assigning employees to the plants. □

EXAMPLE 2.31

An assembly operation in a manufacturing plant involves four steps, which can be performed in any order. If the manufacturer wishes to experimentally compare the assembly times for each possible ordering of the steps, how many orderings will the experiment involve?

Solution

The number of orderings is the permutation of $n = 4$ things taken $r = 4$ at a time. (All steps must be accomplished each time.) This turns out to be

$$P_4^4 = \frac{4!}{0!} = 4! = 4 \cdot 3 \cdot 2 \cdot 1 = 24,$$

since $0! = 1$ by definition. □

THEOREM 2.7

The number of distinct subsets, or **combinations**, of size r selected from n distinct objects is given by ($r \leq n$):

$$\binom{n}{r} = \frac{n!}{r!(n-r)!}$$

Proof   The number of *ordered* subsets of size r, selected from n distinct objects, is given by P_r^n. The number of *unordered* subsets of size r is denoted by $\binom{n}{r}$. Since any particular set of r objects can be ordered among themselves in $P_r^r = r!$ ways, it follows that

$$\binom{n}{r}r! = P_r^n$$

or

$$\binom{n}{r} = \frac{1}{r!} P_r^n = \frac{n!}{r!(n-r)!}.$$

EXAMPLE 2.32

In Example 2.30, suppose that three employees are to be selected from the ten to go to the *same* plant. In how many ways can the selection be made?

Solution   Here order is not important, and we merely want to know how many subsets of size $r = 3$ can be selected from $n = 10$ people. The result is

$$\binom{10}{3} = \frac{10!}{3!7!} = \frac{10 \cdot 9 \cdot 8}{1 \cdot 2 \cdot 3} = 120. \quad \square$$

EXAMPLE 2.33

Refer to Example 2.32. If 2 of the 10 employees are female and 8 are male, what is the probability that exactly one female gets selected among the three?

Solution   We have seen that there are $\binom{10}{3} = 120$ ways to select 3 employees from the 10. Similarly, there are $\binom{2}{1} = 2$ ways to select 1 female from the 2 available and $\binom{8}{2} = 28$ ways to select two males from the 8 available. If selections are made at random (that is, all subsets of 3 employees are equally likely to be chosen), then the probability of selecting exactly one female is

$$\frac{\binom{2}{1}\binom{8}{2}}{\binom{10}{3}} = \frac{2(28)}{120} = \frac{7}{15}. \quad \square$$

THEOREM 2.8

The number of ways of *partitioning* n distinct objects into k groups containing $n_1, n_2, \ldots, n_k$ objects, respectively, is

$$\frac{n!}{n_1!n_2! \cdots n_k!}$$

where

$$\sum_{i=1}^{k} n_i = n.$$

Proof   The partitioning of n objects into k groups can be done by first selecting a subset of size n_1 from the n objects, then selecting a subset of size n_2 from the $n - n_1$ objects that remain, and so on until all groups are filled. The number of ways of doing this is

$$\binom{n}{n_1}\binom{n - n_1}{n_2}\cdots\binom{n - n_1 - \cdots - n_{k-1}}{n_k} = \frac{n!}{n_1!n_2!\cdots n_k!}.$$

EXAMPLE 2.34

Suppose that 10 employees are to be divided among three jobs with 3 employees going to job I, 4 to job II and 3 to job III. In how many ways can the job assignments be made?

Solution   This problem involves a partitioning of the $n = 10$ employees into groups of size $n_1 = 3$, $n_2 = 4$ and $n_3 = 3$, and can be accomplished in

$$\frac{n!}{n_1!n_2!n_3!} = \frac{10!}{3!4!3!} = \frac{10 \cdot 9 \cdot 8 \cdot 7 \cdot 6 \cdot 5}{3 \cdot 2 \cdot 1 \cdot 3 \cdot 2 \cdot 1} = 4200$$

ways. (Notice the *large* number of ways this task can be accomplished!)   □

Exercises

2.66   Seven applicants have applied for two jobs. How many ways can the jobs be filled if
(a) the first person chosen receives a higher salary than the second?
(b) there are no differences between the jobs?

2.67   A package of six lightbulbs contains two defective bulbs. If three bulbs are selected for use, find the probability that none are defective.

2.68   How many four-digit serial numbers can be formed if no digit is to be repeated within any one number? (The first digit may be a zero.)

2.69   A fleet of eight taxis is to be divided up among three airports, A, B, and C, with 2 going to A, 5 to B and 1 to C. How many ways can this be done?

2.70   Refer to Exercise 2.69. What is the probability that the specific cab driven by Jones ends up at airport C?

Common Discrete
Probability Distributions

About This Chapter

Random variables, the numerical outcomes of experiments, can be nicely divided
into two categories for practical convenience. Those that arise from count data,
like the number of defective items per batch or the number of bacteria per cubic
centimer, are called *discrete* random variables. Probability distributions commonly used to model discrete random variables are discussed in this chapter.
The second category of random variables is the subject of Chapter 4.

Contents

3.1   Introduction

In Chapter 2 we presented the basic concepts of random variables and probability distributions, and a few specific distributions were used in the examples. You might wonder, at this point, how specific distributions are chosen to serve as models for various observed phenomena. Conveniently, it turns out that some basic distributions can be developed that will serve as models for a large number of practical problems. In this chapter we consider some fundamental discrete distributions, looking at the theoretical assumptions that underlie these distributions as well as the means, variances, and applications of the distributions.

3.2   The Bernoulli Distribution

Consider the inspection of a single item taken from an assembly line. Suppose a 0 is recorded if the item is nondefective, and a 1 is recorded if the item is defective. If X is the random variable denoting the condition of the inspected item, then $X = 0$ with probability $(1 - p)$ and $X = 1$ with probability p, where p denotes the probability of observing a defective item. The probability distribution of X is then given by

$$p(x) = p^x(1 - p)^{1-x}, \qquad x = 0, 1$$

where $p(x)$ denotes the probability that $X = x$. Such a random variable is said to have a *Bernoulli* distribution or to represent the outcome of a single Bernoulli trial. Any random variable denoting the presence or absence of a certain condition in an observed phenomenon will possess a distribution of this type. Frequently, one of the outcomes is termed "success" and the other "failure."

   Suppose that we repeatedly observe items of this type, and record a value of X for each item observed. What is the average value of X we would expect to see? By Definition 2.13 we have that the expected value of X is given by

$$E(X) = \sum_x xp(x)$$

$$= 0p(0) + 1p(1)$$

$$= 0(1 - p) + 1(p) = p.$$

Thus, if 10% of the items are defective, we expect to observe an *average* of 0.1 defective per item inspected. (In other words, we would expect to see one defective for every ten items inspected.)

   For the Bernoulli random variable, X, the variance (see Theorem 2.2) is

$$V(X) = E(X^2) - [E(X)]^2$$

$$= \sum_x x^2 p(x) - p^2$$

$$= 0(1 - p) + 1(p) - p^2$$

$$= p - p^2 = p(1 - p)$$

The Bernoulli random variable will be used as a building block to form other probability distributions, such as the binomial distribution of Section 3.3. The properties of the Bernoulli distribution are summarized here.

THE BERNOULLI DISTRIBUTION

$$p(x) = p^x(1-p)^{1-x}, \qquad x = 0, 1, \quad \text{for} \quad 0 \le p \le 1$$

$$E(X) = p, \qquad V(X) = p(1-p).$$

3.3   *The Binomial Distribution*

Instead of inspecting a single item, as we do with the Bernoulli random variable, suppose we now independently inspect n items and record values for $X_1, X_2, \ldots, X_n$, where $X_i = 1$ if the ith inspected item is defective and $X_i = 0$ otherwise. We have, in fact, observed a sequence of n independent Bernoulli random variables, for which we assume that p remains constant. One especially interesting function of $X_1, \ldots, X_n$ is the sum

$$Y = \sum_{i=1}^{n} X_i,$$

which denotes the number of defectives among the n sampled items.

To see how to evaluate the probability that Y takes on a specific value, let's look at the special case $n = 3$ and consider $P(Y = 2)$. The outcomes of the experiment that result in two defectives among the three sampled items are $(X_1 = 1, X_2 = 1, X_3 = 0)$, $(X_1 = 1, X_2 = 0, X_3 = 1)$ and $(X_1 = 0, X_2 = 1, X_3 = 1)$. The probability of the first of these is

$$P(X_1 = 1, X_2 = 1, X_3 = 0) = P(X_1 = 1)P(X_2 = 1)P(X_3 = 0)$$
$$= p^2(1-p)$$

since the trials are independent and the probability of a defective, p, is the same for all trials. Since the other two outcomes resulting in $Y = 2$ have identical probabilities, we have $P(Y = 2) = P(X_1 = 1, X_2 = 1, X_3 = 0) + P(X_1 = 1, X_2 = 0, X_3 = 1) + P(X_1 = 0, X_2 = 1, X_3 = 1) = 3p^2(1-p)$.

For general n, the probability that Y takes on a specific value, say y, is given by the term $p^y(1-p)^{n-y}$ multiplied by the number of possible outcomes resulting in exactly y defectives being observed. This number is

$$\binom{n}{y} = \frac{n!}{y!(n-y)!}$$

where $n! = n(n - 1) \cdots 1$ and $0! = 1$. (Note that $\binom{3}{2} = 3!/2!1! = 3$, as in the numerical example given above.) Thus, in general,

$$P(Y = y) = p(y) = \binom{n}{y} p^y (1 - p)^{n-y}, \qquad y = 0, 1, \ldots, n.$$

The probability distribution given above is referred to as the *binomial* distribution.

To summarize, a random variable Y possesses a binomial distribution if:

(1) the experiment consists of a fixed number, n, of identical trials;
(2) each trial can result in one of only two possible outcomes, called "success" or "failure";
(3) the probability of "successes", p, is constant from trial to trial;
(4) the trials are independent;
(5) Y is defined to be the number of successes among the n trials.

Many experimental situations result in a random variable that can be adequately modeled by the binomial. In addition to counts of the number of defectives in a sample of n items, examples may include counts of the number of employees favoring a certain retirement policy out of n employees interviewed, the number of pistons in an eight-cylinder engine that are misfiring, and the number of electronic systems sold this week out of the n that are manufactured.

The following example illustrates the use of the aforementioned formula.

EXAMPLE 3.1

Suppose that a large lot of fuses contains 10% defectives. If four fuses are randomly sampled from the lot, find the probability that exactly one fuse is defective. Find the probability that at least one fuse, in the sample of four, is defective.

Solution

We assume that the four trials are independent and that the probability of observing a defective is the same (0.1) for each trial. This would be approximately true if the lot is indeed large. Thus, the binomial distribution provides a reasonable model for this experiment and we have, with Y denoting the number of defectives,

$$p(1) = \binom{4}{1}(0.1)^1(0.9)^3 = 0.2916.$$

To find $P(Y \geq 1)$ observe that

$$P(Y \geq 1) = 1 - P(Y = 0) = 1 - p(0)$$

$$= 1 - \binom{4}{0}(0.1)^0(0.9)^4$$

$$= 1 - (0.9)^4$$

$$= 0.3439. \quad \square$$

Discrete distributions, like the binomial, can arise in situations where the underlying problem involves a continuous random variable. The following example provides an illustration.

EXAMPLE 3.2

Refer to the exponential model for battery lifelengths from Section 2.3. It was shown that the probability of a lifelength, X, exceeding four hours is 0.135. If three such batteries are in use in independently operating systems, find the probability that only one of the batteries lasts four hours or more.

Solution   Letting Y denote the number of batteries lasting four hours or more, we can reasonably assume Y to have a binomial distribution with $p = 0.135$. Hence,

$$P(Y = 1) = p(1) = \binom{3}{1}(0.135)^1(0.865)^2$$

$$= 0.303. \quad \square$$

There are numerous ways of finding $E(Y)$ and $V(Y)$ for a binomially distributed random variable Y. We might use the basic definition and compute

$$E(Y) = \sum_y yp(y)$$

$$= \sum_{y=0}^{n} y\binom{n}{y}p^y(1-p)^{n-y}$$

but working this into a closed-form solution is a little tricky. Another approach is to use the result of Theorem 2.3 on linear functions of random variables.

The binomial Y arose as a sum of independent Bernoulli random variables, $X_1, \ldots, X_n$, and so

$$E(Y) = E\left[\sum_{i=1}^{n} X_i\right] = \sum_{i=1}^{n} E(X_i)$$

$$= \sum_{i=1}^{n} p = np$$

since it was shown in Section 3.2 that, for a Bernoulli X_i, $E(X_i) = p$. Also, by Theorem 2.3 with all a_i's equal to 1,

$$V(Y) = \sum_{i=1}^{n} V(X_i) = \sum_{i=1}^{n} p(1-p) = np(1-p).$$

EXAMPLE 3.3

Refer to Example 3.1. Suppose that the four fuses sampled from the lot were shipped to a customer before being tested, on a guarantee basis. Assume that the cost of making the shipment good is given by $C = 3Y^2$, where Y denotes the number of defectives in the shipment of four. Find the expected repair cost.

Solution   We know that

$$E(C) = E(3Y^2) = 3E(Y^2)$$

and it now remains to find $E(Y^2)$. We have from Theorem 2.2, that

$$V(Y) = E(Y - \mu)^2 = E(Y^2) - \mu^2.$$

Since $V(Y) = np(1 - p)$ and $\mu = E(Y) = np$, we see that

$$
\begin{aligned}
E(Y^2) &= V(Y) + \mu^2 \\
&= np(1 - p) + (np)^2.
\end{aligned}
$$

For Example 3.1, $p = 0.1$ and $n = 4$, and hence

$$
\begin{aligned}
E(C) = 3E(Y^2) &= 3[np(1 - p) + (np)^2] \\
&= 3[(4)(0.1)(0.9) + (4)^2(0.1)^2] \\
&= 1.56.
\end{aligned}
$$

If the costs were originally in dollars, we could expect to pay an average of $1.56 in repair costs for each shipment of four fuses.   □

Table 2 of the Appendix gives cumulative binomial probabilities for selected values of n and p. The entries in the table are values of

$$\sum_{y=0}^{a} p(y) = \sum_{y=0}^{a} \binom{n}{y} p^y(1 - p)^{n-y}.$$

The following example illustrates the use of Table 2.

EXAMPLE 3.4
An industrial firm supplies 10 manufacturing plants with a certain chemical. The probability that any one firm calls in an order on a given day is 0.2, and this is the same for all 10 plants. Find the probability that, on the given day, the number of plants calling in orders is: (a) at most 3; (b) at least 3; (c) exactly 3.

Solution   Let Y denote the number of plants calling in orders on the day in question. If the plants order independently, then Y can be modeled to have a binomial distribution with $p = 0.2$.

(a)   We then have

$$
\begin{aligned}
P(Y \le 3) &= \sum_{y=0}^{3} p(y) \\
&= \sum_{y=0}^{3} \binom{10}{y}(0.2)^y(0.8)^{10-y} \\
&= 0.879
\end{aligned}
$$

from Table 2(b).

(b) Note that

$$P(Y \geq 3) = 1 - P(Y \leq 2)$$

$$= 1 - \sum_{y=0}^{2} \binom{10}{y} (0.2)^y (0.8)^{10-y}$$

$$= 1 - 0.678 = 0.322.$$

(c) Observe that

$$P(Y = 3) = P(Y \leq 3) - P(Y \leq 2)$$
$$= 0.879 - 0.678 = 0.201$$

from results just established. □

We now move on to a discussion of other discrete random variables, but the binomial distribution, summarized here, will be used frequently throughout the text.

THE BINOMIAL DISTRIBUTION

$$p(y) = \binom{n}{y} p^y (1-p)^{n-y}, \qquad y = 0, 1, \ldots, n, \quad \text{for} \quad 0 \leq p \leq 1.$$

$$E(Y) = np \qquad V(Y) = np(1-p)$$

Exercises

3.1   Let X denote a random variable having a binomial distribution with $p = 0.2$ and $n = 4$. Find
(a) $P(X = 2)$ (b) $P(X \geq 2)$
(c) $P(X \leq 2)$ (d) $E(X)$
(e) $V(X)$.

3.2   Let X denote a random variable having a binomial distribution with $p = 0.4$ and $n = 20$. Use Table 2 of the Appendix to evaluate
(a) $P(X \leq 6)$ (b) $P(X \geq 12)$
(c) $P(X = 8)$.

3.3   A machine that fills boxes of cereal underfills a certain percentage, p. If 25 boxes are randomly selected from the output of this machine, find the probability that no more than two are underfilled when
(a) $p = 0.1$ (b) $p = 0.2$.

3.4   In testing the lethal concentration of a chemical found in polluted water it is found that a certain concentration will kill 20% of the fish that are subjected

to it for 24 hours. If 20 fish are placed in a tank containing this concentration of chemical, find the probability that after 24 hours,
(a) exactly 14 survive.   (b) at least 10 survive.
(c) at most 16 survive.

3.5   Refer to Exercise 3.4.
(a) Find the number expected to survive, out of 20.
(b) Find the variance of the number of survivors, out of 20.

3.6   A missile protection system consists of n radar sets operating independently, each with probability 0.9 of detecting an aircraft entering a specified zone. (All radar sets cover the same zone.) If an airplane enters the zone, find the probability that it will be detected if:
(a) $n = 2$.   (b) $n = 4$.

3.7   Refer to Exercise 3.6. How large must n be if it is desired to have a probability of 0.99 of detecting an aircraft entering the zone?

3.8   A complex electronic system is built with a certain number of backup components in its subsystems. One subsystem has four identical components, each with probability 0.2 of failing in less than 1000 hours. The subsystem will operate if any two of the four components are operating. Assuming that the components operate independently, find the probability that:
(a) exactly two of the four components last longer than 1000 hours.
(b) the subsystem operates longer than 1000 hours.

3.9   An oil exploration firm is to drill ten wells, with each well having probability 0.1 of successfully producing oil. It costs the firm $10,000 to drill each well. A successful well will bring in oil worth $500,000.
(a) Find the firm's expected gain from the ten wells.
(b) Find the standard deviation of the firm's gain.

3.10   A firm sells four items randomly selected from a large lot known to contain 10% defectives. Let Y denote the number of defectives among the four sold. The purchaser of the items will return the defectives for repair, and the repair cost is given by

$$C = 3Y^2 + Y + 2.$$

Find the expected repair cost.

3.11   In Example 2.11 on page 27, the weekly demand (in hundred of gallons) for kerosene was a random variable, X, with density function

$$f(x) = \begin{cases} x, & 0 \le x \le 1, \\ \frac{1}{2}, & 1 < x \le 2, \\ 0, & \text{elsewhere.} \end{cases}$$

Find the probability that the demand will exceed 150 gallons for at least two out of three randomly selected weeks.

3.12   From a large lot of new tires, n are to be sampled by a potential buyer and the number of defectives, X, is to be observed. If at least one defective is observed in the sample of n, the entire lot is to be rejected by the potential buyer. Find n so that the probability of detecting at least one defective is

approximately 0.90 if
(a) 10% of the lot is defective.
(b) 5% of the lot is defective.

3.13   The lifelength, X, for a certain type of resistor has a probability density function given by

$$f(x) = \begin{cases} \frac{1}{3}e^{-x/3}, & x > 0 \\ 0, & \text{elsewhere} \end{cases}$$

with measurements in hundreds of hours. If 5 such resistors are operating independently, in a system, find the probability that at least one will fail before 500 hours has elapsed.

3.14   Ten motors are packaged for sale in a certain warehouse. The motors sell for $100 each, but a "double-your-money-back" guarantee is in effect for any defectives the purchaser might receive. Find the expected net gain for the seller if the probability of any one motor being defective is 0.08. (Assume the quality of any one motor is independent of that of the others.)

3.4   *The Geometric Distribution*

Suppose a series of test firings of a rocket engine can be represented by a sequence of independent Bernoulli random variables with $X_i = 1$ if the ith trial results in a successful firing and $X_i = 0$ otherwise. Assume that the probability of a successful firing is constant for the trials, and let this probability be denoted by p. For this problem we might be interested in the number of the trial on which the first successful firing occurs. If Y denotes the number of the trial on which the first success occurs, then

$$\begin{aligned} P(Y = y) = p(y) &= P(X_1 = 0, X_2 = 0, \ldots, X_{y-1} = 0, X_y = 1) \\ &= P(X_1 = 0)P(X_2 = 0)\cdots P(X_{y-1} = 0)P(X_y = 1) \\ &= (1 - p)^{y-1}p, \qquad y = 1, 2, \ldots, \end{aligned}$$

because of the independence of the trials. This formula is referred to as the *geometric probability distribution*.

In addition to the rocket-firing example just given, here are other situations that result in a random variable whose probabilities can be modeled by a geometric distribution: the number of customers contacted before the first sale is made, the number of years a dam is in service before it overflows, and the number of automobiles going through a radar check before the first speeder is detected.

The following example illustrates the use of the geometric distribution.

EXAMPLE 3.5

Suppose that 30% of the applicants for a certain industrial job have advanced training in computer programming. Applicants are interviewed sequentially and are selected at random from the pool. Find the probability that the first applicant having advanced training in programming is found on the fifth interview.

Solution   The probability of finding a suitably trained applicant will remain relatively constant from trial to trial if the pool of applicants is reasonably large. It then makes sense to define Y as the number of the trial on which the first applicant having advanced training in programming is found, and model Y as having a geometric distribution. Thus,

$$P(Y = 5) = p(5) = (0.7)^4(0.3)$$
$$= 0.072. \quad \square$$

The calculation of the $E(Y)$ for a geometrically distributed Y gives some insight into why the distribution is called geometric. One way to view this is the following. From the basic definition,

$$E(Y) = \sum_y yp(y) = \sum_{y=1}^{\infty} yp(1-p)^{y-1}$$
$$= p \sum_{y=1}^{\infty} y(1-p)^{y-1}$$
$$= p[1 + 2(1-p) + 3(1-p)^2 + \cdots].$$

The infinite series can be split up into a triangular array of series as follows:

$$E(Y) = p[1 + (1-p) + (1-p)^2 + \cdots$$
$$+ (1-p) + (1-p)^2 + \cdots$$
$$+ (1-p)^2 + \cdots$$
$$+ \quad].$$

Each line on the right side is an infinite, decreasing geometric progression with common ratio $(1-p)$. Thus, the first line inside the bracket sums to $1/p$, the second to $(1-p)/p$, the third to $(1-p)^2/p$, and so on. On accumulating these totals, we then have

$$E(Y) = p\left[\frac{1}{p} + \frac{1-p}{p} + \frac{(1-p)^2}{p} + \cdots\right]$$
$$= 1 + (1-p) + (1-p)^2 + \cdots$$
$$= \frac{1}{1-(1-p)} = \frac{1}{p}.$$

This answer for $E(Y)$ should seem intuitively realistic. For example, if 10% of a certain lot of items are defective, and if an inspector looks at randomly selected items one at a time, then he should expect to wait until the tenth trial to see the first defective.

The variance of the geometric distribution is more cumbersome to derive by direct methods, and so the derivation will not be given here. The result, however, is simply

$$V(Y) = \frac{1-p}{p^2}.$$

EXAMPLE 3.6

Refer to Example 3.5 and let Y denote the number of the trial on which the first applicant having advanced training in computer programming is found. Suppose that the first applicant with advanced training is offered the position, and the applicant accepts. If each interview costs $30.00, find the expected value and variance of the total cost of interviewing until the job is filled. Within what interval would this cost be expected to fall?

Solution   Since Y is the number of the trial on which the interviewing process ends, the total cost of interviewing is $C = 30Y$. Now,

$$E(C) = 30E(Y) = 30\left(\frac{1}{p}\right)$$

$$= 30\left(\frac{1}{0.3}\right) = 100,$$

and

$$V(C) = (30)^2 V(Y) = \frac{900(1-p)}{p^2}$$

$$= \frac{900(0.7)}{(0.3)^2}$$

$$= 7000.$$

The standard deviation of C is then $\sqrt{V(C)} = \sqrt{7000} = 83.67$. Tchebysheff's Theorem (see Section 2.9) says that C will lie within two standard deviations of its mean at least 75% of the time. Thus, it is quite likely that C will be between

$$100 - 2(83.67) \quad \text{and} \quad 100 + 2(83.67)$$

or

$$-67.34 \quad \text{and} \quad 267.34.$$

Since the lower bound is negative, that end of the interval is meaningless. However, we can still say that it is quite likely that C will be less than $267.34 on any such interviewing process. □

THE GEOMETRIC DISTRIBUTION

$$p(y) = p(1 - p)^{y-1}, \qquad y = 1, 2, \ldots, \quad \text{for} \quad 0 < p < 1.$$

$$E(Y) = \frac{1}{p}, \qquad V(Y) = \frac{1 - p}{p^2}$$

3.5 *The Negative Binomial Distribution*

In Section 3.4 we saw that the geometric distribution models the probabilistic behavior of the number of the trial on which the first "success" occurs in a sequence of independent Bernoulli trials. But what if we were interested in the number of the trial for the second success, or third success, or, in general, the rth success? The distribution governing the probabilistic behavior in these cases is called the *negative binomial distribution.*

Let Y denote the number of the trial on which the rth success occurs in a sequence of independent Bernoulli trials with p denoting the common probability of "success." We can derive the distribution of Y from known facts. Now,

$$\begin{aligned} P(Y = y) &= P[\text{1st } (y - 1) \text{ trials contain } (r - 1) \\ &\quad \text{successes and } y\text{th trial is a success}] \\ &= P[\text{1st } (y - 1) \text{ trials contain } (r - 1) \\ &\quad \text{successes}] \, P[y\text{th trial is a success}]. \end{aligned}$$

Since the trials are independent, the joint probability can be written as a product of probabilities. The first probability statement is identical to that resulting in a binomial model, and hence,

$$\begin{aligned} P(Y = y) = p(y) &= \binom{y - 1}{r - 1} p^{r-1}(1 - p)^{y-r} \cdot p \\ &= \binom{y - 1}{r - 1} p^r (1 - p)^{y-r}, \qquad y = r, r + 1, \ldots. \end{aligned}$$

EXAMPLE 3.7

　　　　Refer to Example 3.5. Suppose that three jobs requiring advanced programming training are open. Find the probability that the third qualified applicant is found on the fifth interview.

Solution　　　　Again, we assume independent trials with 0.3 being the probability of finding a qualified candidate on any one trial. Let Y denote the number of the trial on which the third qualified candidate is found. Then, Y can reasonably be assumed to have a negative binomial distribution, at least approximately, so that

$$P(Y = 5) = p(5) = \binom{4}{2}(0.3)^3(0.7)^2$$

$$= 6(0.3)^3(0.7)^2$$

$$= .079 \quad \square$$

The expected value, or mean, and variance for the negative binomially distributed Y is most easily found by analogy with the geometric distribution. Recall that Y denotes the number of the trial on which the rth success occurs. Let W_1 denote the number of the trial on which the first success occurs, W_2 the number of trials between the first success and the second success, including the trial of the second success, W_3 the number of trials between the second success and the third success, and so forth. The results of the trials are then as diagramed next (F standing for failure and S for success).

$$\underbrace{FF\cdots FS}_{W_1} \quad \underbrace{F\cdots FS}_{W_2} \quad \underbrace{F\cdots FS}_{W_3}$$

It is easy to observe that $Y = \sum_{i=1}^{r} W_i$, where the W_i's are independent and each has a geometric distribution. Thus,

$$E(Y) = \sum_{i=1}^{r} E(W_i) = \sum_{i=1}^{r} \left(\frac{1}{p}\right) = \frac{r}{p}$$

and

$$V(Y) = \sum_{i=1}^{r} V(W_i) = \sum_{i=1}^{r} \frac{1-p}{p^2} = \frac{r(1-p)}{p^2}.$$

EXAMPLE 3.8

A large stockpile of used pumps contains 20% that are unusable and need repair. A repairman is sent to the stockpile with 3 repair kits. He selects pumps at random and tests them one at a time. If a pump works, he goes on to the next one. If a pump doesn't work, he uses one of his repair kits on it. Suppose that it takes 10 minutes to test a pump if it works, and 30 minutes to test and repair a pump that doesn't work. Find the expected value and variance of the total time it takes the repairman to use up his 3 kits.

Solution   Letting Y denote the number of the trial on which the 3rd defective pump is found, we see that Y has a negative binomial distribution with $p = 0.2$. The total time, T, taken to use up the three repair kits is

$$T = 10(Y - 3) + 3(30) = 10Y + 3(20).$$

(Each test takes 10 minutes, but the repairing takes 20 extra minutes.)

It follows that

$$E(T) = 10E(Y) + 3(20)$$

$$= 10\left(\frac{3}{0.2}\right) + 3(20)$$

$$= 150 + 60 = 210$$

and

$$V(T) = (10)^2 V(Y)$$

$$= (10)^2 \left[\frac{3(0.8)}{(0.2)^2}\right]$$

$$= 100[60]$$

$$= 6000.$$

Thus, the total time to use up the kits has an expected value of 210 minutes, with a standard deviation of $\sqrt{6000} = 77.46$ minutes.   □

The negative binomial distribution is used to model a wide variety of phenomena, from numbers of defects per square yard in fabrics to numbers of individuals in an insect population after many generations.

THE NEGATIVE BINOMIAL DISTRIBUTION

$$p(y) = \binom{y-1}{r-1} p^r (1-p)^{y-r}, \qquad y = r, r+1, \ldots, \quad \text{for} \quad 0 \le p \le 1.$$

$$E(Y) = \frac{r}{p}, \qquad V(Y) = \frac{r(1-p)}{p^2}$$

Exercises

3.15   Let Y denote a random variable having a geometric distribution, with probability of success on any trial denoted by p.
(a) Find $P(Y \ge 2)$ if $p = 0.1$.
(b) Find $P(Y > 4 \mid Y > 2)$ for general p. Compare with the unconditional probability $P(Y > 2)$.

3.16   Let Y denote a negative binomial random variable with $p = 0.4$. Find $P(Y \ge 4)$ if
(a) $r = 2$.   (b) $r = 4$.

3.17   Suppose that 10% of the engines manufactured on a certain assembly line are defective. If engines are randomly selected one at a time and tested, find the probability that the first nondefective engine is found on the second trial.

3.18 Refer to Exercise 3.17. Find the probability that the third nondefective engine is found
(a) on the fifth trial.
(b) on or before the fifth trial.

3.19 Refer to Exercise 3.17. Given that the first two engines are defective, find the probability that at least two more engines must be tested before the first nondefective is found.

3.20 Refer to Exercise 3.17. Find the mean and variance of the number of the trial on which
(a) the first nondefective engine is found.
(b) the third nondefective engine is found.

3.21 The employees of a firm that manufactures insulation are being tested for indications of asbestos in their lungs. The firm is requested to send three employees who have positive indications of asbestos on to a medical center for further testing. If 40% of the employees have positive indications of asbestos in their lungs, find the probability that ten employees must be tested in order to find three positives.

3.22 Refer to Exercise 3.21. If each test costs $20, find the expected value and variance of the total cost of conducting the tests to locate three positives. Do you think it is highly likely that the cost of completing these tests would exceed $350?

3.23 The supply office for a large construction firm has three welding units of Brand A in stock. If a welding unit is requested, the probability is 0.7 that the request will be for this particular brand. On a typical day, five requests for welding units come to the office. Find the probability that all three Brand A units will be in use on that day.

3.24 Refer to Exercise 3.23. If the supply office also stocks three welding units that are not Brand A, find the probability that exactly one of these units will be left immediately after the third Brand A unit is requested.

3.6　*The Poisson Distribution*

A number of probability distributions came about through limiting arguments applied to other distributions. One such very useful distribution is called the *Poisson.*

Consider the development of a probabilistic model for the number of accidents occurring at a particular highway intersection in a period of one week. We can think of the time interval as being split up into n subintervals such that

$$P \text{ (one accident in a subinterval)} = p$$

$$P \text{ (no accidents in a subinterval)} = 1 - p.$$

Note that we are assuming the same value of p holds for all subintervals and the probability of more than one accident in any one subinterval is zero. If the occurrence of accidents can be regarded as independent from subinterval to subinterval, then the total number of accidents in the time period (which equals the total number of subintervals containing one accident) will have a binomial distribution.

Although there is no unique way to choose the subintervals and we therefore know neither n nor p, it seems reasonable to assume that as n increases, p should decrease. Thus we went to look at the limit of the binomial probability distribution as $n \to \infty$ and $p \to 0$. However, the mean number of accidents per time period should be fixed, and not subject to changes with n and p. Thus, we want to take the limit under the restriction that the mean, np in the binomial case, remains constant at a value we will call λ.

Now, with $np = \lambda$ or $p = \lambda/n$, we have

$$\lim_{n \to \infty} \binom{n}{y} \left(\frac{\lambda}{n}\right)^y \left(1 - \frac{\lambda}{n}\right)^{n-y}$$

$$= \lim_{n \to \infty} \frac{\lambda^y}{y!} \left(1 - \frac{\lambda}{n}\right)^n \frac{n(n-1) \cdots (n-y+1)}{n^y} \left(1 - \frac{\lambda}{n}\right)^{-y}$$

$$= \frac{\lambda^y}{y!} \lim_{n \to \infty} \left(1 - \frac{\lambda}{n}\right)^n \left(1 - \frac{\lambda}{n}\right)^{-y} \left(1 - \frac{1}{n}\right) \left(1 - \frac{2}{n}\right) \cdots \left(1 - \frac{y-1}{n}\right).$$

Noting that

$$\lim_{n \to \infty} \left(1 - \frac{\lambda}{n}\right)^n = e^{-\lambda}$$

and that all other terms involving n tend to unity, we have the limiting distribution

$$p(y) = \frac{\lambda^y}{y!} e^{-\lambda}, \qquad y = 0, 1, 2, \ldots .$$

Recall that λ denotes the mean number of occurrences in one time period (a week for the example under consideration) and hence if t nonoverlapping time periods were considered the mean would be λt.

The above distribution, called the *Poisson*, can be used to model counts in areas or volumes, as well as in time. For example, we may use this distribution to model the number of flaws in a square yard of textile, the number of bacteria colonies in a cubic centimeter of water, or the number of times a machine fails in the course of a workday.

We illustrate the use of the Poisson distribution in the following example.

EXAMPLE 3.9

For a certain manufacturing industry, the number of industrial accidents averages three per week. Find the probability that no accidents will occur in a given week.

Solution   If accidents tend to occur independently of one another, and if they occur at a constant rate over time, the Poisson model provides an adequate representation of the probabilities. Thus,

$$p(0) = \frac{3^0}{0!} e^{-3} = e^{-3} = 0.05. \quad \square$$

Table 3 of the Appendix gives values for cumulative Poisson probabilities of the form

$$\sum_{y=0}^{a} e^{-\lambda} \frac{\lambda^y}{y!}.$$

The following example illustrates the use of Table 3.

EXAMPLE 3.10
          Refer to Example 3.9 and let Y denote the number of accidents in the given week. Find $P(Y \leq 4)$, $P(Y \geq 4)$ and $P(Y = 4)$.

Solution   From Table 3 we have

$$P(Y \leq 4) = \sum_{y=0}^{4} \frac{(3)^y}{y!} e^{-3} = 0.815.$$

Also,

$$P(Y \geq 4) = 1 - P(Y \leq 3)$$
$$= 1 - 0.647 = 0.353$$

and

$$P(Y = 4) = P(Y \leq 4) - P(Y \leq 3)$$
$$= 0.815 - 0.647 = 0.168. \quad \square$$

The mean of the Poisson distribution is easily found if one remembers a simple Taylor series result for the expansion of e^x, namely

$$e^x = 1 + x + \frac{x^2}{2!} + \frac{x^3}{3!} + \cdots.$$

Then,

$$E(Y) = \sum_y y p(y) = \sum_{y=0}^{\infty} y \frac{\lambda^y}{y!} e^{-\lambda}$$
$$= \lambda e^{-\lambda} \sum_{y=1}^{\infty} \frac{\lambda^{y-1}}{(y-1)!}$$
$$= \lambda e^{-\lambda} \left(1 + \lambda + \frac{\lambda^2}{2!} + \frac{\lambda^3}{3!} + \cdots \right)$$
$$= \lambda e^{-\lambda} e^{\lambda} = \lambda.$$

It can also be shown that

$$V(Y) = \lambda,$$

but this will be left as an exercise for the interested reader.

EXAMPLE 3.11

The manager of an industrial plant is planning to buy a new machine of either type A or type B. For each day's operation, the number of repairs, X, that machine A requires is a Poisson random variable with mean $0.10t$, where t denotes the time (in hours) of daily operation. The number of daily repairs, Y, for machine B is Poisson with mean $0.12t$. The daily cost of operating A is $C_A(t) = 10t + 30X^2$; for B it is $C_B(t) = 8t + 30Y^2$. Assume that the repairs take negligible time and each night the machines are to be cleaned, so that they operate like new machines at the start of each day. Which machine minimizes the expected daily cost if a day consists of

(a) ten hours?
(b) twenty hours?

Solution   The expected cost for A is

$$\begin{aligned}
E[C_A(t)] &= 10t + 30E(X^2) \\
&= 10t + 30[V(X) + (E(X))^2] \\
&= 10t + 30[0.10t + 0.01t^2] \\
&= 13t + 0.3t^2.
\end{aligned}$$

Similarly,

$$\begin{aligned}
E[C_B(t)] &= 8t + 30E(Y^2) \\
&= 8t + 30[0.12t + 0.0144t^2] \\
&= 11.6t + 0.432t^2
\end{aligned}$$

For part (a),

$$E[C_A(10)] = 13(10) + 0.3(10)^2 = 160$$

and

$$E[C_B(10)] = 11.6(10) + 0.432(10)^2 = 159.2,$$

which results in the choice of machine B.
For part (b),

$$E[C_A(20)] = 380$$

and

$$E[C_B(20)] = 404.8,$$

which results in the choice of machine A. In conclusion, B is more economical for short time periods because of its smaller hourly operating cost. However, for long time periods, A is more economical because it tends to be repaired less frequently. $\square$

THE POISSON DISTRIBUTION

$$p(y) = \frac{\lambda^y}{y!} e^{-\lambda}, \qquad y = 0, 1, 2, \ldots .$$

$$E(Y) = \lambda, \qquad V(Y) = \lambda$$

Exercises

3.25 Let Y denote a random variable having a Poisson distribution with mean $\lambda = 2$. Find
(a) $P(Y = 4)$.   (b) $P(Y \geq 4)$.
(c) $P(Y < 4)$.   (d) $P(Y \geq 4 \mid Y \geq 2)$.

3.26 Customer arrivals at a checkout counter in a department store have a Poisson distribution with an average of 8 per hour. For a given hour, find the probability that
(a) exactly 8 customers arrive.
(b) no more than 3 customers arrive.
(c) at least 2 customers arrive.

3.27 Refer to Exercise 3.26. If it takes approximately 10 minutes to service each customer, find the mean and variance of the total service time connected to the customer arrivals for one hour. (Assume that an unlimited number of servers are available, so that no customer has to wait for service.) Is it highly likely that total service time would exceed 200 minutes?

3.28 Refer to Exercise 3.26. Find the probability that exactly two customers arrive in the two-hour period of time
(a) between 2:00 PM and 4:00 PM (one continuous two-hour period).
(b) between 1:00 PM and 2:00 PM and between 3:00 PM and 4:00 PM (two separate one-hour periods for a total of two hours).

3.29 The number of imperfections in the weave of a certain textile has a Poisson distribution with a mean of 4 per square yard.
(a) Find the probability that a one-square-yard sample will contain at least one imperfection.
(b) Find the probability that a three-square-yard sample will contain at least one imperfection.

3.30 Refer to Exercise 3.29. The cost of repairing the imperfections in the weave is $10 per imperfection. Find the mean and standard deviation of the repair costs for an eight-square-yard bolt of the textile in question.

3.31 The number of bacteria colonies of a certain type in samples of polluted water has a Poisson distribution with a mean of 2 per cubic centimeter.
(a) If four one-cubic-centimeter samples are independently selected from this water, find the probability that at least one sample will contain one or more bacteria colonies.
(b) How many one-cubic-centimeter samples should be selected in order to have a probability of approximately 0.95 of seeing at least one bacteria colony?

3.32   Let Y have a Poisson distribution with mean λ. Find $E[Y(Y-1)]$ and use the result to show that $V(Y) = \lambda$.

3.33   A food manufacturer has in use an extruder (a machine that produces bite-sized foods like cookies and many snack foods), which produces revenue for the firm at the rate of \$200 per hour, when in operation. However, the extruder breaks down on the average of two times for every ten hours of operation. If Y denotes the number of breakdowns during the time of operation, the revenue generated by the machine is given by

$$R = 200t - 50Y^2,$$

where t denotes hours of operation. The extruder will be shut down for routine maintenance on a regular schedule, and operates like a new machine after this maintenance. Find the optimal maintenance interval, t_0, so that the expected revenue is maximized between shutdowns.

3.34   The number of cars entering a parking lot is a random variable having a Poisson distribution with a mean of 4 per hour. The lot holds only 12 cars.
  (a) Find the probability that the lot fills up in the first hour. (Assume all cars stay in the lot longer than one hour.)
  (b) Find the probability that fewer than 12 cars arrive during an eight-hour day.

3.7   *The Hypergeometric Distribution*

The distributions already discussed in this chapter have as their basic building block a series of *independent* Bernoulli trials. The examples, such as sampling from large lots, depict situations in which the trials of the experiment do generate, for all practical purposes, independent outcomes.

Suppose that we have a relatively small lot consisting of N items, of which k are defective. If two items are sampled sequentially, then the outcome for the second draw is very much influenced by what happened on the first draw, provided that the first item drawn remains out of the lot. A new distribution must be developed to handle this situation involving *dependent* trials.

In general, suppose a lot consists of N items, of which k are of one type (called successes) and $N - k$ are of another type (called failures). Suppose that n items are sampled randomly and sequentially from the lot, with none of the sampled items being replaced. (This is called sampling *without replacement*.) Let $X_i = 1$ if the ith draw results in a success and $X_i = 0$ otherwise, $i = 1, \ldots, n$, and let Y denote the total number of successes among the n sampled items. To develop the probability distribution for Y, let us start by looking at a special case for $Y = y$. Now, one way for y successes to occur is to have

$$X_1 = 1, X_2 = 1, \ldots, X_y = 1, X_{y+1} = 0, \ldots, X_n = 0.$$

We know from Section 2.4 that

$$P(X_1 = 1, X_2 = 1) = P(X_1 = 1)P(X_2 = 1 | X_1 = 1)$$

and this result can be extended to give

$$P(X_1 = 1, X_2 = 1, \ldots, X_y = 1, X_{y+1} = 0, \ldots, X_n = 0)$$
$$= P(X_1 = 1)P(X_2 = 1 | X_1 = 1)P(X_3 = 1 | X_2 = 1, X_1 = 1) \cdots$$
$$P(X_n = 0 | X_{n-1} = 0, \ldots, X_{y+1} = 0, X_y = 1, \ldots, X_1 = 1).$$

Now,

$$P(X_1 = 1) = \frac{k}{N}$$

if the item is randomly selected, and similarly

$$P(X_2 = 1 | X_1 = 1) = \frac{k - 1}{N - 1}$$

since, at this point, one of the k successes has been removed. Using this idea repeatedly, we see that

$$P(X_1 = 1, \ldots, X_y = 1, X_{y+1} = 0, \ldots, X_n = 0)$$
$$= \left(\frac{k}{N}\right)\left(\frac{k-1}{N-1}\right) \cdots \left(\frac{k-y+1}{N-y+1}\right)\left(\frac{N-k}{N-y}\right) \cdots \left(\frac{N-k-n+y+1}{N-n+1}\right)$$

provided $y \leq k$. A more compact way to write the above expression is to employ factorials, arriving at the formula

$$\frac{\dfrac{k!}{(k-y)!} \cdot \dfrac{(N-k)!}{(N-k-n+y)!}}{\dfrac{N!}{(N-n)!}}$$

(The reader can check the equivalence of the two expressions.)

Any specified arrangement of y successes and $(n - y)$ failures will have the same probability as the one derived above for all successes followed by all failures; the terms will merely be rearranged. Thus, to find $P(Y = y)$ we need only to count how many of these arrangements are possible. Just as in the binomial case, the number of such arrangements is $\binom{n}{y}$. Hence, we have

$$P(Y = y) = \binom{n}{y} \frac{\dfrac{k!}{(k-y)!} \cdot \dfrac{(N-k)!}{(N-k-n+y)!}}{\dfrac{N!}{(N-n)!}}$$
$$= \frac{\binom{k}{y}\binom{N-k}{n-y}}{\binom{N}{n}}.$$

(We will call $\binom{b}{a} = 0$ if $a > b$.) This formula is referred to as the *hypergeometric* probability distribution. Note that it arises from a situation quite similar to the binomial, except that the trials are *dependent*.

Experiments that result in a random variable possessing a hypergeometric distribution usually involve counting the number of "successes" in a sample taken from a small lot. Examples could include counting the number of males that show up on a committee of five randomly selected from among twenty employees and counting the number of Brand A alarm systems sold in three sales from a warehouse containing two Brand A and four Brand B systems.

EXAMPLE 3.12

A personnel director selects two employees for a certain job from a group of six employees, of which one is female and five are male. Find the probability that the female is selected for one of the jobs.

Solution   If the selections are made at random, and if Y denotes the number of females selected, then the hypergeometric distribution would provide a good model for the behavior of Y. Hence,

$$P(Y = 1) = p(1) = \frac{\binom{1}{1}\binom{5}{1}}{\binom{6}{2}} = \frac{1 \cdot 5}{15} = \frac{1}{3}.$$

Here, $N = 6$, $k = 1$, $n = 2$, and $y = 1$.

It might be instructive to see this calculation from basic principles, letting $X_i = 1$ if the ith draw results in the female and $X_i = 0$ otherwise. Then,

$$
\begin{aligned}
P(Y = 1) &= P(X_1 = 1, X_2 = 0) + P(X_1 = 0, X_2 = 1) \\
&= P(X_1 = 1)P(X_2 = 0 \mid X_1 = 1) + P(X_1 = 0)P(X_2 = 1 \mid X_1 = 0) \\
&= \left(\frac{1}{6}\right)\left(\frac{5}{5}\right) + \left(\frac{5}{6}\right)\left(\frac{1}{5}\right) \\
&= \frac{1}{3}. \quad \square
\end{aligned}
$$

The hypergeometric formula is somewhat complicated to manipulate. Thus, we will not derive the mean and variance, but state the results:

THE HYPERGEOMETRIC DISTRIBUTION

$$p(y) = \frac{\binom{k}{y}\binom{N-k}{n-y}}{\binom{N}{n}}, \qquad y = 0, 1, \ldots, k, \quad \text{with} \quad \binom{b}{a} = 0 \quad \text{if} \quad a > b.$$

$$E(Y) = n\left(\frac{k}{N}\right), \qquad V(Y) = n\left(\frac{k}{N}\right)\left(1 - \frac{k}{N}\right)\left(\frac{N-n}{N-1}\right)$$

Exercises

3.35   From a box containing 4 white and 3 red balls, 2 balls are selected at random, without replacement. Find the probability that:
(a) exactly one white ball is selected.
(b) at least one white ball is selected.
(c) two white balls are selected, given that at least one white ball is selected.
(d) the second ball drawn is white.

3.36   A warehouse contains 10 printing machines, 4 of which are defective. A company randomly selects five of the machines for purchase. What is the probability that all five of the machines are nondefective?

3.37   Refer to Exercise 3.36. The company purchasing the machines returns the defective ones for repair. If it costs $50 to repair each machine, find the mean and variance of the total repair cost. In what interval would you expect the repair costs on these five machines to lie? (Use Tchebysheff's Theorem.)

3.38   A corporation has a pool of 6 firms, 4 of which are local, from which they can purchase certain supplies. If 3 firms are randomly selected without replacement, find the probability that
(a) at least one selected firm is not local.
(b) all three selected firms are local.

3.39   A foreman has 10 employees from whom he must select 4 to perform a certain undesirable task. Among the 10 employees, 3 belong to a minority ethnic group. The foreman selected all three minority employees (plus one other) to perform the undesirable task. The minority group then protested to the union steward that they were discriminated against by the foreman. The foreman claimed that the selection was completely at random. What do you think?

3.40   Two assembly lines (line I and line II) have the same rate of defectives in their production of voltage regulators. Five regulators are sampled from each line and tested. Among the total of ten tested regulators there were 4 defectives. Find the probability that exactly 2 of the defectives came from line I.

3.8   *The Multinomial Distribution*

The distributions considered thus far in Chapter 3 have been rooted in sequences of Bernoulli trials, having only two possible outcomes. Of course, one realistically has to consider more than two possible outcomes for certain experimental situations, and we will now develop a model that takes into account the possibility of there being k outcomes on any particular trial.

Suppose that an experiment consists of n independent trials, much like the binomial case, but that each trial can result in any one of k possible outcomes. For example, a customer checking out of a grocery store may choose any one of k

checkout counters. Now, suppose the probability that a particular trial results in outcome i is denoted by p_i, $i = 1, \ldots, k$, and p_i remains constant from trial to trial. Let Y_i, $i = 1, \ldots, k$, denote the number of the n trials resulting in outcome i. In developing a formula for $P(Y_1 = y_1, \ldots, Y_k = y_k)$ we first call attention to the fact that, because of independence of trials, the probability of having y_1 outcomes of type 1 through y_k outcomes of type k in *a particular order* will be

$$p_1^{y_1} p_2^{y_2} \cdots p_k^{y_k}.$$

It only remains to count the number of such orderings, and this number turns out to be

$$\frac{n!}{y_1! y_2! \cdots y_k!},$$

where

$$\sum_{i=1}^{k} y_i = n.$$

Hence,

$$P(Y_1 = y_1, \ldots, Y_k = y_k) = \frac{n!}{y_1! y_2! \cdots y_k!} p_1^{y_1} p_2^{y_2} \cdots p_k^{y_k}.$$

This is called the *multinomial* probability distribution. Note that if $k = 2$, we are back into the binomial case.

The following example illustrates the computations.

EXAMPLE 3.13

Suppose that items under inspection are subject to two types of defects. About 70% of the items in a large lot are judged to be defect free, whereas 20% have a type A defect alone and 10% have a type B defect alone. (None have both types of defects.) If six of these items are randomly selected from the lot, find the probability that three have no defects, one has a type A defect and two have type B defects.

Solution   If we can assume that the outcomes are independent from trial to trial (item to item in our sample), which they would nearly be in a large lot, then the multinomial distribution provides a useful model. Letting Y_1, Y_2 and Y_3 denote the number of trials resulting in zero, type A and type B defectives, respectively, we have $p_1 = 0.7$, $p_2 = 0.2$ and $p_3 = 0.1$. It follows that

$$P(Y_1 = 3, Y_2 = 1, Y_3 = 2) = \frac{6!}{3! 1! 2!} (0.7)^3 (0.2)(0.1)^2$$

$$= 0.042. \quad \square$$

Each Y_i in the multinomial case will have a marginal distribution that is binomial, and for which means and variances were derived in Section 3.3.

THE MULTINOMIAL DISTRIBUTION

$$P(Y_1 = y_1, \ldots, Y_k = y_k) = \frac{n!}{y_1! y_2! \cdots y_k!} p_1^{y_1} p_2^{y_2} \cdots p_k^{y_k},$$

$$\text{where} \quad \sum_{i=1}^{k} y_i = n \quad \text{and} \quad \sum_{i=1}^{k} p_i = 1$$

$$E(Y_i) = np_i, \qquad V(Y_i) = np_i(1 - p_i), \qquad i = 1, \ldots, k.$$

Exercises

3.41   Customers leaving a subway station can exit through any one of three gates. Assuming that any one customer is equally likely to select any one of the three gates, find the probability that, among four customers,
(a) 2 select gate A, 1 selects gate B and 1 selects gate C.
(b) all four select the same gate.
(c) all three gates are used.

3.42   In a large lot of manufactured items, 10% contain exactly one defect and 5% contain more than one defect. If 10 items are randomly selected from this lot for sale, the repair costs total

$$Y_1 + 3Y_2,$$

where Y_1 denotes the number among the ten having one defect and Y_2 the number with two or more defects. Find the expected value of the repair costs.

3.43   Among a large number of applicants for a certain position, 60% have only a high school education, 30% have some college training, and 10% have completed a college degree. If 5 applicants are selected to be interviewed, find the probability that at least one will have completed a college degree. What assumptions are necessary for your answer to be valid?

3.44   Refer to Exercise 3.42. If Y denotes the number of items containing at least one defect, among the ten sampled items, find the probability that
(a) Y is exactly 2.   (b) Y is at least 1.

3.9   *The Moment-Generating Function*

We saw in earlier sections that if $g(Y)$ is a function of a random variable Y with probability distribution given by $p(y)$, then

$$E[g(Y)] = \sum_{y} g(y)p(y).$$

A special function with many theoretical uses in probability theory is the expected value of e^{tY}, for a random variable Y, and this expected value is called the *moment-generating function* (mgf). We denote mgf's by $M(t)$, and thus

$$M(t) = E(e^{tY}).$$

One use for this special function is that it does, in fact, generate moments, or expected values of powers, of Y. To see this, we differentiate $M(t)$ with respect to t, and assume the differentiation can be moved inside the expected value (which it can if the expected value exists). Thus,

$$\frac{dM(t)}{dt} = M^{(1)}(t) = E(Ye^{tY}).$$

Now, if we set $t = 0$, we have

$$M^{(1)}(0) = E(Y).$$

Going on to the second derivative,

$$M^{(2)}(t) = E(Y^2 e^{tY})$$

and

$$M^{(2)}(0) = E(Y^2).$$

In general,

$$M^{(k)}(0) = E(Y^k).$$

The mgf is very useful for the purpose of finding moments because it is often easier to evaluate $M(t)$ than to find the moments of the random variable directly. Other theoretical uses of the mgf will be seen in later chapters.

EXAMPLE 3.14

Evaluate the moment-generating function for the geometric distribution and use it to find the mean and variance of this distribution.

Solution   We have, for the geometric random variable Y,

$$M(t) = E(e^{tY}) = \sum_{y=1}^{\infty} e^{ty} p(1-p)^{y-1}$$

$$= pe^t \sum_{y=1}^{\infty} (1-p)^{y-1}(e^t)^{y-1}$$

$$= pe^t \sum_{y=1}^{\infty} [(1-p)e^t]^{y-1}$$

$$= pe^t\{1 + [(1-p)e^t] + [(1-p)e^t]^2 + \cdots\}$$

$$= pe^t \left[\frac{1}{1 - (1-p)e^t}\right],$$

since the series is a geometric progression with common ratio $(1-p)e^t$.

To evaluate the mean we have

$$M^{(1)}(t) = \frac{[1 - (1 - p)e^t]pe^t - pe^t[-(1 - p)e^t]}{[1 - (1 - p)e^t]^2}$$

$$= \frac{pe^t}{[1 - (1 - p)e^t]^2}$$

and

$$M^{(1)}(0) = \frac{p}{[1 - (1 - p)]^2} = \frac{1}{p}.$$

To evaluate the variance we first need

$$E(Y^2) = M^{(2)}(0).$$

Now,

$$M^{(2)}(t) = \frac{[1 - (1 - p)e^t]^2 pe^t - pe^t\{2[1 - (1 - p)e^t](-1)(1 - p)e^t\}}{[1 - (1 - p)e^t]^4}$$

and

$$M^{(2)}(0) = \frac{p^3 + 2p^2(1 - p)}{p^4} = \frac{p + 2(1 - p)}{p^2}.$$

Hence,

$$V(Y) = E(Y^2) - [E(Y)]^2$$

$$= \frac{p + 2(1 - p)}{p^2} - \frac{1}{p^2} = \frac{p + 2(1 - p) - 1}{p^2} = \frac{1 - p}{p^2}. \quad \square$$

Exercises

3.45 Find the moment-generating function for the Bernoulli random variable.

3.46 Show that the moment-generating function for the binomial random variable is given by

$$M(t) = [pe^t + (1 - p)]^n.$$

Use this result to derive the mean and variance for the binomial distribution.

3.47 Show that the moment-generating function for the Poisson random variable with mean λ is given by

$$M(t) = e^{\lambda(e^t - 1)}.$$

Use this result to derive the mean and variance for the Poisson distribution.

3.48   If X is a random variable with moment-generating function $M(t)$ and Y is a function of X given by $Y = aX + b$, show that the moment-generating function for Y is $e^{tb}M(at)$.

3.49   Use the result of Exercise 3.48 to show that

$$E(Y) = aE(X) + b$$

and

$$V(Y) = a^2 V(X).$$

3.10   *Conclusion*

Recall that a probability distribution is a model designed to represent the relative frequency behavior of a random variable. We have outlined a few common models that occur frequently in practice. However, this by no means exhausts the supply of possible models. In many instances the probability distribution will not have a nice mathematical formula, such as those given earlier in this chapter, and it may be necessary to simply list the possible values and their probabilities in tabular form. The following example illustrates this point.

EXAMPLE 3.15

Figure 3.1 represents an electrical circuit. Current flows from A to B if there is at least one closed path through the relays 1, 2 and 3.

Suppose that each relay closes properly, when a switch is thrown, with probability p and remains open with probability $(1 - p)$. The relays operate independently. Let Y denote the number of closed paths from A to B after the switch is thrown. Find the probability distribution for Y.

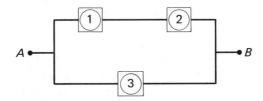

Figure 3.1

Solution   Note, first of all, that Y can take on only the values 0, 1, and 2. We will number the top path through relays 1 and 2 as path I, and the bottom path as path II. Because of independence, path I closes properly with probability p^2 and remains open with probability $1 - p^2$. Similarly, path II closes properly with probability p. Now,

$$P(Y = 0) = P(\text{path I is open and path II is open})$$
$$= (1 - p^2)(1 - p),$$

$$P(Y = 1) = P(\text{path I is open and path II is closed,}$$
$$\text{or path I is closed and path II is open})$$
$$= (1 - p^2)p + (1 - p)p^2,$$

and

$$P(Y = 2) = P(\text{path I is closed and path II is closed})$$
$$= p^2 \cdot p = p^3.$$

For any given value of p, numerical results can be easily evaluated. Y represents a discrete random variable, but it does not have one of the standard distributions discussed earlier in this chapter. □

In summary, the Bernoulli random variable is the basic building block for a number of probability distributions, including the binomial, geometric, and negative binomial. The Poisson distribution, which models counts in some restricted region of time, area, or space, can be obtained as a limiting case of the binomial.

In some cases, dependent trials can be modeled by the hypergeometric distribution.

The multinomial distribution extends the ideas of the binomial distribution to the case in which more than two outcomes may be possible on each trial.

These distributions are the most common of the discrete probability distributions, and serve as very useful models for a variety of practical problems.

Supplementary Exercises

3.50   The proportion of impurities, X, in certain ore samples is a random variable having probability density function

$$f(x) = \begin{cases} 12x^2(1 - x), & 0 \le x \le 1, \\ 0, & \text{elsewhere.} \end{cases}$$

If four such samples are independently selected, find the probability that:
(a) exactly one has a proportion of impurities exceeding 0.5.
(b) at least one has a proportion of impurities exceeding 0.5.

3.51   There are two entrances to a parking lot. Cars arrive at entrance I according to a Poisson distribution with an average of three per hour, and at entrance II according to a Poisson distribution with an average of four per hour. Find the probability that exactly three cars arrive at the parking lot in a given hour.

3.52   For a certain section of a pine forest, the number of diseased trees per acre, Y, has a Poisson distribution with mean $\lambda = 10$. The diseased trees are sprayed with an insecticide at a cost of $3.00 per tree, plus a fixed overhead cost for equipment rental of $50.00. Letting C denote the total spraying cost for a randomly selected acre, find the expected value and standard deviation for C. Within what interval would you expect C to lie with probability at least 0.75?

3.53   A certain type of bacteria cell divides at a constant rate, λ, over time. (That is, the probability that a cell will divide in a small interval of time, t, is approximately λt.) Given that a population starts out at time zero with k cells of this type and cell divisions are independent of one another, the size of the population at time t, $Y(t)$, has the probability distribution

$$P[Y(t) = n] = \binom{n-1}{k-1} e^{-\lambda kt}(1 - e^{-\lambda t})^{n-k}.$$

(a) Find the expected value of $Y(t)$ in terms of λ and t.
(b) If, for a certain type of bacteria cell, $\lambda = 0.1$ per second and the population starts out with 2 cells at time zero, find the expected population size after 5 seconds.

3.54   Find the moment generating function for the negative binomial distribution. Use the result to derive the mean and variance of this distribution.

3.55   Vehicles arriving at an intersection can turn right or left, or continue straight ahead. In a study of traffic patterns at this intersection over a long period of time, engineers have noted that 40% of the vehicles turn left, 25% turn right, and the remainder continue straight ahead.

(a) For the next five cars entering this intersection, find the probability that one turns left, one turns right, and three continue straight ahead.
(b) For the next five cars entering the intersection, find the probability that at least one turns right.
(c) If 100 cars enter the intersection in a day, find the expected value and variance of the number turning left. What assumptions are necessary for your answer to be valid?

3.56   The probability that any one vehicle will turn left at a particular intersection is 0.2. The left-turn lane at this intersection has room for three vehicles. If five vehicles arrive at this intersection while the light is red, find the probability that the left-turn lane will hold all of the vehicles that want to turn left.

3.57   Refer to Exercise 3.56. Find the probability that six cars must arrive at the intersection while the light is red in order to fill up the left-turn lane.

3.58   For any probability function $p(y)$, $\sum_y p(y) = 1$ if the sum is taken over all possible values, y, that the random variable in question can assume. Show that this is true for

(a) the binomial distribution.
(b) the geometric distribution.
(c) the Poisson distribution.

Common Continuous Probability Distributions

About This Chapter

Random variables that are not discrete, like measurements of life length or weight, can often be classified as *continuous*. This is the second category of random variables we will discuss. Probability distributions commonly used to model continuous random variables are presented in this chapter.

Contents

The basic ideas of both discrete and continuous random variables were introduced in Chapter 2, with some specific discrete distributions being discussed in detail in Chapter 3. We now continue in this same vein with a discussion of some common continuous distributions. You will see that the continuous distributions do not arise out of a specific set of assumptions quite as neatly as do the discrete distributions. Generally speaking, an appropriate continuous distribution for a specific problem is chosen by considering a number of theoretical points as well as by viewing data to see what type of function would appear to work well, as in the lifelength example of Chapter 2.

In succeeding sections, we will discuss the uniform, exponential, gamma, normal, and beta distributions.

Consider an experiment that consists of observing events occurring in a certain time frame, such as buses arriving at a bus stop or telephone calls coming into a switchboard. Suppose we know that one such event has occurred in the time interval (a, b). (A bus arrived between 8:00 and 8:10.) It may then be of interest to place a probability distribution on the actual time of occurrence of the event under observation, which we will denote by X. Certainly, X must be a continuous random variable and must lie between a and b. A very simple model assumes that X is equally likely to lie in any small subinterval, say of length d, no matter where that subinterval lies within (a, b). This assumption leads to the *uniform* probability distribution, which has probability density function given by

$$f(x) = \frac{1}{b - a}, \qquad a \le x \le b$$

$$= 0, \qquad \text{elsewhere.}$$

This density function is graphed in Figure 4.1.

If we consider any subinterval $(c, c + d)$ contained entirely within (a, b), we have

$$P(c \le X \le c + d) = \int_c^{c+d} f(x)\, dx$$

$$= \int_c^{c+d} \frac{1}{b - a}\, dx$$

$$= \frac{(c + d) - c}{b - a} = \frac{d}{b - a},$$

which does not depend on the location, c, of the subinterval.

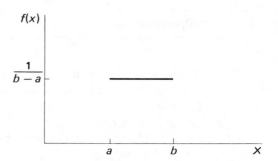

Figure 4.1   The Uniform
Probability Density Function

The uniform model works well for events that tend to occur "randomly" in time or space. In fact, there is a relationship between the uniform distribution and the Poisson distribution introduced in Section 3.6. Suppose the number of events occurring in an interval, say $(0, t)$, has a Poisson distribution. If exactly one of these events is known to have occurred in the interval (a, b), with $a \geq 0$ and $b \leq t$, then the probability distribution of the actual time of occurrence for this event is uniform over (a, b).

Paralleling the material presented in Chapter 3, we now look at the mean and variance of the uniform distribution. From Definition 2.17, we see that

$$E(X) = \int_{-\infty}^{\infty} xf(x)\,dx = \int_{a}^{b} x\left(\frac{1}{b-a}\right)dx$$

$$= \left(\frac{1}{b-a}\right)\left(\frac{b^2-a^2}{2}\right) = \frac{a+b}{2}.$$

It should seem intuitively reasonable that the mean value of a uniformly distributed random variable should lie at the midpoint of the interval.

Recalling from Theorem 2.2 that $V(X) = E(X-\mu)^2 = E(X^2) - \mu^2$, we have, for the uniform case,

$$E(X^2) = \int_{-\infty}^{\infty} x^2 f(x)\,dx$$

$$= \int_{a}^{b} x^2\left(\frac{1}{b-a}\right)dx$$

$$= \left(\frac{1}{b-a}\right)\left(\frac{b^3-a^3}{3}\right) = \frac{b^2+ab+a^2}{3}.$$

Thus,

$$V(X) = \frac{b^2+ab+a^2}{3} - \left(\frac{a+b}{2}\right)^2$$

$$= \frac{1}{12}\left[4(b^2+ab+a^2) - 3(a+b)^2\right]$$

$$= \frac{1}{12}(b-a)^2.$$

This result is not that intuitive, but we do see that the variance only depends upon the length of the interval (a, b).

EXAMPLE 4.1

The failure of a certain component part of an industrial operation causes the operation to be shut down until a new part is delivered. Delivery time, X, is uniformly distributed over the interval one to five days. The cost, C, of this failure and shutdown consists of a fixed cost, c_0, for the new part and a cost that increases proportional to X^2, so that

$$C = c_0 + c_1 X^2.$$

Find the expected cost of a single component failure.

Solution   We know that

$$E(C) = c_0 + c_1 E(X^2)$$

and so it remains to find $E(X^2)$. This could be found directly from the definition or by using the variance and the fact that

$$E(X^2) = V(X) + \mu^2.$$

Using the latter approach,

$$E(X^2) = \frac{(b-a)^2}{12} + \left(\frac{a+b}{2}\right)^2$$

$$= \frac{(5-1)^2}{12} + \left(\frac{1+5}{2}\right)^2 = \frac{31}{3}.$$

Thus,

$$E(C) = c_0 + c_1\left(\frac{31}{3}\right). \quad \square$$

We now summarize the properties of the uniform distribution.

THE UNIFORM DISTRIBUTION

$$f(x) = \frac{1}{b-a}, \qquad a \le x \le b,$$

$$= 0, \qquad \text{elsewhere.}$$

$$E(X) = \frac{a+b}{2}, \qquad V(X) = \frac{(b-a)^2}{12}$$

Exercises

4.1   Suppose X has a uniform distribution over the interval (a, b).
(a) Find $F(X)$.
(b) Find $P(X > c)$, for some point c, between a and b.
(c) If $a \leq c \leq d \leq b$, find $P(X > d \mid X > c)$.

4.2   Arrivals of customers at a certain checkout counter follow a Poisson distribution. It is known that during a given 30-minute period, one customer arrived at the counter. Find the probability that he arrived during the last five minutes of the 30-minute period.

4.3   Refer to Exercise 4.2. Find the conditional probability that the customer arrived during the last five minutes of the 30-minute period, given that there were no arrivals during the first ten minutes of the period.

4.4   In tests of stopping distances for automobiles, those automobiles traveling at 30 miles per hour before the brakes are applied tend to travel distances that appear to be uniformly distributed between two points, a and b. Find the probability that one of these automobiles
(a) stops closer to a than to b.
(b) stops so that the distance to a is more than three times the distance to b.

4.5   Refer to Exercise 4.4. Suppose three automobiles are used in a test of the type discussed there. Find the probability that exactly one of the three travels past the midpoint between a and b.

4.6   The cycle time for trucks hauling concrete to a highway construction site is uniformly distributed over the interval 50 to 70 minutes.
(a) Find the expected value and variance for these cycle times.
(b) How many trucks would you expect to have to schedule to this job so that a truckload of concrete can be dumped at the site every 15 minutes?

4.3   *The Exponential Distribution*

The lifelength data of Chapter 2 displayed a probabilistic behavior that was not uniform, but rather one in which the probability over intervals of constant length decreased as the intervals moved further and further to the right. We saw that an exponential curve seemed to fit this data rather well, and now discuss this exponential probability distribution in more detail. In general, the exponential density function is given by

$$f(x) = \frac{1}{\theta} e^{-x/\theta}, \qquad x \geq 0$$

$$= 0, \qquad \text{elsewhere}$$

where θ is a constant that determines the rate at which the curve decreases. (Constants, like θ, which determine the specific nature of the density function are called

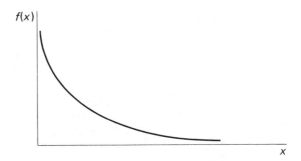

Figure 4.2   An Exponential
Probability Density
Function

parameters.) An exponential density function with $\theta = 2$ was sketched in Figure 2.9, and, in general, the exponential functions have the form shown in Figure 4.2.

Finding expected values for the exponential case requires the evaluation of a certain type of integral called a gamma (Γ) function. The function $\Gamma(n)$ is defined by

$$\Gamma(n) = \int_0^\infty x^{n-1} e^{-x} \, dx \; .$$

Upon integrating by parts, it can be shown that $\Gamma(n) = (n-1)\Gamma(n-1)$ and, hence, that

$$\Gamma(n) = (n-1)!$$

if n is a positive integer.

Suppose that a constant term, θ, appears in the exponent and we wish to evaluate

$$\int_0^\infty x^{n-1} e^{-x/\theta} \, dx.$$

By a transformation of variable techniques we can show that

$$\int_0^\infty x^{n-1} e^{-x/\theta} \, dx = \Gamma(n)\theta^n.$$

Using the above result we see that, for the exponential distribution,

$$E(X) = \int_{-\infty}^\infty xf(x) \, dx = \int_0^\infty x\left(\frac{1}{\theta}\right) e^{-x/\theta} \, dx$$

$$= \frac{1}{\theta} \int_0^\infty xe^{-x/\theta} \, dx$$

$$= \frac{1}{\theta} \Gamma(2)\theta^2 = \theta.$$

Thus, the parameter θ is actually the mean of the distribution.

To evaluate the variance of the exponential distribution, first we can find

$$E(X^2) = \int_0^\infty x^2 \left(\frac{1}{\theta}\right) e^{-x/\theta} \, dx$$

$$= \frac{1}{\theta} \Gamma(3)\theta^3 = 2\theta^2.$$

It follows that

$$V(X) = E(X^2) - \mu^2$$
$$= 2\theta^2 - \theta^2 = \theta^2,$$

and θ becomes the standard deviation as well as the mean.

The moment-generating function for the exponential distribution is, likewise, easily evaluated as follows:

$$M(t) = E(e^{tX}) = \int_0^\infty e^{tx} \left(\frac{1}{\theta}\right) e^{-x/\theta} dx$$

$$= \frac{1}{\theta} \int_0^\infty e^{-x(1-\theta t)/\theta} dx$$

$$= \frac{1}{\theta} \Gamma(1) \left(\frac{\theta}{1-\theta t}\right) = \frac{1}{1-\theta t}.$$

We could have obtained the mean from this result, since

$$E(X) = M'(0) = -(1 - \theta t)^{-2}(-\theta)\Big]_{t=0}$$
$$= \theta.$$

The distribution function for the exponential case has a simple form, seen to be

$$F(t) = P(X \le t) = \int_0^t \frac{1}{\theta} e^{-x/\theta} dx$$

$$= -e^{-x/\theta}\Big]_0^t = 1 - e^{-t/\theta}.$$

EXAMPLE 4.2

A certain manufacturing plant has three production lines, all making use of a specific bulk product. The amount of product used in one day can be modeled as having an exponential distribution with a mean of 4 (measurements in tons), for each of the three lines. If the lines operate independently, find the probability that exactly two of the three lines use more than 4 tons on a given day.

Solution   The probability that any given line uses more than four tons is, with X denoting the amount used,

$$P(X > 4) = \int_4^\infty f(x)\,dx = \int_4^\infty \frac{1}{4} e^{-x/4} dx$$

$$= -e^{-x/4}\Big]_4^\infty = e^{-1} = 0.37.$$

(Note that $P(X > 4) \neq 0.5$)

Knowledge of the distribution function could allow us to evaluate this immediately as

$$P(X > 4) = 1 - P(X \le 4) = 1 - (1 - e^{-4/4})$$
$$= e^{-1}.$$

Now, assuming the three lines operate independently, the problem is to find the probability of two successes out of three tries where 0.37 denotes the probability of success. This is a binomial problem, and the solution is

$$P(\text{exactly 2 use more than 4 tons}) = \binom{3}{2}(0.37)^2(0.63)$$
$$= 3(0.37)^2(0.63)$$
$$= 0.26. \quad \square$$

EXAMPLE 4.3

Consider a particular line in the plant of Example 4.2. How much of the bulk product should be stocked for that line so that the chance of running out of product is only 0.05?

Solution   Let a denote the amount to be stocked. Since the amount to be used, X, has an exponential distribution, we have

$$P(X > a) = \int_a^\infty \frac{1}{4} e^{-x/4} \, dx = e^{-a/4}.$$

We want to choose a so that

$$P(X > a) = e^{-a/4} = 0.05,$$

and solving this equation yields

$$a = 11.98. \quad \square$$

As in the uniform case, there is a relationship between the exponential distribution and the Poisson distribution. Suppose events are occurring in time according to a Poisson distribution with a rate of λ events per hour. Thus, in t hours the number of events, say Y, will have a Poisson distribution with mean value λt. Suppose we start at time zero and ask the question "How long do I have to wait to see the first event occur?" Let X denote the length of time until this first event. Then,

$$P(X > t) = P(Y = 0 \text{ on the interval } (0, t))$$
$$= (\lambda t)^0 e^{-\lambda t}/0! = e^{-\lambda t}$$

and

$$P(X \le t) = 1 - P(X > t) = 1 - e^{-\lambda t}.$$

We see that $P(X < t) = F(t)$, the distribution function for X, has the form of an exponential distribution function with $\lambda = (1/\theta)$. Upon differentiating, we see that the probability density function of X is given by

$$f(t) = \frac{dF(t)}{dt} = \frac{d(1 - e^{-\lambda t})}{dt}$$

$$= \lambda e^{-\lambda t}$$

$$= \frac{1}{\theta} e^{-t/\theta}, \qquad t > 0,$$

and X has an exponential distribution. Actually, we need not start at time zero for it can be shown that the waiting time from the occurrence of any one event until the occurrence of the next event will have an exponential distribution, for events occurring according to a Poisson distribution.

Besides probability density and distribution functions, there is another function that is of use in studying properties of continuous distributions, especially in working with lifelength data. Suppose X denotes the lifelength of a component with density function $f(x)$ and distribution function $F(x)$. The *failure rate function*, $\gamma(t)$, is defined as

$$\gamma(t) = \frac{f(t)}{1 - F(t)}, \qquad t > 0.$$

For an intuitive look at what $\gamma(t)$ is measuring, suppose dt denotes a very small interval around the point t . Then, $f(t)\, dt$ is approximately the probability that X takes on a value in $(t, t + dt)$. Also, $1 - F(t) = P(X > t)$. Thus,

$$\gamma(t)\, dt = \frac{f(t)\, dt}{1 - F(t)}$$

$$\approx P(X \in (t, t + dt)|X > t).$$

In other words, $\gamma(t)$ represents the probability of failure at time t, given that the component has survived up to time t.

For the exponential case,

$$\gamma(t) = \frac{f(t)}{1 - F(t)} = \frac{\dfrac{1}{\theta} e^{-t/\theta}}{e^{-t/\theta}} = \frac{1}{\theta},$$

or X has a *constant* failure rate. It is unlikely that many individual components have a constant failure rate over time (most fail more frequently as they age) but it may be true of some systems that undergo regular preventive maintenance.

We here summarize the properties of the exponential distribution.

THE EXPONENTIAL DISTRIBUTION

$$f(x) = \frac{1}{\theta} e^{-x/\theta}, \qquad x > 0$$

$$= 0, \qquad \text{elsewhere.}$$

$$E(X) = \theta, \qquad V(X) = \theta^2$$

Exercises

4.7   Suppose Y has an exponential density function with mean θ. Show that $P(Y > a + b \mid Y > a) = P(Y > b)$. This is referred to as the "memoryless" property of the exponential distribution.

4.8   The magnitudes of earthquakes recorded in a region of North America can be modeled by an exponential distribution with mean 2.4, as measured on the Richter scale. Find the probability that the next earthquake to strike this region will
(a) exceed 3.0 on the Richter scale.
(b) fall between 2.0 and 3.0 on the Richter scale.

4.9   Refer to Exercise 4.8. Out of the next ten earthquakes to strike this region, find the probability that at least one will exceed 5.0 on the Richter scale.

4.10 A pumping station operator observes that the demand for water at a certain hour of the day can be modeled as an exponential random variable with a mean of 100 cfs (cubic feet per second).
(a) Find the probability that the demand will exceed 200 cfs on a randomly selected day.
(b) What is the maximum water-producing capacity that the station should keep on line for this hour so that the demand will exceed this production capacity with a probability of only 0.01?

4.11 Suppose customers arrive at a certain checkout counter at the rate of two every minute.
(a) Find the mean and variance of the waiting time between successive customer arrivals.
(b) If a clerk takes 3 minutes to serve the first customer arriving at the counter, what is the probability that at least one more customer is waiting when the service of the first customer is completed?

4.12 The length of time, X, to complete a certain key task in house construction is an exponentially distributed random variable with a mean of 10 hours. The cost, C, of completing this task is related to the square of the time to completion by the formula

$$C = 100 + 40X + 3X^2.$$

(a) Find the expected value and variance of C.
(b) Would you expect C to exceed 2000 very often?

4.4   *The Gamma Distribution*

Many sets of data, of course, will not have relative frequency curves with the smooth decreasing trend found in the exponential model. It is, perhaps, more common to see distributions that have low probabilities for intervals close to zero, with the probability increasing for a while as the interval moves to the right (in the positive direction) and then decreasing as the interval moves to the extreme positive side. That is, the relative frequency curves appear as in Figure 4.3.

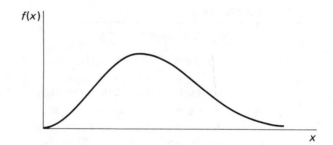

Figure 4.3   A Common
Relative Frequency
Curve

A class of functions that serve as good models for this type of behavior is the *gamma* class. The gamma probability density function is given by

$$f(x) = \frac{1}{\Gamma(\alpha)\beta^\alpha} x^{\alpha-1} e^{-x/\beta}, \qquad x > 0$$

$$= 0, \qquad \text{elsewhere,}$$

where α and β are parameters that determine the specific shape of the curve. Note immediately that the gamma density reduces to the exponential when $\alpha = 1$. The constant $\Gamma(\alpha)\beta^\alpha$ is simply the correct one to make $\int_0^\infty f(x)\,dx = 1$. Recall from Section 4.3 that $\int_0^\infty x^{\alpha-1} e^{-x/\beta}\,dx = \Gamma(\alpha)\beta^\alpha$. The parameter α need not be an integer, but α and β must both be positive. Some typical gamma densities are shown in Figure 4.4.

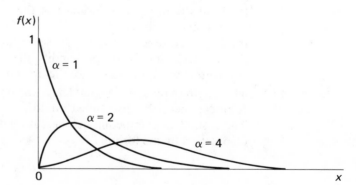

Figure 4.4   The
Gamma Density
Function, $\beta = 1$

The derivation of expectations here is very similar to the exponential case of Section 4.3. We have

$$E(X) = \int_{-\infty}^{\infty} xf(x)\,dx = \int_{0}^{\infty} x\,\frac{1}{\Gamma(\alpha)\beta^{\alpha}}\,x^{\alpha-1}e^{-x/\beta}\,dx$$

$$= \frac{1}{\Gamma(\alpha)\beta^{\alpha}} \int_{0}^{\infty} x^{\alpha}e^{-x/\beta}\,dx$$

$$= \frac{1}{\Gamma(\alpha)\beta^{\alpha}} \Gamma(\alpha+1)\beta^{\alpha+1} = \alpha\beta.$$

Similar manipulations yield $E(X^2) = \alpha(\alpha+1)\beta^2$ and, hence,

$$V(X) = E(X^2) - \mu^2$$
$$= \alpha(\alpha+1)\beta^2 - \alpha^2\beta^2 = \alpha\beta^2.$$

The moment-generating function has similar form to that of the exponential and works out to be

$$M(t) = (1 - \beta t)^{-\alpha}.$$

We now consider another use of the moment-generating function. A very useful property is the fact that moment-generating functions are unique, that is, two different distributions cannot have the same moment-generating function. In other words, if we can find the moment generating function for a random variable and recognize it as coming from a specific distribution, then the random variable *must* have that specific distribution.

To show how this idea works, we look at the sum of two independent exponential random variables with the same mean, and observe that the sum must have a gamma distribution. More specifically, let X_1 and X_2 be independent exponential random variables with common mean θ. Let $Y = X_1 + X_2$. We can directly evaluate the mgf of Y since

$$M_Y(t) = E(e^{tY}) = E(e^{t(X_1+X_2)}) = E(e^{tX_1}e^{tX_2})$$
$$= E(e^{tX_1})E(e^{tX_2}).$$

(See Theorem 2.4.) Thus,

$$M_Y(t) = M_{X_1}(t)M_{X_2}(t)$$
$$M_Y(t) = (1 - \theta t)^{-1}(1 - \theta t)^{-1} = (1 - \theta t)^{-2}.$$

Upon inspection, we see that the mgf of Y has the form of a gamma mgf. Thus, Y must have a gamma distribution with $\alpha = 2$ and $\beta = \theta$.

This idea can be extended to the fact that if $Y = \sum_{i=1}^{n} X_i$ where the X_i's are independent exponential random variables with common mean θ, then Y will have a gamma distribution with $\alpha = n$ and $\beta = \theta$.

EXAMPLE 4.4

A certain electronic system having lifelength, X_1, with an exponential distribution and mean 400 hours, is supported by an identical backup system with lifelength X_2. The backup system takes over immediately when the primary system fails. If the systems operate independently, find the probability distribution and expected value for the total lifelength of the primary and backup system.

Solution   Letting Y denote the total lifelength, we have $Y = X_1 + X_2$ where X_1 and X_2 are independent exponential random variables, each with mean $\theta = 400$. By the results found above, Y will then have a gamma distribution with $\alpha = 2$ and $\beta = 400$, that is,

$$f_Y(y) = \frac{1}{\Gamma(2)(400)^2} \, y e^{-y/400}, \qquad y > 0.$$

The mean value is given by

$$E(Y) = \alpha\beta = 2(400) = 800,$$

which is an intuitive answer.   □

The failure rate function, $\gamma(t)$, for the gamma case is not easily displayed since $F(t)$ is quite cumbersome. However, for $\alpha > 1$, this function will increase but is always bounded above by $1/\beta$. A typical form is shown in Figure 4.5.

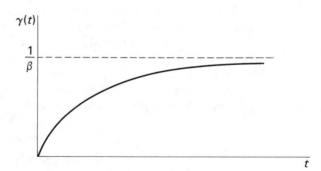

Figure 4.5   The Failure Rate Function for the Gamma Distribution ($\alpha > 1$)

The properties of the gamma distribution are summarized here.

THE GAMMA DISTRIBUTION

$$f(x) = \frac{1}{\Gamma(\alpha)\beta^\alpha} x^{\alpha - 1} e^{-x/\beta}, \qquad x > 0$$

$$= 0, \qquad \text{elsewhere.}$$

$$E(X) = \alpha\beta, \qquad V(X) = \alpha\beta^2$$

Exercises

4.13 Let Y denote a random variable having the gamma distribution with parameters α and β. Show that the moment generating function for Y is given by

$$M(t) = (1 - \beta t)^{-\alpha}.$$

4.14 Four-week summer rainfall totals in a certain section of the midwestern United States have a relative frequency histogram that appears to fit closely to a gamma distribution with $\alpha = 1.6$ and $\beta = 2.0$.
(a) Find the mean and variance of this distribution of four-week rainfall totals.
(b) Find an interval that will include the rainfall total for a selected four-week period with probability at least 0.75.

4.15 Annual incomes for engineers in a certain industry have approximately a gamma distribution with $\alpha = 440$ and $\beta = 50$.
(a) Find the mean and variance of these incomes.
(b) Would you expect to find many engineers in this industry with an annual income exceeding $35,000?

4.16 The weekly downtime, Y, (in hours) for a certain industrial machine has approximately a gamma distribution with $\alpha = 3$ and $\beta = 2$. The loss, in dollars, to the industrial operation as a result of this downtime is given by

$$L = 30Y + 2Y^2.$$

(a) Find the expected value and variance of L.
(b) Find an interval in which L will be on approximately 89% of the weeks that the machine is in use.

4.17 Refer to Exercise 4.11. Find the mean, variance, and probability density function of the waiting time between the opening of the counter and
(a) the arrival of the second customer.
(b) the arrival of the third customer.

4.18 Refer to Exercise 4.12. Suppose two houses are to be built and each will involve the completion of a certain key task. The task has an exponentially distributed time to completion with a mean of 10 hours. Assuming the completion times are independent for the two houses, find the mean, variance, and probability density function of
(a) the *total* time to complete both tasks.
(b) the *average* time to complete the two tasks.

4.19 The total sustained load on the concrete footing of a planned building is the sum of the dead load plus the occupancy load. Suppose the dead load, X_1, has a gamma distribution with $\alpha_1 = 50$ and $\beta_1 = 2$ while the occupancy load, X_2, has a gamma distribution with $\alpha_2 = 20$ and $\beta_2 = 2$. (Units are in kips.)
(a) Find the mean, variance, and probability density function of the total sustained load on the footing.

(b) Find a value for the sustained load that should only be exceeded with probability less than 1/16.

4.20   A forty-year history of maximum river flows for a certain small river in the United States shows a relative frequency histogram that can be modeled by a gamma density function with $\alpha = 1.6$ and $\beta = 150$. (Measurements are in cubic feet per second).

(a) Find the mean and standard deviation of the annual maximum river flows.

(b) Within what interval will the maximum annual flow fall with probability at least 8/9?

4.5   *The Normal Distribution*

Perhaps the most widely used of all the continuous probability distributions is the one referred to as the normal distribution. The normal probability density function has the familiar symmetric "bell" shape as indicated in Figure 4.6. The curve is centered at the mean value, μ, and its spread is, of course, measured by the variance, σ^2. These two parameters, μ and σ^2, completely determine the shape and location of the normal density function, whose functional form is given by

$$f(x) = \frac{1}{\sqrt{2\pi}\sigma} e^{-(x-\mu)^2/2\sigma^2}, \qquad -\infty < x < \infty.$$

The actual derivations of the facts that $E(X) = \mu$ and $V(X) = \sigma^2$, using the density function and standard definitions, are somewhat complicated and are not presented here. We will look at their derivation through the use of the moment-generating function a little later.

The basic reason that the normal distribution works well as a model for many different types of measurements generated in real experiments will be discussed in some detail in Chapter 5. For now we simply say that any time responses tend to be averages of independent quantities, the normal distribution will quite likely provide a reasonably good model for their relative frequency

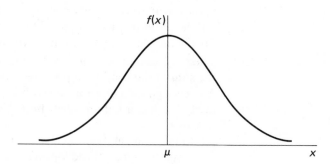

Figure 4.6   A Normal
Density Function

behavior. Many naturally occurring measurements tend to have relative frequency distributions closely resembling the normal curve, probably because nature tends to "average out" the affects of the many variables that relate to a particular response. For example, heights of adult American males tend to have a distribution that shows many measurements clumped closely about a mean height, with relatively few very short or very tall males in the population. In other words, the relative frequency distribution is close to normal.

In contrast, lifelengths of biological organisms or electronic components tend to have relative frequency distributions that are *not* normal, or close to normal. This often results from the fact that lifelength measurements are a product of "extreme" behavior, not "average" behavior. A component may fail because of one extremely hard shock rather than the average affect of many shocks. Thus, the normal distribution is not often used to model lifelengths, and consequently we will not discuss the failure rate function for this distribution.

Returning to properties of the normal distribution, we now take a look at the moment-generating function. Recall that the mgf is given by

$$M(t) = E(e^{tX}) = \int_{-\infty}^{\infty} e^{tx} f(x) \, dx$$

$$= \frac{1}{\sqrt{2\pi}\sigma} \int_{-\infty}^{\infty} e^{tx} e^{-(x-\mu)^2/2\sigma^2} \, dx.$$

This integral can be evaluated with little difficulty, but rather than going through the details here we will leave them as an exercise for the interested reader.

The result turns out to be

$$M(t) = E(e^{tX}) = e^{\mu t + t^2\sigma^2/2}.$$

We can now easily see that

$$E(X) = M'(0) = (\mu + t\sigma^2)e^{\mu t + t^2\sigma^2/2}\Big]_{t=0}$$

$$= \mu.$$

Using $M''(0)$ to find $E(X^2)$, we can similarly show that $V(X) = \sigma^2$.

A very useful property of the normal distribution is that any linear function of a normally distributed random variable will again be normally distributed. That is, if X has a normal distribution and $Y = aX + b$ for constants a and b, then Y will also be normally distributed. The mgf provides us with a convenient tool to prove this result. If X is normal with mean μ and variance σ^2, then

$$M_X(t) = e^{\mu t + t^2\sigma^2/2}.$$

Now,

$$M_Y(t) = E(e^{tY}) = E(e^{t(aX+b)})$$

$$= E(e^{taX}e^{tb})$$

$$= e^{tb}E(e^{(at)X})$$

and $E(e^{(at)X})$ is simply the mgf for X with t replaced by (at). Thus,

$$M_Y(t) = e^{tb} e^{\mu(at) + (at)^2 \sigma^2/2}$$
$$= e^{t(a\mu + b) + t^2(a\sigma)^2/2}.$$

Comparing the form of $M_Y(t)$ to $M_X(t)$, we see that Y must have a normal distribution with mean $(a\mu + b)$ and variance $(a\sigma)^2 = a^2\sigma^2$. (We could have derived the mean and variance of Y directly.)

An application of this result shows us how to obtain a standardized (or standard) normal random variable from any normally distributed variable. Again, suppose X has a normal distribution with mean μ and variance σ^2. Let

$$Z = \frac{X - \mu}{\sigma}.$$

Note that Z is of the form $aX + b$ where $a = 1/\sigma$ and $b = -\mu/\sigma$. Thus, Z is normally distributed with mean $a\mu + b = (1/\sigma)(\mu) + (-\mu/\sigma) = 0$ and variance $a^2\sigma^2 = 1$. The random variable Z is said to have a *standard normal distribution*.

Since any normally distributed random variable can be transformed to the standard normal, probabilities can be evaluated for any normal distribution simply by having a table of standard normal integrals available. Such a table is given in Table 4 of the Appendix. Table 4 gives numerical values for

$$P(0 \le Z \le z) = \int_0^z \frac{1}{\sqrt{2\pi}} e^{-x^2/2} dx.$$

Values of the integral are given for z between 0.00 and 3.09.

EXAMPLE 4.5

If Z denotes a standard normal random variable, find
(a) $P(Z \le 1)$.   (b) $P(Z > 1)$.
(c) $P(Z < -1.5)$.   (d) $P(-1.5 \le Z \le 0.5)$.

Solution

This example merely provides practice in reading Table 4. We see that:
(a) $P(Z \le 1) = P(Z \le 0) + P(0 \le Z \le 1)$
$$= 0.5 + 0.3413 = 0.8413.$$

(b) $P(Z > 1) = 0.5 - P(0 \le Z \le 1)$
$$= 0.5 - 0.3413 = 0.1587.$$

(c) $P(Z < -1.5) = P(Z > 1.5)$
$$= 0.5 - P(0 \le Z \le 1.5)$$
$$= 0.5 - 0.4332 = 0.0668.$$

(d) $P(-1.5 \le Z \le 0.5) = P(-1.5 \le Z \le 0) + P(0 \le Z \le 0.5)$
$$= P(0 \le Z \le 1.5) + P(0 \le Z \le 0.5)$$
$$= 0.4332 + 0.1915$$
$$= 0.6247. \quad \square$$

The next example illustrates how the standardization works to allow Table 4 to be used for any normally distributed random variable.

EXAMPLE 4.6

A firm that manufactures and bottles apple juice has a machine that automatically fills 16 ounce bottles. There is, however, some variation in the ounces of liquid dispensed into each bottle by the machine. Over a long period of time, the average amount dispensed into the bottles was 16 ounces, but there is a standard deviation of one ounce in these measurements. If the ounces of fill per bottle can be assumed to be normally distributed, find the probability that the machine will dispense more than 17 ounces of liquid in any one bottle.

Solution

Let X denote the ounces of liquid dispensed into one bottle by the filling machine. Then, X is assumed to be normally distributed with mean 16 and standard deviation 1. Hence,

$$P(X > 17) = P\left(\frac{X - \mu}{\sigma} > \frac{17 - \mu}{\sigma}\right) = P\left(Z > \frac{17 - 16}{1}\right)$$

$$= P(Z > 1) = 0.1587.$$

The answer is found from Table 4 since $Z = (X - \mu)/\sigma$ has a *standard* normal distribution.   □

EXAMPLE 4.7

Suppose that another machine, similar to the one of Example 4.6, operates so that ounces of fill have a mean equal to the dial setting for "amount of liquid," but have a standard deviation of 1.2 ounces. Find the proper setting for the dial so that 17-ounce bottles will overflow only 5% of the time. Assume that the amounts dispensed have a normal distribution.

Solution

Letting X denote the amount of liquid dispensed, we are now looking for a μ-value such that

$$P(X > 17) = 0.05.$$

Now,

$$P(X > 17) = P\left(\frac{X - \mu}{\sigma} > \frac{17 - \mu}{\sigma}\right)$$

$$= P\left(Z > \frac{17 - \mu}{1.2}\right).$$

From Table 4, we know that if

$$P(Z > z_0) = 0.05$$

then $z_0 = 1.645$. Thus, it must be that

$$\frac{17 - \mu}{1.2} = 1.645$$

and

$$\mu = 17 - 1.2(1.645) = 15.026. \quad \square$$

As mentioned earlier, we will make much more use of the normal distribution in later chapters, especially those that look into the basic notions of statistical inference. The basic properties are summarized here.

THE NORMAL DISTRIBUTION

$$f(x) = \frac{1}{\sqrt{2\pi}\sigma} e^{-(x-\mu)^2/2\sigma^2}, \quad -\infty < x < \infty.$$

$$E(X) = \mu, \quad V(X) = \sigma^2$$

Exercises

4.21   Use Table 4 of the Appendix to find the following probabilities for a standard normal random variable, Z.
(a) $P(0 \le Z \le 1.2)$ (b) $P(-0.9 \le Z \le 0)$
(c) $P(0.3 \le Z \le 1.56)$ (d) $P(-0.2 \le Z \le 0.2)$
(e) $P(-2.00 \le Z \le -1.56)$

4.22   For a standard normal random variable, Z, use Table 4 of the Appendix to find a number, z_0, such that
(a) $P(Z \le z_0) = 0.5$.   (b) $P(Z \le z_0) = 0.8749$.
(c) $P(Z \ge z_0) = 0.117$.   (d) $P(Z \ge z_0) = 0.617$.
(e) $P(-z_0 \le Z \le z_0) = 0.90$. (f) $P(-z_0 \le Z \le z_0) = 0.95$.

4.23   The weekly amount spent for maintenance and repairs in a certain company has approximately a normal distribution with a mean of $400 and a standard deviation of $20. If $450 is budgeted to cover repairs for next week, what is the probability that the actual costs will exceed the budgeted amount?

4.24   Refer to Exercise 4.23. How much should be budgeted weekly for maintenance and repairs so that the budgeted amount will be exceeded with probability only 0.1?

4.25   A machining operation produces steel shafts having diameters that are normally distributed with a mean of 1.005 inches and a standard deviation of 0.01 inch. Specifications call for diameters to fall within the interval 1.00 ± 0.02 inches. What percentage of the output of this operation will fail to meet specifications?

4.26   Refer to Exercise 4.25. What should be the mean diameter of the shafts produced in order to minimize the fraction not meeting specifications?

4.27   Wires manufactured for use in a certain computer system are specified to have resistances between 0.12 and 0.14 ohms. The actual measured resistances of the wires produced by Company A have a normal probability distribution with a mean of 0.13 ohm and a standard deviation of 0.005 ohm.

(a) What is the probability that a randomly selected wire from Company A's production will meet the specifications?

(b) If four such wires are used in the system and all are selected from Company A, what is the probability that all four will meet the specifications?

4.28   A machine for filling cereal boxes has a standard deviation of 1 ounce on ounces of fill per box. What setting of the mean ounces of fill per box will allow 16-ounce boxes to overflow only 1% of the time? Assume that the ounces of fill per box are normally distributed.

4.29   Refer to Exercise 4.28. Suppose the standard deviation, σ, is not known but can be fixed at certain levels by carefully adjusting the machine. What is the largest value of σ that will allow the actual value dispensed to be within one ounce of the mean with probability at least 0.95?

4.30   Suppose X_1 and X_2 are independent normally distributed random variables. Let $E(X_1) = \mu_1$, $E(X_2) = \mu_2$, $V(X_1) = \sigma_1^2$ and $V(X_2) = \sigma_2^2$. Show, by the use of moment-generating functions, that

$$U = a_1 X_1 + a_2 X_2,$$

for real numbers a_1 and a_2, has a normal distribution with

$$E(U) = a_1\mu_1 + a_2\mu_2$$

and

$$V(U) = a_1^2\sigma_1^2 + a_2^2\sigma_2^2.$$

4.31   A certain type of elevator has a maximum weight capacity, X_1, which is normally distributed with a mean and standard deviation of 5000 and 300 pounds, respectively. For a certain building equipped with this type of elevator, the elevator loading, X_2, is a normally distributed random variable with a mean and standard deviation of 4000 and 400 pounds, respectively. For any given time that the elevator is in use, find the probability that it will be overloaded, assuming X_1 and X_2 are independent.

4.6   *The Beta Distribution*

Except for the uniform distribution of Section 4.2, the continuous distributions discussed thus far are defined as nonzero functions over an infinite interval. It is of value to have at our disposal another class of distributions that can be used to model phenomena constrained to a finite interval of possible values. One such class, the beta distributions, is very useful for modeling the probabilistic behavior of certain random variables, such as proportions, constrained to fall in the interval (0, 1). (Actually, any finite interval can be transformed to (0, 1).) The beta distribution has the functional form

$$f(x) = \frac{\Gamma(\alpha + \beta)}{\Gamma(\alpha)\Gamma(\beta)} x^{\alpha - 1}(1 - x)^{\beta - 1}, \qquad 0 < x < 1$$

$$= 0, \qquad \text{elsewhere,}$$

where α and β are positive constants. The constant term in $f(x)$ is necessary so that

$$\int_0^1 f(x)\,dx = 1.$$

In other words,

$$\int_0^1 x^{\alpha - 1}(1 - x)^{\beta - 1}\,dx = \frac{\Gamma(\alpha)\Gamma(\beta)}{\Gamma(\alpha + \beta)}$$

for positive α and β. This is a handy result to keep in mind. The graphs of some common beta curves are shown in Figure 4.7.

The expected value of a beta random variable is easily found, since

$$E(X) = \int_0^1 x \frac{\Gamma(\alpha + \beta)}{\Gamma(\alpha)\Gamma(\beta)} x^{\alpha - 1}(1 - x)^{\beta - 1}\,dx$$

$$= \frac{\Gamma(\alpha + \beta)}{\Gamma(\alpha)\Gamma(\beta)} \int_0^1 x^{\alpha}(1 - x)^{\beta - 1}\,dx$$

$$= \frac{\Gamma(\alpha + \beta)}{\Gamma(\alpha)\Gamma(\beta)} \cdot \frac{\Gamma(\alpha + 1)\Gamma(\beta)}{\Gamma(\alpha + \beta + 1)}$$

$$= \frac{\alpha}{\alpha + \beta}.$$

(Recall that $\Gamma(n + 1) = n\Gamma(n)$.) Similar manipulations reveal that

$$V(X) = \frac{\alpha\beta}{(\alpha + \beta)^2(\alpha + \beta + 1)}.$$

We illustrate the use of this density function in an example.

EXAMPLE 4.8

A gasoline wholesale distributor has bulk storage tanks holding a fixed supply. The tanks are filled every Monday. Of interest to the wholesaler is the proportion of this supply that is sold during the week. Over many weeks, this proportion has been observed to be modeled fairly well by a beta distribution with

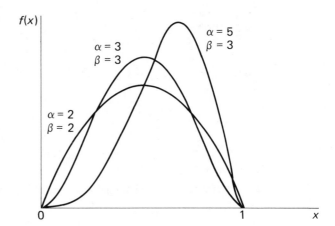

Figure 4.7   The Beta
Density Function

$\alpha = 4$ and $\beta = 2$. Find the expected value of this proportion. Is it highly likely that the wholesaler will sell at least 90% of his stock in a given week?

Solution   By the results given above, with X denoting the proportion of the total supply sold in a given week,

$$E(X) = \frac{\alpha}{\alpha + \beta} = \frac{4}{6} = \frac{2}{3}.$$

For the second part, we are interested in

$$P(X > 0.9) = \int_{0.9}^{1} \frac{\Gamma(4 + 2)}{\Gamma(4)\Gamma(2)} x^3(1 - x)\, dx$$

$$= 20 \int_{0.9}^{1} (x^3 - x^4)\, dx$$

$$= 20(0.004) = 0.08.$$

It is *not* very likely that 90% of the stock will be sold in a given week.   □

The basic properties of the beta distribution are summarized here.

THE BETA DISTRIBUTION

$$f(x) = \frac{\Gamma(\alpha + \beta)}{\Gamma(\alpha)\Gamma(\beta)} x^{\alpha - 1}(1 - x)^{\beta - 1}, \qquad 0 < x < 1$$

$$= 0, \qquad \text{elsewhere.}$$

$$E(X) = \frac{\alpha}{\alpha + \beta}, \qquad V(X) = \frac{\alpha\beta}{(\alpha + \beta)^2(\alpha + \beta + 1)}$$

Exercises

4.32   Suppose X has a probability density function given by

$$f(x) = \begin{cases} kx^3(1 - x)^2, & 0 \le x \le 1, \\ 0, & \text{elsewhere.} \end{cases}$$

(a) Find the value of k that makes this a probability density function.
(b) Find $E(X)$ and $V(X)$.

4.33   If X has a beta distribution with parameters α and β, show that

$$V(X) = \frac{\alpha\beta}{(\alpha + \beta)^2(\alpha + \beta + 1)}.$$

4.34   During any eight-hour shift, the proportion of time, X, that a sheet-metal stamping machine is down for maintenance or repairs has a beta distribution with $\alpha = 1$ and $\beta = 2$. That is,

$$f(x) = \begin{cases} 2(1 - x), & 0 \le x \le 1, \\ 0, & \text{elsewhere.} \end{cases}$$

The cost (in hundreds of dollars) of this downtime, due to lost production and cost of maintenance and repair, is given by

$$C = 10 + 20X + 4X^2.$$

(a) Find the mean and variance of C.
(b) Find an interval in which C will lie with probability at least 0.75.

4.35   The percentage of impurities per batch in a certain type of industrial chemical is a random variable, X, having the probability density function

$$f(x) = \begin{cases} 12x^2(1 - x), & 0 \le x \le 1, \\ 0, & \text{elsewhere.} \end{cases}$$

(a) Suppose a batch with more than 40% impurities cannot be sold. What is the probability that a randomly selected batch will not be allowed to be sold?
(b) Suppose the dollar value of each batch is given by

$$V = 5 - 0.5X.$$

Find the expected value and variance of V.

4.36   In order to study the disposal of pollutants emerging from a power plant, the prevailing wind direction was measured for a large number of days. The direction is measured on a scale of 0° to 360°, but by dividing each daily direction by 360, the measurements can be rescaled to the interval (0, 1). These rescaled measurements, X, are found to follow a beta distribution with $\alpha = 4$ and $\beta = 2$. Find $E(X)$. To what angle does this mean correspond?

4.7   *Distribution of Certain Functions of Random Variables*

It is sometimes necessary, and at other times simply convenient, to look at a function of a random variable rather than at the original variable itself. We have already seen examples in which a cost function may involve X^2, rather than simply X, for some appropriate random variable. It may be of interest to find the distribution of these functions, such as X^2, instead of merely looking at their expected value.

   If the functions of interest are increasing or decreasing over the region for which the original variable has a nonzero density function, then these distributions are, generally, easily found. For example, suppose that X has a nonzero density function, $f_X(x)$, for $x > 0$ and that $Y = X^2$. How will we find the distribution of Y? Often we can evaluate the distribution function for Y directly, since

$$F_Y(y) = P(Y \le y) = P(X^2 \le y) = P(X \le \sqrt{y})$$
$$= F_X(\sqrt{y}).$$

   The density function, $f_Y(y)$, can then be found by differentiating $F_X(\sqrt{y})$ with respect to y. (Note that the above equalities will not hold if X can take on negative values.)

EXAMPLE 4.9

   Suppose that the in-service operating time of a certain machine is denoted by X, with probability density function

$$f(x) = \frac{x}{2}, \qquad 0 \le x \le 2$$

$$= 0, \qquad \text{elsewhere,}$$

with time in weeks. (The machine is stopped and completely overhauled every two weeks, unless it breaks down in the interim.) The productive output of the machine is related to the square of its in-service operating time. Let $Y = X^2$ and find the probability density function for Y.

Solution   Since X takes on only positive values,

$$F_Y(y) = F_X(\sqrt{y}).$$

Now,

$$F_X(x) = \int_0^x \frac{t}{2} dt = \frac{x^2}{4}, \qquad 0 \le x \le 2$$

and, hence,

$$F_Y(y) = \frac{(\sqrt{y})^2}{4} = \frac{y}{4}, \qquad 0 \le y \le 4.$$

By differentiating, we see that

$$f_Y(y) = \frac{1}{4}, \qquad 0 \le y \le 4$$

or Y has a uniform distribution over $(0, 4)$. $\square$

Sometimes transformations provide a mathematically convenient way to handle properties of certain probability density functions. As an illustration we consider a new family of densities, called the *Weibull*. A Weibull density function has the form

$$f(x) = \frac{\gamma}{\theta} x^{\gamma-1} e^{-x^\gamma/\theta}, \qquad x > 0$$

$$= 0, \qquad \text{elsewhere,}$$

for positive parameters θ and γ. For $\gamma = 1$, this becomes an exponential density. For $\gamma > 1$, the functions look something like the gamma functions of Section 4.4, but have somewhat different mathematical properties. We can integrate directly to see that

$$F(x) = \int_0^x \frac{\gamma}{\theta} t^{\gamma-1} e^{-t^\gamma/\theta} \, dt$$

$$= -e^{-t^\gamma/\theta} \Big]_0^x = 1 - e^{-x^\gamma/\theta}, \qquad x > 0.$$

A convenient way to look at properties of the Weibull density is to use the transformation $Y = X^\gamma$. Then

$$F_Y(y) = P(Y \le y) = P(X^\gamma \le y) = P(X \le y^{1/\gamma})$$
$$= F_X(y^{1/\gamma}) = 1 - e^{-(y^{1/\gamma})^\gamma/\theta}$$
$$= 1 - e^{-y/\theta}, \qquad y > 0.$$

Hence,

$$f_Y(y) = \frac{dF_Y(y)}{dy} = \frac{1}{\theta} e^{-y/\theta}, \qquad y > 0$$

and Y has the familiar exponential density.

If we want to find $E(X)$, for an X having the Weibull distribution, then

$$E(X) = E(Y^{1/\gamma}) = \int_0^\infty y^{1/\gamma} \frac{1}{\theta} e^{-y/\theta} \, dy$$

$$= \frac{1}{\theta} \int_0^\infty y^{1/\gamma} e^{-y/\theta} \, dy$$

$$= \frac{1}{\theta} \Gamma\left(1 + \frac{1}{\gamma}\right) \theta^{(1 + 1/\gamma)} = \theta^{1/\gamma} \Gamma\left(1 + \frac{1}{\gamma}\right).$$

The above result follows from recognizing the integral to be of the gamma type.

If we let $\gamma = 2$ in the Weibull density, we see that $Y = X^2$ has an exponential distribution. To reverse the idea outlined above, if we start with an exponentially distributed random variable, Y, then the square root of Y will have a Weibull distribution with $\gamma = 2$. We can illustrate empirically by taking the square roots of the data from an exponential distribution, given in Table 2.1. These square roots are given in Table 4.1.

0.637	0.828	2.186	1.313	2.868
1.531	1.184	1.223	0.542	1.459
0.733	0.484	2.006	1.823	1.709
2.256	1.207	1.032	0.880	0.872
2.364	1.305	1.623	1.360	0.431
1.601	0.719	1.802	1.526	1.032
0.152	0.715	1.668	2.535	0.914
1.826	0.474	1.230	1.793	0.617
1.868	1.525	0.577	2.746	0.984
1.126	1.709	1.274	0.578	2.119

Table 4.1   Square Roots of the Lifelengths of Table 2.1

A relative frequency histogram for these data is given in Figure 4.8. Notice that the exponential form has now disappeared and that the curve given by the Weibull density with $\gamma = 2$, $\theta = 2$ (seen in Figure 4.9) is a much more plausible model for these observations.

The Weibull distribution is commonly used as a model for lifelengths because of the properties of its failure rate function. In this case,

$$\gamma(t) = \frac{f(t)}{1 - F(t)} = \frac{\dfrac{\gamma}{\theta} t^{\gamma - 1} e^{-t^\gamma/\theta}}{e^{-t^\gamma/\theta}}$$

$$= \frac{\gamma}{\theta} t^{\gamma - 1},$$

which, for $\gamma > 1$, is a monotonically increasing function with no upper bound. By appropriate choice of γ, this failure rate function can be made to model many sets of lifelength data seen in practice.

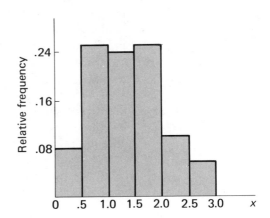

Figure 4.8   Relative Frequency Histogram for the Data of Table 4.1

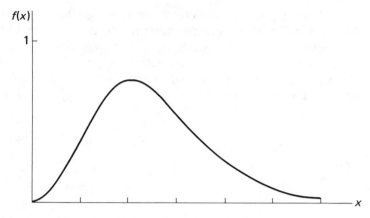

Figure 4.9   The Weibull Density Function $\gamma = 2$, $\theta = 2$

Exercises

4.37   Refer to Example 4.1. If $c_0 = 10$ and $c_1 = 2$, find the probability density function for $C = c_0 + c_1 X^2$, the cost of a failure and shutdown.

4.38   A process for refining sugar yields up to one ton of pure sugar per day, but the actual amount produced, X, is a random variable with probability density function by

$$f(x) = \begin{cases} 2x, & 0 \le x \le 1 \\ 0, & \text{elsewhere.} \end{cases}$$

The company is paid at the rate of $300 per ton for the refined sugar, but it also has a fixed $100 per day overhead cost. Thus, the daily profit, in hundreds of dollars, is given by

$$U = 3X - 1.$$

(a) Find the probability density function for U.
(b) Use the answer in (a) to find the mean and variance of U.
(c) Find the mean and variance of U using only the probability density function for X. Compare to the answer in (b).

4.39   Resistors being used in the construction of an aircraft guidance system have lifelengths that follow a Weibull distribution with $\gamma = 2$ and $\theta = 10$, with measurements in thousands of hours.
(a) Find the probability that a randomly selected resistor of this type has a lifelength that exceeds 5000 hours.
(b) If three resistors of this type are operating independently, find the probability that exactly one of the three burns out prior to 5000 hours of use.

4.40 Refer to Exercise 4.39. Find the mean and variance of the lifelength of a resistor of the type discussed.

4.41 Maximum wind-gust velocities in summer thunderstorms were found to follow a Weibull distribution with $\gamma = 2$ and $\theta = 400$ (measurements in feet per second). Engineers designing structures in the areas in which these thunderstorms are found are interested in finding a gust velocity that will only be exceeded with probability 0.01. Find such a value.

4.42 The velocities of gas particles can be modeled by the Maxwell distribution, with probability density function given by

$$f(v) = 4\pi \left(\frac{m}{2\pi KT} \right)^{3/2} v^2 e^{-v^2(m/2KT)}, \qquad v > 0$$

where m is the mass of the particle, K is Boltzmann's constant, and T is the absolute temperature.
(a) Find the mean velocity of these particles.
(b) The kinetic energy of a particle is given by $(1/2)mV^2$. Find the mean kinetic energy for a particle.

4.8 Conclusion

In this chapter, we have surveyed some of the most common continuous probability distributions, and have not attempted to produce an exhaustive list of all density functions likely to come up in applied work. Keep in mind the fact that these functions are used as *models* for the probabilistic behavior of certain observed phenomena, and will not exactly reproduce the true behavior of the measurements under study in any particular case.

The density functions of Chapter 4 are sometimes combined with the discrete distributions of Chapter 3 to produce other classes of distributions. To illustrate, suppose X has a binomial distribution. (X might represent the number of defectives found among n sampled items from a day's production.) But the parameter, p, varies from day to day according to a uniform distribution on the interval $(0, 1)$. That is, the fraction of defectives produced changes from day to day, and appears to be uniformly distributed. How can we find the probability that x defectives will be observed among the n sampled items?

The binomial distribution is now really a conditional distribution for fixed p. That is,

$$P(X = x \mid p) = \binom{n}{x} p^x (1 - p)^{n-x}.$$

Then, from the results of Chapter 2, the joint distribution of X and p is

$$P(X = x \mid p)f(p) = \binom{n}{x} p^x (1 - p)^{n-x} (1)$$

$$x = 0, 1, \ldots, n; \qquad 0 \le p \le 1.$$

It then also follows that the marginal distribution of X is found by integrating the joint probability function over the range of p values. That is,

$$P(X = x) = \int_0^1 \binom{n}{x} p^x (1 - p)^{n-x} \, dp$$

$$= \binom{n}{x} \int_0^1 p^x (1 - p)^{n-x} \, dp$$

$$= \binom{n}{x} \frac{\Gamma(x + 1)\Gamma(n - x + 1)}{\Gamma(n + 2)}$$

$$= \frac{n!}{x!(n - x)!} \frac{x!(n - x)!}{(n + 1)!} = \frac{1}{n + 1}$$

The result follows by recognizing the integral to be in the form of a beta function. Notice that the final answer is intuitively appealing since, if we know nothing about p other than the fact that it moves about uniformly, it seems reasonable to have all possible values of X equally likely. We will see other distributions generated by combining known distributions in later chapters.

Supplementary Exercises

4.43   The yield force of a steel reinforcing bar of a certain type is found to be normally distributed with a mean of 8500 pounds and a standard deviation of 80 pounds. If three such bars are to be used on a certain project, find the probability that all three will have yield forces in excess of 8700 pounds.

4.44   An engineer has observed that the gap times between vehicles passing a certain point on a highway have an exponential distribution with a mean of ten seconds.
   (a) Find the probability that the next gap observed will be no longer than one minute.
   (b) Find the probability density function for the sum of the next four gap times to be observed. What assumptions are necessary for this answer to be correct?

4.45   The proportion of time, per day, that all checkout counters in a super-market are busy is a random variable, X, having probability density function

$$f(x) = \begin{cases} kx^2(1 - x)^4, & 0 \le x \le 1, \\ 0, & \text{elsewhere.} \end{cases}$$

   (a) Find the value of k that makes this a probability density function.
   (b) Find the mean and variance of X.

4.46   A plant manager figures that his daily profit, X, from sales of a certain product is a normally distributed random variable with a mean of \$50 and a standard deviation of $3. These profit figures disregard daily overhead costs, Y, which have a gamma distribution with $\alpha = 4$ and $\beta = 2$. If X and Y are independent, find the expected value and variance of his daily net gain. Would you think it highly likely that his net gain for tomorrow will exceed $70?

4.47 If the lifelength, X, for a certain type of battery has a Weibull distribution with $\gamma = 2$ and $\theta = 3$ (with measurements in years) find the probability that the battery lasts less than 4 years given that it is now 2 years old.

4.48 The time (in hours) it takes a manager to interview an applicant has an exponential distribution with $\theta = 1/2$. Three applicants arrive at 8:00 AM, and interviews begin. A fourth applicant arrives at 8:45 AM. What is the probability that he has to wait before seeing the manager?

4.49 For the daily output of a certain industrial operation let Y_1 denote the amount of sales and Y_2 the costs, with figures in thousands of dollars. Assume that Y_1 has probability density function

$$f(y) = \begin{cases} (1/6)y^3 e^{-y}, & y > 0, \\ 0, & \text{elsewhere} \end{cases}$$

and Y_2 has density

$$f_2(y) = \begin{cases} (1/2)e^{-y/2}, & y > 0, \\ 0, & \text{elsewhere.} \end{cases}$$

The daily profit is given by $U = Y_1 - Y_2$.
(a) Find $E(U)$.
(b) Assuming Y_1 and Y_2 are independent, find $V(U)$.
(c) Would you anticipate that the daily profit would drop below zero very often? Why?

4.50 A builder of houses has to order some supplies that have a waiting time for delivery, Y, uniformly distributed over the interval one to four days. Since he can get by without them for two days, the cost of the delay is a fixed $100 for any waiting time up to two days. However, after two days the cost of the delay is $100 plus $20 per day for any time beyond two days. That is, if the waiting time is 3.5 days, the cost of the delay is $100 + $20(1.5) = $130. Find the expected value of the builder's cost due to waiting for the supplies.

4.51 There is a relationship between incomplete gamma integrals and sums of Poisson probabilities given by

$$\frac{1}{\Gamma(\alpha)} \int_\lambda^\infty y^{\alpha-1}e^{-y}\,dy = \sum_{y=0}^{\alpha-1} \frac{\lambda^y e^{-\lambda}}{y!}$$

for integer values of α.
   If Y has a gamma distribution with $\alpha = 2$ and $\beta = 1$, find $P(Y > 1)$ by using the above equality and Table 3 of the Appendix.

4.52 Refer to Exercise 4.16. Find the probability that the downtime for a given week will not exceed 10 hours.

4.53   Suppose that plants of a certain species are randomly dispensed over a region, with a mean density of λ plants per unit area. That is, the number of plants in a region of area A has a Poisson distribution with mean λA. For a randomly selected plant in this region, let R denote the distance to the *nearest* neighboring plant.

(a) Find the probability density function for R. [Hint: Note that $P(R > r)$ is the same as the probability of seeing no plants in a circle of radius r.]

(b) Find $E(R)$.

5

Statistics and Sampling Distributions

About This Chapter

In the process of making an inference from a sample to a population we usually calculate one or more statistics, such as the arithmetic mean (or average). Since samples are randomly selected, the values that such statistics assume may change from sample to sample. Thus, sample statistics are, themselves, random variables and their behavior can be modeled by probability distributions. The probability distribution of a sample statistic is called its *sampling distribution.*

Contents

The preceding four chapters dealt primarily with probabilistic models and properties of probability distributions. Now we want to connect those ideas more closely to *statistics*. Statistics is concerned with the process of observing a *sample* from some potentially large group of measurements, called a *population*, and then using the information in the sample to infer something about the behavior of the total population. For example, the lifelength data exhibited in Chapter 2 could constitute a sample of lifetimes from the potentially very large population of lifelength measurements that could result if *all* batteries of that particular type were tested. We have seen that these 50 sample observations do give us some useful information about the behavior of battery lifelengths, but now we want to formalize the connection between sample data and population quantities.

Typically, we want to calculate certain functions of sample observations for use in making inferences. We call these functions *statistics.*

A **statistic** is a function of observable random variables, and perhaps known constants, which contain no unknown parameters.

The remainder of this chapter deals with certain common statistics and some of their elementary properties.

5.2 *Displaying Data*

Before computing certain statistics that are important for statistical inference, it is often helpful to display the data under analysis in some convenient form. We saw a relative frequency histogram presented in Section 2.6 for the data on battery lifelengths. This visual display not only helps us gain some practical insight into the way the lifelengths seem to behave, but it also helps us in selecting an appropriate theoretical model for the random variable under study. In this section we expand the discussion of graphical techniques to include cumulative frequency plots, stem-and-leaf displays, and box-and-whisker plots.

Table 5.1 shows percentages of investment for pollution control for fifteen manufacturing industries:

Table 5.1 Percentage of Total Plant and Equipment Investment for Pollution Control (15 manufacturing industries for 1977) (Source: *World Almanac and Book of Facts*, 1979.)

17	02	07	04	08
17	04	04	14	03
03	02	04	10	01

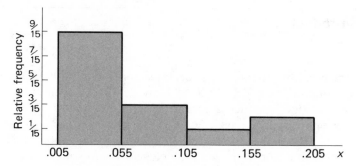

Figure 5.1   Relative Frequency Histogram for Data
of Table 5.1

A relative frequency histogram for these data is shown in Figure 5.1. The range of these numbers (approximately 0 to 20) is broken up into a convenient number of classes, or subintervals, and the class boundaries are chosen so that no observed number falls on a boundary. The height of the bar over each class represents the fraction of observations found in that class. Thus, $9/15 = 0.60$ of the observations fall into the first class, $3/15 = 0.20$ fall into the second class, and so on.

In addition to the relative frequency of observations within each class, we could compute the cumulative frequency of observations up to each class boundary. This plot is shown in Figure 5.2. Note that 60% of the observations are less than 5.5%, 80% are less than 10.5%, 87% are less than 15.5%, and 100% are less than 20.5%.

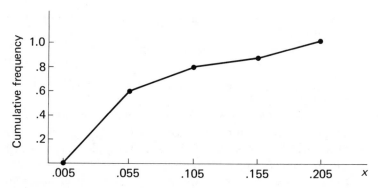

Figure 5.2   Cumulative Frequency Plot for Data of
Table 5.1

A cumulative frequency plot for the lifelength data of Table 2.1 is shown in Figure 5.3.

The *stem-and-leaf* display gives a visual presentation very similar to the relative frequency histogram, and actually provides somewhat more information. We illustrate its construction by using the data of Table 5.1. The left-most digit in each number provides a convenient starting point for breaking the numbers into groups. We have one group of observations starting with 0 and another starting with 1. Thus, we use 0 and 1 to form the *stem*, and write them in a vertical

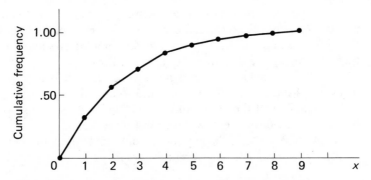

Figure 5.3   Cumulative Frequency Plot for Data of
Table 2.1

array as follows:

$$\begin{array}{c|c} 0 & \\ 1 & \end{array}$$

For each observation, we then record the second digit as a *leaf* on the appropriate
row of the *stem*. The first observation, 17, gives us

$$\begin{array}{c|c} 0 & \\ 1 & 7 \end{array}$$

and adding the second and third yields

$$\begin{array}{c|c} 0 & 3 \\ 1 & 77 \end{array}$$

The complete stem-and-leaf display is shown in Figure 5.4.

Figure 5.4   Stem-and-Leaf Display for the $\begin{array}{c|l} 0 & 3\ 2\ 4\ 2\ 7\ 4\ 4\ 4\ 8\ 3\ 1 \\ 1 & 7\ 7\ 4\ 0 \end{array}$
Data of Table 5.1

     Since most of the observations have a first digit of zero, we could stretch
the stem to two 0 categories and two 1 categories with second digits of 0 through
4 going on the upper row and digits of 5 through 9 on the lower row. The stretched
display is shown in Figure 5.5. Since it is easy to order the observations in any row,
we also show the ordered stem-and-leaf display.

Figure 5.5   Stretched
Stem-and-Leaf Display
for the Data of Table 5.1

$$\begin{array}{c|l} 0 & 3\ 2\ 4\ 2\ 4\ 4\ 4\ 3\ 1 \\ 0 & 7\ 8 \\ 1 & 4\ 0 \\ 1 & 7\ 7 \end{array} \qquad \begin{array}{c|l} 0 & 1\ 2\ 2\ 3\ 3\ 4\ 4\ 4\ 4 \\ 0 & 7\ 8 \\ 1 & 0\ 4 \\ 1 & 7\ 7 \end{array}$$

                                      Unordered   Ordered

Note that the stem-and-leaf display gives the same general picture as the relative frequency histogram, except that it is turned on its side. This display avoids the difficulty of choosing appropriate class boundaries and has the added advantage of showing the actual observations in the display.

Neither stems nor leaves have to be restricted to single digits. If the data in Table 5.1 had been 117, 117, 103, and so on, the stem could consist of 10 and 11 rather than 0, 1. If the data had been 17.2, 17.4, 13.6, and so on, the leaves could be 72, 74, 36, etc., on stems as given in Figure 5.5.

A stem-and-leaf display for the data in Table 2.1, rounded to two decimal places for convenience, is given in Figure 5.6.

```
0 | 02, 19, 23, 27, 29, 33, 33, 41, 51, 52, 54, 68, 76, 77, 84, 97
1 | 06, 06, 27, 40, 46, 51, 51, 62, 70, 72, 85
2 | 13, 32, 33, 34, 56, 63, 78, 92, 92
3 | 21, 25, 32, 33, 49, 81
4 | 02, 49, 78
5 | 09, 59
6 | 43
7 | 54
8 | 22
```

Figure 5.6   Stem-and-Leaf Display of Data from Table 2.1
(rounded to two decimal places and ordered)

The next type of graphical display will depend on certain statistics easily obtained from the sample data. The first of these statistics is the *median*, which is defined to be the number located at position $(n + 1)/2$ when n observations are ordered from smallest to largest. For the data of Table 5.1, $n = 15$ and the location of the median is $(15 + 1)/2 = 8$. Counting to the eighth value in the ordered stem-and-leaf display of Figure 5.5 yields the value 04 as the median.

If n is even, as in Figure 5.6 where $n = 50$, then the median location is still $(n + 1)/2$, which is $(50 + 1)/2 = 25.5$ in this particular case. The additional 0.5 tells us to take the median to be the midpoint between the 25th and 26th ordered values. Referring again to Figure 5.6, we see that the median is midway between 1.70 and 1.72, or is equal to 1.71.

The median splits the sample data in the middle, and it is sometimes convenient to split each of these sets again to find the *quartiles*. The quartile location is given by:

$$\text{quartile location} = \frac{\text{median location (rounded down to nearest integer)} + 1}{2}.$$

For the data of Table 5.1 with median location 8, the quartile location is $(8 + 1)/2 = 4.5$. The *lower quartile*, Q_1, is then taken as the midpoint between the fourth and fifth ordered observations. The *upper quartile*, Q_3, is taken as the midpoint between the fourth and fifth ordered observations *counting down from the largest observation*. Looking at the ordered stem-and-leaf display of Figure 5.5, we see that $Q_1 = 03$ since both the fourth and fifth observations equal 0.3. Also, $Q_3 = 09$ since the fourth observation from the largest is 10 and the fifth is 08.

The *box-and-whisker plot* conveniently displays this information on quartiles and the median, along with the extreme values in the data set. This plot is constructed by marking off Q_1 and Q_3 on a real number line and constructing a narrow rectangle with these values at the ends. (See Figure 5.7.) The median is then marked by a line through the rectangle. One straight line connects the rectangle to the *smallest* value in the data set and another connects the rectangle to the *largest* value. Figure 5.7 shows a box-and-whisker plot for the data of Table 5.1. In Figure 5.1, the fact that the median, Q_1, and the smallest value are relatively close together shows that most of the observations are bunched at the low end of the scale.

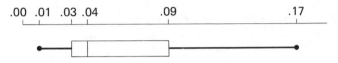

Figure 5.7   Box-and-Whisker Plot for Data of
Table 5.1

Box-and-whisker plots are often convenient graphical displays for comparing two sets of data. Figure 5.8 shows a stem-and-leaf display, along with a box-and-whisker plot, for percentages of investment for pollution control in 1978 for the same fifteen industries as in Table 5.1. The median has increased over its value in 1977 and the observations are slightly more spread out at the lower end of the scale. Q_3 has decreased, but the largest value has increased

```
0 | 1 2 2 3 3 3 4
0 | 5 5 7 7 9
1 | 0 2
1 | 9
```

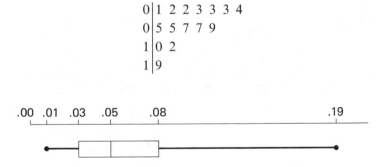

Figure 5.8   Percentage of Total Plant and Equipment
Investment for Pollution Control (15 manufacturing
industries for 1978)
(Source: *World Almanac and Book of Facts*, 1979)

Refer once more to the data of Figure 5.6 (lifelength of batteries). We have already seen that the median location is 25.5 and the median equals 1.71. The

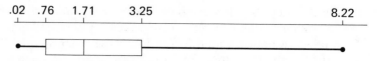

Figure 5.9   Box-and-Whisker Plot for Data on Figure 5.6

quartile location is then $(25 + 1)/2 = 13$, which yields $Q_1 = 0.76$ and $Q_3 = 3.25$. A box-and-whisker plot for these data is given in Figure 5.9.

Again, we see that most of the measurements are close to zero, with a long tail to the right indicating a few relatively large measurements.

We now turn our attention to some other common statistics: the sample mean and variance.

5.3   *The Sample Mean and Variance*

In keeping with the notions of random variables that we have been developing, let $X_1, \ldots, X_n$ denote a sample of n observations. The quantity X_i, denoting the ith sample observation, is a random variable before the sample is observed, but may take on the specific value x_i $(X_i = x_i)$ when the observation is taken. We generally assume that the sampled values are independent of one another, and that they come from the same population. Thus, $X_1, \ldots, X_n$ can be said to be independent random variables with a common probability distribution. Under these conditions, $X_1, \ldots, X_n$ are referred to as a *random sample*.

Probably the most frequently used statistic is the arithmetic average of the sample values, or the *sample mean*, given by

$$\bar{X} = \frac{1}{n} \sum_{i=1}^{n} X_i.$$

If we now assume that X_i comes from a population with mean μ and variance σ^2, that is, $E(X_i) = \mu$ and $V(X_i) = \sigma^2$, then properties of expectations for linear functions (see Theorem 2.3) allow us to show that

$$E(\bar{X}) = \frac{1}{n} \sum_{i=1}^{n} E(X_i) = \mu$$

and

$$V(\bar{X}) = \frac{1}{n^2} \sum_{i=1}^{n} V(X_i) = \frac{1}{n^2} (n\sigma^2) = \frac{\sigma^2}{n}.$$

(Note that the second result depends upon $X_1, \ldots, X_n$ being independent.) Thus we see that, on the average, the sample mean should be close to the population mean and the variance of the sample mean should be considerably smaller than the variance of the population.

Another common statistic is the sample variance, S^2, given by

$$S^2 = \frac{\sum\limits_{i=1}^{n} (X_i - \bar{X})^2}{n - 1}.$$

Again, note that after the sample is observed, S^2 will take on a specific value, say s^2. Observe that S^2 is essentially an average of the square of deviations about the sample mean, whereas $\sigma^2 = E(X_i - \mu)^2$ is the average of the square of deviations about the population mean. There are a number of equivalent ways of writing S^2, such as

$$S^2 = \frac{\sum\limits_{i=1}^{n} (X_i - \bar{X})^2}{n - 1} = \left(\frac{1}{n-1}\right)\left[\sum\limits_{i=1}^{n} X_i^2 - n\bar{X}^2\right]$$

$$= \left(\frac{1}{n-1}\right)\left[\sum\limits_{i=1}^{n} X_i^2 - \frac{1}{n}\left(\sum\limits_{i=1}^{n} X_i\right)^2\right].$$

Again using the properties of expectations of linear functions, we can show that $E(S^2) = \sigma^2$, so that on the average the sample value of S^2 should be close to the population variance, σ^2.

EXAMPLE 5.1

Calculate $\bar{x}$ and s^2 for the fifty lifelength observations in Table 2.1. Also, approximate the variance of $\bar{X}$.

Solution   Using

$$s^2 = \frac{1}{n-1}\left[\sum\limits_{i=1}^{n} x_i^2 - \frac{1}{n}\left(\sum\limits_{i=1}^{n} x_i\right)^2\right]$$

we have

$$s^2 = \frac{1}{49}\left[440.2332 - \frac{1}{50}(113.296)^2\right]$$

$$= 3.745$$

or

$$s = 1.935.$$

Note that for the exponential model

$$f(x) = \frac{1}{2}e^{-x/2}, \qquad x > 0$$

$V(X) = \sigma^2 = 4$, which is quite close to the observed s^2 value.

Also, $V(\bar{X}) = \sigma^2/n$ can be approximated by $3.745/50 = 0.075$. $\square$

To illustrate the behavior of $\bar{X}$ and S^2, we have selected one hundred samples each of size $n = 25$ from an exponential distribution with a mean of 10. That is, the probabilistic model for the population is given by

$$f(x) = \begin{cases} \frac{1}{10}e^{-x/10}, & x > 0 \\ 0, & \text{elsewhere.} \end{cases}$$

For this model, $E(X) = \mu = 10$ and $V(X) = \sigma^2 = (10)^2$, or $\sigma = 10$. The value for $\bar{X}$ and S^2 was calculated for each of the 100 samples. The average of the 100 $\bar{x}$'s turned out to be 9.88 and the average of the 100 values of s is 9.70. Note that both are reasonably close to 10. The standard deviation for the 100 values of $\bar{x}$ was calculated and found to be 2.17. Theoretically, the standard deviation of $\bar{X}$ is

$$\sqrt{V(\bar{X})} = \frac{\sigma}{\sqrt{n}} = \frac{10}{\sqrt{25}} = 2.0,$$

which is not far from the observed 2.17. A relative frequency histogram for the 100 values of $\bar{x}$ is shown in Figure 5.10. We pursue the notions connected with the shape of this distribution in the following section.

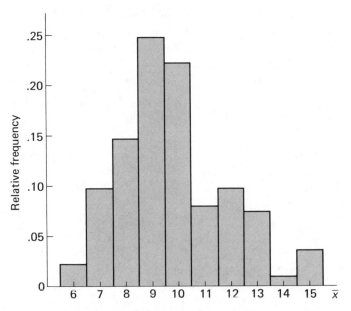

Figure 5.10   Relative Frequency Histogram for $\bar{x}$
from 100 Samples Each of Size 25

Exercises

5.1   Concentrations of uranium 238 were measured in twelve soil samples from a certain region, with the following results in pCi/g :

0.76, 1.90, 1.84, 2.42, 2.01, 1.77, 1.89, 1.56, 0.98, 2.10, 1.41, 1.32.

(a) Construct a stem-and-leaf display and box-and-whisker plot.
(b) Calculate $\bar{x}$ and s^2 for these data.
(c) If another soil sample is randomly selected from this region, find an interval in which the uranium concentration measurement should lie with probability at least 0.75. (Assume the sample mean and variance are good approximations to the population mean and variance. Use Tchebysheff's Theorem.)

5.2   The following data shows the percent change in production of crude petroleum, 1976 to 1977, for selected countries in America, Western Europe, and the Middle East:

$$-1.4, +0.3, +8.0, -13.6, -4.1, -2.1, +8.1, -7.5, -2.0,$$
$$+4.5, 0.0, +205.2, -0.2, -6.5, -7.0, -7.6, +7.7, +4.5.$$

(Source: *The World Almanac and Book of Facts, 1979*)
(a) Construct a stem-and-leaf display and box-and-whisker plot.
(b) Calculate $\bar{x}$ and s^2, the sample mean and variance.
(c) Construct a relative frequency histogram for the data. Do the calculations in (a) look reasonable?
(d) If another country is chosen at random from America, Western Europe, or the Middle East, find an interval in which its change in petroleum production should lie with probability at least 0.89.

5.3   Refer to Exercise 5.2. The figure $+205.2$ is from the United Kingdom, and is exceptionally high because a major new source of petroleum was located in the North Sea. Eliminate this unusual figure and answer the questions of Exercise 5.2 with the reduced data set. Note the effect that this large value has on the mean and variance.

5.4   Show that

$$s^2 = \frac{1}{n-1} \sum_{i=1}^{n} (x_i - \bar{x})^2$$
$$= \frac{1}{n-1} \left[\sum_{i=1}^{n} x_i^2 - \frac{1}{n} \left(\sum_{i=1}^{n} x_i \right)^2 \right].$$

5.5   If $X_1, \ldots, X_n$ is a random sample with $E(X_i) = \mu$ and $V(X_i) = \sigma^2$, show that $E(S^2) = \sigma^2$, where

$$S^2 = \frac{1}{n-1} \sum_{i=1}^{n} (X_i - \bar{X})^2.$$

[Hint: Write $\sum_{i=1}^{n}(X_i - \bar{X})^2 = \sum_{i=1}^{n}[(X_i - \mu) - (\bar{X} - \mu)]^2$. Square the term in brackets and carry out the summation.]

5.4   *The Sampling Distribution of $\bar{X}$*

In Section 5.3 we saw that the average value of $\bar{X}$ is equal to μ, the population mean, and the variance of $\bar{X}$ is σ^2/n. This tells us that an observed value of $\bar{X}$ is likely to be close to μ, but tells us little about the probability distribution of $\bar{X}$. In addition to the mean and variance of $\bar{X}$, it would be nice to know what fraction of the time, in repeated sampling, values of $\bar{X}$ are likely to lie within a certain prescribed interval.

The probability distribution that arises from looking at many independent values of $\bar{X}$, for a fixed sample size, selected from the same population is called the *sampling distribution* of $\bar{X}$. It turns out that when n is large the sampling distribution of $\bar{X}$ can be approximated rather closely, even if the distribution of the population from which we are sampling is unknown. This approximate sampling distribution is normal and the formal statement of this result is called the *Central Limit Theorem*.

THEOREM 5.1   The Central Limit Theorem

If a random sample of size n is drawn from a population with mean μ and variance σ^2, then the sample mean, $\bar{X}$, has approximately a normal distribution with mean μ and variance σ^2/n. That is, the distribution function of

$$\frac{\bar{X} - \mu}{\sigma/\sqrt{n}}$$

tends to a standard normal distribution function as $n \to \infty$.

We sometimes abbreviate the above statement to the phrase "$\bar{X}$ is asymptotically normal with mean μ and variance σ^2/n."

We can observe this behavior of $\bar{X}$ by looking at the following results from a computer simulation. Samples of size n were drawn from a population having the probability density function

$$f(x) = \begin{cases} \frac{1}{10}e^{-x/10}, & x > 0 \\ 0, & \text{elsewhere.} \end{cases}$$

The sample mean was computed for each sample. The relative frequency histogram of these mean values for 1000 samples of size $n = 5$ is shown in Figure 5.11. Figures 5.12 and 5.13 show similar results for 1000 samples of size $n = 25$ and $n = 100$, respectively. Although all the relative frequency histograms have a sort of bell shape, notice that the tendency is toward a symmetric normal curve as n gets larger and larger. A smooth curve drawn through the bar graph of Figure 5.13

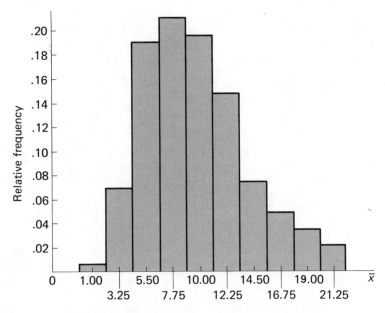

Figure 5.11   Relative Frequency Histogram for $\bar{x}$ from
1000 Samples of Size $n = 5$

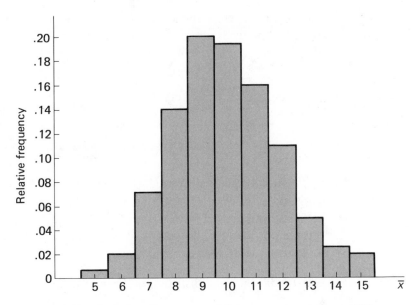

Figure 5.12   Relative Frequency Histogram for $\bar{x}$ from 1000
Samples of Size $n = 25$

would be nearly identical to a normal density function with mean 10 and variance $(10)^2/100 = 1$.

The Central Limit Theorem provides a very useful result for statistical inference, for we now not only know that $\bar{X}$ has mean μ and variance σ^2/n if the population has mean μ and variance σ^2, but we also know that the probability

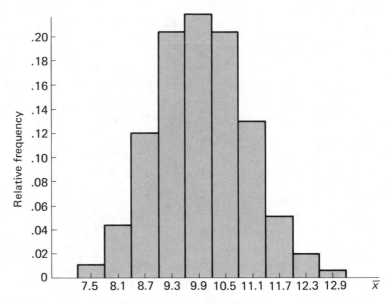

Figure 5.13   Relative Frequency Histogram for $\bar{x}$ from 1000 Samples of Size $n = 100$

distribution for $\bar{X}$ is approximately normal. For example, suppose we wish to find an interval (a, b) such that

$$P(a \leq \bar{X} \leq b) = 0.95.$$

This probability is equivalent to

$$P\left(\frac{a - \mu}{\sigma/\sqrt{n}} \leq \frac{\bar{X} - \mu}{\sigma/\sqrt{n}} \leq \frac{b - \mu}{\sigma/\sqrt{n}}\right) = 0.95$$

for constants μ and σ. Since $(\bar{X} - \mu)/(\sigma/\sqrt{n})$ has approximately a standard normal distribution, the above equality can be approximated by

$$P\left(\frac{a - \mu}{\sigma/\sqrt{n}} \leq Z \leq \frac{b - \mu}{\sigma/\sqrt{n}}\right) = 0.95,$$

where Z has a standard normal distribution. From Table 4, we know that

$$P(-1.96 \leq Z \leq 1.96) = 0.95$$

and, hence,

$$\frac{a - \mu}{\sigma/\sqrt{n}} = -1.96, \qquad \frac{b - \mu}{\sigma/\sqrt{n}} = 1.96,$$

or

$$a = \mu - 1.96\sigma/\sqrt{n}, \qquad b = \mu + 1.96\sigma/\sqrt{n}.$$

EXAMPLE 5.2

A certain machine used to fill bottles with liquid has been observed over a long period of time, and the variance in the amounts of fill is found to be approximately $\sigma^2 = 1$ oz. However, the mean ounces of fill, μ, depends on an adjustment that may change from day to day, or operator to operator. If $n = 25$ observations on ounces of fill dispensed are to be taken on a given day (all with the same machine setting) find the probability that the sample mean will be within 0.3 ounce of the true population mean for that setting.

Solution   We will assume $n = 25$ is large enough for the sample mean, $\bar{X}$, to have approximately a normal distribution. Then

$$P(|\bar{X} - \mu| \le 0.3) = P[-0.3 \le (\bar{X} - \mu) \le 0.3]$$

$$= P\left[-\frac{0.3}{\sigma/\sqrt{n}} \le \frac{\bar{X} - \mu}{\sigma/\sqrt{n}} \le \frac{0.3}{\sigma/\sqrt{n}}\right]$$

$$= P\left[-0.3\sqrt{25} \le \frac{\bar{X} - \mu}{\sigma/\sqrt{n}} \le 0.3\sqrt{25}\right]$$

$$= P\left[-1.5 \le \frac{\bar{X} - \mu}{\sigma/\sqrt{n}} \le 1.5\right].$$

Since $(\bar{X} - \mu)/(\sigma/\sqrt{n})$ has approximately a standard normal distribution, the above probability is approximately

$$P[-1.5 \le Z \le 1.5] = 0.8664$$

using Table 4 of the Appendix for the standard normal random variable Z.   □

EXAMPLE 5.3

In the setting of Example 5.2, how many observations should be taken in the sample so that $\bar{X}$ would be with in 0.3 oz of μ with probability 0.95?

Solution   Now we want

$$P[|\bar{X} - \mu| \le 0.3 \ ] = P[-0.3 \le (\bar{X} - \mu) \le 0.3] = 0.95.$$

We know that since $\sigma = 1$,

$$P\left[-0.3\sqrt{n} \le \frac{\bar{X} - \mu}{\sigma/\sqrt{n}} \le 0.3\sqrt{n}\right]$$

is approximately equal to

$$P[-0.3\sqrt{n} \le Z \le 0.3\sqrt{n}]$$

(on a standard normal random variable Z). But, using Table 4 of the Appendix,

$$P[-1.96 \le Z \le 1.96] = 0.95,$$

and it must follow that

$$0.3\sqrt{n} = 1.96$$

or

$$n = \left(\frac{1.96}{0.3}\right)^2 = 42.68.$$

Thus, 43 observations will be needed to satisfy the desired conditions.   □

Exercises

5.6   Shear strength measurements for spot welds of a certain type have been found to have a standard deviation of approximately 10 psi. If 100 test welds are to be measured, find the approximate probability that the sample mean will be within 1 psi of the true population mean.

5.7   Refer to Exercise 5.6. How many test welds should be used in the sample if the sample mean is to be within 1 psi of the population mean with probability approximately 0.95?

5.8   The soil acidity is measured by a quantity called the pH, which may range from 0 to 14 for soils ranging from low to high acidity. Many soils have an average pH in the 5 to 8 range. A scientist wants to estimate the average pH for a large field from n randomly selected core samples, and measuring the pH in each sample. If the scientist selects $n = 40$ samples, find the approximate probability that the sample mean of the 40 pH measurements will be within 0.2 units of the true average pH for the field.

5.9   Suppose the scientist of Exercise 5.8 would like the sample mean to be within 0.1 of the true mean with probability 0.90. How many core samples should he take?

5.10   Many bulk products, such as iron ore, coal, and raw sugar, are sampled for quality by a method that requires many small samples to be taken periodically as the material is moving along a conveyor belt. The small samples are then aggregated and mixed to form one composite sample. Let Y_i denote the volume of the ith small sample from a particular lot, and suppose $Y_1, \ldots, Y_n$ constitutes a random sample with each Y_i having mean μ and variance σ^2. The average volume of the samples, μ, can be set by adjusting the size of the sampling device. Suppose the variance of sampling volumes, σ^2, is known to be approximately 4 for a particular situation (measurements are to be in cubic inches). It is required that the total volume of the composite sample exceed 200 cubic inches with probability approximately 0.95 when $n = 50$ small samples are selected. Find a setting for μ that will allow the sampling requirements to be satisfied.

5.11   The service times for customers coming through a checkout counter in a retail store are independent random variables with a mean of 1.5 minutes and a variance of 1.0. Approximate the probability that 100 customers can be serviced in less than 2 hours of total service time.

5.12   Refer to Exercise 5.11. Find the number of customers, n, such that the probability of servicing all n customers in less than 2 hours is approximately 0.1.

5.13   Suppose that $X_1, \ldots, X_{n_1}$ and $Y_1, \ldots, Y_{n_2}$ constitute independent random samples from populations with means μ_1 and μ_2 and variances σ_1^2 and σ_2^2, respectively. Then, the central limit theorem can be extended to show that $\bar{X} - \bar{Y}$ is approximately normally distributed, for large n_1 and n_2, with mean $\mu_1 - \mu_2$ and variance $(\sigma_1^2/n_1 + \sigma_2^2/n_2)$.

Water flow through soils depends, among other things, on the porosity (volume proportion due to voids) of the soil. To compare two types of sandy soil, $n_1 = 50$ measurements are to be taken on the porosity of soil A and $n_2 = 100$ measurements are to be taken on soil B. Assume that $\sigma_1^2 = 0.01$ and $\sigma_2^2 = 0.02$. Find the approximate probability that the difference between the sample means will be within 0.05 units of the true difference between the population means, $\mu_1 - \mu_2$.

5.14   Refer to Exercise 5.13. Suppose samples are to be selected with $n_1 = n_2 = n$. Find the value of n that will allow the difference between the sample means to be within 0.04 units of $\mu_1 - \mu_2$ with probability approximately 0.90.

5.15   An experiment is designed to test whether operator A or B gets the job of operating a new machine. Each operator is timed on 50 independent trials involving the performance of a certain task on the machine. If the sample means for the 50 trials differ by more than one second, the operator with the smaller mean gets the job. Otherwise, the experiment is considered to end in a tie. If the standard deviations of times for both operators are assumed to be 2 seconds, what is the probability that operator A gets the job even though both operators have equal ability?

5.5   *Other Sampling Distributions Based on the Normal Distribution*

The beauty of the Central Limit Theorem lies in the fact that $\bar{X}$ will have approximately a normal sampling distribution no matter what the shape of the probabilistic model for the population, so long as n is large and σ^2 is finite. For many other statistics, additional assumptions are needed before useful sampling distributions can be derived. A common assumption is that the probabilistic model for the population is itself normal. That is, we assume that if the population of measurements of interest could be viewed in histogram fashion, that histogram would have roughly the shape of a normal curve. (This, incidentally, is not a bad assumption for many sets of measurements one is likely to come across in real-world experimentation.)

First note that if $X_1, \ldots, X_n$ are independent normally distributed random variables with common mean μ and variance σ^2, then $\bar{X}$ will be *precisely* normally distributed with mean μ and variance σ^2/n. No approximating distribution is needed in this case, since we saw in Chapter 4 that linear functions of independent normal random variables are again normal.

Under this normality assumption a sampling distribution can be derived for S^2, but we do not present the derivation here. It turns out that $(n-1)S^2/\sigma^2$ has a sampling distribution that is a special case of the gamma density function. If we let $(n-1)S^2/\sigma^2 = U$, then U will have the probability density function given by

$$f(u) = \begin{cases} \dfrac{1}{\Gamma\left(\dfrac{n-1}{2}\right)2^{(n-1)/2}} \, u^{(n-1)/2-1}e^{-u/2}, & u > 0 \\ 0, & \text{elsewhere.} \end{cases}$$

The gamma density function with $\alpha = v/2$ and $\beta = 2$ is called a chi-square density function with v degrees of freedom, denoted by $\chi^2_{(v)}$. Thus, $(n-1)S^2/\sigma^2$ has a $\chi^2_{(n-1)}$ distribution.

Specific values that cut off certain right-hand tail areas under the $\chi^2_{(v)}$ density function are given in Table 6 of the Appendix. The value cutting off a tail area of α is denoted by $\chi^2_{(v)}(\alpha)$. A typical χ^2 density function is shown in Figure 5.14.

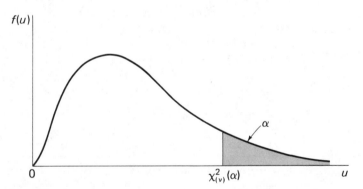

Figure 5.14   A χ^2 Distribution (Probability Density Function)

EXAMPLE 5.4

For the machine dispensing liquid into bottles in Example 5.2, the variance, σ^2, in the ounces of fill was known to be approximately unity. For a sample of size $n = 10$ bottles, find two positive numbers, b_1 and b_2, so that the sample variance, S^2, among the amounts of fill will satisfy

$$P[b_1 \leq S^2 \leq b_2] = 0.90.$$

Assume that the population of amounts of liquid dispensed per bottle is approximately normally distributed.

Solution   Under the normality assumption, $(n - 1)S^2/\sigma^2$ has a $\chi^2_{(n-1)}$ distribution. Since

$$P[b_1 \le S^2 \le b_2] = P\left[\frac{(n-1)b_1}{\sigma^2} \le \frac{(n-1)S^2}{\sigma^2} \le \frac{(n-1)b_2}{\sigma^2}\right],$$

the desired values can be found by setting $(n - 1)b_2/\sigma^2$ equal to the value that cuts off an area of 0.05 in the upper tail of the $\chi^2_{(n-1)}$ distribution, and $(n - 1)b_1/\sigma^2$ equal to the value that cuts off an area of 0.05 in the lower tail. Using Table 6 of the Appendix yields, with $n - 1 = 9$ degrees of freedom,

$$\frac{(n-1)b_2}{\sigma^2} = 16.919 = \chi^2_9(0.05)$$

and

$$\frac{(n-1)b_1}{\sigma^2} = 3.325 = \chi^2_9(0.95).$$

Thus,

$$b_2 = 16.919(1)/9 = 1.880$$

and

$$b_1 = 3.325(1)/9 = 0.369.$$

Note that this is not the only interval that would satisfy the desired condition

$$P[b_1 \le S^2 \le b_2] = 0.90$$

but is the one that cuts off equal tail areas under the appropriate χ^2 distribution.

□

Still assuming that $X_1, \ldots, X_n$ are independent with a common normal distribution, we have seen that $\sqrt{n}(\bar{X} - \mu)/\sigma$ has a standard normal distribution. What will happen if σ is replaced by S? In other words, what is the sampling distribution of

$$\frac{\bar{X} - \mu}{S/\sqrt{n}}?$$

Certainly this distribution should center about zero, and it doesn't appear that it should be far different in shape from the standard normal. In fact, the sampling distribution has a form known as the t distribution (or Student's t-distribution) with $(n - 1)$ degrees of freedom. Figure 5.15 shows a density function for the t distribution.

Table 5 of the Appendix contains values of t_α, that value of t that cuts off an area of α in the upper tail of the density function. Only upper-tail values are needed, since the curve is symmetric. The functional form of the t probability density function is not given here. One can see from the tabled values that the t-distribution becomes equivalent to the standard normal as $n \to \infty$.

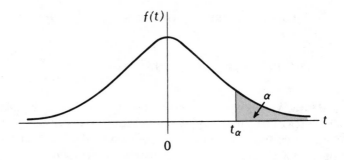

Figure 5.15   A t Distribution
(Probability Density Function)

EXAMPLE 5.5

A random sample of $n = 6$ measurements is to be taken on the tensile strength of a certain type of wire. The measurements are assumed to come from a normally distributed population, but σ^2 is unknown. The variance of $\bar{X}$ can then be approximated by S^2/n, and a numerical value for this approximation can be found after the sampling is completed. Find the probability that $\bar{X}$ will be within two approximate standard deviations of μ.

Solution

We want to find

$$P\left[\frac{-2S}{\sqrt{n}} \leq (\bar{X} - \mu) \leq \frac{2S}{\sqrt{n}}\right] = P\left[-2 \leq \frac{\bar{X} - \mu}{S/\sqrt{n}} \leq 2\right].$$

Since $\sqrt{n}(\bar{X} - \mu)/S$ has a t distribution with $n - 1 = 5$ degrees of freedom, we can use Table 5 of the Appendix to approximate the answer. The area between -2 and 2 cannot be found precisely, but we see that the area to the right of 2.015 is 0.05. Thus, the area under the t-distribution (5 degrees of freedom) between -2.015 and 2.015 is 0.90, and

$$P\left[-2 \leq \frac{\bar{X} - \mu}{S/\sqrt{n}} \leq 2\right]$$

will be slightly less than 0.90.   □

Theoretically, the t-distribution arises in the following way. Suppose Z has a standard normal distribution and U has a $\chi^2_{(v)}$ distribution, with Z and U independent. Then

$$T = \frac{Z}{\sqrt{U/v}}$$

has a t-distribution with v degrees of freedom. Setting

$$Z = \frac{\bar{X} - \mu}{\sigma/\sqrt{n}}$$

and

$$U = \frac{(n-1)S^2}{\sigma^2}$$

produces

$$T = \frac{\bar{X} - \mu}{\sigma/\sqrt{n}} \bigg/ \sqrt{\frac{(n-1)S^2}{\sigma^2(n-1)}}$$

$$= \frac{\bar{X} - \mu}{S/\sqrt{n}}$$

and, hence, the result indicated above.

Both the χ^2 and t distributions will be used extensively throughout the remaining chapters on statistical inference.

There is one more common sampling distribution related to normally distributed sample variables, but this one involves two independently selected samples. Suppose that one random sample contains n_1 normally distributed random variables with common variance σ^2 and a second random sample contains n_2 normally distributed variables with the same common variance, σ^2. We might then want to compare the sample variances by looking at the ratio S_1^2/S_2^2. The sampling distribution of S_1^2/S_2^2 is known as the F distribution with $v_1 = n_1 - 1$ and $v_2 = n_2 - 1$ degrees of freedom. We will use the notation $F_{v_2}^{v_1}(\alpha)$ to indicate that value of the F distribution, with v_1 degrees of freedom in the numerator and v_2 in the denominator, which cuts off an area of α in the right-hand tail. Figure 5.16 shows an F probability density function. Certain values of $F_{v_2}^{v_1}(0.05)$ and $F_{v_2}^{v_1}(0.01)$ are given in Tables 7 and 8 of the Appendix.

Theoretically, the F distribution arises in the following way. Suppose U_1 has a $\chi^2_{(v_1)}$ distribution and U_2 has a $\chi^2_{(v_2)}$ distribution, with U_1 and U_2 independent.

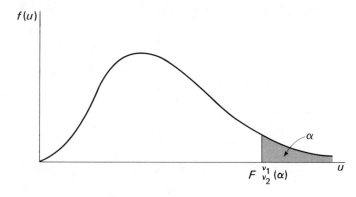

Figure 5.16   An F Distribution (Probability Density Function)

Then

$$\frac{U_1/v_1}{U_2/v_2} = F$$

has the F distribution with v_1 and v_2 degrees of freedom. For two independent random samples from normal populations with common variance, $(n_1 - 1)S_1^2/\sigma^2$ and $(n_2 - 1)S_2^2/\sigma^2$ have χ^2 distributions, and are independent of one another. Thus,

$$\frac{(n_1 - 1)S_1^2/\sigma^2(n_1 - 1)}{(n_2 - 1)S_2^2/\sigma^2(n_2 - 1)} = \frac{S_1^2}{S_2^2} = F$$

has an F distribution, as indicated above.

Only the upper-tail areas of the F distribution are tabled, but the corresponding lower-tail areas can be found, since

$$1 - \alpha = P\left(\frac{U_1/v_1}{U_2/v_2} \geq F_{v_2}^{v_1}(1 - \alpha)\right)$$

$$= P\left(\frac{U_2/v_2}{U_1/v_1} \leq \frac{1}{F_{v_2}^{v_1}(1 - \alpha)}\right)$$

and

$$P\left(\frac{U_2/v_2}{U_1/v_1} \leq F_{v_1}^{v_2}(\alpha)\right) = 1 - \alpha.$$

Thus,

$$F_{v_1}^{v_2}(\alpha) = \frac{1}{F_{v_2}^{v_1}(1 - \alpha)}.$$

EXAMPLE 5.6

Suppose the $n_1 = 6$ observations of Example 5.5 result in a sample variance S_1^2. Now, $n_2 = 10$ independent measurements are to be taken on the tensile strength of a similar type of wire, resulting in a sample variance of S_2^2. Assume the population variances are equal for the two groups of measurements.

(a) Find a number b_1 such that

$$P\left(\frac{S_1^2}{S_2^2} < b_1\right) = 0.95.$$

(b) Find a number b_2 such that

$$P\left(\frac{S_1^2}{S_2^2} > b_2\right) = 0.95.$$

Solution   Since, under these normality conditions, S_1^2/S_2^2 has an F distribution,

$$b_1 = F_9^5(0.05) = 3.48$$

using Table 7.

Similarly,

$$b_2 = F_9^5(0.95) = \frac{1}{F_5^9(0.05)} = \frac{1}{4.77} = 0.21. \quad \square$$

Exercises

5.16   The efficiency (in lumens per watt) of light bulbs of a certain type have a population mean of 9.5 and standard deviation of 0.5, according to production specifications. The specifications for a room in which eight of these bulbs are to be installed call for the average efficiency of the eight bulbs to exceed 10. Find the probability that this specification for the room will be met, assuming efficiency measurements are normally distributed.

5.17   Refer to Exercise 5.16. What should the mean efficiency per bulb equal if the specification for the room is to be met with probability approximately 0.80? (Assume the variance of efficiency measurements remains at 0.5.)

5.18   The Environmental Protection Agency is concerned with the problem of setting criteria for the amount of certain toxic chemicals to be allowed in freshwater lakes and rivers. A common measure of toxicity for any pollutant is the concentration of the pollutant that will kill half of the test species in a given amount of time (usually 96 hours for fish species). This measure is called the LC50 (lethal concentration killing 50% of the test species).

Studies of the effects of copper on a certain species of fish (say species A) show the variance of LC50 measurements to be approximately 1.9, with concentration measured in milligrams per liter. If $n = 10$ studies on LC50 for copper are to be completed, find the probability that the sample mean LC50 will differ from the true population mean by no more than 0.5 units. Assume that the LC50 measurements are approximately normal in their distribution.

5.19   If, in Exercise 5.18, it is desired that the sample mean differ from the population mean by no more than 0.5 with probability 0.95, how many tests should be run?

5.20   (a) If U has a $\chi_{(v)}^2$ distribution, find $E(U)$ and $V(U)$.
(b) Find $E(S^2)$ and $V(S^2)$ when S^2 is calculated from a random sample, $X_1, \ldots, X_n$, from a normal distribution with mean μ and variance σ^2.

5.21   Refer to Exercise 5.18. If $n = 20$ observations are to be taken on LC50 measurements, with $\sigma^2 = 1.9$, find two numbers, a and b, such that $P(a \leq S^2 \leq b) = 0.90$. ($S^2$ is the sample variance of the 20 measurements.)

5.22   Ammeters produced by a certain company are marketed under the specification that the standard deviation of gauge readings is no larger than 0.2 amp. Ten independent readings on a test circuit of constant current, using one of these ammeters, gave a sample variance of 0.065. Does this suggest that the ammeter used does not meet the company's specification?

[Hint: Find the approximate probability of a sample variance exceeding 0.065 if the true variance of the population is 0.04.]

5.23   Refer to Exercise 5.16. Suppose that the true standard deviation of efficiency measureme..ts is not known, and must be estimated from the sample by S. If a random sample of $n = 8$ efficiencies is to be selected, find two statistics, g_1 and g_2, such that

$$P(g_1 \leq (\bar{Y} - \mu) \leq g_2) = 0.90.$$

[Hint: Make use of the t distribution.]

5.24   Let S_1^2 denote a sample variance for a random sample of 10 LC50 measurements for copper and S_2^2 a sample variance for an independent random sample of 8 LC50 measurements for lead, all samples using the same species of fish. The LC50 measurements are approximately normally distributed. If the population variances are equal, find two numbers, a and b, such that

$$P(a \leq S_1^2/S_2^2 \leq b) = 0.90.$$

5.25   Refer to Exercise 5.24. Answer the same questions if the population variance for lead is twice that for copper.

5.6   *A Useful Method of Approximating Distributions*

We saw in the Central Limit Theorem of Section 5.3 that $\sqrt{n}(\bar{X} - \mu)/\sigma$ has, approximately, a standard normal distribution for large n, under certain general conditions. This notion of asymptotic normality actually extends to a large class of functions of $\bar{X}$ or, for that matter, to functions of *any* asymptotically normal random variable. The result holds because of properties of Taylor series expansions of functions, roughly illustrated as follows. Suppose $\bar{X}$ is a statistic based on a random sample of size n from a population with mean μ and finite variance σ^2. In addition, suppose we are interested in the behavior of a function of $\bar{X}$, say $g(\bar{X})$, where $g(x)$ is a real-valued function such that $g'(x)$ exists and is not zero in a neighborhood of μ. We can then write

$$g(\bar{X}) = g(\mu) + g'(\mu)(\bar{X} - \mu) + R,$$

where R denotes the remainder term for the Taylor series. Rearranging terms and multiplying through by $\sqrt{n}$ yields

$$\sqrt{n}[g(\bar{X}) - g(\mu)] = \sqrt{n}g'(\mu)(\bar{X} - \mu) + \sqrt{n}R.$$

Now, the $\sqrt{n}R$ term will usually get small quite rapidly as n tends to infinity, so it can be ignored. Since the distribution of $\sqrt{n}(\bar{X} - \mu)$ tends toward a normal distribution with mean zero and variance σ^2, $\sqrt{n}g'(\mu)(\bar{X} - \mu)$ will tend toward a normal distribution with zero mean and variance $[g'(\mu)]^2\sigma^2$. Thus, the term on the left side will also tend toward the same normal distribution. In summary,

$$\frac{\sqrt{n}[g(\bar{X}) - g(\mu)]}{|g'(\mu)|\sigma}$$

has a distribution function that will converge to the standard normal distribution function as $n \to \infty$. An example of the use of this property is given next.

EXAMPLE 5.7

The current, I, in an electrical circuit is related to the voltage, E, and the resistance, R, by Ohm's Law, $I = E/R$. Suppose that for circuits of a certain type, E is constant but the resistance, R, varies slightly from circuit to circuit. The resistance is to be measured independently in n circuits, yielding measurements $X_1, \ldots, X_n$. If $E(X_i) = \mu$ and $V(X_i) = \sigma^2$, $i = 1, \ldots, n$, approximate the distribution of $E/\bar{X}$, an approximation to the average current.

Solution

In this case, $g(\bar{X}) = E/\bar{X}$, for a constant E. Thus,

$$g'(\mu) = -\frac{E}{\mu^2}$$

and

$$\sqrt{n}\left[\frac{E}{\bar{X}} - \frac{E}{\mu}\right]\bigg/\left(\frac{E\sigma}{\mu^2}\right)$$

has approximately a standard normal distribution for large n. If μ and σ were known, at least approximately, one could make probability statements about the behavior of $E/\bar{X}$ by using the table of normal curve areas. □

Exercises

5.26   Refer to Example 5.7. Circuits of a certain type have resistances with a mean, μ, of 6 ohms and a standard deviation, σ, of 0.5 ohm. Twenty-five such circuits are to be used in a system, each with voltage, E, of 120. A specification calls for the average current in the twenty-five circuits to exceed 19 amps. Find the approximate probability that the specification will be met.

5.27   The distance, d, traveled by a particle, starting from rest, in t seconds is given by $d = \frac{1}{2}at^2$, where a is the acceleration. An engineer desires to study the acceleration of gravel particles rolling down an incline 10 meters in length. Observations on 100 particles showed the average time to travel the 10 meters was 20 seconds, and the standard deviation of these measurements was 1.6 seconds. Approximate the mean and variance of the average acceleration for these 100 particles.

5.28   A fuse used in an electric current has a lifelength, X, which is exponentially distributed with mean θ (measurements in hundreds of hours). The *reliability* of the fuse at time t is given by

$$R(t) = P(X > t) = \int_t^\infty \frac{1}{\theta} e^{-x/\theta} \, dx$$

$$= e^{-t/\theta}.$$

If the lifelengths, $X_1, \ldots, X_{100}$, of one hundred such fuses are to be measured, $e^{-t/\theta}$ can be approximated by $e^{-t/\bar{X}}$. Assuming θ is close to 4, approximate the probability that $e^{-t/\bar{X}}$ will be within 0.05 of $e^{-t/\theta}$ for $t = 5$.

5.7   *Conclusion*

It is important to remember that some of the sampling distributions we commonly deal with are exact and some are approximate. If the random sample under consideration comes from a population that can be closely modeled by a normal distribution, then $\bar{X}$ will have a normal distribution and $(n - 1)S^2/\sigma^2$ a χ^2 distribution with *no* approximation involved. However, the Central Limit Theorem states that $\sqrt{\mu}(\bar{X} - \mu)/\sigma$ will have *approximately* a normal distribution for large n, regardless of the probabilistic model for the population itself.

Sampling distributions for statistics will be used throughout the remainder of the text for the purpose of relating sample quantities (statistics) to parameters of the population.

Supplementary Exercises

5.29   Twenty-five lamps are connected so that when one lamp fails, another takes over immediately. (Only one lamp is on at any one time.) The lamps operate independently, and each has mean life of 50 hours and a standard deviation of four hours. If the system is not checked for 1300 hours after the first lamp is turned on, what is the probability that a lamp will be burning at the end of the 1300-hour period?

5.30   Suppose that $X_1, \ldots, X_{40}$ denotes a random sample of measurements on the proportion of impurities in samples of iron ore. Suppose that each X_i has probability density function,

$$f(x) = \begin{cases} 3x^2, & 0 \le x \le 1, \\ 0, & \text{elsewhere.} \end{cases}$$

The ore is to be rejected by a potential buyer if $\bar{X} > 0.7$. Find the approximate probability that the ore will be rejected, based on the 40 measurements.

5.31   Suppose that $X_1, \ldots, X_n$ and $Y_1, \ldots, Y_m$ are independent random samples, with the X_i's being normally distributed with mean μ_1 and variance σ_1^2 and the Y_i's being also normally distributed but with mean μ_2 and variance σ_2^2. The difference between the sample means, $\bar{X} - \bar{Y}$, will again be normally distributed (see Chapter 4).

(a) Find $E(\bar{X} - \bar{Y})$.   (b) Find $V(\bar{X} - \bar{Y})$.

5.32   Refer to Exercise 5.18. Suppose that the effects of copper on a second species (say species B) of fish produce a variance of LC50 measurements of 0.8. If the population means of LC50's for the two species are equal, find the probability that, with random samples of ten measurements from each species, the sample mean for species A exceeds the sample mean for species B by at least one unit.

5.33   If Y has an exponential distribution with mean θ, show that $U = 2Y/\theta$ has a χ^2 distribution with 2 degrees of freedom.

5.34   A plant supervisor is interested in budgeting for weekly repair costs for a certain type of machine. These repair costs, over the past years, tend to have an exponential distribution with a mean of 20 for each machine studied. Let $Y_1, \ldots, Y_5$ denote the repair costs for five of these machines for next week. Find a number, c, such that $P(\sum_{i=1}^{5} Y_i > c) = 0.05$, assuming the machines operate independently.

5.35   The *coefficient of variation* for a sample of values $Y_1, \ldots, Y_n$ is defined by

$$\text{C.V.} = \frac{S}{\bar{Y}}.$$

This gives the standard deviation as a proportion of the mean, and is sometimes an informative quantity. For example, a value of 10 for S has little meaning for us unless we can compare it to something else. If S is observed to be 10 and $\bar{Y}$ is observed to be 1000, then the amount of variation is small relative to the mean. However, if S is observed to be 10 and $\bar{Y}$ is 5, then the variance is quite large relative to the mean. If we were studying the *precision* of a measuring instrument, the first case (C.V. = 10/1000) might give quite acceptable precision but the second case (C.V. = 2) would be quite unacceptable.

If $Y_1, \ldots, Y_{10}$ denotes a random sample of size 10 from a normal distribution with mean 0 and variance σ^2, find two numbers, a and b, such that

$$P\left(a \le \frac{S}{\bar{Y}} \le b\right) = 0.90.$$

5.36   Suppose that T has a t distribution with v degrees of freedom. Show that T^2 has an F distribution with 1 and v degrees of freedom.

5.37   If U_1/U_2 has an F distribution with v_1 and v_2 degrees of freedom in the numerator and denominator, respectively, find $E(U_1/U_2)$.

5.38   If Y has a $\chi^2_{(n)}$ distribution, then Y can be represented as

$$Y = \sum_{i=1}^{n} X_i,$$

where X_i has a $\chi^2_{(1)}$ distribution and the X_i's are independent. It is not surprising, then, that Y will be approximately normally distributed for large n. Use this fact in the solution of the following.

A machine in a heavy-equipment factory produces steel rods of length Y, where Y is a normally distributed random variable with a mean of 6 inches and a variance of 0.2. The cost, C, of repairing a rod that is not exactly 6 inches in length is given by

$$C = 4(Y - \mu)^2$$

where $\mu = E(Y)$. If 50 rods with independent lengths are produced in a given day, approximate the probability that the total cost for repairs exceed $48.

Estimation

About This Chapter

We now formally introduce the ideas of statistical inference by looking at the techniques of *estimation*. Sample statistics will be employed to estimate population parameters, such as means or proportions. By making use of the sampling distribution of the statistic employed, we can construct intervals (confidence intervals), which should include the unknown parameter value with high probability.

Contents

6.1   *Introduction*

We have seen that probabilistic models for populations usually contain some unknown parameters. We have also seen, in Chapter 5, that certain functions of sample observations, i.e., statistics, have sampling distributions that may contain some of these same unknown parameters. Thus, it seems that we should be able to use certain statistics to obtain information on population parameters. For example, suppose a probabilistic model for a population of measurements is left unspecified except for the fact that it has mean μ and finite variance σ^2. A random sample, $X_1, \ldots X_n$, from this population gives rise to a sample mean $\bar{X}$ that, according to Section 5.3, will tend to have a normal distribution with mean μ and variance σ^2/n. How can we make use of this information to say something more specific about the unknown parameter μ? In this chapter we answer this question with a type of statistical inference called *estimation*. Chapter 7 will, in turn, consider *tests of hypotheses*.

DEFINITION 6.1   An **estimator** is a rule, or formula, which tells us how to use the sample data to estimate an unknown parameter of the population.

In the above example it seems obvious that the sample mean, $\bar{X}$, could be used as an *estimator* of μ. But $\bar{X}$ will take on different numerical values from sample to sample and so some open questions remain. What is the magnitude of the difference between $\bar{X}$ and μ likely to be? How does this difference behave as n gets larger and larger? In short, what properties does $\bar{X}$ have as an estimator of μ? This chapter provides answers for some of these basic questions regarding estimation.

6.2   *Properties of Point Estimators*

The statistics that will be used as estimators will, of course, have sampling distributions. Sometimes, as in the case of the sample mean from large samples, the sampling distribution is known, at least approximately. In other cases, the sampling distribution may not be completely specified, but we can still calculate the mean and variance of the estimator. We might, then, logically ask "What properties would we like this mean and variance to possess?"

Let the symbol θ denote an arbitrary population parameter, such as μ or σ^2, and let $\hat{\theta}$ denote an estimator of θ. We are then concerned with properties of $E(\hat{\theta})$ and $V(\hat{\theta})$. Now, different samples result in different numerical values for $\hat{\theta}$, but we would hope that some of these values underestimate θ and that some over-estimate θ, so that the average value of $\hat{\theta}$ is close to θ. If $E(\hat{\theta}) = \theta$, then $\hat{\theta}$ is said to be an *unbiased* estimator of θ.

DEFINITION 6.2   An estimator, $\hat{\theta}$, is **unbiased** for estimating θ if

$$E(\hat{\theta}) = \theta.$$

For an unbiased estimator, $\hat{\theta}$, the sampling distribution of the estimator has mean value θ. How do we want the possible values for $\hat{\theta}$ to spread out to either side of θ for this unbiased estimator? Intuitively, it would be desirable for all possible values of $\hat{\theta}$ to be very close to θ. That is, we want the variance of $\hat{\theta}$ to be as small as possible. At the level of this text it is not possible to prove that some of our estimators do indeed have the smallest variance among all unbiased estimators, but we will use this variance criterion for comparing estimators. That is, if $\hat{\theta}_1$ and $\hat{\theta}_2$ are both unbiased estimators of θ, then we would choose as the better estimator the one possessing the smaller variance. (See Figure 6.1.)

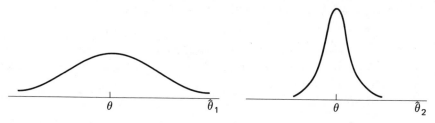

Figure 6.1   Two Unbiased Estimators, $\hat{\theta}_1$ and $\hat{\theta}_2$, with $V(\hat{\theta}_2) < V(\hat{\theta}_1)$

EXAMPLE 6.1

Suppose $X_1, \ldots, X_5$ denotes a random sample from some population with $E(X_i) = \mu$ and $V(X_i) = \sigma^2$, $i = 1, \ldots, 5$. The following are suggested as estimators for μ:

$$\hat{\theta}_1 = X_1, \qquad \hat{\theta}_2 = \frac{1}{2}(X_1 + X_5), \qquad \hat{\theta}_3 = \frac{1}{2}(X_1 + 2X_5)$$

$$\hat{\theta}_4 = \bar{X} = \frac{1}{5}(X_1 + X_2 + \cdots + X_5).$$

Which estimator would you use and why?

Solution   Looking at the means of these estimators, we have $E(\hat{\theta}_1) = \mu$, $E(\hat{\theta}_2) = \mu$, $E(\hat{\theta}_3) = \frac{3}{2}\mu$ and $E(\hat{\theta}_4) = \mu$. Thus, $\hat{\theta}_1$, $\hat{\theta}_2$ and $\hat{\theta}_4$ are all unbiased.

Looking at variances, we have

$$V(\hat{\theta}_1) = V(X_1) = \sigma^2$$

$$V(\hat{\theta}_2) = \frac{1}{4}[V(X_1) + V(X_5)] = \frac{\sigma^2}{2}$$

and

$$V(\hat{\theta}_4) = V(\bar{X}) = \frac{\sigma^2}{5}.$$

Thus, $\hat{\theta}_4$ would be chosen as the best estimator since it is unbiased and has smallest variance from among the three unbiased estimators.   □

We give a method for finding good point estimators in Section 6.5. But, in the meantime, we discuss further details of estimation for intuitively reasonable point estimators.

Exercises

6.1   Suppose X_1, X_2, X_3 denotes a random sample from the exponential distribution with density function

$$f(x) = \begin{cases} \dfrac{1}{\theta} e^{-x/\theta}, & x > 0 \\ 0, & \text{elsewhere.} \end{cases}$$

Consider the following four estimators of θ:

$$\hat{\theta}_1 = X_1$$

$$\hat{\theta}_2 = \frac{X_1 + X_2}{2}$$

$$\hat{\theta}_3 = \frac{X_1 + 2X_2}{3}$$

$$\hat{\theta}_4 = \bar{X}$$

(a) Which of the above estimators are unbiased for θ?
(b) Among the unbiased estimators of θ, which has smallest variance?

6.2   The reading on a voltage meter connected to a test circuit is uniformly distributed over the interval $(\theta, \theta + 1)$, where θ is the true but unknown voltage of the circuit. Suppose that $X_1, \ldots, X_n$ denotes a random sample of readings from this voltage meter.
(a) Show that $\bar{X}$ is a biased estimator of θ.
(b) Find a function of $\bar{X}$ that is an unbiased estimator of θ.

6.3   The number of breakdowns per week for a certain minicomputer is a random variable, X, having a Poisson distribution with mean λ. A random sample, $X_1, \ldots, X_n$, of observations on the number of breakdowns per week is available.
(a) Find an unbiased estimator of λ.
(b) The weekly cost of repairing these breakdowns is

$$C = 3Y + Y^2.$$

Show that

$$E(C) = 4\lambda + \lambda^2.$$

(c) Find an unbiased estimator of $E(C)$ that makes use of $X_1, \ldots, X_n$.

6.4   The *bias, B*, of an estimator, $\hat{\theta}$, is given by

$$B = |\hat{\theta} - E(\hat{\theta})|.$$

The *mean squared error*, or MSE, of an estimator, θ, is given by

$$\text{MSE} = E(\hat{\theta} - \theta)^2.$$

Show that

$$\text{MSE}(\hat{\theta}) = V(\hat{\theta}) + B^2.$$

(Note that $\text{MSE}(\hat{\theta}) = V(\hat{\theta})$ if $\hat{\theta}$ is an unbiased estimator of θ. Otherwise, $\text{MSE}(\hat{\theta}) > V(\hat{\theta})$.)

6.5   Refer to Exercise 6.2. Find $\text{MSE}(\bar{X})$ when $\bar{X}$ is used to estimate θ.

6.6   Suppose $X_1, \ldots, X_n$ is a random sample from a normal distribution with mean μ and variance σ^2.
(a) Show that $S = \sqrt{S^2}$ is a biased estimator of σ.
(b) Adjust S to form an unbiased estimator of σ.

6.7   For a certain new model of microwave oven, it is desired to set a guarantee period so that only 5% of the ovens sold will have had a major failure in this length of time. Assuming length of time until the first major failure for an oven of this type is normally distributed with mean μ and variance σ^2, the guarantee period should end at $\mu - 1.645\sigma$. Use the results of Exercise 6.6 to find an unbiased estimator of $\mu - 1.645\sigma$ based upon a random sample, $X_1, \ldots, X_n$, of measurements on time until the first major failure.

6.8   Suppose that $\hat{\theta}_1$ and $\hat{\theta}_2$ are each unbiased estimators of θ, with $V(\hat{\theta}_1) = \sigma_1^2$ and $V(\hat{\theta}_2) = \sigma_2^2$. A new unbiased estimator for θ can be formed by

$$\hat{\theta}_3 = a\hat{\theta}_1 + (1 - a)\hat{\theta}_2$$

$(0 \leq a \leq 1)$. If $\hat{\theta}_1$ and $\hat{\theta}_2$ are independent, how should a be chosen so as to minimize $V(\hat{\theta}_3)$?

6.3   *Confidence Intervals: The Single Sample Case*

After knowing something about the mean and variance of $\hat{\theta}$ as an estimator of θ, it would be nice to know something about how small the distance between $\hat{\theta}$ and θ is likely to be. Answers to this kind of question require knowledge of the sampling distribution of $\hat{\theta}$ beyond the behavior of $E(\hat{\theta})$ and $V(\hat{\theta})$, and lead to *confidence intervals*.

The idea behind the construction of confidence intervals is as follows. If $\hat{\theta}$ is an estimator of θ (which has a known sampling distribution), then one can find two quantities that depend on $\hat{\theta}$, say $g_1(\hat{\theta})$ and $g_2(\hat{\theta})$, such that

$$P[g_1(\hat{\theta}) \le \theta \le g_2(\hat{\theta})] = 1 - \alpha$$

for some small positive number α. Then we can say that $(g_1(\hat{\theta}), g_2(\hat{\theta}))$ forms an interval that has probability $1 - \alpha$ of capturing the true θ. This interval is referred to as a confidence interval with confidence coefficient $(1 - \alpha)$. The quantity $g_1(\hat{\theta})$ is called the *lower confidence limit* and $g_2(\hat{\theta})$ the *upper confidence limit*. We generally want $(1 - \alpha)$ to be near unity and $(g_1(\theta), g_2(\theta))$ to be as short an interval as possible for a given sample size. We illustrate the construction of confidence intervals for some common parameters here, and other cases will be considered in Chapters Eight through Eleven.

6.3.1   *General Distribution: Large Sample Confidence Interval for μ*

Suppose we are interested in estimating a mean, μ, for a population with variance σ^2, assumed, for the moment, to be known. We select a random sample, $X_1, \ldots, X_n$, from this population and compute $\bar{X}$ as a point estimator of μ. If n is large (say $n \ge 30$ as a rule of thumb) then $\bar{X}$ has approximately a normal distribution with mean μ and variance σ^2/n, or

$$Z = \frac{\bar{X} - \mu}{\sigma/\sqrt{n}}$$

has a standard normal distribution. Now, for any prescribed α, we can find from Table 4 in the Appendix a value $z_{\alpha/2}$ such that

$$P[-z_{\alpha/2} \le Z \le +z_{\alpha/2}] = 1 - \alpha.$$

Rewriting this probability statement, we have

$$1 - \alpha = P\left[-z_{\alpha/2} \le \frac{\bar{X} - \mu}{\sigma/\sqrt{n}} \le +z_{\alpha/2}\right]$$

$$= P\left[-z_{\alpha/2}\frac{\sigma}{\sqrt{n}} \le \bar{X} - \mu \le +z_{\alpha/2}\frac{\sigma}{\sqrt{n}}\right]$$

$$= P\left[\bar{X} - z_{\alpha/2}\frac{\sigma}{\sqrt{n}} \le \mu \le \bar{X} + z_{\alpha/2}\frac{\sigma}{\sqrt{n}}\right]$$

The interval,

$$\left(\bar{x} - z_{\alpha/2}\frac{\sigma}{\sqrt{n}}, \bar{x} + z_{\alpha/2}\frac{\sigma}{\sqrt{n}}\right)$$

forms a realization of a large sample confidence interval for μ with confidence coefficient $(1 - \alpha)$.

If σ is unknown it can be replaced by s, the sample standard deviation, with no serious loss in accuracy for the large sample case.

EXAMPLE 6.2

Consider once again the fifty lifelength observations of Table 2.1, on p. 23. Using these as the sample, find a confidence interval for the mean lifelength of batteries of this type, with confidence coefficient 0.95.

Solution

From Example 5.1 we see that $\bar{x} = 2.266$ and $s = 1.935$. Using the confidence interval

$$\bar{x} \pm z_{\alpha/2} \frac{\sigma}{\sqrt{n}}$$

with $(1 - \alpha) = 0.95$, we see that $z_{\alpha/2} = z_{0.025} = 1.96$ (from Table 4 of the Appendix). Substituting s for σ, this interval yields

$$2.266 \pm 1.96 \frac{1.935}{\sqrt{50}}$$

$$2.266 \pm 0.536$$

or

$$(1.730, 2.802).$$

Thus, we are quite confident that the true mean lies between 1.730 and 2.802. □

Take a careful look at the interpretation of confidence interval statements. The *interval* is random; the parameter is fixed. Before sampling, there is a probability of $(1 - \alpha)$ that the interval will include the true parameter value. After sampling, the resulting realization of the confidence interval either includes the parameter value or fails to include it, but we are quite confident that it will include the true parameter value if $(1 - \alpha)$ is large. The following computer simulation illustrates the behavior of a confidence interval for a mean in repeated sampling.

We started the simulation by selecting random samples of size $n = 100$ from a population having an exponential distribution with a mean value of $\mu = 10$. That is,

$$f(x) = \frac{1}{10} e^{-x/10}, \qquad x > 0$$

$$= 0, \qquad\qquad \text{elsewhere.}$$

For each sample, a 95% confidence interval for μ was constructed by calculating $\bar{x} \pm 1.96s/\sqrt{n}$. The sample mean, standard deviation, lower confidence limit, and upper confidence limit are given in Table 6.1 for each of 100 samples generated. There are seven intervals that do *not* include the true mean value. (These are marked with an asterisk.) Thus, we found that 93 out of 100 intervals include the true mean in our simulation, whereas the theory says that 95 out of 100 should include μ. This is fairly good agreement between theory and application. Later in the chapter we will see other simulations that generate similar results.

Table 6.1 Large Sample Confidence Intervals ($n = 100$)

Sample	LCL	Mean	UCL	S
1	7.26064	8.6714	10.0822	7.1977
2	7.59523	9.5291	11.4630	9.8668
3	7.68938	9.3871	11.0849	8.6619
4	8.94686	11.1785	13.4100	11.3856
5	7.96793	10.1508	12.3336	11.1369
6	7.61223	10.0101	12.4080	12.2340
7	7.55475	9.2754	10.9961	8.7791
8	7.48558	9.1436	10.8016	8.4593
9	7.71919	9.5219	11.3245	9.1973
10	7.95952	9.7012	11.4428	8.8859
11	7.34959	8.7958	10.2420	7.3785
12	8.71580	10.8458	12.9759	10.8675
*13	6.41955	8.1029	9.7863	8.5885
14	7.27538	8.9598	10.6441	8.5938
15	8.30285	10.2902	12.2776	10.1398
16	9.48735	11.5540	13.6206	10.5441
17	8.35947	10.8521	13.3448	12.7176
18	7.63421	9.9196	12.2049	11.6599
19	7.97129	10.1196	12.2679	10.9608
20	8.86613	10.9223	12.9785	10.4906
21	7.16061	9.2142	11.2679	10.4778
22	6.99569	9.2782	11.5607	11.6454
23	8.13781	10.2701	12.4024	10.8791
24	7.70300	9.4910	11.2790	9.1226
25	9.61738	11.9111	14.2048	11.7026
26	7.23197	9.2257	11.2194	10.1720
27	7.85056	9.9053	11.9601	10.4836
28	8.82373	11.1849	13.5462	12.0470
29	8.36303	10.4008	12.4387	10.3970
30	8.74332	10.4288	12.1144	8.5996
31	7.80013	9.7064	11.6127	9.7259
32	7.88003	10.0706	12.2611	11.1763
33	7.01555	8.6994	10.3833	8.5913
34	8.31036	10.3074	12.3045	10.1891
35	7.91383	9.8344	11.7549	9.7986
36	8.80795	10.5208	12.2337	8.7390
37	7.27322	9.1728	11.0725	9.6919
38	7.47957	9.1333	10.7871	8.4375
39	7.77926	9.8034	11.8275	10.3272
40	7.09624	9.0955	11.0947	10.2001
41	8.32909	10.1639	11.9986	9.3610
42	8.23895	10.2593	12.2797	10.3080
43	8.44813	10.4284	12.4087	10.1034
44	7.11788	8.8708	10.6237	8.9436
45	8.14050	10.0992	12.0580	9.9936
46	7.53466	9.4198	11.3050	9.6183
47	8.93450	11.0165	13.0986	10.6227
48	7.43185	8.9012	10.3705	7.4965
49	7.83028	9.7367	11.6432	9.7268
50	7.61207	9.3698	11.1275	8.9680

Table 6.1 (*continued*)

Sample	LCL	Mean	UCL	S
51	7.97829	9.7442	11.5101	9.0098
52	8.97313	11.2890	13.6049	11.8158
*53	5.99726	7.7422	9.4871	8.9027
54	7.51538	9.4089	11.3025	9.6609
55	8.59019	10.4373	12.2843	9.4238
56	8.49077	10.3914	12.2920	9.6971
57	8.12970	10.4056	12.6814	11.6115
*58	6.85175	8.3456	9.8395	7.6217
59	8.87405	10.9482	13.0225	10.5827
60	8.70548	10.2597	11.8140	7.9298
61	6.37467	8.3475	10.3203	10.0653
62	8.64835	10.6703	12.6923	10.3161
63	8.37157	10.6196	12.8676	11.4696
64	7.76632	9.6919	11.6174	9.8241
65	9.19745	11.5565	13.9155	12.0359
66	7.54964	9.1818	10.8140	8.3275
67	8.57961	10.8918	13.2039	11.7967
68	8.23986	10.0088	11.7778	9.0254
69	8.08091	9.9399	11.7989	9.4846
70	7.52910	9.2224	10.9156	8.6391
71	7.52705	9.4949	11.4628	10.0401
72	8.61466	10.7728	12.9310	11.0110
73	9.13542	11.2654	13.3953	10.8670
*74	6.73171	8.1351	9.5386	7.1604
75	7.78546	10.1938	12.6021	12.2874
76	8.04925	9.6668	11.2843	8.2526
77	7.61919	9.6068	11.5943	10.1407
*78	5.91167	7.7383	9.5649	9.3194
79	8.36219	10.4003	12.4384	10.3984
80	8.78276	11.0946	13.4065	11.7953
81	7.75108	9.4840	11.2170	8.8415
82	8.41534	10.4168	12.4183	10.2117
83	7.56210	9.1461	10.7300	8.0815
*84	6.51658	8.0757	9.6349	7.9549
85	8.73332	10.7988	12.8643	10.5381
86	7.10357	8.9350	10.7664	9.3439
87	7.46386	9.5521	11.6403	10.6541
88	7.40553	9.0024	10.5993	8.1473
89	7.70464	9.6524	11.6002	9.9376
90	8.16395	10.3755	12.5870	11.2834
91	8.08567	9.8488	11.6120	8.9958
92	8.45424	10.2642	12.0741	9.2344
*93	6.78362	8.1950	9.6064	7.2010
94	8.56442	10.6626	12.7608	10.7050
95	7.49852	9.2474	10.9962	8.9226
96	8.01983	10.9016	13.7833	14.7028
97	7.40014	9.1321	10.8640	8.8363
98	7.80386	9.6444	11.4849	9.3903
99	8.47046	10.3403	12.2101	9.5399
100	8.08183	10.0133	11.9447	9.8542

6.3.2   *Binomial Distribution: Large Sample Confidence Interval for p*

Estimating the parameter, p, for the binomial distribution is analogous to the estimation of a population mean. As seen in Section 3.3, this is because the random variable, Y, having a binomial distribution with n trials can be written as

$$Y = \sum_{i=1}^{n} X_i,$$

where X_i are independent Bernoulli random variables with common mean p. Thus, $E(Y) = np$ or $E(Y/n) = p$, and Y/n is an unbiased estimator of p. Recall that $V(Y) = np(1 - p)$ and, hence,

$$V(Y/n) = \frac{p(1 - p)}{n}.$$

Note that $Y/n = \sum_{i=1}^{n} X_i/n = \bar{X}$, with the X_i's having $E(X_i) = p$ and $V(X_i) = p(1 - p)$. The Central Limit Theorem then applies to Y/n, the sample fraction of successes, and we have that Y/n is approximately normally distributed with mean p and variance $p(1 - p)/n$. The large sample confidence interval for p is then constructed by comparison with the corresponding result for μ.

The interval

$$\frac{y}{n} \pm z_{\alpha/2} \sqrt{\frac{p(1 - p)}{n}}$$

forms a realization of a large sample confidence interval for p with confidence coefficient $1 - \alpha$.

Since p is unknown, y/n can be used to estimate p in the standard deviation.

EXAMPLE 6.3

In certain water-quality studies it is important to check for the presence or absence of various types of microorganisms. Suppose 20 out of 100 randomly selected samples of a fixed volume show the presence of a particular microorganism. Estimate the true probability, p, of finding this microorganism in a sample of this same volume, with a 90% confidence interval.

Solution

We assume that the number of samples showing the presence of the microorganism, out of n randomly selected samples, can be reasonably modeled by the binomial distribution. Using the confidence interval

$$\frac{y}{n} \pm z_{\alpha/2} \sqrt{\frac{p(1 - p)}{n}},$$

we have $1 - \alpha = 0.90$, $z_{\alpha/2} = z_{0.05} = 1.645$, $y = 20$ and $n = 100$. Thus, the interval estimate of p is

$$0.20 \pm 1.645 \sqrt{\frac{0.2(0.8)}{100}}$$

or

$$0.20 \pm 0.066.$$

We are reasonably confident that the true probability, p, is somewhere between 0.134 and 0.266. □

6.3.3 *Normal Distribution: Confidence Interval for μ*

If the samples we are dealing with are not large enough to ensure a somewhat normal sampling distribution for $\bar{X}$, then the above results are not valid. What can we do in that case? One approach is to use techniques that do not depend upon distributional assumptions (so called distribution-free techniques). This will be considered in Chapter 11. Another approach, which we will pursue here, is to make an additional assumption concerning the nature of the probabilistic model for the population. For samples occurring in many real problems it is appropriate to assume that the random variable under study has a normal distribution. We can then develop an exact confidence interval for the mean, μ.

Suppose that $X_1, \ldots, X_n$ denotes a random sample of size n from a normal distribution, with $E(X_i) = \mu$ and $V(X_i) = \sigma^2$. We then know, from Section 5.4, that $(\bar{X} - \mu)/S/\sqrt{n}$ has a t distribution with $(n - 1)$ degrees of freedom. Thus, from Table 5 of the Appendix, we can find a value $t_{\alpha/2}$, which cuts off an area of $\alpha/2$ in the right-hand tail of a t distribution with known degrees of freedom. Thus

$$P\left(-t_{\alpha/2} \leq \frac{\bar{X} - \mu}{S/\sqrt{n}} \leq t_{\alpha/2}\right) = 1 - \alpha$$

for some prescribed α. Reworking this inequality just as in the normal case given above, we have

$$P\left(\bar{X} - t_{\alpha/2} \frac{S}{\sqrt{n}} \leq \mu \leq \bar{X} + t_{\alpha/2} \frac{S}{\sqrt{n}}\right) = 1 - \alpha.$$

If $X_1, \ldots, X_n$ denotes a random sample from a normal distribution, then

$$\bar{x} \pm t_{\alpha/2} \frac{S}{\sqrt{n}}$$

provides a realization of an exact confidence interval for μ with confidence coefficient $(1 - \alpha)$.

EXAMPLE 6.4

Suppose that $n = 16$ measurements on the tensile strength of a certain type of wire give $\bar{x} = 27.30$ psi and $s = 1.20$. Find a 95% confidence interval estimate of μ, the true mean tensile strength of wire of this type.

Solution   Suppose that it is reasonable to assume that if many wire specimens were tested, their relative frequency distribution would be nearly normal. A confidence interval based on the t distribution can then be employed. With $1 - \alpha = 0.95$ and $n - 1 = 15$ degrees of freedom, we have $t_{0.025} = 2.131$. Thus,

$$\bar{x} \pm t_{\alpha/2} \frac{s}{\sqrt{n}}$$

becomes

$$27.3 \pm 2.131 \frac{1.2}{\sqrt{16}}$$

or

$$27.30 \pm 0.64.$$

We are confident that the interval 26.66 to 27.94 will include the true mean.   □

6.3.4 *Normal Distribution: Confidence Interval for σ^2*

Still under the assumption that the random sample $X_1, \ldots, X_n$ comes from a normal distribution, we know from Section 5.4 that $(n - 1)S^2/\sigma^2$ has a χ_v^2 distribution, with $v = n - 1$ degrees of freedom. We can employ this fact to establish a confidence interval for σ^2. Using Table 6 of the Appendix we can find two values, $\chi_v^2(\alpha/2)$ and $\chi_v^2(1 - \alpha/2)$, such that

$$1 - \alpha = P\left[\chi_v^2(1 - \alpha/2) \leq \frac{(n - 1)S^2}{\sigma^2} \leq \chi_v^2(\alpha/2) \right]$$

$$= P\left[\frac{(n - 1)S^2}{\chi_v^2(\alpha/2)} \leq \sigma^2 \leq \frac{(n - 1)S^2}{\chi_v^2(1 - \alpha/2)} \right].$$

If $X_1, \ldots, X_n$ denotes a random sample from a normal distribution, then

$$\frac{(n - 1)s^2}{\chi_v^2(\alpha/2)}, \qquad \frac{(n - 1)s^2}{\chi_v^2(1 - \alpha/2)}$$

provides a realization of an exact confidence interval for σ^2 with confidence coefficient $1 - \alpha$.

EXAMPLE 6.5

       In laboratory work it is desirable to run careful checks on the variability of readings produced on standard samples. In a study of the amount of calcium in drinking water undertaken as part of a water quality assessment, the same standard was run through the laboratory six times at random intervals. The six readings, in parts per million, were 9.54, 9.61, 9.32, 9.48, 9.70, 9.26.
       Estimate σ^2, the population variance for readings on this standard, in a 90% confidence interval.

Solution　　　　We must first calculate the sample variance, s^2, as

$$s^2 = \left(\sum_{i=1}^{n} x_i^2 - n\bar{x}^2\right)\left(\frac{1}{n-1}\right)$$

$$= [539.9341 - 6(9.485)^2]\left(\frac{1}{5}\right).$$

$$= (539.9341 - 539.7914)\left(\frac{1}{5}\right)$$

$$= \frac{0.1427}{5} = 0.0285.$$

Using Table 6 of the Appendix, we have that

$$\chi_5^2(0.95) = 1.1455, \qquad \chi_5^2(0.05) = 11.0705.$$

Thus, the confidence interval for σ^2 becomes

$$\left[\frac{(n-1)s^2}{\chi_v^2(0.05)}, \frac{(n-1)s^2}{\chi_v^2(0.95)}\right]$$

or

$$\left[\frac{0.1427}{11.0705}, \frac{0.1427}{1.1455}\right]$$

or

$$[0.0129, 0.1246].$$

Note that this is a fairly wide interval, primarily because n is so small.　□

CONFIDENCE INTERVALS FROM SINGLE SAMPLES
General Distribution: Large sample confidence interval for μ

$$\bar{X} \pm z_{\alpha/2}\sigma/\sqrt{n} \qquad (\sigma \text{ can be estimated by } S)$$

Binomial Distribution: Large sample confidence interval for p

$$\frac{Y}{n} \pm z_{\alpha/2}\sqrt{\frac{p(1-p)}{n}} \qquad (p \text{ can be estimated by } Y/n)$$

Normal Distribution: Confidence interval for μ

$$\bar{X} \pm t_{\alpha/2}S/\sqrt{n}$$

Normal Distribution: Confidence interval for σ^2

$$\frac{(n-1)S^2}{\chi_v(\alpha/2)}, \qquad \frac{(n-1)S^2}{\chi_v(1-\alpha/2)} \qquad (v = n-1)$$

Exercises

6.9   For a random sample of 50 measurements on the breaking strength of cotton threads, the mean breaking strength was found to be 210 grams and the standard deviation 18 grams. Obtain a confidence interval for the true mean breaking strength of cotton threads of this type, with confidence coefficient 0.90.

6.10   A random sample of 40 engineers was selected from among the large number employed by a corporation engaged in seeking new sources of petroleum. The hours worked in a particular week was determined for each engineer selected. These data had a mean of 46 hours and a standard deviation of 3 hours. For that particular week, estimate the mean hours worked for all engineers in the corporation, with a 95% confidence coefficient.

6.11   An important property of plastic clays is the percent of shrinkage on drying. For a certain type of plastic clay, 45 test specimens showed an average shrinkage percentage of 18.4 and a standard deviation of 1.2. Estimate the true average percent of shrinkage for specimens of this type in a 98% confidence interval.

6.12   Since we know that a confidence interval for a mean μ will be of the form $\bar{x} \pm z_{\alpha/2}\sigma/\sqrt{n}$, we can sometimes choose the sample size to ensure a certain accuracy before carrying out an experiment. If we desire an interval of length $2B$, that is, an interval $\bar{x} - B$ to $\bar{x} + B$, then we can find n by solving the equation

$$z_{\alpha/2}\frac{\sigma}{\sqrt{n}} = B.$$

That is,

$$n = \left[\frac{z_{\alpha/2}\sigma}{B}\right]^2.$$

If σ is known, at least approximately, and the confidence coefficient is given, then we can find n.

Refer to Exercise 6.9. How many measures on breaking strength should be used in the next experiment if the estimate is to be within 4 grams of the true mean breaking strength, with confidence coefficient 0.90?

6.13   Refer to Exercise 6.10. How many engineers should be sampled if it is desired to estimate the mean number of hours worked to within 0.5 hour with confidence coefficient 0.95?

6.14   Refer to Exercise 6.11. How many specimens should be tested if it is desired to estimate the percent of shrinkage to within 0.2 with confidence coefficient 0.98?

6.15   Upon testing 100 resistors manufactured by Company A, it is found that 12 fail to meet the tolerance specifications. Find a 95% confidence interval for the true fraction of resistors manufactured by Company A that fail to meet the tolerance specification. What assumptions are necessary for your answer to be valid?

6.16   Refer to Exercise 6.15. If it is desired to estimate the true proportion failing to meet tolerance specifications to within 0.05, with confidence coefficient 0.95, how many resistors should be tested?

6.17   Careful inspection of 70 precast concrete supports to be used in a construction project revealed 28 with hairline cracks. Estimate the true proportion of supports of this type with cracks in a 98% confidence interval.

6.18   Refer to Exercise 6.17. Suppose it is desired to estimate the true proportion of cracked supports to within 0.1, with confidence coefficient 0.98. How many supports should be sampled in order to achieve the desired accuracy?

6.19   In conducting an inventory and audit of parts in a certain stockroom, it was found that, for 60 items sampled, the audit value exceeded the book value on 45 items. Estimate, with confidence coefficient 0.90, the true fraction of items in the stockroom for which the audit value exceeds the book value.

6.20   The Environmental Protection Agency has collected data on the LC50 (concentration killing 50% of the test animals in a specified time interval) measurements for certain chemicals likely to be found in freshwater rivers and lakes. For a certain species of fish, the LC50 measurements for DDT in 12 experiments yielded the following:

$$16, \ 5, \ 21, \ 19, \ 10, \ 5, \ 8, \ 2, \ 7, \ 2, \ 4, \ 9.$$

(Measurements are in parts per million). Assuming such LC50 measurements to be approximately normally distributed, estimate the true mean LC50 for DDT with confidence coefficient 0.90.

6.21   The warpwise breaking strength measured on five specimens of a certain cloth gave a sample mean of 180 psi and a standard deviation of 5 psi. Estimate the true mean warpwise breaking strength for cloth of this type in a 95% confidence interval. What assumption is necessary for your answer to be valid?

6.22   Answer Exercise 6.21 if the same sample data had resulted from a sample of:
(a) 10 specimens.   (b) 100 specimens.

6.23   Fifteen resistors were randomly selected from the output of a process supposedly producing 10-ohm resistors. The fifteen resistors actually showed a sample mean of 9.8 ohms and a sample standard deviation of 0.5 ohm. Find a 95% confidence interval for the true mean resistance of the resistors produced by this process. Assume resistance measurements are approximately normally distributed.

6.24   Refer to Exercise 6.20. The variance of LC50 measurements is important because it may reflect an ability (or inability) to reproduce similar results in identical experiments. Find a 95% confidence interval for σ^2, the true variance of the LC50 measurements for DDT.

6.25   Refer to Exercise 6.23. Again, variability of the resistances is an important quantity to study, as it reflects upon the stability of the manufacturing process. Estimate σ^2, the true variance of the resistance measurements, in a 90% confidence interval.

6.4   *Confidence Intervals: The Multiple Sample Case*

All methods for confidence intervals discussed in the preceding section considered only the case in which a single random sample was selected to estimate a single parameter. In many problems, more than one population and, hence, more than one sample is involved. For example, we may desire to estimate the difference between mean daily yields for two industrial processes for producing a certain liquid fertilizer. Or we may want to compare the rates of defectives produced on two or more assembly lines within a factory.

6.4.1   *General Distribution: Large Sample Confidence Interval for Linear Function of Means*

First we consider estimating a linear combination of means from a number of populations. Suppose we are interested in three populations, numbered 1, 2, and 3, with unknown means μ_1, μ_2 and μ_3, respectively, and variances σ_1^2, σ_2^2, and σ_3^2. If a random sample of size n_i is selected from the population with mean μ_i, $i = 1, 2, 3$, then any linear function of the form

$$\theta = a_1\mu_1 + a_2\mu_2 + a_3\mu_3$$

can be estimated unbiasedly by

$$\hat{\theta} = a_1\bar{X}_1 + a_2\bar{X}_2 + a_3\bar{X}_3,$$

where $\bar{X}_i$ is the mean of the sample from population i. Also, if the samples are independent of one another,

$$V(\hat{\theta}) = a_1^2 V(\bar{X}_1) + a_2^2 V(\bar{X}_2) + a_3^2 V(\bar{X}_3)$$
$$= a_1^2\left(\frac{\sigma_1^2}{n_1}\right) + a_2^2\left(\frac{\sigma_2^2}{n_2}\right) + a_3^2\left(\frac{\sigma_3^2}{n_3}\right),$$

and, so long as all of the n_i's are reasonably large, $\hat{\theta}$ will have approximately a normal distribution.

The interval

$$\hat{\theta} \pm z_{\alpha/2}\sqrt{V(\hat{\theta})}$$

will provide a large sample confidence interval for θ with confidence coefficient $(1 - \alpha)$.

EXAMPLE 6.6

A company has three machines for stamping sheet metal located in three different factories around the country. If μ_i denotes the average downtime (in minutes) per day for the ith machine, $i = 1, 2, 3$, then the expected daily cost for downtime on these three machines is

$$C = 3\mu_1 + 5\mu_2 + 2\mu_3.$$

Investigation of company records for 100 randomly selected days on each of these machines showed the following:

$$n_1 = 100 \qquad n_2 = 100 \qquad n_3 = 100$$
$$\bar{x}_1 = 12 \qquad \bar{x}_2 = 9 \qquad \bar{x}_3 = 14$$
$$s_1^2 = 6 \qquad s_2^2 = 4 \qquad s_3^2 = 5$$

Estimate C in a 95% confidence interval.

Solution

We have seen above that an unbiased estimator of C is

$$\hat{C} = 3\bar{X}_1 + 5\bar{X}_2 + 2\bar{X}_3$$

with variance

$$V(\hat{C}) = 9\left(\frac{\sigma_1^2}{100}\right) + 25\left(\frac{\sigma_2^2}{100}\right) + 4\left(\frac{\sigma_3^2}{100}\right).$$

We obtained an observed value of $\hat{C}$ equal to

$$3(12) + 5(9) + 2(14) = 109.$$

Since the σ_i^2's are unknown, we can approximate them with s_i^2's and find an approximate variance of $\hat{C}$ to be

$$9\left(\frac{6}{100}\right) + 25\left(\frac{4}{100}\right) + 4\left(\frac{5}{100}\right) = 1.74.$$

Thus, a realization of the 95% confidence interval for C is

$$109 \pm 1.96\sqrt{1.74}$$

or

$$109 \pm 2.58. \quad \square$$

The most common type of linear function that one is likely to come across is the simple difference of the form $\mu_1 - \mu_2$. Estimation of this difference is a special case of the more general linear function approach given above. The best estimator of $\mu_1 - \mu_2$ from independent random samples would be $\bar{X}_1 - \bar{X}_2$.

The interval

$$(\bar{x}_1 - \bar{x}_2) \pm z_{\alpha/2} \sqrt{\frac{\sigma_1^2}{n_1} + \frac{\sigma_2^2}{n_2}}$$

forms a realization of a large sample confidence interval for $\mu_1 - \mu_2$ with confidence coefficient $(1 - \alpha)$.

EXAMPLE 6.7

From the data given in Example 6.6, find a 90% confidence interval for $\mu_1 - \mu_2$, the difference in true mean downtimes for machines 1 and 2.

Solution   Using the formula given above with s_i^2 estimating σ_i^2, we have

$$(\bar{x}_1 - \bar{x}_2) \pm 1.645 \sqrt{\frac{s_1^2}{n_1} + \frac{s_2^2}{n_2}}$$

yielding

$$(12 - 9) \pm 1.645 \sqrt{\frac{6}{100} + \frac{4}{100}}$$

or

$$3 \pm 0.52. \quad \square$$

6.4.2 *Binomial Distribution: Large Sample Confidence Interval for Linear Function of Proportions*

Since we have seen that sample proportions behave like sample means, and that for large samples the sample proportions will tend to have normal distributions, we can adapt the above methodology to include estimation of linear functions of sample proportions. Again, the most common practical problem concerns the estimation of the difference between two proportions. If Y_i has a binomial distribution with sample size n_i and probability of success p_i, then $p_1 - p_2$ can be estimated by $Y_1/n_1 - Y_2/n_2$.

The interval

$$\left(\frac{y_1}{n_1} - \frac{y_2}{n_2}\right) \pm z_{\alpha/2} \sqrt{\frac{p_1(1 - p_1)}{n_1} + \frac{p_2(1 - p_2)}{n_2}}$$

forms a realization of a large sample confidence interval for $p_1 - p_2$ with confidence coefficient $(1 - \alpha)$.

Note that p_i in the variance can be estimated by y_i/n_i.

EXAMPLE 6.8

We want to compare the proportion of defective electric motors turned out by two shifts of workers. From the large number of motors produced in a given week, $n_1 = 50$ motors were selected from the output of shift I and $n_2 = 40$ motors were selected from the output of shift II. The sample from shift I revealed 4 to be defective and the sample from shift II showed 6 faulty motors. Estimate the true difference between proportions of defective motors produced in a 95% confidence interval.

Solution   Starting with

$$\left(\frac{y_1}{n_1} - \frac{y_2}{n_2}\right) \pm 1.96 \sqrt{\frac{p_1(1 - p_1)}{n_1} + \frac{p_2(1 - p_2)}{n_2}}$$

and estimating p_i by y_1/n_i, we have as an approximate 95% confidence interval

$$\left(\frac{4}{50} - \frac{6}{40}\right) \pm 1.96 \sqrt{\frac{0.08(0.92)}{50} + \frac{0.15(0.85)}{40}}$$

or

$$-0.07 \pm 0.13$$

Since the interval overlaps zero, there does not appear to be any significant difference between the rates of defectives for the two shifts.   □

More general linear functions of sample proportions are sometimes of interest, as will be the case in the following example.

EXAMPLE 6.9

The personnel director of a large company wants to compare two different aptitude tests that are supposed to be equivalent in terms of which aptitudes they measure. He has reason to suspect that the degree of difference in test scores is not the same for women and men. Thus, he sets up an experiment in which one hundred men and one hundred women, of nearly equal aptitude, are selected to take the tests. Fifty men take test I and 50 independently selected men take test II. Likewise, 50 women take test I and 50 independently selected women take test II. The proportions, out of 50, receiving passing scores are recorded for each of the four groups, and the data are as follows:

	Test I	Test II
Male	0.7	0.9
Female	0.8	0.9

If p_{ij} denotes the true probability of passing in row i and column j, the director wants to estimate $(p_{12} - p_{11}) - (p_{22} - p_{21})$ to see if the change in probability for males is different from the corresponding change for females. Estimate this quantity in a 95% confidence interval.

Solution   If $\hat{p}_{ij}$ denotes the observed proportion passing the test, out of 50, in row i and column j, then

$$(p_{12} - p_{11}) - (p_{22} - p_{21})$$

is estimated by

$$(\hat{p}_{12} - \hat{p}_{11}) - (\hat{p}_{22} - \hat{p}_{21}),$$

which is observed to be

$$(0.9 - 0.7) - (0.9 - 0.8) = 0.1$$

Because of the independence of the samples, the estimated variance of $(\hat{p}_{12} - \hat{p}_{11}) - (\hat{p}_{22} - \hat{p}_{21})$ is

$$\frac{\hat{p}_{12}(1 - \hat{p}_{12})}{50} + \frac{\hat{p}_{11}(1 - \hat{p}_{11})}{50} + \frac{\hat{p}_{22}(1 - \hat{p}_{22})}{50} + \frac{\hat{p}_{21}(1 - \hat{p}_{21})}{50}$$

which is observed to be

$$\frac{1}{50}[(0.9)(0.1) + (0.7)(0.3) + (0.9)(0.1) + (0.8)(0.2)] = 0.011.$$

The interval estimate is then

$$0.1 \pm 1.96\sqrt{0.011}$$

or

$$0.1 \pm 0.20.$$

Since this interval overlaps zero there is really no reason to suspect that the change for males is different from the change for females.   □

6.4.3   *Normal Distribution: Confidence Interval for Linear Function of Means*

We must make some additional assumptions for the estimation of linear functions of means in small samples (where the Central Limit Theorem does not take over to produce normality). If we have k populations, and k independent random samples, we assume that all populations have approximately normal distributions with a common unknown variance, σ^2. This assumption should be considered carefully, and if it does not seem reasonable, the methods outlined below should not be employed. The arguments for producing confidence intervals parallel those given for the interval based on the t distribution in Section 6.3.

Suppose once again that we have three populations, numbered 1, 2, and 3, all assumed approximately normal in distribution. The populations have means μ_1, μ_2 and μ_3, respectively, and common variance, σ^2. We want to estimate a linear function of the form

$$\theta = a_1\mu_1 + a_2\mu_2 + a_3\mu_3.$$

The best estimator is still

$$\hat{\theta} = a_1\bar{X}_1 + a_2\bar{X}_2 + a_3\bar{X}_3$$

where $\bar{X}_i$ is the mean of the random sample from population i. Now,

$$V(\hat{\theta}) = a_1^2 V(\bar{X}_1) + a_2^2 V(\bar{X}_2) + a_3^2 V(\bar{X}_3)$$

$$= \sigma^2\left[\frac{a_1^2}{n_1} + \frac{a_2^2}{n_2} + \frac{a_3^2}{n_3}\right].$$

The problem now is to choose the best estimator of the common variance σ^2 from the three sample variances, s_i^2, based on respective sample sizes n_1, n_2, and n_3. It can be shown that an unbiased and minimum variance estimator of σ^2 is

$$\frac{\displaystyle\sum_{i=1}^{3} (n_i - 1)S_i^2}{\displaystyle\sum_{i=1}^{3} (n_i - 1)} = S_p^2.$$

(The subscript p denotes "pooled.") Since $\hat{\theta}$ will have a normal distribution and $\sum_{i=1}^{3}(n_i - 1)S_p^2/\sigma^2$ will have a χ^2 distribution with $\sum_{i=1}^{3}(n_i - 1)$ degrees of freedom,

$$T = \frac{\hat{\theta} - \theta}{S_p\sqrt{\dfrac{a_1^2}{n_1} + \dfrac{a_2^2}{n_2} + \dfrac{a_3^2}{n_3}}}$$

will have a t distribution with $\sum_{i=1}^{3}(n_i - 1)$ degrees of freedom. (See Chapter 5.) We can then use this statistic to derive a confidence interval for θ.

If all random samples come from normal distributions, then the interval

$$\hat{\theta} \pm t_{\alpha/2}S_p\sqrt{\frac{a_1^2}{n_1} + \frac{a_2^2}{n_2} + \frac{a_3^2}{n_3}}$$

provides an exact confidence interval for θ, with confidence coefficient $(1 - \alpha)$. Here $\theta = a_1\mu_1 + a_2\mu_2 + a_3\mu_3$ and $\hat{\theta} = a_1\bar{X}_1 + a_2\bar{X}_2 + a_3\bar{X}_3$.

For the special case of estimating a simple difference of the form $\mu_1 - \mu_2$, the estimator, $\hat{\theta}$, becomes $\bar{X}_1 - \bar{X}_2$.

If both random samples come from normal distributions, then the interval

$$(\bar{x}_1 - \bar{x}_2) \pm t_{\alpha/2} s_p \sqrt{\frac{1}{n_1} + \frac{1}{n_2}}$$

provides a realization of an exact confidence interval for $\mu_1 - \mu_2$, with confidence coefficient $(1 - \alpha)$.

A little reflection will show that it is easy to generalize the above result to linear functions of more than three means.

EXAMPLE 6.10

Copper produced by sintering (heating without melting) a powder under certain conditions is then measured for porosity (the volume fraction due to voids) in a certain laboratory. A sample of $n_1 = 4$ independent porosity measurements shows a mean of $\bar{x}_1 = 0.22$ and a variance of $s_1^2 = 0.0010$. A second laboratory repeats the same process on an identical powder and gets $n_2 = 5$ independent porosity measurements with $\bar{x}_2 = 0.17$ and $s_2^2 = 0.0020$. Estimate the true difference between the population means $(\mu_1 - \mu_2)$ for these two laboratories, with confidence coefficient 0.95.

Solution

First we assume that the population of porosity measurements in either laboratory could be modeled by a normal distribution, and that the population variances are approximately equal. Then, a confidence interval based on the t distribution can be used, with

$$s_p^2 = \frac{(n_1 - 1)s_1^2 + (n_2 - 1)s_2^2}{n_1 + n_2 - 2}$$

$$= \frac{3(0.001) + 4(0.002)}{7} = 0.0016$$

or

$$s_p = 0.04.$$

Using

$$(\bar{x}_1 - \bar{x}_2) + t_{\alpha/2} s_p \sqrt{\frac{1}{n_1} + \frac{1}{n_2}}$$

we have, with $\alpha/2 = 0.025$ and 7 degrees of freedom,

$$(0.22 - 0.17) \pm (2.365)(0.04) \sqrt{\frac{1}{4} + \frac{1}{5}}$$

or

$$0.05 \pm 0.06.$$

Since the interval overlaps zero, we would say that there is not much evidence of any difference between the two population means.   □

EXAMPLE 6.11

A third laboratory sinters a slightly different copper powder and then takes $n_3 = 10$ independent observations on the porosity. These yield a mean of $\bar{x}_3 = 0.12$ and a variance of $s_3^2 = 0.0018$. Compare the population mean for this powder with the mean for the type powder used in Example 6.10. (Estimate the difference in a 95% confidence interval.)

Solution

Again, we assume normality for the population of measurements that could be obtained for this third laboratory, and we assume the variances for these porosity measurements would be approximately equal for all three laboratories. Since the first two samples are conducted with the same type powder, we assume that they have a common population mean, μ. We can estimate this parameter by using a weighted average of the first two sample means, namely

$$\frac{n_1 \bar{x}_1 + n_2 \bar{x}_2}{n_1 + n_2}.$$

This weighted average is unbiased and will have smaller variance than the simple average $(\bar{x}_1 + \bar{x}_2)/2$. Now, to estimate $\mu - \mu_3$ we take

$$\frac{n_1}{n_1 + n_2}\bar{x}_1 + \frac{n_2}{n_1 + n_2}\bar{x}_2 - \bar{x}_3 = \frac{4}{9}(0.22) + \frac{5}{9}(0.17) - 0.12 = 0.0722$$

The pooled estimate of σ^2 is

$$s_p^2 = \frac{\sum\limits_{i=1}^{3} (n_i - 1)s_i^2}{\sum\limits_{i=1}^{3} (n_i - 1)} = \frac{3(0.0010) + 4(0.0020) + 9(0.0018)}{16}$$

$$= 0.0017$$

and $s_p = 0.0412$.

Now, the confidence interval estimate, with $\alpha/2 = 0.025$ and 16 degrees of freedom, is

$$\left(\frac{4}{9}\bar{x}_1 + \frac{5}{9}\bar{x}_2 - \bar{x}_3\right) \pm t_{\alpha/2}s_p\sqrt{\frac{(4/9)^2}{n_1} + \frac{(5/9)^2}{n_2} + \frac{(-1)^2}{n_3}},$$

yielding

$$0.0722 \pm (2.120)(0.0412)\sqrt{\frac{(4/9)^2}{4} + \frac{(5/9)^2}{5} + \frac{1}{10}}$$

or

$$0.0722 \pm 0.0401.$$

This interval would suggest that the second type of powder seems to give a lower mean porosity than the first. ☐

6.4.4   *Normal Distribution: Confidence Interval for σ_1^2/σ_2^2*

When two sambles from normally distributed populations are available in an experimental situation, it is sometimes of interest to compare the population variances. We generally do this by estimating the *ratio* of the population variances, σ_1^2/σ_2^2.

We saw in Section 5.4 that a ratio of independent χ^2 random variables, each divided by its degrees of freedom, will have an F distribution. Now, suppose that two independent random samples from normal distributions with respective sizes n_1 and n_2 yield sample variances of s_1^2 and s_2^2. If the populations in question have variances σ_1^2 and σ_2^2 respectively, then

$$F = \frac{S_1^2/\sigma_1^2}{S_2^2/\sigma_2^2}$$

will have an F distribution with $v_1 = n_1 - 1$ and $v_2 = n_2 - 1$ degrees of freedom. This fact allows us to construct a confidence interval for σ_2^2/σ_1^2.

If both random samples come from normal distributions, then the interval

$$\left[\frac{s_2^2}{s_1^2} \frac{1}{F_{v_1}^{v_2}(\alpha/2)}, \frac{s_2^2}{s_1^2} F_{v_2}^{v_1}(\alpha/2) \right]$$

provides a realization of an exact confidence interval for σ_2^2/σ_1^2, with confidence coefficient $(1 - \alpha)$.

Values for $F_{v_2}^{v_1}(\alpha/2)$ can be found in Tables 7 and 8.

EXAMPLE 6.12

A random sample of $n_1 = 10$ observations on breaking strengths of a certain glass gave $s_1^2 = 2.31$ (measurements were made in pounds per square inch). An independent random sample of $n_2 = 16$ measurements on a second machine, but with the same kind of glass, gave $s_2^2 = 3.68$. Estimate the true variance ratio, σ_2^2/σ_1^2, in a 90% confidence interval.

Solution   It is, of course, necessary to assume that the measurements in both populations can be modeled by normal distributions. Then, the above confidence interval will yield

$$\left[\frac{s_2^2}{s_1^2} \frac{1}{F_9^{15}(0.05)}, \frac{s_2^2}{s_1^2} F_{15}^9(0.05) \right]$$

or, using Table 7,

$$\left[\frac{3.68}{2.31} \left(\frac{1}{3.01} \right), \frac{3.68}{2.31} (2.59) \right]$$

or

$$(0.53, 4.13).$$

Notice the wide interval includes unity, so there is no real evidence that σ_2^2 differs from σ_1^2. □

CONFIDENCE INTERVALS FROM MULTIPLE INDEPENDENT SAMPLES

General Distributions: Large Sample Confidence Interval for $\theta = \sum_{i=1}^{K} a_i \mu_i$:

$$\hat{\theta} \pm z_{\alpha/2} \sqrt{V(\hat{\theta})}$$

where

$$\hat{\theta} = \sum_{i=1}^{K} a_i \bar{X}_i$$

and

$$V(\hat{\theta}) = \sum_{i=1}^{K} a_i^2 \left(\frac{\sigma_i^2}{n_i}\right) \qquad (\sigma_i^2 \text{ can be estimated by } S_i^2)$$

Binomial Distributions: Large Sample Confidence Interval for $\theta = \sum_{i=1}^{K} a_i \hat{p}_i$:

$$\theta \pm z_{\alpha/2} \sqrt{V(\theta)}$$

where

$$\theta = \sum_{i=1}^{K} a_i \hat{p}_i,$$

$$\hat{p}_i = Y_i/n_i,$$

and

$$V(\theta) = \sum_{i=1}^{K} a_i^2 \left(\frac{p_i(1 - p_i)}{n_i}\right) \qquad (p_i \text{ can be estimated by } \hat{p}_i)$$

Normal Distributions with Common Variance: Confidence Interval for $\hat{\theta} = \sum_{i=1}^{K} a_i \mu_i$:

$$\hat{\theta} \pm t_{\alpha/2} S_p \sqrt{\sum_{i=1}^{K} a_i^2/n_i}$$

where

$$S_p^2 = \frac{\sum_{i=1}^{K} (n_i - 1)S_i^2}{\sum_{i=1}^{K} (n_i - 1)}$$

and $t_{\alpha/2}$ depends on $\sum_{i=1}^{K} (n_1 - 1)$ degrees of freedom.

Normal Distributions: Confidence Interval for σ_2^2/σ_1^2:

$$\frac{S_2^2}{S_1^2} \frac{1}{F_{v_1}^{v_2}(\alpha/2)}, \qquad \frac{S_2^2}{S_1^2} F_{v_2}^{v_1}(\alpha/2)$$

where $v_1 = n_1 - 1$ and $v_2 = n_2 - 1$.

Exercises

6.26   The abrasive resistance of rubber is increased by adding a silica filler and a coupling agent to chemically bond the filler to the rubber polymer chains. Fifty specimens of rubber made with a type I coupling agent gave a mean resistance measure of 92, the variance of the measurements being 20. Forty specimens of rubber made with a type II coupling agent gave a mean of 98 and a variance of 30 on resistance measurements. Estimate the true difference between mean resistances to abrasion in a 95% confidence interval.

6.27   Refer to Exercise 6.26. Suppose a similar experiment is to be run again with an equal number of specimens from each type of coupling agent. How many specimens should be used if we want to estimate the true difference between mean resistances to within 1 unit with a confidence coefficient of 0.95?

6.28   Two different types of coating for pipes are to be compared with respect to their ability to aid in resistance to corrosion. The amount of corrosion on a pipe specimen is quantified by measuring the maximum pit depth. For coating A, 35 specimens showed an average maximum pit depth of 0.18 cm. The standard deviation of these maximum pit depths was 0.02 cm. For coating B, the maximum pit depths in 30 specimens had a mean of 0.21 cm and a standard deviation of 0.03 cm. Estimate the true difference between mean depths in a 90% confidence interval. Do you think coating B does a better job of inhibiting corrosion?

6.29   Bacteria in water samples are sometimes difficult to count, but their presence can easily be detected by culturing. In fifty independently selected water samples from a certain lake, 43 contained a certain harmful bacteria. After adding a chemical to the lake water, another fifty water samples showed only 22 with the harmful bacteria. Estimate the true difference between the proportions of samples containing the harmful bacteria with a 95% confidence coefficient. Does the chemical appear to be effective in reducing the amount of bacteria?

6.30   Refer to Exercise 6.29. How many samples should be selected before and after the chemical is added it if we want to estimate the true difference between proportions to within 0.1 with a 95% confidence coefficient? (Assume the sample sizes are to be equal.)

6.31   A large firm made up of several companies has instituted a new quality-control inspection policy. Among 30 artisans sampled in Company A, only 5 objected to the new policy. Among 35 artisans sampled in Company B, 10 objected to the policy. Estimate the true difference between the proportions *favoring* the new policy for the two companies, with confidence coefficient 0.98.

6.32   A measurement of physiological activity important to runners is the rate of oxygen consumption. *Research Quarterly*, May 1979, reports on the differences between oxygen consumption rates for college males trained by two different methods, one involving continuous training for a period of time each day and the other involving intermittent training of about the same overall duration. The means, standard deviations, and sample sizes are as follows:

Continuous Training	Intermittent Training
$n_1 = 9$	$n_2 = 7$
$\bar{y}_1 = 43.71$	$\bar{y}_2 = 39.63$
$s_1 = 5.88$	$s_2 = 7.68$

(The measurements are in ml/kg min) If the measurements are assumed to come from normally distributed populations, estimate the difference between the population means with confidence coefficient 0.95.

6.33   Refer to Exercise 6.20, which gives LC50 measurements for DDT. Another common insecticide, Diazinon, gave LC50 measurements of 7.8, 1.6, and 1.3 in the three independent experiments. Estimate the difference between the mean LC50 for DDT and the mean LC50 for Diazinon in a 90% confidence interval. What assumptions are necessary for your answer to be valid?

6.34   *Research Quarterly*, May 1979, reports on a study of impulses applied to the ball by tennis rackets of various construction. Three measurements on ball impulses were taken on each type of racket. For a Classic (wood) racket the mean was 2.41 and the standard deviation was 0.02. For a Yamaha (graphite) racket, the mean was 2.22 and the standard deviation was 0.07. Estimate the difference between true mean impulses for the two rackets with confidence coefficient 0.95. What assumptions are necessary for the method used to be valid?

6.35   Refer to Exercise 6.34. Find the estimate of the difference between the mean impulses (95% confidence coefficient), assuming the sample means and variances given there were provided by samples:
(a) of size 10,   (b) of size 100.

6.36   Seasonal ranges (in hectares) for alligators were monitored on a lake outside of Gainesville, Florida by biologists from the Florida Game and Fish Commission. Six alligators monitored in the spring showed ranges of 8.0, 12.1, 8.1, 18.1, 18.2, and 31.7. Four different alligators monitored in the summer showed ranges of 102.0, 81.7, 54.7, and 50.7. Estimate the difference between mean spring and summer ranges on a 95% confidence interval, assuming the data to come from normally distributed populations.

6.37   Refer to Exercise 6.32. Find a 90% confidence interval on the ratio of the true variances for the two training methods. Does it appear that intermittent training gives more variable results?

6.38   Refer to Exercises 6.20 and 6.33. Find a 90% confidence interval for the ratio of the variance of DDT LC50's to that of Diazinon LC50's.

6.39   An electric circuit contains three resistors, each of a different type. Tests on 10 type I resistors showed a sample mean resistance of 9.1 ohms with a sample standard deviation of 0.2 ohm. Tests on 8 type II resistors yielded a sample mean of 14.3 ohms and a sample standard deviation of 0.4 ohm, while tests on 12 type III resistors yielded a sample mean of 5.6 ohms and a sample standard deviation of 0.1 ohm. Find a 95% confidence interval for $\mu_I + \mu_{II} + \mu_{III}$, the expected resistance for the circuit. What assumptions are necessary for your answer to be valid?

6.5   *The Method of Maximum Likelihood*

The estimators presented in previous sections of this chapter were justified merely by the fact that they seemed reasonable. For instance, our intuition says that a sample mean should be a good estimator of a population mean, or a sample proportion should somehow resemble the corresponding population proportion. There are, however, general methods for driving estimators for unknown parameters of population models. One widely used method is called the *method of maximum likelihood.*

As the name implies, this method strives to estimate the unknown parameter, or parameters, by choosing as the estimators those values that would maximize the probability of the observed result. Suppose, for example, that a box contains four balls, of which an unknown number θ are white ($4 - \theta$ are nonwhite). We are to sample two balls at random and count X, the number of white balls in the sample. We know the probability distribution of X to be given by

$$P(X = x) = p(x) = \frac{\binom{\theta}{x}\binom{4 - \theta}{2 - x}}{\binom{4}{2}}.$$

Now, suppose we observe that $X = 1$. What value of θ will maximize the probability of this event? From the above distribution, we have

$$p(1\,|\,\theta = 0) = 0$$

$$p(1\,|\,\theta = 1) = \frac{\binom{1}{1}\binom{3}{1}}{\binom{4}{2}} = \frac{3}{6} = \frac{1}{2}$$

$$p(1\,|\,\theta = 2) = \frac{2}{3}$$

$$p(1\,|\,\theta = 3) = \frac{1}{2}$$

$$p(1\,|\,\theta = 4) = 0.$$

Hence, $\theta = 2$ maximizes the probability of the observed sample, so we would choose this value, 2, as the maximum likelihood estimate for θ, given we observed that $X = 1$. You can show for yourself that if $X = 2$, then 4 will be the maximum likelihood estimate of θ.

If the form of the probability distribution is not too complicated, we can generally use methods of calculus to find the functional form of the maximum likelihood estimator, instead of working out specific numerical cases. We illustrate with the following examples.

EXAMPLE 6.13

Suppose that in a sequence of n independent, identical Bernoulli trials, Y successes are observed. Find the maximum likelihood estimator of p, the probability of successes on any single trial.

Solution

The probability, or *likelihood*, of observing Y successes in n Bernoulli trials is given by the binomial distribution,

$$p(y) = \binom{n}{y} p^y (1 - p)^{n-y}.$$

We now have to find the value of p that will maximize this function, that is, we must solve for p as a function of y and n. Since we want to treat this probability, or likelihood, as a function of p, we will change notation slightly and denote the probability of the observable result $Y = y$ by

$$L(p) = \binom{n}{y} p^y (1 - p)^{n-y}$$

where L stands for likelihood.

Since $\ln L(p)$ is a monotone function of $L(p)$, both $\ln L(p)$ and $L(p)$ will have their maxima at the same value of p. In many cases, it is easier to maximize $\ln L(p)$, so that is the approach we follow here.

Now,

$$\ln L(p) = \ln \binom{n}{y} + y \ln p + (n - y) \ln(1 - p)$$

is a continuous function of p $(0 < p < 1)$, and, thus, the maximum value can be found by setting the first derivative equal to zero. We have

$$\frac{\partial \ln L(p)}{\partial p} = \frac{y}{p} - \frac{n - y}{1 - p}.$$

Setting

$$\frac{y}{\hat{p}} - \frac{n - y}{1 - \hat{p}} = 0$$

we find

$$\hat{p} = \frac{y}{n},$$

and hence we take Y/n as the maximum likelihood estimator of p. In this case, as well as in many others, the maximum likelihood estimator agrees with our intuitive estimator given earlier in this chapter. $\square$

We now look at an example that we have not yet considered.

EXAMPLE 6.14

Suppose we are to observe n independent lifelength measurements, $X_1, \ldots, X_n$, from components known to have lifelengths exhibiting a Weibull model, given by

$$f(x) = \frac{\gamma x^{\gamma - 1}}{\theta} e^{-x^{\gamma}/\theta}, \qquad x > 0$$

$$= 0, \qquad \text{elsewhere.}$$

Assuming γ is known, find the maximum likelihood estimator of θ.

Solution   In analogy with the discrete case given above, we write the likelihood, $L(\theta)$, as the joint density function of $X_1, \ldots, X_n$, or

$$L(\theta) = f(x_1, x_2, \ldots, x_n)$$
$$= f(x_1)f(x_2) \cdots f(x_n)$$
$$= \frac{\gamma x_1^{\gamma - 1}}{\theta} e^{-x_1^{\gamma}/\theta} \cdots \frac{\gamma x_n^{\gamma - 1}}{\theta} e^{-x_n^{\gamma}/\theta}$$
$$= \left(\frac{\gamma}{\theta}\right)^n (x_1, x_2, \ldots, x_n)^{\gamma - 1} e^{-\sum_{i=1}^{n} x_i^{\gamma}/\theta}$$

Now,

$$\ln L(\theta) = n \ln \gamma - n \ln \theta + (\gamma - 1) \ln(x_1 \cdots x_n) - \frac{1}{\theta} \sum_{i=1}^{n} x_i^{\gamma}.$$

To find the θ that maximizes $L(\theta)$, we take

$$\frac{\partial \ln L(\theta)}{\partial \theta} = -\frac{n}{\theta} + \frac{1}{\theta^2} \sum_{i=1}^{n} x_i^{\gamma}$$

and setting this derivative equal to zero, we get

$$-\frac{n}{\hat{\theta}} + \frac{1}{\hat{\theta}^2} \sum_{i=1}^{n} x_i^{\gamma} = 0$$

or

$$\hat{\theta} = \frac{1}{n} \sum_{i=1}^{n} x_i^{\gamma}.$$

Thus, we take $(1/n) \sum_{i=1}^{n} X_i^{\gamma}$ as the maximum likelihood estimator of θ. The interested reader can check to see that this estimator is unbiased for θ.   □

The maximum likelihood estimators shown in Examples 6.13 and 6.14 are both unbiased, but this is not always the case. For example, if X has a geometric distribution, as given in Chapter 3, then the maximum likelihood estimator of p, the probability of a success on any one trial, is $1/X$. In this case $E(1/X) \neq p$, so this estimator is not unbiased for p.

Many times the maximum likelihood estimator is simple enough that we can use its probability distribution to find a confidence interval, either exact or approximate, for the parameter in question. We illustrate the construction of an exact confidence interval for a nonnormal case with the exponential distribution. Suppose $X_1, \ldots, X_n$ represents a random sample from a population modeled by the density function

$$f(x) = \frac{1}{\theta} e^{-x/\theta}, \qquad x > 0$$

$$= 0, \qquad \text{elsewhere.}$$

Since this exponential density is a special case of the Weibull with $\gamma = 1$, we know from Example 6.14 that the maximum likelihood estimator of θ is $(1/n) \sum_{i=1}^{n} X_i$. We also know that $\sum_{i=1}^{n} X_i$ will have a gamma distribution but we do not have percentage points of most gamma distributions in standard sets of tables, except for the special case of the χ^2 distribution. Thus, we shall try to transform $\sum_{i=1}^{n} X_i$ into something that has a χ^2 distribution.

Let $U_i = 2X_i/\theta$. Then

$$F_U(u) = P(U_i \leq u) = P\left(\frac{2X_i}{\theta} \leq u\right)$$

$$= P\left(X_i \leq \frac{u\theta}{2}\right) = 1 - e^{-(1/\theta)(u\theta/2)}$$

$$= 1 - e^{-u/2}.$$

Hence,

$$f_U(u) = \frac{1}{2} e^{-u/2}$$

and U_i has an exponential distribution with mean 2, which is equivalent to the χ_2^2 distribution. It then follows that

$$\sum_{i=1}^{n} U_i = \frac{2}{\theta} \sum_{i=1}^{n} X_i$$

has a χ^2 distribution with $2n$ degrees of freedom. Thus, a confidence interval for θ with confidence coefficient $(1 - \alpha)$ can be formed by finding a $\chi_{2n}^2 (\alpha/2)$ and a $\chi_{2n}^2 (1 - \alpha/2)$ value and writing

$$(1 - \alpha) = P\left[\chi_{2n}^2(1 - \alpha/2) \leq \frac{2}{\theta} \sum_{i=1}^{n} X_i \leq \chi_{2n}^2(\alpha/2)\right]$$

$$= P\left[\frac{1}{\chi_{2n}^2(\alpha/2)} \leq \frac{\theta}{2 \sum_{i=1}^{n} X_i} \leq \frac{1}{\chi_{2n}^2(1 - \alpha/2)}\right]$$

$$= P\left[\frac{2 \sum_{i=1}^{n} X_i}{\chi_{2n}^2(\alpha/2)} \leq \theta \leq \frac{2 \sum_{i=1}^{n} X_i}{\chi_{2n}^2(1 - \alpha/2)}\right].$$

EXAMPLE 6.15

Consider the first ten observations from Table 2.1 on lifelengths of batteries. These are as follows: 0.406, 2.343, 0.538, 5.088, 5.587, 2.563, 0.023, 3.334, 3.491, and 1.267. Using these observations as a realization of a random sample of lifelength measurements from an exponential distribution with mean θ, find a 95% confidence interval for θ.

Solution   Using

$$\left[\frac{2 \sum\limits_{i=1}^{n} x_i}{\chi_{2n}^2(\alpha/2)}, \frac{2 \sum\limits_{i=1}^{n} x_i}{\chi_{2n}^2(1 - \alpha/2)} \right]$$

as the confidence interval for θ, we have

$$\sum_{i=1}^{10} x_i = 24.640$$

$$\chi_{20}^2(0.975) = 9.591$$

and

$$\chi_{20}^2(0.025) = 34.170$$

Hence, the realization of the confidence interval becomes

$$\left[\frac{2(24.640)}{34.170}, \frac{2(24.640)}{9.591} \right]$$

or $(1.442, 5.138)$. We are reasonably confident that this interval includes the true value of θ.

It is informative to compare the exact intervals for the mean, θ, from the exponential distribution with what would have been generated if we had falsely assumed the random variables to have a normal distribution and used $\bar{x} \pm t_{\alpha/2} s/\sqrt{n}$ as a confidence interval. Table 6.2 shows 100 95% confidence intervals generated by exact methods (using the χ^2 table) for samples of size $n = 5$ from an exponential distribution with $\theta = 10$. Note that five of the intervals do not include the true θ, as expected. Four miss on the low side, and one misses on the high side.

Table 6.3 repeats the process of generating confidence intervals for θ, with the same samples of size $n = 5$, but now using $\bar{x} \pm t_{\alpha/2} s/\sqrt{n}$ with $\alpha/2 = 0.025$ and four degrees of freedom. Now note that ten of the intervals do not include the true θ, twice the number expected. Also, the intervals that miss the true $\theta = 10$ all miss on the low side. That, coupled with the fact that the lower bounds are frequently negative even though $\theta > 0$, seems to indicate that the intervals based on normality are too far left, as compared to the true intervals based on the χ^2 distribution.

The lesson to be learned here is that one should be careful of inflicting the normality assumption on data, especially if a more reasonable and mathematically tractable model is available.

Before we leave the section on maximum likelihood estimation, we will show how we can carry out the estimation of certain functions of parameters. In general, if we have a maximum likelihood estimator, say Y, for a parameter

Table 6.2   Exact Exponential Confidence Intervals ($n = 5$)

Sample	LCL	UCL	Sample	LCL	UCL
1	2.03600	12.8439	51	9.10805	57.4570
*2	1.49454	9.4281	52	4.20731	26.5413
3	4.15706	26.2243	53	5.08342	32.0681
4	3.07770	19.4153	54	5.04982	31.8561
5	5.89943	37.2158	55	3.60932	22.7689
6	6.49541	40.9755	56	5.84841	36.8940
7	2.19705	13.8598	57	5.19353	32.7627
8	2.37724	14.9965	58	4.18032	26.3710
9	5.90726	37.2652	59	4.66717	29.4422
10	7.67249	48.4009	60	5.39428	34.0291
11	6.64161	41.8977	61	6.06969	38.2899
12	4.78097	30.1601	62	3.45198	21.7764
13	3.17174	20.0085	63	5.19596	32.7781
*14	1.51473	9.5555	64	4.79768	30.2655
15	3.70163	23.3513	65	5.76487	36.3669
16	3.69998	23.3408	66	4.15674	26.2223
17	6.90343	43.5494	67	8.96348	56.5450
18	2.36005	14.8881	68	6.74431	42.5456
19	6.53294	41.2122	69	5.36919	33.8709
20	4.04756	25.5335	70	3.77090	23.7883
21	5.61737	35.4365	71	5.42996	34.2542
22	4.07102	25.6815	72	2.7016	17.0429
23	4.65284	29.3518	73	4.2962	27.1020
24	4.58284	28.9103	74	2.3106	14.5761
25	3.80908	24.0291	75	7.6502	48.2602
26	4.22984	26.6834	76	7.4693	47.1190
27	5.17128	32.6223	77	8.5458	53.9103
28	8.77035	55.3266	78	2.9840	18.8243
29	2.54689	16.0667	79	9.2678	58.4647
30	5.27866	33.2998	80	4.2078	26.5442
31	7.26216	45.8124	81	8.0267	50.6353
32	2.27762	14.3680	82	9.9686	62.8854
33	4.63549	29.2424	83	2.2581	14.2447
34	3.80281	23.9895	84	9.9971	63.0651
35	1.98777	12.5396	*85	10.2955	64.9478
36	4.63779	29.2569	86	6.0830	38.3740
37	7.36773	46.4784	87	3.0037	18.9483
38	3.55928	22.4533	88	2.3759	14.9881
39	2.99137	18.8707	89	4.0007	25.2376
40	5.79160	36.5356	*90	1.1737	7.4044
41	5.62684	35.4962	91	3.8375	24.2081
42	3.95994	24.9808	92	2.9560	18.6473
43	2.30394	14.5341	93	4.9714	31.3616
44	7.40844	46.7352	94	3.0063	18.9648
45	3.06875	19.3588	95	4.1684	26.2958
46	2.99999	18.9251	96	4.6269	29.1879
47	3.95912	24.9756	97	3.8026	23.9883
48	3.01418	19.0146	98	6.0056	37.8858
49	2.69137	16.9782	*99	1.5153	9.5592
50	4.28299	27.0187	100	7.0408	44.4161

Table 6.3 Confidence Intervals Based on the
Normal Distributions ($n = 5$)

Sample	LCL	Mean	UCL	S
*1	1.975	4.1704	6.3656	1.7682
*2	−1.069	3.0613	7.1916	3.3269
3	−1.550	8.5150	18.5800	8.1074
4	−1.019	6.3041	13.6277	5.8991
5	4.183	12.0839	19.9850	6.3644
6	3.838	13.3046	22.7712	7.6253
7	−3.036	4.5002	12.0368	6.0707
*8	0.010	4.8693	9.7289	3.9144
9	1.004	12.0999	23.1954	8.9374
10	4.917	15.7156	26.5146	8.6986
11	8.340	13.6041	18.8683	4.2404
12	−0.397	9.7929	19.9832	8.2083
13	1.042	6.4967	11.9513	4.3937
*14	−0.274	3.1026	6.4790	2.7197
15	2.542	7.5821	12.6217	4.0594
16	3.398	7.5787	11.7597	3.3678
17	6.994	14.1404	21.2868	5.7564
*18	1.244	4.8341	8.4245	2.8920
19	−6.383	13.3815	33.1458	15.9202
20	1.122	8.2907	15.4591	5.7742
21	−3.593	11.5061	26.6049	12.1621
22	−0.433	8.3387	17.1102	7.0654
23	−5.925	9.5305	24.9856	12.4491
24	−11.200	9.3871	29.9740	16.5828
25	−4.166	7.8022	19.7701	9.6402
26	1.564	8.6640	15.7640	5.7191
27	3.818	10.5924	17.3667	5.4567
28	−3.492	17.9644	39.4208	17.2832
29	−0.656	5.2168	11.0900	4.7308
30	1.837	10.8123	19.7876	7.2296
31	2.581	14.8751	27.1690	9.9027
32	−1.941	4.6653	11.2716	5.3214
33	−10.734	9.4949	29.7238	16.2943
34	−2.725	7.7893	18.3035	8.4692
*35	−0.546	4.0716	8.6890	3.7193
36	0.841	9.4996	18.1584	6.9747
37	−1.467	15.0914	31.6496	13.3376
38	2.144	7.2905	12.4370	4.1455
39	−2.991	6.1272	15.2452	7.3446
40	−4.714	11.8630	28.4403	13.3530
41	4.356	11.5255	18.6946	5.7747
42	−4.436	8.1112	20.6585	10.1069
*43	1.221	4.7192	8.2178	2.8181
44	−0.877	15.1748	31.2261	12.9294
45	0.865	6.2858	11.7065	4.3665
46	0.751	6.1449	11.5392	4.3451
47	−1.325	8.1095	17.5442	7.5997
48	−1.116	6.1740	13.4641	5.8722
49	−2.837	5.5128	13.8623	6.7256

Table 6.3 (*continued*)

Sample	LCL	Mean	UCL	S
50	2.529	8.7729	15.0168	5.0294
51	− 3.559	18.6561	40.8713	17.8944
52	− 2.949	8.6179	20.1847	9.3171
53	1.648	10.4124	19.1769	7.0598
54	− 2.852	10.3436	23.5391	10.6290
55	1.645	7.3930	13.1407	4.6298
56	2.344	11.9794	21.6150	7.7615
57	− 8.525	10.6380	29.8011	15.4359
58	− 0.781	8.5626	17.9059	7.5260
59	2.364	9.5598	16.7556	5.7962
60	− 1.314	11.0491	23.4128	9.9589
61	1.465	12.4326	23.3998	8.8341
62	− 2.978	7.0707	17.1193	8.0941
63	− 6.065	10.6429	27.3514	13.4586
64	− 4.378	9.8271	24.0327	11.4426
65	3.155	11.8082	20.4612	6.9700
66	0.298	8.5143	16.7307	6.6184
67	− 4.655	18.3600	41.3751	18.5387
68	3.14	13.8144	24.4798	8.5910
69	− 2.948	10.9978	24.9433	11.2331
70	0.332	7.7240	15.1161	5.9544
71	− 3.383	11.1222	25.6275	11.8840
72	1.027	5.5338	10.0406	3.6302
73	− 1.720	8.7999	19.3194	8.4735
74	− 0.755	4.7328	10.2205	4.4203
75	− 4.753	15.6699	36.0924	16.4503
76	− 12.223	15.2994	42.8221	22.1695
77	− 5.102	17.5045	40.1115	18.2099
78	0.504	6.1122	11.7204	4.5175
79	0.042	18.9833	37.9249	15.2575
80	− 0.873	8.6188	18.1102	7.6453
81	7.232	16.4411	25.6501	7.4179
82	− 0.289	20.4187	41.1267	16.6803
*83	− 0.684	4.6252	9.9343	4.2765
84	1.162	20.4771	39.7917	15.5579
85	− 13.471	21.0884	55.6473	27.8373
86	− 0.086	12.4599	25.0060	10.1059
87	− 3.659	6.1524	15.9641	7.9033
88	− 4.660	4.8666	14.3930	7.6735
89	0.914	8.1946	15.4755	5.8648
*90	0.826	2.4042	3.9824	1.2712
91	− 0.416	7.8603	16.1361	6.6662
92	− 0.093	6.0547	12.2023	4.9519
93	2.451	10.1830	17.9150	6.2281
94	− 6.613	6.1578	18.9282	10.2866
95	− 0.470	8.5382	17.5461	7.2559
96	− 0.036	9.4772	18.9902	7.6627
97	− 2.201	7.7889	17.7785	8.0466
98	2.279	12.3014	22.3234	8.0727
*99	1.383	3.1038	4.8248	1.3862
100	?.804	14.4218	31.6476	13.8754

θ, then almost any continuous function of θ, say $g(\theta)$, will have maximum likelihood estimator $g(Y)$. Rather than going deeper into the theory here, we illustrate with an example.

Suppose $X_1, \ldots, X_n$ again denote independent life length measurements from a population modeled by the exponential distribution with mean θ. The *reliability* of each component is defined by

$$R(t) = P(X_i > t).$$

In the exponential case,

$$R(t) = \int_t^\infty \frac{1}{\theta} e^{-x/\theta} \, dx = e^{-t/\theta}.$$

Suppose we want to estimate $R(t)$ from $X_1, \ldots, X_n$. We know that the maximum likelihood estimator of θ is $\bar{X}$, and, hence, the maximum likelihood estimator of $R(t) = e^{-t/\theta}$ is $e^{-t/\bar{X}}$.

Now we can use the results from Section 5.5 to find an approximate confidence interval for $R(t)$ if n is large. Let

$$g(\theta) = e^{-t/\theta}.$$

Then $g'(\theta) = (t/\theta^2)e^{-t/\theta}$ and, since $\bar{X}$ is approximately normally distributed with mean θ and standard deviation $\theta/\sqrt{n}$ (since $V(X_i) = \theta^2$), it follows that

$$\sqrt{n} \frac{[g(\bar{X}) - g(\theta)]}{|g'(\theta)|\theta} = \frac{\sqrt{n}\left[e^{-t/\bar{X}} - e^{-t/\theta}\right]}{\left(\dfrac{t}{\theta}\right)e^{-t/\theta}}$$

tends to a standard normal random variable as $n \to \infty$. Thus, for large n, $e^{-t/\bar{X}}$ is approximately normally distributed with mean $e^{-t/\theta}$ and standard deviation $(1/\sqrt{n})(t/\theta)e^{-t/\theta}$. Note that this is only a large sample approximation, as $E(e^{-t/\bar{X}}) \neq e^{-t/\theta}$. This result can be used to form an approximate confidence interval for $R(t) = e^{-t/\theta}$ of the form

$$e^{-t/\bar{x}} \pm z_{\alpha/2} \frac{1}{\sqrt{n}}\left(\frac{t}{\bar{x}}\right)e^{-t/\bar{x}}$$

using $\bar{x}$ as an approximation to θ in the standard deviation.

EXAMPLE 6.16

Using the fifty observations given in Table 2.1 as a realization of a random sample from an exponential distribution, estimate $R(5) = P(X_i > 5) = e^{-5/\theta}$ in an approximate 95% confidence interval.

Solution   For $(1 - \alpha) = 0.95$, $z_{\alpha/2} = 1.96$. Using the method indicated above, the interval becomes

$$e^{-t/\bar{x}} \pm (1.96) \frac{1}{\sqrt{n}} \left(\frac{t}{\bar{x}}\right) e^{-t/\bar{x}}$$

or

$$e^{-5/2.267} \pm (1.96) \frac{1}{\sqrt{50}} \left(\frac{5}{2.267}\right) e^{-5/2.267}$$

$$0.110 \pm 0.067$$

$$(0.043, 0.177)$$

For these data the true value of θ was two, and $R(5) = e^{-5/2} = 0.082$ is well within this interval.   □

Exercises

6.40   If $X_1, \ldots, X_n$ denotes a random sample from a Poisson distribution with mean λ, find the maximum likelihood estimator of λ.

6.41   Refer to Exercise 6.40. Since $V(X_i) = \lambda$ in the Poisson case, it follows from the Central Limit Theorem that $\bar{X}$ will be approximately normally distributed with mean λ and variance λ/n, for large n.
   (a) Use the above facts to construct a large sample confidence interval for λ.
   (b) Suppose that 100 reinforced concrete trusses were examined for cracks. The average number of cracks per truss was observed to be 4. Construct an approximate 95% confidence interval for the true mean number of cracks per truss for trusses of this type. What assumptions are necessary for your answer to be valid?

6.42   Suppose $X_1, \ldots, X_n$ denotes a random sample from the normal distribution with mean μ and variance σ^2. Find the maximum likelihood estimators of μ and σ^2.

6.43   Suppose $X_1, \ldots, X_n$ denotes a random sample from the gamma distribution with a known α but unknown β. Find the maximum likelihood estimator of β.

6.44   The stress resistances for specimens of a certain type of plastic tend to have a gamma distribution with $\alpha = 2$, but β may change with certain changes in the manufacturing process. For eight specimens independently selected from a certain process, the resistances (in psi) were:

$$29.2 \quad 28.1 \quad 30.4 \quad 31.7 \quad 28.0 \quad 32.1 \quad 30.1 \quad 29.7$$

Find a 95% confidence interval for β. [Hint: Use the methodology outlined for Example 6.15.]

6.45   If X denotes the number of the trial on which the first defective is found in a series of independent quality control tests, find the maximum likelihood estimator of p, the true probability of observing a defective.

6.6   *Bayes Estimators*

In all previous sections on estimation, population parameters were treated as unknown constants. However, it is sometimes convenient and sometimes necessary to treat an unknown parameter as a random variable in its own right. For example, the proportion of defectives, p, produced by an assembly line may change from day to day, or even hour to hour. Thus, it may be possible to model this changing behavior by allowing p to possess a probability density function, say $g(p)$. Even though we may not be able to choose the correct value of p for a given hour, we can find

$$P(a \le p \le b) = \int_a^b g(p)\, dp.$$

Similarly, the mean daily cost of production for the assembly line in question may vary from day to day, and could be assigned an appropriate probability density function to model the day-to-day variation.

Suppose we are to observe a random sample, $Y_1, \ldots, Y_n$, from a probability density function with a single unknown parameter, θ. If θ is a constant, then the density function is completely specified as $f(y|\theta)$. Note that $f(y|\theta)$ is now a *conditional* density function for y *given* a fixed value of θ. The joint conditional density function for the random sample is given by

$$f(y_1, \ldots, y_n|\theta) = f(y_1|\theta) \cdots f(y_n|\theta).$$

Next, suppose θ varies according to a probability density function, $g(\theta)$. This density function, $g(\theta)$, is referred to as the *prior* density for θ because it is assigned prior to the actual collection of data in a sample.

Knowledge of the above density functions allows us to compute

$$f(\theta|y_1, \ldots, Y_n) = \frac{f(y_1, \ldots, y_n, \theta)}{f(y_1, \ldots, y_n)}$$

$$= \frac{f(y_1, \ldots, y_n|\theta)g(\theta)}{\int_{-\infty}^{\infty} f(y_1, \ldots, y_n|\theta)g(\theta)\, d\theta}.$$

The density function $f(\theta|y_1, \ldots, y_n)$ is the conditional density of θ given the sample data, and is called the *posterior* density function for θ. We will call the *mean* of the posterior density function the *Bayes estimator* of θ. The computations are illustrated in the following example.

EXAMPLE 6.17

Let Y denote the number of defectives observed in a random sample of n items produced by a given machine in one day. The proportion, p, of defectives produced by this machine varies from day to day according to the probability density function

$$g(p) = \begin{cases} 1, & 0 \le p \le 1, \\ 0, & \text{elsewhere.} \end{cases}$$

(In other words, p is uniformly distributed over the interval $(0, 1)$.) Find the Bayes estimator of p.

Solution   For a given p, Y will have a binomial distribution given by

$$f(y|p) = \binom{n}{y} p^y (1 - p)^{n-y}, \qquad y = 0, 1, \ldots, n$$

Then

$$f(y, p) = f(y|p)g(p)$$

$$= \binom{n}{y} p^y (1 - p)^{n-y}(1), \qquad \begin{matrix} y = 0, 1, \ldots, n \\ 0 \le p \le 1. \end{matrix}$$

Now,

$$f(y) = \int_{-\infty}^{\infty} f(y, p)\, dp$$

$$= \int_0^1 \binom{n}{y} p^y (1 - p)^{n-y}\, dp$$

$$= \binom{n}{y} \int_0^1 p^y (1 - p)^{n-y}\, dp$$

$$= \binom{n}{y} \frac{y!(n - y)!}{(n + 1)!}$$

$$= \frac{1}{n + 1}, \qquad y = 0, 1, \ldots, n.$$

The above integral is evaluated by recognizing it as a beta function and referring to the beta density function of Chapter 4. Note that $f(y)$ says that each possible value of y has the same unconditional probability of occurring, since nothing is known about p other than the fact that it is in the interval $(0, 1)$.

It follows that

$$f(p|y) = \frac{f(y, p)}{f(y)}$$

$$= (n + 1)\binom{n}{y} p^y (1 - p)^{n-y}$$

$$= \frac{(n + 1)!}{y!(n - y)!} p^y (1 - p)^{n-y}, \qquad 0 \le p \le 1,$$

which is another beta density function.

The Bayes estimate of p is taken to be the mean of this posterior density function, namely

$$\int_0^1 pf(p|y)\,dp = \int_0^1 p\,\frac{(n+1)!}{y!(n-y)!}\,p^y(1-p)^{n-y}\,dp$$

$$= \frac{y+1}{n+2}.$$

(Check Section 4.6 to find the mean of a beta density function.) Recall that the simple maximum likelihood estimator of p, when p is fixed but unknown, is Y/n. □

Exercises

6.46 Refer to Example 6.17. Suppose that

$$g(p) = \begin{cases} 2, & 0 \le p \le \frac{1}{2}, \\ 0, & \text{elsewhere.} \end{cases}$$

If two items are produced on a given day and one is defective, find the Bayes estimate of p.

6.47 Let Y denote the number of defects per yard for a certain type of fabric. For a given mean, λ, Y has a Poisson distribution. But λ varies from yard to yard according to the density function

$$g(\lambda) = \begin{cases} e^{-\lambda}, & \lambda > 0, \\ 0, & \text{elsewhere.} \end{cases}$$

Find the Bayes estimator of λ.

6.48 Suppose the life length, Y, of a certain component has probability density function

$$f(y|\theta) = \frac{\theta^\alpha}{\Gamma(\alpha)}\,y^{\alpha-1}e^{-y\theta}, \qquad y > 0,$$

$$= 0, \qquad \text{elsewhere.}$$

Also, suppose θ has a prior density function given by

$$g(\theta) = \begin{cases} e^{-\theta}, & \theta > 0, \\ 0, & \text{elsewhere.} \end{cases}$$

For a single observation, Y, show that the Bayes estimator of θ is given by $(\alpha + 2)/(Y + 1)$.

6.7   *Prediction Intervals*

Previous sections of this chapter have considered the problem of *estimating* parameters, or population constants. A similar problem is that of *predicting* a value for a future observation of a random variable. Given a set of *n* lifelength measurements on components of a certain type, it may be of interest to form an interval (a prediction interval) in which we think the next observation on the lifelength of a similar component is quite likely to lie.

For independent random variables having a common normal distribution, a prediction interval is easily derived using the *t* distribution. Suppose we are to observe independent, identically distributed normal random variables, and then use the information to predict where X_{n+1} might lie. We know from previous discussions that $\bar{X}_n - X_{n+1}$ is normally distributed with mean zero and variance $(\sigma^2/n) + \sigma^2 = \sigma^2(1 + (1/n))$. If we use the variables $X_1, \ldots, X_n$ to calculate S^2 as an estimator of σ^2, then

$$T = \frac{\bar{X}_n - X_{n+1}}{S\sqrt{1 + \dfrac{1}{n}}}$$

will have a *t* distribution with $(n-1)$ degrees of freedom. Thus,

$$1 - \alpha = P\left[-t_{\alpha/2} \leq \frac{\bar{X}_n - X_{n+1}}{S\sqrt{1 + \dfrac{1}{n}}} \leq t_{\alpha/2} \right]$$

$$= P\left[\bar{X}_n - t_{\alpha/2}S\sqrt{1 + \dfrac{1}{n}} \leq X_{n+1} \leq \bar{X}_n + t_{\alpha/2}S\sqrt{1 + \dfrac{1}{n}} \right].$$

The interval

$$\bar{X}_n \pm t_{\alpha/2}S\sqrt{1 + \dfrac{1}{n}}$$

forms a realization of prediction interval for X_{n+1}, with coverage probability $1 - \alpha$.

EXAMPLE 6.18

Ten independent observations are taken on bottles coming off a machine designed to fill them to 16 ounces. The $n = 10$ observations show a mean of $\bar{x} = 16.1$ oz and a standard deviation of $s = 0.01$ oz. Find a 95% prediction interval for the ounces of fill in the next bottle to be observed.

Solution   Assuming a normal probability model for ounces of fill, the interval

$$\bar{x} \pm t_{0.025}s\sqrt{1 + \dfrac{1}{n}}$$

will provide the answer. We obtain

$$16.1 \pm (2.262)(0.01)\sqrt{1 + \frac{1}{10}}$$

with $t_{0.025}$ based on 9 degrees of freedom, which yields

$$16.1 \pm 0.024$$

or

$$(16.076, 16.124).$$

We are quite confident that the next observation will lie in this interval. □

Note that the prediction interval will *not* become arbitrarily small with increasing n. In fact, if n is very large the term $1/n$ might be ignored, resulting in an interval of the form $\bar{x} \pm t_{\alpha/2}s$. There will be a certain amount of error in predicting the value of a specific random variable no matter how much information is available to estimate μ and σ^2.

This type of prediction interval is sometimes used as the basis for control charts when "sampling by variables." That is, if n observations on some important variable are made while a process is in control, then the next observation should lie in the interval $\bar{x} \pm t_{\alpha/2}s\sqrt{1 + 1/n}$. If it doesn't, then there may be some reason to suspect that the process has gone out of control. (Usually more than one observation would have to be observed outside of the appropriate interval before an investigation into causes of the abnormality would be launched.)

Exercises

6.49   Refer to Exercise 6.20. Suppose a new experiment is to be run for the purpose of obtaining an LC50 measurement for DDT. Use the data for Exercise 6.20 to develop a 90% prediction interval for this new observation.

6.50   Refer to Exercise 6.23. If a resistor of this type is to be used in a circuit, find a 95% prediction interval for the amount of resistance it will actually produce.

6.51   Refer to Exercise 6.11. If a portion of this plastic clay is to be used on a specific job, find a 95% prediction interval for its percent of shrinkage.

6.8   Conclusion

We have developed confidence intervals for individual means and proportions, linear functions of means and proportions, individual variances and ratios of variances. In a few cases, we have shown how to calculate confidence intervals for other functions of parameters. We also touched on the notion of a prediction interval for a random variable. All of these intervals were two-sided, in the sense that they provided both an upper and a lower bound. Occasionally, a one-sided interval is in order. Suppose that the standard process for producing a certain detergent yields μ_0 pounds per minute. A new process is suggested that may increase the mean yield. Suppose n independent observations, $X_1, \ldots, X_n$, on yield per minute are observed on the new process. What is then of interest is a lower bound on the mean, μ_N, for the new process. The lower bound will allow us to see if μ_N is likely to be larger than μ_0, which is the comparison of interest. A one-sided confidence interval for μ_N, if $X_1, \ldots, X_n$ come from a common normal distribution, is given by

$$P\left(\bar{x} - t_\alpha \frac{s}{\sqrt{n}} \leq \mu_N\right) = 1 - \alpha.$$

In other words,

$$\bar{x} - t_\alpha \frac{s}{\sqrt{n}}$$

will form the realization of a bound, which should be smaller than μ_N with probability $1 - \alpha$. If $\mu_0 < \bar{x} - t_\alpha s/\sqrt{n}$ for some small α, we would be inclined to say that μ_N is probably larger than μ_0.

Supplementary Exercises

6.52 The diameter measurements of an armored electric cable, taken at 10 points along the cable, yield a sample mean of 2.1 centimeters and a sample standard deviation of 0.3 centimeter. Estimate the average diameter of the cable in a confidence interval with a confidence coefficient of 0.90. What assumption is necessary for your answer to be valid?

6.53 Suppose the sample mean and standard deviation of Exercise 6.49 had come from a sample of 100 measurements. Construct a 90% confidence interval for the average diameter of the cable. What assumption must necessarily be made?

6.54 The Rockwell hardness measure of steel ingots is produced by pressing a diamond point into the steel and measuring the depth of penetration. A sample of 15 Rockwell hardness measurements on specimens of steel gave a sample mean of 65 and a sample variance of 90. Estimate the true mean hardness in a 95% confidence interval, assuming the measurements to come from a normal distribution.

6.55 Refer to Exercise 6.54. Twenty specimens were sampled from a slightly different steel and yielded Rockwell hardness measurements with a mean of 72 and a variance of 94. Estimate the difference between the mean hardnesses for the two varieties of steel in a 95% confidence interval.

6.56 It is desired to estimate the proportion of defective items produced by a certain assembly line to within 0.1 with confidence coefficient 0.95. What is the smallest sample size that will guarantee this accuracy no matter where the true proportion of defectives might lie? [Hint: Find the value of p that maximizes the variance, $p(1 - p)/n$, and choose the n that corresponds to it.]

6.57 Suppose that in a large-sample estimate of $\mu_1 - \mu_2$ for two populations with respective variances σ_1^2 and σ_2^2, a *total* of n observations are to be selected. How should these n observations be allocated to the two populations so that the length of the resulting confidence interval will be minimized?

6.58 Refer to Exercise 6.26. Suppose the sample variances given there are good estimates of the population variances. Using the allocation scheme of Exercise 6.54, find the number of measurements to be taken on each coupling agent in order to estimate the true difference in means to within 1 unit with confidence coefficient 0.95. Compare the answer to that of Exercise 6.27.

6.59 A factory operates with two machines of type A and one machine of type B. The weekly repair costs, Y, for type A machines are normally distributed with mean μ_1 and variance σ^2. The weekly repair costs, X, for machines of type B are also normally distributed but with mean μ_2 and variance $3\sigma^2$. The expected repair cost per week for the factory is then $2\mu_1 + \mu_2$. Suppose $Y_1, \ldots, Y_n$ denotes a random sample on costs for type A machines and $X_1, \ldots, X_m$ denotes an independent random sample on costs for type B machines. Use these data to construct a 95% confidence interval for $2\mu_1 + \mu_2$.

6.60 In polycrystalline aluminum the number of grain nucleation sites per unit volume is modeled as having a Poisson distribution with mean λ. Fifty unit-volume test specimens subjected to annealing under regime A showed an average of 20 sites per unit volume. Fifty independently selected unit-volume test specimens subjected to annealing regime B showed an average of 23 sites per unit volume. Find an approximate 95% confidence interval for the difference between the mean site frequencies for the two annealing regimes. Would you say that regime B tends to increase the number of nucleation sites?

6.61 A random sample of n items is selected from the large number of items produced by a certain production line in one day. The number of defectives, X, is observed. Find the maximum likelihood estimator of the ratio, R, of the number of defective to good items.

7

Hypothesis Testing

About This Chapter

The second formal manner of making inferences from sample to population is through *tests of hypotheses*. This methodology is basic to the scientific method, as it allows for hypotheses to be substantiated or refuted by looking at sample statistics. Again, the sampling distributions of the statistics involved play a key role in the development.

Contents

One method of using sample data to formulate inferences about a population parameter, as seen in Chapter 6, is to produce a confidence interval estimate of the parameter in question. But it often happens that an experimenter is only interested in checking a claim, or hypothesis, concerning the value of a parameter, and is basically not interested in the location or length of the confidence interval itself. For example, if an electronic component is guaranteed to possess a mean lifelength of at least 200 hours, then an investigator may only be interested in checking the hypothesis that the mean really is 200 hours or more against the alternative that the mean is less than 200 hours. A confidence interval on the mean is not, in itself, of great interest, although it can provide a mechanism for checking, or *testing*, the hypothesis of interest.

Hypothesis testing arises as a natural consequence of the scientific method. The scientist observes nature, formulates a theory, and then tests theory against observation. In the context of our problems, the experimenter theorizes that a population parameter takes on a certain value, or set of values. A sample is then selected from the population in question and observation is compared with theory. If the observations seriously disagree with the theory, then the experimenter may reject the hypothesis. If not, the experimenter concludes that either the theory is true or that the sample did not detect the difference between the real and hypothesized value of the population parameter.

Note that hypothesis testing requires a decision when comparing the observed sample with theory. How do we decide whether the sample disagrees with the hypothesis? When should we reject the hypothesis, and when should we not reject? What is the probability that we will make a wrong decision? What function of the sample observations should we employ in our decision-making process? The answers to these questions lie in a study of statistical hypothesis testing.

7.2   *Hypothesis Testing: The Single Sample Case*

In this section we present tests of hypotheses concerning the mean of an unspecified distribution, the probability of success in a binomial distribution, and the mean and variance of a normal distribution. The first two tests require large samples, and are approximate in nature, while the second two are exact tests for any sample size.

7.2.1   *General Distribution: Testing the Mean*

One of the most common and, at the same time, easiest hypothesis-testing situations to consider is that of testing a population mean when a large random sample from the population in question is available for observation. Denoting the population mean by μ and the mean of the sample of size n by $\bar{X}$, we know from Chapter 6 that $\bar{X}$ is a good point estimator of μ. Therefore, it seems intuitively reasonable that our decision about μ should be based on $\bar{X}$, with extra information provided by the population variance σ^2, or its estimator S^2.

Suppose it is claimed that μ takes on the specific value μ_0, and we wish to test the validity of this claim. How can we tie this testing notion into the notion of a confidence interval established in Chapter 6? Upon reflection, it may seem reasonable that if the resulting confidence interval for μ does *not* contain μ_0, then we should *reject* the hypothesis that $\mu = \mu_0$. On the other hand, if μ_0 is within the confidence limits, then we cannot reject it as a highly plausible value for μ. Now, if μ_0 is not within the interval $\bar{X} \pm z_{\alpha/2}\, \sigma/\sqrt{n}$, then either

$$\mu_0 < \bar{X} - z_{\alpha/2}\,\frac{\sigma}{\sqrt{n}}$$

or

$$\mu_0 > \bar{X} + z_{\alpha/2}\,\frac{\sigma}{\sqrt{n}}.$$

The former equation can be rewritten as

$$\frac{\bar{X} - \mu_0}{\sigma/\sqrt{n}} > z_{\alpha/2}$$

and the latter as

$$\frac{\bar{X} - \mu_0}{\sigma/\sqrt{n}} < -z_{\alpha/2}.$$

Assuming a large sample, so that $\bar{X}$ has approximately a normal distribution, we see that the hypothesized value μ_0 is rejected if

$$|Z| = \left| \frac{\bar{X} - \mu_0}{\sigma/\sqrt{n}} \right| > z_{\alpha/2},$$

for some prescribed α, where Z has approximately a standard normal distribution. Whereas $1 - \alpha$ was called the confidence coefficient in estimation problems, α is referred to as the *significance level* in hypothesis-testing problems.

EXAMPLE 7.1

The depth setting on a certain drill press is two inches. One could then hypothesize that the average depth of all holes drilled by this machine is $\mu = 2$ inches. To check this hypothesis (and the accuracy of the depth gauge) a random sample of $n = 100$ holes drilled by this machine were measured and found to have a sample mean of $\bar{x} = 2.005$ inches with a standard deviation of $s = 0.03$ inch. With $\alpha = 0.05$, can the hypothesis be rejected based on this sample data?

Solution   With $n = 100$, it is assumed that $\bar{X}$ will be approximately normal in distribution. Thus, we reject the hypothesis $\mu = 2$ if

$$|Z| = \left| \frac{\bar{X} - \mu_0}{\sigma/\sqrt{n}} \right| > z_{\alpha/2} = 1.96.$$

Now,

$$\frac{\bar{x} - \mu_0}{s/\sqrt{n}} = \frac{2.005 - 2.000}{0.03/\sqrt{100}} = 1.67.$$

Since the observed value of $(\bar{x} - \mu_0)/s/\sqrt{n}$ is less than 1.96, we cannot reject the hypothesis that 2 is a plausible value of μ. (The 95% confidence interval for μ would include the value 2.)   □

To introduce some standard notation and terminology into the hypothesis testing problems, we will refer to the hypothesis being tested as the *null hypothesis*, denoted by H_0. The alternative of interest is simply the *alternative hypothesis*, denoted by H_a. The quantity calculated from the observed sample upon which the decision is based is called the *test statistic*. The set of values of the test statistic that lead to rejection of the null hypothesis is called the *rejection region* (or *critical region*). We summarize these concepts in Table 7.1, illustrating in terms of testing a population mean with a large sample.

	Terminology	Example
	Null hypothesis, H_0	$H_0 : \mu = \mu_0$
	Alternative hypothesis, H_a	$H_a : \mu \neq \mu_0$
Table 7.1 Components of an Hypothesis Testing Problem	Test statistic	$Z = \dfrac{\bar{X} - \mu_0}{\sigma/\sqrt{n}}$
	Rejection region	$|Z| > z_{\alpha/2}$

It is sometimes of interest to have a more specific alternative hypothesis in mind, such as in testing $H_0 : \mu = \mu_0$ versus the alternative $H_a : \mu < \mu_0$. Such hypotheses might be appropriate if we want to test that the mean ounces of fill dispensed by a machine filling cereal boxes is 16, versus the alternative that the mean is less than 16. In this problem, it is important to detect a serious underfilling ($\mu < 16$) situation, but if μ is slightly over 16 ounces no serious harm results. In fact, the null hypothesis here could just as well be $\mu \geq \mu_0$, since we are only interested in checking to see if there is any evidence to suggest that μ is less than μ_0.

For testing $H_0 : \mu \geq \mu_0$ versus $H_a : \mu < \mu_0$ we only need consider the analogous one-sided confidence interval for μ. Here it is important to establish an upper confidence limit for μ, so we look at the one-sided upper limit $\bar{X} + z_\alpha \sigma/\sqrt{n}$. (See Section 6.6.) We reject H_0 in favor of H_a if $\mu_0 > \bar{X} + z_\alpha \sigma/\sqrt{n}$ or, equivalently, if

$$\frac{\bar{X} - \mu_0}{\sigma/\sqrt{n}} < -z_\alpha.$$

Notice that we still have the same test statistic but that the rejection region has changed somewhat. The corresponding rejection region for testing $H_0: \mu \leq \mu_0$ versus $H_a: \mu > \mu_0$ is given by

$$\frac{\bar{X} - \mu_0}{\sigma/\sqrt{n}} > +z_\alpha.$$

EXAMPLE 7.2

A vice president for a large corporation claims that the number of service calls on equipment sold by that corporation is no more than 15 per week, on the average. To check his claim, service records were checked for $n = 36$ randomly selected weeks, with the result that $\bar{x} = 17$ and $s^2 = 9$ for the sample data. Does the sample evidence contradict the vice-president's claim at the 5% significance level?

Solution

We are testing

$$H_0: \mu \leq 15 \qquad \text{vs.} \qquad H_a: \mu > 15.$$

Using as test statistic

$$Z = \frac{\bar{X} - \mu_0}{\sigma/\sqrt{n}}$$

and substituting s for σ, we have

$$\frac{\bar{x} - \mu_0}{s/\sqrt{n}} = \frac{17 - 15}{3/\sqrt{36}} = 4.$$

With $\alpha = 0.05$, $z_\alpha = 1.645$. Since the test statistic exceeds z_α, we have sufficient evidence to reject the null hypothesis. It does appear that the number of service calls exceeds 15, on the average. □

In thinking about the above hypothesis testing problems we see that there are two ways that errors can be made in the decision process. We can reject the null hypothesis when it is true, called a *Type I error*, or we can fail to reject the null hypothesis when some alternative value is true, called a *Type II error*. Looking at the one-sided test $H_0: \mu = \mu_0$ versus $H_a: \mu < \mu_0$, we reject H_0 if

$$\frac{\bar{X} - \mu_0}{\sigma/\sqrt{n}} < -z_\alpha.$$

Now, the probability that we reject H_0 when H_0 is true is simply

$$P[\text{Reject } H_0 | H_0 \text{ True}] = P\left[\frac{\bar{X} - \mu_0}{\sigma/\sqrt{n}} < -z_\alpha\right] = \alpha,$$

if μ_0 is the true mean of $\bar{X}$. So, we see that

$$\alpha = P[\text{Type I error}].$$

Thus, in the case of a simple null hypothesis like $\mu = \mu_0$, the significance level, α, is the same as the probability of a Type I error.

We will denote the probability of a Type II error by β. That is,

$$\beta = P[\text{Type II error}]$$
$$= P[\text{Do not reject } H_0 | H_a \text{ is true}].$$

For the large sample test of a mean, we can show α and β as in Figure 7.1.

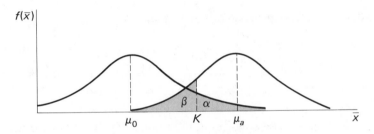

Figure 7.1 α and β for a Statistical Test

Referring to Figure 7.1, if μ_0 is the true value of μ under H_0 and μ_a is a specific alternative value of interest, then the area to the right of K under the normal curve centered at μ_0 is α. The area to the left of K under the curve centered at μ_a is β, for that particular alternative. How do we find the point denoted by K? Recall that for testing $H_0: \mu = \mu_0$ versus $H_a: \mu > \mu_0$, we reject H_0 if

$$\frac{\bar{X} - \mu_0}{\sigma/\sqrt{n}} > z_\alpha.$$

Thus,

$$\alpha = P\left[\frac{\bar{X} - \mu_0}{\sigma/\sqrt{n}} > z_\alpha\right]$$

$$= P\left[\bar{X} > \mu_0 + z_\alpha \frac{\sigma}{\sqrt{n}}\right],$$

and, therefore, $K = \mu_0 + z_\alpha(\sigma/\sqrt{n})$.

We show how to calculate β in the following example.

EXAMPLE 7.3

In a power generating plant, pressure in a certain line is supposed to maintain an average of 100 psi over any four-hour period. If the average pressure exceeds 103 psi for a four-hour period, serious complications can evolve. During a given four-hour period $n = 30$ measurements (assumed random) are to be taken. For testing $H_0 : \mu = 100$ versus $H_a : \mu = 103$, α is to be 0.01. If $\sigma = 4$ psi for these measurements, calculate the probability of a Type II error.

Solution   For testing $H_0 : \mu = 100$ vs. $H_a : \mu = 103$, we reject H_0 if

$$\frac{\bar{X} - \mu_0}{\sigma/\sqrt{n}} > z_{0.01} = 2.33,$$

or if

$$\bar{X} > \mu_0 + z_{0.01} \frac{\sigma}{\sqrt{n}}$$

$$= 100 + 2.33 \left(\frac{4}{\sqrt{30}} \right) = 101.7.$$

Now, if the true mean is really 103, then

$$\beta = P[\bar{X} < 101.7] = P\left[\frac{\bar{X} - \mu_a}{\sigma/\sqrt{n}} < \frac{101.7 - 103}{4/\sqrt{30}} \right]$$

$$= P[Z < -1.78] = 0.0375.$$

Under these conditions, the chance of observing a sample mean that is not in the rejection region when the true average pressure is 103 psi is quite small. Thus, the operation can confidently continue if the sample mean of the tests supports H_0.   □

Notice that for a fixed sample size, increasing the size of the rejection region will increase α and decrease β. In many practical problems, a specific value for an alternative will not be known, and consequently β cannot be calculated. In those cases, we want to choose an appropriate significance level, α, and a test statistic that will make β as small as possible. Fortunately, most of the test statistics we use in this text have the property that, for fixed α and fixed sample size, β is nearly as small as possible. In that sense, we are using the best possible test statistics.

7.2.2   *Binomial Distribution: Testing the Probability of Success*

Just as in the case of interval estimation, the large sample test for a mean can be easily transformed into a test for a binomial proportion. Recall that if Y has a binomial distribution with mean np, then Y/n is approximately normal, for large n, with mean p and variance $p(1 - p)/n$. We illustrate with the following example.

EXAMPLE 7.4

A machine in a certain factory must be repaired if it produces more than 10% defectives among the large lot of items it produces in a day. A random sample of 100 items from the day's production contains 15 defectives, and the foreman says that the machine must be repaired. Does the sample evidence support his decision? Use $\alpha = 0.01$.

Solution   We want to test $H_0 : p = 0.10$ versus the alternative $H_a : p > 0.10$, where p denotes the proportion of defectives in the population. The test statistic will be based upon Y/n, where Y denotes the number of defectives observed. We will reject H_0 in favor of H_a if Y/n is suitably large. Following the procedure for testing a mean, we reject H_0 if

$$Y/n > K$$

or

$$\frac{Y/n - p_0}{\sqrt{\dfrac{p_0(1 - p_0)}{n}}} > z_\alpha.$$

Note that p_0 can be used in the variance of Y/n since we are assuming H_0 is true when we perform the test. Our observed value of the test statistic is

$$\frac{y/n - p_0}{\sqrt{\dfrac{p_0(1 - p_0)}{n}}} = \frac{0.15 - 0.10}{\sqrt{\dfrac{(0.1)(0.9)}{100}}} = \frac{5}{3} = 1.67.$$

Now, $z_{0.01} = 2.33$ and since $1.67 < 2.33$, we will not reject H_0. It is quite likely that a sample fraction of 15% could occur even if p is in the neighborhood of 0.10. The evidence does not support the foreman's decision at the 0.01 significance level. The α value should be chosen to be quite small here since a Type I error (rejecting H_0 when it is true) has serious consequences, namely, the machine would unnecessarily be shut down for repairs. $\square$

7.2.3   *Normal Distribution: Testing the Mean*

If the sample size is not large enough to allow $\bar{X}$ to have approximately a normal distribution, then additional assumptions must be made on the nature of the probabilistic model for the population. Just as in the case of estimation, one common procedure is to assume, whenever it can be justified, that the population measurements fit the normal distribution reasonably well. Then, $\bar{X}$, the sample mean for a random sample of size n, will have a normal distribution, and

$$\frac{\bar{X} - \mu}{S/\sqrt{n}}$$

will have a t distribution with $(n - 1)$ degrees of freedom. Thus, the hypothesis-testing procedures for the population mean will be as outlined above except that the test statistic

$$T = \frac{\bar{X} - \mu_0}{S/\sqrt{n}}$$

will have a t distribution, rather than a normal distribution, under $H_0 : \mu = \mu_0$. For testing $H_0 : \mu = \mu_0$ versus $H_a : \mu \neq \mu_0$ the test statistic $T = (\bar{X} - \mu_0)/S/\sqrt{n}$ is calculated for the observed sample, and H_0 is rejected if $|T| \geq t_{\alpha/2}$, where $t_{\alpha/2}$ is the point cutting off an area of $\alpha/2$ in the upper tail of the t distribution with $(n - 1)$ degrees of freedom. (See Table 5.) Corresponding one-sided tests can be conducted in a manner analogous to the large sample case. The following examples indicate the methodology.

EXAMPLE 7.5

A corporation sets its annual budget for a new plant on the basis of the assumption that the average weekly cost for repairs is to be $\mu = \$1200$. To see if this claim is realistic, $n = 10$ weekly repair cost figures are obtained from similar plants. The sample is assumed to be random, and yields $\bar{x} = 1290$ and $s = 110$. Since a departure from the assumed average in either direction would be important to detect for budgeting purposes, it is desired to test $H_0 : \mu = 1200$ versus $H_a : \mu \neq 1200$. Use $\alpha = 0.05$ and carry out the test.

Solution   Assuming normality of weekly repair costs, the test statistic is

$$T = \frac{\bar{X} - \mu_0}{S/\sqrt{n}},$$

and the rejection region starts at $t_{\alpha/2} = t_{0.025} = 2.262$ for $n - 1 = 9$ degrees of freedom. The observed value of the test statistic is

$$t = \frac{\bar{x} - \mu_0}{s/\sqrt{n}} = \frac{1290 - 1200}{110/\sqrt{10}} = 2.587,$$

which is greater than 2.262. Therefore, we reject the null hypothesis. There is reason to suspect the 1200 is not a good assumed value of μ, and perhaps more investigation into these repair costs should be made before the budget is set. $\square$

The following illustrates a one-sided alternative testing situation.

EXAMPLE 7.6

Muzzle velocities of eight shells tested with a new gunpowder yield a sample mean of $\bar{x} = 2959$ feet per second and a standard deviation, $s = 39.4$. The manufacturer claims that the new gunpowder produces an average velocity of no less than 3000 feet per second. Does the sample provide enough evidence to contradict the manufacturer's claim? Use $= 0.05$.

Solution   Here, we are interested in testing $H_0: \mu \geq 3000$ versus $H_a: \mu < 3000$, since we want to see if there is evidence to refute the manufacturer's claim. Assuming that muzzle velocities can be reasonably modeled by a normal probability distribution, the test statistic is

$$T = \frac{\bar{X} - \mu_0}{S/\sqrt{n}},$$

observed to be

$$t = \frac{\bar{x} - \mu_0}{s/\sqrt{n}} = \frac{2959 - 3000}{39.4/\sqrt{8}} = -2.943.$$

The rejection region starts at $-t_{0.05} = -1.895$ for 7 degrees of freedom. Since $t < -t_\alpha$, we reject the null hypothesis, and say that there appears to be good reason to doubt the manufacturer's claim.

7.2.4 *Normal Distribution: Testing the Variance*

The variance of the underlying normal distributions in the above examples was assumed to be unknown, which is generally the case. If it is desired to test an hypothesis on the variance, σ^2, it can be done by making use of the statistics used in constructing the confidence interval for σ^2. Recall that, for a random sample of size n from a normal distribution,

$$\frac{(n-1)S^2}{\sigma^2}$$

has a $\chi^2_{(n-1)}$ distribution. Following the same principles as above, for testing $H_0: \sigma^2 = \sigma_0^2$ versus $H_a: \sigma^2 \neq \sigma_0^2$ we calculate a value for the statistic $(n-1)S^2/\sigma_0^2$ and reject H_0, at level α, if this statistic is larger than $\chi^2_{(n-1)}(\alpha/2)$ or smaller than $\chi^2_{(n-1)}(1 - \alpha/2)$. Suitable one-sided tests can also be employed.

EXAMPLE 7.7

A machined engine part produced by a certain company is claimed to have diameter variance no larger than 0.0002 inches. A random sample of 10 such parts gave a sample variance of $s^2 = 0.0003$. Assuming normality of diameter measurement, is there evidence here to refute the company's claim? Use $\alpha = 0.05$.

Solution   The test statistic is

$$\frac{(n-1)S^2}{\sigma_0^2}$$

which is observed to be

$$\frac{(n-1)s^2}{\sigma_0^2} = \frac{9(0.0003)}{0.0002} = 13.5.$$

Here, we are testing $H_0:\sigma^2 \le 0.0002$ versus $H_a:\sigma^2 > 0.0002$. Thus, we reject H_0 if $(n-1)S^2/\sigma_0^2$ is larger than $\chi_9^2(0.05) = 16.919$. Since this is not the case, we do not have sufficient evidence to refute the company's claim.

Many other exact small sample tests could be illustrated for other distributions, but these give the general idea for some commonly used cases. We will consider the small sample tests for a binomial parameter in Chapter 12, in the context of lot acceptance sampling.

SUMMARY OF SINGLE SAMPLE TESTS

	Null Hypothesis (H_0)	Alternative Hypothesis (H_a)	Test Statistic	Rejection Region
General Distribution (Large Sample)	$\mu = \mu_0$ $\mu \le \mu_0$ $\mu \ge \mu_0$	$\mu \ne \mu_0$ $\mu > \mu_0$ $\mu < \mu_0$	$Z = \dfrac{\bar{X} - \mu_0}{\sigma/\sqrt{n}}$	$\|z\| > z_{\alpha/2}$ $z > z_\alpha$ $z < -z_\alpha$
Binomial Distribution (Large Sample)	$p = p_0$ $p \le p_0$ $p \ge p_0$	$p \ne p_0$ $p > p_0$ $p < p_0$	$Z = \dfrac{Y/n - p_0}{\sqrt{\dfrac{p_0(1 - p_0)}{n}}}$	$\|z\| > z_{\alpha/2}$ $z > z_\alpha$ $z < -z_\alpha$
Normal Distribution	$\mu = \mu_0$ $\mu \le \mu_0$ $\mu \ge \mu_0$	$\mu \ne \mu_0$ $\mu > \mu_0$ $\mu < \mu_0$	$T = \dfrac{\bar{X} - \mu_0}{S/\sqrt{n}}$ $(n-1)$ d.f.	$\|t\| > t_{\alpha/2}$ $t > t_\alpha$ $t < -t_\alpha$
Normal Distribution	$\sigma^2 = \sigma_0^2$	$\sigma^2 \ne \sigma_0^2$	$\dfrac{(n-1)S^2}{\sigma_0^2}$	$\dfrac{(n-1)s^2}{\sigma_0^2} < \chi^2(1 - \alpha/2)$ or $> \chi^2(\alpha/2)$
	$\sigma^2 \le \sigma_0^2$	$\sigma^2 > \sigma_0^2$		$\dfrac{(n-1)s^2}{\sigma_0^2} > \chi^2(\alpha)$
	$\sigma^2 \ge \sigma_0^2$	$\sigma^2 < \sigma_0^2$	$(n-1)$ d.f.	$\dfrac{(n-1)s^2}{\sigma_0^2} < \chi^2(1 - \alpha)$

Exercises

7.1   The output voltage for a certain electric circuit is specified to be 130. A sample of 40 independent readings on the voltage for this circuit gave a sample mean of 128.6 and a standard deviation of 2.1. Test the hypothesis that the average output voltage is 130 against the alternative that it is less than 130. Use a 5% significance level.

7.2   Refer to Exercise 7.1. If the voltage falls as low as 128 serious consequences may result. For testing $H_0:\mu = 130$ versus $H_a:\mu = 128$ find the probability of a Type II error, β, for the rejection region used in Exercise 7.1.

7.3   The Rockwell hardness index for steel is determined by pressing a diamond point into the steel and measuring the depth of penetration. For 50 specimens of a certain type of steel, the Rockwell hardness index averaged 62 with a standard deviation of 8. The manufacturer claims that this steel has an average hardness index of at least 64. Test this claim at the 1% significance level.

7.4   Refer to Exercise 7.3. The steel is sufficiently hard for a certain use so long as the mean Rockwell hardness measure does not drop below 60. Using the rejection region found in Exercise 7.3, find β for the specific alternative $\mu = 60$.

7.5   The pH of water coming out of a certain filtration plant is specified to be 7.0. Thirty water samples independently selected from this plant show a mean pH of 6.8 and a standard deviation of 0.9. Is there any reason to doubt that the plant's specification is being maintained? Use $\alpha = 0.05$.

7.6   A manufacturer of resistors claims that 10% fail to meet the established tolerance limits. A random sample of resistance measurements for 60 such resistors reveal 8 to lie outside the tolerance limits. Is there sufficient evidence to refute the manufacturer's claim, at the 5% significance level?

7.7   For a certain type of electronic surveillance system the specifications state that the system will function for more than 1000 hours with probability at least 0.90. Checks on 40 such systems show that five failed prior to 1000 hours of operation. Does this sample provide sufficient information to conclude that the specification is not being met? Use $\alpha = 0.01$.

7.8   The hardness of a certain rubber (in degrees Shore) is claimed to be 65. Fourteen specimens are tested, resulting in an average hardness measure of 63.1 and a standard deviation of 1.4. Is there sufficient evidence to reject the claim, at the 5% level of significance? What assumption is necessary for your answer to be valid?

7.9   Certain rockets are manufactured with a range of 2500 meters. It is theorized that the range will be reduced after the rockets are in storage for some time. Six of these rockets are stored for a certain period of time and then tested. The ranges found in the tests are as follows: 2490, 2510, 2360, 2410, 2300, 2440. Does the range appear to be shorter after storage? Test at the 1% significance level.

7.10   For screened coke the porosity factor is measured by the difference in weight between dry and soaked coke. A certain supply of coke is claimed to have a porosity factor of 1.5 kilograms. Ten samples are tested, resulting in a mean porosity factor of 1.9 kilograms and a variance of 0.04. Is there sufficient evidence to indicate that the coke is more porous than is claimed? Use $\alpha = 0.05$ and assume the porosity measurements are approximately normally distributed.

7.11   The stress resistance of a certain plastic is specified to be 30 psi. The results from ten specimens of this plastic show a mean of 27.4 psi and a standard deviation of 1.1 psi. Is there sufficient evidence to doubt the specification, at the 5% significance level? What assumption are you making?

7.12   The dispersion, or variance, of haul times on a construction project are of great importance to the project foreman, since highly variable haul times cause problems in scheduling jobs. The foreman of the truck crews states that the range of haul times should not exceed 40 minutes. (The range is the difference between the longest and shortest times.) Assuming these haul times to be approximately normally distributed, the project foreman takes the statement on the range to mean that the standard deviation, σ, should be approximately 10 minutes. Fifteen haul times are actually measured, and show a mean of 142 minutes and a standard deviation of 12 minutes. Can the claim of $\sigma = 10$ be refuted at the 5% significance level?

7.13   Aptitude tests should produce scores with a large amount of variation so that an administrator can distinguish between persons with low aptitude and those with high aptitude. The standard test used by a certain industry has been producing scores with a standard deviation of 5 points. A new test is tried on 20 prospective employees and produces a sample standard deviation of 8 points. Are scores from the new test significantly more variable than scores from the standard? Use $\alpha = 0.05$.

7.14   Refer to Exercise 7.9. The variation in ranges is also of importance. New rockets have a standard deviation of range measurements equal to 20 meters. Does it appear that storage increases the variability of these ranges? Use $\alpha = 0.05$.

7.3 *Hypothesis Testing: The Multiple Sample Case*

Just as we developed confidence interval estimates for linear functions of means when k samples from k different populations are available, we could develop the corresponding hypothesis tests. However, most tests on population means come down to tests on simple differences of the form $\mu_1 - \mu_2$. Thus, we will only consider this case. (The more general case of testing equality of k means will be covered in a discussion of analysis of variance in Chapter 10.)

7.3.1 *General Distributions: Testing the Difference Between Two Means*

We know from Chapter 6 that in the large sample case, the estimator $\bar{X}_1 - \bar{X}_2$ has approximately a normal distribution. Hence, for testing $H_0: \mu_1 - \mu_2 = D_0$ versus $H_a: \mu_1 - \mu_2 \neq D_0$, we can use as a test statistic

$$Z = \frac{(\bar{X}_1 - \bar{X}_2) - D_0}{\sqrt{\dfrac{\sigma_1^2}{n_1} + \dfrac{\sigma_2^2}{n_2}}}.$$

We reject H_0 for $|Z| \geq z_{\alpha/2}$, for a specified α. Similar one-sided tests can be constructed in the obvious way. If σ_1^2 and σ_2^2 are unknown, they can simply be estimated by the sample variances S_1^2 and S_2^2, respectively.

EXAMPLE 7.8

A study was conducted to compare the length of time it took men and women to perform a certain assembly-line task. Independent samples of 50 men and 50 women were employed in an experiment in which each person was timed on the same identical task. The results were as follows:

Men	Women
$n_1 = 50$	$n_2 = 50$
$\bar{x}_1 = 42$ sec	$\bar{x}_2 = 38$ sec
$s_1^2 = 18$	$s_2^2 = 14$

Do the data present sufficient evidence to suggest a difference between the true mean completion times for men and women at the 5% significance level?

Solution   Since we are interested in detecting a difference in either direction, we want to test $H_0: \mu_1 - \mu_2 = 0$ (no difference) versus $H_a: \mu_1 - \mu_2 \neq 0$. The test statistic is calculated to be

$$z = \frac{(\bar{x}_1 - \bar{x}_2) - D_0}{\sqrt{\dfrac{s_1^2}{n_1} + \dfrac{s_2^2}{n_2}}} = \frac{42 - 38}{\sqrt{\dfrac{18}{50} + \dfrac{14}{50}}} = 5.$$

Now, $z_{0.025} = 1.96$ and since $|z| > 1.96$, we reject H_0. It does appear that the difference in times between men and women is significant. $\square$

7.3.2   *Normal Distributions: Testing the Difference Between Two Means*

As before, the small sample case necessitates an assumption on the nature of the probabilistic model for the random variables in question. If both populations seem to have normal distributions, and if the two variances are equal ($\sigma_1^2 = \sigma_2^2 = \sigma^2$), then t tests on hypotheses concerning $\mu_1 - \mu_2$ can be constructed. For testing $H_0: \mu_1 - \mu_2 = D_0$ versus $H_a: \mu_1 - \mu_2 \neq D_0$ the test statistic to be employed is

$$T = \frac{(\bar{X}_1 - \bar{X}_2) - D_0}{S_p \sqrt{\dfrac{1}{n_1} + \dfrac{1}{n_2}}},$$

where

$$S_p^2 = \frac{(n_1 - 1)S_1^2 + (n_2 - 1)S_2^2}{n_1 + n_2 - 2}.$$

T has a t distribution with $n_1 + n_2 - 2$ degrees of freedom when H_0 is true. As in the large sample case, we reject H_0 whenever $|T| > t_{\alpha/2}$. Corresponding one-sided tests are easily obtained.

EXAMPLE 7.9

The designer of a new sheet-metal stamping machine claims that his new machine can turn out a certain product faster than the machine now in use. Nine independent trials of stamping the same item on each machine gave the following results on times to completion:

Standard Machine	New Machine
$n_1 = 9$	$n_2 = 9$
$\bar{x}_1 = 35.22$ seconds	$\bar{x}_2 = 31.56$ seconds
$(n_1 - 1)s_1^2 = 195.50$	$(n_2 - 1)s_2^2 = 160.22$

At the 5% significance level, can the designer's claim be substantiated?

Solution   We are interested, here, in testing $H_0: \mu_1 - \mu_2 \leq 0$ versus $H_a: \mu_1 - \mu_2 > 0$ (or $\mu_2 < \mu_1$). The test statistic, T, is calculated as

$$t = \frac{(\bar{x}_1 - \bar{x}_2) - D_0}{s_p \sqrt{\dfrac{1}{n_1} + \dfrac{1}{n_2}}} = \frac{35.22 - 31.56}{4.71 \sqrt{\dfrac{1}{9} + \dfrac{1}{9}}} = 1.65,$$

since

$$s_p^2 = \frac{(n_1 - 1)s_1^2 + (n_2 - 1)s_2^2}{n_1 + n_2 - 2} = \frac{195.50 + 160.22}{16} = 22.24.$$

Since $t_{0.05} = 1.746$, with 16 degrees of freedom, we cannot reject H_0. There is no real evidence here to substantiate the designer's claim. $\square$

7.3.3 *Normal Distributions: Testing the Difference Between Means for Paired Samples*

The two-sample t-test just given works only in the case of *independent* samples. On many occasions, however, two samples will arise in a dependent fashion. A commonly occurring example involves the situation in which repeated observations are taken on the *same* sampling unit, such as counting the number of accidents in various plants both before and after a safety awareness program is effected. The counts in one plant may be independent of the counts in another, but the two counts (before and after) within any one plant will be dependent. Thus, we must develop a mechanism for analyzing measurements that occur in pairs.

Let $(X_1, Y_1), \ldots, (X_n, Y_n)$ denote a random sample of paired observations. That is, (X_i, Y_i) denote two measurements taken in the same sampling unit, such as counts of accidents within a plant before and after a safety awareness program is put into effect, or lifelengths of two components within the same machine. Suppose it is of interest to test an hypothesis concerning the difference between $E(X_i)$ and $E(Y_i)$. The two-sample tests developed earlier in this chapter cannot be used for this purpose because of the dependence between X_i and Y_i. Observe, however, that $E(X_i) - E(Y_i) = E(X_i - Y_i)$. Thus, the comparison of $E(X_i)$ with $E(Y_i)$ can be made through looking at the mean of the differences, $(X_i - Y_i)$. Letting $X_i - Y_i = D_i$, the hypothesis $E(X_i) - E(Y_i) = 0$ is equivalent to the hypothesis $E(D_i) = 0$.

In order to construct a test statistic with a known distribution, we assume $D_1, \ldots, D_n$ is a random sample of *differences*, each possessing a normal distribution with mean μ_D and variance σ_D^2. To test $H_0 : \mu_D = 0$ versus the alternative $H_a : \mu_D \neq 0$, we employ the test statistics

$$T = \frac{\bar{D} - 0}{S_D / \sqrt{n}},$$

where

$$\bar{D} = \frac{1}{n} \sum_{i=1}^{n} D_i$$

and

$$S_D^2 = \frac{1}{n-1} \sum_{i=1}^{n} (D_i - \bar{D})^2.$$

Since $D_1, \ldots, D_n$ have normal distributions, T will have a t-distribution with $n - 1$ degrees of freedom when H_0 is true. Thus, we have reduced the problem to that of a one-sample t test. Example 7.10 illustrates the use of this procedure.

EXAMPLE 7.10

Two methods of determining the percentage of iron in ore samples are to be compared by subjecting 12 ore samples to each method. The results of the experiment are as follows:

Ore Sample	Method A	Method B	d_i
1	38.25	38.27	−0.02
2	31.68	31.71	−0.03
3	26.24	26.22	+0.02
4	41.29	41.33	−0.04
5	44.81	44.80	+0.01
6	46.37	46.39	−0.02
7	35.42	35.46	−0.04
8	38.41	38.39	+0.02
9	42.68	42.72	−0.04
10	46.71	46.76	−0.05
11	29.20	29.18	+0.02
12	30.76	30.79	−0.03

Do the data show that method B has a higher average percentage than method A? Use $\alpha = 0.05$.

Solution   We wish to test $H_0 : \mu_D \geq 0$ versus $H_a : \mu_D < 0$, since μ_D will be negative if method B has the larger mean. For the given data

$$\bar{d} = \frac{1}{12}(-0.20) = -0.0167$$

and

$$s_D^2 = \frac{\sum\limits_{i=1}^{n} d_i^2 - \frac{1}{n}\left(\sum\limits_{i=1}^{n} d_i\right)^2}{n-1}$$

$$= \frac{0.0112 - \frac{1}{12}(-0.20)^2}{11}$$

$$= 0.0007.$$

It follows that

$$t = \frac{\bar{d} - 0}{s_d/\sqrt{n}} = \frac{-0.0167}{\sqrt{0.0007}/\sqrt{12}} = -2.1586.$$

Since $\alpha = 0.05$ and $n - 1 = 11$ degrees of freedom, the rejection region consists of those values of t smaller than $-t_{0.05} = -1.796$. Hence, we reject the null hypothesis that $\mu_D \geq 0$ and conclude that the data supports the alternative, $\mu_D < 0$. □

7.3.4 *Normal Distributions: Testing the Ratio of Variances*

One can compare the variances of two normal populations by looking at the ratio of sample variances. For testing $H_0 : \sigma_1^2 = \sigma_2^2$ (or $\sigma_1^2/\sigma_2^2 = 1$) versus $H_a : \sigma_1^2 \neq \sigma_2^2$, we look at S_1^2/S_2^2 and reject if this statistic is either very large or very small. The precise rejection region can be found by observing that

$$F = \frac{S_1^2}{S_2^2}$$

has an F distribution when $H_0 : \sigma_1^2 = \sigma_2^2$ is true. Thus, we reject H_0 for $F > F_{v_2}^{v_1}(\alpha/2)$ or $F < F_{v_2}^{v_1}(1 - \alpha/2)$. A one-sided test can always be constructed with the larger S_i^2 in the numerator, so that only the upper-tail critical F value needs to be found.

EXAMPLE 7.11

Suppose that the machined engine part of Example 7.7 is to be compared, with respect to diameter variance, with a similar part manufactured by a competitor. The former showed $s_1^2 = 0.0003$ for a sample of $n_1 = 10$ diameter measurements. A sample of $n_2 = 20$ of the competitors showed $s_2^2 = 0.0001$. Is there evidence to say that $\sigma_2^2 < \sigma_1^2$ at the 5% significance level? Assume normality for both populations.

Solution   We are interested in testing $H_0: \sigma_1^2 \le \sigma_2^2$ versus $H_a: \sigma_1^2 > \sigma_2^2$. The statistic $F = S_1^2/S_2^2$, which has an F distribution if $\sigma_1^2 = \sigma_2^2$, is calculated to be

$$\frac{s_1^2}{s_2^2} = \frac{0.0003}{0.0001} = 3.$$

We reject H_0 if $F > F_{v_2}^{v_1}(\alpha) = F_{19}^{9}(0.05) = 2.42$. Since the observed ratio is 3, we reject H_0. It looks like the second manufacturer has less variability in the diameter measurements.   □

The comparison of binomial parameters will be discussed in the context of the χ^2 tests presented in the next section.

SUMMARY OF TWO-SAMPLE TESTS

	Null Hypothesis (H_0)	Alternative Hypothesis (H_a)	Test Statistic	Rejection Region
General Distribution (Large Sample)	$\mu_1 - \mu_2 = D_0$ $\mu_1 - \mu_2 \le D_0$ $\mu_1 - \mu_2 \ge D_0$	$\mu_1 - \mu_2 \ne D_0$ $\mu_1 - \mu_2 > D_0$ $\mu_1 - \mu_2 < D_0$	$Z = \dfrac{(\bar{X}_1 - \bar{X}_2) - D_0}{\sqrt{\dfrac{\sigma_1^2}{n_1} + \dfrac{\sigma_2^2}{n_2}}}$	$\|z\| > z_{\alpha/2}$ $z > z_\alpha$ $z < -z_\alpha$
Normal Distributions	$\mu_1 - \mu_2 = D_0$ $\mu_1 - \mu_2 \le D_0$ $\mu_1 - \mu_2 \ge D_0$	$\mu_1 - \mu_2 \ne D_0$ $\mu_1 - \mu_2 > D_0$ $\mu_1 - \mu_2 < D_0$	$T = \dfrac{(\bar{X}_1 - \bar{X}_2) - D_0}{S_p\sqrt{\dfrac{1}{n_1} + \dfrac{1}{n_2}}}$ $(n_1 + n_2 - 2)$ d.f.	$\|t\| > t_{\alpha/2}$ $t > t_\alpha$ $t < -t_\alpha$
Normal Distributions (Paired Samples)	$\mu_D = \mu_{D0}$ $\mu_D \le \mu_{D0}$ $\mu_D \ge \mu_{D0}$	$\mu_D \ne \mu_{D0}$ $\mu_D > \mu_{D0}$ $\mu_D < \mu_{D0}$	$T = \dfrac{\bar{D} - \mu_{D0}}{S_D/\sqrt{n}}$ $(n - 1)$ d.f.	$\|t\| > t_{\alpha/2}$ $t > t_\alpha$ $t < -t_\alpha$
Normal Distributions	$\sigma_1^2 = \sigma_2^2$	$\sigma_1^2 \ne \sigma_2^2$	$F = \dfrac{S_1^2}{S_2^2}$	$\dfrac{s_1^2}{s_2^2} > F_{v_2}^{v_1}(\alpha/2)$ or $< F_{v_2}^{v_1}(1 - \alpha/2)$
	$\sigma_1^2 \le \sigma_2^2$	$\sigma_1^2 > \sigma_2^2$		$\dfrac{s_1^2}{s_2^2} > F_{v_2}^{v_1}(\alpha)$
	$\sigma_1^2 \ge \sigma_2^2$	$\sigma_1^2 < \sigma_2^2$		$\dfrac{s_2^2}{s_1^2} > F_{v_1}^{v_2}(\alpha)$

$$v_1 = (n_1 = -1)\text{ d.f. numerator}$$
$$v_2 = (n_2 = -1)\text{ d.f. denominator}$$

Exercises

7.15   Two different designs for a laboratory are to be compared with respect to the average amount of light produced on table surfaces. Forty independent measurements (in foot candles) are taken in each laboratory, with the following results:

Design I	Design II
$n_1 = 40$	$n_2 = 40$
$\bar{x}_1 = 28.9$	$\bar{x}_2 = 32.6$
$S_1^2 = 15.1$	$S_2^2 = 15.8$

Is there sufficient evidence to suggest that the designs differ with respect to the average amount of light produced? Use $\alpha = 0.05$.

7.16   Shear strength measurements derived from unconfined compression tests for two types of soils gave the following results (measurements in tons per square foot).

Soil Type I	Soil Type II
$n_1 = 30$	$n_2 = 35$
$\bar{x}_1 = 1.65$	$\bar{x}_2 = 1.43$
$S_1 = 0.26$	$S_2 = 0.22$

Do the soils appear to differ with respect to average shear strength, at the 1% significance level?

7.17   A study was conducted by the Florida Game and Fish Commission to assess the amounts of chemical residues found in the brain tissue of brown pelicans. For DDT, random samples of $n_1 = 10$ juveniles and $n_2 = 13$ nestlings gave the following results (measurements in parts per million):

Juveniles	Nestlings
$n_1 = 10$	$n_2 = 13$
$\bar{y}_1 = 0.041$	$\bar{y}_2 = 0.026$
$s_1 = 0.017$	$s_2 = 0.006$

Test the hypothesis that there is no difference between mean amounts of DDT found in juveniles and nestlings versus the alternative that the juveniles have a larger mean. Use $\alpha = 0.05$. (This test has important implications regarding the build-up of DDT over time.)

7.18   The strength of concrete depends, to some extent, on the method used for drying. Two different drying methods showed the following results for independently tested specimens (measurements in psi):

Method I	Method II
$n_1 = 7$	$n_2 = 10$
$\bar{x}_1 = 3250$	$\bar{x}_2 = 3240$
$S_1 = 210$	$S_2 = 190$

Do the methods appear to produce concrete with different mean strengths? Use $\alpha = 0.05$. What assumptions are necessary in order for your answer to be valid?

7.19   Refer to Exercise 7.9. Another group of six rockets, of the same type, were stored for the same length of time but in a different manner. The ranges for these six were: 2410, 2500, 2360, 2290, 2310, 2340. Do the storage methods produce significantly different mean ranges? Use $\alpha = 0.05$ and assume range measurements to be approximately normally distributed.

7.20   The average depth of bedrock at two possible construction sites is to be compared by driving five piles at random locations within each site. The results, with depths in feet, are as follows:

Site A	Site B
$n_1 = 5$	$n_2 = 5$
$\bar{x}_1 = 142$	$\bar{x}_2 = 134$
$s_1 = 14$	$s_2 = 12$

Do the average depths of bedrock differ for the two sites, at the 10% significance level? What assumptions are you making?

7.21   Gasoline mileage is to be compared for two automobiles, A and B, by testing each automobile on five brands of gasoline. Each car used one tank of each brand, with the following results (in miles per gallon):

Brand	Auto A	Auto B
1	28.3	29.2
2	27.4	28.4
3	29.1	28.2
4	28.7	28.0
5	29.4	29.6

Is there evidence to suggest a difference between true average mileage figure for the two automobiles? Use a 5% significance level.

7.22   The two drying methods for concrete introduced in Exercise 7.18 were used on seven different mixes, with each mix of concrete subjected to each drying method. The resulting strength test measurements (in psi) are given below. Is there evidence of a difference between average strengths for the two drying methods, at the 10% significance level?

Mix	Method I	Method II
A	3160	3170
B	3240	3220
C	3190	3160
D	3520	3530
E	3480	3440
F	3220	3210
G	3120	3120

7.23   Two procedures for sintering copper are to be compared by testing each procedure on six different types of powder. The measurement of interest is the porosity (volume percentage due to voids) of each test specimen. The results of the tests were as follows:

Powder	Procedure I	Procedure II
1	21	23
2	27	26
3	18	21
4	22	24
5	26	25
6	19	16

Is there evidence of a difference between true average porosity measurements for the two procedures? Use $\alpha = 0.05$.

7.24   Refer to Exercise 7.18. Do the variances for strength measurements differ for the two drying methods? Test at the 10% significance level.

7.25   Refer to Exercises 7.9 and 7.19. Is there sufficient evidence to say that the variances among range measurements differ for the two storage methods? Use $\alpha = 0.10$.

7.26   Refer to Exercise 7.20. Does site A have significantly more variation among depth measurements than site B? Use $\alpha = 0.05$.

7.4 χ^2 *Tests on Frequency Data*

In Section 7.2, we saw how to construct tests of hypotheses concerning a binomial parameter, p, in the large sample case. In that case, the test statistic was based on Y, the *number* (or *frequency*) of successes in n trials of an experiment. The observation of interest there was a frequency count, rather than a continuous measurement such as a lifelength, reaction time, velocity, or weight. Now we want to take a detailed look at three types of situations in which hypothesis testing problems arise with frequency, or count, data. All of the results in this section are approximations that only work well when samples are reasonably large. More about what we mean by "large" will be stated later.

7.4.1   *Testing Parameters of the Multinomial Distribution*

The first of the three situations involves testing an hypothesis concerning the parameters of a multinomial distribution. (See Section 3.8 for a description of this distribution and some of its properties.) Suppose we have n observations (trials) from a multinomial distribution with k possible outcomes per trail. Let X_i, $i = 1, \ldots, k$, denote the number of trials resulting in outcome i, with p_i denoting the probability that any one trial will result in outcome i. Recall that $E(X_i) = np_i$. Suppose we want to test the hypothesis that the p_i's have specified values, that is, $H_0: p_1 = p_{10}$, $p_2 = p_{20}, \ldots, p_k = p_{k0}$. The alternative will be the most general one that simply states "at least one equality fails to hold." To test the validity of this hypothesis we can compare the observed count in cell i, X_i, with what we would expect that count to be if H_0 were true, namely $E(X_i) = np_{i0}$. So, we will base our test statistic upon $X_i - E(X_i)$, $i = 1, \ldots, k$. Now, we don't know if these differences are large or small unless we can standardize them in some way. It turns out that a good statistic to use squares these differences and divides them by $E(X_i)$, resulting in the test statistic

$$X^2 = \sum_{i=1}^{k} \frac{[X_i - E(X_i)]^2}{E(X_i)}.$$

In repeated sampling from a multinomial distribution for which H_0 is true, X^2 will have approximately a $\chi^2_{(k-1)}$ distribution. We would reject the null hypothesis for large values of X^2 $(X^2 > \chi^2_{(k-1)}(\alpha))$ since X^2 will be large if there are large discrepancies between X_i and $E(X_i)$.

EXAMPLE 7.12

The ratio of number of items produced in a factory by three shifts, first, second, and third, is $4:2:1$ due primarily to the decreased number of employees on the later shifts. This means that $4/7$ of the items produced come from the first shift, $2/7$ from the second, and $1/7$ from the third. It is hypothesized that the number of defectives produced should follow this same ratio. A sample of 50 defective items was traced back to the shift that produced them, with the following results:

	Shift		
	1	2	3
Number of Defectives	20	16	14

Test the hypothesis indicated above, with $\alpha = 0.05$.

Solution   Using the X^2 statistic with X_i replaced by its observed value we have, for $H_0: p_1 = 4/7, p_2 = 2/7, p_3 = 1/7,$

$$\sum_{i=1}^{3} \frac{[X_i - E(X_i)]^2}{E(X_i)} = \frac{[20 - 50(4/7)]^2}{50(4/7)} + \frac{[16 - 50(2/7)]^2}{50(2/7)} + \frac{[14 - 50(1/7)]^2}{50(1/7)}$$

$$= 9.367.$$

Now, $\chi_2^2(0.05) = 5.991$ and since our observed X^2 is larger than this critical χ^2 value, we reject H_0. It looks like the later shifts are producing a higher fraction of defectives. □

7.4.2 *Testing Equality Among Binomial Parameters*

The second situation in which a χ^2 statistic can be used on frequency data is in the testing of equality among binomial parameters for k separate populations. In this case, k independent random samples are selected that result in k binomially distributed random variables, $Y_1, \ldots, Y_k$, where Y_i is based on n_i trials with success probability p_i on each trial. The problem is to test the null hypothesis $H_0: p_1 = p_2 = \cdots = p_k$, against the alternative of at least one inequality. We now really have $2k$ cells to consider, as outlined in Figure 7.2.

	Observation					
	1	2	3	$\cdots$	k	
Successes	y_1	y_2	y_3		y_k	y
Failures	$n_1 - y_1$	$n_2 - y_2$	$n_3 - y_3$		$n_k - y_k$	$n - y$
Total	n_1	n_2	n_3		n_k	n

$$n = \sum_{i=1}^{k} n_i \qquad y = \sum_{i=1}^{k} y_i$$

Figure 7.2   Cells for K Binomial Observations

As in the case of testing multinomial parameters, the test statistic should be constructed by comparing the observed cell frequencies with the expected cell frequencies. However, the null hypothesis does not specify values for $p_1, p_2, \ldots, p_k$ and, hence, the expected cell frequencies must be estimated. The expected cell frequencies and their estimators will now be discussed.

Since each Y_i has a binomial distribution, we know from Chapter 3 that

$$E(Y_i) = n_i p_i$$

and

$$E(n_i - Y_i) = n_i - n_i p_i = n_i(1 - p_i).$$

Under the null hypothesis that $p_1 = p_2 = \cdots = p_k = p$, the common value of p should be estimated by pooling the data from all k samples. The minimum variance unbiased estimator of p is

$$\frac{1}{n} \sum_{i=1}^{k} Y_i = \frac{Y}{n} = \frac{\text{total number of successes}}{\text{total sample size}}.$$

The estimators of the expected cell frequencies are then taken to be

$$\hat{E}(Y_i) = n_i \left(\frac{Y}{n} \right)$$

and

$$\hat{E}(n_i - Y_i) = n_i \left(1 - \frac{Y}{n} \right) = n_i \left(\frac{n - Y}{n} \right).$$

In each case, note that the estimate of an expected cell frequency is found by the following rule:

$$\text{estimated expected cell frequency} = \frac{(\text{column total})(\text{row total})}{\text{overall total}}.$$

To test $H_0: p_1 = p_2 = \cdots = p_k = p$, we make use of the statistic

$$X^2 = \sum_{i-1}^{k} \left\{ \frac{[Y_i - \hat{E}(Y_i)]^2}{\hat{E}(Y_i)} + \frac{[(n_i - Y_i) - \hat{E}(n_i - Y_i)]^2}{\hat{E}(n_i - Y_i)} \right\}.$$

This statistic has approximately a $\chi^2_{(k-1)}$ distribution, so long as the sample sizes are reasonably large.

We illustrate with an example.

EXAMPLE 7.13

A chemical company is experimenting with four different mixtures of a chemical designed to kill a certain species of insect. Independent random samples of 200 insects each are subjected to one of the four chemicals, and the number of insects dead after one hour of exposure is counted. The results are as follows:

	1	2	3	4	Total
Dead	124 (141)	147 (141)	141 (141)	152 (141)	564
Not Dead	76 (59)	52 (59)	59 (59)	48 (59)	236
Total	200	200	200	200	

We want to test the hypothesis that the rate of kill is the same for all four mixtures. Test this claim at the 5% level of significance.

Solution   We use testing $H_0: p_1 = p_2 = p_3 = p_4 = p$ where p_i denotes the probability that an insect subjected to chemical i dies in the indicated length of time. Now, the estimated cell frequencies under H_0 are found by:

$$\frac{(n_1)(y)}{n} = \frac{1}{n}(\text{column 1 total})(\text{row 1 total})$$

$$= \frac{1}{800}(200)(564) = \frac{1}{4}(564) = 141,$$

$$\frac{n_1(n-y)}{n} = \frac{1}{800}(200)(236) = \frac{1}{4}(236) = 59,$$

and so on. Note that in this case all estimated expected frequencies in any one row are equal. Calculating an observed value for X^2, we get

$$\frac{[124 - 141]^2}{141} + \cdots + \frac{[48 - 59]^2}{59} = 10.72.$$

Since $\chi_3^2(0.05) = 7.815$, we reject the hypothesis of equal kill rates for the four chemicals.   □

7.4.3 *Contingency Tables*

The third type of experimental situation that makes use of a similar χ^2 test again makes use of the multinomial distribution. However, this time the cells arise from a double classification scheme. For example, employees could be classified according to sex and according to marital status, which results in four cells as follows:

	Male	Female
Married		
Unmarried		

A random sample of n employees would then give random frequencies to the four cells. In these two-way classifications a common question to ask is, "Does the row criterion depend upon the column criterion?" In other words, "Is the row criterion *contingent* upon the column criterion?" In this context, the two-way tables, like the one just illustrated, are referred to as *contingency* tables. We might want to know whether or not the marital status depends upon the sex of the employee, or if these two classification criteria seem to be independent of one another.

   The null hypothesis in these two-way tables is that the row criterion and the column criterion are independent of each other. The alternative is simply that they are *not* independent. In looking at a 2 × 2 table, an array such as

5	15
10	30

would support the hypothesis of independence since, within each column, the chance of being in row 1 is about 1 out of 3. That is, the chance of being in row 1 does *not* depend upon which column you happen to be in. On the other hand, an array like

5	30
10	15

would support the alternative hypothesis of dependence.

   In general, the cell frequencies and cell probabilities would look as follows:

Row	Column 1	$\cdots$	j	c	
1	$X_{11}; p_{11}$			$X_{1c}; p_{1c}$	$X_{1\cdot}$
$\vdots$	$\vdots$				
i		$\cdots$	$X_{ij}; p_{ij}$		$X_{i\cdot}$
r	$X_{r1}; p_{r1}$			$X_{rc}; p_{rc}$	
	$X_{\cdot 1}$		$X_{\cdot j}$		n

We will let $X_{i\cdot}$ denote the frequency total for row i and $X_{\cdot j}$ the total for column j. Also, $p_{i\cdot}$ will denote the probability of being in row i and $p_{\cdot j}$ the probability of being in column j.

   Under the null hypothesis of independence between rows and columns, $p_{ij} = p_{i\cdot} p_{\cdot j}$. Also, $E(X_{ij}) = np_{ij} = np_{i\cdot}p_{\cdot j}$. Now $p_{i\cdot}$ and $p_{\cdot j}$ must be estimated, and the best estimators are

$$\hat{p}_{i\cdot} = \frac{X_{i\cdot}}{n}, \qquad \hat{p}_{\cdot j} = \frac{X_{\cdot j}}{n}.$$

Thus, the best estimator of an expected cell frequency is

$$\hat{E}(X_{ij}) = \left(n \frac{X_{i\cdot}}{n} \right)\left(\frac{X_{\cdot j}}{n} \right) = \frac{X_{i\cdot} X_{\cdot j}}{n},$$

Once again we see that the estimate of an expected cell frequency is given by

$$\frac{x_i.x_{.j}}{n} = \frac{1}{n}(\text{row } i \text{ total})(\text{column } j \text{ total}).$$

The test statistic for testing the independence hypothesis is

$$X^2 = \sum_{ij} \frac{[X_{ij} - \hat{E}(X_{ij})]^2}{\hat{E}(X_{ij})},$$

which has approximately a $\chi^2_{(r-1)(c-1)}$ distribution, where r is the number of rows and c the number of columns in the table.

EXAMPLE 7.14

A sample of 200 machined parts is selected from the one-week output of a machine shop that employs three machinists. The parts are inspected to determine whether or not they are defective, and are categorized according to which machinist did the work. The results are as follows:

	Machinist			
	A	B	C	
Defective	10 (9.92)	8 (10.88)	14 (11.2)	32
Nondefective	52 (52.08)	60 (57.12)	56 (58.8)	168
	62	68	70	200

Is the defective nondefective classification independent of machinist? Conduct a test at the 1% significance level.

Solution   First we must find the estimated expected cell frequencies as follows:

$$\frac{x_1.x_{.1}}{n} = \frac{(32)(62)}{200} = 9.92$$

$$\frac{x_1.x_{.2}}{n} = \frac{(32)(68)}{200} = 10.88$$

$$\vdots$$

$$\frac{x_2.x_{.3}}{n} = \frac{(168)70}{200} = 58.8$$

(These numbers are shown in parentheses on the table.) Now, the test statistic is observed to be

$$\frac{(10 - 9.22)^2}{9.22} + \cdots + \frac{(56 - 58.8)^2}{58.8} = 1.74.$$

In this case, the degrees of freedom are given by

$$(r - 1)(c - 1) = (2 - 1)(3 - 1) = 2$$

and

$$\chi_2^2(0.01) = 9.21.$$

Thus, we cannot reject the null hypothesis of independence between machinists and defective/nondefective classification. There is not sufficient evidence to say that the rate of defectives produced differs among machinists.   □

Recall that all of the above test statistics have only a χ^2 distribution, approximately, for large samples. A rough guideline for "large" is that each cell should contain an observed frequency count of at least five.

Exercises

7.27   Two types of defects, A and B, are frequently seen in the output of a certain manufacturing process. Each item can be classified into one of the four classes AB, $A\bar{B}$, $\bar{A}B$, $\overline{AB}$, where $\bar{A}$ denotes the absence of the A-type defect. For 100 inspected items, the following frequencies were observed:

$$
\begin{array}{ll}
AB & 48 \\
A\bar{B} & 18 \\
\bar{A}B & 21 \\
\overline{AB} & 13 \\
\end{array}
$$

Test the hypothesis that the four categories, in the order listed, occur in the ratio $5:2:2:1$. (Use $\alpha = 0.05$.)

7.28   Vehicles can turn right, turn left, or continue straight ahead at a certain intersection. It is hypothesized that half of the vehicles entering this intersection will continue straight ahead. Of the other half, equal proportions will turn right and left. Fifty vehicles were observed to have the following behavior:

	Straight	Left Turn	Right Turn
Frequency	28	12	10

Test the stated hypothesis at the 10% level of significance.

7.29   A manufacturer of stereo amplifiers has three assembly lines. We want to test the hypothesis that the three lines do not differ with respect to the number of defectives produced. Independent samples of 30 amplifiers each are selected from the output of the lines, and the number of defectives is observed. The data are as follows:

Line	I	II	III
No. of Defectives	6	5	9
Sample Size	30	30	30

Conduct a test of the hypothesis given above at the 5% significance level.

7.30 Two inspectors are asked to rate independent samples of textiles from the same loom. Inspector A reports that 18 out of 25 samples fall in the top category while inspector B reports that 20 out of 25 samples merit the top category. Do the inspectors appear to differ in their assessments? Use $\alpha = 0.05$.

7.31 Two chemicals, A and B, are designed to protect pine trees from a certain disease. One hundred trees are sprayed with chemical A and one hundred are sprayed with chemical B. All trees are subjected to the disease, with the following results:

	A	B
Infected	20	16
Sample Size	100	100

Do the chemicals appear to differ in their ability to protect the trees? Test at the 1% significance level.

7.32 Refer to Exercise 7.27. Test the hypothesis that the type A defects occur independently of the type B defects. Use $\alpha = 0.05$.

7.33 The *Sociological Quarterly* for Spring 1978, reports on a study of the relationship between athletic involvement and academic achievement for college students. The 852 students sampled were categorized according to amount of athletic involvement and grade-point averages at graduation, with results as follows:

		Athletic Involvement			
		None	1–3 Semesters	4 or more semesters	
GPA	Below mean	290	94	42	
	Above mean	238	125	63	
		528	219	105	852

(a) Do final grade-point averages appear to be independent of athletic involvement? (Use $\alpha = 0.05$.)

(b) For students with 4 or more semesters of athletic involvement, is the proportion with GPA's above the mean significantly different, at the 0.05 level, from the proportion with GPA's below the mean?

7.34 A new sick-leave policy is being introduced into a firm. A sample of employee opinions showed the following breakdowns by sex and opinion:

	Favor	Oppose	Undecided
Male	31	44	6
Female	42	36	8

Does the reaction to the new policy appear to be related to sex? Test at the 5% significance level.

7.35 A sample of 150 people are observed using one of four entrances to a commercial building. The data are as follows:

Entrance	1	2	3	4
No. of People	42	36	31	41

(a) Test the hypothesis that all four entrances are used equally often. Use $\alpha = 0.05$.
(b) Entrances 1 and 2 are on a subway level while 3 and 4 are on ground level. Test the hypothesis that subway and ground-level entrances are used equally often, again with $\alpha = 0.05$.

7.5   *Goodness-of-Fit Tests*

Thus far our main emphasis in the text has been that of choosing a probabilistic model for a measurement, or a set of measurements, taken on some natural phenomenon. We have talked about the basic probabilistic manipulations one can make, and discussed estimation of certain unknown parameters, as well as testing hypotheses concerning these unknown parameters. Up to this point, we have not discussed any rigorous way of checking to see if the data we observe do, in fact, agree with the underlying probabilistic model we assumed for these data. That subject, called testing goodness of fit, will be discussed in this section. Goodness-of-fit testing is a broad subject, with entire textbooks devoted to it. We will merely skim the surface by presenting two techniques that have wide applicability and are fairly easy to calculate: the χ^2 goodness-of-fit test for discrete distributions and the Kolmogorov–Smirnov (K-S) test for continuous distributions.

Let Y denote a discrete random variable that can take on values $y_1, y_2, \ldots$. Under the null hypothesis, H_0, we assume a probabilistic model for Y. That is, we assume $P(Y = y_i) = p_i$ where p_i may be completely specified or may be a function of other unknown parameters. For example, we could assume a Poisson model for Y, and thus

$$P(Y = y_i) = p_i = \lambda^{y_i} e^{-\lambda} / y_i!$$

In addition, we could assume λ is specified at λ_0 or we could assume nothing is known about λ, in which case λ would have to be estimated from the sample data. The alternative hypothesis is the general one that the model in H_0 does not fit.

The sample will consist of n independently observed values of the random variable, Y. For this sample, let F_i denote the number of times $Y = y_i$ is observed. Thus, F_i is the frequency count for the value y_i. Under the null hypothesis that $P(Y = y_i) = p_i$, the expected frequency can be calculated as $E(F_i) = np_i$.

After the sample is taken, we will have an observed value of F_i in hand. At that point, we can compare the observed value of F_i with what is expected under the null hypothesis. The test statistic will be based upon the differences $[F_i - E(F_i)]$, as in previously discussed χ^2 tests. In many cases, one or more parameters will have to be estimated from sample data. In those cases, $E(F_i)$ is also estimated and referred to as $\hat{E}(F_i)$, the estimated expected frequency.

For certain samples, many of the frequency counts, F_i, may be quite small. (In fact, many may be zero.) When this occurs, consecutive values of y_i are grouped together and the corresponding probabilities added, since

$$P(Y = y_i \text{ or } Y = y_j) = p_i + p_j.$$

It follows that the frequencies F_i and F_j can be added, since $E(F_i + F_j) = n(p_i + p_j)$. As a handy rule of thumb, values of Y should be grouped so that the observed frequency count is at least five in every cell. After this grouping is completed, let k denote the number of cells obtained.

The test statistic for the null hypothesis that $P(Y = y_i) = p_i$, $i = 1, 2, \ldots$, is given by

$$X^2 = \sum_{i=1}^{k} \frac{[F_i - \hat{E}(F_i)]^2}{\hat{E}(F_i)}.$$

For large n, this statistic has approximately a χ^2 distribution with degrees of freedom given by

$$(k - 1) - (\text{number of parameters estimated}).$$

Thus, if one parameter is estimated, the statistic would possess $(k - 2)$ degrees of freedom.

We illustrate this procedure with a Poisson example.

EXAMPLE 7.15

The number of accidents per week, Y, in a certain factory was checked for a random sample of $n = 50$ weeks with the following results:

y	Frequency
0	32
1	12
2	6
3 or more	0

Test the hypothesis that Y follows a Poisson distribution, with $\alpha = 0.05$.

Solution H_0 states that Y has a probability distribution given by

$$P(y_i) = \frac{\lambda^{y_i} e^{-\lambda}}{y_i!}, \qquad y_i = 0, 1, 2, \ldots.$$

Since λ is unknown it must be estimated, and the best estimation is $\hat{\lambda} = \bar{Y}$. For the given data, $\bar{y} = [0(32) + 1(12) + 2(6)]/50 = 24/50 = 0.48$.

Using the guideline that each cell in a χ^2 test should have five or more observations, we must group the "two or more" category into one cell, giving us a total of three cells, indexed by the values $Y = 0$, $Y = 1$ and $Y \geq 2$. The corresponding probabilities for observing a value in these cells are

$$P_0 = P[Y = 0] = e^{-\lambda}$$
$$P_1 = P[Y = 1] = \lambda e^{-\lambda}$$

and

$$p_2 = P[Y \geq 2] = 1 - e^{-\lambda} - \lambda e^{-\lambda}.$$

If F_0, F_1, F_2 denote the observed frequencies in the respective cells, then

$$E(F_i) = np_i$$

and

$$\hat{E}(F_i) = n\hat{p}_i$$

where $\hat{p}_i$ denotes p_i with λ replaced by $\hat{\lambda}$. The observed values of the estimated expected frequencies then become

$$50e^{-0.48} = 30.95$$
$$50(0.48)e^{-0.48} = 14.85$$

and

$$50[1 - e^{-0.48} - 0.48e^{-0.48}] = 4.20.$$

The observed value of X^2 is then

$$\frac{[32 - 30.95]^2}{30.95} + \frac{[12 - 14.85]^2}{14.85} + \frac{[6 - 4.20]^2}{4.20} = 1.35.$$

The test statistic has one degree of freedom since $k = 3$ and one parameter is estimated. Now, $\chi_1^2(0.05) = 3.841$ and, hence, we do not have sufficient evidence to reject H_0. The data do appear to fit the Poisson model reasonably well. $\square$

It is possible to construct χ^2 tests for goodness of fit to continuous distributions but the procedure is a little more subjective, since the continuous random variable does not provide natural cells into which the data can be grouped. For the continuous case we choose to use the Kolmogorov–Smirnov (K-S) statistic, which actually compares the empirical distribution function of a random sample with a theoretical hypothesized distribution function.

Before we define the K-S statistic, let us define the *empirical distribution function*. Suppose Y is a continuous random variable having distribution function $F(y)$. A random sample of n realizations of Y yields the observations $y_1, \ldots, y_n$. It is convenient to reorder these observed values from smallest to largest, and we denote the ordered y_i's by $y_{(1)} \leq y_{(2)} \leq \cdots \leq y_{(n)}$. That is, if $y_1 = 7$, $y_2 = 9$ and $y_3 = 3$, then $y_{(1)} = 3$, $y_{(2)} = 7$ and $y_{(3)} = 9$. Now, the empirical distribution function is given by

$$F_n(y) = \text{fraction of the sample less than or equal to } y$$

$$= \begin{cases} \dfrac{(i-1)}{n} & \text{if} \quad y_{(i-1)} \leq y < y_{(i)}, \, i = 1, \ldots, n \\[2mm] 1 & \text{if} \quad y \geq y_{(n)}, \end{cases}$$

where we let $y_0 = -\infty$.

Suppose a continuous random variable, Y, is assumed, under the null hypothesis, to have a distribution function given by $F(y)$. The alternate hypothesis is that $F(y)$ is *not* the true distribution function for Y. After a random sample of n values of Y is observed, $F(y)$ should be "close" to $F_n(y)$ provided the null hypothesis is true. Our statistic, then, must measure the closeness of $F(y)$ to $F_n(y)$ over the whole range of y values. (See Figure 7.3 for a typical plot of $F(y)$ and $F_n(y)$.)

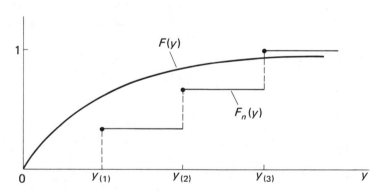

Figure 7.3   A Plot of $F_n(y)$ and $F(y)$

The K-S statistic, D, is based upon the *maximum* distance between $F(y)$ and $F_n(y)$. That is,

$$D = \max_y |F(y) - F_n(y)|.$$

The null hypothesis is rejected if D is "too large."

Because $F(y)$ and $F_n(y)$ are nondecreasing and $F_n(y)$ is constant between sample observations, the maximum deviation between $F_n(y)$ and $F(y)$ will occur either at one of the observation points, $y_1 \cdots y_n$, or immediately to the left of one of these points. To find the observed value of D, then, it is only necessary to check

$$D^+ = \max_{1 \leq i \leq n} \left[\frac{i}{n} - F(y_i) \right]$$

and

$$D^- = \max_{1 \leq i \leq n} \left[F(y_i) - \frac{i-1}{n} \right]$$

since

$$D = \max(D^+, D^-).$$

If H_0 hypothesizes the *form* of $F(y)$ but leaves some parameters unspecified, then these unknown parameters must be estimated from the sample data before the test can be carried out.

Values cutting off upper-tail areas of 0.15, 0.10, 0.05, 0.025, and 0.01 for a slightly modified form of D are given by Stephens (1974) and are reproduced in Table 7.2 for three cases. These cases are for the null hypotheses of a fully specified $F(y)$, a normal $F(y)$ with unknown mean and variance, and an exponential $F(y)$ with unknown mean.

Table 7.2   Upper-Tail Percentage Points of Modified D

	Modified Form of D	Tail Area				
		0.15	0.10	0.05	0.025	0.01
Specified $F(y)$	$(D)(\sqrt{n} + 0.12 + 0.11/\sqrt{n})$	1.138	1.224	1.358	1.480	1.626
Normal $F(y)$ Unknown μ, σ^2	$(D)(\sqrt{n} - 0.01 + 0.85/\sqrt{n})$	0.775	0.819	0.895	0.955	1.035
Exponential $F(y)$ Unknown θ	$(D - 0.2/n)(\sqrt{n} + 0.26 + 0.5/\sqrt{n})$	0.926	0.990	1.094	1.190	1.308

We illustrate the use of all three cases by use of suitable examples.

EXAMPLE 7.16
Consider the first ten observations of Table 2.1 on p. 23 to be a random sample from a continuous distribution. Test the hypothesis that these data are from an exponential distribution with mean 2, at the 0.05 significance level.

Solution   We must order the ten observations and then find, for each $y_{(i)}$, the value of $F(y_i)$, where H_0 states that $F(y)$ is exponential with $\theta = 2$. Thus,

$$F(y_i) = 1 - e^{-y_i/2}.$$

The data and pertinent calculations are given in Table 7.3.

Table 7.3   Data and Calculations for Example 7.15

i	$y_{(i)}$	$F(y_i)$	i/n	$(i-1)/n$	$i/n - F(y_i)$	$F(y_i) - (i-1)/n$
1	0.023	0.0114	0.1	0	0.0886	0.0114
2	0.406	0.1838	0.2	0.1	0.0162	0.0838
3	0.538	0.2359	0.3	0.2	0.0641	0.0359
4	1.267	0.4693	0.4	0.3	-0.0693	0.1693
5	2.343	0.6901	0.5	0.4	-0.1901	0.2901
6	2.563	0.7224	0.6	0.5	-0.1224	0.2224
7	3.334	0.8112	0.7	0.6	-0.1112	0.2112
8	3.491	0.8255	0.8	0.7	-0.0255	0.1255
9	5.088	0.9215	0.9	0.8	-0.0215	0.1215
10	5.587	0.9388	1.0	0.9	0.0612	0.0388

D^+ is the maximum value in column 6 and D^- the maximum in column 7. Thus, $D^+ = 0.0886$ and $D^- = 0.2901$, giving $D = 0.2901$. To find the critical value from Table 7.2, we need to calculate

$$(D)\left(\sqrt{n} + 0.12 + \frac{0.11}{\sqrt{n}}\right) = (0.2901)(3.317) = 0.9623.$$

At the $0.05 = \alpha$ significance level, the rejection region starts at 1.358. Thus, we do not reject the null hypothesis. Notice we are saying that we cannot reject the exponential model ($\theta = 2$) as a plausible model for this data. This does not imply that the exponential is the *best* model for these data, as numerous other possible null hypotheses would not be rejected either.   □

EXAMPLE 7.17

The following data are an ordered sample of observations on the amount of pressure (in pounds per square inch) needed to fracture a certain type of glass. Test the hypothesis that these data fit a Weibull distribution with $\gamma = 2$ but unknown θ.

04.90	08.60	11.42	15.46	19.19	20.69
40.29	41.19	43.55	44.62	53.56	77.61

Solution   We see the form of the Weibull probability density function in Section 4.7. We also see there that, if $\gamma = 2$, then Y^2 will have an exponential distribution under the null hypothesis that Y has a Weibull distribution. Hence, we want to test the hypothesis that Y^2 has an exponential distribution with unknown θ. The best estimator of θ is the average of the Y^2 values, observed to be 1446.93. $F(y)$ is then estimated to be

$$\hat{F}(y) = 1 - e^{-y/1446.93}.$$

The information needed to complete the test is given in Table 7.4.

Table 7.4   Data and Calculations for Example 7.16

i	$u_i = y_{(i)}^2$	$\hat{F}(u_i)$	i/n	$i/n - \hat{F}(u_i)$	$\hat{F}(u_i) - (i-1)/n$
1	24.01	0.0165	0.0833	0.0668	0.0165
2	73.96	0.0498	0.1667	0.1169	-0.0335
3	130.42	0.0862	0.2500	0.1638	-0.0805
4	239.01	0.1523	0.3333	0.1810	-0.0977
5	538.26	0.2247	0.4167	0.1920	-0.1086
6	428.08	0.2561	0.5000	0.2439	-0.1606
7	1623.28	0.6743	0.5833	-0.0910	0.1743
8	1696.62	0.6904	0.6667	-0.0237	0.1071
9	1896.60	0.7304	0.7500	0.0196	0.0637
10	1990.94	0.7474	0.8333	0.0859	-0.0026
11	2868.67	0.8623	0.9167	0.0544	0.0290
12	6023.31	0.9844	1.0000	0.0156	0.0677

From the last two columns, we see that $D = 0.2439$. Thus, the modified D is

$$\left(D - \frac{0.2}{n}\right)\left(\sqrt{n} + 0.26 + \frac{0.5}{\sqrt{n}}\right) = (0.2439 - 0.0167)(3.8684)$$

$$= 0.8789.$$

If we select $\alpha = 0.05$, we have from Table 7.2 that the critical value is 1.094. Thus, we cannot reject the null hypothesis that the data fit a Weibull distribution with $\gamma = 2$. □

EXAMPLE 7.18

Soil-water flux measurements (in centimeters/day) were taken at 20 experimental plots in a field. The soil-water flux was measured in a draining soil profile in which steady-state soil-water flow conditions had been established. Theory and empirical evidence have suggested that the measurements should fit a normal distribution. The data recorded as y_i in Table 7.5 are the logarithms of the actual measurements. Test the hypothesis that the data come from a normal distribution. Use $\alpha = 0.05$.

Solution   The basic idea of the K-S test in this case is to transform the observed data to new observations that should look like standard normal variates, if the null hypothesis is true. If random variable, Y, has a normal distribution with mean μ and variance σ^2, then $(Y - \mu)/\sigma$ will have a standard normal distribution. Since μ and σ are unknown we will estimate them by $\bar{y}$ and s, respectively. Then we transform each y_i value to a u_i, where

$$u_i = \frac{y_i - \bar{y}}{s},$$

and test to see if the u_i's fit a standard normal distribution. The $F(u_i)$ values in Table 7.5 come from cumulative probabilities under a standard normal curve, and can be obtained from a table such as Table 4 of the Appendix, or a computer subroutine.

Table 7.5   Data and Calculations for Example 7.17

i	$y_{(i)}$	$u_i = \dfrac{y_{(i)} - \bar{y}}{s}$	i/n	$F(u_i)$	$i/n - F(u_i)$	$F(u_i) - (i-1)/n$
1	0.3780	−2.0224	0.0500	0.0216	0.0284	0.0216
2	0.5090	−1.5215	0.1000	0.0641	0.0359	0.0141
3	0.6230	−1.0856	0.1500	0.1388	0.0112	0.0388
4	0.6860	−0.8448	0.2000	0.1991	0.0009	0.0491
5	0.7350	−0.6574	0.2500	0.2555	−0.0055	0.0555
6	0.7520	−0.5924	0.3000	0.2768	0.0232	0.0268
7	0.7580	−0.5695	0.3500	0.2845	0.0655	−0.0155
8	0.8690	−0.1451	0.4000	0.4423	−0.0423	0.0923
9	0.8890	−0.0686	0.4500	0.4726	−0.0226	0.0726
10	0.8890	−0.0686	0.5000	0.4726	0.0274	0.0226
11	0.8990	−0.0304	0.5500	0.4879	0.0621	−0.0121
12	0.9370	0.1149	0.6000	0.5457	0.0543	−0.0043
13	0.9820	0.2869	0.6500	0.6129	0.0371	0.0129
14	1.0220	0.4399	0.7000	0.6700	0.0300	0.0200
15	1.0370	0.4972	0.7500	0.6905	0.0595	−0.0095
16	1.0880	0.6922	0.8000	0.7556	0.0444	0.0056
17	1.1230	0.8260	0.8500	0.7956	0.0544	−0.0044
18	1.2060	1.1434	0.9000	0.8736	0.0264	0.0236
19	1.3340	1.6328	0.9500	0.9487	0.0013	0.0487
20	1.4230	1.9730	1.0000	0.9758	0.0242	0.0258

From Table 7.5, we see that $D = 0.0923$. Using Table 7.2, the modified D is

$$(D)\left(\sqrt{n} - 0.10 + \frac{0.85}{\sqrt{n}}\right) = (0.0923)(4.6522)$$

$$= 0.4294.$$

From Table 7.2, the critical value at the 5% significance level is 0.895, and thus, we do not reject the null hypothesis. The data appears to fit the normal distribution. Figure 7.4 shows graphically how $F_n(u)$ and $F(u)$ compare. The figure is a plot of the empirical distribution function for $n = 20$ soil-water flux measurements and normal distribution function. The statistics D^- and D^+ are illustrated in the inset. □

Example 7.18 has a more appropriate sample size for a goodness-of-fit test. Samples of size less than 20 do not allow for much discrimination among distributions, that is, many different distributions may all appear to fit equally well.

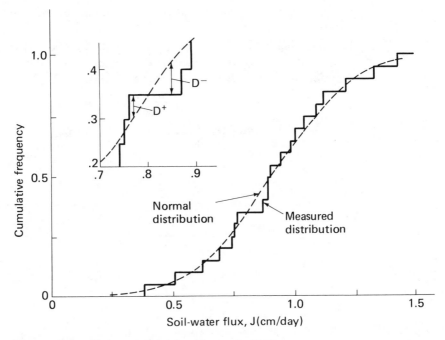

Figure 7.4 $F(u)$ and $F_n(u)$ for Example 7.17

There are numerous goodness-of-fit statistics that could be considered in addition to the Kolmogorov-Smirnov. Some of these are the Cramér-von Mises, the Anderson-Darling and the Watson statistics. The interested reader can look into these procedures by referring to the references given in the bibliography, particularly the 1974 paper by Stephens.

Exercises

7.36   For fabric coming off a certain loom, the number of defects per square yard is counted on 50 sample specimens, each one square yard in size. The results are as follows:

Number of Defects	Frequency of Observation
0	0
1	3
2	5
3	10
4	14
5	8
6 or more	10

Test the hypothesis that the data come from a Poisson distribution. Use $\alpha = 0.05$.

7.37   The following data show the frequency counts for 400 observations on the number of bacterial colonies within the field of a microscope, using samples of milkfilm. (Source: Bliss and Owens, *Biometrics*, 9, 1953.)

Number of Colonies per Field	Frequency of Observations
0	56
1	104
2	80
3	62
4	42
5	27
6	9
7	9
8	5
9	3
10	2
11	0
19	1
	400

Test the hypothesis that the data fit the Poisson distribution. (Use $\alpha = 0.05$.)

7.38   The number of accidents experienced by machinists in a certain industry were observed for a certain period of time with the following results. (Source: Bliss and Fisher, *Biometrics*, 9, 1953.)

Accidents per Machinist	0	1	2	3	4	5	6	7	8
Frequency of Observation (Number of Machinists)	296	74	26	8	4	4	1	0	1

At the 5% level of significance, test the hypothesis that the data came from a Poisson distribution.

7.39   Counts on the number of items per cluster (or colony or group) must necessarily be greater than or equal to one. Thus, the Poisson distribution does not generally fit these kinds of counts. For modeling counts on phenomena such as number of bacteria per colony, number of people per household, and number of animals per litter, the *logarithmic series* distribution often proves useful. This discrete distribution has probability function given by

$$p(y) = -\frac{1}{\ln(1-\alpha)}\frac{\alpha^y}{y}, \qquad y = 1, 2, 3, \ldots, 0 < \alpha < 1,$$

where α is an unknown parameter.

(a) Show that the maximum likelihood estimator, $\hat{\alpha}$, of α satisfies the equation

$$\bar{y} = \frac{\hat{\alpha}}{-(1-\hat{\alpha})\ln(1-\hat{\alpha})},$$

where $\bar{y}$ is the mean of the sampled observations $y_1, \ldots, y_n$.

(b) The following data give frequencies of observation for counts on the number of bacteria per colony, for a certain type of soil bacteria. (Source: Bliss and Fisher, *Biometrics*, 9, 1953.)

Bacteria per Colony	1	2	3	4	5	6	7 or more
Number of Colonies Observed	359	146	57	41	26	17	29

Test the hypothesis that these data fit a logarithmic series distribution. Use $\alpha = 0.05$. (Note that $\bar{y}$ must be approximated because we do not have exact information on counts greater than six.)

7.40 The following data are observed LC50 values on copper in a certain species of fish (measurements in parts per million):

0.075	0.10	0.23	0.46	0.10	0.15	1.30	0.29
0.31	0.32	0.33	0.54	0.85	1.90	9.00	

It has been hypothesized that the natural logarithms of these data fit the normal distribution. Check this claim at the 5% significance level.

7.41 The time (in seconds) between vehicle arrivals at a certain intersection was measured for a certain time period with the following results:

9.0	10.1	10.2	9.3	9.5	9.8	14.2	16.1
8.9	10.5	10.0	18.1	10.6	16.8	13.6	11.1

(a) Test the hypothesis that these data come from an exponential distribution. Use $\alpha = 0.05$.

(b) Test the hypothesis that these data come from an exponential distribution with a mean of 12 seconds. Use $\alpha = 0.05$.

7.6   *Conclusion*

For the simple cases that we have considered, hypothesis testing problems parallel estimation problems in that similar statistics are used. Some exceptions are noted, such as the χ^2 tests on frequency data and goodness-of-fit tests. These latter tests are not motivated by confidence intervals.

This might prompt the question of how one chooses appropriate test statistics. We did not discuss a general method of choosing a test statistic as we did for choosing an estimator (maximum likelihood principle). General methods of choosing test statistic with good properties do, however, exist. The reader interested in the theory of hypothesis testing should consult a text on mathematical statistics, and look up topics such as likelihood ratio tests, the Neyman-Pearson Lemma, and uniformly most powerful tests.

The tests given in this chapter have some intuitive appeal, as well as good theoretical properties.

Supplementary Exercises

7.42   Refer to Exercise 6.9. In order to be used in a certain product, the mean breaking strength of the threads must be at least 215 grams. Should these threads be used in that product?

7.43   Refer to Exercise 6.10. It is claimed that the engineers working for this corporation average at least 45 hours a week. Test this claim at the 5% significance level.

7.44   Refer to Exercise 6.15. Company A claims that no more than 8% of its resistors fail to meet the tolerance specification. Test this claim at the 10% significance level.

7.45   Refer to Exercise 6.20. A standard states that the average LC50 for DDT should be 10 parts per million. Do the data cast doubt on this standard? Test at the 5% significance level.

7.46   Refer to Exercise 6.23. Do you think the process is producing 10-ohm resistors, on the average?

7.47   Refer to Exercises 6.23 and 6.25. The claim is made that the standard deviation of the resistors produced by this process will not exceed 0.4 ohm. Can this claim be refuted at the 10% significance level?

7.48   Refer to Exercise 6.26. Is there evidence that the mean resistance to abrasion differs for the two coupling agents? Use $\alpha = 0.05$.

7.49   Refer to Exercise 6.28. Do the mean pit depths appear to differ for the two types of coating? Test at the 10% level of significance.

7.50   Refer to Exercise 6.29. Does the addition of the chemical significantly reduce the proportion of samples containing the harmful bacteria? Use $\alpha = 0.025$.

7.51 Refer to Exercise 6.31. Is there a significant difference, at the 5% level, between the proportions favoring the new policy for the two companies?

7.52 Refer to Exercise 6.37. Is there a significant difference between the mean oxygen consumptions, at the 5% level?

7.53 Refer to Exercise 6.33. Is there evidence of a significant difference between the mean impulses for the two rackets, at the 5% significance level?

7.54 Refer to Exercises 6.32 and 6.37. Is there evidence to suggest that intermittent training gives more variable results? Use $\alpha = 0.05$.

7.55 Refer to Exercises 6.20, 6.33, and 6.38. Does the variance of LC50's for DDT differ significantly from that for Diazinon, at the 10% level?

7.56 An interesting and practical use of the χ^2 test comes about in the testing for segregation of species of plants or animals. Suppose that two species of plants, say A and B, are growing on a test plot. To assess whether or not the species tend to segregate, n plants are randomly sampled from the plot, and the species of each sampled plant *and* the species of its *nearest* neighbor is recorded. The data are then arranged on a table as follows:

| | | Nearest Neighbor | |
		A	B
Sampled Plant	A	a	b
	B	c	d
			n

If a and d are large relative to b and c, we would be inclined to say that the species tend to segregate. (Most of A's neighbors are of type A, and most of B's neighbors are of type B.) If b and c are large compared to a and d we would say that the species tend to be overly mixed. In either of these cases (segregation or overmixing) a χ^2 test should yield a large value and the hypothesis of random mixing would be rejected. For each of the following cases, test the hypothesis of random mixing (or, equivalently, the hypothesis that the species of a sampled plant is independent of the species of its nearest neighbor). Use $\alpha = 0.05$ in each case.

(a) $a = 20, b = 4, c = 8, d = 18$ (b) $a = 4, b = 20, c = 18, d = 8$

(c) $a = 20, b = 4, c = 18, d = 8$

Simple Regression

About This Chapter

In previous chapters we have estimated and tested hypotheses concerning a population mean by making use of a set of measurements on a single variable from that population. Frequently, however, the mean of one variable is dependent upon one or more related variables. For example, the average amount of energy required to heat houses of a certain size depends upon the air temperature during the days of the study. In this chapter we begin to build models in which the mean of one variable can be written as a linear function of another variable. This is sometimes referred to as the *regression* of one variable upon another.

Contents

Many engineering applications involve *modeling* the relationships among sets of variables. For example, a chemical engineer may want to model the yield of a chemical process as a function of the temperature and pressure at which the reactions take place. An electrical engineer may be interested in modeling the daily peak load of a power plant as a function of the time of year and number of customers. An environmental engineer may want to model the dissolved oxygen of samples from a large lake as a function of the algal and nitrogen content of the sample.

One method of modeling the relationship between variables is called *regression analysis.* In this chapter we discuss this important topic.

8.2   *Probabilistic Models*

A problem facing every power plant is the estimation of the daily peak power load. Suppose we wanted to model the peak power load as a function of the high temperature for the day. The first question to be answered is this: "Does an exact relationship exist between these variables?" That is, is it possible to predict the exact peak load if the high temperature is known? We might see that this is not possible for several reasons. Peak load depends on other factors beside the high temperature. For example, the number of customers the plant services, the geographical location of the plant, the capacity of the plant, and the average temperature over the day, all probably affect the daily peak power load. However, even if all these factors were included in a model, it is still unlikely that we would be able to predict *exactly* the peak load. There will almost certainly be some variation in peak load due strictly to *random phenomena* that cannot be modeled or explained.

If we were to construct a model that hypothesized an exact relationship between variables, it would be called a *deterministic model.* For example, if we believe that y, peak load (in megawatts) will be exactly five times x, the high temperature (degrees Fahrenheit), we write

$$y = 5x.$$

This represents a deterministic relationship between the variables y and x. It implies that y can always be determined exactly when the value of x is known. There is no allowance for error in this prediction.

Probably the primary usefulness of deterministic models is in the description of physical laws. For example, Ohm's law describes the relationship between current and resistance in a deterministic manner. Newton's laws of motion are other examples of deterministic models. However, it should be noted that in all examples, the laws hold precisely only under ideal conditions. Laboratory experiments rarely reproduce these laws exactly. There will usually be random error

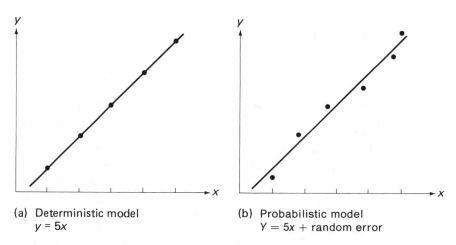

(a) Deterministic model
  $y = 5x$

(b) Probabilistic model
  $Y = 5x + \text{random error}$

Figure 8.1   Deterministic and Probabilistic Models

introduced by the experimenter that will cause the laws to provide only approximations to reality.

Returning to the peak power load example, if we believe there will be unexplained variation in peak power load, we will discard the deterministic model and use a model that accounts for this *random error*. This *probabilistic model* includes both a deterministic component and a random error component. For example, if we hypothesize that the peak load, Y, now a random variable, is related to the high temperature x by

$$Y = 5x + \text{random error,}$$

we are hypothesizing a *probabilistic relationship* between Y and x. Note that the deterministic component of this probabilistic model is $5x$.

Figure 8.1(a) shows possible peak loads for five different values of x, the high temperature, when the model is deterministic. All the peak loads must fall exactly on the line because the deterministic model leaves no room for error.

Figure 8.1(b) shows a possible set of responses for the same values of x when we are using a probabilistic model. Note that the deterministic part of the model (the straight line itself) is the same. Now, however, the inclusion of a random error component allows the peak loads to vary from this line. Since we believe that the peak load will vary randomly for a given value of x, the probabilistic model provides a more realistic model for Y than does the deterministic model.

GENERAL FORM OF PROBABILISTIC MODELS $Y = $ deterministic component + random error where Y is the random variable to be predicted. We will always assume that the mean value of the random error equals zero. This is equivalent to assuming that the mean value of Y, $E(Y)$, equals the deterministic component of the model, i.e.,

$$E(Y) = \text{deterministic component.}$$

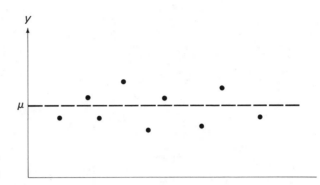

Figure 8.2   The Proba-
bilistic Model $Y = \mu + \varepsilon$

In the last two chapters we discussed the simplest form of a probabilistic model. We showed how to make inferences about the mean of Y, $E(Y)$ when

$$E(Y) = \mu$$

where μ is a constant. However, we realized that this did not imply that Y would equal μ exactly, but instead would be equal to μ plus or minus a random error. In particular, if we assume that Y is normally distributed with mean μ and variance σ^2, then we may write the probabilistic model

$$Y = \mu + \varepsilon$$

where the random component ε (epsilon) is normally distributed with mean 0 and variance σ^2. This model is shown in Figure 8.2.

The purpose of this chapter is to generalize this model to allow $E(Y)$ to be a function of other variables. For example, if we want to model daily peak power load Y as a function of the high temperature x for the day, we might hypothesize that the mean of Y is a straight-line function of x, as shown in the following box.

THE STRAIGHT-LINE PROBABILISTIC MODEL

$$Y = \beta_0 + \beta_1 x + \varepsilon$$

where Y = dependent variable (variable to be modeled)
          x = independent* variable (variable used as a predictor of Y)
          ε = random error component

β_0(beta zero) = y-intercept of the line, that is, point at which the line intercepts or cuts through the y-axis (see Figure 8.3)

β_1(beta one) = slope of the line, that is, amount of increase (or decrease) in the mean of Y for every 1 unit increase in x (see Figure 8.3)

---

* The word independent should not be interpreted in a probabilistic sense, as defined in Chapter 2. The phrase *independent variable* is used in regression analysis to refer to a predictor variable for the response Y.

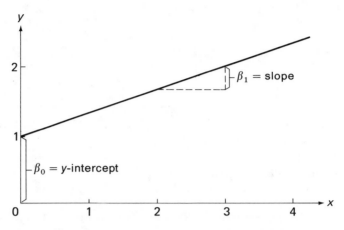

Figure 8.3   Straight-Line Probabilistic Model

Note that we use the Greek symbols, β_0 and β_1, to represent the y-intercept and slope of the model, as we used the Greek symbol, μ, to represent the constant mean in the model $Y = \mu + \varepsilon$. In each case, these symbols represent population parameters with numerical values that will need to be estimated using sample data.

It is helpful to think of regression analysis as a five-step procedure:

Step 1. Hypothesize the form for $E(Y)$, the mean of Y (deterministic component of the model).

Step 2. Use the sample data to estimate unknown parameters in the model.

Step 3. Specify the probability distribution of ε, the random error component, and estimate any unknown parameters of this distribution.

Step 4. Statistically check the adequacy of the model.

Step 5. When satisfied with the model's adequacy, use it for prediction, estimation, and so on.

In this chapter, we skip the more difficult step 1 and introduce the concepts of regression analysis via the straight-line model. In Chapter 9 we discuss how to build more complex models.

8.3   *Fitting the Model: The Least Squares Approach*

Suppose we want to estimate the mean daily peak load for a power plant given the sample of peak loads for ten days in Table 8.1. We hypothesize the model

$$Y = \mu + \varepsilon$$

and wish to use the sample data to estimate μ. One method, the *least-squares approach*, chooses the estimator that minimizes the sum of squared errors (SSE).

Day	Peak Load (y_i)
1	214
2	152
3	156
4	129
5	254
6	266
7	210
8	204
9	213
10	150

Table 8.1   Sample of 10 Days Peak Power Load

That is, we choose the estimator $\hat{\mu}$ so that

$$\text{SSE} = \sum_{i=1}^{n} (y_i - \hat{\mu})^2$$

is minimized. The form of this estimator can be obtained by differentiating SSE with respect to $\hat{\mu}$, setting it equal to zero, and solving for $\hat{\mu}$. Thus

$$\frac{d(\text{SSE})}{d\hat{\mu}} = -2 \sum_{i=1}^{n} (y_i - \hat{\mu}) = 0.$$

Simplifying,

$$-2 \sum_{i=1}^{n} y_i + 2n\hat{\mu} = 0.$$

Solving for $\hat{\mu}$,

$$\hat{\mu} = \frac{\sum_{i=1}^{n} y_i}{n} = \bar{y}.$$

Thus, the sample mean $\bar{Y}$ is the estimator that minimizes the sum of squared errors, and is called the *least-squares estimator* of μ.

For the peak power load data in Table 8.1, we calculate

$$\bar{y} = \frac{1948}{10} = 194.8$$

and

$$\text{SSE} = \sum_{i=1}^{n} (y_i - \bar{y})^2 = 19{,}263.6.$$

We know that no other estimate of μ will yield as small an SSE as this.

Now suppose we decide that the main peak power load can be modeled as a function of the high temperature x for the day. Specifically, we model the mean peak power load, $E(Y)$, as a straight-line function of x. Thus we record the high temperature for the days in Table 8.1, and obtain the data in Table 8.2. A plot of this data, called a *scattergram*, is shown in Figure 8.4.

Day	High Temperature, x	Peak Power Load, y
1	95	214
2	82	152
3	90	156
4	81	129
5	99	254
6	100	266
7	93	210
8	95	204
9	93	213
10	87	150

Table 8.2   Data for Peak Power Load, *y*, and High Temperature, *x*, for Ten Days

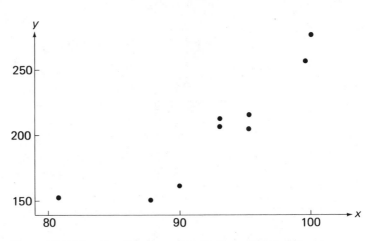

Figure 8.4(a)   Scattergram for Data in Table 8.2

We hypothesize the straight-line probabilistic model

$$Y = \beta_0 + \beta_1 x + \varepsilon$$

and want to use the sample data to estimate the y-intercept β_0 and the slope β_1. We use the same principle to estimate β_0 and β_1 in the straight-line model that we used to estimate μ in the constant mean model: the least-squares approach. Thus, we choose the estimate

$$\hat{y} = \hat{\beta}_0 + \hat{\beta}_1 x$$

so that

$$SSE = \sum_{i=1}^{n} (y_i - \hat{y})^2 = \sum_{i=1}^{n} (y_i - \hat{\beta}_0 - \hat{\beta}_1 x_i)^2$$

is minimized. We differentiate SSE with respect to $\hat{\beta}_0$ and $\hat{\beta}_1$, set the results equal to zero, and then solve for $\hat{\beta}_0$ and $\hat{\beta}_1$.

$$\frac{\partial(SSE)}{\partial \hat{\beta}_0} = -2 \sum_{i=1}^{n} (y_i - \hat{\beta}_0 - \hat{\beta}_1 x_i) = 0$$

$$\frac{\partial(SSE)}{\partial \hat{\beta}_1} = -2 \sum_{i=1}^{n} x_i(y_i - \hat{\beta}_0 - \hat{\beta}_1 x_i) = 0$$

and the solution is

$$\hat{\beta}_1 = \frac{\sum_{i=j}^{n} (x_i - \bar{x})(y_i - \bar{y})}{\sum_{i=j}^{n} (x_i - \bar{x})^2} = \frac{SS_{xy}}{SS_{xx}}$$

$$\hat{\beta}_0 = \bar{y} - \hat{\beta}_1 \bar{x}.$$

For the data in Table 8.3 we find

$$SS_{xy} = \sum_{i=1}^{n} (x_i - \bar{x})(y_i - \bar{y}) = \sum_{i=1}^{n} x_i y_i - \frac{\left(\sum_{i=1}^{n} x_i\right)\left(\sum_{i=1}^{n} y_i\right)}{n}$$

$$= 180{,}798 - \frac{(915)(1948)}{10} = 2556$$

$$SS_{xx} = \sum_{i=1}^{n} (x_i - \bar{x})^2 = \sum_{i=1}^{n} x_i^2 - \frac{\left(\sum_{i=1}^{n} x_i\right)^2}{n}$$

$$= 84{,}103 - \frac{(915)^2}{10} = 380.5$$

and

$$\bar{x} = \frac{915}{10} = 91.5$$

$$\bar{y} = 194.8.$$

Then the least-squares estimates are

$$\hat{\beta}_1 = \frac{SS_{xy}}{SS_{xx}} = \frac{2556}{380.5} = 6.7175$$

$$\hat{\beta}_0 = \bar{y} - \hat{\beta}_1 \bar{x} = 194.8 - (6.7175)(91.5)$$

$$= -419.85.$$

Table 8.3   Data, Predicted Values, and Errors for the Peak Power Load Data

x	y	$\hat{y} = \hat{\beta}_0 + \hat{\beta}_1 x$	$(y - \hat{y})$	$(y_i - \hat{y})^2$
95	214	218.31	−4.31	18.58
82	152	130.98	21.02	441.84
90	156	184.72	−28.72	824.84
81	129	124.27	4.73	22.37
99	254	245.18	8.82	77.79
100	266	251.90	14.10	198.81
93	210	204.88	5.12	26.21
95	204	218.31	−14.31	204.78
93	213	204.88	8.12	65.93
87	150	164.57	−14.57	212.28
				SSE = 2093.43

The least-squares line is therefore

$$\hat{y} = -419.85 + 6.7175x$$

as shown in Figure 8.4(b). Note that the errors are the vertical distances between the observed points and the prediction line, $(y_i - \hat{y}_i)$. The predicted values, $\hat{y}_i$, the error, $(y_i - \hat{y}_i)$, and the squared error, $(y_i - \hat{y}_i)^2$ are shown in Table 8.3. You can see that the sum of squared errors, SSE, is 2093.43. We know that no other straight line will yield as small an SSE as this one.

To summarize, we have defined the best-fitting straight line to be the one that satisfies the least-squares criterion, that is, the sum of squared errors will be smaller than for any other straight-line model. This line is called the *least-squares*

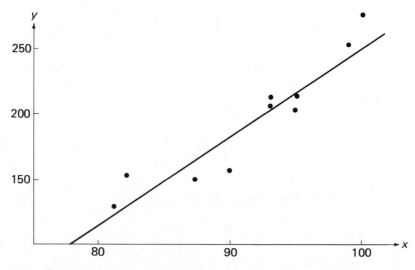

Figure 8.4(b)   Scattergram and Least Squares Line for Data in Table 8.2

line, and its equation is called the *least-squares prediction equation*. The prediction equation can be determined by substituting the sample values of x and y into the formulas given in the box.

FORMULAS FOR THE LEAST SQUARES LINE

$$\text{Slope: } \hat{\beta}_1 = \frac{SS_{xy}}{SS_{xx}}$$

$$y\text{-intercept: } \hat{\beta}_0 = \bar{y} - \hat{\beta}_1 \bar{x}$$

where

$$SS_{xy} = \sum_{i=1}^{n} x_i y_i - \frac{\left(\sum_{i=1}^{n} x_i\right)\left(\sum_{i=1}^{n} y_i\right)}{n}$$

$$SS_{xx} = \sum_{i=1}^{n} x_i^2 - \frac{\left(\sum_{i=1}^{n} x_i\right)^2}{n}$$

n = number of pairs of observations (sample size)

Exercises

8.1   Use the method of least squares to fit a straight line to the following six data points:

x	1	2	3	4	5	6
y	1	2	2	3	5	5

(a) What are the least-squares estimates of β_0 and β_1?
(b) Plot the data points and graph the least-squares line. Does the line pass through the data points?

8.2   Use the method of least squares to fit a straight line to the following data points:

x	-2	-1	0	1	2
y	4	3	3	1	-1

(a) What are the least-squares estimates of β_0 and β_1?
(b) Plot the data points and graph the least-squares line. Does the line pass through the data points?

8.3   The elongation of a steel cable is assumed to be linearly related to the amount of force applied. Five identical specimens of cable gave the following results when varying forces were applied:

Force (x)	1.0	1.5	2.0	2.5	3.0
Elongation (y)	3.0	3.8	5.4	6.9	8.4

Use the method of least squares to fit the line

$$Y = \beta_0 + \beta_1 x + \varepsilon.$$

8.4   A company wants to model the relationship between its sales and the sales for the industry as a whole. For the following data, fit a straight line by the method of least squares.

Year	Company Sales y (millions of \$)	Industry Sales x (millions of \$)
1972	0.5	10
1973	1.0	12
1974	1.0	13
1975	1.4	15
1976	1.3	14
1977	1.6	15

8.5   It is thought that abrasion loss in certain steel specimens should be a linear function of the Rockwell hardness measure. A sample of eight specimens gave the following results:

Rockwell Hardness (x)	60	62	63	67	70	74	79	81
Abrasion loss (y)	251	245	246	233	221	202	188	170

Fit a straight line to these measurements.

8.6   A new manufactured ammeter is to be checked against a standard meter. Fit a straight line to the following measurements:

x (standard)	15.1	15.5	16.2	16.3	16.7	16.9
y (new meter)	15.0	15.7	16.0	16.2	16.8	16.9

8.7   A study is made of the number of parts assembled as a function of the time spent on the job. Twelve employees are divided into three groups, corresponding to three time intervals, with the following results:

Time (x)	Number of parts assembled (y)
10 minutes	27, 32, 26, 34
15 minutes	35, 30, 42, 47
20 minutes	45, 50, 52, 49

Fit the model

$$Y = \beta_0 + \beta_1 x + \varepsilon$$

by the method of least squares.

8.8   Laboratory experiments designed to measure LC50 values for the effect of certain toxicants on fish are run by basically two different methods. One method has water continuously flowing through laboratory tanks and the other has static water conditions. For purposes of establishing criteria for toxicants, the Environmental Protection Agency (EPA) wants to adjust all results to the flow-through condition. Thus, a model is needed to relate the two types of observations. Observations on certain toxicants examined under both static and flow-through conditions yielded the following (measurements in parts per million):

Toxicant	LC50 flow-through (y)	LC50 static (x)
1	23.00	39.00
2	22.30	37.50
3	9.40	22.20
4	9.70	17.50
5	0.15	0.64
6	0.28	0.45
7	0.75	2.62
8	0.51	2.36
9	28.00	32.00
10	0.39	0.77

Fit the model $Y = \beta_0 + \beta_1 x + \varepsilon$ by the method of least squares.

8.4   *The Probability Distribution of the Random Error Component*

We have now completed the first two steps of regression modeling: we have hypothesized the form of $E(Y)$, and used the sample data to estimate unknown parameters in the model. The hypothesized model relating peak power load Y to daily high temperature x is

$$Y = \beta_0 + \beta_1 x + \varepsilon$$

and the least squares estimate of $E(Y) = \beta_0 + \beta_1 x$ is

$$\hat{y} = -419.85 + 6.7175x.$$

Step 3.   Specify the probability distribution of the random error term, and estimate any unknown parameters of this distribution.

Recall that when we wanted to make inferences about a population mean and had only a small sample with which to work, we used a t-statistic, and assumed that the data were normally distributed. Similarly, when we want to make inferences about the parameters of a regression model, we need to assume that the error component ε is normally distributed, and the assumption is most important when the sample size is small. The mean of ε is zero, since the deterministic component of the model describes $E(Y)$. Finally, we assume that the variance of ε is σ^2, a constant for all values of x, and that the errors associated with different observations are independent.

The assumptions about the probability distribution of ε are summarized in the box, and are shown in Figure 8.5.

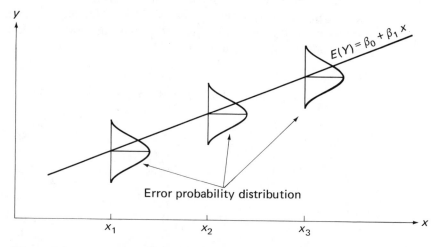

Figure 8.5   The Probability Distribution of ε

PROBABILITY DISTRIBUTION OF THE RANDOM ERROR COMPONENT, ε   The error component is normally distributed with mean zero and constant variance σ^2. The errors associated with different observations are independent.

Various techniques exist for testing the validity of the assumptions, and there are some alternative techniques to be used when they appear to be invalid. These techniques often require us to return to Step 2 and to use a method other than least squares to estimate the model parameters. Much current statistical research is devoted to alternative methodologies. Most are beyond the scope of this text, but we will mention a few in later chapters. In actual practice, the assumptions need not hold exactly in order for the least squares techniques to be useful.

Note that the probability distribution of ε would be completely specified if the variance, σ^2, were known. To estimate σ^2, we make use of the SSE for the least squares model. The estimate s^2 of σ^2 is calculated by dividing SSE by the number of degrees of freedom associated with the error component. We use 2 df to estimate the y-intercept and slope in the straight-line model, leaving $(n - 2)$ df for the error variance estimation. Thus

$$s^2 = \frac{SSE}{n - 2}$$

where

$$SSE = \sum_{i=1}^{n} (y_i - \hat{y}_i)^2 = SS_{yy} - \hat{\beta}_1 SS_{xy}$$

and

$$SS_{yy} = \sum_{i=1}^{n} (y_i - \bar{y})^2 = \sum_{i=1}^{n} y_i^2 - \frac{\left(\sum_{i=1}^{n} y_i\right)^2}{n}.$$

In our peak power load example, we calculated SSE $= 2093.43$ for the least squares line. Recalling that there were $n = 10$ data points, we have $n - 2 = 8$ df for estimating σ^2. Thus,

$$s^2 = \frac{SSE}{n - 2} = \frac{2093.43}{8} = 261.68$$

is the estimated variance, and

$$s = \sqrt{261.68} = 16.18$$

is the estimated standard deviation of ε.

You may be able to obtain an intuitive feeling for s by recalling that about 95% of the observations from a normal distribution lie within two standard deviations of the mean. Thus, we expect approximately 95% of the observations to fall within $2s$ of the estimated mean $\hat{y} = \hat{\beta}_0 + \hat{\beta}_1 x$. For our peak power load example, note that all ten observations fall within $2s = 2(16.18) = 32.36$ of the least-squares line. In Section 8.8 we show how to use the estimated standard deviation to evaluate the prediction error when $\hat{y}$ is used to predict a value of y to be observed for a given value of x.

Exercises

8.9   Calculate SSE and s^2 for the data of Exercise
    (a) 8.1   (b) 8.2
    (c) 8.3   (d) 8.4
    (e) 8.5   (f) 8.6
    (g) 8.7   (h) 8.8

8.10 Matis and Wehrly (*Biometrics*, 35, No. 1, March, 1979) report the following data on the proportion of green sunfish that survive a fixed level of thermal pollution for varying lengths of time.

Proportion of survivors (y)	1.00	0.95	0.95	0.90	0.85	0.70	0.65	0.60	0.55	0.40
Scaled time (x)	0.10	0.15	0.20	0.25	0.30	0.35	0.40	0.45	0.50	0.55

(a) Fit the linear model $Y = \beta_0 + \beta_1 x + \varepsilon$ by the method of least squares.
(b) Plot the data points and graph the line found in (a). Does the line fit through the points?
(c) Compute SSE and s^2.

8.5 *Assessing the Adequacy of the Model: Making Inferences about the Slope β_1*

Step 4. Statistically check the adequacy of the model.

Now that we have specified the probability distribution of ε and estimated the variance σ^2, we are prepared to make statistical inferences about the model's adequacy for describing the mean $E(Y)$ and for predicting the values of Y for given values of x.

Refer again to the peak power load example and suppose that the daily peak load is *completely unrelated* to the high temperature that day. The implication is that the mean $E(Y) = \beta_0 + \beta_1 x$ does not change as x changes. In this straight-line model this means that the true slope, β_1, is equal to zero (see Figure 8.6). Note that if β_1 is equal to zero, the model is just $Y = \beta_0 + \varepsilon$, the constant mean model used in previous chapters. Therefore, to test the null hypothesis that x contributes no information for the prediction of Y against the alternative hypothesis that these variables are linearly related with a slope differing from

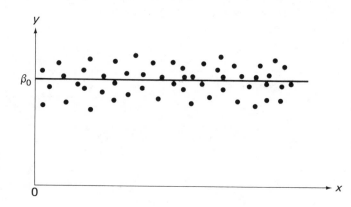

Figure 8.6 Graph of the Model $Y = \beta_0 + \varepsilon$

zero, we test

$$H_0: \beta_1 = 0 \qquad \text{vs.} \qquad H_a: \beta_1 \neq 0.$$

If the data support the research hypothesis, we conclude that x does contribute information for the prediction of Y using the straight-line model (although the true relationship between $E(Y)$ and x could be more complex than a straight line). Thus, to some extent, this is a test of the adequacy of the hypothesized model.

The appropriate test statistic is found by considering the sampling distribution of $\hat{\beta}_1$, the least-squares estimator of the slope β_1.

SAMPLING DISTRIBUTION OF $\hat{\beta}_1$ If we assume that the error components are independent normal random variables with mean zero and constant variance σ^2, the sampling distribution of the least-squares estimator, $\hat{\beta}_1$, of the slope will be normal, with mean β_1 (the true slope) and standard deviation

$$\sigma_{\hat{\beta}_1} = \frac{\sigma}{\sqrt{SS_{xx}}} \qquad \text{(see Figure 8.7).}$$

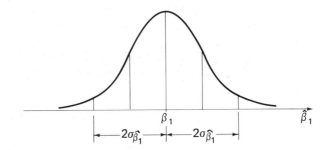

Figure 8.7   Sampling Distribution of $\hat{\beta}_1$

Note: Proof of the unbiasedness of $\hat{\beta}_1$ and a derivation of its standard deviation are given next.

PROOF OF UNBIASEDNESS OF $\hat{\beta}_1$ Recall that

$$\hat{\beta}_1 = \frac{SS_{xy}}{SS_{xx}} = \frac{\sum\limits_{i=1}^{n} (x_i - \bar{x})(\bar{Y}_i - \bar{Y})}{\sum\limits_{i=1}^{n} (x_i - \bar{x})^2}.$$

Using the facts:

1. $Y_i = \beta_0 + \beta_1 x_1 + \varepsilon_i$
2. $\bar{Y} = \beta_0 + \beta_1 \bar{x} + \bar{\varepsilon}$
3. x_i's are fixed*

---

* If the independent variable X is random, we use expectations *conditional* on the observed values of X.

we find

$$E(\hat{\beta}_1) = E\left\{\frac{\sum\limits_{i=1}^{n} (x_i - \bar{x})(Y_i - \bar{Y})}{\sum\limits_{i=1}^{n} (x_i - \bar{x})^2}\right\}$$

$$= \frac{1}{\sum\limits_{i=1}^{n} (x_i - \bar{x})^2} \sum\limits_{i=1}^{n} (x_1 - \bar{x})E(Y_i - \bar{Y})$$

$$= \frac{1}{SS_{xx}} \sum\limits_{i=1}^{n} (x_i - \bar{x})E[(\beta_0 + \beta_1 x_i + \varepsilon_i) - (\beta_0 + \beta_1 \bar{x} + \bar{\varepsilon})]$$

$$= \frac{1}{SS_{xx}} \sum\limits_{i=1}^{n} (x_i - \bar{x})[\beta_1(x_i - \bar{x})]$$

$$= \frac{SS_{xx}}{SS_{xx}} \beta_1$$

$$= \beta_1$$

showing that $\hat{\beta}_1$ is an unbiased estimator of β_1.

DERIVATION OF THE VARIANCE OF $\hat{\beta}_1$ Using the formula derived for the variance of a linear function,

$$\sigma_{\hat{\beta}_1}^2 = \text{Var}(\hat{\beta}_1) = \text{Var}\left\{\frac{\sum\limits_{i=1}^{n} (x_i - \bar{x})(Y_i - \bar{Y})}{\sum\limits_{i=1}^{n} (x_i - \bar{x})^2}\right\}$$

$$= \frac{1}{\left[\sum\limits_{i=1}^{n} (x_i - \bar{x})^2\right]^2} \text{Var}\left\{\sum\limits_{i=1}^{n} (x_i - \bar{x})(Y_i - \bar{Y})\right\}$$

$$= \frac{1}{SS_{xx}^2}\left[\sum\limits_{i=1}^{n} (x_i - \bar{x})^2 \text{Var}(Y_i - \bar{Y})\right.$$

$$\left. + \sum\limits_{i=1}^{n}\sum\limits_{\substack{j=1 \\ i \neq j}}^{n} (x_i - \bar{x})(x_j - \bar{x})\text{Cov}\{(Y_i - \bar{Y}),(Y_j - \bar{Y})\}\right]$$

Now,

$$\text{Var}(Y_i - \bar{Y}) = \text{Var}\{(\beta_0 + \beta_1 x_i + \varepsilon_i) - (\beta_0 + \beta_1 \bar{x} + \bar{\varepsilon})\}$$

$$= \text{Var}\{\varepsilon_i - \bar{\varepsilon}\} = \sigma^2 + \frac{\sigma^2}{n} - 2\frac{\sigma^2}{n}$$

$$= \sigma^2 - \frac{\sigma^2}{n}$$

and

$$\text{Cov}\{(Y_i - \bar{Y}),(Y_j - \bar{Y})\} = \text{Cov}\{(\varepsilon_i - \bar{\varepsilon}),(\varepsilon_j - \bar{\varepsilon})\}$$
$$= -\text{Cov}(\varepsilon_i,\bar{\varepsilon}) - \text{Cov}(\varepsilon_j,\bar{\varepsilon}) + \text{Var}(\bar{\varepsilon})$$
$$= -\frac{\sigma^2}{n} - \frac{\sigma^2}{n} + \frac{\sigma^2}{n}$$
$$= -\frac{\sigma^2}{n},$$

where we have used:

(1) $\text{Var}(\varepsilon_i) = \sigma^2$

(2) $\text{Cov}(\varepsilon_i,\varepsilon_j) = 0, i \neq j$

(3) $\text{Var}(\bar{\varepsilon}) = \text{Var}\left(\dfrac{\sum\limits_{i=1}^{n} \varepsilon_i}{n}\right) = \dfrac{1}{n^2} \sum\limits_{i=1}^{n} \text{Var}(\varepsilon_i)$

$$= \frac{n\sigma^2}{n^2} = \frac{\sigma^2}{n}$$

(4) $\text{Cov}(\varepsilon_i,\bar{\varepsilon}) = \text{Cov}\left(\varepsilon_i, \dfrac{\sum\limits_{j=1}^{n} \varepsilon_j}{n}\right) = \dfrac{\text{Var}(\varepsilon_i)}{n} = \dfrac{\sigma^2}{n}$

Thus

$$\sigma_{\hat{\beta}_1}^2 = \frac{1}{\text{SS}_{xx}^2}\left[\sum_{i=1}^{n}(x_i - \bar{x})^2\left(\sigma^2 - \frac{\sigma^2}{n}\right) - \sum_{\substack{i=1 \\ i \neq j}}^{n}\sum_{j=1}^{n}(x_i - \bar{x})(x_j - \bar{x})\left(-\frac{\sigma^2}{n}\right)\right]$$

$$= \frac{1}{\text{SS}_{xx}^2}\left\{\text{SS}_{xx}\sigma^2 - \frac{\sigma^2}{n}\left[\sum_{i=1}^{n}(x_i - \bar{x})\right]^2\right\}$$

$$= \frac{\sigma^2}{\text{SS}_{xx}} \qquad \text{using } \sum_{i=1}^{n}(x_i - \bar{x}) = 0.$$

The standard error of $\hat{\beta}_1$ is therefore $\sigma_{\hat{\beta}_1} = \sigma/\sqrt{\text{SS}_{xx}}$.

Since the standard deviation of ε, σ, will usually be unknown, the appropriate test statistic will generally be a Student's t statistic formed as follows:

$$t = \frac{\hat{\beta}_1 - (\text{Hypothesized value of } \beta_1)}{s_{\hat{\beta}_1}}$$

where $s_{\hat{\beta}_1} = s/\sqrt{\text{SS}_{xx}}$, the estimated standard deviation of the sampling distribution of $\hat{\beta}_1$. We will usually be testing the null hypothesis $H_0 : \beta_1 = 0$, so that the t-statistic becomes

$$t = \frac{\hat{\beta}_1}{s/\sqrt{\text{SS}_{xx}}}.$$

For the peak power load example, we choose $\alpha = 0.05$, and since $n = 10$, our rejection region is

$$t < -t_{0.025, 10-2} = -2.306$$

$$t > t_{0.025, 8} = 2.306.$$

We previously calculated $\hat{\beta}_1 = 6.7175$, $s = 16.18$, and $SS_{xx} = 380.5$. Thus

$$t = \frac{\hat{\beta}_1}{s/\sqrt{SS_{xx}}} = \frac{6.7175}{16.18/\sqrt{380.5}} = 8.10.$$

A TEST OF MODEL UTILITY

One-tailed test	*Two-tailed test*
$H_0: \beta_1 = 0$	$H_0: \beta_1 = 0$
$H_a: \beta_1 < 0 \quad$ (or $H_a: \beta_1 > 0$)	$H_a: \beta_1 \neq 0$
Test statistic:	Test statistic:
$t = \dfrac{\hat{\beta}_1}{s_{\hat{\beta}_1}} = \dfrac{\hat{\beta}_1}{s/\sqrt{SS_{xx}}}$	$t = \dfrac{\hat{\beta}_1}{s_{\hat{\beta}_1}} = \dfrac{\hat{\beta}_1}{s/\sqrt{SS_{xx}}}$
Rejection region:	Rejection region:
$t < -t_{\alpha, n-2}$	$t < -t_{\alpha/2, n-2} \quad$ or $\quad t > t_{\alpha/2, n-2}$
(or $t > t_{\alpha, n-2}$ when $H_a: \beta_1 > 0$)	

Assumptions: The four assumptions about ε listed in Section 12.3.

Since this calculated t value falls in the upper-tail rejection region, we reject the null hypothesis and conclude that the slope β_1 is not zero. The sample evidence indicates that the peak power load tends to increase as a day's high temperature increases.

What conclusion can be drawn if the calculated t value does not fall in the rejection region? We know from previous discussions of the philosophy of hypothesis testing that such a t value does not lead us to accept the null hypothesis. That is, we do not conclude that $\beta_1 = 0$. Additional data might indicate that β_1 differs from zero, or a more complex relationship may exist between x and Y, requiring the fitting of a model other than the straight-line model. We discuss several such models in Chapter 9.

Another way to make inferences about the slope β_1 is to estimate it using a confidence interval. This interval is formed as shown next.

A 100(1 − α) *PERCENT CONFIDENCE INTERVAL FOR THE SLOPE* $\hat{\beta}_1$

$$\hat{\beta}_1 \pm t_{\alpha/2,\, n-2} s_{\hat{\beta}_1}$$

where

$$s_{\hat{\beta}_1} = \frac{s}{\sqrt{SS_{xx}}}.$$

Assumptions: The four assumptions about ε listed in Section 8.4.

For the peak power load example, a 95% confidence interval for the slope β_1 is

$$\hat{\beta}_1 \pm t_{0.025,8} s_{\hat{\beta}_1} = 6.7175 \pm 2.306\left(\frac{16.18}{\sqrt{380.5}}\right)$$

$$= 6.7175 \pm 1.913 = (4.80, 8.63).$$

Exercises

8.11   Refer to Exercise 8.1. Is there sufficient evidence to say that the slope of the line is significantly different from zero? Use $\alpha = 0.05$.

8.12   Refer to Exercise 8.2. Estimate β_1 in a confidence interval with confidence coefficient 0.90.

8.13   Refer to Exercise 8.3. Estimate the amount of elongation per unit increase in force. Use a confidence coefficient of 0.95.

8.14   Refer to Exercise 8.4. Does industry sales appear to contribute any information to the prediction of company sales? Test at the 10% level of significance.

8.15   Refer to Exercise 8.5. Does Rockwell hardness appear to be linearly related to abrasion loss? Use $\alpha = 0.05$.

8.16   Refer to Exercise 8.6. If the new ammeter is functioning correctly, the slope of the line relating x to y should be unity. Test the hypothesis that the new ammeter is functioning correctly, employing a 5% significance level.

8.17   Refer to Exercise 8.7. Estimate the increase in expected number of parts assembled per 5-minute increase in time spent on the job. Use a 95% confidence coefficient.

8.18   Refer to Exercise 8.8. Does it appear that flow-through LC50's are linearly related to static LC50's? Use $\alpha = 0.05$.

8.19   It is well-known that large bodies of water have a mitigating effect on the temperature of the surrounding land masses. On a cold night in central Florida, temperatures were recorded at equal distances along a transect running in the down-wind direction from a large lake. The data are as follows:

Site (x)	1	2	3	4	5	6	7	8	8	10
Temperature (y)	37.00	36.25	35.41	34.92	34.52	34.45	34.40	34.00	33.62	33.90

(a) Fit the linear model $Y = \beta_0 + \beta_1 x + \varepsilon$ by the method of least squares.
(b) Find SSE and s^2.
(c) Does it appear that temperatures decrease significantly as distance from the lake increases? Use $\alpha = 0.05$.

8.6   *The Coefficient of Correlation: Another Measure of Model Utility*

A common joint probability density function used to model the joint behavior of continuous random variables X and Y is the *bivariate normal*. This density function is given by

$$f(x, y) = \frac{1}{2\pi\sigma_1\sigma_2\sqrt{1 - \rho^2}} e^{-Q/2}, \qquad \begin{array}{l} -\infty < x < \infty \\ -\infty < y < \infty, \end{array}$$

where

$$Q = \frac{1}{1 - \rho^2}\left[\frac{(x - \mu_1)^2}{\sigma_1^2} - 2\rho\frac{(x - \mu_1)(y - \mu_2)}{\sigma_1\sigma_2} + \frac{(y - \mu_2)^2}{\sigma_2^2}\right].$$

For this distribution the marginal distributions will both be normal, with X having mean μ_1 and variance σ_1^2 while Y has mean μ_2 and variance σ_2^2.

One parameter of this frequency is of particular interest in the context of simple regression modeling: the correlation coefficient, ρ. The reason for this importance is most easily understood by considering the conditional expectation of Y for given $X = x$,

$$E(Y|X = x) = \mu_Y + \rho\sigma_Y\left(\frac{x - \mu_x}{\sigma_x}\right)$$

where μ_y and μ_x are the unconditional means of Y and X respectively, and σ_y and σ_x are the corresponding standard deviations. This may be rewritten in the more familiar form of a simple regression model.

$$E(Y|X = x) = \beta_0 + \beta_1 x$$

where

$$\beta_0 = \mu_y - \rho\frac{\mu_x\sigma_y}{\sigma_x}$$

$$\beta_1 = \rho\frac{\sigma_y}{\sigma_x}.$$

Since σ_y/σ_x is a positive quantity, the sign of the slope β_1 and the correlation coefficient ρ will always agree, and β_1 will be zero if and only if ρ is zero. It should not be surprising then that inferences concerning the slope in a straight-line model relating bivariate normal random variables are equivalent to inferences about the correlation coefficient ρ. In addition, ρ will always have a numerical value between -1 and $+1$.

The sample correlation coefficient r can be computed from the least-squares slope, $\hat{\beta}_1$, by inverting the above formula and substituting sample estimators:

$$r = \hat{\beta}_1 \frac{s_x}{s_y}$$

where s_y and s_x are the sample standard deviations of y and x. The calculation formula for r is

$$r = \frac{SS_{xy}}{\sqrt{SS_{xx}SS_{yy}}}.$$

Note that r is computed using the same quantities used in fitting the least-squares line. Since both r and $\hat{\beta}_1$ provide information about the utility of the model, it is not surprising that there is a similarity in their computational formulas. Particularly, note that SS_{xy} appears in the numerators of both expressions and, since both denominators are always positive, r and $\hat{\beta}_1$ will always be of the same sign (either both positive or both negative). A value of r near or equal to zero implies little or no linear relationship between y and x. In contrast, the closer r is to 1 or -1, the stronger the linear relationship between y and x. And, if $r = 1$ or $r = -1$, all the points fall exactly on the least-squares line. Positive values of r imply that y increases as x increases; negative values imply that y decreases as x increases. Each of these situations is portrayed in Figure 8.8 on p. 260.

In the peak power load example we related peak daily power usage, y, to the day's maximum temperature, x. For this data (Table 8.2) we found

$$SS_{xy} = 2556$$

and

$$SS_{xx} = 380.5,$$

where

$$SS_{yy} = \sum_{i=1}^{n} (y_i - \bar{y})^2 = 19,263.6$$

and, therefore,

$$r = \frac{2556}{\sqrt{(380.5)(19,263.6)}} = 0.94.$$

The fact that the value of r is positive and near 1 indicates that the peak power load tends to increase as the daily maximum temperature increases, *for this sample of ten days*. This is the same conclusion we reached upon finding that the least-squares slope, $\hat{\beta}_1$, was positive.

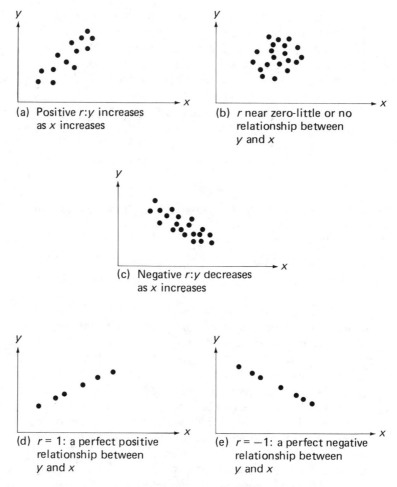

(a) Positive r:y increases
as x increases

(b) r near zero-little or no
relationship between
y and x

(c) Negative r:y decreases
as x increases

(d) r = 1: a perfect positive
relationship between
y and x

(e) r = −1: a perfect negative
relationship between
y and x

Figure 8.8   Values of r and Their Implications

If we want to use the sample information to test the null hypothesis that the normal random variables X and Y are uncorrelated, that is, $H_0:\rho = 0$, we can use the results of the test that the slope of the straight-line model is zero, that is, $H_0:\beta_1 = 0$. The test given in Section 8.2 for the latter hypothesis is identical to the one used for the former hypothesis. When we tested the null hypothesis $H_0:\beta_1 = 0$ in connection with the peak power load example, the data led to a rejection of the null hypothesis at the $\alpha = 0.05$ level. This implies that the null hypothesis of a zero linear correlation between the two variables (maximum temperature and peak power load) can also be rejected at the $\alpha = 0.05$ level. The only real difference between the least squares slope $\hat{\beta}_1$ and the coefficient of correlation r is the measurement scale. Therefore, the information they provide about the utility of the least-squares model is to some extent redundant. However, the test for correlation requires the additional assumption that the variables X and Y have a bivariate normal distribution, while the test of slope does not ever require that x be a random variable. For example, we could use the straight-line model to describe the relationship between the yield of a chemical process, Y, and the temperature at which the reaction takes place, x, even if the temperature were controlled and therefore nonrandom. However, the correlation coefficient would have no meaning in this case, since the bivariate normal distribution requires that both variables be marginally normal.

We close the section with a caution: do not infer a causal relationship on the basis of high sample correlation. Although it is probably true that a high maximum daily temperature *causes* an increase in peak power demand, the same would not necessarily be true of the relationship between availability of oil and peak power load, even though they are probably positively correlated. That is, we would not be willing to state that low availability of oil *causes* a lower peak power load. Rather, the scarcity of oil tends to cause an increase in conservation awareness, which in turn tends to cause a decrease in peak power load. Thus, a large sample correlation only indicates that the two variables tend to change together, but causality must be determined by considering other factors in addition to the size of the correlation.

8.7   *The Coefficient of Determination*

Another way to measure the contribution of x in predicting Y is to consider how much the errors of prediction of Y were reduced by using the information provided by x. If you do not use x, the best prediction for any value of Y would be $\bar{y}$, and the sum of squares of the deviations of the observed y values of $\bar{y}$ is the familiar

$$SS_{yy} = \sum(y_i - \bar{y})^2.$$

On the other hand, if you use x to predict Y, the sum of squares of the deviations of the y values about the least-squares line is

$$SSE = \sum(y_i - \hat{y}_i)^2.$$

Then, the reduction in the sum of squares of deviations that can be attributed to x, expressed as a proportion of SS_{yy}, is

$$\frac{SS_{yy} - SSE}{SS_{yy}}.$$

It can be shown that this quantity is equal to the square of the simple linear coefficient of correlation.

DEFINITION 8.1   The square of the coefficient of correlation is called the **coefficient of determination.** It represents the proportion of the sum of squares of deviations of the y values about their mean that can be attributed to a linear relation between Y and x.

$$r^2 = \frac{SS_{yy} - SSE}{SS_{yy}} = 1 - \frac{SSE}{SS_{yy}}.$$

Note that r^2 is always between 0 and 1, because r is between -1 and $+1$. Thus, $r^2 = 0.60$ means that 60% of the sum of squares of deviations of the observed y values about their mean is attributable to the linear relation between Y and x.

EXAMPLE 8.1

Calculate and interpret the coefficient of determination for the peak power load example.

Solution   We have previously calculated

$$SS_{yy} = 19,263.6$$

$$SSE = 2093.4$$

so that

$$r^2 = \frac{SS_{yy} - SSE}{SS_{yy}} = \frac{19263.6 - 2093.4}{19263.6}$$

$$= 0.89. \quad \Box$$

Note that we could obtained $r^2 = (0.94)^2 = 0.89$ more simply using the correlation coefficient calculated in the previous section. However, use of the above formula is worthwhile because it reminds us that r^2 represents the fraction reduction in variability from SS_{yy} to SSE. In the peak power load example, this fraction is 0.89, meaning that the sample variability of the peak loads about their mean is reduced by 89% when the mean peak load is modeled as a linear function of daily high temperature. Remember, though, that this statement only holds true for the sample at hand. We have no way of knowing how much of the population variability can be explained by the linear model.

Exercise

8.20   Compute r and r^2 for the data of Exercise
    (a) 8.1   (b) 8.2
    (c) 8.5   (d) 8.6
    (e) 8.7   (f) 8.8
    Interpret these numerical values in each case.

8.8   *Using the Model for Estimation and Prediction*

If we are satisfied that a useful model has been found to describe the relationship between peak power load and maximum daily temperature, we are ready to accomplish the original objective in constructing the model.

Step 5.   When satisfied that the model is adequate, use it for prediction, estimation, and so on.

The most common uses of a probabilistic model for making inferences can be divided into two categories. The first is the use of the model for estimating the mean value of Y, $E(Y)$, for a specific value of x. For our peak power load example, we may want to estimate the mean peak power load for days during which the maximum temperature is 90°F. The second use of the model entails predicting a particular value for a given x. That is, we may want to predict the peak power load for a particular day during which the maximum temperature will be 90°F.

In the first case we are attempting to estimate the mean value of Y over a very large number of days. In the second case, we are trying to predict the Y value for a single day. Which of these model uses, estimating the mean value of Y or predicting an individual value of Y (for the same value of x), can be accomplished with the greater accuracy?

Before answering this question, first we consider the problem of choosing an estimator (or predictor) of the mean (or individual) Y value. We use the least-squares model

$$\hat{y} = \hat{\beta}_0 + \hat{\beta}_1 x$$

both to estimate the mean value of Y and predict a particular value of Y for a given value of x. For our example, we found

$$\hat{y} = -419.85 + 6.7175x$$

so that the estimated mean peak power load for all days when $x = 90$ (maximum temperature is 90°F) is

$$\hat{y} = -419.85 + 6.7175(90) = 184.72.$$

The identical value is used to predict the Y value when $x = 90$. That is, both the estimated mean and the predicted value of Y are $\hat{y} = 184.72$ when $x = 90$, as shown in Figure 8.9.

The difference between the uses of these two models lies in the relative precision of the estimate and prediction. The precisions are measured by the expected squared distances between the estimator-predictor $\hat{y}$ and the quantity being estimated or predicted. In the case of estimation, we are trying to estimate

$$E(Y) = \beta_0 + \beta_1 x_p,$$

where x_p is the particular value of x at which the estimate is being made. The estimator is

$$\hat{Y} = \hat{\beta}_0 + \hat{\beta}_1 x_p$$

so that the sources of error in estimating $E(Y)$ are the estimators $\hat{\beta}_0$ and $\hat{\beta}_1$. The variance can be shown to be

$$\sigma_{\hat{Y}}^2 = E\{[\hat{Y} - E(\hat{Y})]^2\} = \sigma^2 \left[\frac{1}{n} + \frac{(x_p - \bar{x})^2}{SS_{xx}} \right].$$

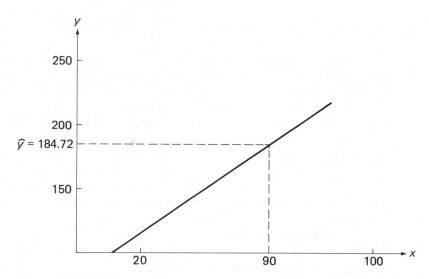

Figure 8.9   Estimated Mean Value and Predicted Individual Value of Peak Power Load, Y, for $x = 90$

In the case of predicting for a particular y value, we are trying to predict

$$Y_p = \beta_0 + \beta_1 x_p + \varepsilon_p$$

where ε_p is the error associated with the particular Y value, Y_p. Thus, the sources of prediction error are the estimators $\hat{\beta}_0$ and $\hat{\beta}_1$, *and* the error ε_p. The variance associated with ε_p is σ^2, and it can be shown that this is the additional term in the expected squared prediction error:

$$\sigma^2_{(Y-\hat{Y})} = E[(\hat{Y} - Y_p)^2] = \sigma^2 + \sigma^2_{\hat{Y}}$$

$$= \sigma^2\left[1 + \frac{1}{n} + \frac{(x_p - \bar{x})^2}{SS_{xx}}\right].$$

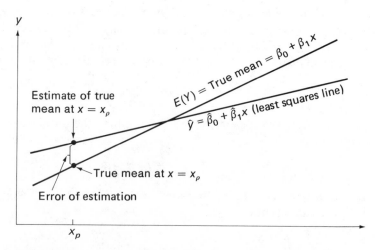

Figure 8.10   Error of Estimating the Mean Value of Y for a Given Value of x

The sampling errors associated with the estimator and predictor are summarized next. Figures 8.10 and 8.11 graphically depict the difference between the error of estimating a mean value of Y and the error of predicting a future value of Y for $x = x_p$. Note that the error of estimation is just the vertical difference between the least-squares line and the true line of means, $E(Y) = \beta_0 + \beta_1 x$. However, the error in predicting some future value of Y is the sum of two errors: the error of estimating the mean of Y, $E(Y)$, shown in Figure 8.10, plus the random error ε_p that is a component of the value Y_p to be predicted. Note that both errors will be smallest when $x_p = \bar{x}$. The farther x_p lies from the mean, the larger the errors of estimation and prediction.

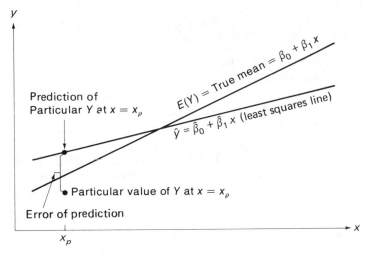

Figure 8.11   Error of Predicting a Future Value of Y for a Given Value of x

---

SAMPLING ERRORS FOR THE ESTIMATOR OF THE MEAN OF Y AND THE PREDICTOR OF AN INDIVIDUAL Y

1.   The standard deviation of the sampling distribution of the estimator $\hat{Y}$ of the mean value of Y at a fixed x is

$$\sigma_{\hat{Y}} = \sigma \sqrt{\frac{1}{n} + \frac{(x - \bar{x})^2}{SS_{xx}}},$$

where σ is the standard deviation of the random error ε.

2.   The standard deviation of the prediction error for the predictor $\hat{Y}$ of an individual Y value at a fixed x is

$$\sigma_{(Y - \hat{Y})} = \sigma \sqrt{1 + \frac{1}{n} + \frac{(x - \bar{x})^2}{SS_{xx}}},$$

where σ is the standard deviation of the random error ε.

The true value of σ will rarely be known. Thus, we estimate σ by s and calculate the estimation and prediction intervals as shown next.

A 100(1 − α) *PERCENT CONFIDENCE INTERVAL FOR THE MEAN VALUE OF y AT A FIXED x*

$$\hat{y} \pm t_{\alpha/2,n-2}(\text{Estimated standard deviation of } \hat{Y})$$

or

$$\hat{y} \pm t_{\alpha/2,n-2}s\sqrt{\frac{1}{n} + \frac{(x - \bar{x})^2}{SS_{xx}}}.$$

EXAMPLE 8.2

Find a 95% confidence interval for the mean peak power load when the maximum daily temperature is 90°F.

Solution   A 95% confidence interval for estimating the mean peak load at a high temperature of 90° is given by

$$\hat{y} \pm t_{\alpha/2,\,n-2}s\sqrt{\frac{1}{n} + \frac{(x - \bar{x})^2}{SS_{xx}}}.$$

We have previously calculated $\hat{y} = 184.72$, and $s = 16.18$, and $\bar{x} = 91.5$, and $SS_{xx} = 380.5$. With $n = 10$ and $\alpha = 0.05$, $t_{0.025,8} = 2.306$ and thus the 95% confidence interval is

$$\hat{y} \pm t_{\alpha/2,\,n-2}s\sqrt{\frac{1}{n} + \frac{(x - \bar{x})^2}{SS_{xx}}},$$

$$184.72 \pm (2.306)(16.18)\sqrt{\frac{1}{10} + \frac{(90 - 91.5)^2}{380.5}},$$

or

$$184.72 \pm 12.14.$$

Thus, we can be 95% confident that the mean peak power load is between 172.58 and 196.86 megawatts for days with a maximum temperature of 90°F.   □

A 100(1 − α) *PERCENT PREDICTION INTERVAL* FOR AN INDIVIDUAL Y AT A FIXED x*

$$\hat{y} \pm t_{\alpha/2,\,n-2}[\text{Estimated standard deviation of } (Y - \hat{Y})]$$

or

$$\hat{y} \pm t_{\alpha/2,\,n-2}s\sqrt{1 + \frac{1}{n} + \frac{(x - \bar{x})^2}{SS_{xx}}}.$$

---

* The term prediction interval is used when the interval is intended to enclose the value of a random variable. The term confidence interval is reserved for estimation of population parameters (such as the mean).

EXAMPLE 8.3

Predict the peak power load for a day during which the maximum temperature is 90°F.

Solution

Using the same values as in the previous example, we find

$$\hat{y} \pm t_{\alpha/2, n-2} s \sqrt{1 + \frac{1}{n} + \frac{(x - \bar{x})^2}{SS_{xx}}},$$

$$184.72 \pm (2.306)(16.18) \sqrt{1 + \frac{1}{10} + \frac{(90 - 91.5)^2}{380.5}},$$

or

$$184.72 \pm 39.24.$$

Thus, we are 95% confident that the peak power load will be between 145.48 and 223.96 on a particular day when the high temperature is 90°F.   □

A comparison of the confidence interval for the mean peak power load and the prediction interval for a single day's peak power load for a maximum temperature of 90°F. ($x = 90$) is illustrated in Figure 8.12. It is important to note that the prediction interval for an individual value of Y will always be wider than the corresponding confidence interval for the mean value of Y.

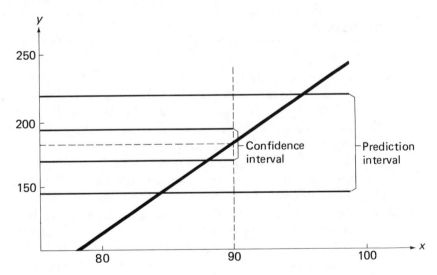

Figure 8.12   A 95% Confidence Interval for Mean Peak Power Load and a Prediction Interval for Peak Power Load When $x = 90$

Be careful not to use the least-squares prediction equation to estimate the mean value of Y or to predict a particular value of Y for values of x that fall outside the range of the values of x contained in your sample data. The model might provide a good fit to the data over the range of x values contained in the sample but a very

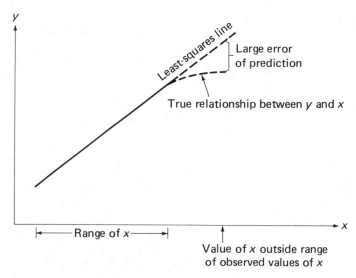

Figure 8.13   The Danger of Using a Model to Predict Outside the Range of the Sample Values of x

poor fit for values of x outside this region (see Figure 8.13). Failure to heed this warning may lead to errors of estimation and prediction that are much larger than expected.

Exercises

8.21   Refer to Exercise 8.1.
(a) Estimate the mean value of Y for $x = 2$ in a 95% confidence interval.
(b) Find a 95% prediction interval for a response, Y, at $x = 2$.

8.22   Refer to Exercise 8.3. Estimate the expected elongation for a force of 1.8, using a 90% confidence interval.

8.23   Refer to Exercise 8.4. If in 1978 the industry sales figure is 16, find a 95% prediction interval for the company sales figure. Do you see any possible difficulties with the solution to this problem?

8.24   Refer to Exercise 8.5. Estimate, in a 95% confidence interval, the mean abrasion loss for steel specimens with a Rockwell hardness measure of 75. What assumptions are necessary for your answer to be valid?

8.25   Refer again to Exercise 8.5. Predict, in a 95% prediction interval, the abrasion loss for a particular steel specimen with a Rockwell hardness measure of 75. What assumptions are necessary for your answer to be valid?

8.26   Refer to Exercise 8.6. Predict the reading on the new meter for circuit showing 16.0 on the old meter. Use a prediction coefficient of 0.90.

8.27   Refer to Exercise 8.7. Estimate, in a 90% confidence interval, the expected number of parts assembled by employees working for 12 minutes.

8.28   Refer to Exercise 8.8. Find a 95% prediction interval for a flow-through measurement corresponding to a static measurement of 21.0.

8.29   Refer to Exercise 8.3. If no force is applied, the expected elongation should be zero (that is, $\beta_0 = 0$). Construct a test of $H_0: \beta_0 = 0$ versus $H_a: \beta_0 \neq 0$ using the data of Exercise 8.3.

8.9   Conclusion

Many engineering problems involve modeling the relationship between a dependent variable, Y, and one or more independent variables. In this chapter, we have discussed the case of a single independent variable, x. The regression analysis presented here only considers the situation in which $E(Y)$ is a linear function of x, but the general steps to follow are:

Step 1.   Hypothesize the form of $E(Y)$.

Step 2.   Use the sample data to estimate unknown parameters in the model.

Step 3.   Specify the probability distribution of the random component of the model.

Step 4.   Statistically check the adequacy of the model.

Step 5.   When satisfied with the model's adequacy, use it for prediction and estimation.

In Chapter 9, we consider the situation in which there may be multiple independent variables.

Supplementary Exercises

8.30   The data in the table give the mileages per gallon obtained by a test automobile when using gasolines of varying levels of octane.

Mileage, y (miles per gallon)	Octane, x
13.0	89
13.2	93
13.0	87
13.6	90
13.3	89
13.8	95
14.1	100
14.0	98

(a) Calculate r and r^2.

(b) Do the data provide sufficient evidence to indicate a correlation between octane level and miles per gallon for the test automobile?

8.31   Two different elements, nickel and iron, can be used in bonding zircaloy components. An experiment was conducted to determine whether there is a correlation between the strengths of the bonds for the two elements. Two pairs of components were randomly selected from each of seven different batches of the zircaloy components. One pair in each batch was bonded by nickel and the other pair by iron, and the strength of the bond was determined for each pair by measuring the amount of pressure (in thousands of pounds per square inch) required to separate the bonded pair. The data from the experiment are shown below:

Batch	Nickel	Iron
1	71.3	76.2
2	71.8	73.1
3	80.3	86.9
4	77.0	82.4
5	77.4	78.5
6	79.9	88.2
7	70.1	75.1

(a) Find the correlation coefficient for the data.

(b) Find the coefficient of determination and interpret it.

(c) Is there sufficient evidence to indicate that the correlation between the strengths of the bonds of the two elements differs from 0? Use $\alpha = 0.05$.

8.32   Labor and material costs are two basic components in analyzing the cost of construction. Changes in the component costs, of course, will lead to changes in total construction costs.

Month	Construction Cost* Y	Index of All Construction Materials[†] X
January	193.2	180.0
February	193.1	181.7
March	193.6	184.1
April	195.1	185.3
May	195.6	185.7
June	198.1	185.9
July	200.9	187.7
August	202.7	189.6

* Source United States Department of Commerce, Bureau of the Census
[†] Source: United States Department of Labor, Bureau of Labor Statistics. Tables were given in Tables E-1 (p. 43) and E-2 (p. 44), respectively, in *Construction Review.* United States Department of Commerce, Oct. 1976, 22 (8).

(a) Use the data in the table to find a measure of the importance of the materials component. Do this by determining the fraction of reduction in the variability of the construction cost index that can be explained by a linear relationship between the construction cost index and the material cost index.

(b) Do the data provide sufficient evidence to indicate a nonzero correlation between Y and X?

8.33 Use the method of least squares and the sample data in the table to model the relationship between the number of items produced by a particular manufacturing process and the total variable cost involved in production. Find the coefficient of determination and explain its significance in the context of this problem.

Total Output y	Total Variable Cost x dollars
10	10
15	12
20	20
20	21
25	22
30	20
30	19

8.34 Does a linear relationship exist between the Consumer Price Index (CPI) and the Dow Jones Industrial Average (DJA)? A random sample of 10 months selected from the past several years produced the following corresponding DJA and CPI data:

DJA y	CPI x
660	13.0
638	14.2
639	13.7
597	15.1
702	12.6
650	13.8
579	15.7
570	16.0
725	11.3
738	10.4

(a) Find the least-squares line relating the DJA, y, to the CPI, x.
(b) Do the data provide sufficient evidence to indicate that x contributes information for the prediction of Y? Test using $\alpha = 0.05$.
(c) Find a 95% confidence interval for β_1 and interpret your result.
(d) Suppose you want to estimate the value of the DJA when the CPI is at 15.0. Should you calculate a 95% prediction interval for a particular value of the DJA, or a 95% confidence interval for the mean value of the DJA? Explain the difference.
(e) Calculate both intervals considered in part d when the CPI is 15.0.

8.35   Will the national 55 mile per hour highway speed limit provide a substantial savings in fuel? To investigate the relationship between automobile gasoline consumption and driving speed, a small economy car was driven twice over the same stretch of an interstate freeway at each of six different speeds. The numbers of miles per gallon measured for each of the twelve trips are shown below:

Miles per hour	50	55	60	65	70	75
Miles per gallon	34.8, 33.6	34.6, 34.1	32.8, 31.9	32.6, 30.0	31.6, 31.8	30.9, 31.7

(a) Fit a least-squares line to the data.
(b) Is there sufficient evidence to conclude there is a linear relationship between speed and gasoline consumption?
(c) Construct a 90% confidence interval for β_1.
(d) Construct a 95% confidence interval for miles per gallon when the speed is 72 miles per hour.
(e) Construct a 95% prediction interval for miles per gallon when the speed is 58 miles per hour.

8.36   At temperatures approaching absolute zero (273 degrees below zero Celsius), helium exhibits traits that defy many laws of conventional physics. An experiment has been conducted with helium in solid form at various temperatures near absolute zero. The solid helium is placed in a dilution refrigerator along with a solid impure substance, and the fraction (in weight) of the impurity passing through the solid helium is recorded. (The phenomenon of solids passing directly through solids is known as *quantum tunnelling*.) The data are given in the table.

Temperature x °C	Proportion of Impurity Passing Through Helium y
− 262.0	.315
− 265.0	.202
− 256.0	.204
− 267.0	.620
− 270.0	.715
− 272.0	.935
− 272.4	.957
− 272.7	.906
− 272.8	.985
− 272.9	.987

(a) Fit a least squares line to the data.
(b) Test the null hypothesis, $H_0: \beta_1 = 0$, against the alternative hypothesis, $H_a: \beta_1 < 0$, at the $\alpha = 0.01$ level of significance.

(c) Compute r^2 and interpret your results.

(d) Find a 95% prediction interval for the percentage of the solid impurity passing through solid helium at $-273°C$. (Note that this value of x is outside the experimental region, where use of the model for prediction may be dangerous.)

8.37 The data in the table were collected to calibrate a new instrument for measuring interocular pressure. The interocular pressure for each of ten glaucoma patients was measured by the new instrument and by a standard, reliable, but more time-consuming method.

Patient	Reliable Method x	New Instrument y
1	20.2	20.0
2	16.7	17.1
3	17.1	17.2
4	26.3	25.1
5	22.2	22.0
6	21.8	22.1
7	19.1	18.9
8	22.9	22.2
9	23.5	24.0
10	17.0	18.1

(a) Fit a least-squares line to the data.

(b) Calculate r and r^2. Interpret each of these qualities.

(c) Predict the pressure measured by the new instrument when the reliable method gives a reading of 20.0. Use a 90% prediction interval.

8.38 A study was conducted to determine whether there is a linear relationship between the breaking strength, y, of wooden beams and the specific gravity, x, of the wood. Ten randomly selected beams of the same cross-sectional dimensions were stressed until they broke. The breaking strengths and the density of the wood are shown below for each of the ten beams:

Beam	Specific Gravity x	Strength y
1	0.499	11.14
2	0.558	12.74
3	0.604	13.13
4	0.441	11.51
5	0.550	12.38
6	0.528	12.60
7	0.418	11.13
8	0.480	11.70
9	0.406	11.02
10	0.467	11.41

(a) Fit the model $Y = \beta_0 + \beta_1 x + \varepsilon$.

(b) Test $H_0 : \beta_1 = 0$ against the alternative hypothesis, $H_a : \beta_1 \neq 0$.

(c) Estimate the mean strength for beams with specific gravity 0.590 using a 90% confidence interval.

8.39   The octane number, y, of refined petroleum is related to the temperature, x, of the refining process, but is also related to the particle size of the catalyst. An experiment with a small particle catalyst gave a fitted least-squares line of

$$\hat{y} = 9.360 + 0.115x$$

with $n = 31$ and $V(\hat{\beta}_1) = (0.0225)^2$. An independent experiment with a large particle catalyst gave

$$\hat{y} = 4.265 + 0.190x$$

with $n = 11$ and $V(\hat{\beta}_1) = (0.0202)^2$. (*Source*: Gweyson and Cheasley, *Petroleum Refiner*, August, 1959, p. 135)

(a) Test the hypotheses that the slopes are significantly different from zero, with each test at the 5% significance level.

(b) Test, at the 5% level, that the two types of catalyst produce the same slope in the relationship between octane number and temperature.

Multiple Regression Analysis

About This Chapter

Following up on the work of Chapter 8, we now proceed to build models in which the mean of one variable can be written as a linear function of numerous related variables. For example, the average amount of energy required to heat a house depends not only on the air temperature but also on the size of the house, the amount of insulation, and the type of heating unit, among other things. We will use *multiple regression* models for estimating means and for predicting future values of key variables under study.

Contents

Most practical applications of regression analysis utilize models that are more complex than the simple straight-line model. For example, a realistic probabilistic model for a power plant's peak power load would include more than just the daily high temperature. Factors such as humidity, day of the week, and season are a few of the many variables that might be related to peak load. Thus, we would want to incorporate these and other potentially important independent variables into the model in order to make accurate predictions.

Probabilistic models that include terms involving x^2, x^3 (or higher-order terms), or more than one independent variable are called *multiple regression models*. The general form of these models is

$$Y = \beta_0 + \beta_1 x_1 + \beta_2 x_2 + \cdots + \beta_k x_k + \varepsilon.$$

The dependent variable Y is now written as a function of k independent variables, $x_1, x_2, \ldots, x_k$. The random error term is added to allow for deviation between the deterministic part of the model, $\beta_0 + \beta_1 x_1 + \cdots + \beta_k x_k$, and the value of the dependent variable, Y. The random component makes the model probabilistic rather than deterministic. The value of the coefficient β_i determines the contribution of the independent variable x_i, and β_0 is the Y-intercept. The coefficients β_0, $\beta_1, \ldots, \beta_k$ will usually be unknown, since they represent population parameters.

At first glance it might appear that the regression model shown above would not allow for anything other than straight-line relationships between Y and the independent variables, but this is not true. Actually, $x_1, x_2, \ldots, x_k$ can be functions of variables as long as the functions do not contain unknown parameters. For example, the yield, Y, of a chemical process could be a function of the independent variables

$$x_1 = \text{temperature at which the reaction takes place}$$

$$x_2 = (\text{temperature})^2 = x_1^2$$

$$x_3 = \text{pressure at which the reaction takes place.}$$

We might hypothesize the model

$$E(Y) = \beta_0 + \beta_1 x_1 + \beta_2 x_1^2 + \beta_3 x_3.$$

Although this model contains a second order (or "quadratic") term, x_1^2, and therefore is curvilinear, the model is still *linear in the unknown parameters*, β_0, β_1, β_2 and β_3. Multiple regression models that are linear in the unknown parameters (the β's) are called *linear models*, even though they may contain nonlinear independent variables.

The same steps we followed in developing a straight-line model are applicable to the multiple regression model.

Step 1.   First, hypothesize the form of the model. This involves the choice of the independent variables to be included in the model.

Step 2.   Next, estimate the unknown parameters $\beta_0, \beta_1, \ldots, \beta_k$.

Step 3.   Then, specify the probability distribution of the random error component, ε, and estimate its variance, σ^2.

Step 4.   The fourth step is to check the adequacy of the model.

Step 5.   Finally, use the fitted model to estimate the mean value of Y or to predict a particular value of Y for given values of the independent variables.

First we consider steps 2–5, leaving the more difficult problem of model construction until last.

9.2   *Fitting the Model: The Least Squares Approach*

The method of fitting multiple regression models is identical to that of fitting the simple straight-line model: the method of least squares. That is, we choose the estimated model

$$\hat{y} = \hat{\beta}_0 + \hat{\beta}_1 x_1 + \cdots + \hat{\beta}_k x_k$$

that minimizes

$$\text{SSE} = \sum_{i=1}^{n} (y_i - \hat{y})^2.$$

As in the case of the simple linear model, the sample estimates $\hat{\beta}_0, \hat{\beta}_1, \ldots, \hat{\beta}_k$ are obtained as a solution of a set of simultaneous linear equations.

The primary difference between fitting the simple and multiple regression models is computational difficulty. The $(k + 1)$ simultaneous linear equations that must be solved to find the $(k + 1)$ estimated coefficients $\hat{\beta}_0, \hat{\beta}_1, \ldots, \hat{\beta}_k$ are difficult (sometimes nearly impossible) to solve with a pocket or desk calculator. Consequently, we resort to the use of computers. Many computer packages have been developed to fit a multiple regression model using the method of least squares. We will present output from one of the more popular computer packages instead of presenting the tedious hand calculations required to fit the models. The computer output we will use is from the Statistical Analysis System (SAS). Since the regression output of the SAS is similar to that of most other package regression programs, you should have little trouble interpreting regression output from other packages. We demonstrate the SAS regression procedure with the example below.

Recall the peak power load data from Chapter 8, repeated in Table 9.1. We previously used a straight-line model to describe the peak power load daily high temperature relationship. Now suppose we want to hypothesize a curvilinear relationship:

$$Y = \beta_0 + \beta_1 x + \beta_2 x^2 + \varepsilon.$$

Daily High Temperature (x)	Peak Power Load (Y)
95	214
82	152
90	156
81	129
99	254
100	266
93	210
95	204
93	213
87	150

Table 9.1   Peak   Power
Load Data

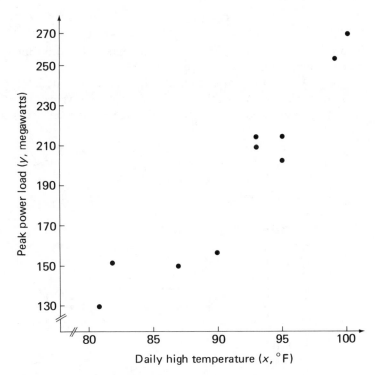

Figure 9.1   Scattergram of Power Load Data, Table 9.1

Note that the scattergram in Figure 9.1 provides some support for the inclusion of the term $\beta_2 x^2$ in the model, since there appears to be some curvature present in the relationship.

Part of the output from the SAS multiple regression routine for the peak power load data is reproduced in Figure 9.2. The least-square estimates of the β parameters appear in the column labeled ESTIMATE. You can see that $\hat{\beta}_0 = 1784.18$, $\hat{\beta}_1 = -42.386$, and $\hat{\beta}_2 = 0.272$. Therefore, the equation that minimizes the

SOURCE	DF	SUM OF SQUARES	MEAN SQUARE	F VALUE	PR > F
MODEL	2	18088.53450617	9044.26725399	53.88	0.0001
ERROR	7	1175.06549383	167.86649912	R-SQUARE	STD DEV
CORRECTED TOTAL	9	19263.60000000		0.939001	12.95633046

PARAMETER	ESTIMATE	T FOR H0: PARAMETER = 0	PR > |T|	STD ERROR OF ESTIMATE
INTERCEPT	1784.18832525	1.89	0.1007	944.12303144
X	−42.38624074	−2.02	0.0833	21.00078538
X * X	0.27216065	2.34	0.0519	0.11634003

Figure 9.2   Computer Output for the Peak Power Load Example

SSE for the data is

$$\hat{y} = 1784.188 - 42.386x + 0.272x^2.$$

The value of the SSE, 1175.065, also appears in the printout. We will discuss the rest of the printout as the chapter progresses.

Note that the graph of the multiple regression model (Figure 9.3) provides a good fit to the data of Table 9.1. However, before we can more formally measure the utility of the model, we need to estimate the variance of the error component, ε.

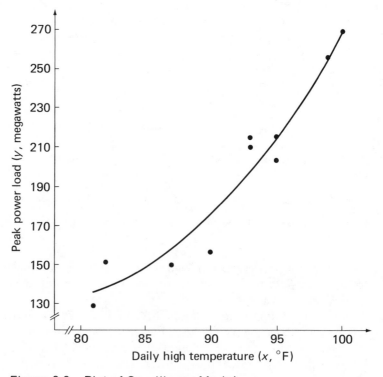

Figure 9.3   Plot of Curvilinear Model

9.3   *Estimation of σ^2, the Variance of ε*

The specification of the probability distribution of the random error component, ε, of the multiple regression model follows the same general outline as for the straight-line model. We assume that ε is normally distributed with mean zero and constant variance σ^2 for any set of values for the independent variables $x_1, x_2, \ldots, x_k$. Furthermore, the errors are assumed to be independent. Given these assumptions, the remaining task in specifying the probability distribution of ε is to estimate σ^2.

For example, in the quadratic model describing peak power load as a function of daily high temperature, we found a minimum SSE = 1175.065. Now we want to use this quantity to estimate the variance of ε. Recall that the estimator for the straight-line model was $s^2 = \text{SSE}/(n - 2)$ and note that the denominator is $n - $ (number of estimated β parameters), which is $n - (2)$ in the straight-line model. Since we must estimate one more parameter, β_2, for the quadratic model $Y = \beta_0 + \beta_1 x + \beta_2 x^2 + \varepsilon$, the estimate of σ^2 is

$$s^2 = \frac{\text{SSE}}{n - 3}.$$

That is, the denominator becomes $(n - 3)$ because there are now three β parameters in the model.

The numerical estimate for this example is

$$s^2 = \frac{\text{SSE}}{10 - 3} = \frac{1175.065}{7} = 167.87$$

where s^2 is called the mean square for error, or MSE. This estimate of σ^2 is shown in Figure 9.2 in the column titled MEAN SQUARE and the row titled ERROR.

For the general multiple regression model

$$Y = \beta_0 + \beta_1 x_1 + \beta_2 x_2 + \cdots + \beta_k x_k + \varepsilon$$

we must estimate the $(k + 1)$ parameters $\beta_0, \beta_1, \beta_2, \ldots, \beta_k$. Thus, the estimator of σ^2 is the SSE divided by the quantity $n - $ (number of estimated β parameters).

ESTIMATOR OF σ^2 FOR MULTIPLE REGRESSION MODEL WITH k INDEPENDENT VARIABLES

$$\text{MSE} = \frac{\text{SSE}}{n - (\text{Number of estimated } \beta \text{ parameters})}$$

$$= \frac{\text{SSE}}{n - (k + 1)}.$$

We use the estimator of σ^2 both to check the adequacy of the model (Sections 9.4 and 9.5) and to provide a measure of the reliability of predictors and estimates when the model is used for those purposes (Section 9.6). Thus, you can see that the estimation of σ^2 plays an important part in the development of a regression model.

9.4   *A Test of Model Adequacy: The Coefficient of Determination*

To find a statistic that measures how well a multiple regression model fits a set of data, we use the multiple regression equivalent of r^2, the coefficient of determination for the straight-line model (Chapter 8). Thus, we define the *multiple coefficient of determination*, R^2, as

$$R^2 = 1 - \frac{\sum\limits_{i=1}^{n} (y_i - \hat{y}_i)^2}{\sum\limits_{i=1}^{n} (y_i - \bar{y})^2} = 1 - \frac{\text{SSE}}{\text{SS}_{yy}},$$

where $\hat{y}_i$ is the predicted value of Y_i for the model. Just as for the simple linear model, R^2 represents the fraction of the sample variation of the y values (measured by SS_{yy}) that is explained by the least squares prediction equation. Thus, $R^2 = 0$ implies a complete lack of fit of the model to the data, and $R^2 = 1$ implies a perfect fit, with the model passing through every data point. In general, the larger the value of R^2, the better the model fits the data.

To illustrate, the value of $R^2 = 0.939$ for the peak power load data is indicated on Figure 9.2. This value of R^2 implies that using the independent variable daily high temperature in a quadratic model results in a 93.9% reduction in the total *sample* variation (measured by SS_{yy}) of peak power load, Y. Thus, R^2 is a sample statistic that tells us how well the model fits the data, and thereby represents a measure of the adequacy of the model.

The fact that R^2 is a sample statistic implies that it can be used to make inferences about the utility of the entire model for predicting the population of y values at each setting of the independent variables. In particular, for the peak power load data, the test

$$H_0: \beta_1 = \beta_2 = 0$$

H_a: at least one of the coefficients is nonzero

would formally test the global utility of the model. The test statistic used to test this null hypothesis is

$$\text{Test statistic:} \quad F = \frac{R^2/k}{(1 - R^2)/[n - (k + 1)]},$$

where n is the number of data points and k is the number of parameters in the model not including β_0. The test statistic F will have the F probability distribution with k degrees of freedom in the numerator and $[n - (k + 1)]$ degrees of freedom in the denominator. The tail values of the F distribution are given in tables in the Appendix.

The F test statistic becomes large as the coefficient of determination, R^2, becomes large. To determine how large F must be before we can conclude at a given significance level that the model is useful for predicting Y, we set up the rejection region as follows:

$$\text{Rejection region:}\quad F > F^k_{n-(k+1)}(\alpha).$$

For the electrical usage example ($n = 10, k = 2, n - (k + 1) = 7$, and $\alpha = 0.05$), we reject $H_0 : \beta_1 = \beta_2 = 0$ if

$$F > F^2_7(0.05)$$

or

$$F > 4.74.$$

From the computer printout (Figure 9.2), we find that the computed F is 53.88. Since this value greatly exceeds the tabulated value of 4.74, we conclude that at least one of the model coefficients β_1 and β_2 is nonzero. Therefore, this global F test indicates that the quadratic model $Y = \beta_0 + \beta_1 x + \beta_2 x^2 + \varepsilon$ is useful for predicting peak load.

TESTING THE UTILITY OF A MULTIPLE REGRESSION MODEL: THE GLOBAL F TEST

$$H_0 : \beta_1 = \beta_2 = \cdots = \beta_k = 0$$

H_a: At least one of the β parameters does not equal zero

$$\text{Test statistic:}\quad F = \frac{R^2/k}{(1 - R^2)/[n - (k + 1)]}$$

Assumptions: See Section 8.4 for the four assumptions about the random component ε.

$$\text{Rejection region:}\quad F > F^k_{n-(k+1)}(\alpha)$$

where

n = number of data points

k = number of β parameters in the model, excluding β_0.

EXAMPLE 9.1

A study is conducted to determine the effects of company size and presence or absence of a safety program on the number of work-hours lost due to work-related accidents. A total of 40 companies are selected for the study, 20 randomly chosen from companies having no active safety programs, and the other 20 from companies who have enacted active safety programs. Each company is monitored for a 1-year period, and the following model is proposed:

$$E(Y) = \beta_0 + \beta_1 x_1 + \beta_2 x_2$$

where

$$Y = \text{lost work-hours over the 1-year study period}$$

$$x_1 = \text{number of employees}$$

$$x_2 = \begin{cases} 1 & \text{if an active safety program is used} \\ 0 & \text{if no active safety program is used.} \end{cases}$$

The variable x_2 is called a *dummy* or *indicator variable*. Dummy variables are used to represent categorical or qualitative independent variables, like "presence or absence of a safety program." Note that the coefficient β_2 of the dummy variable x_2 represents the expected difference in lost work-hours between companies with safety programs and those without safety programs, assuming the companies have the same number of employees. For example, the expected number of lost work-hours for a company with 500 employees and no safety program is, according to the model,

$$E(Y) = \beta_0 + \beta_1(500) + \beta_2(0)$$
$$= \beta_0 + 500\beta_1$$

while the expected lost work-hours for a company with 500 employees and an active safety program is

$$E(Y) = \beta_0 + \beta_1(500) + \beta_2(1)$$
$$= \beta_0 + 500\beta_1 + \beta_2.$$

You can see that the difference in the means is β_2. Thus, the use of the dummy variable allows us to assess the effect of a qualitative variable on the mean response.
    The data are shown in Table 9.2.

(a)   Test the utility of the model by testing $H_0: \beta_1 = \beta_2 = 0$.
(b)   Give and interpret the least-squares coefficients $\hat{\beta}_1$ and $\hat{\beta}_2$.

Solution   (a) The computer printout corresponding to the least-squares fit of the model

$$Y = \beta_0 + \beta_1 x_1 + \beta_2 x_2 + \varepsilon$$

is shown in Figure 9.4. We want to use this information to test

$$H_0: \beta_1 = \beta_2 = 0$$

H_a: At least one β is non-zero, that is,
        the model is useful for predicting Y.

Table 9.2

Number of Employees (x_1)	Safety Program (x_2) $\begin{pmatrix} x_2 = 0, \text{no program} \\ x_2 = 1, \text{active program} \end{pmatrix}$	Lost Hours Due to Accidents (y) (Annually in thousands of hours)
6490	0	121
7244	0	169
7943	0	172
6478	0	116
3138	0	53
8747	0	177
2020	0	31
4090	0	94
3230	0	72
8786	0	171
1986	0	23
9653	0	177
9429	0	178
2782	0	65
8444	0	146
6316	0	129
2363	0	40
7915	0	167
6928	0	115
5526	0	123
3077	1	44
6600	1	73
2732	1	8
7014	1	90
8321	1	71
2422	1	37
9581	1	111
9326	1	89
6818	1	72
4831	1	35
9630	1	86
2905	1	40
6308	1	44
1908	1	36
8542	1	78
4750	1	47
6056	1	56
7052	1	75
7794	1	46
1701	1	6

SOURCE	DF	SUM OF SQUARES	MEAN SQUARE	F VALUE	PR > F
MODEL	2	90081.33870451	45040.66935226	113.14	0.0001
ERROR	37	14729.43629549	398.09287285	R-SQUARE	STD DEV
CORRECTED TOTAL	39	104810.77500000		0.859466	19.95226486

PARAMETER	ESTIMATE	T FOR H0: PARAMETER = 0	PR > |T|	STD ERROR OF ESTIMATE
INTERCEPT	31.64928263	3.70	0.0007	8.55394667
X1	0.01427173	11.69	0.0001	0.00122109
X2	−58.20151703	−9.22	0.0001	6.31085100

Figure 9.4 Computer Printout of Least-Squares Fit for the Safety Program Example

Test statistic:

$$F = \frac{R^2/k}{(1 - R^2)/[n - (k + 1)]} = \frac{R^2/2}{(1 - R^2)/37}$$

Rejection region: For $\alpha = 0.05$,

$$F > F^2_{37}(0.05) = 3.25.$$

The value of R^2, shaded on the printout, is 0.86. Then

$$F = \frac{0.86/2}{(1 - 0.86)/37} = 113.6.$$

Thus, we can be very confident that this model contributes information for the prediction of lost work-hours, since $F = 113.6$ greatly exceeds the tabled value, 3.25. The F value is also given on the printout (shaded), so we do not have to perform the calculation. Also, using the printout value helps to avoid rounding errors; note the difference between our calculated F value and the printout value.

We should be careful not to be too excited about this very large F value, since we have only concluded that the model contributes *some* information about Y. The width of the prediction intervals and confidence intervals are better measures of the amount of information the model provides about Y. Note that the standard deviation of this model (shaded on the printout) is 19.95. Since most (usually 90% or more) of the values of Y will fall within two standard deviations of the predicted value, we have the notion that the model predictions will usually be accurate to within about 40 thousand hours. We will make these notions more precise in Section 9.5, but the standard deviation helps us obtain a preliminary idea of the amount of information the model contains about Y.

(b) The estimated values of β_1 and β_2 are shown shaded on the printout, Figure 9.4. The least-squares model is

$$\hat{y} = 31.649 + 0.0143x_1 - 58.202x_2.$$

The coefficient $\hat{\beta}_1 = 0.0143$ represents the estimated slope of the number of lost hours (in thousands) versus number of employees. In other words, we estimate that, on average, each employee loses 14.3 work-hours (0.0143 thousand hours) annually due to accidents. Note that this slope applies both to plants with and plants without safety programs. We will show how to construct models that allow the slopes to differ later in this chapter.

The coefficient $\hat{\beta}_2 = -58.2$ is *not* a slope, because it is the coefficient of the dummy variable x_2. Instead, $\hat{\beta}_2$ represents the estimated mean change in lost hours between plants with no safety programs ($x_2 = 0$) and plants with safety programs ($x_2 = 1$), assuming both plants have the same number of employees. Our estimate indicates that an average of 58.2 thousand fewer work-hours are lost by plants with safety programs than by those without them. □

9.5 *Estimating and Testing Hypotheses About Individual β Parameters*

After determining that the model is useful by testing and rejecting $H_0: \beta_1 = \beta_2 = \cdots \beta_k = 0$, we may be interested in making inferences about particular β parameters that have practical significance. For example, in the peak power load example we fit the model

$$E(Y) = \beta_0 + \beta_1 x + \beta_2 x^2,$$

where Y is the peak load and x is the daily high temperature. A test of particular interest would be

$H_0: \beta_2 = 0$ (no quadratic relationship exists)

$H_a: \beta_2 > 0$ (the peak power load increases at an increasing rate as the daily high temperature increases).

A test of this hypothesis can be performed using a Student's t test. The t test utilizes a test statistic analogous to that used to make inferences about the slope of the simple straight-line model (Section 8.5). The t statistic is formed by dividing the sample estimate $\hat{\beta}_2$ of the population coefficient β_2 by the estimated standard deviation of the repeated sampling distribution of $\hat{\beta}_2$:

$$\text{Test statistic:} \quad t = \frac{\hat{\beta}_2}{s_{\hat{\beta}_2}}.$$

We use the symbol $s_{\hat{\beta}_2}$ to represent the estimated standard deviation of $\hat{\beta}_2$. Most computer packages list the estimated standard deviation $s_{\hat{\beta}_i}$ for each of the estimated model coefficients β_i. In addition, they usually give the calculated t values for each coefficient in the model.

The rejection region for the test is found in exactly the same way as the rejection regions for the t tests in previous chapters. That is, we consult the t-table in the Appendix to obtain an upper-tail value of t. This is a value t_α such that $P(t > t_\alpha) = \alpha$. Then we can use this value to construct rejection regions for either one- or two-tailed tests. To illustrate, in the power load example, the error degrees

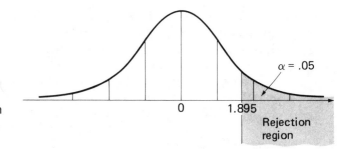

Figure 9.5   Rejection
Region for Test of
$H_0: \beta_2 = 0$

of freedom is $(n - 3) = 7$, the denominator of the estimate of σ^2. Then the rejection region (shown in Figure 9.5) for a one-tailed test with $\alpha = 0.05$ is

$$\text{Rejection region:}\quad t > t_{\alpha, n-3}$$

$$t > 1.895.$$

In Figure 9.6, we again show a portion of the computer printout for the peak power load example.

The estimated standard deviations for the model coefficient appear under the column STD ERROR OF ESTIMATE. The t statistic for testing the null hypothesis that the true coefficients are equal to zero appear under the column headed T FOR H0: PARAMETER $= 0$. The t value corresponding to the test of the null hypothesis $H_0: \beta_2 = 0$ is the last one in the column, that is, $t = 2.34$. Since this value is greater than 1.895, we conclude that the quadratic term $\beta_2 x^2$ makes a contribution to the predicted value of peak power load.

The SAS printout shown in Figure 9.6 also lists the two-tailed significance levels for each t value. These values appear under the column headed PR $> |T|$. The significance level 0.0519 corresponds to the quadratic term, and this implies that we would reject $H_0: \beta_2 = 0$ in favor of $H_a: \beta_2 \neq 0$ at any α level larger than 0.0519. Since our alternative was one-sided, $H_a: \beta_2 > 0$, the significance level is half that given in the printout, that is, $\frac{1}{2}(0.0519) = 0.02595$. Thus, there is evidence at the $\alpha = 0.05$ level that the peak power load increases more quickly per unit increase in daily high temperature for high temperature than for low ones.

SOURCE	DF	SUM OF SQUARES	MEAN SQUARE	F VALUE	PR > F
MODEL	2	18088.53450617	9044.26725309	53.88	0.0001
ERROR	7	1175.06549383	167.86649912	R-SQUARE	STD DEV
CORRECTED TOTAL	9	19263.60000000		0.939001	12.95633046

PARAMETER	ESTIMATE	T FOR H0: PARAMETER = 0	PR > |T|	STD ERROR OF ESTIMATE
INTERCEPT	1784.18832525	1.89	0.1227	944.12303144
X	−42.38624074	−2.02	0.0933	21.00078538
X * X	0.27216065	2.34	0.0519	0.11634003

Figure 9.6   Computer Printout for the Peak Power Load Example

We can also form a confidence interval for the parameter β_2 as follows:

$$\hat{\beta}_2 \pm t_{\alpha/2,\, n-3} s_{\hat{\beta}_2} = 0.272 \pm (1.895)(0.116)$$

or, $(0.052, 0.492)$. Note that the t value 1.895 corresponds to $\alpha/2 = 0.05$ and $(n - 3) = 7$ df. This interval constitutes a 90% confidence interval for β_2 and represents an estimate of the rate of curvature in mean peak power load as the daily high temperature increases. Note that all values in the interval are positive, reconfirming the conclusion of our test.

Testing an hypothesis about a single β parameter that appears in any multiple regression model is accomplished in exactly the same manner as described for the quadratic electrical usage model. The form of that test is shown here.

TEST OF AN INDIVIDUAL PARAMETER COEFFICIENT IN THE MULTIPLE REGRESSION MODEL

One-tailed test	Two-tailed test
$H_0: \beta_i = 0$	$H: \beta_i = 0$
$H_a: \beta_i < 0$ (or $H_a: \beta_i > 0$)	$H_a: \beta_i \neq 0$

Test statistic: Test statistic:

$$t = \frac{\hat{\beta}_i}{s_{\hat{\beta}_i}} \qquad\qquad t = \frac{\hat{\beta}_i}{s_{\hat{\beta}_i}}$$

Rejection region: Rejection region:

$$t < -t_{\alpha,\, n-(k+1)} \qquad\qquad t < -t_{\alpha/2,\, n-(k+1)}$$

(or $t > t_{\alpha,\, n-(k+1)}$ or

when $H_a: \beta_i > 0$)

$$t > t_{\alpha/2,\, n-(k+1)}$$

where

n = number of observations

k = number of β parameters in the model, excluding β_0.

Assumptions: See Section 8.4 for the assumptions about the probability distribution for the random error component ε.

If all the tests of model utility indicate that the model is useful for predicting Y, can we conclude that the best prediction model has been found? Unfortunately, we cannot. There is no way of knowing (without further analysis) whether the addition of other independent variables will improve the utility of the model, as Example 9.1 indicates.

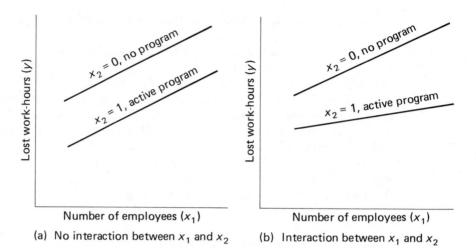

Figure 9.7   Examples of No Interaction and Interaction Models

EXAMPLE 9.2

Refer to Example 9.1 in which we modeled a plant's lost work-hours as a function of number of employees and the presence or absence of a safety program. Suppose a safety engineer believes that safety programs tend to help larger companies even more than smaller ones. Thus, instead of a relationship like that shown in Figure 9.7(a), in which the rate of increase in mean lost work-hours per employee is the same for companies with and without safety programs, the engineers believes that the relationship is like that shown in Figure 9.7(b). Note that although the mean number of lost work-hours is smaller for companies with safety programs no matter how many employees the company has, the magnitude of the difference becomes greater as the number of employees increases. When the slope of the relationship between $E(Y)$ and one independent variable (x_1) depends on the value of a second independent variable (x_2), as is the case here, we say that x_1 and x_2 *interact*. The model for mean lost work-hours that includes interaction is written

$$E(Y) = \beta_0 + \beta_1 x_1 + \beta_2 x_2 + \beta_3 x_1 x_1.$$

Note that the increase in mean lost work-hours, $E(Y)$, for each person increase in number of employees, x_1, is no longer given by the constant β_1, but is now $\beta_1 + \beta_3 x_2$. That is, the amount that $E(Y)$ increases for each 1-unit increase in x_1 is dependent on whether the company has a safety program. Thus, the two variables x_1 and x_2 interact to affect Y.

The forty data points listed in Table 9.2 were used to fit the model with interaction. A portion of the computer printout is shown in Figure 9.8. Test the hypothesis that the effect of safety programs on mean lost work-hours is greater for larger companies.

Solution   The interaction model is

$$E(Y) = \beta_0 + \beta_1 x_1 + \beta_2 x_2 + \beta_3 x_1 x_2$$

SOURCE	DF	SUM OF SQUARES	MEAN SQUARE	F VALUE	PR > F
MODEL	3	97768.02245857	32589.34081952	166.58	0.0001
ERROR	36	7042.75254143	195.63201504		
CORRECTED TOTAL	39	104810.77500000		R-SQUARE	STD DEV
				0.932805	13.98685151

PARAMETER	ESTIMATE	T FOR H0: PARAMETER = 0	PR > |T|	STD ERROR OF ESTIMATE
INTERCEPT	−0.73740471	−0.09	0.9263	7.91534430
X1	0.01969038	16.19	0.0001	0.00121656
X2	5.36521029	0.48	0.6307	11.06397237
X1 * X2	−0.01073185	−6.27	0.0001	0.00171208

Figure 9.8   Computer Printout for the Safety Program Example

so that the slope of $E(Y)$ versus x_1 is β_1 for companies with no safety programs and $\beta_1 + \beta_3$ for those with safety programs. Our research hypothesis is that the slope is smaller for companies with safety programs, so we will test

$$H_0: \beta_3 = 0 \qquad H_a: \beta_3 < 0$$

$$\text{Test statistic:} \quad t = \frac{\hat{\beta}_3}{s_{\hat{\beta}_3}}$$

Rejection region: for $\alpha = 0.05$,
$$t < -t_{0.05, \, n-(k+1)}, \quad \text{or} \quad t < -t_{0.05, \, 36} = -1.645.$$

The t value corresponding to the test for β_3 is indicated in Figure 9.8. The value, $t = -6.27$, is less than -1.645 and therefore falls in the rejection region. Thus, the safety engineer can conclude that the larger the company, the greater the benefit of the safety program in terms of reducing the mean number of lost work-hours.   □

Exercises

9.1   Suppose that you fit the model

$$Y = \beta_0 + \beta_1 x_1 + \beta_2 x_2 + \beta_3 x_1 x_2 + \beta_4 x_1^2 + \beta_5 x_2^2 + \varepsilon$$

to $n = 30$ data points and that

$$\text{SSE} = 0.37 \qquad R^2 = 0.89$$

(a) Do the values of SSE and R^2 suggest that the model provides a good fit to the data? Explain.

(b) Is the model of any use in predicting y? Test the null hypothesis that

$$E(Y) = \beta_0,$$

that is,

$$H_0 : \beta_1 = \beta_2 = \cdots = \beta_5 = 0$$

against the alternative hypothesis that

H_a: At least one of the parameters $\beta_1, \beta_2, \ldots, \beta_5$ is nonzero.

Use $\alpha = 0.05$.

9.2   In hopes of increasing the company's share of the fine food market, researchers for a meat-processing firm that prepares meats for exclusive restaurants are working to improve the quality of its hickory-smoked hams. One of their studies concerns the effect of time spent in the smokehouse on the flavor of the ham. Hams that were in the smokehouse for varying amounts of time were each subjected to a taste test by a panel of ten food experts. The following model was thought to be appropriate by the researchers:

$$Y = \beta_0 + \beta_1 t + \beta_2 t^2 + \varepsilon$$

where

Y = Mean of the taste scores for the ten experts

t = Time in the smokehouse (hours)

Assume the least squares model estimated using a sample of twenty hams is

$$\hat{y} = 20.3 + 5.2t - 0.0025t^2$$

and that $s_{\hat{\beta}_2} = 0.0011$. The coefficient of determination is $R^2 = 0.79$.
(a) Is there evidence to indicate that the overall model is useful? Test at $\alpha = 0.05$.
(b) Is there evidence to indicate the quadratic term is important in this model? Test at $\alpha = 0.05$.

9.3   Because the coefficient of determination R^2 always increases when a new independent variable is added to the model, it is tempting to include many variables in a model to force R^2 to be near 1. However, doing so reduces the degrees of freedom available for estimating σ^2, which adversely affects our ability to make reliable inferences. As an example, suppose you want to use eighteen economic indicators to predict next year's GNP. You fit the model

$$Y = \beta_0 + \beta_1 x_1 + \beta_2 x_2 + \cdots + \beta_{17} x_{17} + \beta_{18} x_{18} + \varepsilon$$

where Y = GNP and $x_1, x_2, \ldots, x_{18}$ are indicators. Only 20 years of data ($n = 20$) are used to fit the model, and you obtain $R^2 = 0.95$. Test to see whether this impressive looking R is large enough for you to infer that this model is useful, that is, that at least one term in the model is important for predicting GNP. Use $\alpha = 0.05$.

9.4 A utility company of a major city gave the average utility bills listed in the table at the top of page 356 for a standard-size home during the last year.

(a) Plot the points in a scattergram.

(b) Use the methods of Chapter 11 to fit the model

$$Y = \beta_0 + \beta_1 x + \varepsilon.$$

What do you conclude about the utility of this model?

(c) Hypothesize another model that might better describe the relationship between the average utility bill and average temperature. If you have access to a computer package, fit the model and test its utility.

9.5 To project personnel needs for the Christmas shopping season, a department store wants to project sales for the season. The sales for the previous Christmas season are an indication of what to expect for the current season. However, the projection should also reflect the current economic environment by taking into consideration sales for a more recent period. The following model might be appropriate:

$$y = \beta_0 + \beta_1 x_1 + \beta_2 x_2 + \varepsilon$$

where

$$x_1 = \text{Previous Christmas sales}$$

$$x_2 = \text{Sales for August of current year}$$

$$y = \text{Sales for upcoming Christmas}$$

(All units are in thousands of dollars.) Data for 10 previous years were used to fit the prediction equation, and the following were calculated:

$$\hat{\beta}_1 = 0.62 \qquad s_{\hat{\beta}_1} = 0.273$$
$$\hat{\beta}_2 = 0.55 \qquad s_{\hat{\beta}_2} = 0.181$$

Use these results to determine whether there is evidence to indicate that the mean sales this Christmas are related to this year's August sales in the proposed model.

9.6 Suppose you fit the second-order model,

$$Y = \beta_0 + \beta_1 x + \beta_2 x^2 + \varepsilon$$

to $n = 30$ data points. Your estimate of β_2 is $\hat{\beta}_2 = 0.35$ and the standard error of the estimate is $s_{\hat{\beta}_2} = 0.13$.

(a) Test the null hypothesis that the mean value of Y is related to x by the (*first-order*) linear model

$$E(Y) = \beta_0 + \beta_1 x.$$

$(H_0:\beta_2 = 0)$ against the alternative hypothesis that the true relationship is given by the quadratic model (a *second-order* linear model),

$$E(Y) = \beta_0 + \beta_1 x + \beta_2 x^2$$

$(H_a:\beta_2 \neq 0)$. Use $\alpha = 0.05$.

(b) Suppose you wanted only to determine whether the quadratic curve opens upward, that is, as x increases, the slope of the curve increases. Give the test statistic and the rejection region for the test for $\alpha = 0.05$. Do the data support the theory that the slope of the curve increases as x increases? Explain.

(c) What is the value of the F statistic for testing the null hypothesis that $\beta_2 = 0$?

(d) Could the F statistic in part (c) be used to conduct the tests in parts (a) and (b)? Explain.

9.7 How is the number of degrees of freedom available for estimating σ^2 (the variance of ε) related to the number of independent variables in a regression model?

9.8 An employer has found that factory workers who are with the company longer tend to invest more in a company investment program per year than workers with less time with the company. The following model is believed to be adequate in modeling the relationship of annual amount invested, Y, to years working for the company, x:

$$Y = \beta_0 + \beta_1 x + \beta_2 x^2 + \varepsilon.$$

The employer checks the records for a sample of fifty factory employees for a previous year, and fits the above model to get $\hat{\beta}_2 = 0.0015$ and $s_{\hat{\beta}_2} = 0.00712$. The basic shape of a quadratic model depends upon whether $\beta_2 < 0$ or $\beta_2 > 0$. Test to see whether the employer can conclude that $\beta_2 > 0$. Use $\alpha = 0.05$.

9.6   *Model Building: Testing Portions of a Model*

In Section 9.4 we discussed testing all the parameters in a multiple regression model using the coefficient of determination, R^2. Then, in Section 9.5, a t-test for individual model parameters was presented. We will now develop a test of sets of β-parameters representing a *portion of* the model. In doing so, we will also present some useful techniques in constructing multiple regression models.

An example will best demonstrate the need for such a test for portions of a regression model, as well as the flexibility of multiple regression models. Suppose a construction firm wishes to compare the performance of its three sales engineers using the mean profit per sales dollar. The sales engineers bid on jobs in two states, so that the true mean profit per sales dollar is to be considered a function of two factors: sales engineer and state. The six means are symbolically represented by μ_{ij}, with the i subscript used for sales engineer ($i = 1, 2, 3$), and the j subscript for state ($j = 1, 2$). The mean values are presented in Table 9.3.

		State	
		S_1	S_2
Sales Engineer	E_1	μ_{11}	μ_{12}
	E_2	μ_{21}	μ_{22}
	E_3	μ_{31}	μ_{32}

Table 9.3 Mean Profit per Sales Dollar for Six Sales Engineer-State Combinations

Since both sales engineers and state are *qualitative* factors, dummy variables will be used to represent them in the multiple regression model (see Example 9.1). Thus, we define

$$x_1 = \begin{cases} 1 & \text{if state} = S_2 \\ 0 & \text{if state} = S_1 \end{cases}$$

to represent the state effect in the model, and

$$x_2 = \begin{cases} 1 & \text{if sales engineer} = E_2 \\ 0 & \text{if sales engineer} = E_1 \text{ or } E_3 \end{cases}$$

$$x_3 = \begin{cases} 1 & \text{if sales engineer} = E_3 \\ 0 & \text{if sales engineer} = E_1 \text{ or } E_2 \end{cases}$$

to represent the sales engineer effect. Note that two dummy variables are defined to represent the three sales engineers. The reason for this will be apparent when we write the model, which, using Y = profit per sales dollar, is

$$\overset{\text{State}}{E(Y) = \beta_0 + \overbrace{\beta_1 x_1}} + \overbrace{\beta_2 x_2 + \beta_3 x_3}^{\text{Sales Engineer}} + \overbrace{\beta_4 x_1 x_2 + \beta_5 x_1 x_3}^{\substack{\text{State} \times \text{Sales} \\ \text{Engineer Interaction}}}$$

Note that there are six parameters in the model: β_0, β_1, β_2, β_3, β_4 and β_5: one corresponding to each mean in Table 9.3. The correspondence is shown in Table 9.4. Other definitions of dummy variables can be used, which will generate a different correspondence between the means μ_{ij} and the β-parameters of the model.

Table 9.4 Correspondence Between Six Sales Engineer—State Means (μ_{ij}) and Model Parameters (β's)

$$\mu_{11} = E(Y|E_1, S_1) = E(Y|x_1 = x_2 = x_3 = 0) = \beta_0$$

$$\mu_{12} = E(Y|E_1, S_2) = E(Y|x_1 = 1, x_2 = x_3 = 0) = \beta_0 + \beta_1$$

$$\mu_{21} = E(Y|E_2, S_1) = E(Y|x_1 = 0, x_2 = 1, x_3 = 0) = \beta_0 + \beta_2$$

$$\mu_{22} = E(Y|E_2, S_2) = E(Y|x_1 = 1, x_2 = 1, x_3 = 0) = \beta_0 + \beta_1 + \beta_2 + \beta_4$$

$$\mu_{31} = E(Y|E_3, S_1) = E(Y|x_1 = x_2 = 0, x_3 = 1) = \beta_0 + \beta_3$$

$$\mu_{32} = E(Y|E_3, S_2) = E(Y|x_1 = 1, x_2 = 0, x_3 = 1) = \beta_0 + \beta_3 + \beta_5$$

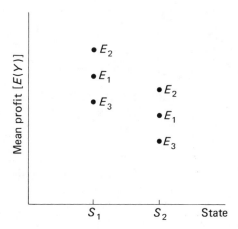

Figure 9.9   Relative Performance of Sales Engineers is the Same in both States: Effects are Additive

However, the use of one fewer dummy variable than the number of factor levels (that is, one dummy variable for the 2 states, and two dummy variables for the 3 sales engineers) will yield an exact correspondence between the *number* of means and the *number* of model parameters. Fewer dummy variables will result in too few model parameters, and more dummy variables will yield more model parameters than necessary to generate the six mean profit values.

Now, suppose the construction firm wishes to test whether the relative performance of the three sales engineers is the same in both states, as shown in Figure 9.9. Thus, although the level of profit may shift between states, the shift is the same for all three sales engineers. Therefore, the *relative* position of the engineers' mean profits is the same. This phenomenon is referred to as *additivity* of the state and sales engineer effects, and results in a simplification of the model. The interaction terms, $\beta_4 x_1 x_2$ and $\beta_5 x_1 x_3$, are now unnecessary, since only β_1 is needed to represent the additive effect of state, as shown in Table 9.5. Note that the difference between the state means for each sales engineer is the same, β_1.

Table 9.5   Representation of Mean Profit in the Additive Model: $E(Y) = \beta_0 + \beta_1 x_1 + \beta_2 x_2 + \beta_3 x_3$

Sales Engineer	State	Mean
E_1	S_1	$\mu_{11} = \beta_0$
E_1	S_2	$\mu_{12} = \beta_0 + \beta_1$
E_2	S_1	$\mu_{21} = \beta_0 + \beta_2$
E_2	S_2	$\mu_{22} = \beta_0 + \beta_1 + \beta_2$
E_3	S_1	$\mu_{31} = \beta_0 + \beta_3$
E_3	S_2	$\mu_{32} = \beta_0 + \beta_1 + \beta_3$

If the sales engineers perform differently in the two states, their mean profits will not maintain the same relative positions. An example of this *nonadditive* relationship between state and sales engineer is shown in Figure 9.10. This more

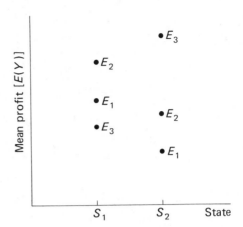

Figure 9.10   Relative Performance of Sales Engineers Is Not the Same in Two States: Effects Are Nonadditive

complex relationship requires all six model parameters

$$E(Y) = \beta_0 + \beta_1 x_1 + \beta_2 x_2 + \beta_3 x_3 + \beta_4 x_1 x_2 + \beta_5 x_1 x_3$$

to describe it. Thus you can see that the difference between an additive and a nonadditive relationship is the interaction terms, $\beta_4 x_1 x_2$ and $\beta_5 x_1 x_3$. If β_4 and β_5 are zero, the effects are additive; otherwise, the state sales engineer effects are nonadditive.

We will call the interaction model the complete model, and the reduced model the main effects model. Now, suppose we wanted to use some data to test which of these models is more appropriate. This can be done by testing the hypothesis that the β parameters for the interaction terms equal zero:

$$H_0: \beta_4 = \beta_5 = 0$$

H_a: at least one interaction β parameter differs from zero.

In Section 9.5 we presented the t test for a single coefficient, and in Section 9.4 we gave the F test for *all* the β parameters (except β_0) in the model. Now we need a test for *some* of the β parameters in the model. The test procedure is intuitive: first, we use the method of least squares to fit the main effects model, and calculate the corresponding sum of squares for error, SSE_1 (the sum of squares of the deviations between observed and predicted y values). Next, we fit the interaction model, and calculate its sum of squares for error, SSE_2. Then, we compare SSE_1 to SSE_2 by calculating the difference $SSE_1 - SSE_2$. If the interaction terms contribute to the model, then SSE_2 should be much smaller than SSE_1, and the difference $SSE_1 - SSE_2$ will be large. That is, the larger the difference, the greater the weight of evidence that the variables sales engineer and state interact to affect the mean profit per sales dollar in the construction job.

The sum of squares for error will always decrease when new terms are added to the model. The question is whether this decrease is large enough to conclude that it is due to more than just an increase in the number of model terms and to chance. To test the null hypothesis that the interaction terms β_4

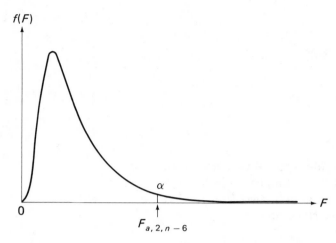

Figure 9.11   Rejection Region for the F Test
$H_0: \beta_4 = \beta_5 = 0$

and β_5 simultaneously equal zero, we use an F statistic calculated as follows:

$$F = \frac{(\text{SSE}_1 - \text{SSE}_2)/2}{\text{SSE}_2/[n - (5 + 1)]}$$

$$= \frac{\text{Drop in SSE/Number of } \beta \text{ parameters being tested}}{s^2 \text{ for complete model}}.$$

When the assumptions listed in Section 9.3 about the error term ε are satisfied and the β parameters for interaction are all zero (H_0 is true), this F statistic has an F distribution with $v_1 = 2$ and $v_2 = n - 6$ degrees of freedom. Note that v_1 is the number of β parameters being tested and v_2 is the number of degrees of freedom associated with s^2 in the complete model.

If the interaction terms *do* contribute to the model (H_a is true), we expect the F statistic to be large. Thus, we use a one-tailed test and reject H_0 when F exceeds some critical value, F_α, as shown in Figure 9.11.

EXAMPLE 9.3

The profit per sales dollar, Y, for the six combinations of sales engineers and states is shown in Table 9.6. Note that the number of construction jobs per combination varies from one for levels (E_1, S_2) to three for levels (E_1, S_1). A total of twelve jobs are sampled.

(a)   Assume the interaction between E and S is negligible. Fit the model for $E(Y)$ with interaction terms omitted.

(b)   Fit the complete model for $E(Y)$, allowing for the fact that interactions might occur.

(c)   Test the hypothesis that the interaction terms do not contribute to the model.

| | State | |
	S_1	S_2
	$0.065	
E_1	0.073	$0.036
	0.068	
Sales	0.078	0.050
Engineer E_2	0.082	0.043
E_3	0.048	0.061
	0.046	0.062

Table 9.6   Profit Data for Combinations of Sales Engineers and States

Solution   (a)   The SAS printout for the main effects model

$$E(Y) = \beta_0 + \overbrace{\beta_1 x_1 + \beta_2 x_2}^{\substack{E \\ \text{main effect}}} + \overbrace{\beta_3 x_3}^{\substack{S \\ \text{main effect}}}$$

is given in Figure 9.12. The least-squares prediction equation is

$$\hat{y} = 0.0645 + 0.0067 x_1 - 0.00230 x_2 - 0.0158 x_3.$$

SOURCE	DF	SUM OF SQUARES	MEAN SQUARE	F VALUE	PR > F
MODEL	3	0.00085826	0.00028609	1.51	0.2838
ERROR	8	0.00151241	0.00018905		
CORRECTED TOTAL	11	0.00237067		R-SQUARE	STD DEV
				0.362032	0.01374959

PARAMETER	ESTIMATE	T FOR HO: PARAMETER = 0	PR > |T|	STD ERROR OF ESTIMATE
INTERCEPT	0.06445455	8.98	0.0001	0.00718049
X1	0.00670455	0.67	0.5190	0.00994093
X2	-0.00229545	-0.23	0.8232	0.00994093
X3	-0.01581818	-1.91	0.0928	0.00829131

X1	X2	X3	PREDICTED VALUE	LOWER 95% CL FOR MEAN	UPPER 95% CL FOR MEAN
0	1	1	0.04634091	0.02782807	0.06485375

Figure 9.12   SAS Printout for Main Effects Model of Example 9.3

(b)   The complete model SAS printout is given in Figure 9.13. Recall that the complete model is

$$E(Y) = \beta_0 + \beta_1 x_1 + \beta_2 x_2 + \beta_3 x_3 + \beta_4 x_1 x_3 + \beta_5 x_2 x_3.$$

SOURCE	DF	SUM OF SQUARES	MEAN SQUARE	F VALUE	PR > F
MODEL	5	0.00230300	0.00046060	40.84	0.0001
ERROR	6	0.00006767	0.00001128		
CORRECTED TOTAL	11	0.00237067		R-SQUARE	STD DEV
				0.971457	0.00335824

PARAMETER	ESTIMATE	T FOR HO: PARAMETER = 0	PR > |T|	STD ERROR OF ESTIMATE
INTERCEPT	0.06866667	35.42	0.0001	0.00193888
X1	0.01133333	3.70	0.0101	0.00306564
X2	−0.02166667	−7.07	0.0004	0.00306564
X3	−0.03266667	−8.42	0.0002	0.00387776
X1 * X3	−0.00083333	−0.16	0.8763	0.00512980
X2 * X3	0.04716667	9.19	0.0001	0.00512980

X1	X2	X3	X1 * X3	X2 * X3	PREDICTED VALUE	LOWER 95% CL FOR MEAN	UPPER 95% CL FOR MEAN
0	1	1	0	1	0.06150000	0.05568948	0.06731052

Figure 9.13   SAS Printout for Complete Model (Includes Interaction) of Example 9.3

The least-squares prediction equation is

$$\hat{y} = 0.0687 + 0.0113x_1 - 0.0217x_2 - 0.0327x_3 - 0.0008x_1x_3 + 0.0472x_2x_3.$$

(c) Referring to the printouts shown in Figures 9.12 and 9.13, we find the following:

$$\text{Main effects model:}\quad SSE_1 = 0.00151241$$

$$\text{Interaction model:}\quad SSE_2 = 0.00006767.$$

The test statistic is

$$F = \frac{(SSE_1 - SSE_2)/2}{SSE_2/(12 - 6)} = \frac{(0.00151241 - 0.00006767)/2}{0.00006767/6}$$

$$= \frac{0.00072237}{0.00001128} = 64.04.$$

The critical value of F for $\alpha = 0.05$, $v_1 = 2$, and $v_2 = 6$ is found in the F table of the Appendix to be

$$F_6^2(0.05) = 5.14.$$

Since the calculated $F = 64.04$ greatly exceeds 5.14, we are quite confident in concluding that the interaction terms contribute to the prediction of Y, profit per sales dollar. They should be retained in the model. □

The F test can be used to determine whether *any* set of terms should be included in a model by testing the null hypothesis that a particular set of β parameters simultaneously equal zero. For example, we may want to test to determine whether a set of quadratic terms for quantitative variables or a set of main effect terms for a qualitative variable should be included in a model. The F test appropriate for testing the null hypothesis that all of a set of β parameters are equal to zero is summarized below.

F TEST FOR TESTING THE NULL HYPOTHESIS: SET OF β PARAMETERS EQUAL ZERO

$$\text{Reduced model:} \quad E(Y) = \beta_0 + \beta_1 x_1 + \cdots + \beta_g x_g$$

$$\text{Complete model:} \quad E(Y) = \beta_0 + \beta_1 x_1 + \cdots + \beta_g x_g$$
$$+ \beta_{g+1} x_{g+1} + \cdots + \beta_k x_k$$

$$H_0: \beta_{g+1} = \beta_{g+2} = \cdots = \beta_k = 0$$

H_a: At least one of the β parameters under test is nonzero

$$\text{Test statistic:} \quad F = \frac{(\text{SSE}_1 - \text{SSE}_2)/(k - g)}{\text{SSE}_2/[n - (k + 1)]}$$

where

$$\text{SSE}_1 = \text{sum of squared errors for the reduced model}$$

$$\text{SSE}_2 = \text{sum of squared errors for the complete model}$$

$$k - g = \text{number of } \beta \text{ parameters specified in } H_0$$

$$k + 1 = \text{number of } \beta \text{ parameters in the complete model}$$

$$n = \text{total sample size}$$

$$\text{Rejection region:} \quad F > F_{v_2}^{v_1}(\alpha)$$

where

$$v_1 = k - g = \text{degrees of freedom for the numerator}$$

$$v_2 = n - (k + 1) = \text{degrees of freedom for the denominator}$$

Exercises

9.9   Suppose you fit the regression model

$$Y = \beta_0 + \beta_1 x_1 + \beta_2 x_2 + \beta_3 x_3 + \beta_4 x_4 + \varepsilon$$

to $n = 25$ data points and you wish to test the null hypothesis, $\beta_1 = \beta_2 = 0$.
(a) Explain how you would find the quantities necessary for the F statistic.
(b) How many degrees of freedom would be associated with F?

9.10 An insurance company is experimenting with three different training programs, A, B, and C, for its salespeople. The following main-effects model is proposed:

$$E(Y) = \beta_0 + \beta_1 x_1 + \beta_2 x_2 + \beta_3 x_3$$

where

$$Y = \text{monthly sales (in thousands of dollars)}$$

$$x_1 = \text{number of months experience}$$

$$x_2 = \begin{cases} 1 & \text{if training program } B \text{ was used} \\ 0 & \text{otherwise} \end{cases}$$

$$x_3 = \begin{cases} 1 & \text{if training program } C \text{ was used} \\ 0 & \text{otherwise.} \end{cases}$$

Training program A is the base level.

(a) What hypothesis would you test to determine whether the mean monthly sales differ for salespeople trained by the three programs?

(b) After experimenting with fifty salespeople over a 5-year period, the complete model is fit, with the result

$$\hat{y} = 10 + 0.5x_1 + 1.2x_2 - 0.4x_3 \qquad \text{SSE} = 140.5$$

Then the reduced model $E(Y) = \beta_0 + \beta_1 x_1$ is fit to the same data, with the result

$$\hat{y} = 11.4 + 0.4x_1 \qquad \text{SSE} = 183.2$$

Test the hypothesis you formulated in part (a). Use $\alpha = 0.05$.

9.11 In an attempt to reduce the number of work-hours lost due to accidents, a company tested three safety programs, A, B, and C, each at three of the company's nine factories. The proposed complete model is

$$E(Y) = \beta_0 + \beta_1 x_1 + \beta_2 x_2 + \beta_3 x_3$$

where

$$Y = \text{Total work-hours lost due to accidents for a 1-year period beginning 6 months after the plan is instituted}$$

$$x_1 = \text{Total work-hours lost due to accidents during the year before the plan was instituted}$$

$$x_2 = \begin{cases} 1 & \text{if program } B \text{ is in effect} \\ 0 & \text{otherwise} \end{cases}$$

$$x_3 = \begin{cases} 1 & \text{if program } C \text{ is in effect} \\ 0 & \text{otherwise.} \end{cases}$$

After the programs have been in effect for 18 months, the complete model is fit to the $n = 9$ data points, with the result

$$\hat{y} = -2.1 + 0.88x_1 - 150x_2 + 35x_3 \qquad SSE = 1{,}527.27.$$

Then the reduced model $E(Y) = \beta_0 + \beta_1 x_1$ is fit, with the result

$$\hat{y} = 15.3 + 0.84x_1 \qquad SSE = 3{,}113.14.$$

Test to see whether the mean work-hours lost differ for the three programs. Use $\alpha = 0.05$.

9.12   The following model was proposed for testing salary discrimination against women in a state university system:

$$E(Y) = \beta_0 + \beta_1 x_1 + \beta_2 x_2 + \beta_3 x_1 x_2 + \beta_4 x_2^2$$

where

$$Y = \text{annual salary (in thousands of dollars)}$$

$$x_1 = \begin{cases} 1 & \text{if female} \\ 0 & \text{if male} \end{cases}$$

$$x_2 = \text{experience (years)}.$$

Below is a portion of the computer printout that results from fitting this model to a sample of 200 faculty members in the university system:

SOURCE	DF	SUM OF SQUARES	MEAN SQUARE
MODEL	4	2351.70	587.92
ERROR	195	783.90	4.02
TOTAL	199	3135.60	R-SQUARE
			0.7500

The reduced model $E(Y) = \beta_0 + \beta_2 x_2 + \beta_4 x_2^2$ is fit to the same data and the resulting computer printout is partially reproduced below:

SOURCE	DF	SUM OF SQUARES	MEAN SQUARE
MODEL	2	2340.37	1170.185
ERROR	197	795.23	4.04
TOTAL	199	3135.60	R-SQUARE
			0.7464

Do these data provide sufficient evidence to support the claim that the mean salary of faculty members is dependent upon sex? Use $\alpha = 0.05$.

9.7   *Using the Model for Estimation and Prediction*

In Section 8.8 we discussed the use of the least-squares line for estimating the mean value of Y, $E(Y)$, for some value of x, say $x = x_p$. We also showed how to use the same fitted model to predict, when $x = x_p$, some value of Y to be observed in the future. Recall that the least-squares line yielded the same value for both the estimate of $E(Y)$ and the prediction of some future value of Y. That is, both are the result of substituting x_p into the prediction equation $\hat{y}_p = \hat{\beta}_0 + \hat{\beta}_1 x_p$ and calculating $\hat{y}_p$. There the equivalence ends. The confidence interval for the mean $E(Y)$ was narrower than the prediction interval for Y, because of the additional uncertainty attributable to the random error ε when predicting some future value of Y.

These same concepts carry over to the multiple regression model. For example, suppose we want to estimate the mean peak power load for a given daily high temperature $x_p = 90$ degrees. Assuming the quadratic model represents the true relationship between peak power load and maximum temperature, we want to estimate

$$E(Y) = \beta_0 + \beta_1 x_p + \beta_2 x_p^2$$
$$= \beta_0 + \beta_1 90 + \beta_2 (90)^2.$$

Substituting into the least-squares prediction equation, the estimate of $E(Y)$ is

$$\hat{y} = \hat{\beta}_0 + \hat{\beta}_1 90 + \hat{\beta}_2 (90)^2$$
$$= 1784.188 - 42.3862(90) + 0.27216(90)^2$$
$$= 173.93.$$

x	ESTIMATED MEAN VALUE	LOWER 95% CL FOR MEAN	UPPER 95% CL FOR MEAN
90	173.92791187	159.14624576	188.70957799

Figure 9.14   SAS Printout for Estimated Value and Corresponding Confidence Interval for $x = 90$

To form a confidence interval for the mean, we need to know the standard deviation of the sampling distribution for the estimator $\hat{y}$. For multiple regression models, the form of this standard deviation is rather complex. However, most regression computer programs allow us to obtain the confidence intervals for mean values of Y for any given combination of values of the independent variables. This portion of the computer output for the peak power load examples is shown in Figure 9.14. The mean value and corresponding 95% confidence interval for $x = 90$ are shown in the columns labeled ESTIMATED MEAN VALUE, LOWER 95% CL FOR MEAN, and UPPER 95% CL FOR MEAN. Note that

$$\hat{y} = 173.93,$$

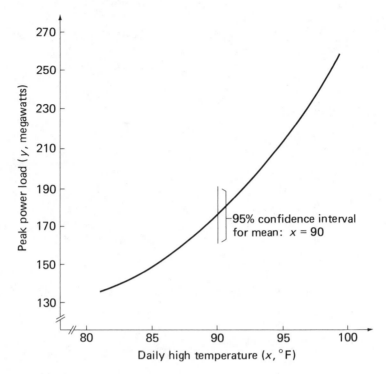

Figure 9.15   Confidence Interval for Mean Peak Power Load

which agrees with our earlier calculation. The 95% confidence interval for the true mean of Y is shown to be 159.15 to 188.71 (see Figure 9.15).

If we were interested in predicting the electrical usage for a particular day on which the high temperature is 90 degrees, $\hat{y} = 173.93$ would be used as the predicted value. However, the prediction interval for a particular value of Y will be wider than the confidence interval for the mean value. This is reflected by the printout shown in Figure 9.16, which gives the predicted value of Y and corresponding 95% prediction interval when $x = 90$. The prediction interval for $x = 90$ is 139.91 to 207.94 (see Figure 9.17).

Unfortunately, not all computer packages have the capability to produce confidence intervals for means and prediction intervals for particular Y values. This is a rather serious oversight, since the estimation of mean values and the prediction of particular values represent the culmination of our model building efforts: using the model to make inferences about the dependent variable Y.

x	PREDICTED VALUE	LOWER 95% CL INDIVIDUAL	UPPER 95% CL INDIVIDUAL
90	173.92791187	139.91131797	207.94450577

Figure 9.16   SAS Printout for Predicted Value and Corresponding Prediction Interval for $x = 90$

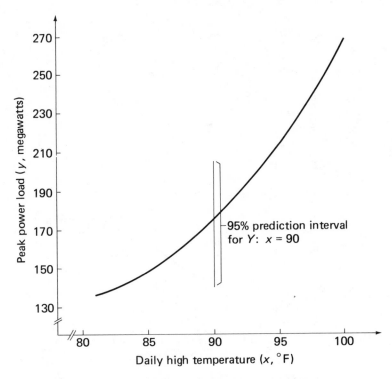

Figure 9.17   Prediction Interval for Electrical Usage

9.8   *Multiple Regression: An Example*

Many companies manufacture products that are at least partially chemically produced (e.g., steel, paint, gasoline). In many instances, the quality of the finished product is a function of the temperature and pressure at which the chemical reactions take place.

Suppose you wanted to model the quality, Y, of a product as a function of the temperature, x_1, and the pressure x_2, at which it is produced. Four inspectors independently assign a quality score between 0 and 100 to each product, and then the quality, y, is calculated by averaging the four scores. An experiment is conducted by varying temperature between 80 and 100°F and pressure between 50 and 60 pounds per square inch. The resulting data ($n = 27$) are given in Table 9.7.

Step 1
The first step is to hypothesize a model relating product quality to the temperature and pressure at which it was manufactured. A model that will allow us to find the setting of temperature and pressure that maximize quality is the equation for a *paraboloid*. The visualization of the paraboloid appropriate for this application is an inverted bowl-shaped surface, and the corresponding mathematical model for the mean quality at any temperature-pressure setting is

$$E(Y) = \beta_0 + \beta_1 x_1 + \beta_2 x_2 + \beta_3 x_1^2 + \beta_4 x_2^2 + \beta_5 x_1 x_2.$$

Table 9.7   Temperature, Pressure, and Quality of the Finished Product

x_1, °F	x_2, pounds per square inch	y	x_1, °F	x_2, pounds per square inch	y	x_1, °F	x_2, pounds per square inch	y
80	50	50.8	90	50	63.4	100	50	46.6
80	50	50.7	90	50	61.6	100	50	49.1
80	50	49.4	90	50	63.4	100	50	46.4
80	55	93.7	90	55	93.8	100	55	69.8
80	55	90.9	90	55	92.1	100	55	72.5
80	55	90.9	90	55	97.4	100	55	73.2
80	60	74.5	90	60	70.9	100	60	38.7
80	60	73.0	90	60	68.8	100	60	42.5
80	60	71.2	90	60	71.3	100	60	41.4

This model is also referred to as a *complete second-order model*, because it contains all first and second order terms in x_1 and x_2. Note that a model with only first-order terms (a plane) would have no curvature, so that the mean quality could not reach a maximum within the experimental region of temperature-pressure even if the data indicate the probable existence of such a value. The inclusion of second-order terms allows curvature in the three-dimensional response surface traced by mean quality, so that a maximum mean quality can be reached if the experimental data indicate one exists.

Step 2
Next we use the least-squares technique to estimate the model coefficients $\beta_0, \beta_1, \ldots, \beta_5$ of the paraboloid, using the data in Table 9.7. The least squares model is (see SAS printout, Figure 9.19)

$$\hat{y} = -5127.90 + 31.10x_1 + 139.75x_2 - 0.133x_1^2 - 1.14x_2^2 - 0.146x_1x_2.$$

A three-dimensional graph of this model is shown in Figure 9.18.

Step 3
The next step is to specify the probability distribution of ε, the random error component. We assume that ε is normally distributed, with a mean of zero and a constant variance σ^2. Furthermore, we assume that the errors are independent. The estimate of the variance σ^2 is given in the SAS printout as

$$s^2 = \text{MSE} = \frac{\text{SSE}}{n - (k + 1)} = \frac{\text{SSE}}{27 - (5 + 1)} = 2.818.$$

Step 4
Next we want to evaluate the adequacy of the model. First, note that $R^2 = 0.993$. This implies that 99.3% of the variation in y, observed quality ratings for the

* Recall from your analytic geometry that the order of a term is the sum of the exponents of the variables in the term. Thus, $\beta_5 x_1 x_2$ is a second-order term, as is $\beta_3 x_1^2$. The term $\beta_i x_1^2 x_2$ is a third-order term.

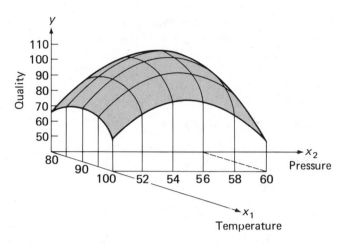

Figure 9.18   Plot of Second-Order Least-Squares
Model for Product Quality Example

SOURCE	DF	SUM OF SQUARES	MEAN SQUARE	F VALUE	PR > F
MODEL	5	8402.26453714	1680.45290743	596.32	0.0001
ERROR	21	59.17842582	2.81802028		
CORRECTED TOTAL	26	8461.44296296		R-SQUARE	STD DEV
				0.993006	1.67869601

PARAMETER	ESTIMATE	T FOR HO: PARAMETER = 0	PR > T	STD ERROR OF ESTIMATE
INTERCEPT	−5127.89907417	−46.49	0.0001	110.29601483
X1	31.09638889	23.13	0.0001	1.34441322
X2	139.74722222	44.50	0.0001	3.14005411
X1 * X1	−0.13338889	−19.46	0.0001	0.00685325
X2 * X2	−1.14422222	−41.74	0.0001	0.02741299
X1 * X2	−0.14550000	−15.01	0.0001	0.00969196

Figure 9.19   SAS Printout for the Product Quality Example

27 experiments, is accounted for by the model. The statistical significance of this can be tested:

$$H_0: \beta_1 = \beta_2 = \beta_3 = \beta_4 = \beta_5 = 0$$

H_α: At least one model coefficient is nonzero

Test statistic: $$F = \frac{R^2/k}{(1 - R^2)/[n - (k + 1)]}$$

Rejection region: For $\alpha = 0.05$,

$$F > F_{n-(k+1)}^{k}(\alpha) = F_{21}^{5}(0.05),$$

that is, $F > 2.57.$

The test statistic is given on the SAS printout. Since $F = 596.32$ greatly exceeds the tabulated value, we conclude that the model does contribute information about product quality.

Step 5
The culmination of the modeling effort is to use the model for estimation and/or prediction. In this example, suppose the manufacturer is interested in estimating the mean product quality for the setting of temperature and pressure at which the estimated model reaches a maximum. To find this setting, we solve the equations:

$$\frac{\partial \hat{y}}{\partial x_1} = \hat{\beta}_1 + 2\hat{\beta}_3 x_1 + \hat{\beta}_5 x_2 = 0$$

$$\frac{\partial \hat{y}}{\partial x_2} = \hat{\beta}_2 + 2\hat{\beta}_4 x_2 + \hat{\beta}_5 x_1 = 0$$

for x_1 and x_2, obtaining $x_1 = 86.25°$ and $x_2 = 55.58$ pounds per square inch. The fact that $\partial^2 \hat{y}/\partial x_1^2 = \hat{\beta}_3 < 0$ and $\partial^2 \hat{y}/\partial x_2^2 = \hat{\beta}_4 < 0$ assures that this setting of x_1 and x_2 corresponds to a maximum value of $\hat{y}$.

To obtain an estimated mean quality for this temperature-pressure combination, we use the least-squares model:

$$\hat{y} = \hat{\beta}_0 + \hat{\beta}_1(86.25) + \hat{\beta}_2(55.58) + \hat{\beta}_3(86.25)^2 + \hat{\beta}_4(55.58)^2 + \hat{\beta}_5(86.25)(55.58).$$

The estimated mean value is given in Figure 9.20, a partial reproduction of the SAS regression printout for this example. The estimated mean quality is 96.9, and a 95% confidence interval is 95.5 to 98.3. Thus, we are confident that the mean quality rating will be between 95.5 and 98.3 when the product is manufactured at 86.25°F and 55.58 pounds per square inch.

X1	X2	PREDICTED VALUE	LOWER 95% CL FOR MEAN	UPPER 95% CL FOR MEAN
86.25	55.58	96.87401860	95.46463236	98.28340483

Figure 9.20   Partial SAS Printout for Product Quality Example

9.9   *Conclusion*

We have discussed some of the methodology of *multiple regression analysis*, a technique for modeling a dependent variable Y as a function of several independent variables $x_1, x_2, \ldots, x_k$. The steps we follow in constructing and using multiple regression models are much the same as those for the simple straight-line models:

1. The form of the probabilistic model is hypothesized.
2. The model coefficients are estimated using least squares.
3. The probability distribution of ε is specified and σ^2 is estimated.
4. The adequacy of the model is checked.
5. If the model is deemed useful, it may be used to make estimates and to predict values of Y to be observed in the future.

We stress that this is not intended to be a complete coverage of multiple regression analysis. Whole texts have been devoted to this topic. However, we have presented the core necessary for a basic understanding of multiple regression. If you are interested in a more extensive coverage, consult the references.

Supplementary Exercises

9.13 After a regression model is fit to a set of data, a confidence interval for the mean value of Y at a given setting of the independent variables will *always* be narrower than the corresponding prediction interval for a particular value of y at the same setting of the independent variables. Why?

9.14 Before accepting a job, a computer at a major university estimates the cost of running the job in order to see if the user's account contains enough money to cover the cost. As part of the job submission, the user must specify estimated values for two variables: central processing unit (CPU) time and number of lines printed. While the CPU time required and the number of lines printed do not account for the complete cost of the run, it is thought that knowledge of their values should allow a good prediction of job cost. The following model is proposed to explain the relationship of CPU time and lines printed to job cost:

$$E(Y) = \beta_0 + \beta_1 x_1 + \beta_2 x_2 + \beta_3 x_1 x_2$$

where

$$Y = \text{job cost (in dollars)}$$
$$x_1 = \text{number of lines printed}$$
$$x_2 = \text{CPU time}$$

Records from twenty previous runs were used to fit this model. The SAS printout is shown below:

SOURCE	DF	SUM OF SQUARES	MEAN SQUARE	F VALUE	PR > F
MODEL	3	43.25090461	14.41696820	84.96	0.0001
ERROR	16	2.71515039	0.16969690		
CORRECTED TOTAL	19	45.96605500		R-SQUARE	STD DEV
				0.940931	0.41194283

PARAMETER	ESTIMATE	T FOR H0: PARAMETER = 0	PR > |T|	STD ERROR OF ESTIMATE
INTERCEPT	0.04564705	0.22	0.8313	0.21082636
X1	0.00078505	5.80	0.0001	0.00013537
X2	0.23737262	7.50	0.0001	0.03163301
X1 * X2	−0.00003809	−2.99	0.0086	0.00001273

X1	X2	PREDICTED VALUE	LOWER 95% CL FOR MEAN	UPPER 95% CL FOR MEAN
2000	42	8.38574865	7.32284845	9.44864885

Portion of SAS Printout for Exercise 9.14

(a) Identify the least-squares model that was fit to the data.

(b) What are the values of SSE and s^2 (estimate of σ^2) for the data?

(c) What do we mean by the statement: This value of SSE (see part (b)) is minimum?

9.15 Refer to Exercise 9.14 and the portion of the SAS printout shown.

(a) Is there evidence that the model is useful (as a whole) for predicting job cost? Test at $\alpha = 0.05$.

(b) Is there evidence that the variables x_1 and x_2 interact to affect Y? Test at $\alpha = 0.01$.

(c) What assumptions are necessary for the validity of the tests conducted in parts (a) and (b)?

9.16 Refer to Exercise 9.14 and the portion of the SAS printout shown. Use a 95% confidence interval to estimate the mean cost of computer jobs that require 42 seconds of CPU time and print 2000 lines.

9.17 The EPA wants to model the gas mileage ratings, Y, of automobiles as a function of their engine size, x. A quadratic model,

$$Y = \beta_0 + \beta_1 x + \beta_2 x^2$$

is proposed. A sample of fifty engines of varying sizes is selected and the miles per gallon rating of each is determined. The least-squares model is

$$\hat{y} = 51.3 - 10.1x + 0.15x^2.$$

The size, x, of the engine is measured in hundreds of cubic inches. Also $s_{\beta_2} = 0.0037$ and $R^2 = 0.93$.

(a) Sketch this model between $x = 1$ and $x = 4$.

(b) Is there evidence that the quadratic term in the model is contributing to the prediction of the miles per gallon rating, Y? Use $\alpha = 0.05$.

(c) Use the model to estimate the mean miles per gallon rating for all cars with 350 cubic inch engines ($x = 3.5$).

(d) Suppose a 95% confidence interval for the quantity estimated in part (c) is (17.2, 18.4). Interpret this interval.

(e) Suppose you purchase an automobile with a 350 inch engine and determine that the miles per gallon rating is 14.7. Is the fact that this value lies outside the confidence interval given in part (d) surprising? Explain.

9.18 To increase the motivation and productivity of workers, an electronics manufacturer decides to experiment with a new pay incentive structure at one of two plants. The experimental plan will be tried at plant A for 6 months, while workers at plant B will remain on the original pay plan. To evaluate the effectiveness of the new plan, the average assembly time for part of an electronic system was measured for employees at both plants at the beginning and end of the 6-month period. Suppose the following model was proposed:

$$Y = \beta_0 + \beta_1 x_1 + \beta_2 x_2 + \varepsilon$$

where

$Y =$ Assembly time (hours) at end of 6-month period

$x_1 =$ Assembly time (hours) at beginning of 6-month period

$x_2 = \begin{cases} 1 & \text{if plant A} \\ 0 & \text{if plant B.} \end{cases}$ (dummy variable)

A sample of $n = 42$ observations yielded

$$\hat{y} = 0.11 + 0.98x_1 - 0.53x_2$$

where

$$s_{\hat{\beta}_1} = 0.231 \qquad s_{\hat{\beta}_2} = 0.48.$$

Test to see whether, after allowing for the effect of initial assembly time, plant A had a lower mean assembly time than plant B. Use $\alpha = 0.01$. [*Note*: When the $(0, 1)$ coding is used to define a dummy variable, the coefficient of the variable represents the difference between the mean response at the two levels represented by the variable. Thus, the coefficient β_2 is the difference in mean assembly time between plant A and plant B at the end of the 6-month period, and $\hat{\beta}_2$ is the sample estimator of that difference.]

9.19   One factor that must be considered in developing a shipping system that is beneficial to both the customer and the seller is time of delivery. A manufacturer of farm equipment can ship its products by either rail or truck. Quadratic models are thought to be adequate in relating time of delivery to distance traveled for both modes of transportation. Consequently, it has been suggested that the following model be fit:

$$E(Y) = \beta_0 + \beta_1 x_1 + \beta_2 x_2 + \beta_3 x_1 x_2 + \beta_4 x_2^2$$

where

$$Y = \text{Shipping time}$$

$$x_1 = \begin{cases} 1 & \text{if rail} \\ 0 & \text{if truck} \end{cases}$$

$$x_2 = \text{Distance to be shipped}$$

(a) What hypothesis would you test to determine whether the data indicate that the quadratic distance term is useful in the model, i.e., whether curvature is present in the relationship between mean delivery time and distance?

(b) What hypothesis would you test to determine whether there is a difference in mean delivery time by rail and by truck?

9.20   Refer to Exercise 9.19. Suppose the complete second-order model is fit to a total of fifty observations on delivery time. The sum of squared errors is $SSE = 226.12$. Then, the reduced model

$$E(Y) = \beta_0 + \beta_2 x_2 + \beta_4 x_2^2$$

is fit to the same data, and $SSE = 259.34$. Test to see whether the data indicate that the mean delivery time differs for rail and truck deliveries.

9.21   Many companies must accurately estimate their costs before a job is begun in order to acquire a contract and make a profit. For example, a heating and plumbing contractor may base cost estimates for new homes on the total area of the house, the number of baths in the plans, and whether central air conditioning is to be installed.

(a) Write a first-order model relating the mean cost of material and labor, $E(Y)$, to the area, number of baths, and central air conditioning variables.

(b) Write a complete second-order model for the mean cost as a function of the same three variables.

(c) How would you test the research hypothesis that the second-order terms are useful for predicting mean cost?

9.22 Refer to Exercise 9.21. The contractor samples twenty-five recent jobs and fits both the complete second-order modeling (part (b) and the reduced main-effects model in part (a), so that a test can be conducted to determine whether the additional complexity of the second-order model is necessary. The resulting SSE and R^2 are given in the table.

	SSE	R^2
First-order	8.548	0.950
Second-order	6.133	0.964

(a) Is there sufficient evidence to conclude that the second-order terms are important for predicting the mean cost?

(b) Suppose the contractor decides to use the main-effects model to predict costs. Use the global F test to determine whether the main-effects model is useful for predicting costs.

9.23 Plastics made under different environmental conditions are known to have differing strengths. A scientist would like to know which combination of temperature and pressure yields a plastic with a high breaking strength. A small preliminary experiment was run at two pressure levels and two temperature levels. The following model was proposed:

$$E(Y) = \beta_0 + \beta_1 x_1 + \beta_2 x_2 + \beta_3 x_1 x_2$$

where

$$Y = \text{Breaking strength (pounds)}$$

$$x_1 = \text{Temperature (}^\circ\text{F)}$$

$$x_2 = \text{Pressure (pounds per square inch).}$$

A sample of $n = 16$ observations yielded

$$\hat{y} = 226.8 + 4.9x_1 + 1.2x_2 - 0.7x_1 x_2$$

with

$$s_{\hat{\beta}_1} = 1.11 \qquad s_{\hat{\beta}_2} = 0.27 \qquad s_{\hat{\beta}_3} = 0.34.$$

Do the data indicate there is an interaction between temperature and pressure? Test using $\alpha = 0.05$.

9.24   Air pollution regulations for power plants are often written so that the maximum amount of pollutant that can be omitted is increased as the plant's output increases. Suppose the following data are collected over a period of time:

Output, x (megawatts)	Sulfur dioxide omission Y, (parts per million)
525	143
452	110
626	173
573	161
422	105
712	240
600	165
555	140
675	210

(a) Plot the data in a scattergram.
(b) Use the least-squares method to fit a straight line relating sulfur dioxide emission to output. Plot the least-squares line on the scattergram.
(c) Use a computer program to fit a second-order (quadratic) model relating sulfur dioxide emission to output.
(d) Conduct a test to determine whether the quadratic model provides a better description of the relationship between sulfur dioxide and output than the linear model.
(e) Use the quadratic model to estimate the mean sulfur dioxide emission when the power output is 500 megawatts. Use a 95% confidence interval.

The Analysis of Variance

We have now developed the techniques necessary to extend the two-sample hypothesis testing results of Chapter 7 to cases involving more than two samples. More specifically, we will now construct tests of the equality of two or more means for sampling situations analogous to both the unpaired and paired samples of Chapter 7. The tools of multiple regression analysis will be used in this development.

Contents

10.1   Introduction

We learned how to compare two means in Chapter 7, and we now want to extend the hypothesis testing ideas developed there to the cases in which we might have three or more means to compare. For example, a reliability engineer may wish to compare the mean lifelengths of three brands of capacitors. Or, a chemical engineer may desire to compare the average yields of four processes designed to produce an industrial chemical.

In this chapter we present a method (involving an F-test) for testing the equality of two or more means. We then show how this analysis can be handled through the linear regression techniques developed in Chapters 8 and 9. The remainder of the chapter deals with procedures for estimating individual means and differences between means, and with testing and estimation procedures for more complex experimental designs.

10.2   Analysis of Variance for the Completely Randomized Design

The two-sample t-test of Section 7.3 was designed to test the hypothesis that two population means are equal versus the alternative that they differ. Recall that, in order to use that test, the experiment must have resulted in two independent random samples, one sample from each of the populations under study. As an illustration, Example 7.9 reports results from a random sample of nine measurements on stamping times for a standard machine and an independently selected random sample of nine measurements from a new machine. This is a simple example of a *completely randomized design*.

DEFINITION 10.1   *A* **completely randomized design** is a plan for collecting data in which a random sample is selected from each population of interest, and the samples are independent.

The stamping time example consists of only two populations, but Definition 10.1 allows any finite number of populations. For example, suppose mean tensile strengths are to be compared for steel specimens coming from three processes, each involving a different percentage of carbon. If random samples of tensile strength measurements are taken on specimens from each process, and the samples are independent, then the resulting experiment would be a completely randomized design.

The populations of interest in experimental design problems are generally referred to as *treatments*. Thus, the stamping time problem has two treatments (standard machine and new machine) whereas the tensile strength problem has three treatments (one for each percentage of carbon in the steel).

The notation we will employ for the k-population (or k-treatment) problem is summarized in Table 10.1.

Table 10.1   Notation for a Completely Randomized Design

Populations (Treatments)

	1	2	3	$\cdots$	k
Mean	μ_1	μ_2	μ_3	$\cdots$	μ_k
Variance	σ_1^2	σ_2^2	σ_3^2	$\cdots$	σ_k^2

Independent Random Samples

Sample Size	n_1	n_2	n_3	$\cdots$	n_k
Sample Totals	T_1	T_2	T_3	$\cdots$	T_k
Sample Means	$\bar{y}_1$	$\bar{y}_2$	$\bar{y}_3$	$\cdots$	$\bar{y}_k$

Total sample size $= n = n_1 + n_2 + n_3 + \cdots + n_k$
Overall sample total $= \sum y = T_1 + T_2 + \cdots + T_k$
Overall sample mean $= \bar{y} = \sum y/n$
Sum of squares of all n measurements $= \sum y^2$

The method we will present to analyze data from a completely randomized design (as well as many other designs) is called the *analysis of variance*. The basic inference problem for which analysis of variance provides an answer is the test of the null hypothesis

$$H_0: \mu_1 = \mu_2 = \cdots = \mu_k$$

versus the alternative

$$H_a: \text{at least two treatment means differ.}$$

To see how we might formulate a test statistic for the null hypothesis indicated above, let us once again look at the two-sample problem involving the stamping times. Example 7.9 provides the following data:

$$n_1 = 9 \qquad\qquad n_2 = 9$$

$$\bar{y}_1 = 35.33 \text{ seconds} \qquad\qquad \bar{y}_2 = 31.56 \text{ seconds}$$

$$(n_1 - 1)s_1^2 = 195.50 \qquad\qquad (n_2 - 1)s_2^2 = 160.22$$

If we want to test $H_0: \mu_1 = \mu_2$ versus $H_a: \mu_1 \neq \mu_2$, the t-test can be used, with the statistic calculated as follows:

$$t = \frac{(\bar{y}_1 - \bar{y}_2)}{s_p \sqrt{\dfrac{1}{n_1} + \dfrac{1}{n_2}}}.$$

(The s_p here is the square root of the "pooled" s_p^2 given by

$$s_p^2 = \frac{(n_1 - 1)s_1^2 + (n_2 - 1)s_2^2}{n_1 + n_2 - 2}.\Bigg)$$

The value of this statistic is calculated in Example 7.9 to be $t = 1.65$. The critical value with $\alpha = 0.05$ and 16 degrees of freedom is $t_{0.025} = 2.120$, and hence we cannot reject H_0.

The t-test as presented above cannot be extended to a test of the equality of more than two means. However, if we square the t-statistic we obtain, after some algebra,

$$t^2 = \frac{(\bar{y}_1 - \bar{y}_2)^2}{s_p^2 \left(\dfrac{1}{n_1} + \dfrac{1}{n_2} \right)} = \frac{\displaystyle\sum_{i=1}^{2} n_i(\bar{y}_i - \bar{y})^2}{s_p^2}.$$

In repeated sampling, this quantity can be shown to have an F-distribution with $v_1 = 1$ and $v_2 = n_1 + n_2 - 2$ degrees of freedom in the numerator and denominator, respectively. Thus, we could have tested the above hypothesis by calculating

$$\frac{\displaystyle\sum_{i=1}^{2} n_i(\bar{y}_i - \bar{y})^2}{s_p^2} = \frac{n_1(\bar{y}_1 - \bar{y})^2 + n_2(\bar{y}_2 - \bar{y})^2}{s_p^2} = \frac{60.28}{22.23} = 2.71$$

and comparing the value to $F_{16}^{1}(0.05) = 4.49$. Again, we would not reject H_0.

Now, the second approach can be generalized to k populations quite easily. In general, the numerator must have a divisor of $(k - 1)$, so that for testing

$$H_0 : \mu_1 = \mu_2 = \cdots = \mu_k$$

versus

$$H_a : \text{at least two treatment means differ,}$$

we use the test statistic

$$F = \frac{\displaystyle\sum_{i=1}^{k} n_i(\bar{y}_i - \bar{y})^2/(k - 1)}{s_p^2},$$

where

$$s_p^2 = \frac{\displaystyle\sum_{i=1}^{k} (n_i - 1)s_i^2}{n - k}.$$

By inspecting this ratio, we can see that large deviations among the sample means will cause the numerator to be large, and thus may provide evidence for rejection of the null hypothesis. The denominator is an average within-sample variance, and is not affected by differences among the sample means.

The usual analysis of variance notation is given as follows:

$$\text{SST} = \text{sum of squares for treatments}$$

$$= \sum_{i=1}^{k} n_i(\bar{y}_i - \bar{y})^2$$

$$\text{SSE} = \text{sum of squares for error}$$
$$= s_p^2(n - k)$$

$$\text{TSS} = \text{total sum of squares}$$
$$= \text{SST} + \text{SSE}$$

$$\text{MST} = \text{treatment mean square} = \frac{\text{SST}}{k - 1}$$

and

$$\text{MSE} = \text{error mean square} = \frac{\text{SSE}}{n - k} = s_p^2.$$

Thus, the F-ratio for testing $H_0: \mu_1 = \mu_2 = \cdots = \mu_k$ is given by

$$F = \frac{\text{MST}}{\text{MSE}}.$$

Given below are formulas for SST and TSS that minimize computational difficulties, but which are equivalent to those given above, are provided in Table 10.2.

Table 10.2   Calculation Formulas for the Completely Randomized Design

$$\text{TSS} = \sum y^2 - \frac{(\sum y)^2}{n}$$

$$\text{SST} = \sum_{i=1}^{k} \frac{T_i^2}{n_i} - \frac{(\sum y)^2}{n}$$

$$\text{SSE} = \text{TSS} - \text{SST}$$

As in the two-sample t-test, the population probability distributions must be normal and the population variances must be equal in order for $F = \text{MST/MSE}$ to have an F-distribution. The basic analysis of variance F-test is summarized below.

TEST TO COMPARE k TREATMENT MEANS FOR A COMPLETELY RANDOMIZED DESIGN

$$H_0: \mu_1 = \mu_2 = \cdots = \mu_k$$

H_a: at least two treatment means differ

$$\text{Test statistic:} \quad F = \frac{\text{MST}}{\text{MSE}}$$

Assumptions:
1. Each population has a normal probability distribution.
2. The k population variances are equal.

$$\text{Rejection region:}\quad F > F_{n-k}^{k-1}(\alpha).$$

The analysis of variance (ANOVA) summary table is usually written as suggested in Table 10.3.

Table 10.3 ANOVA for Completely Randomized Design

Source	d.f.	S.S.	M.S.	F ratio
Treatments	$k-1$	SST	MST	MST/MSE
Error	$n-k$	SSE	MSE	
Total	$n-1$	TSS		

EXAMPLE 10.1

Specimens were randomly selected from three production processes for steel, with each process using a different percentage of carbon. Independent observations on tensile strength were made, with one observation coming from each specimen. The data are as follows (with measurements in thousand psi):

Process:	A	B	C
	32.1	38.9	42.8
	34.2	40.2	44.6
	29.6	41.4	
		39.5	
Totals:	95.9	160.0	87.4

Is there sufficient evidence to say that the mean tensile strengths differ for the three processes? Use $\alpha = 0.05$.

Solution Using the calculation formulas on p. 320, we have

$$\text{TSS} = \sum y^2 - \frac{(\sum y)^2}{n} = 13{,}300.67 - \frac{(343.3)^2}{9}$$

$$= 205.68$$

$$\text{SST} = \sum_{i=1}^{3} \frac{T_i^2}{n_i} - \frac{(\sum y)^2}{n} = \frac{(95.9)^2}{3} + \frac{(160.0)^2}{4} + \frac{(87.4)^2}{2} - \frac{(343.3)^2}{9}$$

$$= 190.00$$

and

$$SSE = TSS - SST = 15.68.$$

The test statistic then has the value

$$F = \frac{MST}{MSE} = \frac{SST/(k-1)}{SSE/(n-k)} = \frac{190.00/2}{15.68/6} = 36.35.$$

Since $F_6^2(0.05) = 5.14$, we reject the hypothesis that the mean tensile strengths for the three processes are equal.

The ANOVA table is as follows:

Source	d.f.	S.S.	M.S.	F ratio
Treatments	2	190.00	95.000	36.35
Error	6	15.68	2.613	
Total	8	205.68		

We will show in Section 10.3 that the analysis just given can be conducted through regression models. In Section 10.4 we will discuss estimation of treatment means.

Exercises

10.1   Independent random samples were selected from three normally distributed populations with common (but unknown) variance, σ^2. The data shown below:

Sample 1	Sample 2	Sample 3
3.1	5.4	1.1
4.3	3.6	0.2
1.2	4.0	3.0
	2.9	

(a) Compute the appropriate sums of squares and mean squares and fill in the appropriate entries in the analysis of variance table shown below:

ANOVA Table

Source	d.f.	SS	MS	F
Treatments				
Error				
Total				

(b) Test the hypothesis that the population means are equal (that is, $\mu_1 = \mu_2 = \mu_3$) against the alternative hypothesis that at least one mean is different from the other two. Test using $\alpha = 0.05$.

10.2   A partially completed ANOVA table for a completely randomized design is shown below:

Source	d.f.	SS	MS	F
Treatments	4	24.7		
Error				
Total	34	62.4		

(a) Complete the ANOVA table.
(b) How many treatments are involved in the experiment?
(c) Do the data provide sufficient evidence to indicate a difference among the population means? Test using $\alpha = 0.01$.

10.3   Some varieties of nematodes (round worms that live in the soil and frequently are so small they are invisible to the naked eye) feed upon the roots of lawn grasses and other plants. This pest, which is particularly troublesome in warm climates, can be treated by the application of nematicides. Data collected on the percentage of kill for nematodes for four particular rates of application (dosages given in pounds of active ingredient per acre) are as follows:

Rate of Application			
2	3	5	7
86	87	94	90
82	93	99	85
76	89	97	86
		91	

Do the data provide sufficient evidence to indicate a difference in the mean percentage of kill for the four different rates of application of nematicide? Use $\alpha = 0.05$.

10.4 It has been hypothesized that treatment (after casting) of a plastic used in optic lenses will improve wear. Four different treatments are to be tested. To determine whether any differences in mean wear exist among treatments, twenty-eight castings from a single formulation of the plastic were made and seven castings were randomly assigned to each of the treatments. Wear was determined by measuring the increase in "haze" after 200 cycles of abrasion (better wear being indicated by small increases).

| | Treatment | | |
A	B	C	D
9.16	11.95	11.47	11.35
13.29	15.15	9.54	8.73
12.07	14.75	11.26	10.00
11.97	14.79	13.66	9.75
13.31	15.48	11.18	11.71
12.32	13.47	15.03	12.45
11.78	13.06	14.86	12.38

(a) Is there evidence of a difference in mean wear among the four treatments? Use $\alpha = 0.05$.
(b) Estimate the mean difference in haze increase between treatments B and C using a 99% confidence interval.
(c) Find a 90% confidence interval for the mean wear for lenses receiving treatment A.

10.5 The concentration of a catalyst used in producing grouted sand is thought to affect its strength. An experiment designed to investigate the effects of three different concentrations of the catalyst utilized five specimens of grout per concentration. The strength of a grouted sand was determined by placing the test specimen in a press and applying pressure until the specimen broke. The pressure required to break the specimens, expressed in pounds per square inch, are shown below.

| Concentration of Catalyst | | |
35%	40%	45%
5.9	6.8	9.9
8.1	7.9	9.0
5.6	8.4	8.6
6.3	9.3	7.9
7.7	8.2	8.7

Do the data provide sufficient evidence to indicate a difference in mean strength of the grouted sand among the three concentrations of catalyst? Test using $\alpha = 0.05$.

10.6 Several companies are experimenting with the concept of paying production workers (generally paid by the hour) on a salary basis. It is believed that absenteeism and tardiness will increase under this plan, yet some companies feel that the working environment and overall productivity will improve. Fifty production workers under the salary plan are monitored at company A, and likewise, fifty under the hourly plan at company B. The number of work-hours missed due to tardiness or absenteeism over a 1-year period is recorded for each worker. The results are partially summarized in the table.

Source	d.f.	SS	MS	F
Company		3,237.2		
Error		16,167.7		
Total	99			

(a) Fill in the missing information above.
(b) Is there evidence at the $\alpha = 0.05$ level of significance that the mean number of hours missed differs for employees of the two companies?

10.7 One of the selling points of golf balls is their durability. An independent testing laboratory is commissioned to compare the durability of three different brands of golf balls. Balls of each type will be put into a machine that hits the balls with the same force that a golfer does on the course. The number of hits required until the outer covering cracks is recorded for each ball, with the results given in the table below. Ten balls from each manufacturer are randomly selected for testing.

| | Brand | |
A	B	C
310	261	233
235	219	289
279	263	301
306	247	264
237	288	273
284	197	208
259	207	245
273	221	271
219	244	298
301	228	276

Is there evidence that the mean durabilities of the three brands differ? Use $\alpha = 0.05$.

10.8 Eight independent observations on percent copper content were taken on each of four castings of bronze. The sample means for each casting are as follows:

$$
\begin{array}{lcccc}
\text{Casting:} & 1 & 2 & 3 & 4 \\
\text{Means:} & 80 & 81 & 86 & 90 \\
\text{SSE} = 700
\end{array}
$$

Is there sufficient evidence to say that there are differences among the mean percentages of copper for the four castings? Use $\alpha = 0.01$.

10.9   Three thermometers are used regularly in a certain laboratory. To check the relative accuracies of the thermometers, they are randomly and independently placed in a cell kept at zero degrees centigrade. Each thermometer is placed in the cell four times, with the following results:

Thermometer	1	2	3
Reading	0.10	−0.20	0.90
(Degrees C)	0.90	0.80	0.20
	−0.80	−0.30	0.30
	−0.20	0.60	−0.30

Are there significant differences among the means for the three thermometers? Use $\alpha = 0.05$.

10.10   Casts of aluminum were subjected to four standard heat treatments and their tensile strengths measured. Five measurements were taken on each treatment, with the following results (in 1000 psi):

Treatment:	A	B	C	D
	35	41	42	31
	31	40	49	32
	40	43	45	30
	36	39	47	32
	32	45	48	34

Perform an analysis of variance. Do the mean tensile strengths differ from treatment to treatment, at the 5% significance level?

10.3   *A Linear Model for the Completely Randomized Design*

The analysis of variance, as presented in Section 10.2, can be produced through the regression techniques given in Chapters 8 and 9. This approach is particularly beneficial if a computer program for multiple regression is available.

Consider the experiment of Example 10.1 involving three treatments. If we let Y denote the response variable for the measurement on one specimen, we can model Y as

$$Y = \beta_0 + \beta_1 x_1 + \beta_2 x_2 + \varepsilon$$

where

$$x_1 = \begin{cases} 1 & \text{if the response is from treatment B} \\ 0 & \text{otherwise,} \end{cases}$$

$$x_2 = \begin{cases} 1 & \text{if the response is from treatment C} \\ 0 & \text{otherwise,} \end{cases}$$

and ε is the random error, with $E(\varepsilon) = 0$ and $V(\varepsilon) = \sigma^2$. For a response, Y_A, from treatment A, $x_1 = 0$ and $x_2 = 0$ and, hence

$$E(Y_A) = \beta_0 = \mu_A.$$

For a response, Y_B, from the treatment B, $x_1 = 1$ and $x_2 = 0$, so that

$$E(Y_B) = \beta_0 + \beta_1 = \mu_B.$$

It follows that

$$\beta_1 = \mu_B - \mu_A.$$

In like manner,

$$E(Y_C) = \beta_0 + \beta_2 = \mu_C$$

and thus

$$\beta_2 = \mu_C - \mu_A.$$

The null hypothesis of interest in the analysis of variance, namely $H_0: \mu_A = \mu_B = \mu_C$, is now equivalent to $H_0: \beta_1 = \beta_2 = 0$.

For fitting the above model by the method of least squares, the data would be arrayed as follows:

y	x_1	x_2
32.1	0	0
34.2	0	0
29.6	0	0
38.9	1	0
40.2	1	0
41.4	1	0
39.5	1	0
42.8	0	1
44.6	0	1

The method of least squares will give

$$\hat{\beta}_0 = \bar{y}_A,$$

$$\hat{\beta}_1 = \bar{y}_B - \bar{y}_A,$$

and

$$\hat{\beta}_2 = \bar{y}_C - \bar{y}_A.$$

The error sum of squares for this model, denoted by SSE_2, turns out to be

$$\text{SSE}_2 = \text{TSS} - \text{SST} = 15.68.$$

Under $H_0 : \beta_1 = \beta_2 = 0$, the reduced model becomes $Y = \beta_0 + \varepsilon$. The error sum of squares, when this model is fit by the method of least squares, is denoted by SSE_1 and is computed to be

$$\text{SSE}_1 = \text{TSS} = 205.68.$$

The F-test discussed in Section 9.6 for testing $H_0 : \beta_1 = \beta_2 = 0$ has the form

$$F = \frac{(\text{SSE}_1 - \text{SSE}_2)/2}{\text{SSE}_2/(n-3)},$$

which is equivalent to

$$F = \frac{[\text{TSS} - (\text{TSS} - \text{SST})]/2}{\text{SSE}_2/(n-3)} = \frac{\text{SST}/2}{\text{SSE}_2/(n-3)} = \frac{\text{MST}}{\text{MSE}}.$$

Thus, the F-test arising from the regression formulation is equivalent to the analysis of variance F-test as given in Section 10.2.

All of the analysis of variance problems discussed in this chapter can be formulated in terms of regression problems, as shown in Sections 10.6 and 10.8.

Exercises

10.11 Refer to Exercise 10.1. Answer part (b) by writing the appropriate linear model and using regression techniques.

10.12 Refer to Exercise 10.3. Test the assumption of equal percentages of kill for the four rates of application by writing a linear model and using regression techniques.

10.13 Refer to Exercise 10.9. Write a linear model for this experiment. Test for significant differences among the three means by making use of regression techniques.

10.4   *Estimation for the Completely Randomized Design*

Confidence intervals for treatment means and differences between treatment means can be produced by the methods introduced in Chapter 7. Recall that we are assuming all treatment populations to be normally distributed with a common variance. Thus, the confidence intervals based upon the t-distribution can be employed. The common population variance, σ^2, is estimated by the pooled sample variance, $s^2 = \text{MSE}$.

Since we have k means in an analysis of variance problem, we may want to construct a number of confidence intervals based on the same set of experimental data. For example, we may want to construct confidence intervals for all k means individually or for all possible differences between pairs of means. If such multiple intervals are to be used, we must use extreme care in selecting the confidence coefficients for the individual intervals so that the *experimentwise* error rate remains small.

For example, suppose that we construct two confidence intervals,

$$\bar{Y}_A \pm t_{\alpha/2}\frac{s}{\sqrt{n}} \quad \text{and} \quad \bar{Y}_B \pm t_{\alpha/2}\frac{s}{\sqrt{n}}.$$

Now, $P(\bar{Y}_A \pm t_{\alpha/2}s/\sqrt{n} \text{ includes } \mu_A) = 1 - \alpha$ and $P(\bar{Y}_B \pm t_{\alpha/2}s/\sqrt{n} \text{ includes } \mu_B) = 1 - \alpha$. But,

$$P\left(\bar{Y}_A \pm t_{\alpha/2}\frac{s}{\sqrt{n}} \text{ includes } \mu_A \text{ and } \bar{Y}_B \pm t_{\alpha/2}\frac{s}{\sqrt{n}} \text{ includes } \mu_B\right) < 1 - \alpha$$

and so the simultaneous coverage probability is *less than* the $(1 - \alpha)$ confidence coefficient that we used on each interval.

If c intervals are to be constructed on one set of experimental data, then one method of keeping the simultaneous coverage probability (or confidence coefficient) at a value of *at least* $1 - \alpha$ is make the individual confidence coefficients as close as possible to $1 - (\alpha/c)$. This technique for multiple confidence intervals is outlined in the following summary.

CONFIDENCE INTERVALS FOR MEANS IN THE COMPLETELY RAN-DOMIZED DESIGN   Suppose c intervals are to be constructed from one set of data.

$$\text{Single treatment mean, } \mu_i \text{:} \bar{y}_i \pm t_{\alpha/2c}\frac{s}{\sqrt{n_i}}$$

Difference between two treatment means, $\mu_i - \mu_j$:

$$(\bar{y}_i - \bar{y}_j) \pm t_{\alpha/2c}s\sqrt{\frac{1}{n_i} + \frac{1}{n_j}}$$

Note that $s = \sqrt{\text{MSE}}$ and all t-values depend on $n - k$ degrees of freedom.

EXAMPLE 10.2

Using the data of Example 10.1, construct confidence intervals for all three possible differences between treatment means so that the simultaneous confidence coefficient is at least 0.95.

Solution   Since there are three intervals to construct ($c = 3$), each interval should be of the form

$$(\bar{y}_i - \bar{y}_j) \pm t_{0.05/2(3)}s\sqrt{\frac{1}{n_i} + \frac{1}{n_j}}.$$

Now, $t_{0.05/2(3)} = t_{0.05/6}$ is approximately $t_{0.01}$. (This is as close as we can get with Table 5 given in the Appendix.) With $n - k = 6$ degrees of freedom, the tabled value is $t_{0.01} = 3.143$.

The three intervals are then constructed as follows:

$$\mu_A - \mu_B: (\bar{y}_A - \bar{y}_B) \pm t_{0.01}s\sqrt{\frac{1}{n_A} + \frac{1}{n_B}}$$

$$(31.97 - 40.00) \pm (3.143)\sqrt{2.61}\sqrt{\frac{1}{3} + \frac{1}{4}}$$

$$-8.03 \pm 3.88$$

$$\mu_A - \mu_C: (\bar{y}_A - \bar{y}_C) \pm t_{0.01}s\sqrt{\frac{1}{n_A} + \frac{1}{n_C}}$$

$$(31.97 - 43.70) \pm (3.143)\sqrt{2.61}\sqrt{\frac{1}{3} + \frac{1}{2}}$$

$$-11.73 \pm 4.64$$

$$\mu_B - \mu_C: (\bar{y}_B - \bar{y}_C) \pm t_{0.01}s\sqrt{\frac{1}{n_B} + \frac{1}{n_C}}$$

$$(40.00 - 43.70) \pm (3.143)\sqrt{2.61}\sqrt{\frac{1}{4} + \frac{1}{2}}$$

$$-3.70 \pm 4.40.$$

In interpreting these results, we would be inclined to say that μ_A and μ_B differ (since the observed interval does not overlap zero), μ_A and μ_C differ, but μ_B and μ_C do not differ. Our combined confidence level for making all three statements is at least 0.95.

If the $t_{0.025}$ value (with 6 degrees of freedom) had been used in place of the $t_{0.01}$ value, the interval on $\mu_B - \mu_C$ would have been -3.70 ± 3.43, and we would say that μ_B and μ_C differ. However, in doing this our combined confidence level is reduced to something below 0.95. $\square$

Exercises

10.14   Refer to Exercise 10.1.
   (a) Find a 90% confidence interval for $(\mu_2 - \mu_3)$. Interpret the interval.
   (b) What would happen to the width of the confidence interval in part (c) if you quadrupled the number of observations in the two samples?

(c) Find a 95% confidence interval for μ_2.

(d) Approximately how many observations would be required if you wished to be able to estimate a population mean correct to within 0.4 with probability equal to 0.95?

10.15 Refer to Exercise 10.2.

(a) Suppose that $\bar{y}_1 = 3.7$ and $\bar{y}_2 = 4.1$. Do the data provide sufficient evidence to indicate a difference between μ_1 and μ_2? Assume that there are seven observations for each treatment. Test using $\alpha = 0.10$.

(b) Refer to part (a). Find a 90% confidence interval for $(\mu_1 - \mu_2)$.

(c) Refer to part (a). Find a 90% confidence interval for μ_1.

10.16 Refer to Exercise 10.3.

(a) Estimate the true difference in mean percentage of kill between rate 2 and rate 5. Use a 90% confidence interval.

(b) Construct confidence intervals for the six possible differences between treatment means, with simultaneous confidence close to 0.90.

10.17 Refer to Exercise 10.5.

(a) Find a 95% confidence interval for the difference in mean strength for specimens produced with a 35% concentration of catalyst versus those containing a 45% concentration of catalyst.

(b) Construct confidence intervals for the three treatment means, with simultaneous confidence coefficient approximately 0.90.

10.18 Refer to Exercise 10.8. Casting 1 is a standard and 2, 3, and 4 involve slight modifications to the process. Compare the standard with each of the modified processes by producing three confidence intervals with simultaneous confidence coefficient approximately 0.90.

10.5 *Analysis of Variance for the Randomized Block Design*

In the completely randomized design only one source of variation, the treatment-to-treatment variation, is specifically considered in the design and analyzed after the data is collected. That is, observations are taken from each of k treatments, and then a test and confidence intervals are constructed to analyze how the treatment means may differ.

Most often, however, the responses of interest are subject to sources of variation in addition to the treatments under study. Suppose, for example, that an engineer is studying the gas mileage resulting from four brands of gasoline. If more than one automobile is used in the study, then automobiles would form another important source of variation. To control for this additional variation, it would be crucially important to run each brand of gasoline at least once in each automobile. In this type of experiment, the brands of gasoline are the *treatments* and the automobiles are called the *blocks*. If the order of running the brands in each automobile is randomized, the resulting design is called a *randomized block design*. Letting the brands be denoted by A, B, C, and D and the automobiles by I, II and III, the structure of the design might look like Figure 10.1.

	I	II	III
	B	A	D
	A	C	B
	C	B	A
	D	D	C

Figure 10.1   Typical Randomized Block Design

For auto I, brand B was run first, followed in order by A, C, and D.

DEFINITION 10.2   A **randomized block design** is a plan for collecting data in which each of k treatments is measured once in each of b blocks. The order of the treatments within the blocks is random.

The blocking helps the experimenter control a source of variation in responses so that any true treatment differences are more likely to show up in the analysis. Suppose that the gasoline mileage study did, in fact, use more than one automobile, but that we had not blocked on automobiles as indicated above. Assuming that we still take three measurements on each treatment, as indicated in Figure 10.2, two undesirable conditions might result.

A	B	C	D
—	—	—	—
—	—	—	—
—	—	—	—

Figure 10.2   A Completely Randomized Design for the Gasoline Mileage Study

Table 10.4   Notation for the Results of Randomized Block Experiment Treatments

		1	2	$\cdots$	k	Totals
Blocks	1	y_{11}	y_{12}	$\cdots$	y_{1k}	B_1
	2	y_{21}	y_{22}	$\cdots$	y_{2k}	B_2
	$\vdots$	$\vdots$	$\vdots$	$\cdots$	$\vdots$	$\vdots$
	b	y_{b1}	y_{b2}	$\cdots$	y_{bk}	B_b
Totals		T_1	T_2	$\cdots$	T_k	

Total sample size $= n = bk$

Overall sample total $= \sum y = T_1 + T_2 + \cdots + T_k$
$$= B_1 + B_2 + \cdots + B_b$$

Overall sample mean $= \sum y/n$

Sum of squares of all n measurements $= \sum y^2$

Note that there are k treatments and b blocks.

First, the auto-to-auto variation would add to the variance of the measurements within each sample, and, hence, inflate the MSE. The F-test could then turn out to be nonsignificant even when differences do exist among the true treatment means. Second, all of the A responses could turn out to be from automobile I and all of the B responses from automobile II. If the mean for A and the mean for B are significantly different, we still don't know how to interpret the result. Are the brands really different or are the automobiles different with respect to gas mileage? A randomized block design will help us avoid both of these difficulties.

After the measurements are completed in a randomized block design, as shown in Figure 10.1, they can be rearranged into a two-way table, as given in Table 10.4.

The total sum of squares (TSS) can now be partitioned into a treatment sum of squares (SST), a block sum of squares (SSB), and an error sum of squares (SSE). The computation formulas are given in Table 10.5.

$$\text{TSS} = \sum y^2 - \frac{(\sum y)^2}{n}$$

$$\text{SST} = \frac{1}{b} \sum_{i=1}^{k} T_i^2 - \frac{(\sum y)^2}{n}$$

$$\text{SSB} = \frac{1}{k} \sum_{i=1}^{b} B_i^2 - \frac{(\sum y^2)}{n}$$

$$\text{SSE} = \text{TSS} - \text{SST} - \text{SSB}$$

$$\text{MST} = \frac{\text{SST}}{k-1}$$

$$\text{MSB} = \frac{\text{SSB}}{b-1}$$

Table 10.5 Calculation Formulas for the Randomized Block Design

$$\text{MSE} = \frac{\text{SSE}}{n-k-b+1} = \frac{\text{SSE}}{(b-1)(k-1)}$$

The test of the null hypothesis that the k treatment means, $\mu_1, \mu_2, \ldots, \mu_k$, are equal is, once again, an F-test constructed as the ratio of MST to MSE. In an analogous fashion, we could construct a test of the hypothesis that the block means are equal. The resulting F-test for this case would be the ratio of MSB to MSE.

TEST TO COMPARE k TREATMENT MEANS FOR A RANDOMIZED BLOCK DESIGN

$$H_0 : \mu_1 = \mu_2 = \cdots = \mu_k$$

H_a: At least two treatment means differ

Test statistic: $F = \dfrac{\text{MST}}{\text{MSE}}$

Assumptions:
1. Each population (treatment-block combination) has a normal probability distribution.
2. The variances of the probability distributions are equal.

Rejection region: $F > F_{(b-1)(k-1)}^{k-1}(\alpha)$

The analysis of variance summary table for a randomized block design is given in Table 10.6.

Table 10.6   ANOVA for a Randomized Block Design

Source	d.f.	S.S.	M.S.	F ratio
Treatments	$k-1$	SST	MST	MST/MSE
Blocks	$b-1$	SSB	MSB	MSB/MSE
Errors	$(b-1)(k-1)$	SSE	MSE	
Total	$bk-1$	TSS		

EXAMPLE 10.3

Four chemical treatments for fabric are to be compared with regard to their ability to resist stains. Two different types of fabric are available for the experiment, so it is decided to apply each chemical to a sample of each type of fabric. The result is a randomized block design with four treatments and two blocks. The measurements are as follows:

		Block (Fabric)		
		1	2	Totals
	1	5	9	14
Treatment	2	3	8	11
(Chemicals)	3	8	13	21
	4	4	6	10
Totals		20	36	56

Is there evidence of significant differences among the treatment means? Use $\alpha = 0.05$.

Solution   For these data, the computations (see Table 10.4) are as follows:

$$\text{TSS} = 464 - \frac{(56)^2}{8} = 464 - 392 = 72,$$

$$\text{SST} = \frac{1}{2}\left[(14)^2 + (11)^2 + (21)^2 + (10)^2\right] - \frac{(56)^2}{8}$$

$$= 429 - 392 = 37,$$

$$\text{SSB} = \frac{1}{4}[(20)^2 + (36)^2] - \frac{(56)^2}{8} = 424 - 392 = 32,$$

$$\text{SSE} = \text{TSS} - \text{SST} - \text{SSB} = 72 - 37 - 32 = 3.$$

The ANOVA summary table then becomes

Source	d.f.	S.S.	M.S.	F-ratio
Treatments	3	37	$\frac{37}{3} = 12.33$	$\frac{12.33}{1} = 12.33$
Blocks	1	32	$\frac{32}{1} = 32$	$\frac{32}{1} = 32$
Error	3	3	$\frac{3}{3} = 1$	
Total	7			

Since $F_3^3(0.05) = 9.28$ and our observed F-ratio for treatments is 12.33, we reject $H_0 : \mu_1 = \mu_2 = \mu_3 = \mu_4$ and say that there is significant evidence of at least one treatment difference.

We also see in this summary table that the F-ratio for blocks is 32. Since $F_3^1(0.05) = 10.13$, we say that there is evidence of a difference between the block (fabric) means. That is, the fabrics seem to differ with respect to their ability to resist stains when treated with these chemicals.   □

Now we turn to a brief discussion of how the randomized block experiment can be analyzed by a linear model, and then consider estimation of means for this design.

Exercises

10.19 A randomized block design was conducted to compare the mean responses for three treatments, A, B, and C, in four blocks. The data are shown below:

		Block		
Treatment	1	2	3	4
A	3	6	1	2
B	5	7	4	6
C	2	3	2	2

(a) Compute the appropriate sums of squares and mean squares and fill in the entries in the analysis of variance table shown below:

ANOVA Table

Source	d.f.	SS	MS	F
Treatment				
Block				
Error				
Total				

(b) Do the data provide sufficient evidence to indicate a difference among treatment means? Test using $\alpha = 0.05$.

(c) Do the data provide sufficient evidence to indicate that blocking was effective in reducing the experimental error? Test using $\alpha = 0.05$.

10.20 The analysis of variance for a randomized block design produced the ANOVA table entries shown below:

ANOVA Table

Source	d.f.	SS	MS	F
Treatment	3	27.1		
Block	5		14.90	
Error		33.4		
Total				

(a) Complete the ANOVA table.

(b) Do the data provide sufficient evidence to indicate a difference among the treatment means? Test using $\alpha = 0.01$.

(c) Do the data provide sufficient evidence to indicate that blocking was a useful design strategy to employ for this experiment? Explain.

10.21 An evaluation of diffusion bonding of zircaloy components is performed. The main objective is to determine which of three elements—nickel, iron, or copper—is the best bonding agent. A series of zircaloy components are bonded using each of the possible bonding agents. Since there is a great deal of variation in components machined from different ingots, a randomized block design is used, blocking on the ingots. A pair of components from each ingot are bonded together using each of the three agents, and the pressure (in units of 1,000 pounds per square inch) required to separate the bonded components is measured. The following data are obtained.

Ingot	Bonding Agent		
	Nickel	Iron	Copper
1	67.0	71.9	72.2
2	67.5	68.8	66.4
3	76.0	82.6	74.5
4	72.7	78.1	67.3
5	73.1	74.2	73.2
6	65.8	70.8	68.7
7	75.6	84.9	69.0

Is there evidence of a difference in pressure required to separate the components among the three bonding agents? Use $\alpha = 0.05$.

10.22 A construction firm employs three cost estimators. Usually, only one estimator works on each potential job, but it is advantageous to the company if the estimators are consistent enough so that it does not matter which of the three estimators is assigned to a particular job. To check on the consistency of the estimators, several jobs are selected and all three estimators are asked to make estimates. The estimates for each job by each estimator are given in the table.

Estimates (in thousands of dollars)

Job	Estimator		
	A	B	C
1	27.3	26.5	28.2
2	66.7	67.3	65.9
3	104.8	102.1	100.8
4	87.6	85.6	86.5
5	54.5	55.6	55.9
6	58.7	59.2	60.1

(a) Do these estimates provide sufficient evidence that the means for the estimators differ? Use $\alpha = 0.05$.

(b) Present the complete ANOVA summary table for this experiment.

10.23 A power plant, which uses water from the surrounding bay for cooling its condensors, is required by EPA to determine whether discharging its heated water into the bay has a detrimental effect on the flora (plant life) in the water. The EPA requests that the power plant make its investigation at three strategically chosen locations, called *stations*. Stations 1 and 2 are located near the plant's discharge tubes, while Station 3 is located farther out in the bay. During one randomly selected day in each of four months, a diver is sent down to each of the stations, randomly samples a square meter area of the bottom, and counts the number of blades of the different types of grasses present. The results are as follows for one important grass type:

Month	Station 1	2	3
May	28	31	53
June	25	22	61
July	37	30	56
August	20	26	48

(a) Is there sufficient evidence to indicate that the mean number of blades found per square meter per month differs for the three stations? Use $\alpha = 0.05$.

(b) Is there sufficient evidence to indicate that the mean number of blades found per square meter differs across the 4 months? Use $\alpha = 0.05$.

10.24 From time to time, one branch office of a company must make shipments to a certain branch office in another state. There are three package delivery services between the two cities where the branch offices are located. Since the price structures for the three delivery services are quite similar, the company wants to compare the delivery times. The company plans to make several different types of shipments to its branch office. To compare the carriers, each shipment will be sent in triplicate, one with each carrier. The results listed in the table are the delivery times in hours.

Shipment	Carrier I	II	III
1	15.2	16.9	17.1
2	14.3	16.4	16.1
3	14.7	15.9	15.7
4	15.1	16.7	17.0
5	14.0	15.6	15.5

Is there evidence of a difference in mean delivery times among the three carriers? Use $\alpha = 0.05$.

10.25 Due to increased energy shortages and costs, utility companies are stressing ways in which home and apartment utility bills can be cut. One utility company reached an agreement with the owner of a new apartment complex to conduct a test of energy saving plans for apartments. The tests were to be conducted before the apartments were rented. Four apartments were chosen that were identical in size, amount of shade, and direction faced. Four plans were to be tested, one on each apartment. The thermostat was set at 75°F in each apartment and the monthly utility bill was recorded for each of the 3 summer months. The results are listed in the table.

| | | Treatment | | |
Month	1	2	3	4
June	$74.44	$68.75	$71.34	$65.47
July	89.96	73.47	83.62	72.33
August	82.00	71.23	79.98	70.87

Treatment 1:   No insulation
Treatment 2:   Insulation in walls and ceilings
Treatment 3:   No insulation; awnings for windows
Treatment 4:   Insulation and awnings for windows
(a) Is there evidence that the mean monthly utility bills differ for the four treatments? Use $\alpha = 0.01$.
(b) Is there evidence that blocking is important, that is, that the mean bills differ for the 3 months? Use $\alpha = 0.05$.

10.26 A chemist runs an experiment to study the effect of four treatments on the glass transition temperature of a particular polymer compound. Raw material used to make this polymer is bought in small batches. The material is thought to be fairly uniform within a batch but variable between batches. Therefore, each treatment was run on samples from each batch with the following results:

Temperature (in °K)

| | | Treatment | | |
Batch	I	II	III	IV
1	576	584	562	543
2	515	563	522	536
3	562	555	550	530

(a) Do the data provide sufficient evidence to indicate a difference in mean temperature among the four treatments? Use $\alpha = 0.05$.
(b) Is there sufficient evidence to indicate a difference in mean temperature among the three batches? Use $\alpha = 0.05$.
(c) If the experiment is conducted again in the future, would you recommend any changes in its design?

10.6   *A Linear Model for the Randomized Block Design*

Section 10.3 contains a discussion of the regression approach to the analysis of a completely randomized design. A similar linear model can be written for the randomized block design.

Letting Y denote a response from the randomized block design of Example 10.3, we can write

$$Y = \beta_0 + \beta_1 x_1 + \beta_2 x_2 + \beta_3 x_3 + \beta_4 x_4 + \varepsilon,$$

where

$$x_1 = \begin{cases} 1 & \text{if the response is from treatment 1} \\ 0 & \text{otherwise,} \end{cases}$$

$$x_2 = \begin{cases} 1 & \text{if the response is from treatment 2} \\ 0 & \text{otherwise,} \end{cases}$$

$$x_3 = \begin{cases} 1 & \text{if the response is from treatment 3} \\ 0 & \text{otherwise,} \end{cases}$$

$$x_4 = \begin{cases} 1 & \text{if the response is from treatment 4} \\ 0 & \text{otherwise,} \end{cases}$$

and ε is the random error term. The error sum of squares for this model is denoted by SSE_2. Testing the null hypothesis that the four treatment means are equal is now equivalent to testing $H_0: \beta_2 = \beta_3 = \beta_4 = 0$. The reduced model is then

$$Y = \beta_0 + \beta_1 x_1 + \varepsilon,$$

which, when fit by the method of least squares, will produce an error sum of squares denoted by SSE_1.

The F-test for $H_0: \beta_2 = \beta_3 = \beta_4 = 0$ versus the alternative that at least one β_i, $i = 2, 3, 4$, is different from zero then has the form

$$F = \frac{(SSE_1 - SSE_2)/(k - 1)}{SSE_2/(b - 1)(k - 1)}$$

$$= \frac{SST/(k - 1)}{SSE_2/(b - 1)(k - 1)} = \frac{MST}{MSE}.$$

This test is equivalent to the F-test for equality of treatment means given in Section 10.5.

The SAS regression printouts for the two models are shown in Figure 10.3. The sum of squared errors (SSE) for the complete and reduced model are boxed:

$$\text{Reduced model:} \quad SSE_1 = 40$$

$$\text{Complete model:} \quad SSE_2 = 3.$$

Then

$$F = \frac{(40 - 3)/3}{3/3} = 12.33,$$

which is exactly the same F value calculated in Example 10.3. The regression approach leads us to the same conclusion as did the ANOVA approach: there is evidence that the mean stain resistances of the four chemicals differ.

(a) Complete Model

SOURCE	DF	SUM OF SQUARES	MEAN SQUARE	F VALUE
MODEL	4	69.00000000	17.25000000	17.25
ERROR	3	3.00000000	1.00000000	PR > F
CORRECTED TOTAL	7	72.00000000		0.0207

R-SQUARE	C.V.	STD DEV	Y MEAN
0.958333	14.2857	1.00000000	7.00000000

PARAMETER	ESTIMATE	T FOR H0: PARAMETER = 0	PR > |T|	STD ERROR OF ESTIMATE
INTERCEPT	5.00000000	6.32	0.0080	0.79056942
X1	4.00000000	5.66	0.0109	0.70710678
X2	−1.50000000	−1.50	0.2306	1.00000000
X3	3.50000000	3.50	0.0395	1.00000000
X4	−2.00000000	−2.00	0.1393	1.00000000

(b) Reduced Model

SOURCE	DF	SUM OF SQUARES	MEAN SQUARE	F VALUE
MODEL	1	32.00000000	32.00000000	4.80
ERROR	6	40.00000000	6.66666667	PR > F
CORRECTED TOTAL	7	72.00000000		0.0710

R-SQUARE	C.V.	STD DEV	Y MEAN
0.444444	36.8856	2.58198890	7.00000000

PARAMETER	ESTIMATE	T FOR H0: PARAMETER = 0	PR > |T|	STD ERROR OF ESTIMATE
INTERCEPT	5.00000000	3.87	0.0082	1.29099445
X1	4.00000000	2.19	0.0710	1.82574186

Figure 10.3   SAS Printouts for Complete and Reduced Models, Example 10.3

The randomized block design is only one of many types of block designs. When there are two sources of nuisance variation, it is necessary to block on both sources to eliminate this unwanted variability. Blocking in two directions can be accomplished by using a Latin square design.

In order to evaluate the toxicity of certain compounds in water, samples must be preserved for long periods of time. Suppose an experiment is being conducted to evaluate the Maximum Holding Time (MHT) for four different preservatives used to treat a mercury-base compound. The MHT is defined as the time that elapses before the solution loses 10% of its initial concentration. Both the level of the initial concentration and the analyst who measures the MHT are sources of variation, so an experimental design that blocks on both is necessary in order to allow the difference in mean MHT between preservatives to be more accurately estimated. A Latin square design is constructed wherein each preservative is applied exactly *once* to each initial concentration, and is analyzed *exactly once* by each analyst. You can see why the design must be "square," since the single application of each treatment level at each block level requires that the number of levels of each block *equal* the number of treatment levels. Thus, to apply the Latin square design using four different preservatives, we must employ four initial concentrations and four analysts. The design would be constructed as shown in Figure 10.4, where P_i = Preservative i ($i = 1, 2, 3, 4$). Note that each preservative appears exactly once in each row (initial concentration) and each column (analyst). The resulting design is a 4×4 Latin square. A Latin square design for three treatments will require a 3×3 configuration and, in general, p treatments will require a $p \times p$ array of experimental units. If more observations are desired per treatment, the experimenter would utilize several Latin square configurations in one experiment. In the example above, it would be necessary to run two Latin squares to obtain eight observations per treatment.

A comparison of mean MHT for any pair of preservatives would eliminate the variability due to initial concentration and to analysts, because each preservative was applied with equal frequency (once) at each level of both blocking factors. Consequently, the block effects would be canceled when comparing mean MHT for any pair of preservatives.

The linear model for the Latin square design is an extension of that for the randomized block design. For the MHT example, the model is

$$Y = \beta_0 + \overbrace{\beta_1 x_1 + \beta_2 x_2 + \beta_3 x_3}^{\text{Initial Concentration}} + \overbrace{\beta_4 x_4 + \beta_5 x_5 + \beta_6 x_6}^{\text{Analyst}}$$

$$+ \overbrace{\beta_7 x_7 + \beta_8 x_8 + \beta_9 x_9}^{\text{Preservative}} + \varepsilon$$

where Y = MHT.

$$x_1 = \begin{cases} 1 & \text{if Initial Concentration 1} \\ 0 & \text{otherwise} \end{cases} \qquad x_4 = \begin{cases} 1 & \text{if Analyst 1} \\ 0 & \text{otherwise} \end{cases}$$

$$x_2 = \begin{cases} 1 & \text{if Initial Concentration 2} \\ 0 & \text{otherwise} \end{cases} \qquad x_5 = \begin{cases} 1 & \text{if Analyst 2} \\ 0 & \text{otherwise} \end{cases}$$

$$x_3 = \begin{cases} 1 & \text{if Initial Concentration 3} \\ 0 & \text{otherwise} \end{cases} \qquad x_6 = \begin{cases} 1 & \text{if Analyst 3} \\ 0 & \text{otherwise} \end{cases}$$

$$x_7 = \begin{cases} 1 & \text{if Preservative 1} \\ 0 & \text{otherwise} \end{cases}$$

$$x_8 = \begin{cases} 1 & \text{if Preservative 2} \\ 0 & \text{otherwise} \end{cases}$$

$$x_9 = \begin{cases} 1 & \text{if Preservative 3} \\ 0 & \text{otherwise} \end{cases}$$

Thus, dummy variables are used to represent the block effects, as well as the treatments. To test the null hypothesis of no treatment differences, we test $H_0: \beta_7 = \beta_8 = \beta_9 = 0$ by fitting complete and reduced models, just as we did for the randomized block design. There are equivalent ANOVA formulas (not

Analyst

		1	2	3	4
	1	P_1	P_2	P_3	P_4
	2	P_2	P_3	P_4	P_1
Initial Concentration	3	P_3	P_4	P_1	P_2
	4	P_4	P_1	P_2	P_3

Figure 10.4   A Latin
Square Design

presented here) similar to those presented in Section 10.5 for the randomized block design for calculating the F-test statistic for treatment (and block) differences.

In summary, there are many types of block designs for comparing treatment means while controlling sources of nuisance variation. As with the randomized block and Latin square designs, other block designs can be most easily analyzed using the linear model approach, with dummy variables representing both block and treatment effects. Then the complete and reduced model approach is used to test for treatment and block effects on the mean response.

Note that, in order for the F-tests given above to be valid, we must still make the usual assumptions about the normality of population measurements and equal variances across all treatment-block combinations.

Exercises

10.27   Refer to Exercise 10.19. Answer parts (b) and (c) by fitting a linear model to the data and using regression techniques.

10.28   Refer to Exercise 10.23. Answer part (a) by fitting a linear model to the data and using regression techniques.

10.29   Suppose that three automobile engine designs are being compared to determine differences in mean time between breakdowns.
   (a)   Show how three test automobiles and three different test drivers could be used in a 3×3 Latin square design aimed at comparing the engine designs.
   (b)   Write the linear model for the design in part (a).
   (c)   What null hypothesis would you test in order to determine whether the mean time between breakdowns differs for the engine designs?

10.7   Estimation for the Randomized Block Design

As in the case of the completely randomized design, we may want to estimate the mean for a particular treatment, or the difference between the means of two treatments, after conducting the initial F-test. Since we will generally be interested in c intervals simultaneously, we will want to set the confidence coefficient of each individual interval at $(1 - \alpha/c)$. This will guarantee that the probability of all c intervals simultaneously covering the parameters being estimated is at least $1 - \alpha$. A summary of the estimation procedure is given below.

CONFIDENCE INTERVALS FOR MEANS IN THE RANDOMIZED BLOCK DESIGN   Suppose c intervals are to be constructed from one set of data.

$$\text{Single treatment mean, } \mu_i : \bar{y}_i \pm t_{\alpha/2c} s \sqrt{\frac{1}{b}}$$

Difference between two treatment means, $\mu_i - \mu_j$:

$$(\bar{y}_i - \bar{y}_j) \pm t_{\alpha/2c} s \sqrt{\frac{1}{b} + \frac{1}{b}}$$

Note that $s = \sqrt{\text{MSE}}$ and all t-values depend upon $(k - 1)(b - 1)$ degrees of freedom, where k is the number of treatments and b the number of blocks.

EXAMPLE 10.4

Refer to the four chemical treatments and two blocks (fabrics) of Example 10.3. It is of interest to estimate simultaneously all possible differences between treatment means. Construct confidence intervals for these differences with a simultaneous confidence coefficient of at least 0.90, approximately.

Solution   Since there are four treatment means, μ_1, μ_2, μ_3 and μ_4, there will be $c = 6$ differences of the form $\mu_i - \mu_j$. Since the simultaneous confidence coefficient is to be $1 - \alpha = 0.90$, $\alpha/2c$ becomes $0.10/2(6) = 0.008$. The closest tabled t-values in Table 5 of the Appendix has a tail area of 0.01, and so we will use $t_{0.01}$ as an approximation to $t_{0.008}$.

For the data of Example 10.3, the four sample treatment means are

$$\bar{y}_1 = 7.0, \qquad \bar{y}_2 = 5.5, \qquad \bar{y}_3 = 10.5 \qquad \text{and} \qquad \bar{y}_4 = 5.0.$$

Also, $s = \sqrt{\text{MSE}} = \sqrt{1} = 1$ and $b = 2$. Thus, any interval of the form

$$(\bar{y}_i - \bar{y}_j) \pm t_{0.01} s \sqrt{\frac{1}{b} + \frac{1}{b}}$$

will become

$$(\bar{y}_i - \bar{y}_j) \pm (4.541)(1) \sqrt{\frac{1}{2} + \frac{1}{2}}$$

or

$$(\bar{y}_i - \bar{y}_j) \pm 4.541,$$

since the degrees of freedom are $(b - 1)(k - 1) = 3$. The six confidence intervals are as follows:

Parameter	Interval
$\mu_1 - \mu_2$	$(\bar{y}_1 - \bar{y}_2) \pm 4.541$ or 1.5 ± 4.541
$\mu_1 - \mu_3$	$(\bar{y}_1 - \bar{y}_3) \pm 4.451$ or -3.5 ± 4.541
$\mu_1 - \mu_4$	$(\bar{y}_1 - \bar{y}_4) \pm 4.541$ or 2.0 ± 4.541
$\mu_2 - \mu_3$	$(\bar{y}_2 - \bar{y}_3) \pm 4.541$ or -5.0 ± 4.541
$\mu_2 - \mu_4$	$(\bar{y}_2 - \bar{y}_4) \pm 4.541$ or 0.5 ± 4.541
$\mu_3 - \mu_4$	$(\bar{y}_3 - \bar{y}_4) \pm 4.541$ or 5.5 ± 4.541

The sample data would suggest that μ_2 and μ_3 are significantly different, and μ_3 and μ_4 are significantly different, since these intervals do not overlap zero.   □

Exercises

10.30   Refer to Exercise 10.21.
   (a) Form a 95% confidence interval to estimate the true mean difference in pressure between nickel and iron. Interpret this interval.
   (b) Form confidence intervals on the three possible differences between the means for the bonding agents, using a simultaneous confidence coefficient of approximately 0.90.

10.31   Refer to Exercise 10.22. Use a 90% confidence interval to estimate the true difference between the mean responses given by estimators B and C.

10.32   Refer to Exercise 10.23. What are the significant differences among the station means? (Use a simultaneous confidence coefficient of 0.90.)

10.33   Refer to Exercise 10.24.
   (a) Use a 99% confidence interval to estimate the difference between the mean delivery time for carriers I and II.
   (b) What assumptions are necessary for the validity of the procedures you used in parts (a) and (b)?

10.8   The Factorial Experiment

The response of interest, Y, is, in many experimental situations, related to one or more other variables that can be controlled by the experimenter. For example, the yield, Y, in an experimental study of the process of manufacturing a chemical may be related to the temperature, x_1, and pressure, x_2, at which the experiment is run. The variables temperature and pressure can be controlled by the experimenter. In a study of heat loss through ceilings of houses, the amount of heat loss, Y, will be related to the thickness of insulation, x_1, and the temperature differential, x_2, between the inside and outside of the house. Again, the thickness of insulation and the temperature differential can be controlled by the experimenter as he designs the study. The strength, Y of concrete may be related to the amount of aggregate, x_1, the mixing time, x_2, and the drying time, x_3.

The variables that are thought to affect the response of interest and are controlled by the experimenter are called *factors*. The various settings of these factors in an experiment are called *levels*. A factor-level combination then defines a *treatment*. In the chemical yield example, the temperatures of interest may be 90°, 100° and 110°C. These are the three experimental levels of the factor "temperature." The pressure settings (levels) of interest may be 400 and 450 psi. Setting temperature at 90° and pressure at 450 psi would define a particular treatment, and observations on yield could then be obtained for this combination of levels. Note that three levels of temperature and two of pressure would result in $2 \times 3 = 6$ different treatments, if all factor-level combinations are to be used.

An experiment in which treatments are defined by specified factor-level combinations is referred to as a *factorial experiment*. In this section, we assume that r observations on the response of interest are realized from each treatment, with each observation being independently selected. (That is, the factorial experiment is run in a completely randomized design with r observations per treatment.) The objective of the analysis is to decide if, and to what extent, the various factors affect the response variable. Does the yield of chemical increase as temperature increases? Does the strength of concrete decrease as less and less aggregate is used? These are the types of questions we will be able to answer with the results of this section.

We illustrate the concepts and calculations involved in the analysis of variance for a factorial experiment by considering an example consisting of two factors each at two levels. In the production of a certain industrial chemical the yield, Y, depends upon the cooking time, x_1, and the cooling time, x_2. Two cooking times and two cooling times are of interest. Only the relative magnitudes of the levels are important in the analysis of factorial experiments, and thus we can call the two levels of cooking time 0 and 1. That is, x_1 can take on the value 0 or 1. Similarly, we can call the levels of cooling time 0 and 1, that is, x_2 can take on the values 0 or 1. For convenience, we will refer to cooking time as factor A and cooling time as factor B. Schematically, we then have the arrangement of four treatments seen in Figure 10.3, and we will assume that r observations will be available from each.

The analysis of this factorial experiment could be accomplished by writing a linear regression model for the response, Y, as a function of x_1 and x_2, and then

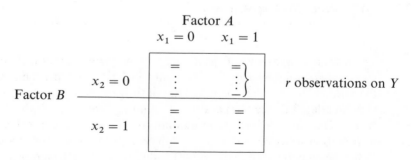

Figure 10.5   A 2 × 2 Factorial Experiment (r observations per treatment)

employing the theory of Chapters 8 and 9. We will proceed by writing the models for illustrative purposes, but we will then present simple calculation formulas that make the actual fitting of the models by least squares unnecessary.

Since Y depends, supposedly, on x_1 and x_2, we could start with the simple model

$$E(Y) = \beta_0 + \beta_1 x_1 + \beta_2 x_2.$$

On Figure 10.4, we see that this model implies that the rate of change on $E(Y)$ as x_1 goes from 0 to 1 is the same (β_1) for each value of x_2. This is referred to as the "no-interaction" case.

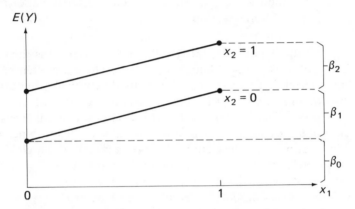

Figure 10.6 $E(Y)$ for a 2 × 2 Factorial Experiment with No Interaction

It is quite likely that the rate of change on $E(Y)$, as x_1 goes from 0 to 1, could be different for different values of x_2. To account for this *interaction* we write the model as

$$E(Y) = \beta_0 + \beta_1 x_1 + \beta_2 x_2 + \beta_3 x_1 x_2.$$

$\beta_3 x_1 x_2$ is referred to as the interaction term. Now, if $x_2 = 0$ we have

$$E(Y) = \beta_0 + \beta_1 x_1$$

and if $x_2 = 1$ we have

$$E(Y) = (\beta_0 + \beta_2) + (\beta_1 + \beta_3)x_1.$$

The slope (rate of change) when $x_2 = 0$ is β_1 but the slope when $x_2 = 1$ changes to $\beta_1 + \beta_3$. Figure 10.7 on p. 348 depicts a possible "interaction" case.

One way to proceed with an analysis of this 2 × 2 factorial experiment is as follows. First, test the hypothesis $H_0: \beta_3 = 0$. If you reject this hypothesis, thus establishing that there is evidence of interaction, *do not* proceed with tests on β_1 and β_2. The significance of β_3 is enough to establish the fact that there are some differences among the treatment means. It may then be best to simply estimate the individual treatment means, or differences between means, by the methods given in Section 10.4.

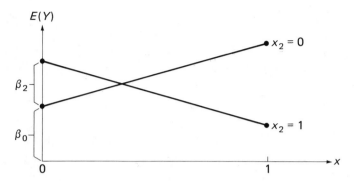

Figure 10.7 $E(Y)$ for a 2 $\times$ 2 Factorial Experiment with Interaction

If the hypothesis $H_0:\beta_3 = 0$ is not rejected, it is then appropriate to test the hypotheses $H_0:\beta_2 = 0$ and $H_0:\beta_1 = 0$. These are often referred to as tests of "main effects." The test of $\beta_2 = 0$ actually compares the observed mean of all observations at $x_2 = 1$ with the corresponding mean at $x_2 = 0$, regardless of the value of x_1. That is, each level of B is averaged over all levels of A, and then the levels of B are compared. This is a reasonable procedure when there is no evidence of interaction, since the change in response from low to high level of B is essentially the same for each level of A. Similarly, the test of $\beta_1 = 0$ compares the mean response at the high level of factor A ($x_1 = 1$) with that at the low level of A ($x_1 = 0$), with the means computed over all levels of factor B.

Using the method of fitting complete and reduced models (Section 9.6) the analysis would be completed by fitting the models given below and calculating the SSE for each:

1. $Y = \beta_0 + \beta_1 x_1 + \beta_2 x_2 + \beta_3 x_1 x_2 + \varepsilon, \quad \text{SSE}_1,$
2. $Y = \beta_0 + \beta_1 x_1 + \beta_2 x_2 + \varepsilon, \quad \text{SSE}_2,$
3. $Y = \beta_0 + \beta_1 x_1 + \varepsilon, \quad \text{SSE}_3,$
4. $Y = \beta_0 + \varepsilon, \quad \text{SSE}_4.$

Now,

$$\text{SSE}_2 - \text{SSE}_1 = \text{SS}(A \times B),$$

the sum of squares for the $A \times B$ interaction. Also,

$$\text{SSE}_3 - \text{SSE}_2 = \text{SS}(B)$$

the sum of squares due to factor B, and

$$\text{SSE}_4 - \text{SSE}_3 = \text{SS}(A),$$

the sum of squares due to factor A. This approach works well if a computer is available for fitting the indicated models.

The sums of squares shown above can be calculated by the direct formulas given in Table 10.7. Table 10.7 shows the general formulas for any two-factor factorial experiment with r observations per cell, assuming that there are a levels of factor A and b levels of factor B. That is, the data must follow the format given in Figure 10.8.

$$n = abr = \text{total number of observations}$$

$$\text{TSS} = \sum y^2 - \frac{(\sum y)^2}{n}$$

$$\text{SST} = \sum_{ij} \frac{T_{ij}^2}{r} - \frac{(\sum y)^2}{n}$$

$$\text{SS}(A) = \sum_{i=1}^{a} \frac{A_i^2}{br} - \frac{(\sum y)^2}{n}$$

$$\text{SS}(B) = \sum_{i=1}^{b} \frac{B_j^2}{ar} - \frac{(\sum y)^2}{n}$$

$$\text{SS}(A \times B) = \text{SST} - \text{SS}(A) - \text{SS}(B)$$

$$\text{SSE} = \text{TSS} - \text{SST}$$

Table 10.7   Calculation Formulas for a Two-Factor Factorial Experiment with _r_ Observations per Cell

		Factor A				
	1	2	3	$\cdots$	a	Totals
1	— — — T_{11}	— — — T_{12}	— — — T_{13}		— — — T_{1a}	B_1
2	— — — T_{21}	— — — T_{22}	— — — T_{23}		— — — T_{2a}	B_2
Factor B 3	— — — T_{31}	— — — T_{32}	— — — T_{33}		— — — T_{3a}	B_3
$\vdots$						
	— — — T_{b1}	— — — T_{b2}	— — — T_{b3}		— — — T_{ba}	B_b
Totals	A_1	A_2	A_3		A_a	$\sum_y$

T_{ij} = total of observations in row i and column j.

Figure 10.8   A General Two-Factor Factorial Experiment with _r_ Observations per Cell

Notice that the treatment sum of squares is now partitioned into a sum of squares for A, a sum of squares for B and an interaction sum of squares. The degrees of freedom for the latter three sums of squares are $(a - 1)$, $(b - 1)$ and $(a - 1)(b - 1)$, respectively. These facts are shown on the analysis of variance table given in Table 10.8.

Table 10.8   ANOVA for a Two-Factor Factorial Experiment in a Completely Randomized Design

Source	d.f.	S.S.	M.S.	F-ratio
Treatments	$ab - 1$	SST	$MST = \dfrac{SST}{ab - 1}$	
Factor A	$a - 1$	SS(A)	$MS(A) = \dfrac{SS(A)}{a - 1}$	MS(A)/MSE
Factor B	$b - 1$	SS(B)	$MS(B) = \dfrac{SS(B)}{b - 1}$	MS(B)/MSE
$A \times B$ Interaction	$(a - 1)(b - 1)$	SS($A \times B$)	$MS(A \times B) = \dfrac{SS(A \times B)}{(a - 1)(b - 1)}$	MS($A \times B$)/MSE
Error	$ab(r - 1)$	SSE	$MSE = \dfrac{SSE}{ab(r - 1)}$	
Total	$n - 1$	TSS		

We illustrate the calculations and F-tests in the following example.

EXAMPLE 10.5

For the chemical experiment with two cooking times (factor A) and two cooling times (factor B), the yields are as given below, with $r = 2$ observations per treatment.

$$
\begin{array}{c|c|c|c}
 & \multicolumn{2}{c}{A} & \\
 & x_1 = 0 & x_1 = 1 & \\
\hline
x_2 = 0 & \begin{matrix} 9 \\ 8 \\ \overline{17} \end{matrix} & \begin{matrix} 5 \\ 6 \\ \overline{11} \end{matrix} & 28 \\
\hline
x_2 = 1 & \begin{matrix} 8 \\ 7 \\ \overline{15} \end{matrix} & \begin{matrix} 3 \\ 4 \\ \overline{7} \end{matrix} & 22 \\
\hline
 & 32 & 18 & 50
\end{array}
$$

with B labelling the rows ($x_2 = 0$, $x_2 = 1$).

Perform an analysis of variance.

Solution   Using the computation formulas of Table 10.7, with $a = 2, b = 2$, and $r = 2$, we have:

$$\text{TSS} = 9^2 + 8^2 + \cdots + 3^2 + 4^2 - \frac{(50)^2}{8} = 31.5,$$

$$\text{SST} = \frac{1}{2}\left[(17)^2 + (11)^2 + (15)^2 + (7)^2\right] - \frac{(50)^2}{8} = 29.5,$$

$$\text{SS}(A) = \frac{1}{4}\left[(32)^2 + (18)^2\right] - \frac{(50)^2}{8} = 24.5,$$

$$\text{SS}(B) = \frac{1}{4}\left[(28)^2 + (22)^2\right] - \frac{(50)^2}{8} = 4.5,$$

$$\text{SSE}(A \times B) = \text{SST} - \text{SS}(A) - \text{SS}(B) = 0.5,$$

and

$$\text{SSE} = \text{TSS} - \text{SST} = 2.0.$$

The analysis of variance, using the format of Table 10.8, proceeds as follows:

Source	d.f.	S.S.	M.S.	F
Treatments	3	29.5		
A	1	24.5	24.5	$\dfrac{24.5}{0.5} = 49.0$
B	1	4.5	4.5	$\dfrac{4.5}{0.5} = 9.0$
$A \times B$	1	0.5	0.5	$\dfrac{0.5}{0.5} = 1.0$
Error	4	2.0	0.5	
Total	7	31.5		

Since $F_4^1(0.05) = 7.71$, the interaction effect is not significant. We can then proceed with "main effect" tests for factors A and B. The F-ratio of 49.0 for factor A is highly significant. Thus, there is a significant difference between the mean response at $x_1 = 0$ and that at $x_1 = 1$. Looking at the data, we see that the yield falls off as cooking time goes from the low level to the high level.

The F-ratio of 9.0 for factor B is also significant. The mean yield also seems to decrease as cooling time is changed from the low to the high level.   □

In Example 10.6 we show an analysis in which the interaction term is highly significant.

EXAMPLE 10.6

Suppose a chemical experiment like the one of Example 10.5 (two factors each at two levels) gave the following responses:

		A		
		$x_1 = 0$	$x_1 = 1$	
	$x_2 = 0$	9 8	5 6	28
B				
	$x_2 = 1$	3 4	8 7	22
		24	26	50

Perform an analysis of variance. If the interaction is significant, construct confidence intervals for the six possible differences between treatment means.

Solution   The data involves the same responses as in Example 10.5, with the observations in the lower left and lower right cells interchanged. Thus, we still have

$$\text{TSS} = 9^2 + 8^2 + \cdots + 8^2 + 7^2 - \frac{(50)^2}{8} = 31.5,$$

$$\text{SST} = \frac{1}{2}\left[(17)^2 + (11)^2 + (7)^2 + (15)^2\right] - \frac{(50)^2}{8} = 29.5$$

and

$$\text{SSE} = \text{TSS} - \text{SST} = 2.0.$$

Now,

$$\text{SS}(A) = \frac{1}{4}\left[(24)^2 + (26)^2\right] - \frac{(50)^2}{8} = 0.5,$$

$$\text{SS}(B) = \frac{1}{4}\left[(28)^2 + (22)^2\right] - \frac{(50)^2}{8} = 4.5,$$

and

$$\text{SS}(A \times B) = \text{SST} - \text{SS}(A) - \text{SS}(B) = 24.5.$$

The analysis of variance table is as follows:

Source	d.f.	S.S.	M.S.	*F*
Treatments	3	29.5		
A	1	0.5	0.5	
B	1	4.5	4.5	
A × *B*	1	24.5	24.5	49.0
Error	4	2.0	0.5	
Total	7	31.5		

At the 5% level, the interaction term is highly significant. Hence, we will not make any "main effect" tests, but instead will place confidence intervals on all possible differences between treatment means. For convenience, we will identify the $(x_1 = 0, x_2 = 0)$ combination as treatment 1 with mean μ_1, $(x_1 = 1, x_2 = 0)$ as treatment 2 with mean μ_2, $(x_1 = 0, x_2 = 1)$ as treatment 3 with mean μ_3, and $(x_1 = 1, x_2 = 1)$ as treatment 4 with mean μ_4. To form a confidence interval on $\mu_i - \mu_j$ we follow the format of Section 10.4, which gives the interval to be of the form

$$(\bar{y}_i - \bar{y}_j) \pm t_{\alpha/2c} s \sqrt{\frac{1}{n_i} + \frac{1}{n_j}}.$$

In this problem, $c = 6$ and $n_i = n_j = 2$. Also, $s = \sqrt{\text{MSE}}$ and is based upon 4 degrees of freedom. If we settle for $1 - \alpha = 0.90$, then $\alpha/2c = 0.10/12 \approx 0.01$. From Table 5 in the Appendix, $t_{0.01} = 3.747$, with 4 degrees of freedom. Thus, all six intervals will be of the form

$$(\bar{y}_i - \bar{y}_j) \pm 3.747 \sqrt{0.5} \sqrt{\frac{1}{2} + \frac{1}{2}}$$

or

$$(\bar{y}_i - \bar{y}_j) \pm 2.65.$$

The sample means are given by

$$y_1 = 8.5, \qquad y_2 = 5.5, \qquad y_3 = 4.5, \qquad y_4 = 7.5,$$

and the confidence intervals would then result in:

$$(\bar{y}_1 - \bar{y}_2) \pm 2.65 \quad \text{or} \quad 3.0 \pm 2.65*$$
$$(\bar{y}_1 - \bar{y}_3) \pm 2.65 \quad \text{or} \quad 5.0 \pm 2.65*$$
$$(\bar{y}_1 - \bar{y}_4) \pm 2.65 \quad \text{or} \quad 1.0 \pm 2.65$$
$$(\bar{y}_2 - \bar{y}_3) \pm 2.65 \quad \text{or} \quad 2.0 \pm 2.65$$
$$(\bar{y}_2 - \bar{y}_4) \pm 2.65 \quad \text{or} \quad -2.0 \pm 2.65$$
$$(\bar{y}_3 - \bar{y}_4) \pm 2.65 \quad \text{or} \quad -4.0 \pm 2.65*$$

The significant differences are then between μ_1 and μ_2, μ_1 and μ_3, and μ_3 and μ_4. (See the intervals marked with an asterisk.) In practical terms, the yield is reduced significantly as x_1 goes from 0 to 1 and x_2 remains at 0. Also, the yield is increased as x_1 goes from 0 to 1 and x_2 remains at 1. The yield decreases as x_2 goes from 0 to 1 with x_1 at 0, but there is no significant change in mean yield between x_2 at 0 and x_2 at 1 with x_1 at 1. Since μ_1 and μ_4 do not appear to differ, the best choices for maximizing yield are either $(x_1 = 0, x_2 = 0)$ or $(x_1 = 1, x_2 = 1)$. $\square$

Suppose that the chemical example under discussion had three cooking times (levels of factor A) and two cooling times (levels of factor B). If the three cooking times were equally spaced (such as 20 minutes, 30 minutes, and 40 minutes) then the levels of A could be coded as $x_1 = -1$, $x_1 = 0$ and $x_1 = 1$. Again, only the *relative* magnitudes of the levels are important in the analysis. Since there are now three levels of factor A, a quadratic term in x_1 can be added to the model. Thus, the complete model would have the form

$$E(Y) = \beta_1 + \beta_1 x_1 + \beta_2 x_1^2 + \beta_3 x_2 + \beta_4 x_1 x_2 + \beta_5 x_1^2 x_2.$$

Note that if $x_2 = 0$, we simply have a quadratic model in x_1, given by

$$E(Y) = \beta_0 + \beta_1 x_1 + \beta_2 x_1^2.$$

If $x_2 = 1$, we have another quadratic model in x_1, but the coefficients have changed, and

$$E(Y) = (\beta_0 + \beta_3) + (\beta_1 + \beta_4)x_1 + (\beta_2 + \beta_5)x_1^2.$$

If $\beta_4 = \beta_5 = 0$, the two curves will have the same shape, but if either β_4 or β_5 differs from zero, the curves will differ in shape. Thus, β_4 and β_5 are both components of interaction. (See Figure 10.9.)

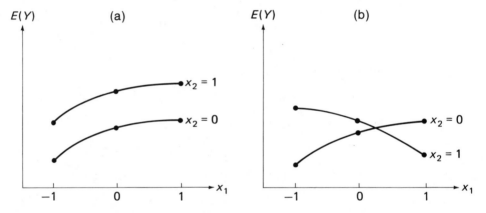

Figure 10.9 $E(Y)$ for a 3 × 2 Factorial Experiment, (a) without Interaction, (b) with Interaction

In the analysis, first we test $H_0: \beta_4 = \beta_5 = 0$ (no interaction). If we reject this hypothesis, then we do no further F-tests but may compare treatment means. If we do not reject the hypothesis of no interaction we proceed with tests of $H_0: \beta_3 = 0$ (no main effect for factor B) and $H_0: \beta_1 = \beta_2 = 0$ (no main effect for factor A). The test of $H_0: \beta_3 = 0$ merely compares the mean responses at the high and low levels of factor B. The test of $H_0: \beta_1 = \beta_2 = 0$ looks for both linear and quadratic trends among the three means for the levels of factor A, averaged across the levels of factor B.

The analysis could be conducted by fitting complete and reduced models, and using the results of Section 9.6, or by using the computational formulas of Table 10.7. We illustrate the latter approach with the following example.

EXAMPLE 10.7

In manufacturing a certain beverage, an important measurement is the percentage of impurities present in the final product. The following data show the percentage of impurities present in samples taken from products manufactured at three different temperatures (factor *A*), and two sterilization times (factor *B*). The three levels of *A* were actually 75°, 100°, and 125°C. The two levels of *B* were actually 15 minutes and 20 minutes. The data are as follows:

		75°	100°	125°	
		14.05	10.55	7.55	
	15 min.	14.93	9.48	6.59	63.15
		28.98	20.03	14.14	
B					
		16.56	13.63	9.23	
	20 min.	15.85	11.75	8.78	75.80
		32.41	25.38	18.01	
		61.39	45.41	32.15	138.95

Perform an analysis of variance.

Using the formulas of Table 10.7, with $a = 3$, $b = 2$ and $r = 2$, we have

$$\text{TSS} = (14.05)^2 + \cdots + (8.78)^2 - \frac{(138.95)^2}{12} = 124.56,$$

$$\text{SST} = \frac{1}{2}[(28.98)^2 + (45.41)^2 + (32.15)^2] - \frac{(138.95)^2}{12} = 121.02,$$

$$\text{SS}(A) = \frac{1}{4}[(61.39)^2 + (45.41)^2 + (32.15)^2] - \frac{(138.95)^2}{12} = 107.18,$$

$$\text{SS}(B) = \frac{1}{6}[(63.15)^2 + (75.80)^2] - \frac{(138.95)^2}{12} = 13.33,$$

$$\text{SS}(A \times B) = \text{SST} - \text{SS}(A) - \text{SS}(B) = 0.50,$$

and

$$\text{SSE} = \text{TSS} - \text{SST} = 3.54.$$

The analysis of variance table then has the form:

Source	d.f.	S.S.	M.S.	*F*-ratio
Treatments	5	121.02		
A	2	107.18	53.59	90.83
B	1	13.33	13.33	22.59
A × *B*	2	0.50	0.25	0.42
Error	6	3.54	0.59	
Total	11	124.56		

Since $F_6^2(0.05) = 5.14$ and $F_6^1(0.05) = 5.99$, it is clear that the interaction is not significant and that the main effects for both factor A and factor B are highly significant. The means for factor A tend to decrease as the temperature goes from low to high, and this decreasing trend is of approximately the same degree for both the low and high levels of factor B.   □

The analyses of factorial experiments with more than two factors proceed along similar lines. However, we will not present those results here. The interested reader should consult a text on experimental design.

Exercises

10.34   In pressure sintering of alumina, two important variables controlled by the experimenter are the pressure and time of sintering. An experiment involving two pressures and two times, with three specimens tested on each pressure-time combination, showed the following densities (in g/cc):

		Pressure	
		100 psi	200 psi
Time	10 min	3.6, 3.5, 3.3	3.8, 3.9, 3.8
	20 min	3.4, 3.7, 3.7	4.1, 3.9, 4.2

(a) Perform an analysis of variance, constructing appropriate tests for interaction and main effects. Use $\alpha = 0.05$.
(b) Estimate the difference between the true densities for specimens sintered for 20 minutes and those sintered for 10 minutes. Use a 95% confidence coefficient.

10.35   The yield percentage, Y, of a chemical process depends upon the temperature at which the process is run and the length of time the process is active. For two levels of temperature and two lengths of time, the yields were as follows (with two observations per treatment):

		Temperature	
		Low	High
Time	Low	24	28
		25	30
	High	26	23
		28	22

(a) Perform an analysis of variance, testing first for interaction. Use $\alpha = 0.05$.

(b) If interaction is significant, construct confidence intervals on the six possible differences between treatment means, using a simultaneous confidence coefficient of approximately 0.90.

10.36 The yield percentage, Y, of a certain precipitate depends upon the concentration of the reactant and the rate of addition of diammonium hydrogen phosphate. Experiments were run at three different concentration levels and three addition rates. The yield percentages, with two observations per treatment, were as follows:

		Concentration of Reactant		
		-1	0	1
	-1	90.1	92.4	96.4
		90.3	91.8	96.8
Addition	0	91.2	94.3	98.2
Rate		92.3	93.9	97.6
	1	92.4	96.1	99.0
		92.5	95.8	98.9

(a) Perform an analysis of variance, constructing all appropriate tests at the 5% significance level.

(b) Estimate the average yield percentage, in a 95% confidence interval, for the treatment at the middle level of both concentration and addition rate.

10.37 In analyzing coal samples for ash content, two types of crucibles and three temperatures were used in a complete factorial arrangement, with the following results:

		Crucible			
		Steel		Silica	
	825	8.7	7.2	9.3	9.1
Temperature	875	9.4	9.6	9.7	9.8
	925	10.1	10.2	10.4	10.7

(Two independent observations were taken on each treatment.) Note that "crucible" is not a quantitative factor, but it can still be considered to have two levels even though the levels cannot be ordered as to high and low.

Perform an analysis of variance, conducting appropriate tests at the 5% significance level. Does there appear to be a difference between the two types of crucible, with respect to average ash content?

10.38   Four different types of heads were tested on each of two sealing machines. Four independent measurements of strain were then made on each head-machine combination. The data are as follows:

		Head		
	1	2	3	4
Machine A	3	2	6	3
	0	1	5	0
	4	1	8	1
	1	3	8	1
Machine B	6	7	2	4
	8	6	0	7
	6	3	1	6
	5	4	2	7

(a) Perform an analysis of variance, making all appropriate tests at the 5% level of significance.

(b) If you were to use machine A, which head type would you recommend for maximum strain resistance in the seals? Why?

10.39   An experiment was conducted to determine the effects of two alloying elements (carbon and manganese) on the ductility of specimens of metal. Two specimens from each treatment were measured, and the data (in work required to break a specimen of standard dimension) are as follows:

		Carbon	
		0.2%	0.5%
Manganese	0.5%	34.5	38.2
		37.5	39.4
	1.0%	36.4	42.8
		37.1	43.4

(a) Perform an analysis of variance, conducting all appropriate tests at the 5% significance level.

(b) Which treatment would you recommend to maximize average breaking strength? Why?

10.9   *Conclusion*

Before measurements are actually made in any experimental investigation, careful attention should be paid to the *design* of the experiment. If the experimental objective is the comparison of k treatment means, and no other major source of variation is present, then a completely randomized design will be adequate. If a second source of variation is present, it can often be controlled through the use of a randomized block design. These two designs serve as an introduction to the topic of design of experiments, but many more complex designs can be considered. The interested reader should consult one of the references on design of experiments.

The analysis of variance for either design considered in this chapter can be carried out through a linear model (regression) approach or through the use of direct calculation formulas. The reader would benefit by trying both approaches on some examples in order to gain familiarity with the concepts and techniques.

The factorial experiment arises in cases for which treatments are defined by various combinations of factor levels. Notice that the factorial arrangement defines the treatments of interest, but is *not* in itself a design. Factorial experiments can be run in completely randomized, randomized block, or other designs, but we only considered the completely randomized design in this chapter. Many more topics dealing with factorial experiments can be found in any of the references on experimental design and analysis of variance.

Supplementary Exercises

10.40   Three methods have been devised to reduce the time spent in transferring materials from one location to another. With no previous information available on the effectiveness of these three approaches, a study is performed. Each approach is tried several times, and the amount of time to completion (in hours) is recorded in the table.

	Method	
A	B	C
8.2	7.9	7.1
7.1	8.1	7.4
7.8	8.3	6.9
8.9	8.5	6.8
8.8	7.6	
	8.5	

(a) What type of experimental design was used?

(b) Is there evidence that the mean time to completion of the task differs for the three methods? Use $\alpha = 0.01$.

(c) Form a 95% confidence interval for the mean time to completion for method B.

10.41   One important consideration in determining which location is best for a new retail business is the amount of traffic that passes the location each business day. Counters are placed at each of four locations on the 5 week-days, and the number of cars passing each location is recorded in the following table.

Day	Location I	II	III	IV
1	453	482	444	395
2	500	605	505	490
3	392	400	383	390
4	441	450	429	405
5	427	431	440	430

(a) What type of design does this represent?
(b) Is there evidence of a difference in the mean number of cars per day at the four locations?
(c) Estimate the difference between the mean numbers of cars that pass locations I and III each weekday.

10.42 Mileage tests were performed to compare three different brands of regular gas. Four different automobiles were used in the experiment, and each brand of gas was used in each car until the mileage was determined. The results are shown in the table.

Miles per Gallon

Brand	Automobile 1	2	3	4
A	20.2	18.7	19.7	17.9
B	19.7	19.0	20.3	19.0
C	18.3	18.5	17.9	21.1

(a) Is there evidence of a difference in the mean mileage rating among the three brands of gasoline? Use $\alpha = 0.05$.
(b) Construct the ANOVA summary table for this experiment.
(c) Is there evidence of a difference in the mean mileage for the four models, that is, is blocking important in this type of experiment? Use $\alpha = 0.05$.
(d) Form a 99% confidence interval for the difference between the mileage ratings of brands B and C.
(e) Form confidence intervals for the three possible differences between the means for the brands, with a simultaneous confidence coefficient of approximately 0.90.

10.43 England has experimented with different 40-hour work weeks to maximize production and minimize expenses. A factory tested a 5-day week (8 hours per day), a 4-day week (10 hours per day), and a $3\frac{1}{3}$-day week (12 hours per day), with the weekly production results shown in the table (in thousands of dollars worth of items produced).

8-Hour Day	10-Hour Day	12-Hour Day
87	75	95
96	82	76
75	90	87
90	80	82
72	73	65
86		

(a) What type of experimental design was employed here?
(b) Construct an ANOVA summary table for this experiment.
(c) Is there evidence of a difference in the mean productivities for the three lengths of workdays?
(d) Form a 90% confidence interval for the mean weekly productivity when 12 hour workdays are used.

10.44 To compare the preferences of technicians for three brands of calculators, each technician was required to perform an identical series of calculations on each of the three calculators, A, B, and C. To avoid the possibility of fatigue, a suitable time period separated each set of calculations and the calculators were used in random order by each technician. A preference rating, based on a 0–100 scale, was recorded for each machine/technician combination. These data are shown here:

Technician	Calculator Brand		
	A	B	C
1	85	90	95
2	70	70	75
3	65	60	80

(a) Do the data provide sufficient evidence to indicate a difference in technician preference among the three brands? Use $\alpha = 0.05$.
(b) Why did the experimenter have each technician test all three calculators? Why not randomly assign three different technicians to each calculator?

10.45 An experiment was conducted to compare the yields of orange juice for six different juice extractors. Because of a possibility of a variation in the amount of juice per orange from one truckload of oranges to another, equal weights of oranges from a single truckload were assigned to each extractor and this process was repeated for fifteen loads. The amount of juice recorded for each extractor for each truckload produced the following sums of squares:

Source	d.f.	SS	MS	F
Extractor		84.71		
Truckload		159.29		
Error		94.33		
Total		339.33		

(a) Complete the ANOVA table.
(b) Do the data provide sufficient evidence to indicate a difference in mean amount of juice extracted by the six extractors? Use $\alpha = 0.05$.

10.46   A farmer wants to determine the effect of five different concentrations of lime on the pH (acidity) of the soil on a farm. Fifteen soil samples are to be used in the experiment, five from each of the three different locations. The five soil samples from each location are then randomly assigned to the five concentrations of lime, and 1 week after the lime is applied, the pH of the soil is measured. The data are shown in the following table:

Location	Lime Concentration				
	0	1	2	3	4
I	3.2	3.6	3.9	4.0	4.1
II	3.6	3.7	4.2	4.3	4.3
III	3.5	3.9	4.0	3.9	4.2

(a) What type of experimental design was used here?
(b) Do the data provide sufficient evidence to indicate that the five concentrations of lime have different mean soil pH levels? Use $\alpha = 0.05$.
(c) Is there evidence of a difference in soil pH levels among locations? Test using $\alpha = 0.05$.

10.47   In the hope of attracting more riders, a city transit company plans to have express bus service from a suburban terminal to the downtown business district. These buses should save travel time. The city decides to perform a study of the effect of four different plans (such as a special bus lane and traffic signal progression) on the travel time for the buses. Travel times (in minutes) are measured for several weekdays during a morning rush-hour trip while each plan is in effect. The results are recorded in the table.

(a) What type of experimental design was employed?
(b) Is there evidence of a difference in the mean travel times for the four plans? Use $\alpha = 0.01$.

	Plan		
1	2	3	4
27	25	34	30
25	28	29	33
29	30	32	31
26	27	31	
	24	36	

(c) Form a 95% confidence interval for the difference between plan 1 (express lane) and plan 3 (a control: no special travel arrangements).

10.48 Five sheets of writing paper are randomly selected from each of three batches produced by a certain company. A measure of brightness is obtained for each sheet, with the following results:

	Batch	
1	2	3
28	34	27
32	36	25
25	32	29
27	38	31
26	39	21

(a) Do the mean brightness measurements seem to differ among the three batches? Use $\alpha = 0.05$.
(b) If you were to select the batch with the largest mean brightness, which would you select? Why?

Nonparametric Statistics

About This Chapter

Many of the inferential techniques of Chapters 6 through 10 required some distributional assumptions on the population of measurements under study. Most often, the population was assumed to be normally distributed. Obviously, this assumption is not met for certain populations of interest. Also, there are occasions when exact numerical measurements are impossible to obtain, as in the case of ranking the appearance of four designs of a building. In these cases we must resort to *nonparametric* statistical techniques. Five of these techniques are presented in this chapter.

Contents

Chapters 7 and 10 presented techniques for making inferences about the mean of a single population and for comparing the means of two or more populations. Most of the techniques discussed in those chapters were based on the assumption that the sampled populations have probability distributions that are approximately normal with equal variances. But how can you analyze data that evolve from populations that do *not* satisfy these assumptions? Or, how can you make comparisons between populations when you cannot assign specific numerical values to your observations?

In this chapter, we present statistical techniques for comparing two or more populations that are based on an ordering of the sample measurements according to their relative magnitudes. These techniques, which require fewer or less stringent assumptions concerning the nature of the probability distributions of the populations, are called *nonparametric statistical methods.* The statistical tests presented in this chapter apply to the same experimental designs as those covered in the introduction to an analysis of variance (Chapter 10). Thus, we will present nonparametric statistical techniques for comparing two or more populations using either a completely randomized or a randomized block design.

The *t* and *F* tests for comparing the means of two or more populations (Chapters 7 and 10) are unsuitable for analyzing some types of experimental data. For these tests to be appropriate, we assumed that the random variables being measured had normal probability distributions with equal variances. Yet in practice, the observations from one population may exhibit much greater variability than those from another, or the probability distributions may be decidedly nonnormal. For example, the distribution might be very flat, peaked, or strongly skewed to the right or left. When any of the assumptions required for the *t* and *F* tests are seriously violated, the computed *t* and *F* statistics may not follow the standard *t* and *F* distributions. If this is true, the tabulated values of *t* and *F* (Tables 5, 7, and 8 in the Appendix) are not applicable, the correct value of α for the test is unknown, and the *t* and *F* tests are of dubious value.

Data that often occur in practical situations for which the *t* and *F* tests are inappropriate are responses that are not susceptible to a meaningful numerical measurement, but can be ranked in order of magnitude. For example, if we want to compare the teaching ability of two college instructors based on subjective evaluations of students, we cannot assign a number that exactly measures the teaching ability of a single instructor. But we can compare two instructors by ranking them according to a subjective evaluation of their teaching abilities. If instructors A and B are evaluated by each of ten students, we have the standard problem of comparing the probability distributions for two populations of ratings: one for instructor A and one for B. However, the *t* test of Chapter 7 would be inappropriate, because the only data that can be recorded are the preference statements of the ten students, that is, each student decides that either A is better than B or vice versa.

Another situation in which the assumption of normality is not generally appropriate involves the measurement of extreme values, like breaking strengths of cables or maximum annual water levels in streams. These sets of data tend to possess a few very large measurements, and the symmetric normal distribution would not provide a good model for the respective populations.

The nonparametric counterparts of the t and F tests compare the probability distributions of the sampled populations, rather than specific parameters of these populations (such as the means or variances). For example, nonparametric tests can be used to compare the probability distribution of the strength measurements for a new cable to the probability distributions of the strength measurements for a cable in current use. If it can be inferred that the distribution from the new cable lies above (to the right of) the other (see Figure 11.1), the implication is that the new cable tends to be stronger than the one in current use. Such an inference might lead to a decision to replace the old cable.

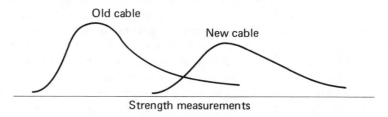

Figure 11.1   Probability Distributions of Strength Measurements for Cables (New cable tends to be stronger.)

Many nonparametric methods use the relative ranks of the sample observations, rather than their actual numerical values. These tests are particularly valuable when we are unable to obtain numerical measurements of some phenomena but are able to rank them in comparison to each other. Statistics based on ranks of measurements are called *rank statistics*. In Sections 11.2 and 11.4, we present rank statistics for comparing two probability distributions using independent samples. In Sections 11.3 and 11.5, the matched-pairs and randomized block design are used to make nonparametric comparisons of populations. Finally, in Section 11.6, we present a nonparametric measure of correlation between two variables: Spearman's rank correlation coefficient.

11.2   *Comparing Two Populations: Wilcoxon Rank Sum Test for Independent Samples*

Suppose two independent random samples are to be used to compare two populations and the t test of Chapter 7 is inappropriate for making the comparison. We may be unwilling to make assumptions about the form of the underlying population probability distributions or we may be unable to obtain exact values of the sample measurements. For either of these situations, if the data can be ranked in order of magnitude, the Wilcoxon rank sum test (developed by Frank Wilcoxon) can be used to test the hypothesis that the probability distributions associated with the two populations are equivalent.

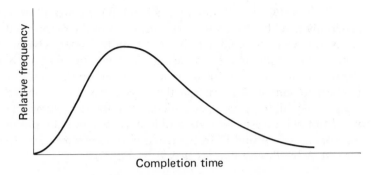

Figure 11.2   Typical Probability Distribution of
Completion Times

For example, suppose an engineer wants to compare completion times for technicians on task A to those on a similar task B. Prior experience has shown that populations of completion time measurements often possess probability distributions that are skewed to the right, as shown in Figure 11.2. Consequently, a t test should not be used to compare the mean completion times for the two tasks, because the normality assumption that is required for the t test may not be valid.

Suppose the engineer randomly assigns seven technicians to each of two groups, one group to receive task A and the other to receive task B. The completion time for each technician is measured. These data (with the exception of the measurement for one technician in group A who was eliminated from the experiment for personal reasons) are shown in Table 11.1.

Table 11.1   Completion Times for Technicians on
Tasks A or B

TASK A Completion Time (seconds)	Rank	TASK B Completion Time (seconds)	Rank
1.96	4	2.11	6
2.24	7	2.43	9
1.71	2	2.07	5
2.41	8	2.71	11
1.62	1	2.50	10
1.93	3	2.84	12
		2.88	13

The population of completion times for either of the tasks, say task A, is that which could conceptually be obtained by giving task A to all possible technicians. To compare the probability distributions for populations A and B, first we rank the sample observations as though they were all drawn from the same population. This is, we pool the measurements from both samples, and then rank the measurements from the smallest (a rank of 1) to the largest (a rank of 13). The results of this ranking process are shown in Table 11.1.

If the two populations were identical, we would expect the ranks to be randomly mixed between the two samples. On the other hand, if one population tends to have larger completion times than the other, we would expect the larger ranks to be mostly in one sample and the smaller ranks mostly in the other. Thus, the test statistic for the Wilcoxon test is based on the totals of the ranks for each of the two samples, that is, on the rank sums. For example, when the sample sizes are equal, the greater the difference in the rank sums, the greater will be the weight of evidence to indicate a difference between the probability distributions for populations A and B. In the reaction times example, we denote the rank sum for task A by T_A and that for task B by T_B. Then

$$T_A = 4 + 7 + 2 + 8 + 1 + 3 = 25$$

and

$$T_B = 6 + 9 + 5 + 11 + 10 + 12 + 13 = 66.$$

The sum of T_A and T_B will always equal $n(n + 1)/2$, where $n = n_1 + n_2$. So, for this example, $n_1 = 6$, $n_2 = 7$, and

$$T_A + T_B = \frac{13(13 + 1)}{2} = 91.$$

Since $T_A + T_B$ is fixed, a small value for T_A implies a large value for T_B (and vice versa) and a large difference between T_A and T_B. Therefore, the smaller the value of one of the rank sums, the greater will be the evidence to indicate that the samples were selected from different populations.

Values that locate the rejection region for the rank sum associated with the smaller sample are given in Table 9 in the Appendix. The columns of the table represent n_1, the first sample size, and the rows represent n_2, the second sample size. The T_L and T_U entries in the table are the boundaries of the lower and upper regions, respectively, for the rank sum associated with the sample that has fewer measurements. If the sample sizes n_1 and n_2 are the same, either rank sum may be used as the test statistic. To illustrate, suppose $n_1 = 8$ and $n_2 = 10$. For a two-tailed test with $\alpha = 0.05$, we consult the table and find that the null hypothesis will be rejected if the rank sum of sample 1 (the sample with fewer measurements), T_A, is less than or equal to $T_L = 54$ or greater than or equal to $T_U = 98$. The Wilcoxon rank sum test is summarized here.

WILCOXON RANK SUM TEST: INDEPENDENT SAMPLES*

One-tailed test	Two-tailed test
H_0: Two sampled populations have identical probability distributions	H_0: Two sampled populations have identical probability distributions

---

* Another statistic used for comparing two populations based on independent random samples is the Mann–Whitney U statistic. The U statistic is a simple function of the rank sums. It can be shown that the Wilcoxon rank sum test and the Mann–Whitney U test are equivalent.

H_a: The probability distribution for population A is shifted to the right of that for B

H_a: The probability distribution for population A is shifted to the left *or* to the right of that for B

Test statistic:

The rank sum T associated with the sample with fewer measurements (if sample sizes are equal, either rank sum can be used)

Test statistic:

The rank sum T associated with the sample with fewer measurements (if the sample sizes are equal, either rank sum can be used)

Rejection region:

Assuming the smaller sample size is associated with distribution A (or, if sample sizes are equal, we use the rank sum T_A), we reject if

$$T_A \geq T_U$$

where T_U is the upper value given by Table 10 of the Appendix for the chosen *one-tailed* α value.

Rejection region:

$T \leq T_L$ or $T \geq T_U$, where T_L is the lower value given by Table 9 in the Appendix for the chosen *two-tailed* α value, and T_U is the upper value from Table 10

[*Note*: If the one-sided alternative is that the probability distribution for A is shifted to the *left* of B (and T_A is the test statistic), we reject if $T_A \leq T_L$.]

Assumptions:

1. The two samples are random and independent
2. The observations obtained can be ranked in order of magnitude. [*Note*: No assumptions have to be made about the shape of the population probability distributions.]

EXAMPLE 11.1

Do the data given in Table 11.1 provide sufficient evidence to indicate a shift in the probability distributions for tasks A and B? That is, can we say that the probability distribution corresponding to task A lies either to the right or left of the probability distribution corresponding to task B? Test at the 0.05 level of significance.

Solution

For this problem we have:

H_0: The two populations of completion times corresponding to task A and task B have the same probability distribution.

H_a: The probability distribution for task A is shifted to the right or left of the probability distribution corresponding to task B.

Test statistic: Since task A has fewer subjects than task B, the test statistic is T_A, the rank sum of task A's completion times.

Rejection region: Since the test is two-sided, we consult part (a) of Table 9 for the rejection region corresponding to $\alpha = 0.05$. We will reject H_0 for $T_A \le T_L$ or $T_A \ge T_U$. Thus, we will reject H_0 if $T_A \le 28$ or $T_A \ge 56$.

Since T_A, the rank sum of task A's completion times in Table 11.1, is 25, it is in the rejection region (see Figure 11.3)*. Therefore, we can conclude that the probability distributions for tasks A and B are not identical. In fact, it appears that task B tends to be associated with completion times that are larger than those associated with task A (because T_A fell in the lower tail of the rejection region).   □

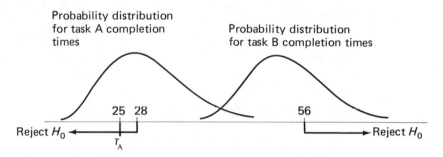

Figure 11.3   Alternative Hypothesis and Rejection Region for Example 11.1

When you apply the Wilcoxon rank sum test in a practical situation, you may encounter one or more ties in the observations. A tie occurs when two of the sample observations are equal. The Wilcoxon rank sum test is still valid if the number of ties is small in comparison with the number of sample measurements, and if you assign to each tied observation the average of the ranks the two observations would have received if the observations had not been tied. For example, suppose the fourth and fifth smallest observations are tied. Since these observations would have received the ranks 4 and 5, you should assign the average of these ranks, 4.5, to both of them and then proceed with the test in the usual manner.

Exercises

11.1   Suppose you wish to compare two treatments, A and B, and you want to determine whether the distribution of the population of B measurements

---

* The figure depicts only one side of the two-sided alternative hypothesis. The other would show distribution A shifted to the right of distribution B.

is shifted to the right of the distribution of the population of A measurements. If $n_1 = 7$, $n_2 = 5$, and $\alpha = 0.05$, give the rejection region for the test.

11.2 Refer to Exercise 11.1. Suppose you wish to detect a shift in the distributions, either A to the right of B or vice versa. Locate the rejection region for the test (assume $n_1 = 7$, $n_2 = 5$, and $\alpha = 0.05$).

11.3 An industrial psychologist claims that the order in which test questions are presented affects a prospective employee's chance of answering correctly. To investigate this assertion, the psychologist randomly divides thirteen applicants into two groups, seven in one and six in the other. The test questions are arranged in order of increasing difficulty on test A, but the order is reversed on test B. One group of applicants is given test A and the other test B. The resulting scores are as shown below:

Test A: 90, 71, 83, 82, 75, 91, 65

Test B: 66, 78, 50, 68, 80, 60

Do the data provide sufficient evidence to indicate a difference between the two tests? Test using $\alpha = 0.05$.

11.4 A major razor blade manufacturer advertises that its twin-blade disposable razor will "get you a lot more shaves" than any single-blade disposable razor on the market. A rival blade company, which has been very successful in selling single-blade razors, wishes to test this claim. Independent random samples of eight single-blade shavers and eight twin-blade shavers are taken, and the number of shaves that each gets before the razor is disposed of is recorded. The results are shown below:

Number of Shaves

Twin Blades	Single Blades
8	10
17	6
9	3
11	7
15	13
10	14
6	5
12	7

(a) Do the data support the twin-blade manufacturer's claim? Use $\alpha = 0.05$.

(b) Do you think that this experiment was designed in the best possible way? If not, what design might have been better?

11.5 Six specimens were independently selected from each of two processes for producing plastic. The ultimate strength measurements (in 1000 psi) for the specimens were as follows:

Plastic A	Plastic B
15.8	18.3
16.3	22.5
18.9	19.6
17.6	21.3
21.4	20.9
16.9	19.8

Do the ultimate strengths for the plastics appear to differ in location? Use $\alpha = 0.05$. (Note that these are *maximum* strength measurements, and such measurements usually do not follow the normal distribution.)

11.6 Counts on the number of defects per square yard for fabrics woven on two different machines were recorded for independently selected samples from each machine. The data are as follows:

Machine A: 3, 0, 4, 9, 25, 10, 8, 14

Machine B: 12, 21, 2, 3, 7

(a) Is there sufficient evidence to suggest a difference in location for the defect populations of the two machines, at the 10% significance level?
(b) Discuss a possible parametric analysis designed to answer the question in (a).

11.7 Electronic components of similar type but from two different suppliers, A and B, are operating in an industrial system. Five new components from each supplier are put into the system at the same time. As the components fail and are replaced, over time, their supplier is duly noted. The sequence of failures, ordered in time, is:

ABBABBBAAA

Is there evidence to suggest a difference between the two suppliers? Use $\alpha = 0.10$.

11.3   *Comparing Two Populations: Wilcoxon Signed Rank Test for the Paired Difference Experiment*

Nonparametric techniques may also be employed to compare two probability distributions when a paired difference design is used. For example, consumer preferences for two competing products are often compared by having each of a sample of consumers rate both products. Thus, the ratings have been paired on each consumer. Here is an example of this type of experiment.

For some paper products, softness of the paper is an important consideration in determining consumer acceptance. One method of determining softness is to have judges give a softness rating to a sample of the products. Suppose each of ten judges is given a sample of two products that a company wants to compare. Each judge rates the softness of each product on a scale from 1 to 10, with higher ratings implying a softer product. The results of the experiment are shown in Table 11.2.

Table 11.2 Softness Ratings of Paper

Judge	Product A	B	Difference (A − B)	Absolute Value of Difference	Rank Absolute Value
1	6	4	2	2	5
2	8	5	3	3	7.5
3	4	5	−1	1	2
4	9	8	1	1	2
5	4	1	3	3	7.5
6	7	9	−2	2	5
7	6	2	4	4	9
8	5	3	2	2	5
9	6	7	−1	1	2
10	8	2	6	6	10

$$T_+ = \text{Sum of positive ranks} = \overline{46}$$
$$T_- = \text{Sum of negative ranks} = 9$$

Since this is a paired difference experiment, we should analyze the differences between the measurements. However, the nonparametric approach requires that we calculate the ranks of the absolute values of the differences between the measurements, that is, the ranks of the differences after removing any minus signs. Note that tied absolute differences are assigned the average of the ranks they would receive if they were unequal but successive measurements. After the absolute differences are ranked, the sum of the ranks of the positive differences, T_+, and the sum of the ranks of the negative differences, T_-, are computed.

Now we are prepared to test the nonparametric hypothesis:

H_0: The probability distributions of the ratings for products A and B are identical.

H_a: The probability distributions of the ratings differ (in location) for the two products. (Note that this is a two-sided alternative and therefore that it implies a two-tailed test.)

Test statistic: $T = $ Smaller of the positive and negative rank sums T_+ and T_-.

The smaller the value of T, the greater will be the evidence to indicate that the two probability distributions differ in location. The rejection region for T can be determined by consulting Table 10 in the Appendix. This table gives a value T_0 for both one- and two-tailed tests for each value of n, the number of matched pairs. For a two-tailed test with $\alpha = 0.05$, we will reject H_0 if $T \leq T_0$. You can see from the table that the value of T_0 that locates the rejection region for the judges' ratings for $\alpha = 0.05$ and $n = 10$ pairs of observations is 8. Therefore, the rejection region for the test (see Figure 11.4) is

Rejection region: $T \leq 8$ for $\alpha = 0.05$.

WILCOXON SIGNED RANK TEST FOR A PAIRED DIFFERENCE EXPERIMENT

One-tailed test	Two-tailed test

H_0: Two sampled populations have identical probability distributions

H_a: The probability distribution for population A is shifted to the right of that for population B

Test statistic:
T_-, the negative rank sum (we assume the differences are computed by subtracting each paired B measurement from the corresponding A measurement)

Rejection region:
$T_- \leq T_0$, where T_0 is found in Table 10 (in the Appendix) for the one-tailed significance level α and the number of untied pairs, n.

H_0: Two sampled populations have identical probability distributions

H_a: The probability distribution for population A is shifted to the right *or* to the left of that for population B

Test statistic:
T, the smaller of the positive and negative rank sums, T_+ and T_-

Rejection region:
$T \leq T_0$, where T_0 is found in Table 10 (in the Appendix) for the two-tailed significance level α and the number of untied pairs, n.

[*Note:* If the alternative hypothesis is that the probability distribution for A is shifted to the left of B, we use T_+ as the test statistic and reject H_0 if $T_+ \leq T_0$.]

Assumptions:
1. A random sample of pairs of observations has been taken.
2. The absolute differences in the paired observations can be ranked. [*Note:* No assumptions have to be made about the form of the population probability distributions.]

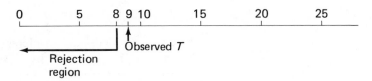

Figure 11.4   Rejection Region for Paired Difference Experiment

Since the smaller rank sum for the paper data, $T_- = 9$, does not fall within the rejection region, the experiment has not provided sufficient evidence to indicate that the two paper products differ with respect to their softness ratings at the $\alpha = 0.05$ level.

Note that if a significance level of $\alpha = 0.10$ had been used, the rejection region would have been $T \le 11$, and we would have rejected H_0. In other words, the samples do provide evidence that the probability distributions of the softness ratings differ at the $\alpha = 0.10$ significance level.

When the Wilcoxon signed rank test is applied to a set of data, it is possible that one (or more) of the paired differences may equal 0. The Wilcoxon test will continue to be valid if the number of zeros is small in comparison to the number of pairs, but to perform the test you must delete the zeros and reduce the number of differences accordingly. For example, if you have $n = 12$ pairs and two of the differences equal 0, you should delete these pairs, rank the remaining $n = 10$ differences, and use $n = 10$ when locating T_0 in Table 10. Ties in ranks are treated in the same manner as for the Wilcoxon rank sum test for a completely randomized design. Assign to each of the tied ranks the average of the ranks the two observations would have received if the observations had not been tied.

The Wilcoxon signed rank test for a paired difference experiment is summarized on page 374.

EXAMPLE 11.2

The president of a corporation must choose between two plans for improving employee safety: plan A and plan B. To aid in reaching a decision, both plans are examined by ten safety experts, each of whom is asked to rate the plans on a scale from one to ten (high ratings imply a better plan). The corporation will adopt plan B, which is more expensive, only if the data provide evidence that the safety experts rate plan B higher than plan A.

The results of the study are shown in Table 11.3. Do the data provide evidence at the $\alpha = 0.05$ level that the distribution of ratings for plan B lies above that for plan A?

Solution   The null and alternative hypotheses are

H_0:   The two probability distributions of ratings are identical

H_a: The ratings of the more expensive plan (B) tend to exceed those of plan A.

Observe that the alternative hypothesis is one-sided (that is, we only wish to detect a shift in the distribution of the B ratings to the right of the distribution

Safety Expert	Plan A	Plan B	Difference (A − B)	Rank of Absolute Difference
1	7	9	−2	4.5
2	4	5	−1	2
3	8	8	0	(Eliminated)
4	9	8	1	2
5	3	6	−3	6
6	6	10	−4	7.5
7	8	9	−1	2
8	10	8	2	4.5
9	9	4	5	9
10	5	9	−4	7.5
			Positive rank sum = $T^+ = 15.5$	

Table 11.3 Ratings by Ten Qualified Safety Experts

Figure 11.5   The Research Hypothesis for Example 11.2: We Expect T_+ to be Small

of A ratings) and therefore it implies a one-tailed test of the null hypothesis (see Figure 11.5). When the alternative hypothesis is true, the B ratings will tend to be larger than their paired A ratings, more negative differences in pairs will occur, T_- will be large, and T_+ will be small. Because Table 10 is constructed to give lower-tail values of T_0, we will use T_+ as the test statistic and reject H_0 for $T_+ \le T_0$. The differences in ratings for the pairs $(A - B)$ are shown in Table 11.3. Note that one of the differences equals 0. Consequently, we eliminate this pair from the ranking and reduce the number of pairs to $n = 9$. Using this value to enter Table 10 in this Appendix, you see that for a one-tailed test with $\alpha = 0.05$ and $n = 9$, $T_0 = 8$. Therefore, the test statistic and rejection region for the test are:

Test statistic: T_+, the positive rank sum

Rejection region: $T_+ \le 8$

Summing the ranks of the positive differences from Table 11.3, we find $T_+ = 15.5$. Since this value exceeds the critical value, $T_0 = 8$, we conclude that this sample provides insufficient evidence at the $\alpha = 0.05$ level to support the research hypothesis. The president cannot conclude that plan B is rated higher than plan A. □

Exercises

11.8   Suppose you wish to test an hypothesis that two treatments, A and B, are equivalent against the alternative that the responses for A tend to be larger than those for B. If $n = 9$ and $\alpha = 0.01$, give the rejection region for a Wilcoxon signed rank test.

11.9   Refer to Exercise 11.8. Suppose you wish to detect a difference in the locations of the distributions of the responses for A and B. If $n = 7$ and $\alpha = 0.10$, give the rejection region for the Wilcoxon signed rank test.

11.10 Economic indices provide measures of economic change. The June 1977 issue of *U.S. News and World Report* listed a sample of economic indices for May 1977 and May 1976 in order to provide a means for measuring economic change over the year:

	May 1977	May 1976
Steel products	99.3	106.4
Automobile products	123.9	118.7
Crude petroleum products	91.0	93.2
Lumber products	117.1	112.6
Freight products	84.8	82.2
Electric power products	169.5	167.0

(a) Conduct a paired difference t test to compare the mean values of these indices for the month of May in 1976 and 1977. Use $\alpha = 0.05$. What assumptions are necessary for the validity of this procedure? Why might these assumptions be doubtful?

(b) Use the Wilcoxon signed rank test to determine whether these data provide evidence that the locations of the probability distributions of all economic indices have changed. Use $\alpha = 0.05$.

11.11 On clear, cold nights in the central Florida citrus region, the precise location of the below-freezing temperatures is important since the methods of protecting trees from freezing conditions are very expensive. One method of locating likely cold spots is by relating temperature to elevation. It is conjectured that, on calm nights, the cold spots will be at low elevation. The highest and lowest spots in a particular grove showed the following minimum temperatures for ten cold nights in a recent winter.

Night	1	2	3	4	5	6	7	8	9	10
High Elevation	32.9	33.2	32.0	33.1	33.5	34.6	32.1	33.1	30.2	29.1
Low Elevation	31.8	31.9	29.2	33.2	33.0	33.9	31.0	32.5	28.9	28.0

(a) Is there sufficient evidence to support the conjecture that low elevations tend to be colder?

(b) Would it be reasonable to use a t test on the above data? Why or why not?

11.12 The following data set lists the number of industrial accidents in twelve manufacturing plants for one-week periods before and after an intensive promotion on safety:

Plant	1	2	3	4	5	6	7	8	9	10	11	12
Before	3	4	6	3	4	5	5	3	2	4	4	5
After	2	1	3	5	4	2	3	3	0	3	1	2

(a) Do the data support the claim that the campaign was successful in reducing accidents? Use $\alpha = 0.05$.

(b) Discuss the problems associated with a parametric analysis designed to answer the question in (a).

11.13 Dental researchers have developed a new material for preventing cavities, a plastic sealant, which is applied to the chewing surfaces of teeth. To determine whether the sealant is effective, it was applied in half of the teeth of each of twelve school-age children. After 5 years, the number of cavities in the sealant-coated teeth and untreated teeth were counted. The results are given in the accompanying table. Is there sufficient evidence to indicate that sealant-coated teeth are less prone to cavities than are untreated teeth? Test using $\alpha = 0.05$.

Child	Sealant-coated	Untreated
1	3	3
2	1	3
3	0	2
4	4	5
5	1	0
6	0	1
7	1	5
8	2	0
9	1	6
10	0	0
11	0	3
12	4	3

11.14 A food vending company currently uses vending machines made by two different manufacturers. Before purchasing new machines, the company wants to compare the two types in terms of reliability. Records for 7 weeks are given in the accompanying table; the data indicate the number of breakdowns per week for each type of machine. The company has the same number of machines of each type. Do the data present sufficient evidence to indicate that one of the machine types is less prone to break-downs than the other? Test using $\alpha = 0.05$.

Week	Machine Type A	B
1	14	12
2	17	13
3	10	14
4	15	12
5	14	9
6	9	11
7	12	11

11.4   *Kruskal–Wallis H Test for Completely Randomized Design*

In Chapter 10 we used an analysis of variance and the F test to compare the means of k populations based on random sampling from populations that were normally distributed with a common variance, σ^2. Now we present a nonparametric technique for comparing the populations that requires no assumptions concerning the population probability distributions.

A quality control engineer in an electronics plant has sampled the output of three assembly lines and recorded the number of defects observed. The samples involve the entire output of the three lines for ten randomly selected hours from a given week. (Different hours were selected for each line.) The number of defects observed could be quite large since a specific inspected component could have many different defects (see Table 11.4). It is quite unlikely that the data would follow a normal distribution, and thus a nonparametric analysis is in order. Our comparison is based on the ranks sums for the three sets of sample data.

Just as with two independent samples (Section 11.2), the ranks are computed for each observation according to the relative magnitude of the measurements when the data for all the samples are combined (see Table 11.4). Ties are treated as they were for the Wilcoxon rank sum and signed rank tests by assigning the average value of the ranks to each of the tied observations.
We test

H_0:   The probability distributions of the number of defects are the same for all three assembly lines.

H_a: At least two of the probability distributions differ in location.

Table 11.4   Number of Defects

Line 1		Line 2		Line 3	
Defects	Rank	Defects	Rank	Defects	Rank
6	5	34	25	13	9.5
38	27	28	19	35	26
3	2	42	30	19	15
17	13	13	9.5	4	3
11	8	40	29	29	20
30	21	31	22	0	1
15	11	9	7	7	6
16	12	32	23	33	24
25	17	39	28	18	14
5	4	27	18	24	16
$R_1 = 120$		$R_2 = 210.5$		$R_3 = 134.5$	

If we denote the three sample rank sums by R_1, R_2, R_3, the test statistic is given by

$$H = \frac{12}{n(n+1)} \sum \frac{R_j^2}{n_j} - 3(n+1),$$

where n_j is the number of measurements in the jth sample and n is the total sample size $(n = n_1 + n_2 + \cdots + n_k)$. For the data in Table 11.4, we have $n_1 = n_2 = n_3 = 10$ and $n = 30$. The rank sums are $R_1 = 120$, $R_2 = 210.5$, and $R_3 = 134.5$. Thus,

$$H = \frac{12}{30(31)} \left[\frac{(120)^2}{10} + \frac{(210.5)^2}{10} + \frac{(134.5)^2}{10} \right] - 3(31)$$

$$= 99.097 - 93 = 6.097.$$

If the null hypothesis is true, the distribution of H in repeated sampling is approximately a χ^2 (chi square) distribution. This approximation for the sampling distribution of H is adequate as long as each of the k sample sizes exceeds five (see the references for more detail). The χ^2 probability distribution is characterized by a single parameter, called the degrees of freedom associated with the distribution. Several χ^2 probability distributions with different degrees of freedom are shown in Figure 11.6. The degrees of freedom corresponding to the approximate sampling distribution of H will always be $(k-1)$, 1 less than the number of probability distributions being compared. Because large values of H support the research hypothesis that the populations have different probability distributions, the rejection region for the test will be located in the upper tail of the χ^2 distribution.

For the data of Table 11.4, the approximate distribution of the test statistic H is a χ^2 with $(k-1) = 2$ d.f. To determine how large H must be before we reject the null hypothesis, we consult Table 6 in the Appendix. Entries in the table give an upper-tail value of χ^2, call it χ_α^2, such that $P(\chi^2 > \chi_\alpha^2) = \alpha$. The columns of the table identify the value of α associated with the tabulated value of χ_α^2, and the rows correspond to the degrees of freedom. Thus, for $\alpha = 0.05$ and d.f. = 2, we

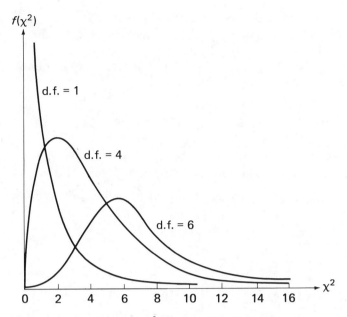

Figure 11.6   Several χ^2 Probability Distributions

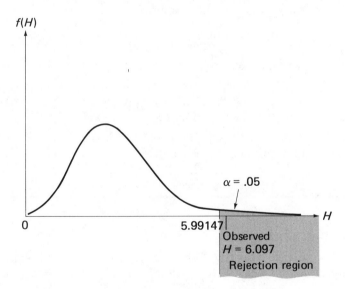

Figure 11.7   Rejection Region for the Comparison of Three Probability Distributions

can reject the null hypothesis that the three probability distributions are the same if

$$H > \chi^2_{0.05,2} \qquad \text{where } \chi^2_{0.05,2} = 5.99147.$$

The rejection region is pictured in Figure 11.7. Since the calculated $H = 6.097$ exceeds the critical value of 5.99147, we conclude that at least one of the three lines tends to have a larger number of defects than the others.

Note that prior to conducting the experiment, we might have decided to compare the defect rates for a specific pair of lines. The Wilcoxon rank sum test presented in Section 11.2 could be used for this purpose.

The Kruskal–Wallis H test for comparing more than two probability distributions is summarized in the box.

KRUSKAL–WALLIS H TEST FOR COMPARING k PROBABILITY DISTRIBUTIONS

H_0: The k probability distributions are identical

H_a: At least two of the k probability distributions differ in location

$$\text{Test statistic:} \quad H = \frac{12}{n(n + 1)} \sum \frac{R_j^2}{n_j} - 3(n + 1)$$

where

n_j = Number of measurements in sample j

R_j = Rank sum for sample j, where the rank of each measurement is computed according to its relative magnitude in the totality of data for the k samples

n = Total sample size = $n_1 + n_2 + \cdots + n_k$

Assumptions:
1. The k samples are random and independent.
2. There are five or more measurements in each sample.
3. The observations can be ranked.

[*Note*: No assumptions have to be made about the shape of the population probability distributions.]

Rejection region: $H > \chi_\alpha^2$ with $(k - 1)$ degrees of freedom.

EXAMPLE 11.3

An electrical engineer wants to compare the lifelengths of four brands of capacitors. He does so by randomly selecting four capacitors of each brand and

	Brand 1	Brand 2	Brand 3	Brand 4
	1	12	8	14
	5	2	9	15
	6	17	3	16
	7	19	11	4
	10	20	13	18
	$R_1 = 29$	$R_2 = 70$	$R_3 = 44$	$R_4 = 67$

Table 11.5   Ranks for Lifelength Data

placing them on test, under identical conditions. Since some of the lifelengths are extremely long, relative to the others, the normal distribution will not serve well as a population model. Thus, a rank analysis is suggested, and the data in Table 11.5 are the ranks of the actual observations. Do the data provide sufficient evidence to indicate that at least one of the brands tends to have longer lifelengths than the others? Test at the 5% level of significance.

Solution The elements of the test are as follows:

H_0: The population probability distributions of lifelengths for the four brands are identical.

H_a: At least two of the brands have probability distributions with different locations.

Test statistic: $H = \dfrac{12}{n(n+1)} \sum \dfrac{R_j^2}{n_j} - 3(n+1)$

$$= \frac{12}{20(21)} \left[\frac{(29)^2}{5} + \frac{(70)^2}{5} + \frac{(44)^2}{5} + \frac{(67)^2}{5} \right] - 3(21)$$

$$= 69.5 - 63 = 6.5$$

Rejection region: Since we are comparing four probability distributions, there are $(4 - 1) = 3$ d.f. associated with the test statistic. Thus, we will reject H_0 if $H > \chi^2_{0.05,3} = 7.81473$.

Since 6.5 is less than 7.81473, we have insufficient evidence to indicate that one or more of the brands tends to have longer lifelengths than the others.

Exercises

11.15 To investigate possible differences among production rates for three production lines turning out similar items, independent random samples of total production figures were obtained for seven days for each line. The data are as follows:

Line 1	Line 2	Line 3
48	41	18
43	36	42
39	29	28
57	40	38
21	35	15
47	45	33
58	32	31

Do the data provide sufficient evidence to indicate any differences in location for the three sets of production figures, at the 5% significance level?

11.16 Refer to Exercise 11.6. Suppose samples from a third machine produced the following data on number of defects per square yard:

Machine C: 22, 24, 26, 25, 28, 30

Is there evidence of significant differences in location among the three sets of defect measurements? Use $\alpha = 0.05$.

11.17 An experiment was conducted to compare the length of time it takes a human to recover from each of the three types of influenza—Victoria A, Texas, and Russian. Twenty-one human subjects were selected at random from a group of volunteers and divided into three groups of seven each. Each group was randomly assigned a strain of the virus and the influenza was induced in the subjects. All the subjects were then cared for under identical conditions, and the recovery time (in days) was recorded. The results are as follows:

Victoria A	Texas	Russian
12	9	7
6	10	3
13	5	7
10	4	5
8	9	6
11	8	4
7	11	8

(a) Do the data provide sufficient evidence to indicate that the recovery times for one (or more) type(s) of influenza tend(s) to be longer than for the other types? Test using $\alpha = 0.05$.

(b) Do the data provide sufficient evidence to indicate a difference in locations of the distributions of recovery times for the Victoria A and Russian types? Test using $\alpha = 0.05$.

11.18 The EPA wants to determine whether temperature changes in the ocean's water caused by a nuclear power plant will have a significant effect on the animal life in the region. Recently hatched specimens of a certain species of fish are randomly divided into four groups. The groups are placed in separate simulated ocean environments that are identical in every way except for water temperature. Six months later, the specimens are weighed. The results (in ounces) are given in the table. Do the data provide sufficient evidence to indicate that one (or more) of the temperatures tend(s) to produce larger weight increases than the other temperatures? Test using $\alpha = 0.10$.

Weights of Specimens

38°F	42°F	46°F	50°F
22	15	14	17
24	21	28	18
16	26	21	13
18	16	19	20
19	25	24	21
	17	23	

11.19 Three different brands of magnetron tubes (the key components in microwave ovens) were subjected to stressful testing, and the number of hours each operated without repair was recorded. Although these times do not represent typical life lengths, they do indicate how well the tubes can withstand extreme stress:

	Brand	
A	B	C
36	49	71
48	33	31
5	60	140
67	2	59
53	55	42

(a) Use the F test for a completely randomized design (Chapter 10) to test the hypothesis that the mean length of life under stress is the same for the three brands. Use $\alpha = 0.05$. What assumptions are necessary for the validity of this procedure? Is there any reason to doubt these assumptions?

(b) Use the Kruskal–Wallis H test to determine whether evidence exists to conclude that the brands of magnetron tubes tend to differ in length of life under stress. Test using $\alpha = 0.05$.

11.5   *The Friedman F_r Test for a Randomized Block Design*

In Section 10.5 we employed an analysis of variance to compare k population means when the data were collected using a randomized block design. The Friedman F_r test* provides another method for testing to detect a shift in location of

---

* The Friedman F_r test is the product of the Nobel prize winning economist, Milton Friedman.

a set of k populations. Like other nonparametric tests, it requires no assumptions concerning the nature of the populations other than that you be able to rank the individual observations.

In Section 11.2, we gave an example where a completely randomized design was used to compare the completion times of technicians assigned to one of two tasks. When the completion time varies greatly from person to person, it may be beneficial to employ a randomized block design. Using the technicians as blocks, we would hope to eleminate the variability among persons and thereby increase the amount of information in the experiment. Suppose that three tasks, A, B, and C, are to be compared using a randomized block design. Each of the technicians is assigned to each task with suitable time lags between the three tasks. The order in which the tasks are completed is randomly determined for each technician. Thus, one task would be completed by a technician, a completion time noted, and after a sufficient length of time the second task completed, and so on.

Suppose that six technicians are chosen and that the completion times for each task are shown in Table 11.6. To compare the three tasks, we rank the observations within each technician (block) and then compute the rank sums for each of the tasks (treatments). Tied observations within blocks are handled in the usual manner by assigning the average value of the rank to each of the tied observations.

Table 11.6   Completion Times for Three Tasks

Technician	Task A	Rank	Task B	Rank	Task C	Rank
1	1.21	1	1.48	2	1.56	3
2	1.63	1	1.85	2	2.01	3
3	1.42	1	2.06	3	1.70	2
4	2.43	2	1.98	1	2.64	3
5	1.16	1	1.27	2	1.48	3
6	1.94	1	2.44	2	2.81	3
		$R_1 = 7$		$R_2 = 12$		$R_3 = 17$

The null and alternative hypotheses are

H_0:   The population of completion times are identically distributed for all three tasks.

H_a: At least two of the tasks have probability distributions of completion times that differ in location.

The Friedman F_r test statistic, which is based on the rank sums for each treatment, is

$$F_r = \frac{12}{bk(k+1)} \sum R_j^2 - 3b(k+1),$$

where b is the number of blocks, k is the number of treatments, and R_j is the jth rank sum. For the data in Table 11.6,

$$F_r = \frac{12}{(6)(3)(4)} [(7)^2 + (12)^2 + (17)^2] - 3(6)(4)$$

$$= 80.33 - 72 = 8.33.$$

As with the Kruskal–Wallis statistic, the Friedman F_r statistic has approximately a χ^2 sampling distribution with $(k-1)$ degrees of freedom. Empirical results show the approximation to be adequate if either b (the number of blocks) or k (the number of treatments) exceeds 5. For the task example, we will use $\alpha = 0.05$ to form the rejection region:

$$F_r > \chi^2_{0.05,2} = 5.99147.$$

Consequently, because the observed value, $F_r = 8.33$, exceeds 5.99147, we conclude that at least two of the three tasks have probability distributions of completion times that differ in location.

The Friedman F_r test for randomized block designs is summarized here.

FRIEDMAN F_r TEST FOR A RANDOMIZED BLOCK DESIGN

H_0:   The probability distributions for the k treatments are identical

H_a: At least two of the probability distributions differ in location

$$\text{Test statistic:} \quad F_r = \frac{12}{bk(k+1)} \sum R_j^2 - 3b(k+1)$$

where
b = Number of blocks
k = Number of treatments
R_j = Rank sum of the jth treatment, where the rank of each measurement is computed relative to its position *within its own block*

Assumptions:
1. The treatments are randomly assigned to experimental units within the blocks.
2. The measurements can be ranked within blocks.
3. Either the number of blocks (b) or the number of treatments (k) should exceed 5 for the χ^2 approximation to be adequate.

[*Note:* No assumptions have to be made about the shape of the population probability distributions.]

Rejection region: $F_r > \chi^2_a$ with $(k-1)$ degrees of freedom.

EXAMPLE 11.4

    Suppose a marketing firm wants to compare the relative effectiveness of three different modes of advertising: direct-mail, newspaper and magazine ads. For fifteen clients, all three modes are used over a 1-year period, and the marketing firm records the year's percentage response to each type of advertising. That is, the firm divides the number of responses to a particular type of advertising by the total number of potential customers reached by the advertisements of that type. The results are shown in Table 11.7. Do these data provide sufficient evidence

Table 11.7   Percent Response to Three Types of Advertising for Fifteen Different Companies

Company	Direct-mail	Rank	Newspaper	Rank	Magazine	Rank
1	7.3	1	15.7	3	10.1	2
2	9.4	2	18.3	3	8.2	1
3	4.3	1	11.2	3	5.1	2
4	11.3	2	19.1	3	6.5	1
5	3.3	1	9.2	3	8.7	2
6	4.2	1	10.5	3	6.0	2
7	5.9	1	8.7	2	12.3	3
8	6.2	1	14.3	3	11.1	2
9	4.3	2	3.1	1	6.0	3
10	10.0	1	18.8	3	12.1	2
11	2.2	1	5.7	2	6.3	3
12	6.3	2	20.2	3	4.3	1
13	8.0	1	14.1	3	9.1	2
14	7.4	2	6.2	1	18.1	3
15	3.2	1	8.9	3	5.0	2
		$R_1 = 20$		$R_2 = 39$		$R_3 = 31$

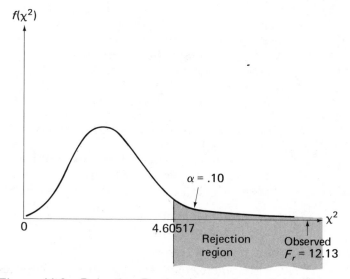

Figure 11.8   Rejection Region for the Advertising Example

to indicate a difference in the locations of the probability distributions of response rates? Use the Friedman F_r test at the $\alpha = 0.10$ level of significance.

Solution   The fifteen companies act as blocks in this experiment; thus, we rank the observations within each company (block), and then compute the rank sums for each of the three types of advertising (treatments). The null and alternative hypotheses are:

H_0:   The probability distributions for the response rates are the same for all three types of advertising.

H_a: At least two of the probability distributions of response rates differ in location.

Friedman F_r test statistic:

$$F_r = \frac{12}{bk(k + 1)} \sum R_j^2 - 3b(k + 1)$$

$$= \frac{12}{(15)(3)(4)} (R_1^2 + R_2^2 + R_3^2) - (3)(15)(4)$$

$$= \frac{12}{(15)(3)(4)} [(20)^2 + (39)^2 + (31)^2] - (3)(15)(4)$$

$$= 192.13 - 180 = 12.13$$

Rejection region: $F_r > \chi_{10.2}^2 = 4.60517$

Since the calculated $F_r = 12.13$ exceeds the critical value of 4.60517 (see Figure 11.8), we conclude that the probability distributions of response rates differ in location for at least two of the three types of advertising.

Clearly, the assumptions that the measurements are ranked within blocks and that the number of blocks (companies) is greater than 5 are satisfied. However, the experimenter must be sure that the treatments are randomly assigned to blocks. For the procedure to be valid, we assume that the three modes of advertising are used in a random order by each company. Note that if this were not true, the difference in the response rates for the three advertising modes might be due to the order in which the modes are used.   □

Exercises

11.20   Corrosion of different metals is a problem in many mechanical devices. Three sealers used to help retard the corrosion of metals were tested to see whether there were any differences among them. Samples of ten different metal compositions were treated with each of the three sealers and the amount of corrosion was measured after exposure to the same environmental conditions for 1 month. The data are given in the table. Is there any evidence of a difference in the abilities of the sealers to prevent corrosion? Test using $\alpha = 0.05$.

Metal	Sealer		
	I	II	III
1	4.6	4.2	4.9
2	7.2	6.4	7.0
3	3.4	3.5	3.4
4	6.2	5.3	5.9
5	8.4	6.8	7.8
6	5.6	4.8	5.7
7	3.7	3.7	4.1
8	6.1	6.2	6.4
9	4.9	4.1	4.2
10	5.2	5.0	5.1

11.21 A serious drought-related problem for farmers is the spread of aflatoxin, a highly toxic substance caused by mold, which contaminates field corn. In higher levels of contamination, aflatoxin is potentially hazardous to animal and possibly human health. (Officials of the FDA have set a maximum limit of 20 parts per billion aflatoxin as safe for interstate marketing.) Three sprays, A, B, and C, have been developed to control aflatoxin in field corn. To determine whether differences exist among the sprays, ten ears of corn are randomly chosen from a contaminated corn field and each is divided into three pieces of equal size. The sprays are then randomly assigned to the pieces for each ear of corn, thus setting up a randomized block design. The table gives the amount (in parts per billion) of aflatoxin present in the corn samples after spraying. Use the Friedman F_r test to determine whether there are differences among the sprays for control of aflatoxin. Test at the $\alpha = 0.05$ level of significance.

Ear	Spray		
	A	B	C
1	21	23	15
2	29	30	21
3	16	19	18
4	20	19	18
5	13	10	14
6	5	12	6
7	18	18	12
8	26	32	21
9	17	20	9
10	4	10	2

11.22 In recent years, domestic car manufacturers have devoted more attention to the small car market. To compare the popularity of four domestic small cars within a city, a local trade organization obtained the information given in the accompanying table from four car dealers—one dealer for each of the four car makes. Is there evidence of differences in location among the probability distributions of the number of cars sold for each type? Use $\alpha = 0.10$.

Number of Small Cars Sold

| | Make of Car | | | |
Month	A	B	C	D
1	9	17	14	8
2	10	20	16	9
3	13	15	19	12
4	11	12	19	11
5	7	18	13	8

11.23 An experiment is conducted to investigate the toxic effect of three chemicals, A, B, and C, on the skin of rats. Three adjacent 1-inch squares are marked on the backs of eight rats and each of the three chemicals is applied to each rat. The squares of skin are then scored from 0 to 10, depending on the degree of irritation. The data are given in the table. Is there sufficient evidence to support the research hypothesis that the probability distributions of skin irritation scores corresponding to the three chemicals differ in location? Use $\alpha = 0.01$.

| | Chemical | | |
Rat	A	B	C
1	6	5	3
2	9	8	4
3	6	9	3
4	5	8	6
5	7	8	9
6	5	7	6
7	6	7	5
8	6	5	7

11.24 One of the byproducts of inflationary times is increased replacement costs of materials. The June 20, 1977 issue of *Business Week* gave a table of ratios of current replacement costs to historical costs in four categories for three well-known pharmaceutical companies. Use the Friedman F_r test to determine whether evidence exists to indicate that the inflationary effects have been felt to different extents by the companies. Test using $\alpha = 0.05$.*

	Gross Assets	Net Assets	Depreciation	Inventory
Bristol-Myers	1.62	1.58	1.64	1.03
Eli-Lilly	1.74	1.41	1.57	1.00
Pfizer	1.84	1.85	1.67	1.16

11.6   *Spearman's Rank Correlation Coefficient*

Suppose that ten applicants for a position as civil engineer are to be ranked from 1 (best) to 10 (worst) by each of two experienced civil engineers, say A and B. We might want to determine whether or not the rankings by the two engineers are related. If an applicant is rated high by engineer A, is he likely to also be rated high by engineer B? Or do high rankings by A correspond to low rankings by B? That is, we wish to determine whether the rankings by the two engineers are correlated.

If the rankings are as shown in the "Perfect Agreement" columns of Table 11.8, we immediately notice that the engineers agree on the rank of every applicant. High ranks correspond to high ranks and low ranks to low ranks. This is an example of *perfect positive correlation* between the ranks.

In contrast, if the rankings appear as shown in the "Perfect Disagreement" columns of Table 11.8, high ranks by one applicant correspond to low ranks by the other. This is an example of *perfect negative correlation*.

Table 11.8   Rankings of Ten Applicants by Two Engineers

Applicant	Perfect Agreement		Perfect Disagreement	
	Eng. A	Eng. B	Eng. A	Eng. B
1	4	4	9	2
2	1	1	3	8
3	7	7	5	6
4	5	5	1	10
5	2	2	2	9
6	6	6	10	1
7	8	8	6	5
8	3	3	4	7
9	10	10	8	3
10	9	9	7	4

* The true α level for this test will only approximately equal 0.05, since the χ^2 distribution provides only a rough approximation when neither the number of blocks nor the number of treatments exceeds 5.

Table 11.9   Rankings of Applicants:
Less Than Perfect Agreement

Applicant	Engineer A	B	Difference Between Rank 1 and Rank 2	d^2
1	4	5	-1	1
2	1	2	-1	1
3	9	10	-1	1
4	5	6	-1	1
5	2	1	1	1
6	10	9	1	1
7	7	7	0	0
8	3	3	0	0
9	6	4	2	4
10	8	8	0	0

$$\sum d^2 = 10$$

In practice, you will rarely see perfect positive or negative correlation between the ranks. In fact, it is quite possible for the ranks to appear as shown in Table 11.9. You will note that these rankings indicate some agreement between the engineers but not perfect agreement, thus indicating a need for a measure of rank correlation.

Spearman's rank correlation coefficient, r_s, provides a measure of correlation between ranks. The formula for this measure of correlation is given below. We also give a formula that is identical to r_s when there are no ties in rankings; this provides a good approximation to r_s when the number of ties is small relative to the number of pairs.

SPEARMAN'S RANK CORRELATION COEFFICIENT

$$r_s = \frac{SS_{uv}}{\sqrt{SS_{uu}SS_{vv}}}$$

where

$$SS_{uv} = \sum (u_i - \bar{u})(v_i - \bar{v}) = \sum u_i v_i - \frac{(\sum u_i)(\sum v_i)}{n}$$

$$SS_{uu} = \sum (u_i - \bar{u})^2 = \sum u_i^2 - \frac{(\sum u_i)^2}{n}$$

$$SS_{vv} = \sum (v_i - \bar{v})^2 = \sum v_i^2 - \frac{(\sum v_i)^2}{n}$$

u_i = Rank of the ith observation in sample 1

v_i = Rank of the ith observation in sample 2

n = Number of pairs of observations (number of observations in each sample)

Shortcut Formula for r_s

$$r_s = 1 - \frac{6 \sum d_i^2}{n(n^2 - 1)}$$

where

$d_i = u_i - v_i$ (difference in the ranks of the ith observations for samples 1 and 2)

Note that if the rankings by the two engineers are identical, as in the second and third columns of Table 11.8, the differences between the ranks, d, will all be zero. Thus,

$$r_s = 1 - \frac{6 \sum d^2}{n(n^2 - 1)} = 1 - \frac{6(0)}{10(99)} = 1.$$

That is, perfect positive correlation between the pairs of ranks is characterized by a Spearman correlation coefficient of $r_s = 1$. When the ranks indicate perfect disagreement, as in the fourth and fifth columns of Table 11.8, $d_i^2 = 330$ and

$$r_s = 1 - \frac{6(330)}{10(99)} = -1.$$

Thus, perfect negative correlation is indicated by $r_s = -1$.

For the data of Table 11.9,

$$r_s = 1 - \frac{6 \sum d^2}{n(n^2 - 1)} = 1 - \frac{6(10)}{10(99)} = 1 - \frac{6}{99} = 0.94.$$

The fact that r_s is close to 1 indicates that engineers A and B tend to agree, but the agreement is not perfect.

The value of r_s will always fall between -1 and $+1$, with $+1$ indicating the perfect positive correlation and -1 indicating perfect negative correlation. The closer r_s falls to $+1$ or -1, the greater the correlation between the ranks. Conversely, the nearer r_s is to 0, the less the correlation. We summarize the properties of r_s.

PROPERTIES OF SPEARMAN'S RANK CORRELATION COEFFICIENT

1. The value of r_s is always between -1 and 1.
2. r_s positive: The ranks of the pairs of sample observations tend to increase together.
3. $r_s = 0$: The ranks are not correlated.
4. r_s negative: The ranks of one variable tend to decrease as the other variable's ranks increase.

You will note that the concept of correlation implies that two responses are obtained for each experimental unit. In the above example, each applicant received two ranks (one by each engineer) and the objective of the study was to determine the degree of positive correlation between the two rankings. Rank correlation methods can be used to measure the correlation between any pair of variables. If two variables are measured on each of n experimental units, we rank the measurements associated with each variable separately. Ties receive the average of the ranks of the tied observations. Then we calculate the value of r_s for the two rankings. This value will measure the rank correlation between the two variables. We illustrate the procedure with Example 11.5.

EXAMPLE 11.5

In a factory producing handcrafted items, certain workers produce many items per day while others produce few. It is hypothesized that those workers producing many items per day have a low quality rating on work produced, while those producing few items have a high quality rating. The data in Table 11.10 show the average number of items produced per day (over a one-month period) by fifteen randomly selected workers. In addition, Table 11.10 shows the average quality rating on inspected items for the same fifteen workers. (High values on the quality rating scale imply high quality work.) Calculate and interpret Spearman's rank correlation coefficient for the data.

Solution

First we rank the number of items produced per day, assigning a 1 to the smallest (12) and a 15 to the largest number (46). Note that the two ties received the averages of their respective ranks. Similarly, we assign ranks to the fifteen quality scores. Since the number of ties is relatively small, we will use the shortcut formula to calculate r_s. The differences between the ranks of the quality scores and the ranks of the number of items produced per day are shown in Table 11.10. The squares of the differences are also given. Thus,

$$r_s = 1 - \frac{6\sum d_i^2}{n(n^2 - 1)} = 1 - \frac{6(795)}{15(15^2 - 1)} = 1 - 1.42 = -0.42.$$

Table 11.10   Data and Calculations for Example 11.5

Worker	Items Produced Per Day	Rank	Quality Score	Rank	d	d^2
1	12	1	7.7	5	−4	16
2	15	2	8.1	9	−7	49
3	35	13	6.9	4	9	81
4	21	7	8.2	10	−3	9
5	20	5.5	8.6	13.5	−8	64
6	17	3	8.3	11.5	−8.5	72.25
7	19	4	9.4	15	−11	121
8	46	15	7.8	6	9	81
9	20	5.5	8.3	11.5	−6	36
10	25	8.5	5.2	1	7.5	56.25
11	39	14	6.4	3	11	121
12	25	8.5	7.9	7	1.5	2.25
13	30	12	8.0	8	4	16
14	27	10	6.1	2	8	64
15	29	11	8.6	13.5	−2.5	6.25
					Total =	795

This negative correlation coefficient indicates that in this sample, an increase in the number of items produced per day is associated with a decrease in the quality rating. Can this conclusion be generalized from the sample to the population? That is, can we conclude that quality scores and the number of items produced per day are negative correlated for the populations of observations for all workers?

If we define ρ_s as the population Spearman rank correlation coefficient, this question can be answered by conducting the test

$H_0: \rho_s = 0$ (no population correlation between ranks)

$H_a: \rho_s < 0$ (negative population correlation between ranks)

Test statistic: r_s, the sample Spearman rank correlation coefficient

To determine a rejection region, we consult Table 11 in the Appendix. Note that the left-hand column gives values of n, the number of pairs of observations. The entries in the table are values for an upper-tail rejection region, since only positive values are given. Thus, for $n = 15$ and $\alpha = 0.05$, the value 0.441 is the boundary of the upper-tail rejection region, so that $P(r_s > 0.441) = 0.05$ when $H_0: \rho_s = 0$ is true. Similarly, for negative values of r_s, $P(r_s < -0.441) = 0.05$ when $\rho_s = 0$. That is, we expect to see $r_s < -0.441$ only 5% of the time when there is really no relationship between the ranks of the variables. The lower-tailed rejection region is therefore

Rejection region: $\alpha = 0.05$ $r_s < -0.441$

Since the calculated $r_s = -0.42$ is not less than -0.441, we cannot reject H_0 at the $\alpha = 0.05$ level of significance. That is, this sample of fifteen workers provides insufficient evidence to conclude that a negative correlation exists between number of items produced and the quality scores of the populations of measurements corresponding to all workers. This does not, of course, mean that no relationship exists. A study using a larger sample of workers and taking other factors into account would be more likely to discover whether production rate and quality are related.   □

A summary of Spearman's nonparametric test for correlation is given here.

SPEARMAN'S NONPARAMETRIC TEST FOR RANK CORRELATION

One-tailed test	Two-tailed test
$H_0: \rho_s = 0$	$H_0: \rho_s = 0$
$H_a: \rho_s > 0$ (or $H_a: \rho_s < 0$)	$H_a: \rho_s \neq 0$
Test statistic: r_s, the sample rank correlation (formulas for calculating r_s are given on page 393)	Test statistic: r_s, the sample rank correlation (formulas for calculating r_s are given on page 393)

Rejection region: Rejection region:

$$r_s > r_{s,\alpha,n}$$ $$r_s < -r_{s,\alpha/2,n} \quad \text{or} \quad r_s > r_{s,\alpha/2n}$$

(or $r_s < -r_{s,\alpha,n}$ when $H_a:\rho_s < 0$)

where $r_{s,\alpha,n}$ is the value from   where $r_{s,\alpha/2,n}$ is the value from
Table 11 corresponding to the   Table 11 corresponding to the
upper-tail area α and n pairs   upper-tail area $\alpha/2$ and n pairs
of observations.   of observations.

EXAMPLE 11.6

Manufacturers of perishable foods often use preservatives to retard spoilage. One concern is that using too much preservative will change the flavor of the food. Suppose an experiment is conducted using samples of a food product with varying amounts of preservative added. The length of time until the food shows signs of spoiling and a taste rating are recorded for each sample. The taste rating is the average rating for three tasters, each of whom rates each sample on a scale from 1 (good) to 5(bad). Twelve sample measurements are shown in Table 11.11. Use a nonparametric test to find out whether the spoilage times and taste ratings are correlated. Use $\alpha = 0.05$.

Table 11.11   Data for Example 11.6

Sample	Time Until Spoilage (Days)	Rank	Taste Rating	Rank
1	30	2	4.3	11
2	47	5	3.6	7.5
3	26	1	4.5	12
4	94	11	2.8	3
5	67	7	3.3	6
6	83	10	2.7	2
7	36	3	4.2	10
8	77	9	3.9	9
9	43	4	3.6	7.5
10	109	12	2.2	1
11	56	6	3.1	5
12	70	8	2.9	4

[*Note*: Tied measurements are assigned the average of the ranks that would be given the measurements if they were different but consecutive.]

Solution   The test is two-tailed, with

$$H_0:\rho_s = 0 \qquad H_a:\rho_s \neq 0$$

$$\text{Test statistic:} \quad r_s = 1 - \frac{6\sum d_i^2}{n(n^2 - 1)}$$

Rejection region: Since the test is two-tailed, we need to halve the α value before consulting Table II. For $\alpha = 0.05$, we calculate $\alpha/2 = 0.025$ and look up

$$r_{s,\alpha/2,n} = r_{s,0.025,12} = 0.591.$$

We will reject H_0 if

$$r_s < -0.591 \qquad \text{or} \qquad r_s > 0.591.$$

The first step in the computation of r_s is to sum the squares of the differences between ranks:

$$\sum d_i^2 = (2 - 11)^2 + (5 - 7.5)^2 + \cdots + (8 - 4)^2 = 536.5.$$

Then

$$r_s = 1 - \frac{6(536.5)}{12(144 - 1)} = -0.876.$$

Since $-0.876 < -0.591$, we reject H_0 and conclude that the preservative does affect the taste of the food. The fact that r_s is negative suggests that the preservative has an adverse effect on the taste.   □

Exercises

11.25 Suppose you wish to detect $\rho_s > 0$ and you have $n = 14$ and $\alpha = 0.01$. Give the rejection region for the test.

11.26 Suppose you wish to detect $\rho_s \neq 0$ and you have $n = 22$ and $\alpha = 0.05$. Give the rejection region for the test.

11.27 Two expect design engineers were asked to rank six designs for a new aircraft. The rankings are shown below:

Design	Engineer I	Engineer II
A	6	5
B	5	6
C	1	2
D	3	1
E	2	4
F	4	3

Do the data present sufficient evidence to indicate a positive correlation in the rankings of the two engineers?

11.28 For a certain factory job that requires great skill, it is thought that productivity on the job should increase as the years of experience increases.

Ten employees were randomly selected from among those who hold this type of job. Data on years of experience and a measure of productivity were found to be as follows:

Employee	Years of Experience	Productivity
1	4	80
2	6	82
3	10	88
4	2	81
5	12	92
6	6	85
7	5	83
8	10	86
9	13	91
10	9	90

Do the data support the conjecture that years of experience is positively correlated with productivity?

11.29 Many large businesses send representatives to college campuses to conduct job interviews. To aid the interviewer, one company decides to study the correlation between the strength of an applicant's references (the company requires three references) and the performance of the applicant on the job. Eight recently hired employees are sampled and independent evaluations of both references and job performance are made on a scale from 1 to 20. The scores are given in the table.

Employee	References	Job Performance
1	18	20
2	14	13
3	19	16
4	13	9
5	16	15
6	11	18
7	20	15
8	9	12

(a) Compute Spearman's rank correlation coefficient for these data.
(b) Is there evidence that strength of references and job performance are positively correlated? Use $\alpha = 0.05$.

11.30 A large manufacturing firm wants to determine whether a relationship exists between the number of work-hours an employee misses per year and the employee's annual wages. A sample of fifteen employees produced the data in the table. Do these data provide evidence that the work-hours missed are related to annual wages? Use $\alpha = 0.05$.

Employee	Work-Hours Missed	Annual Wages (Thousands of dollars)
1	49	12.8
2	36	14.5
3	127	8.3
4	91	10.2
5	72	10.0
6	34	11.5
7	155	8.8
8	11	17.2
9	191	7.8
10	6	15.8
11	63	10.8
12	79	9.7
13	43	12.1
14	57	21.2
15	82	10.9

11.7   *Conclusion*

We have presented several useful nonparametric techniques for comparing two or more populations. Nonparametric techniques are useful when the underlying assumptions for their parametric counterparts are not justified or when it is impossible to assign specific values to the observations. Rank sums are the primary tools of nonparametric statistics. The Wilcoxon rank sum statistic and the Wilcoxon signed rank statistic can be used to compare two populations for either an independent sampling experiment or a paired difference experiment. The Kruskal–Wallis H test is applied when comparing k populations using a completely randomized design. The Friedman F_r test is used to compare k populations when a randomized block design is conducted.

The strength of nonparametric statistics lies in their general applicability. They require few restrictive assumptions, and they may be used for observations that can be ranked but cannot be exactly measured. Therefore, nonparametric tests provide very useful sets of statistical tests to use in conjunction with the parametric tests of Chapters 7 and 10.

Supplementary Exercises

11.31 A study was conducted to determine whether the installation of a traffic light was effective in reducing the number of accidents at a busy intersection. Samples taken 6 months before installation and 5 months after installation of the light yielded the following numbers of accidents per month:

Before	After
12	4
5	2
10	7
9	3
14	8
6	

(a) Is there sufficient evidence to conclude the traffic light aided in reducing the number of accidents? Test using $\alpha = 0.025$.

(b) Explain why this type of data might or might not be suitable for analysis using the t test of Chapter 7.

11.32 A manufacturer of household appliances is considering one of two department store chains to be the sales merchandiser for its product in a particular region of the United States. Before choosing one chain, the manufacturer wants to make a comparison of the product exposure that might be expected for the two chains. Eight locations are selected where both chains have stores and, on a specific day, the number of shoppers entering each store is recorded. The data are shown in the table. Do the data (shown in the table) provide sufficient evidence to indicate that one of the chains tends to have more customers per day than the other? Test using $\alpha = 0.05$.

Location	A	B
1	879	1085
2	445	325
3	692	848
4	1565	1421
5	2326	2778
6	857	992
7	1250	1303
8	773	1215

11.33 A drug company has synthesized two new compounds to be used in sleeping pills. The data in the table represent the additional hours of sleep

Patient	Drug A	Drug B
1	0.4	0.7
2	−0.7	−1.6
3	−0.4	−0.2
4	−1.4	−1.4
5	−1.6	−0.2
6	2.9	3.4
7	4.0	3.7
8	0.1	0.8
9	3.1	0.0
10	1.9	2.0

gained by ten patients through the use of the two drugs. Do the data present sufficient evidence to indicate that one drug is more effective than the other in increasing the hours of sleep? Test using $\alpha = 0.10$.

11.34 Weevils cause millions of dollars worth of damage each year to cotton crops. Three chemicals designed to control weevil populations are applied, one to each of three cotton fields. After 3 months, ten plots of equal size are randomly selected within each field and the percentage of cotton plants with weevil damage is recorded for each. Do the data in the table provide sufficient evidence to indicate a difference in location among the distributions of damage rates corresponding to the three treatments? Use $\alpha = 0.05$.

A	B	C
10.8	22.3	9.8
15.6	19.5	12.3
19.2	18.6	16.2
17.9	24.3	14.1
18.3	19.9	15.3
9.8	20.4	10.8
16.7	23.6	12.2
19.0	21.2	17.3
20.3	19.8	15.1
19.4	22.6	11.3

11.35 (a) Suppose a company wants to study how personality relates to leadership. Four supervisors with different types of personalities are selected. Several employees are then selected from the group supervised by each, and these employees are asked to rate the leader of their group on a scale from 1 to 20 (20 signifies highly favorable). The table shows the resulting data. Is there sufficient evidence to indicate that one or more of the supervisors tend to receive higher ratings than the others? Use $\alpha = 0.05$.

| | Supervisor | | |
I	II	III	IV
20	17	16	8
19	11	15	12
20	13	13	10
18	15	18	14
17	14	11	9
	16		10

(b) Suppose the company is particularly interested in comparing the ratings of the personality types represented by supervisors I and III. Make this comparison using $\alpha = 0.05$.

11.36 A manufacturer wants to determine whether the number of defectives produced by its employees tends to increase as the day progresses. Unknown to the employees, a complete inspection is made of every item produced on one day, and the hourly fraction defective is recorded. The table gives the resulting data. Do they provide evidence that the fraction defective increases as the day progresses? Test at the $\alpha = 0.05$ level.

Hour	Fraction Defective
1	0.02
2	0.05
3	0.03
4	0.08
5	0.06
6	0.09
7	0.11
8	0.10

11.37 An experiment is conducted to compare three calculators, A, B, and C, according to ease of operation. To make the comparison, six randomly selected students are assigned to perform the same sequence of arithmetic operations on each of the three calculators. The order of use of the calculators varies in a random manner from student to student. The times necessary for the completion of the sequence of tasks (in seconds) are recorded in the table. Do the data provide sufficient evidence to indicate that the calculators differ in ease of operation?

Student	Calculator Type A	B	C
1	306	330	300
2	260	265	285
3	281	290	277
4	288	301	305
5	301	309	319
6	262	245	240

11.38 A union wants to determine its members preferences before negotiating with management. Ten union members are randomly selected, and each member completes an extensive questionnaire. The responses to the various aspects of the questionnaire will enable the union to rank in order of importance the items to be negotiated. The rankings are shown in the table. Is there sufficient evidence to indicate that one or more of the items are preferred to the others? Test using $\alpha = 0.05$.

Person	More Pay	Job Stability	Fringe Benefits	Shorter Hours
1	2	1	3	4
2	1	2	3	4
3	4	3	2	1
4	1	4	2	3
5	1	2	3	4
6	1	3	4	2
7	2.5	1	2.5	4
8	3	1	4	2
9	1.5	1.5	3	4
10	2	3	1	4

11.39 A clothing manufacturer employs five inspectors who provide quality control of workmanship. Every item of clothing produced carries with it the number of the inspector who checked it. Thus, the company can evaluate an inspector by keeping records of the number of complaints received about products bearing his or her inspection number. Records for 6 months are given in the table.

Number of Returns

Month	Inspector				
	I	II	III	IV	V
1	8	10	7	6	9
2	5	7	4	12	12
3	5	8	6	10	6
4	9	6	8	10	13
5	4	13	3	7	15
6	4	8	2	6	9

(a) Do these data provide sufficient evidence to indicate a tendency to receive more complaints for one or more of the inspectors' products than for the others? Use $\alpha = 0.10$.

(b) Use the Wilcoxon signed rank test to determine whether evidence exists to indicate that the performances of inspectors I and IV differ. Use $\alpha = 0.05$.

11.40 Performance in a personal interview often determines whether a candidate is offered a job. Suppose the personnel director of a company interviewed six potential job applicants without knowing anything about their backgrounds, and then rated them on a scale from 1 to 10. Independently, the director's supervisor made an evaluation of the background qualifications of each candidate on the same scale. The results are shown in the table. Is there evidence that a candidate's qualification score is positively correlated with interview performance score? Use $\alpha = 0.05$.

Candidate	Qualifications	Interview Performance
1	10	8
2	8	9
3	9	10
4	4	5
5	5	3
6	6	6

11.41 Refer to Exercise 10.4. Perform an appropriate nonparametric analysis of the data given there.

11.42 Refer to Exercise 10.10.
   (a) Perform an appropriate nonparametric analysis of the data given there.
   (b) Discuss the relative merits of a parametric versus a nonparametric analysis in this case.

11.43 Answer the question asked in Exercise 10.21 by performing a nonparametric analysis of the data.

11.44 Refer to Exercise 10.23.
   (a) Perform a nonparametric analysis of the data given there.
   (b) Discuss the relative merits of a parametric versus a nonparametric analysis in this case.

12

Applications to Quality Control

About This Chapter

An important use of statistics is in the area of industrial quality control. Quality of raw material and finished products is maintained by periodic sampling and inspection of representative items. Statistics, like proportion of defectives, are calculated from these sampled items and used in making decisions concerning acceptable or unacceptable quality levels. Many of the statistical techniques discussed earlier in this book are used in quality control, but some modifications are unique to this application.

Contents

Our theme throughout this text has been that many, if not most, experiments result in outcomes that are *not* purely deterministic. That is, a sequence of seemingly identical experiments will give slightly different results due to uncontrolled sources of variation. Because of this variability in outcomes of experiments, we have developed probabilistic models for such outcomes and statistical techniques for making decisions based on such outcomes.

Suppose our "experiment" now becomes the measurement of a quality trait on an item resulting from a production process. The measurement might be the strength of a section of steel cable, the weight of cereal dispensed by a filling machine, the percentage of copper in a casting of bronze, or the diameter of a machined rod for an engine. No matter how carefully a production process is controlled, these quality measurements will vary from item to item, and there will be a probability distribution associated with the population of such measurements.

If all important sources of variation are under control in a production process, then the slight variations among quality measurements usually cause no serious problems. Such a process should produce the same distribution of quality measurements no matter when it is sampled, and thus it can be referred to as a "stable system." For example, a process for producing bronze castings may be regarded as stable as long as the percentages of copper in test samples appear to lie between 80 and 82.

One objective of quality control is to develop a scheme for sampling a process, making the quality measurement of interest on the sampled items, and then making a decision as to whether or not the process is in its stable state, or "in control." If the sample data suggests that the process is "out of control," a cause ("assignable cause") for the abnormality is sought. A common method for making these decisions involves the use of control charts. In the next four sections, we discuss the $\bar{X}$-chart for checking control tendency, the R-chart for checking variability, the p-chart for checking fraction of defectives, and the c-chart for checking number of defects per item.

Before proceeding, some comments as to why these applications merit a separate chapter are in order. First, these are very important and widely used techniques in industry, and every engineer working in industry, even if not directly in quality control, should be aware of how the techniques work. Second, the statistical formulas and methodologies that have become standard in the area of quality control differ somewhat from similar methodologies presented earlier in the text for other purposes. We will develop the control-charting techniques using standard terminology wherever possible.

12.2   *The $\bar{X}$-Chart*

Imagine an industrial process that is running continuously. A standard quality control plan would require sampling one or more items from this process periodically, and making the appropriate quality measurements. Usually, more than one item is measured at each time point to ensure accuracy. The objective of this section is to develop a technique that will help the quality control engineer decide whether the center (or average or location) of the measurements has shifted up or down.

Suppose that n observations are to be made at each time point in which the process is checked. Let X_i denote the ith observation ($i = 1, \ldots, n$) at the specified time point, and $\bar{X}_j$ denote the average of the n observations at time point j. If $E(X_i) = \mu$ and $V(X_i) = \sigma^2$, for a process in control, then $\bar{X}_j$ should be approximately normally distributed with $E(\bar{X}_j) = \mu$ and $V(\bar{X}_j) = \sigma^2/n$. As long as the process remains in control, where will most of the $\bar{X}_j$ values lie? Since we know that $\bar{X}_j$ has approximately a normal distribution, we can find an interval that will have probability $1 - \alpha$ of containing $\bar{X}_j$. This interval is $\mu \pm Z_{\alpha/2}(\sigma/\sqrt{n})$. A common value for $Z_{\alpha/2}$ in most control-charting problems is 3. Thus, the interval $\mu \pm 3(\sigma/\sqrt{n})$ has probability 0.9973 of including $\bar{X}_j$, as long as the process is in control. If μ and σ were known, we could use $\mu - 3(\sigma/\sqrt{n})$ as a lower control limit and $\mu + 3(\sigma/\sqrt{n})$ as an upper control limit. If an $\bar{X}_j$ was observed to fall outside of these limits, we would suspect that the process might be out of control since this event has a very small probability of occurring (0.0027) given that the process is in control. Figure 12.1 shows schematically how the decision process would work.

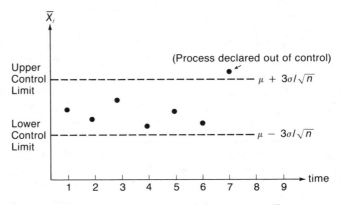

Figure 12.1   Schematic Representation of $\bar{X}$-Chart

Note that if a process is declared to be out of control because $\bar{X}_j$ fell outside of the control limits, there is a positive probability of making an error. However, this probability of error is only 0.0027 for the 3-standard deviation limits used above. (This error is similar to the Type I error of an hypothesis testing problem.)

If a control chart is being started for a new process, μ and σ will not be known and, hence, must be estimated from the data. For establishing control limits, it is generally recommended that at least $k = 20$ time points be sampled before the control limits are calculated. We will now discuss the details of estimating $\mu \pm 3(\sigma/\sqrt{n})$ from k independent samples, each of size n.

For each of the k samples we will compute the mean, $\bar{X}_j$, the sample variance S_j^2, and the range of observations in the sample, R_j. (Recall that the range is simply the difference between the largest and smallest observations in the sample.)

Traditionally, quality control engineers work with

$$S_j'^2 = \left(\frac{n-1}{n}\right) S_j^2$$

rather than S_j^2 itself. This is merely a matter of changing the denominator of the sample variance from $(n-1)$ to n.

To form an unbiased estimator of μ from $\bar{X}_1, \bar{X}_2, \ldots, \bar{X}_k$, we can simply calculate the average of the sample means, $\bar{\bar{X}}$, where

$$\bar{\bar{X}} = \frac{1}{k} \sum_{j=1}^{k} \bar{X}_j.$$

In a similar fashion, we can calculate the average of the S_j' quantities to form

$$\bar{S}' = \frac{1}{k} \sum_{j=1}^{k} S_j'.$$

Now, $\bar{S}'$ is *not* an unbiased estimator of σ, but it can be made unbiased by dividing by a constant, c_2, found in Table 12 of the Appendix. Thus, $\bar{S}'/c_2$ is an unbiased estimator of σ. A good estimator of $\mu \pm 3(\sigma/\sqrt{n})$ then becomes

$$\bar{\bar{X}} \pm 3 \frac{\bar{S}'}{c_2\sqrt{n}}$$

or

$$\bar{\bar{X}} \pm A_1\bar{S}'$$

where

$$A_1 = 3/c_2\sqrt{n}.$$

For convenience, values of A_1 are also in Table 12 of the Appendix. In practice, then, we can use $\bar{\bar{X}} + A_1\bar{S}'$ as the upper control limit and $\bar{\bar{X}} - A_1\bar{S}'$ as the lower control limit. The computations are illustrated in Example 12.1.

EXAMPLE 12.1

We want to start a control chart for a new machine that fills boxes of cereal by weight. Five observations on amount of fill are taken every two hours until twenty such samples are obtained. The data are given in Table 12.1. Calculate upper and lower control limits on the mean.

Solution   The sample means ($\bar{x}_j$) and adjusted standard deviations (s_j') are given on Table 12.1 for each of the twenty samples of size 5. Now, we can calculate

$$\bar{\bar{x}} = \frac{1}{20} \sum_{j=1}^{20} \bar{x}_j = 16.32$$

and

$$\bar{s}' = \frac{1}{20} \sum_{j=1}^{20} \bar{s}_j' = 0.3017$$

Since $n = 5$, we have that $A_1 = 1.596$ from Table 12 of the Appendix. Thus, the realization of the control limit is

$$\bar{\bar{x}} \pm A_1 \bar{s}',$$

$$16.32 \pm 1.596(0.3017),$$

or

$$(15.84, 16.80).$$

Any sample mean below 15.84 or above 16.80, from a sample of size 5, would be declared out of control.

The control limits and data points are plotted in Figure 12.2.

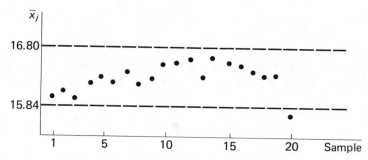

Figure 12.2   An $\bar{x}$-Chart for the Data in Table 12.1

Since the sample mean for sample 20 ($\bar{x}_{20} = 15.12$) falls below the lower control limit, we would declare the process to be out of control at that point. Now we might want to eliminate that sample and recompute the control limits from the remaining 19 samples. Doing these computations results in

$$\bar{\bar{x}} = 16.38$$

$$\bar{s}' = 0.3085$$

and

$$\bar{\bar{x}} \pm A_1 \bar{s}',$$

yielding

$$16.38 \pm 1.596(0.3085)$$

or

$$(15.89, 16.87).$$

All sample means are now within these limits, and they can be used to check the means of future samples. As new data becomes available, the control limits should be recomputed from time to time.   □

Computation of $\bar{s}'$ requires a time consuming effort that can often be avoided by using the ranges (R_j) rather than the adjusted standard deviations (S'_j). R_j denotes the range (difference between the largest and smallest observation) for sample j, $j = 1, \ldots, k$. We can average these ranges to produce

$$\bar{R} = \frac{1}{k} \sum_{j=1}^{k} R_j.$$

Now, the range (or average range) has some relationship to the variation of the data, but $\bar{R}$ is *not* an unbiased estimator of σ. However, it turns out that $\bar{R}/d_2$, where d_2 is found in Table 12 of the Appendix, *is* an unbiased estimator of σ and thus $\mu \pm 3\sigma/\sqrt{n}$ can be estimated by

$$\bar{\bar{X}} \pm 3 \frac{\bar{R}}{d_2\sqrt{n}}$$

or

$$\bar{\bar{X}} \pm A_2\bar{R}$$

where $A_2 = 3/d_2\sqrt{n}$. For convenience, values of A_2 are found in Table 12 of the Appendix.

EXAMPLE 12.2

Using the data in Table 12.1, construct control limits for the mean using the sample ranges.

Table 12.1   Amount of Cereal Dispensed by Filling Machines

Sample						$\bar{x}_j$	$\bar{s}'_j$	r_j(range)
1	16.1,	16.2,	15.9,	16.0,	16.1	16.06	0.1020	0.3
2	16.2,	16.4,	15.8,	16.1,	16.2	16.14	0.1860	0.6
3	16.0,	16.1,	15.7,	16.3,	16.1	16.04	0.1960	0.6
4	16.1,	16.2,	15.9,	16.4,	16.6	16.24	0.2417	0.7
5	16.5,	16.1,	16.5,	16.4,	16.2	16.32	0.1470	0.4
6	16.8,	16.9,	16.1,	16.3,	16.4	16.30	0.3033	0.9
7	16.1,	15.9,	16.2,	16.5,	16.5	16.44	0.2800	0.8
8	15.9,	16.2,	16.8,	16.1,	16.4	16.28	0.3059	0.9
9	15.7,	16.7,	16.1,	16.4,	16.8	16.34	0.4030	1.1
10	16.2,	16.9,	16.1,	17.0,	16.4	16.52	0.3655	0.9
11	16.4,	16.9,	17.1,	16.2,	16.1	16.54	0.3929	1.0
12	16.5,	16.9,	17.2,	16.1,	16.4	16.62	0.3868	1.1
13	16.7,	16.2,	16.4,	15.8,	16.6	16.34	0.3200	0.9
14	17.1,	16.2,	17.0,	16.9,	16.1	16.66	0.4224	1.0
15	17.0,	16.8,	16.4,	16.5,	16.2	16.58	0.2856	0.8
16	16.2,	15.7,	16.6,	16.2,	17.0	16.54	0.3072	0.8
17	17.1,	16.9,	16.2,	16.0,	16.1	16.46	0.4499	1.1
18	15.8,	16.2,	17.1,	16.9,	16.2	16.44	0.4841	1.3
19	16.4,	16.2,	16.7,	16.8,	16.1	16.44	0.2728	0.7
20	15.4,	16.1,	15.0,	15.2,	14.9	15.12	0.1720	0.5

Solution   Using all twenty samples, we have already seen that $\bar{\bar{x}} = 16.32$. The sample realization of $\bar{R}$ is

$$\bar{r} = \frac{1}{20} \sum_{j=1}^{20} r_j = 0.82.$$

Then, $\bar{\bar{X}} \pm A_2\bar{R}$ takes on the value

$$\bar{\bar{x}} \pm A_2\bar{r},$$

$$16.32 \pm (0.577)(0.82)$$

or

$$(15.85, 16.79).$$

The twentieth sample mean still falls outside of the control limits. Recomputing the limits on the 19 samples (excluding sample 20) results in

$$\bar{\bar{x}} \pm A_2\bar{r},$$

$$16.38 \pm (0.577)(0.84),$$

or

$$(15.90, 16.86),$$

and all 19 means now fall within the limits. $\square$

Note that the limits based on $\bar{R}$ are very close to those based on $\bar{S}'$ and the ones based on $\bar{R}$ require far fewer computations. In general, $\bar{R}/d_2$ is not as good as $\bar{S}'/c_2$ as an estimator of σ, but the method employing $\bar{R}$ usually works very well if k is at least 20. The disadvantage of a slight loss in accuracy is offset by the advantage of easy computations.

Exercises

12.1   Production of ammeters is controlled for quality by periodically selecting an ammeter and obtaining four measurements on a test circuit designed to produce 15 amps. The following data were observed for 15 tested ammeters.
(a) Construct control limits for the mean using the sample standard deviations.
(b) Do all observed sample means lie within the limits found in (a)? If not, recalculate the control limits after omitting these samples that are "out of control."

Ammeter	Readings			
1	15.1,	14.9,	14.8,	15.2
2	15.0,	15.0,	15.2,	14.9
3	15.1,	15.1,	15.2,	15.1
4	15.0,	14.7,	15.3,	15.1
5	14.8,	14.9,	15.1,	15.2
6	14.9,	14.9,	15.1,	15.1
7	14.7,	15.0,	15.1,	15.0
8	14.9,	15.0,	15.3,	14.8
9	14.4,	14.5,	14.3,	14.4
10	15.2,	15.3,	15.2,	15.5
11	15.1,	15.0,	15.3,	15.3
12	15.2,	15.6,	15.8,	15.8
13	14.8,	14.8,	15.0,	15.0
14	14.9,	15.1,	14.7,	14.8
15	15.1,	15.2,	14.9,	15.0

12.2   Refer to Exercise 12.1. Repeat both parts (a) and (b) using sample ranges
       instead of sample standard deviations.

12.3   Refer to Exercise 12.1, part (a). How would the control limits change if
       the probability of a sample mean falling outside of the limits, when the
       process is in control, is to be 0.01?

12.4   Refer to Exercises 12.1 and 12.2. The specifications for these ammeters
       require individual readings on the test circuit to be within 15.0 ± 0.4. Do
       the meters seem to be meeting this specification? (Hint: Construct an
       interval in which *individual* measurements will lie with high probability.)

12.5   Bronze castings are controlled for copper content. Ten samples of five
       specimens each gave the following measurements on percentage of copper.

Sample	Percentages of Copper				
1	82,	84,	80,	86,	83
2	90,	91,	94,	90,	89
3	86,	84,	87,	83,	80
4	92,	91,	89,	91,	90
5	84,	82,	83,	81,	84
6	82,	81,	83,	84,	81
7	80,	80,	79,	83,	82
8	79,	83,	84,	82,	82
9	81,	84,	85,	79,	86
10	81,	92,	94,	79,	80

(a) Construct control limits for the mean percentage of copper using the
    sample ranges.

(b) Would you use the limits in (a) as control limits for future samples?
    Why?

12.3   *The R-Chart*

In addition to deciding whether the center of the distribution of quality measurements has shifted up or down, it is frequently of interest to decide if the variability of the process measurements has significantly increased or decreased. A process that suddenly starts turning out highly variable products could cause severe problems in the operation of the industry.

Since we have already established the fact that there is a relationship between the ranges (R_j) and σ, it should seem natural to base our control chart for variability on the R_j's. A control chart for variability could be based on S_j also, but use of ranges provides nearly as much accuracy for much less computation.

Where will most of the range measurements lie if a process is in control? Using the same argument as that employed for the mean, almost all R_j's should be within three standard deviations of the mean of R_j. Now,

$$E(R_j) = d_2\sigma$$

and

$$V(R_j) = d_3^2\sigma^2,$$

where d_2 and d_3 can be found in Table 12 of the Appendix.

The three-standard deviation interval about the mean of R_j then becomes

$$d_2\sigma \pm 3d_3\sigma$$

or

$$\sigma(d_2 \pm 3d_3).$$

There is a high probability (approximately 0.9973) that any one R_j will fall inside this interval if the process is in control.

As in the case of the $\bar{X}$-chart, σ is not known and, hence, must be estimated from the data. The best estimator of σ based on $\bar{R}$ is $\bar{R}/d_2$, and the estimator of $\sigma(d_2 \pm 3d_3)$ then becomes

$$\frac{\bar{R}}{d_2}(d_2 \pm 3d_3)$$

or

$$\bar{R}\left(1 \pm 3\frac{d_3}{d_2}\right)$$

Letting $1 - 3(d_3/d_2) = D_3$ and $1 + 3(d_3/d_2) = D_4$, the control limits take on the form ($\bar{R}D_3$, $\bar{R}D_4$).

D_3 and D_4 are given in Table 12 of the Appendix.

EXAMPLE 12.3

Use the data of Table 12.1 to construct control limits on the variability of the process using ranges.

Solution   From Table 12.1 we have that $\bar{r} = 0.82$, using all twenty samples. From
Table 12 of the Appendix we see that, for samples of size $n = 5$, $D_3 = 0$ and
$D_4 = 2.115$. (The lower bound is set at zero since a range cannot be negative.)
Hence, the realization of the control limits is

$$(\bar{r}D_3, \bar{r}D_4),$$

$$((0.82)(0), (0.82)(2.115)),$$

or

$$(0, 1.73).$$

All twenty sample ranges are well within these limits, so there appear to
be no significant changes in the variability of the process over these twenty time
points. The limits constructed above could now be used to check future samples.
The control limits are plotted in Figure 12.3.   □

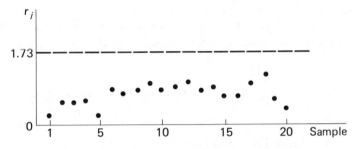

Figure 12.3   An *r*-Chart for the Data in Table 12.1.

Exercises

12.6   Refer to Exercise 12.1. Construct control limits for variability. Does the
process appear to be entirely in control with respect to variability?

12.7   Refer to Exercise 12.5. Construct control limits for variability of the
percentages of copper. Based on all ten samples, would you use these
limits as control limits for future samples? Why?

12.8   Refer to Exercise 12.6. Change the control limits so that a sample will be
falsely declared to be out of control with probability only 0.01.

12.4   *The p-Chart*

The control charting procedures outlined in the preceding sections of this chapter
depend upon quality measurements that possess a continuous probability distribution. Sampling such measurements is commonly referred to as "sampling by
variables." In many quality control situations, however, we merely want to assess

whether or not a certain item is defective. We then observe the number of defective items from a particular sample or series of samples. This is commonly referred to as "sampling by attributes."

As in previous control charting problems, suppose a series of k independent samples, each of size n, is selected from a production process. Let p denote the proportion of defective items in the population (total production for a certain time period) for a process in control and let X_i denote the number of defectives observed in the ith sample. Then, X_i has a binomial distribution, assuming random sampling from large lots, with $E(X_i) = np$ and $V(X_i) = np(1 - p)$. We will usually work with sample fractions of defectives (X_i/n) rather than the observed number of defectives. Where will these sample fractions tend to lie for a process in control? As argued previously, most sample fractions should lie within three standard deviations of their mean, or in the interval

$$p \pm 3 \sqrt{\frac{p(1 - p)}{n}},$$

since $E(X_i/n) = p$ and $V(X_i/n) = p(1 - p)/n$.

Since p is unknown, now we must estimate these control limits, using the data from all k samples. An unbiased estimator of p is

$$\bar{P} = \frac{\sum_{i=1}^{k} X_i}{nk} = \frac{\text{Total number of defectives observed}}{\text{Total sample size}}.$$

Thus, estimated control limits are given by

$$\bar{P} \pm 3 \sqrt{\frac{\bar{P}(1 - \bar{P})}{n}}.$$

The following example illustrates the calculation of these control limits.

EXAMPLE 12.4

A process that produces transistors is sampled every four hours. At each time point 50 transistors are randomly sampled, and the number of defectives, x_i, is observed. The data for 24 samples are given in Table 12.2. Construct a control chart based on these samples.

Solution   From the above data, the observed value of $\bar{P}$ is

$$\bar{p} = \frac{\sum_{i=1}^{k} x_i}{nk} = \frac{52}{50(24)} = 0.04.$$

Thus,

$$\bar{p} \pm 3 \sqrt{\frac{\bar{p}(1 - \bar{p})}{n}}$$

Table 12.2   Data for Example 12.4

Sample	x_i	x_i/n	Sample	x_i	x_i/n
1	3	0.06	13	1	0.02
2	1	0.02	14	2	0.04
3	4	0.08	15	0	0.00
4	2	0.04	16	3	0.06
5	0	0.00	17	2	0.04
6	2	0.04	18	2	0.04
7	3	0.06	19	4	0.08
8	3	0.06	20	1	0.02
9	5	0.10	21	3	0.06
10	4	0.08	22	0	0.00
11	1	0.02	23	2	0.04
12	1	0.02	24	3	0.06

becomes

$$0.04 \pm 3 \sqrt{\frac{(0.04)(0.96)}{50}},$$

$$0.04 \pm 0.08,$$

or

$$(0, 0.12).$$

We set the lower control limit at zero since a fraction of defectives cannot be negative.

All of the observed sample fractions are within these limits, so we would feel comfortable in using them as control limits for future samples. The limits should be recalculated from time to time as new data becomes available.

The control limits and observed data points are plotted in Figure 12.4. ☐

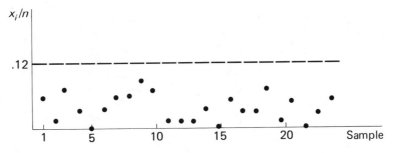

Figure 12.4   A p-Chart for the Data of Table 12.2

Exercises

12.9 Filled bottles of soft drink coming off a production line are checked for underfilling. One hundred bottles are sampled from each half-day's production. The results for twenty such samples are as follows:

Sample	No. of Defectives	Sample	No. of Defectives
1	10	11	15
2	12	12	6
3	8	13	3
4	14	14	2
5	3	15	0
6	7	16	1
7	12	17	1
8	10	18	4
9	9	19	3
10	11	20	6

(a) Construct control limits for the proportion of defectives.
(b) Do all the observed sample fractions fall within the control limits found in (a)? If not, adjust the limits for future use.

12.10 Refer to Exercise 12.9. Adjust the control limits so that a sample fraction will fall outside of the limits with probability .05, when the process is in control.

12.11 Bolts being produced in a certain plant are checked for tolerances. Those not meeting tolerance specifications are considered to be defective. Fifty bolts are gauged for tolerance every hour. The results for thirty hours of sampling are as follows:

Sample	No. Defective	Sample	No. Defective	Sample	No. Defective
1	5	11	3	21	6
2	6	12	0	22	4
3	4	13	1	23	9
4	0	14	1	24	3
5	8	15	2	25	0
6	3	16	5	26	6
7	10	17	5	27	4
8	2	18	4	28	2
9	9	19	3	29	1
10	7	20	1	30	2

(a) Construct control limits for the proportion of defectives based on these data.
(b) Would you use the control limits found in (a) for future samples? Why?

12.5   The c-Chart

In many quality control problems, the particular items being subjected to inspection may have more than one defect, and so we may wish to count defects instead of merely classifying an item as to whether or not it is defective. If C_i denotes the number of defects observed on the ith inspected item, a good working model for many applications is to assume that C_i has a Poisson distribution. We will let the Poisson distribution have a mean of λ for a process in control.

Most of the C_i's should fall within their mean if the process remains in control. Since $E(C_i) = \lambda$ and $V(C_i) = \lambda$, the control limits become

$$\lambda \pm 3\sqrt{\lambda}.$$

If k items are inspected, then an unbiased estimator of λ is given by

$$\bar{C} = \frac{1}{k}\sum_{i=1}^{k} C_i.$$

The estimated control limits then become

$$\bar{C} \pm 3\sqrt{\bar{C}}.$$

The computations are illustrated in Example 12.5.

EXAMPLE 12.5

Twenty rebuilt pumps were sampled from the hydraulics shop of an aircraft rework facility. The numbers of defects recorded are given in Table 12.3.

Table 12.3   Data for Example 12.5

Pump	No. of Defects (c_i)	Pump	No. of Defects (c_i)
1	6	11	4
2	3	12	3
3	4	13	2
4	0	14	2
5	2	15	6
6	7	16	5
7	3	17	0
8	1	18	7
9	0	19	2
10	0	20	1

Use these data to construct control limits for defects per pump.

Solution   Assuming that C_i, the number of defects observed on pump i, has a Poisson distribution, we estimate the mean number of defects per pump by $\bar{C}$ and use

$$\bar{C} \pm 3\sqrt{\bar{C}}$$

as the control limits. Using the data in Table 12.3, we have

$$\bar{c} = \frac{58}{20} = 2.9$$

and hence,

$$\bar{c} \pm 3\sqrt{\bar{c}}$$

becomes

$$2.9 \pm 3\sqrt{2.9},$$
$$2.9 \pm 5.1,$$

or

$$(0, 8.0).$$

Again, the lower limit is raised to zero since a number of defects cannot be negative.

All of the observed counts are within the control limits, so we could use these limits for future samples. Again, the limits should be recomputed from time to time, as new data becomes available.

The control limits and data points are plotted in Figure 12.5.   □

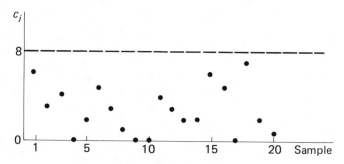

Figure 12.5   A *c*-Chart for the Data of Table 12.3

Exercises

12.12 Woven fabric from a certain loom is controlled for quality by periodically sampling one-square-meter specimens and counting the number of defects. For 15 such samples, the observed number of defects was as follows:

Sample	No. of Defects
1	3
2	6
3	10
4	4
5	7
6	11
7	3
8	9
9	6
10	14
11	4
12	3
13	1
14	4
15	

    (a) Construct control limits for the average number of defects per square meter.

    (b) Do all samples observed seem to be "in control?"

12.13 Refer to Exercise 12.12. Adjust the control limits so that a count for a process in control will fall outside the limits with probability only 0.01, approximately.

12.14 Quality control in glass production involves counting the number of defects observed in samples of a fixed size periodically selected from the production process. For twenty samples, the observed counts on numbers of defects are as follows:

Sample	No. of Defects	Sample	No. of Defects
1	3	11	7
2	0	12	3
3	2	13	0
4	5	14	1
5	3	15	4
6	0	16	2
7	4	17	2
8	1	18	1
9	2	19	0
10	2	20	2

    (a) Construct control limits for defects per sample based on these data.

    (b) Would you adjust the limits in (a) before using them on future samples?

12.15 Suppose variation among defect counts is important in a process like that of Exercise 12.14. Is it necessary to have a separate method to construct control limits for variation? Discuss.

12.6   *Acceptance Sampling by Attributes*

The preceding sections of this chapter dealt with statistical methods for controlling quality of products in an ongoing production process. In this section we discuss the problem of making a decision with regard to the proportion of defective items in a finite lot based on the number of defectives observed in a sample from that lot. Inspection in which a unit of product is classified simply as defective or nondefective is called inspection by *attributes*.

Lots of items, either raw materials or finished products, are sold by a producer to a consumer with some guarantee as to quality. In this section, quality will be determined by the proportion, p, of defective items in the lot. In order to check on the quality characteristics of a lot, the consumer will sample some of the items, test them, and observe the number of defectives. Generally, some defectives are allowable because defective-free lots may be too expensive for the consumer to purchase. But, if the number of defectives is too large, the consumer will reject the lot and return it to the producer.

In the decision to accept or reject the lot, sampling is generally used because the cost of inspecting the entire lot may be too high, the inspection process may be destructive, or the sampling procedure may actually give more accurate results than could be obtained by attempting to inspect the entire lot.

Before sampling inspection takes place for a lot, the consumer must have in mind a proportion, p_0, of defectives that will be acceptable. Thus, if the true proportion of defectives, p, is no greater than p_0 the consumer wants to accept the lot, and if p is greater than p_0 the consumer wants to reject the lot. This maximum proportion of defectives satisfactory to the consumer is called the *acceptable quality level* (AQL).

Note that we now have an hypothesis testing problem in which we are testing $H_0 : p \le p_0$ versus $H_a : p > p_0$. A random sample of n items will be selected from the lot, and the number of defectives, Y, observed. The decision concerning rejection or nonrejection of H_0 (rejecting or accepting the lot) will be based on the observed value of Y.

The probability of a type I error, α, in this problem is the probability that the lot will be rejected by the consumer when, in fact, the proportion of defectives is satisfactory to the consumer. This is referred to as the *producer's risk*. The value of α calculated for $p = p_0$ is the upper limit to the proportion of good lots rejected by the sampling plan being considered. The probability of a type II error, β, calculated for some proportion of defectives p_1, where $p_1 > p_0$, represents the probability that an unsatisfactory lot will be accepted by the consumer. This is referred to as the *consumer's risk*. The value of β calculated for $p = p_1$ is the upper limit to the proportion of bad lots accepted by the sampling plan, for all $p \ge p_1$.

The null hypothesis, $H_0 : p \le p_0$, will be rejected if the observed value of Y is larger than some constant, a. Since the lot is accepted if $Y \le a$, the constant a is called the *acceptance number*. In this context, the significance level, α, is given by

$$\alpha = P(\text{Reject } H_0 \text{ when } p = p_0)$$
$$= P(Y > a \text{ when } p = p_0)$$

and

$$1 - \alpha = P(\text{Not rejecting } H_0 \text{ when } p = p_0)$$
$$= P(\text{Accepting the lot when } p = p_0)$$
$$= P(A).$$

Since p_0 may not be known precisely, it is of interest to see how $P(A)$ behaves as a function of the true p, for a given n and a. A plot of these probabilities is called an *operating characteristic curve*, abbreviated OC curve. We illustrate its calculation with the following numerical example.

EXAMPLE 12.6

One sampling inspection plan calls for $(n = 10, a = 1)$ while another calls for $(n = 25, a = 3)$. Plot the operating characteristic curves for both plans. If the plant using these plans can operate well on 30% defective raw materials, considering the price, but cannot operate efficiently if the proportion gets close to 40%, which plan should they choose?

Solution

We must calculate $P(A) = P(Y \leq a)$ for various values of p in order to plot the OC curves. For $(n = 10, a = 1)$ we have:

$$p = 0, \qquad P(A) = 1$$
$$p = 0.1, \qquad P(A) = 0.736$$
$$p = 0.2, \qquad P(A) = 0.376$$
$$p = 0.3, \qquad P(A) = 0.149$$
$$p = 0.4, \qquad P(A) = 0.046$$
$$p = 0.6, \qquad P(A) = 0.002$$

using Table 2 of the Appendix. For $(n = 25, a = 3)$, we have:

$$p = 0, \qquad P(A) = 1$$
$$p = 0.1, \qquad P(A) = 0.764$$
$$p = 0.2, \qquad P(A) = 0.234$$
$$p = 0.3, \qquad P(A) = 0.033$$
$$p = 0.4, \qquad P(A) = 0.002$$

These values are plotted in Figure 12.6. Note that the $(n = 10, a = 1)$ plan drops slowly, and does not get appreciably small until p is in the neighborhood of 0.4. For p around 0.3, this plan still has a fairly high probability of accepting the lot. The other curve, $(n = 25, a = 3)$ drops much more rapidly, and falls to a small $P(A)$ at $p = 0.3$. It seems like the latter plan would be better for the plant, if they can afford to sample $n = 25$ items out of each lot before making a decision. □

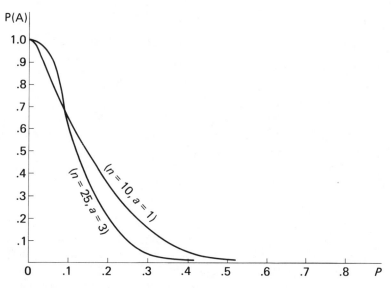

Figure 12.6   Operating Characteristic Curves

There are numerous handbooks that give operating characteristic curves and related properties for a variety of sampling plans, when inspecting by attributes, but one of the most widely used sets of plans is Military Standard 105D (MIL–STD–105D).

Even though the probability of acceptance, as calculated in Example 12.6, generally does not depend upon the lot size, as long as the lot is large compared to the sample size, MIL–STD–105D is constructed so that sample size increases with lot size. The practical reasons for the increasing sample sizes are that small random samples are sometimes difficult to obtain from large lots and that discrimination between good and bad lots may be more important for large lots. The adjustments in sample sizes for large lots are based upon empirical evidence rather than strict probabilistic considerations.

MIL–STD–105D contains plans for three sampling levels, labeled I, II, and III. Generally, sampling or inspection level II is used. Level I gives slightly smaller samples and less discrimination whereas level III gives slightly larger samples and more discrimination. Table 13 gives the code letters for various lot or batch sizes and inspection levels I, II, and III. This code letter is used to enter either Table 14, 15 or 16 to find the sample size and acceptance number to be used for specified values of the AQL.

In addition to having three inspection levels, MIL–STD–105D also has sampling plans for normal, tightened and reduced inspection. These plans are given in Tables 14, 15 and 16, respectively. Normal inspection is designed to protect the producer against the rejection of lots with percent defectives less than the AQL. Tightened inspection is designed to protect the consumer from accepting lots with percent defectives greater than the AQL. Reduced inspection is introduced as an economical plan to be used if the quality history of the lots is good. When sampling a series of lots, rules for switching among normal, tightened and reduced sampling are given in MIL–STD–105D. When using MIL–STD–105D on a single lot, the OC curves for various plans, given in the handbook, should be studied carefully before deciding on the optimal plan for a particular problem.

EXAMPLE 12.7

A lot of size 1000 is to be sampled with normal inspection at level II. If the AQL of interest is 10%, find the appropriate sample size and acceptance number from MIL–STD–105D.

Solution   Entering Table 13 for a lot size 1000, we see that the code letter for level II is J. Since normal inspection is to be used, we enter Table 14 at row J. The sample size is 80 and, moving over to the column headed 10% AQL, we see that the acceptance number is 14. Thus, we sample 80 items and accept the lot if the number of defectives is less than or equal to 14. This plan will have a high probability of accepting any lot with a true percentage of defectives below 10%.   □

12.7   *Acceptance Sampling by Variables*

In acceptance sampling by attributes, one merely records, for each sampled item, whether or not the item is defective. The decision to accept or reject the lot then depends upon the number of defectives observed in the sample. However, if the characteristic under study involves a measurement on each sampled item, one could base the decision to accept or reject on the measurements themselves, rather than simply on the number of items having measurements that do not meet a certain standard.

For example, suppose a lot of manufactured steel rods are checked for quality with the quality measurement being the diameter. Rods are not allowed to exceed ten centimeters in diameter, and a rod with a diameter in excess of ten centimeters is declared defective. In attribute sampling, the decision to accept or reject the lot is based on the number of defective rods observed in a sample. But, this decision could be made on the basis of some function of the actual diameter observations themselves, say the mean of these observations. If the sample mean is close to or in excess of ten centimeters one would expect the lot to contain a high percentage of defectives, whereas if the sample mean is much smaller than ten centimeters one would expect the lot to contain relatively few defectives.

Using actual measurements of the quality characteristic as a basis for acceptance or rejection of a lot is called acceptance sampling by *variables*. Sampling by variables often has advantages over sampling by attributes since the variables method may contain more information for a fixed sample size than the attribute method. Also, when looking at the actual measurements obtained by the variables method the experimenter may gain some insights into the degree of nonconformance and may be able to quickly suggest methods for improving the product.

For acceptance sampling by variables, let

$$U = \text{upper specification limit}$$

and

$$L = \text{lower specification limit.}$$

If X denotes the quality measurement being considered, the U is the maximum allowable value for X on an acceptable item. (U is equal to ten centimeters in the rod diameter example.) Similarly, L is the minimum allowable value for X on an acceptable item. Some problems may specify a U, others an L, and still others both U and L.

As in acceptance sampling by attributes, an AQL is specified for a lot, and a sampling plan is then determined that will give high probability of acceptance to lots with percent defectives lower than the AQL and low probability of acceptance to lots with percent defectives higher than the AQL. In practice an *acceptability constant*, k, is determined such that a lot is accepted if

$$\frac{U - \bar{X}}{S} \geq k$$

or

$$\frac{\bar{X} - L}{S} \geq k,$$

where $\bar{X}$ is the sample mean and S the sample standard deviation of the quality measurements.

As in the case of sampling by attributes, handbooks of sampling plans are available for acceptance sampling by variables. One of the most widely used of these handbooks is Military Standard 414 (MIL–STD–414). Tables 17 and 18 of the Appendix are necessary to illustrate how MIL–STD–414 is used. Table 17A shows which tabled AQL value to use if the problem calls for an AQL not specifically tabled. Table 17B gives the sample size code letter to use with any possible lot size. Sample sizes are tied to lot sizes and different levels of sampling are used, as in MIL–STD–105D. Inspection level IV is recommended for general use.

Table 18 gives the sample size and value of k for a fixed code letter and AQL. Both normal and tightened inspection procedures can be found in this table.

The use of these tables is illustrated in Example 12.8.

EXAMPLE 12.8

The tensile strengths of wires in a certain lot of size 400 are specified to exceed 5 kilograms. We want to set up an acceptance sampling plan with AQL = 1.4%. With inspection level IV and normal inspection, find the appropriate plan from MIL–STD–414.

Solution

Looking first at Table 17A, we see that a desired AQL of 1.4% would correspond to a tabled value of 1.5%. Finding the lot size of 400 for inspection level IV in Table 17B yields a code letter of I.

Now, looking at 17 in row labeled I, we find a sample size of 25. For that same row, the column headed with an AQL of 1.5% gives $k = 1.72$. Thus, we are to sample 25 wires from the lot and accept the lot if

$$\frac{\bar{X} - 5}{S} \geq 1.72,$$

where $\bar{X}$ and S are the mean and standard deviation for the 25 tensile strength measurements. $\square$

MIL–STD–414 also gives a table for reduced inspection, much as in MIL–STD–105D. The handbook provides OC curves for the sampling plans tabled there and, in addition, gives sampling plans based on sample ranges rather than standard deviations.

The theory connected with the development of the sampling plans for inspection by variables is more difficult than that for inspection by attributes, and cannot be fully developed here. However, we will outline the basic approach.

Suppose again that X is the quality measurement under study and U is the upper specification limit. The probability that an item is defective is then given by $P(X > U)$. (This probability also represents the proportion of defective items in the lot.) Now, we only want to accept lots for which $P(X > U)$ is small, say less than or equal to a constant M. But,

$$P(X > U) \le M$$

is equivalent to

$$P\left(\frac{X - \mu}{\sigma} > \frac{U - \mu}{\sigma}\right) \le M$$

where $\mu = E(X)$ and $\sigma^2 = V(X)$. If, in addition, X has a normal distribution then the latter probability statement is equivalent to

$$P\left(Z > \frac{U - \mu}{\sigma}\right) \le M,$$

where Z has a standard normal distribution.

It follows that $P(X > U)$ will be "small" if and only if $(U - \mu)/\sigma$ is "large." Thus,

$$P(X > U) \le M$$

is equivalent to

$$\frac{U - \mu}{\sigma} \ge k^*$$

for some constant k^*. Since μ and σ are unknown, the actual acceptance criterion used in practice becomes

$$\frac{U - \bar{X}}{S} \ge k,$$

where k is chosen so that $P(X > U) \le M$.

For normally distributed X, the $P(X > U)$ can be estimated by making use of the sample information provided by $\bar{X}$ and S, and these estimates are tabled in

MIL–STD–414. These estimates are used in the construction of OC curves. Also, tables are given that show the values of M, in addition to the value of k, for sampling plans designed for specified AQL's.

Exercises

12.16 Construct operating characteristic curves for the following sampling plans, when sampling by attributes:
(a) $n = 10, a = 2$
(b) $n = 10, a = 4$
(c) $n = 20, a = 2$
(d) $n = 20, a = 4$

12.17 Suppose a lot of size 3000 is to be sampled by attributes. An AQL of 4% is specified for acceptable lots. Find the appropriate level II sampling plan under
(a) normal inspection
(b) tightened inspection
(c) reduced inspection

12.18 Fuses of a certain type must not allow the current passing through them to exceed 20 amps. A lot of 1200 of these fuses is to be checked for quality by a lot acceptance sampling plan with inspection by variables. The desired AQL is 2%. Find the appropriate sampling plan for level IV sampling and
(a) normal inspection
(b) tightened inspection

12.19 Refer to Exercise 12.18. If, under normal inspection, the sample mean turned out to be 19.2 amps and the sample standard deviation 0.3 amp, what would you conclude?

12.20 For a lot of 250 gallon cans filled with a certain industrial chemical, each gallon is specified to have a percentage of alcohol in excess of L. If the AQL is specified to be 10%, find an appropriate lot-acceptance sampling plan (level IV inspection) under
(a) normal inspection
(b) tightened inspection

12.8   Conclusion

Quality assurance often necessitates the use of control charts. The construction of control limits is based on standard statistical techniques, sometimes using the sample mean as a measure of central tendency and the variance. More commonly, the range is used as a measure of variability. The normal distribution is employed as a basic model for control limits based on means, whereas the binomial or Poisson distribution is commonly used for counts.

Control limits are usually set so that the chance of stating that a process is out of control when, in fact, it *is* in control is very small, much smaller than the common 0.05 value for Type I errors in statistical tests. This is so because of the often serious and expensive consequences of falsely declaring a process to be out of control.

There are many other adaptations of control charting techniques. Some can be found in the suggested references.

If instead of controlling an ongoing process, one is interested in deciding whether to accept or reject a lot of manufactured items or raw materials, a lot acceptance sampling plan is needed. Inspection for lot acceptance may be by attributes or by variables, and excellent military standard sampling plans are available for both types of inspection.

Supplementary Exercises

12.21 Casts of aluminum are checked for tensile strength by testing four specimens from each batch. The results from tests of ten batches are given below, with measurements in 1000 psi.

Batch	Tensile Strength Measurements			
1	40,	41,	43,	39
2	44,	42,	46,	41
3	32,	34,	33,	31
4	42,	47,	43,	44
5	46,	48,	49,	46
6	47,	49,	48,	46
7	42,	44,	43,	46
8	49,	47,	42,	48
9	48,	47,	32,	31
10	42,	44,	46,	45

(a) Construct control limits for the mean tensile strength, using ranges as a measure of variability.
(b) Do all samples appear to come from a process "in control?"
(c) How would you adjust the limits found in (a) for use in future sampling?

12.22 Refer to Exercise 12.21.
(a) Construct control limits for variability.
(b) Would you use these limits for future studies? If not, how would you adjust them for future use?

12.23 Refer to Exercise 12.21. Adjust the control limits so that a sample mean will fall outside the limits with probability approximately 0.02 when the process is in control.

12.24 Refer to Exercise 12.22. Adjust the control limits so that a sample range will fall outside the limits with probability approximately 0.01 when the process is in control.

12.25 Refer to Exercise 12.5. A specimen will be called "defective" if the percentage of copper is outside the interval (80, 90). Construct control limits for the percentage of specimens that are defective, using these data. Do all of the observed samples appear to be "in control"?

12.26 Occasionally, samples of equal size cannot be obtained at every time point. In that event, the control limits must be computed separately for each sample size. Construct a three-standard deviation limit control chart for the mean, using the sample standard deviations as measures of variability, based on the following data on measures of pollutants in water samples.

Sample	Amount of Pollutant				
1	6.2	7.3	9.2	8.1	
2	5.4	6.8	3.2		
3	20.4	16.8	17.2	16.0	19.1
4	5.7	10.2	9.3		
5	6.8	10.1	7.2	8.4	
6	7.9	10.4	8.6	9.3	
7	17.1	16.8	17.3		
8	16.2	13.9	14.7	16.1	
9	10.2	11.4	13.2	10.9	
10	11.1	12.4	13.2		

(Hint: An unbiased estimate of μ can be found by using a weighted average of the sample means, with weights equal to the sample sizes. The best estimate of σ^2 involves a weighted average of the sample variances s_i^2.)

12.27 Discuss the construction of a p-chart for proportions when the sample sizes vary.

12.28 Discuss the construction of a c-chart when the sample sizes vary.

Appendix

Table 1 Random Numbers

Row \ Column	1	2	3	4	5	6	7	8	9	10	11	12	13	14
1	10480	15011	01536	02011	81647	91646	69179	14194	62590	36207	20969	99570	91291	90700
2	22368	46573	25595	85393	30995	89198	27982	53402	93965	34095	52666	19174	39615	99505
3	24130	48360	22527	97265	76393	64809	15179	24830	49340	32081	30680	19655	63348	58629
4	42167	93093	06243	61680	07856	16376	39440	53537	71341	57004	00849	74917	97758	16379
5	37570	39975	81837	16656	06121	91782	60468	81305	49684	60672	14110	06927	01263	54613
6	77921	06907	11008	42751	27756	53498	18602	70659	90655	15053	21916	81825	44394	42880
7	99562	72905	56420	69994	98872	31016	71194	18738	44013	48840	63213	21069	10634	12952
8	96301	91977	05463	07972	18876	20922	94595	56869	69014	60045	18425	84903	42508	32307
9	89579	14342	63661	10281	17453	18103	57740	84378	25331	12566	58678	44947	05585	56941
10	85475	36857	53342	53988	53060	59533	38867	62300	08158	17983	16439	11458	18593	64952
11	28918	69578	88231	33276	70997	79936	56865	05859	90106	31595	01547	85590	91610	78188
12	63553	40961	48235	03427	49626	69445	18663	72695	52180	20847	12234	90511	33703	90322
13	09429	93969	52636	92737	88974	33488	36320	17617	30015	08272	84115	27156	30613	74952
14	10365	61129	87529	85689	48237	52267	67689	93394	01511	26358	85104	20285	29975	89868
15	07119	97336	71048	08178	77233	13916	47564	81056	97735	85977	29372	74461	28551	90707
16	51085	12765	51821	51259	77452	16308	60756	92144	49442	53900	70960	63990	75601	40719
17	02368	21382	52404	60268	89368	19885	55322	44819	01188	65255	64835	44919	05944	55157
18	01011	54092	33362	94904	31273	04146	18594	29852	71585	85030	51132	01915	92747	64951
19	52162	53916	46369	58586	23216	14513	83149	98736	23495	64350	94738	17752	35156	35749
20	07056	97628	33787	09998	42698	06691	76988	13602	51851	46104	88916	19509	25625	58104
21	48663	91245	85828	14346	09172	30168	90229	04734	59193	22178	30421	61666	99904	32812
22	54164	58492	22421	74103	47070	25306	76468	26384	58151	06646	21524	15227	96909	44592
23	32639	32363	05597	24200	13363	38005	94342	28728	35806	06912	17012	64161	18296	22851
24	29334	27001	87637	87308	58731	00256	45834	15398	46557	41135	10367	07684	36188	18510
25	02488	33062	28834	07351	19731	92420	60952	61280	50001	67658	32586	86679	50720	94953
26	81525	72295	04839	96423	24878	82651	66566	14778	76797	14780	13300	87074	79666	95725
27	29676	20591	68086	26432	46901	20849	89768	81536	86645	12659	92259	57102	80428	25280
28	00742	57392	39064	66432	84673	40027	32832	61362	98947	96067	64760	64584	96096	98253
29	05366	04213	25669	26422	44407	44048	37937	63904	45766	66134	75470	66520	34693	90449
30	91921	26418	64117	94305	26766	25940	39972	22209	71500	64568	91402	42416	07844	69618
31	00582	04711	87917	77341	42206	35126	74087	99547	81817	42607	43808	76655	62028	76630
32	00725	69884	62797	56170	86324	88072	76222	36086	84637	93161	65855	77919	88006	

Source: Abridged from W. H. Beyer, Ed., CRC Standard Mathematical Tables, 24th ed (Cleveland, The Chemical Rubber Company), 1976. Reproduced by permission of the publisher.

Table 1 (Continued)

Row \ Column	1	2	3	4	5	6	7	8	9	10	11	12	13	14
33	69011	65795	95876	55293	18988	27354	26575	08625	40801	59920	29841	80150	12777	48501
34	25976	57948	29888	88604	67917	48708	18912	82271	65424	69774	33611	54262	85963	03547
35	09763	83473	73577	12908	30883	18317	28290	35797	05998	41688	34952	37888	38917	88050
36	91576	42595	27958	30134	04024	86385	29880	99730	55536	84855	29080	09250	79656	73211
37	17955	56349	90999	49127	20044	59931	06115	20542	18059	02008	73708	83517	36103	42791
38	46503	18584	18845	49618	02304	51038	20655	58727	28168	15475	56942	53389	20562	87338
39	92157	89634	94824	78171	84610	82834	09922	25417	44137	48413	25555	21246	35509	20468
40	14577	62765	35605	81263	39667	47358	56873	56307	61607	49518	89656	20103	77490	18062
41	98427	07523	33362	64270	01638	92477	66969	98420	04880	45585	46565	04102	46880	45709
42	34914	63976	88720	82765	34476	17032	87589	40836	32427	70002	70663	88863	77775	69348
43	70060	28277	39475	46473	23219	53416	94970	25832	69975	94884	19661	72828	00102	66794
44	53976	54914	06990	67245	68350	82948	11398	42878	80287	88267	47363	46634	06541	97809
45	76072	29515	40980	07391	58745	25774	22987	80059	39911	96189	41151	14222	60697	59583
46	90725	52210	83974	29992	65831	38857	50490	83765	55657	14361	31720	57375	56228	41546
47	64364	67412	33339	31926	14883	24413	59744	92351	97473	89286	35931	04110	23726	51900
48	08962	00358	31662	25388	61642	34072	81249	35648	56891	69352	48373	45578	78547	81788
49	95012	68379	93526	70765	10592	04542	76463	54328	02349	17247	28865	14777	62730	92277
50	15664	10493	20492	38391	91132	21999	59516	81652	27195	48223	46751	22923	32261	85653
51	16408	81899	04153	53381	79401	21438	83035	92350	36693	31238	59649	91754	72772	02338
52	18629	81953	05520	91962	04739	13092	97662	24822	94730	06496	35090	04822	86774	98289
53	73115	35101	47498	87637	99016	71060	88824	71013	18735	20286	23153	72924	35165	43040
54	57491	16703	23167	49323	45021	33132	12544	41035	80780	45393	44812	12515	98931	91202
55	30405	83946	23792	14422	15059	45799	22716	19792	09983	74353	68668	30429	70735	25499
56	16631	35006	85900	98275	32388	52390	16815	69298	82732	38480	73817	32523	41961	44437
57	96773	20206	42559	78985	05300	22164	24369	54224	35083	19687	11052	91491	60383	19746
58	38935	64202	14349	82674	66523	44133	00697	35552	35970	19124	63318	29686	03387	59846
59	31624	76384	17403	53363	44167	64486	64758	75366	76554	31601	12614	33072	60332	92325
60	78919	19474	23632	27889	47914	02584	37680	20801	72152	39339	34806	08930	85001	87820
61	03931	33309	57047	74211	63445	17361	62825	39908	05607	91284	68833	25570	38818	46920
62	74426	33278	43972	10119	89917	15665	52872	73823	73144	88662	88970	74492	51805	99378
63	09066	00903	20795	95452	92648	45454	09552	88815	16553	51125	79375	97596	16296	66092
64	42238	12426	87025	14267	20979	04508	64535	31355	86064	29472	47689	05974	52468	16834

65	16153	08002	26504	41744	81959	65642	74240	56302	00033	67107	77510	70625	28725	34191
66	21457	40742	29820	96783	29400	21840	15035	34537	33310	06116	95240	15957	16572	06004
67	21581	57802	02050	89728	17937	37621	47075	42080	97403	48626	68995	43805	33386	21597
68	55612	78095	83197	33732	05810	24813	86902	60397	16489	03264	88525	42786	05269	92532
69	44657	66999	99324	51281	84463	60563	79312	93454	68876	25471	93911	25650	12682	73572
70	91340	84979	46949	81973	37949	61023	43997	15263	80644	43942	89203	71795	99533	50501
71	91227	21199	31935	27022	84067	05462	35216	14486	29891	68607	41867	14951	91696	85065
72	50001	38140	66321	19924	72163	09538	12151	06878	91903	18749	34405	56087	82790	70925
73	65390	05224	72958	28609	81406	39147	25549	48542	42627	45233	57202	94617	23772	07896
74	27504	96131	83944	41575	10573	08619	64482	73923	36152	05184	94142	25299	84387	34925
75	37169	94851	39117	89632	00959	16487	65536	49071	39782	17095	02330	74301	00275	48280
76	11508	70225	51111	38351	19444	66499	71945	05422	13442	78675	84081	66938	93654	59894
77	37449	30362	06694	54690	04052	53115	62757	95348	78662	11163	81651	50245	34971	52924
78	46515	70331	85922	38329	57015	15765	97161	17869	45349	61796	66345	81073	49106	79860
79	30986	81223	42416	58353	21532	30502	32305	86482	05174	07901	54339	58861	74818	46942
80	63798	64995	46583	09785	44160	78128	83991	42865	92520	83531	80377	35909	81250	54238
81	82486	84846	99254	67632	43218	50076	21361	64816	51202	88124	41870	52689	51275	83556
82	21885	32906	92431	09060	64297	51674	64126	62570	26123	05155	59194	52799	28225	85762
83	60336	98782	07408	53458	13564	59089	26445	29789	85205	41001	12535	12133	14645	23541
84	43937	46891	24010	25560	86355	33941	25786	54990	71899	15475	95434	98227	21824	19585
85	97656	63175	89303	16275	07100	92063	21942	18611	47348	20203	18534	03862	78095	50136
86	03299	01221	05418	38982	55758	92237	26759	86367	21216	98442	08303	56613	91511	75928
87	79626	06486	03574	17668	07785	76020	79924	25651	83325	88428	85076	72811	22717	50585
88	85636	68335	47539	03129	65651	11977	02510	26113	99447	68645	34327	15152	55230	93448
89	18039	14367	61337	06177	12143	46609	32989	74014	64708	00533	35398	58408	13261	47908
90	08362	15656	60627	36478	65648	16764	53412	09013	07832	41574	17639	82163	60859	75567
91	79556	29068	04142	16268	15387	12856	66227	38358	22478	73373	88732	09443	82558	05250
92	92608	82674	27072	32534	17075	27698	98204	63863	11951	34648	88022	56148	34925	57031
93	23982	25835	40055	67006	12293	02753	14827	23235	35071	99704	37543	11601	35503	85171
94	09915	96306	05908	97901	28395	14186	00821	80703	70426	75647	76310	88717	37890	40129
95	59037	33300	26695	62247	69927	76123	50842	43834	04098	70959	79725	93872	28117	19233
96	42488	78077	69882	61657	34136	79180	97526	43092	73571	73571	80799	76536	71255	64239
97	46764	86273	63003	93017	31204	36692	40202	35275	57306	55543	53203	18098	47625	88684
98	03237	45430	55417	63282	90816	17349	88298	90183	36600	78406	06216	95787	42579	90730
99	86591	81482	52667	61582	14972	90053	89534	76036	49199	43716	97548	04379	46370	28672
100	38534	01715	94964	87288	65680	43772	39560	12918	86537	62738	19636	51132	25739	56947

Table 2   Binomial Probabilities

Tabulated values are $\sum\limits_{x=0}^{k} p(x)$. (Computations are rounded at the third decimal place.)

(a) $n = 5$

k \ p	0.01	0.05	0.10	0.20	0.30	0.40	0.50	0.60	0.70	0.80	0.90	0.95	0.99
0	0.951	0.774	0.590	0.328	0.168	0.078	0.031	0.010	0.002	0.000	0.000	0.000	0.000
1	0.999	0.977	0.919	0.737	0.528	0.337	0.188	0.087	0.031	0.007	0.000	0.000	0.000
2	1.000	0.999	0.991	0.942	0.837	0.683	0.500	0.317	0.163	0.058	0.009	0.001	0.000
3	1.000	1.000	1.000	0.993	0.969	0.913	0.812	0.663	0.472	0.263	0.081	0.023	0.001
4	1.000	1.000	1.000	1.000	0.998	0.990	0.969	0.922	0.832	0.672	0.410	0.226	0.049

(b) $n = 10$

k \ p	0.01	0.05	0.10	0.20	0.30	0.40	0.50	0.60	0.70	0.80	0.90	0.95	0.99
0	0.904	0.599	0.349	0.107	0.028	0.006	0.001	0.000	0.000	0.000	0.000	0.000	0.000
1	0.996	0.914	0.736	0.376	0.149	0.046	0.011	0.002	0.000	0.000	0.000	0.000	0.000
2	1.000	0.988	0.930	0.678	0.383	0.167	0.055	0.012	0.002	0.000	0.000	0.000	0.000
3	1.000	0.999	0.987	0.879	0.650	0.382	0.172	0.055	0.011	0.001	0.000	0.000	0.000
4	1.000	1.000	0.998	0.967	0.850	0.633	0.377	0.166	0.047	0.006	0.000	0.000	0.000
5	1.000	1.000	1.000	0.994	0.953	0.834	0.623	0.367	0.150	0.033	0.002	0.000	0.000
6	1.000	1.000	1.000	0.999	0.989	0.945	0.828	0.618	0.350	0.121	0.013	0.001	0.000
7	1.000	1.000	1.000	1.000	0.998	0.988	0.945	0.833	0.617	0.322	0.070	0.012	0.000
8	1.000	1.000	1.000	1.000	1.000	0.998	0.989	0.954	0.851	0.624	0.264	0.086	0.004
9	1.000	1.000	1.000	1.000	1.000	1.000	0.999	0.994	0.972	0.893	0.651	0.401	0.096

(c) $n = 15$

k \ p	0.01	0.05	0.10	0.20	0.30	0.40	0.50	0.60	0.70	0.80	0.90	0.95	0.99
0	0.860	0.463	0.206	0.035	0.005	0.000	0.000	0.000	0.000	0.000	0.000	0.000	0.000
1	0.990	0.829	0.549	0.167	0.035	0.005	0.000	0.000	0.000	0.000	0.000	0.000	0.000
2	1.000	0.964	0.816	0.398	0.127	0.027	0.004	0.000	0.000	0.000	0.000	0.000	0.000
3	1.000	0.995	0.944	0.648	0.297	0.091	0.018	0.002	0.000	0.000	0.000	0.000	0.000
4	1.000	0.999	0.987	0.836	0.515	0.217	0.059	0.009	0.001	0.000	0.000	0.000	0.000
5	1.000	1.000	0.998	0.939	0.722	0.403	0.151	0.034	0.004	0.000	0.000	0.000	0.000
6	1.000	1.000	1.000	0.982	0.869	0.610	0.304	0.095	0.015	0.001	0.000	0.000	0.000
7	1.000	1.000	1.000	0.996	0.950	0.787	0.500	0.213	0.050	0.004	0.000	0.000	0.000
8	1.000	1.000	1.000	0.999	0.985	0.905	0.696	0.390	0.131	0.018	0.000	0.000	0.000
9	1.000	1.000	1.000	1.000	0.996	0.966	0.849	0.597	0.278	0.061	0.002	0.000	0.000
10	1.000	1.000	1.000	1.000	0.999	0.991	0.941	0.783	0.485	0.164	0.013	0.001	0.000
11	1.000	1.000	1.000	1.000	1.000	0.998	0.982	0.909	0.703	0.352	0.056	0.005	0.000
12	1.000	1.000	1.000	1.000	1.000	1.000	0.996	0.973	0.873	0.602	0.184	0.036	0.000
13	1.000	1.000	1.000	1.000	1.000	1.000	1.000	0.995	0.965	0.833	0.451	0.171	0.010
14	1.000	1.000	1.000	1.000	1.000	1.000	1.000	1.000	0.995	0.965	0.794	0.537	0.140

Table 2 (Continued)

(d) n = 20

k \ p	0.01	0.05	0.10	0.20	0.30	0.40	0.50	0.60	0.70	0.80	0.90	0.95	0.99
0	0.818	0.358	0.122	0.002	0.001	0.000	0.000	0.000	0.000	0.000	0.000	0.000	0.000
1	0.983	0.736	0.392	0.069	0.008	0.001	0.000	0.000	0.000	0.000	0.000	0.000	0.000
2	0.999	0.925	0.677	0.206	0.035	0.004	0.000	0.000	0.000	0.000	0.000	0.000	0.000
3	1.000	0.984	0.867	0.411	0.107	0.016	0.001	0.000	0.000	0.000	0.000	0.000	0.000
4	1.000	0.997	0.957	0.630	0.238	0.051	0.006	0.000	0.000	0.000	0.000	0.000	0.000
5	1.000	1.000	0.989	0.804	0.416	0.126	0.021	0.002	0.000	0.000	0.000	0.000	0.000
6	1.000	1.000	0.998	0.913	0.608	0.250	0.058	0.006	0.000	0.000	0.000	0.000	0.000
7	1.000	1.000	1.000	0.968	0.772	0.416	0.132	0.021	0.001	0.000	0.000	0.000	0.000
8	1.000	1.000	1.000	0.990	0.887	0.596	0.252	0.057	0.005	0.000	0.000	0.000	0.000
9	1.000	1.000	1.000	0.997	0.952	0.755	0.412	0.128	0.017	0.001	0.000	0.000	0.000
10	1.000	1.000	1.000	0.999	0.983	0.872	0.588	0.245	0.048	0.003	0.000	0.000	0.000
11	1.000	1.000	1.000	1.000	0.995	0.943	0.748	0.404	0.113	0.010	0.000	0.000	0.000
12	1.000	1.000	1.000	1.000	0.999	0.979	0.868	0.584	0.228	0.032	0.000	0.000	0.000
13	1.000	1.000	1.000	1.000	1.000	0.994	0.942	0.750	0.392	0.087	0.002	0.000	0.000
14	1.000	1.000	1.000	1.000	1.000	0.998	0.979	0.874	0.584	0.196	0.011	0.000	0.000
15	1.000	1.000	1.000	1.000	1.000	1.000	0.994	0.949	0.762	0.370	0.043	0.003	0.000
16	1.000	1.000	1.000	1.000	1.000	1.000	0.999	0.984	0.893	0.589	0.133	0.016	0.000
17	1.000	1.000	1.000	1.000	1.000	1.000	1.000	0.996	0.965	0.794	0.323	0.075	0.001
18	1.000	1.000	1.000	1.000	1.000	1.000	1.000	0.999	0.992	0.931	0.608	0.264	0.017
19	1.000	1.000	1.000	1.000	1.000	1.000	1.000	1.000	0.999	0.988	0.878	0.642	0.182

(e) n = 25

k \ p	0.01	0.05	0.10	0.20	0.30	0.40	0.50	0.60	0.70	0.80	0.90	0.95	0.99
0	0.778	0.277	0.072	0.004	0.000	0.000	0.000	0.000	0.000	0.000	0.000	0.000	0.000
1	0.974	0.642	0.271	0.027	0.002	0.000	0.000	0.000	0.000	0.000	0.000	0.000	0.000
2	0.998	0.873	0.537	0.098	0.009	0.000	0.000	0.000	0.000	0.000	0.000	0.000	0.000
3	1.000	0.966	0.764	0.234	0.033	0.002	0.000	0.000	0.000	0.000	0.000	0.000	0.000
4	1.000	0.993	0.902	0.421	0.090	0.009	0.000	0.000	0.000	0.000	0.000	0.000	0.000
5	1.000	0.999	0.967	0.617	0.193	0.029	0.002	0.000	0.000	0.000	0.000	0.000	0.000
6	1.000	1.000	0.991	0.780	0.341	0.074	0.007	0.000	0.000	0.000	0.000	0.000	0.000
7	1.000	1.000	0.998	0.891	0.512	0.154	0.022	0.001	0.000	0.000	0.000	0.000	0.000
8	1.000	1.000	1.000	0.953	0.677	0.274	0.054	0.004	0.000	0.000	0.000	0.000	0.000
9	1.000	1.000	1.000	0.983	0.811	0.425	0.115	0.013	0.000	0.000	0.000	0.000	0.000
10	1.000	1.000	1.000	0.994	0.902	0.586	0.212	0.034	0.002	0.000	0.000	0.000	0.000
11	1.000	1.000	1.000	0.998	0.956	0.732	0.345	0.078	0.006	0.000	0.000	0.000	0.000
12	1.000	1.000	1.000	1.000	0.983	0.846	0.500	0.154	0.017	0.000	0.000	0.000	0.000
13	1.000	1.000	1.000	1.000	0.994	0.922	0.655	0.268	0.044	0.002	0.000	0.000	0.000
14	1.000	1.000	1.000	1.000	0.998	0.966	0.788	0.414	0.098	0.006	0.000	0.000	0.000
15	1.000	1.000	1.000	1.000	1.000	0.987	0.885	0.575	0.189	0.017	0.000	0.000	0.000
16	1.000	1.000	1.000	1.000	1.000	0.996	0.946	0.726	0.323	0.047	0.000	0.000	0.000
17	1.000	1.000	1.000	1.000	1.000	0.999	0.978	0.846	0.488	0.109	0.002	0.000	0.000
18	1.000	1.000	1.000	1.000	1.000	1.000	0.993	0.926	0.659	0.220	0.009	0.000	0.000
19	1.000	1.000	1.000	1.000	1.000	1.000	0.998	0.971	0.807	0.383	0.033	0.001	0.000
20	1.000	1.000	1.000	1.000	1.000	1.000	1.000	0.991	0.910	0.579	0.098	0.007	0.000
21	1.000	1.000	1.000	1.000	1.000	1.000	1.000	0.998	0.967	0.766	0.236	0.034	0.000
22	1.000	1.000	1.000	1.000	1.000	1.000	1.000	1.000	0.991	0.902	0.463	0.127	0.002
23	1.000	1.000	1.000	1.000	1.000	1.000	1.000	1.000	0.998	0.973	0.729	0.358	0.026
24	1.000	1.000	1.000	1.000	1.000	1.000	1.000	1.000	1.000	0.996	0.928	0.723	0.222

Table 3   Poisson Distribution Function*

$$F(x; \lambda) = \sum_{k=0}^{x} e^{-\lambda} \frac{\lambda^k}{k!}$$

λ \ x	0	1	2	3	4	5	6	7	8	9
0.02	0.980	1.000								
0.04	0.961	0.999	1.000							
0.06	0.942	0.998	1.000							
0.08	0.923	0.997	1.000							
0.10	0.905	0.995	1.000							
0.15	0.861	0.990	0.999	1.000						
0.20	0.819	0.982	0.999	1.000						
0.25	0.779	0.974	0.998	1.000						
0.30	0.741	0.963	0.996	1.000						
0.35	0.705	0.951	0.994	1.000						
0.40	0.670	0.938	0.992	0.999	1.000					
0.45	0.638	0.925	0.989	0.999	1.000					
0.50	0.607	0.910	0.986	0.998	1.000					
0.55	0.577	0.894	0.982	0.998	1.000					
0.60	0.549	0.878	0.977	0.997	1.000					
0.65	0.522	0.861	0.972	0.996	0.999	1.000				
0.70	0.497	0.844	0.966	0.994	0.999	1.000				
0.75	0.472	0.827	0.959	0.993	0.999	1.000				
0.80	0.449	0.809	0.953	0.991	0.999	1.000				
0.85	0.427	0.791	0.945	0.989	0.998	1.000				
0.90	0.407	0.772	0.937	0.987	0.998	1.000				
0.95	0.387	0.754	0.929	0.981	0.997	1.000				
1.00	0.368	0.736	0.920	0.981	0.996	0.999	1.000			
1.1	0.333	0.699	0.900	0.974	0.995	0.999	1.000			
1.2	0.301	0.663	0.879	0.966	0.992	0.998	1.000			
1.3	0.273	0.627	0.857	0.957	0.989	0.998	1.000			
1.4	0.247	0.592	0.833	0.946	0.986	0.997	0.999	1.000		
1.5	0.223	0.558	0.809	0.934	0.981	0.996	0.999	1.000		
1.6	0.202	0.525	0.783	0.921	0.976	0.994	0.999	1.000		
1.7	0.183	0.493	0.757	0.907	0.970	0.992	0.998	1.000		
1.8	0.165	0.463	0.731	0.891	0.964	0.990	0.997	0.999	1.000	
1.9	0.150	0.434	0.704	0.875	0.956	0.987	0.997	0.999	1.000	
2.0	0.135	0.406	0.677	0.857	0.947	0.983	0.995	0.999	1.000	

* Reprinted by permission from E. C. Molina, *Poisson's Exponential Binomial Limit*, D. Van Nostrand Company, Inc., Princeton, H.J., 1947.

Table 3   (Continued)

λ \ x	0	1	2	3	4	5	6	7	8	9
2.2	0.111	0.355	0.623	0.819	0.928	0.975	0.993	0.998	1.000	
2.4	0.091	0.308	0.570	0.779	0.904	0.964	0.988	0.997	0.999	1.000
2.6	0.074	0.267	0.518	0.736	0.877	0.951	0.983	0.995	0.999	1.000
2.8	0.061	0.231	0.469	0.692	0.848	0.935	0.976	0.992	0.998	0.999
3.0	0.050	0.199	0.423	0.647	0.815	0.916	0.966	0.988	0.996	0.999
3.2	0.041	0.171	0.380	0.603	0.781	0.895	0.955	0.983	0.994	0.998
3.4	0.033	0.147	0.340	0.558	0.744	0.871	0.942	0.977	0.992	0.997
3.6	0.027	0.126	0.303	0.515	0.706	0.844	0.927	0.969	0.988	0.996
3.8	0.022	0.107	0.269	0.473	0.668	0.816	0.909	0.960	0.984	0.994
4.0	0.018	0.092	0.238	0.433	0.629	0.785	0.889	0.949	0.979	0.992
4.2	0.015	0.078	0.210	0.395	0.590	0.753	0.867	0.936	0.972	0.989
4.4	0.012	0.066	0.185	0.359	0.551	0.720	0.844	0.921	0.964	0.985
4.6	0.010	0.056	0.163	0.326	0.513	0.686	0.818	0.905	0.955	0.980
4.8	0.008	0.048	0.143	0.294	0.476	0.651	0.791	0.887	0.944	0.975
5.0	0.007	0.040	0.125	0.265	0.440	0.616	0.762	0.867	0.932	0.968
5.2	0.006	0.034	0.109	0.238	0.406	0.581	0.732	0.845	0.918	0.960
5.4	0.005	0.029	0.095	0.213	0.373	0.546	0.702	0.822	0.903	0.951
5.6	0.004	0.024	0.082	0.191	0.342	0.512	0.670	0.797	0.886	0.941
5.8	0.003	0.021	0.072	0.170	0.313	0.478	0.638	0.771	0.867	0.929
6.0	0.002	0.017	0.062	0.151	0.285	0.446	0.606	0.744	0.847	0.916

	10	11	12	13	14	15	16
2.8	1.000						
3.0	1.000						
3.2	1.000						
3.4	0.999	1.000					
3.6	0.999	1.000					
3.8	0.998	0.999	1.000				
4.0	0.997	0.999	1.000				
4.2	0.996	0.999	1.000				
4.4	0.994	0.998	0.999	1.000			
4.6	0.992	0.997	0.999	1.000			
4.8	0.990	0.996	0.999	1.000			
5.0	0.986	0.995	0.998	0.999	1.000		
5.2	0.982	0.993	0.997	0.999	1.000		
5.4	0.977	0.990	0.996	0.999	1.000		
5.6	0.972	0.988	0.995	0.998	0.999	1.000	
5.8	0.965	0.984	0.993	0.997	0.999	1.000	
6.0	0.957	0.980	0.991	0.996	0.999	0.999	1.000

Table 3   (Continued)

λ \ x	0	1	2	3	4	5	6	7	8	9
6.2	0.002	0.015	0.054	0.134	0.259	0.414	0.574	0.716	0.826	0.902
6.4	0.002	0.012	0.046	0.119	0.235	0.384	0.542	0.687	0.803	0.886
6.6	0.001	0.010	0.040	0.105	0.213	0.355	0.511	0.658	0.780	0.869
6.8	0.001	0.009	0.034	0.093	0.192	0.327	0.480	0.628	0.755	0.850
7.0	0.001	0.007	0.030	0.082	0.173	0.301	0.450	0.599	0.729	0.830
7.2	0.001	0.006	0.025	0.072	0.156	0.276	0.420	0.569	0.703	0.810
7.4	0.001	0.005	0.022	0.063	0.140	0.253	0.392	0.539	0.676	0.788
7.6	0.001	0.004	0.019	0.055	0.125	0.231	0.365	0.510	0.648	0.765
7.8	0.000	0.004	0.016	0.048	0.112	0.210	0.338	0.481	0.620	0.741
8.0	0.000	0.003	0.014	0.042	0.100	0.191	0.313	0.453	0.593	0.717
8.5	0.000	0.002	0.009	0.030	0.074	0.150	0.256	0.386	0.523	0.653
9.0	0.000	0.001	0.006	0.021	0.055	0.116	0.207	0.324	0.456	0.587
9.5	0.000	0.001	0.004	0.015	0.040	0.089	0.165	0.269	0.392	0.522
10.0	0.000	0.000	0.003	0.010	0.029	0.067	0.130	0.220	0.333	0.458

λ	10	11	12	13	14	15	16	17	18	19
6.2	0.949	0.975	0.989	0.995	0.998	0.999	1.000			
6.4	0.939	0.969	0.986	0.994	0.997	0.999	1.000			
6.6	0.927	0.963	0.982	0.992	0.997	0.999	0.999	1.000		
6.8	0.915	0.955	0.978	0.990	0.996	0.998	0.999	1.000		
7.0	0.901	0.947	0.973	0.987	0.994	0.998	0.999	1.000		
7.2	0.887	0.937	0.967	0.984	0.993	0.997	0.999	0.999	1.000	
7.4	0.871	0.926	0.961	0.980	0.991	0.996	0.998	0.999	1.000	
7.6	0.854	0.915	0.954	0.976	0.989	0.995	0.998	0.999	1.000	
7.8	0.835	0.902	0.945	0.971	0.986	0.993	0.997	0.999	1.000	
8.0	0.816	0.888	0.936	0.966	0.983	0.992	0.996	0.998	0.999	1.000
8.5	0.763	0.849	0.909	0.949	0.973	0.986	0.993	0.997	0.999	0.999
9.0	0.706	0.803	0.876	0.926	0.959	0.978	0.989	0.995	0.998	0.999
9.5	0.645	0.752	0.836	0.898	0.940	0.967	0.982	0.991	0.996	0.998
10.0	0.583	0.697	0.792	0.864	0.917	0.951	0.973	0.986	0.993	0.997

λ	20	21	22
8.5	1.000		
9.0	1.000		
9.5	0.999	1.000	
10.0	0.998	0.999	1.000

Table 3   (Continued)

λ \ x	0	1	2	3	4	5	6	7	8	9
10.5	0.000	0.000	0.002	0.007	0.021	0.050	0.102	0.179	0.279	0.397
11.0	0.000	0.000	0.001	0.005	0.015	0.038	0.079	0.143	0.232	0.341
11.5	0.000	0.000	0.001	0.003	0.011	0.028	0.060	0.114	0.191	0.289
12.0	0.000	0.000	0.001	0.002	0.008	0.020	0.046	0.090	0.155	0.242
12.5	0.000	0.000	0.000	0.002	0.005	0.015	0.035	0.070	0.125	0.201
13.0	0.000	0.000	0.000	0.001	0.004	0.011	0.026	0.054	0.100	0.166
13.5	0.000	0.000	0.000	0.001	0.003	0.008	0.019	0.041	0.079	0.135
14.0	0.000	0.000	0.000	0.000	0.002	0.006	0.014	0.032	0.062	0.109
14.5	0.000	0.000	0.000	0.000	0.001	0.004	0.010	0.024	0.048	0.088
15.0	0.000	0.000	0.000	0.000	0.001	0.003	0.008	0.018	0.037	0.070

	10	11	12	13	14	15	16	17	18	19
10.5	0.521	0.639	0.742	0.825	0.888	0.932	0.960	0.978	0.988	0.994
11.0	0.460	0.579	0.689	0.781	0.854	0.907	0.944	0.968	0.982	0.991
11.5	0.402	0.520	0.633	0.733	0.815	0.878	0.924	0.954	0.974	0.986
12.0	0.347	0.462	0.576	0.682	0.772	0.844	0.899	0.937	0.963	0.979
12.5	0.297	0.406	0.519	0.628	0.725	0.806	0.869	0.916	0.948	0.969
13.0	0.252	0.353	0.463	0.573	0.675	0.764	0.835	0.890	0.930	0.957
13.5	0.211	0.304	0.409	0.518	0.623	0.718	0.798	0.861	0.908	0.942
14.0	0.176	0.260	0.358	0.464	0.570	0.669	0.756	0.827	0.883	0.923
14.5	0.145	0.220	0.311	0.413	0.518	0.619	0.711	0.790	0.853	0.901
15.0	0.118	0.185	0.268	0.363	0.466	0.568	0.664	0.749	0.819	0.875

	20	21	22	23	24	25	26	27	28	29
10.5	0.997	0.999	0.999	1.000						
11.0	0.995	0.998	0.999	1.000						
11.5	0.992	0.996	0.998	0.999	1.000					
12.0	0.988	0.994	0.997	0.999	0.999	1.000				
12.5	0.983	0.991	0.995	0.998	0.999	0.999	1.000			
13.0	0.975	0.986	0.992	0.996	0.998	0.999	1.000			
13.5	0.965	0.980	0.989	0.994	0.997	0.998	0.999	1.000		
14.0	0.952	0.971	0.983	0.991	0.995	0.997	0.999	0.999	1.000	
14.5	0.936	0.960	0.976	0.986	0.992	0.996	0.998	0.999	0.999	1.000
15.0	0.917	0.947	0.967	0.981	0.989	0.994	0.997	0.998	0.999	1.000

Table 3   (Continued)

λ \ x	4	5	6	7	8	9	10	11	12	13
16	0.000	0.001	0.004	0.010	0.022	0.043	0.077	0.127	0.193	0.275
17	0.000	0.001	0.002	0.005	0.013	0.026	0.049	0.085	0.135	0.201
18	0.000	0.000	0.001	0.003	0.007	0.015	0.030	0.055	0.092	0.143
19	0.000	0.000	0.001	0.002	0.004	0.009	0.018	0.035	0.061	0.098
20	0.000	0.000	0.000	0.001	0.002	0.005	0.011	0.021	0.039	0.066
21	0.000	0.000	0.000	0.000	0.001	0.003	0.006	0.013	0.025	0.043
22	0.000	0.000	0.000	0.000	0.001	0.002	0.004	0.008	0.015	0.028
23	0.000	0.000	0.000	0.000	0.000	0.001	0.002	0.004	0.009	0.017
24	0.000	0.000	0.000	0.000	0.000	0.000	0.001	0.003	0.005	0.011
25	0.000	0.000	0.000	0.000	0.000	0.000	0.001	0.001	0.003	0.006

	14	15	16	17	18	19	20	21	22	23
16	0.368	0.467	0.566	0.659	0.742	0.812	0.868	0.911	0.942	0.963
17	0.281	0.371	0.468	0.564	0.655	0.736	0.805	0.861	0.905	0.937
18	0.208	0.287	0.375	0.469	0.562	0.651	0.731	0.799	0.855	0.899
19	0.150	0.215	0.292	0.378	0.469	0.561	0.647	0.725	0.793	0.849
20	0.105	0.157	0.221	0.297	0.381	0.470	0.559	0.644	0.721	0.787
21	0.072	0.111	0.163	0.227	0.302	0.384	0.471	0.558	0.640	0.716
22	0.048	0.077	0.117	0.169	0.232	0.306	0.387	0.472	0.556	0.637
23	0.031	0.052	0.082	0.123	0.175	0.238	0.310	0.389	0.472	0.555
24	0.020	0.034	0.056	0.087	0.128	0.180	0.243	0.314	0.392	0.473
25	0.012	0.022	0.038	0.060	0.092	0.134	0.185	0.247	0.318	0.394

	24	25	26	27	28	29	30	31	32	33
16	0.978	0.987	0.993	0.996	0.998	0.999	0.999	1.000		
17	0.959	0.975	0.985	0.991	0.995	0.997	0.999	0.999	1.000	
18	0.932	0.955	0.972	0.983	0.990	0.994	0.997	0.998	0.999	1.000
19	0.893	0.927	0.951	0.969	0.980	0.988	0.993	0.996	0.998	0.999
20	0.843	0.888	0.922	0.948	0.966	0.978	0.987	0.992	0.995	0.997
21	0.782	0.838	0.883	0.917	0.944	0.963	0.976	0.985	0.991	0.994
22	0.712	0.777	0.832	0.877	0.913	0.940	0.959	0.973	0.983	0.989
23	0.635	0.708	0.772	0.827	0.873	0.908	0.936	0.956	0.971	0.981
24	0.554	0.632	0.704	0.768	0.823	0.868	0.904	0.932	0.953	0.969
25	0.473	0.553	0.629	0.700	0.763	0.818	0.863	0.900	0.929	0.950

	34	35	36	37	38	39	40	41	42	43
19	0.999	1.000								
20	0.999	0.999	1.000							
21	0.997	0.998	0.999	0.999	1.000					
22	0.994	0.996	0.998	0.999	0.999	1.000				
23	0.988	0.993	0.996	0.997	0.999	0.999	1.000			
24	0.979	0.987	0.992	0.995	0.997	0.998	0.999	0.999	1.000	
25	0.966	0.978	0.985	0.991	0.991	0.997	0.998	0.999	0.999	1.000

Table 4 Normal Curve Areas

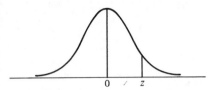

z	0.00	0.01	0.02	0.03	0.04	0.05	0.06	0.07	0.08	0.09
0.0	0.0000	0.0040	0.0080	0.0120	0.0160	0.0199	0.0239	0.0279	0.0319	0.0359
0.1	0.0398	0.0438	0.0478	0.0517	0.0557	0.0596	0.0636	0.0675	0.0174	0.0753
0.2	0.0793	0.0832	0.0871	0.0910	0.0948	0.0987	0.1026	0.1064	0.1103	0.1141
0.3	0.1179	0.1217	0.1255	0.1293	0.1331	0.1368	0.1406	0.1443	0.1480	0.1517
0.4	0.1554	0.1591	0.1628	0.1664	0.1700	0.1736	0.1772	0.1808	0.1844	0.1879
0.5	0.1915	0.1950	0.1985	0.2019	0.2054	0.2088	0.2123	0.2157	0.2190	0.2224
0.6	0.2257	0.2291	0.2324	0.2357	0.2389	0.2422	0.2454	0.2486	0.2517	0.2549
0.7	0.2580	0.2611	0.2642	0.2673	0.2704	0.2734	0.2764	0.2794	0.2823	0.2852
0.8	0.2881	0.2910	0.2939	0.2967	0.2995	0.3023	0.3051	0.3078	0.3106	0.3133
0.9	0.3159	0.3186	0.3212	0.3238	0.3264	0.3289	0.3315	0.3340	0.3365	0.3389
1.0	0.3413	0.3438	0.3461	0.3485	0.3508	0.3531	0.3554	0.3577	0.3599	0.3621
1.1	0.3643	0.3665	0.3686	0.3708	0.3729	0.3749	0.3770	0.3790	0.3810	0.3830
1.2	0.3849	0.3869	0.3888	0.3907	0.3925	0.3944	0.3962	0.3980	0.3997	0.4015
1.3	0.4032	0.4049	0.4066	0.4082	0.4099	0.4115	0.4131	0.4147	0.4162	0.4177
1.4	0.4192	0.4207	0.4222	0.4236	0.4251	0.4265	0.4279	0.4292	0.4306	0.4319
1.5	0.4332	0.4345	0.4357	0.4370	0.4382	0.4394	0.4406	0.4418	0.4429	0.4441
1.6	0.4452	0.4463	0.4474	0.4484	0.4495	0.4505	0.4515	0.4525	0.4535	0.4545
1.7	0.4554	0.4564	0.4573	0.4582	0.4591	0.4599	0.4608	0.4616	0.4625	0.4633
1.8	0.4641	0.4649	0.4656	0.4664	0.4671	0.4678	0.4686	0.4693	0.4699	0.4706
1.9	0.4713	0.4719	0.4726	0.4732	0.4738	0.4744	0.4750	0.4756	0.4761	0.4767
2.0	0.4772	0.4778	0.4783	0.4788	0.4793	0.4798	0.4803	0.4808	0.4812	0.4817
2.1	0.4821	0.4826	0.4830	0.4834	0.4838	0.4842	0.4846	0.4850	0.4854	0.4857
2.2	0.4861	0.4864	0.4868	0.4871	0.4875	0.4878	0.4881	0.4884	0.4887	0.4890
2.3	0.4893	0.4896	0.4898	0.4901	0.4904	0.4906	0.4909	0.4911	0.4913	0.4916
2.4	0.4918	0.4920	0.4922	0.4925	0.4927	0.4929	0.4931	0.4932	0.4934	0.4936
2.5	0.4938	0.4940	0.4941	0.4943	0.4945	0.4946	0.4948	0.4949	0.4951	0.4952
2.6	0.4953	0.4955	0.4956	0.4957	0.4959	0.4960	0.4961	0.4962	0.4963	0.4964
2.7	0.4965	0.4966	0.4967	0.4968	0.4969	0.4970	0.4971	0.4972	0.4973	0.4974
2.8	0.4974	0.4975	0.4976	0.4977	0.4977	0.4978	0.4979	0.4979	0.4980	0.4981
2.9	0.4981	0.4982	0.4982	0.4983	0.4984	0.4984	0.4985	0.4985	0.4986	0.4986
3.0	0.4987	0.4987	0.4987	0.4988	0.4988	0.4989	0.4989	0.4989	0.4990	0.4990

Source: Abridged from Table I of A. Hald. *Statistical Tables and Formulas* (New York: John Wiley & Sons, Inc.), 1952. Reproduced by permission of A. Hald and the publisher.

Table 5   Critical Values of t

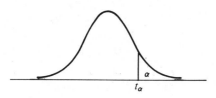

Degrees of Freedom	$t_{0.100}$	$t_{0.050}$	$t_{0.025}$	$t_{0.010}$	$t_{0.005}$
1	3.078	6.314	12.706	31.821	63.657
2	1.886	2.920	4.303	6.965	9.925
3	1.638	2.353	3.182	4.541	5.841
4	1.533	2.132	2.776	3.747	4.604
5	1.476	2.015	2.571	3.365	4.032
6	1.440	1.943	2.447	3.143	3.707
7	1.415	1.895	2.365	2.998	3.499
8	1.397	1.860	2.306	2.896	3.355
9	1.383	1.833	2.262	2.821	3.250
10	1.372	1.812	2.228	2.764	3.169
11	1.363	1.796	2.201	2.718	3.106
12	1.356	1.782	2.179	2.681	3.055
13	1.350	1.771	2.160	2.650	3.012
14	1.345	1.761	2.145	2.624	2.977
15	1.341	1.753	2.131	2.602	2.947
16	1.337	1.746	2.120	2.583	2.921
17	1.333	1.740	2.110	2.567	2.898
18	1.330	1.734	2.101	2.552	2.878
19	1.328	1.729	2.093	2.539	2.861
20	1.325	1.725	2.086	2.528	2.845
21	1.323	1.721	2.080	2.518	2.831
22	1.321	1.717	2.074	2.508	2.819
23	1.319	1.714	2.069	2.500	2.807
24	1.318	1.711	2.064	2.492	2.797
25	1.316	1.708	2.060	2.485	2.787
26	1.315	1.706	2.056	2.479	2.779
27	1.314	1.703	2.052	2.473	2.771
28	1.313	1.701	2.048	2.467	2.763
29	1.311	1.699	2.045	2.462	2.756
∞	1.282	1.645	1.960	2.326	2.576

Source: From M. Merrington, "Table of Percentage Points of the t-Distribution," *Biometrika*, 1941, 32, 300. Reproduced by permission of the *Biometrika* Trustees.

Table 6   Critical Values of χ^2

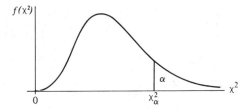

Degrees of Freedom	$\chi^2_{0.995}$	$\chi^2_{0.990}$	$\chi^2_{0.975}$	$\chi^2_{0.950}$	$\chi^2_{0.900}$
1	0.0000393	0.0001571	0.0009821	0.0039321	0.0157908
2	0.0100251	0.0201007	0.0506356	0.102587	0.210720
3	0.0717212	0.114832	0.215795	0.351846	0.584375
4	0.206990	0.297110	0.484419	0.710721	1.063623
5	0.411740	0.554300	0.831211	1.145476	1.61031
6	0.675727	0.872085	1.237347	1.63539	2.20413
7	0.989265	1.239043	1.68987	2.16735	2.83311
8	1.344419	1.646482	2.17973	2.73264	3.48954
9	1.734926	2.087912	2.70039	3.32511	4.16816
10	2.15585	2.55821	3.24697	3.94030	4.86518
11	2.60321	3.05347	3.81575	4.57481	5.57779
12	3.07382	3.57056	4.40379	5.22603	6.30380
13	3.56503	4.10691	5.00874	5.89186	7.04150
14	4.07468	4.66043	5.62872	6.57063	7.78953
15	4.60094	5.22935	6.26214	7.26094	8.54675
16	5.14224	5.81221	6.90766	7.96164	9.31223
17	5.69724	6.40776	7.56418	8.67176	10.0852
18	6.26481	7.01491	8.23075	9.39046	10.8649
19	6.84398	7.63273	8.90655	10.1170	11.6509
20	7.43386	8.26040	9.59083	10.8508	12.4426
21	8.03366	8.89720	10.28293	11.5913	13.2396
22	8.64272	9.54249	10.9823	12.3380	14.0415
23	9.26042	10.19567	11.6885	13.0905	14.8479
24	9.88623	10.8564	12.4011	13.8484	15.6587
25	10.5197	11.5240	13.1197	14.6114	16.4734
26	11.1603	12.1981	13.8439	15.3791	17.2919
27	11.8076	12.8786	14.5733	16.1513	18.1138
28	12.4613	13.5648	15.3079	16.9279	18.9392
29	13.1211	14.2565	16.0471	17.7083	19.7677
30	13.7867	14.9535	16.7908	18.4926	20.5992
40	20.7065	22.1643	24.4331	26.5093	29.0505
50	27.9907	29.7067	32.3574	34.7642	37.6886
60	35.5346	37.4848	40.4817	43.1879	46.4589
70	43.2752	45.4418	48.7576	51.7393	55.3290
80	51.1720	53.5400	57.1532	60.3915	64.2778
90	59.1963	61.7541	65.6466	69.1260	73.2912
100	67.3276	70.0648	74.2219	77.9295	82.3581

Source: From C. M. Thompson, "Tables of the Percentage Points of the χ^2-Distribution." *Biometrika*, 1941, 32, 188–189. Reproduced by permission of the *Biometrika* Trustees.

Table 6   (Continued)

Degrees of Freedom	$\chi^2_{0.100}$	$\chi^2_{0.050}$	$\chi^2_{0.025}$	$\chi^2_{0.010}$	$\chi^2_{0.005}$
1	2.70554	3.84146	5.02389	6.63490	7.87944
2	4.60517	5.99147	7.37776	9.21034	10.5966
3	6.25139	7.81473	9.34840	11.3449	12.8381
4	7.77944	9.48773	11.1433	13.2767	14.8602
5	9.23635	11.0705	12.8325	15.0863	16.7496
6	10.6446	12.5916	14.4494	16.8119	18.5476
7	12.0170	14.0671	16.0128	18.4753	20.2777
8	13.3616	15.5073	17.5346	20.0902	21.9550
9	14.6837	16.9190	19.0228	21.6660	23.5893
10	15.9871	18.3070	20.4831	23.2093	25.1882
11	17.2750	19.6751	21.9200	24.7250	26.7569
12	18.5494	21.0261	23.3367	26.2170	28.2995
13	19.8119	22.3621	24.7356	27.6883	29.8194
14	21.0642	23.6848	26.1190	29.1413	31.3193
15	22.3072	24.9958	27.4884	30.5779	32.8013
16	23.5418	26.2962	28.8454	31.9999	34.2672
17	24.7690	27.5871	30.1910	33.4087	35.7185
18	25.9894	28.8693	31.5264	34.8053	37.1564
19	27.2036	30.1435	32.8523	36.1908	38.5822
20	28.4120	31.4104	34.1696	37.5662	39.9968
21	29.6151	32.6705	35.4789	38.9321	41.4010
22	30.8133	33.9244	36.7807	40.2894	42.7956
23	32.0069	35.1725	38.0757	41.6384	44.1813
24	33.1963	36.4151	39.3641	42.9798	45.5585
25	34.3816	37.6525	40.6465	44.3141	46.9278
26	35.5631	38.8852	41.9232	45.6417	48.2899
27	36.7412	40.1133	43.1944	46.9630	49.6449
28	37.9159	41.3372	44.4607	48.2782	50.9933
29	39.0875	42.5569	45.7222	49.5879	52.3356
30	40.2560	43.7729	46.9792	50.8922	53.6720
40	51.8050	55.7585	59.3417	63.6907	66.7659
50	63.1671	67.5048	71.4202	76.1539	79.4900
60	74.3970	79.0819	83.2976	88.3794	91.9517
70	85.5271	90.5312	95.0231	100.425	104.215
80	96.5782	101.879	106.629	112.329	116.321
90	107.565	113.145	118.136	124.116	128.299
100	118.498	124.342	129.561	135.807	140.169

Table 7 Percentage Points of the F Distribution, α = 0.05

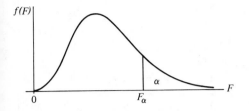

					Numerator Degrees of Freedom				
v_1 v_2	1	2	3	4	5	6	7	8	9
1	161.4	199.5	215.7	224.6	230.2	234.0	236.8	238.9	240.5
2	18.51	19.00	19.16	19.25	19.30	19.33	19.35	19.37	19.38
3	10.13	9.55	9.28	9.12	9.01	8.94	8.89	8.85	8.81
4	7.71	6.94	6.59	6.39	6.26	6.16	6.09	6.04	6.00
5	6.61	5.79	5.41	5.19	5.05	4.95	4.88	4.82	4.77
6	5.99	5.14	4.76	4.53	4.39	4.28	4.21	4.15	4.10
7	5.59	4.74	4.35	4.12	3.97	3.87	3.79	3.73	3.68
8	5.32	4.46	4.07	3.84	3.69	3.58	3.50	3.44	3.39
9	5.12	4.26	3.86	3.63	3.48	3.37	3.29	3.23	3.18
10	4.96	4.10	3.71	3.48	3.33	3.22	3.14	3.07	3.02
11	4.84	3.98	3.59	3.36	3.20	3.09	3.01	2.95	2.90
12	4.75	3.89	3.49	3.26	3.11	3.00	2.91	2.85	2.80
13	4.67	3.81	3.41	3.18	3.03	2.92	2.83	2.77	2.71
14	4.60	3.74	3.34	3.11	2.96	2.85	2.76	2.70	2.65
15	4.54	3.68	3.29	3.06	2.90	2.79	2.71	2.64	2.59
16	4.49	3.63	3.24	3.01	2.85	2.74	2.66	2.59	2.54
17	4.45	3.59	3.20	2.96	2.81	2.70	2.61	2.55	2.49
18	4.41	3.55	3.16	2.93	2.77	2.66	2.58	2.51	2.46
19	4.38	3.52	3.13	2.90	2.74	2.63	2.54	2.48	2.42
20	4.35	3.49	3.10	2.87	2.71	2.60	2.51	2.45	2.39
21	4.32	3.47	3.07	2.84	2.68	2.57	2.49	2.42	2.37
22	4.30	3.44	3.05	2.82	2.66	2.55	2.46	2.40	2.34
23	4.28	3.42	3.03	2.80	2.64	2.53	2.44	2.37	2.32
24	4.26	3.40	3.01	2.78	2.62	2.51	2.42	2.36	2.30
25	4.24	3.39	2.99	2.76	2.60	2.49	2.40	2.34	2.28
26	4.23	3.37	2.98	2.74	2.59	2.47	2.39	2.32	2.27
27	4.21	3.35	2.96	2.73	2.57	2.46	2.37	2.31	2.25
28	4.20	3.34	2.95	2.71	2.56	2.45	2.36	2.29	2.24
29	4.18	3.33	2.93	2.70	2.55	2.43	2.35	2.28	2.22
30	4.17	3.32	2.92	2.69	2.53	2.42	2.33	2.27	2.21
40	4.08	3.23	2.84	2.61	2.45	2.34	2.25	2.18	2.12
60	4.00	3.15	2.76	2.53	2.37	2.25	2.17	2.10	2.04
120	3.92	3.07	2.68	2.45	2.29	2.17	2.09	2.02	1.96
∞	3.84	3.00	2.60	2.37	2.21	2.10	2.01	1.94	1.88

Source: From M. Merrington and C. M. Thompson, "Tables of Percentage Points of the Inverted Beta (F)-Distribution," *Biometrika*, 1943, *33*, 73–88. Reproduced by permission of the *Biometrika* Trustees.

Table 7   (Continued)

v_2 \ v_1	Numerator Degrees of Freedom									
	10	12	15	20	24	30	40	60	120	∞
1	241.9	243.9	245.9	248.0	249.1	250.1	251.1	252.2	253.3	254.3
2	19.40	19.41	19.43	19.45	19.45	19.46	19.47	19.48	19.49	19.50
3	8.79	8.74	8.70	8.66	8.64	8.62	8.59	8.57	8.55	8.53
4	5.96	5.91	5.86	5.80	5.77	5.75	5.72	5.69	5.66	5.63
5	4.74	4.68	4.62	4.56	4.53	4.50	4.46	4.43	4.40	4.36
6	4.06	4.00	3.94	3.87	3.84	3.81	3.77	3.74	3.70	3.67
7	3.64	3.57	3.51	3.44	3.41	3.38	3.34	3.30	3.27	3.23
8	3.35	3.28	3.22	3.15	3.12	3.08	3.04	3.01	2.97	2.93
9	3.14	3.07	3.01	2.94	2.90	2.86	2.83	2.79	2.75	2.71
10	2.98	2.91	2.85	2.77	2.74	2.70	2.66	2.62	2.58	2.54
11	2.85	2.79	2.72	2.65	2.61	2.57	2.53	2.49	2.45	2.40
12	2.75	2.69	2.62	2.54	2.51	2.47	2.43	2.38	2.34	2.30
13	2.67	2.60	2.53	2.46	2.42	2.38	2.34	2.30	2.25	2.21
14	2.60	2.53	2.46	2.39	2.35	2.31	2.27	2.22	2.18	2.13
15	2.54	2.48	2.40	2.33	2.29	2.25	2.20	2.16	2.11	2.07
16	2.49	2.42	2.35	2.28	2.24	2.19	2.15	2.11	2.06	2.01
17	2.45	2.38	2.31	2.23	2.19	2.15	2.10	2.06	2.01	1.96
18	2.41	2.34	2.27	2.19	2.15	2.11	2.06	2.02	1.97	1.92
19	2.38	2.31	2.23	2.16	2.11	2.07	2.03	1.98	1.93	1.88
20	2.35	2.28	2.20	2.12	2.08	2.04	1.99	1.95	1.90	1.84
21	2.32	2.25	2.18	2.10	2.05	2.01	1.96	1.92	1.87	1.81
22	2.30	2.23	2.15	2.07	2.03	1.98	1.94	1.89	1.84	1.78
23	2.27	2.20	2.13	2.05	2.01	1.96	1.91	1.86	1.81	1.76
24	2.25	2.18	2.11	2.03	1.98	1.94	1.89	1.84	1.79	1.73
25	2.24	2.16	2.09	2.01	1.96	1.92	1.87	1.82	1.77	1.71
26	2.22	2.15	2.07	1.99	1.95	1.90	1.85	1.80	1.75	1.69
27	2.20	2.13	2.06	1.97	1.93	1.88	1.84	1.79	1.73	1.67
28	2.19	2.12	2.04	1.96	1.91	1.87	1.82	1.77	1.71	1.65
29	2.18	2.10	2.03	1.94	1.90	1.85	1.81	1.75	1.70	1.64
30	2.16	2.09	2.01	1.93	1.89	1.84	1.79	1.74	1.68	1.62
40	2.08	2.00	1.92	1.84	1.79	1.74	1.69	1.64	1.58	1.51
60	1.99	1.92	1.84	1.75	1.70	1.65	1.59	1.53	1.47	1.39
120	1.91	1.83	1.75	1.66	1.61	1.55	1.50	1.43	1.35	1.25
∞	1.83	1.75	1.67	1.57	1.52	1.46	1.39	1.32	1.22	1.00

Denominator Degrees of Freedom

Table 8   Percentage Points of the F Distribution, $\alpha = 0.01$

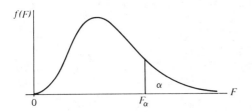

v_1	Numerator Degrees of Freedom								
v_2	1	2	3	4	5	6	7	8	9
1	4,052	4,999.5	5,403	5,625	5,764	5,859	5,928	5,982	6,022
2	98.50	99.00	99.17	99.25	99.30	99.33	99.36	99.37	99.39
3	34.12	30.82	29.46	28.71	28.24	27.91	27.67	27.49	27.35
4	21.20	18.00	16.69	15.98	15.52	15.21	14.98	14.80	14.66
5	16.26	13.27	12.06	11.39	10.97	10.67	10.46	10.29	10.16
6	13.75	10.92	9.78	9.15	8.75	8.47	8.26	8.10	7.98
7	12.25	9.55	8.45	7.85	7.46	7.19	6.99	6.84	6.72
8	11.26	8.65	7.59	7.01	6.63	6.37	6.18	6.03	5.91
9	10.56	8.02	6.99	6.42	6.06	5.80	5.61	5.47	5.35
10	10.04	7.56	6.55	5.99	5.64	5.39	5.20	5.06	4.94
11	9.65	7.21	6.22	5.67	5.32	5.07	4.89	4.74	4.63
12	9.33	6.93	5.95	5.41	5.06	4.82	4.64	4.50	4.39
13	9.07	6.70	5.74	5.21	4.86	4.62	4.44	4.30	4.19
14	8.86	6.51	5.56	5.04	4.69	4.46	4.28	4.14	4.03
15	8.68	6.36	5.42	4.89	4.56	4.32	4.14	4.00	3.89
16	8.53	6.23	5.29	4.77	4.44	4.20	4.03	3.89	3.78
17	8.40	6.11	5.18	4.67	4.34	4.10	3.93	3.79	3.68
18	8.29	6.01	5.09	4.58	4.25	4.01	3.84	3.71	3.60
19	8.18	5.93	5.01	4.50	4.17	3.94	3.77	3.63	3.52
20	8.10	5.85	4.94	4.43	4.10	3.87	3.70	3.56	3.46
21	8.02	5.78	4.87	4.37	4.04	3.81	3.64	3.51	3.40
22	7.95	5.72	4.82	4.31	3.99	3.76	3.59	3.45	3.35
23	7.88	5.66	4.76	4.26	3.94	3.71	3.54	3.41	3.30
24	7.82	5.61	4.72	4.22	3.90	3.67	3.50	3.36	3.26
25	7.77	5.57	4.68	4.18	3.85	3.63	3.46	3.32	3.22
26	7.72	5.53	4.64	4.14	3.82	3.59	3.42	3.29	3.18
27	7.68	5.49	4.60	4.11	3.78	3.56	3.39	3.26	3.15
28	7.64	5.45	4.57	4.07	3.75	3.53	3.36	3.23	3.12
29	7.60	5.42	4.54	4.04	3.73	3.50	3.33	3.20	3.09
30	7.56	5.39	4.51	4.02	3.70	3.47	3.30	3.17	3.07
40	7.31	5.18	4.31	3.83	3.51	3.29	3.12	2.99	2.89
60	7.08	4.98	4.13	3.65	3.34	3.12	2.95	2.82	2.72
120	6.85	4.79	3.95	3.48	3.17	2.96	2.79	2.66	2.56
∞	6.63	4.61	3.78	3.32	3.02	2.80	2.64	2.51	2.41

Denominator Degrees of Freedom

Table 8   (Continued)

ν_2 \ ν_1	Numerator Degrees of Freedom								
	10	12	15	20	24	30	40	60	120
1	6,056	6,106	6,157	6,209	6,235	6,261	6,287	6,313	6,339
2	99.40	99.42	99.43	99.45	99.46	99.47	99.47	99.48	99.49
3	27.23	27.05	26.87	26.69	26.60	26.50	26.41	26.32	26.22
4	14.55	14.37	14.20	14.02	13.93	13.84	13.75	13.65	13.56
5	10.05	9.89	9.72	9.55	9.47	9.38	9.29	9.20	9.11
6	7.87	7.72	7.56	7.40	7.31	7.23	7.14	7.06	6.97
7	6.62	6.47	6.31	6.16	6.07	5.99	5.91	5.82	5.74
8	5.81	5.67	5.52	5.36	5.28	5.20	5.12	5.03	4.95
9	5.26	5.11	4.96	4.81	4.73	4.65	4.57	4.48	4.40
10	4.85	4.71	4.56	4.41	4.33	4.25	4.17	4.08	4.00
11	4.54	4.40	4.25	4.10	4.02	3.94	3.86	3.78	3.69
12	4.30	4.16	4.01	3.86	3.78	3.70	3.62	3.54	3.45
13	4.10	3.96	3.82	3.66	3.59	3.51	3.43	3.34	3.25
14	3.94	3.80	3.66	3.51	3.43	3.35	3.27	3.18	3.09
15	3.80	3.67	3.52	3.37	3.29	3.21	3.13	3.05	2.96
16	3.69	3.55	3.41	3.26	3.18	3.10	3.02	2.93	2.84
17	3.59	3.46	3.31	3.16	3.08	3.00	2.92	2.83	2.75
18	3.51	3.37	3.23	3.08	3.00	2.92	2.84	2.75	2.66
19	3.43	3.30	3.15	3.00	2.92	2.84	2.76	2.67	2.58
20	3.37	3.23	3.09	2.94	2.86	2.78	2.69	2.61	2.52
21	3.31	3.17	3.03	2.88	2.80	2.72	2.64	2.55	2.46
22	3.26	3.12	2.98	2.83	2.75	2.67	2.58	2.50	2.40
23	3.21	3.07	2.93	2.78	2.70	2.62	2.54	2.45	2.35
24	3.17	3.03	2.89	2.74	2.66	2.58	2.49	2.40	2.31
25	3.13	2.99	2.85	2.70	2.62	2.54	2.45	2.36	2.27
26	3.09	2.96	2.81	2.66	2.58	2.50	2.42	2.33	2.23
27	3.06	2.93	2.78	2.63	2.55	2.47	2.38	2.29	2.20
28	3.03	2.90	2.75	2.60	2.52	2.44	2.35	2.26	2.17
29	3.00	2.87	2.73	2.57	2.49	2.41	2.33	2.23	2.14
30	2.98	2.84	2.70	2.55	2.47	2.39	2.30	2.21	2.11
40	2.80	2.66	2.52	2.37	2.29	2.20	2.11	2.02	1.92
60	2.63	2.50	2.35	2.20	2.12	2.03	1.94	1.84	1.73
120	2.47	2.34	2.19	2.03	1.95	1.86	1.76	1.66	1.53
∞	2.32	2.18	2.04	1.88	1.79	1.70	1.59	1.47	1.32

Denominator Degrees of Freedom

Table 9 Critical Values of T_L and T_U for the Wilcoxon Rank Sum Test: Independent Samples

Test statistic is rank sum associated with smaller sample (if equal sample sizes, either rank sum can be used).

(a) $\alpha = 0.025$ one-tailed; $\alpha = 0.05$ two-tailed

n_2 \ n_1	3		4		5		6		7		8		9		10	
	T_L	T_U	T_L	T_U	T_L	T_U	T_L	T_U	T_L	T_U	T_L	T_U	T_L	T_U	T_L	T_U
3	5	16	6	18	6	21	7	23	7	26	8	28	8	31	9	33
4	6	18	11	25	12	28	12	32	13	35	14	38	15	41	16	44
5	6	21	12	28	18	37	19	41	20	45	21	49	22	53	24	56
6	7	23	12	32	19	41	26	52	28	56	29	61	31	65	32	70
7	7	26	13	35	20	45	28	56	37	68	39	73	41	78	43	83
8	8	28	14	38	21	49	29	61	39	73	49	87	51	93	54	98
9	8	31	15	41	22	53	31	65	41	78	51	93	63	108	66	114
10	9	33	16	44	24	56	32	70	43	83	54	98	66	114	79	131

(b) $\alpha = 0.05$ one-tailed; $\alpha = 0.10$ two-tailed

n_2 \ n_1	3		4		5		6		7		8		9		10	
	T_L	T_U	T_L	T_U	T_L	T_U	T_L	T_U	T_L	T_U	T_L	T_U	T_L	T_U	T_L	T_U
3	6	15	7	17	7	20	8	22	9	24	9	27	10	29	11	31
4	7	17	12	24	13	27	14	30	15	33	16	36	17	39	18	42
5	7	20	13	27	19	36	20	40	22	43	24	46	25	50	26	54
6	8	22	14	30	20	40	28	50	30	54	32	58	33	63	35	67
7	9	24	15	33	22	43	30	54	39	66	41	71	43	76	46	80
8	9	27	16	36	24	46	32	58	41	71	52	84	54	90	57	95
9	10	29	17	39	25	50	33	63	43	76	54	90	66	105	69	111
10	11	31	18	42	26	54	35	67	46	80	57	95	69	111	83	127

Source: From F. Wilcoxon and R. A. Wilcox, "Some Rapid Approximate Statistical Procedures," 1964, 20–23. Reproduced with the permission of American Cyanamid Company

Table 10 Critical Values of T_0 in the Wilcoxon Paired Difference Signed-Ranks Test

One-tailed	Two-tailed	$n = 5$	$n = 6$	$n = 7$	$n = 8$	$n = 9$	$n = 10$
$\alpha = 0.05$	$\alpha = 0.10$	1	2	4	6	8	11
$\alpha = 0.025$	$\alpha = 0.05$		1	2	4	6	8
$\alpha = 0.01$	$\alpha = 0.02$			0	2	3	5
$\alpha = 0.005$	$\alpha = 0.01$				0	2	3
		$n = 11$	$n = 12$	$n = 13$	$n = 14$	$n = 15$	$n = 16$
$\alpha = 0.05$	$\alpha = 0.10$	14	17	21	26	30	36
$\alpha = 0.025$	$\alpha = 0.05$	11	14	17	21	25	30
$\alpha = 0.01$	$\alpha = 0.02$	7	10	13	16	20	24
$\alpha = 0.005$	$\alpha = 0.01$	5	7	10	13	16	19
		$n = 17$	$n = 18$	$n = 19$	$n = 20$	$n = 21$	$n = 22$
$\alpha = 0.05$	$\alpha = 0.10$	41	47	54	60	68	75
$\alpha = 0.025$	$\alpha = 0.05$	35	40	46	52	59	66
$\alpha = 0.01$	$\alpha = 0.02$	28	33	38	43	49	56
$\alpha = 0.005$	$\alpha = 0.01$	23	28	32	37	43	49
		$n = 23$	$n = 24$	$n = 25$	$n = 26$	$n = 27$	$n = 28$
$\alpha = 0.05$	$\alpha = 0.10$	83	92	101	110	120	130
$\alpha = 0.025$	$\alpha = 0.05$	73	81	90	98	107	117
$\alpha = 0.01$	$\alpha = 0.02$	62	69	77	85	93	102
$\alpha = 0.005$	$\alpha = 0.01$	55	61	68	76	84	92
		$n = 29$	$n = 30$	$n = 31$	$n = 32$	$n = 33$	$n = 34$
$\alpha = 0.05$	$\alpha = 0.10$	141	152	163	175	188	201
$\alpha = 0.025$	$\alpha = 0.05$	127	137	148	159	171	183
$\alpha = 0.01$	$\alpha = 0.02$	111	120	130	141	151	162
$\alpha = 0.005$	$\alpha = 0.01$	100	109	118	128	138	149
		$n = 35$	$n = 36$	$n = 37$	$n = 38$	$n = 39$	
$\alpha = 0.05$	$\alpha = 0.10$	214	228	242	256	271	
$\alpha = 0.025$	$\alpha = 0.05$	195	208	222	235	250	
$\alpha = 0.01$	$\alpha = 0.02$	174	186	198	211	224	
$\alpha = 0.005$	$\alpha = 0.01$	160	171	183	195	208	
		$n = 40$	$n = 41$	$n = 42$	$n = 43$	$n = 44$	$n = 45$
$\alpha = 0.05$	$\alpha = 0.10$	287	303	319	336	353	371
$\alpha = 0.025$	$\alpha = 0.05$	264	279	295	311	327	344
$\alpha = 0.01$	$\alpha = 0.02$	238	252	267	281	297	313
$\alpha = 0.005$	$\alpha = 0.01$	221	234	248	262	277	292
		$n = 46$	$n = 47$	$n = 48$	$n = 49$	$n = 50$	
$\alpha = 0.05$	$\alpha = 0.10$	389	408	427	446	466	
$\alpha = 0.025$	$\alpha = 0.05$	361	379	397	415	434	
$\alpha = 0.01$	$\alpha = 0.02$	329	345	362	380	398	
$\alpha = 0.005$	$\alpha = 0.01$	307	323	339	356	373	

Source: From F. Wilcoxon and R. A. Wilcox, "Some Rapid Approximate Statistical Procedures," 1964, 28. Reproduced with the permission of American Cyanamid Company.

Table 11   Critical Values of Spearman's Rank Correlation Coefficient

The α values correspond to a one-tailed test of H_0: $\rho_s = 0$. The value should be doubled for two-tailed tests.

n	$\alpha = 0.05$	$\alpha = 0.025$	$\alpha = 0.01$	$\alpha = 0.005$
5	0.900	—	—	—
6	0.829	0.886	0.943	—
7	0.714	0.786	0.893	—
8	0.643	0.738	0.833	0.881
9	0.600	0.683	0.783	0.833
10	0.564	0.648	0.745	0.794
11	0.523	0.623	0.736	0.818
12	0.497	0.591	0.703	0.780
13	0.475	0.566	0.673	0.745
14	0.457	0.545	0.646	0.716
15	0.441	0.525	0.623	0.689
16	0.425	0.507	0.601	0.666
17	0.412	0.490	0.582	0.645
18	0.399	0.476	0.564	0.625
19	0.388	0.462	0.549	0.608
20	0.377	0.450	0.534	0.591
21	0.368	0.438	0.521	0.576
22	0.359	0.428	0.508	0.562
23	0.351	0.418	0.496	0.549
24	0.343	0.409	0.485	0.537
25	0.336	0.400	0.475	0.526
26	0.329	0.392	0.465	0.515
27	0.323	0.385	0.456	0.505
28	0.317	0.377	0.448	0.496
29	0.311	0.370	0.440	0.487
30	0.305	0.364	0.432	0.478

Source: From E. G. Olds, "Distribution of Sums of Squares of Rank Differences for Small Samples." *Annals of Mathematical Statistics.* 1938, 9. Reproduced with the permission of the Editor, *Annals of Mathematical Statistics.*

Table 12 Factors for Computing Control Chart Lines

| Number of Observations in Sample, n | Chart for Averages | | | Chart for Standard Deviations | | | | | | Chart for Ranges | | | | | | | |
| | Factors for Control Limits | | | Factors for Central Line | | Factors for Control Limits | | | | Factors for Central Line | | | Factors for Control Limits | | | |
	A	A_1	A_2	c_2	$1/c_2$	B_1	B_2	B_3	B_4	d_2	$1/d_2$	d_3	D_1	D_2	D_3	D_4
2	2.121	3.760	1.880	0.5642	1.7725	0	1.843	0	3.267	1.128	0.8865	0.853	0	3.686	0	3.276
3	1.732	2.394	1.023	0.7236	1.3820	0	1.858	0	2.568	1.693	0.5907	0.888	0	4.358	0	2.575
4	1.501	1.880	0.729	0.7979	1.2533	0	1.808	0	2.266	2.059	0.4857	0.880	0	4.698	0	2.282
5	1.342	1.596	0.577	0.8407	1.1894	0	1.756	0	2.089	2.326	0.4299	0.864	0	4.918	0	2.115
6	1.225	1.410	0.483	0.8686	1.1512	0.026	1.711	0.030	1.970	2.534	0.3946	0.848	0	5.078	0	2.004
7	1.134	1.277	0.419	0.8882	1.1259	0.105	1.672	0.118	1.882	2.704	0.3698	0.833	0.205	5.203	0.076	1.924
8	1.061	1.175	0.373	0.9027	1.1078	0.167	1.638	0.185	1.815	2.847	0.3512	0.820	0.387	5.307	0.136	1.864
9	1.000	1.094	0.337	0.9139	1.0942	0.219	1.609	0.239	1.761	2.970	0.3367	0.808	0.546	5.394	0.184	1.816
10	0.949	1.028	0.308	0.9227	1.0837	0.262	1.584	0.284	1.716	3.078	0.3249	0.797	0.687	5.469	0.223	1.777
11	0.905	0.973	0.285	0.9300	1.0753	0.299	1.561	0.321	1.679	3.173	0.3152	0.787	0.812	5.534	0.256	1.744
12	0.866	0.925	0.266	0.9359	1.0684	0.331	1.541	0.354	1.646	3.258	0.3069	0.778	0.924	5.592	0.284	1.719
13	0.832	0.884	0.249	0.9410	1.0627	0.359	1.523	0.382	1.618	3.336	0.2998	0.770	1.026	5.646	0.308	1.692
14	0.802	0.848	0.235	0.9453	1.0579	0.384	1.507	0.406	1.594	3.407	0.2935	0.762	1.121	5.693	0.329	1.671
15	0.775	0.816	0.223	0.9490	1.0537	0.406	1.492	0.428	1.572	3.472	0.2880	0.755	1.207	5.737	0.348	1.652
16	0.750	0.788	0.212	0.9523	1.0501	0.427	1.478	0.448	1.552	3.532	0.2831	0.749	1.285	5.779	0.364	1.636
17	0.728	0.762	0.203	0.9551	1.0470	0.445	1.465	0.466	1.534	3.588	0.2787	0.743	1.359	5.817	0.379	1.621
18	0.707	0.738	0.194	0.9576	1.0442	0.461	1.454	0.482	1.518	3.640	0.2747	0.738	1.426	5.854	0.392	1.608
19	0.688	0.717	0.187	0.9599	1.0418	0.477	1.443	0.497	1.503	3.689	0.2711	0.733	1.490	5.888	0.404	1.596
20	0.671	0.697	0.180	0.9619	1.0396	0.491	1.433	0.510	1.490	3.735	0.2677	0.729	1.548	5.922	0.414	1.586
21	0.655	0.679	0.173	0.9638	1.0376	0.504	1.424	0.523	1.477	3.778	0.2647	0.724	1.606	5.950	0.425	1.575
22	0.640	0.662	0.167	0.9655	1.0358	0.516	1.415	0.534	1.466	3.819	0.2618	0.720	1.659	5.979	0.434	1.566
23	0.626	0.647	0.162	0.9670	1.0342	0.527	1.407	0.545	1.455	3.858	0.2592	0.716	1.710	6.006	0.443	1.557
24	0.612	0.632	0.157	0.9684	1.0327	0.538	1.399	0.555	1.445	3.895	0.2567	0.712	1.759	6.031	0.452	1.548
25	0.600	0.619	0.153	0.9696	1.0313	0.548	1.392	0.565	1.435	3.931	0.2544	0.709	1.804	6.058	0.459	1.541
Over 25	$\dfrac{3}{\sqrt{n}}$	$\dfrac{3}{\sqrt{n}}$	—	—	—	‡	∞	‡	∞	—	—	—	—	—	—	—

[1] Reproduced by permission from *ASTM Manual on Quality Control of Materials*, American Society for Testing Materials, Philadelphia, Pa., 1951.

Table 13   Sample Size Code Letters: MIL–STD–105D

Lot or batch size	Special inspection levels				General inspection levels		
	S-1	S-2	S-3	S-4	I	II	III
2–8	A	A	A	A	A	A	B
9–15	A	A	A	A	A	B	C
16–25	A	A	B	B	B	C	D
26–50	A	B	B	C	C	D	E
51–90	B	B	C	C	C	E	F
91–150	B	B	C	D	D	F	G
151–280	B	C	D	E	E	G	H
281–500	B	C	D	E	F	H	J
501–1,200	C	C	E	F	G	J	K
1,201–3,200	C	D	E	G	H	K	L
3,201–10,000	C	D	F	G	J	L	M
10,001–35,000	C	D	F	H	K	M	N
35,001–150,000	D	E	G	J	L	N	P
150,001–500,000	D	E	G	J	M	P	Q
500,001 and over	D	E	H	K	N	Q	R

Table 14 Master Table for Normal Inspection (Single Sampling): MIL–STD–105D

Acceptable quality levels (normal inspection). Each cell shows **Ac** (acceptance number) and **Re** (rejection number).

Sample size code letter	Sample size	0.010	0.015	0.025	0.040	0.065	0.10	0.15	0.25	0.40	0.65	1.0	1.5	2.5	4.0	6.5	10	15	25	40	65	100	150	250	400	650	1,000
A	2	↓	↓	↓	↓	↓	↓	↓	↓	↓	↓	↓	↓	↓	↓	↓	↓	0 1	1 2	2 3	3 4	5 6	7 8	10 11	14 15	21 22	30 31
B	3	↓	↓	↓	↓	↓	↓	↓	↓	↓	↓	↓	↓	↓	↓	↓	0 1	1 2	2 3	3 4	5 6	7 8	10 11	14 15	21 22	30 31	44 45
C	5	↓	↓	↓	↓	↓	↓	↓	↓	↓	↓	↓	↓	↓	↓	0 1	1 2	2 3	3 4	5 6	7 8	10 11	14 15	21 22	30 31	44 45	↑
D	8	↓	↓	↓	↓	↓	↓	↓	↓	↓	↓	↓	↓	↓	0 1	1 2	2 3	3 4	5 6	7 8	10 11	14 15	21 22	30 31	44 45	↑	↑
E	13	↓	↓	↓	↓	↓	↓	↓	↓	↓	↓	↓	↓	0 1	1 2	2 3	3 4	5 6	7 8	10 11	14 15	21 22	30 31	44 45	↑	↑	↑
F	20	↓	↓	↓	↓	↓	↓	↓	↓	↓	↓	↓	0 1	1 2	2 3	3 4	5 6	7 8	10 11	14 15	21 22	30 31	44 45	↑	↑	↑	↑
G	32	↓	↓	↓	↓	↓	↓	↓	↓	↓	↓	0 1	1 2	2 3	3 4	5 6	7 8	10 11	14 15	21 22	30 31	44 45	↑	↑	↑	↑	↑
H	50	↓	↓	↓	↓	↓	↓	↓	↓	↓	0 1	1 2	2 3	3 4	5 6	7 8	10 11	14 15	21 22	30 31	44 45	↑	↑	↑	↑	↑	↑
J	80	↓	↓	↓	↓	↓	↓	↓	↓	0 1	1 2	2 3	3 4	5 6	7 8	10 11	14 15	21 22	30 31	44 45	↑	↑	↑	↑	↑	↑	↑
K	125	↓	↓	↓	↓	↓	↓	↓	0 1	1 2	2 3	3 4	5 6	7 8	10 11	14 15	21 22	30 31	44 45	↑	↑	↑	↑	↑	↑	↑	↑
L	200	↓	↓	↓	↓	↓	↓	0 1	1 2	2 3	3 4	5 6	7 8	10 11	14 15	21 22	30 31	44 45	↑	↑	↑	↑	↑	↑	↑	↑	↑
M	315	↓	↓	↓	↓	↓	0 1	1 2	2 3	3 4	5 6	7 8	10 11	14 15	21 22	30 31	44 45	↑	↑	↑	↑	↑	↑	↑	↑	↑	↑
N	500	↓	↓	↓	↓	0 1	1 2	2 3	3 4	5 6	7 8	10 11	14 15	21 22	30 31	44 45	↑	↑	↑	↑	↑	↑	↑	↑	↑	↑	↑
P	800	↓	↓	↓	0 1	1 2	2 3	3 4	5 6	7 8	10 11	14 15	21 22	30 31	44 45	↑	↑	↑	↑	↑	↑	↑	↑	↑	↑	↑	↑
Q	1,250	↓	↓	0 1	1 2	2 3	3 4	5 6	7 8	10 11	14 15	21 22	30 31	44 45	↑	↑	↑	↑	↑	↑	↑	↑	↑	↑	↑	↑	↑
R	2,000	↓	0 1	1 2	2 3	3 4	5 6	7 8	10 11	14 15	21 22	30 31	44 45	↑	↑	↑	↑	↑	↑	↑	↑	↑	↑	↑	↑	↑	↑

↓ = use first sampling plan below arrow. If sample size equals, or exceeds, lot or batch size, do 100% inspection.

↑ = use first sampling plan above arrow.

Ac = acceptance number.

Re = rejection number.

Table 15 Master Table for Tightened Inspection (Single Sampling)—MIL–STD–105D

Acceptable quality levels (tightened inspection). Each cell gives Ac (acceptance number) and Re (rejection number). ↓ = use first sampling plan below arrow. ↑ = use first sampling plan above arrow.

Sample size code letter	Sample size	0.010	0.015	0.025	0.040	0.065	0.10	0.15	0.25	0.40	0.65	1.0	1.5	2.5	4.0	6.5	10	15	25	40	65	100	150	250	400	650	1,000
A	2	↓	↓	↓	↓	↓	↓	↓	↓	↓	↓	↓	↓	↓	↓	0 1	↓	↓	↓	1 2	2 3	3 4	5 6	8 9	12 13	18 19	27 28
B	3	↓	↓	↓	↓	↓	↓	↓	↓	↓	↓	↓	↓	↓	0 1	↓	↓	↓	1 2	2 3	3 4	5 6	8 9	12 13	18 19	27 28	41 42
C	5	↓	↓	↓	↓	↓	↓	↓	↓	↓	↓	↓	↓	0 1	↓	↓	↓	1 2	2 3	3 4	5 6	8 9	12 13	18 19	27 28	41 42	↑
D	8	↓	↓	↓	↓	↓	↓	↓	↓	↓	↓	↓	0 1	↓	↓	↓	1 2	2 3	3 4	5 6	8 9	12 13	18 19	27 28	41 42	↑	↑
E	13	↓	↓	↓	↓	↓	↓	↓	↓	↓	↓	0 1	↓	↓	↓	1 2	2 3	3 4	5 6	8 9	12 13	18 19	27 28	41 42	↑	↑	↑
F	20	↓	↓	↓	↓	↓	↓	↓	↓	↓	0 1	↓	↓	↓	1 2	2 3	3 4	5 6	8 9	12 13	18 19	27 28	41 42	↑	↑	↑	↑
G	32	↓	↓	↓	↓	↓	↓	↓	↓	0 1	↓	↓	↓	1 2	2 3	3 4	5 6	8 9	12 13	18 19	27 28	41 42	↑	↑	↑	↑	↑
H	50	↓	↓	↓	↓	↓	↓	↓	0 1	↓	↓	↓	1 2	2 3	3 4	5 6	8 9	12 13	18 19	27 28	41 42	↑	↑	↑	↑	↑	↑
J	80	↓	↓	↓	↓	↓	↓	0 1	↓	↓	↓	1 2	2 3	3 4	5 6	8 9	12 13	18 19	27 28	41 42	↑	↑	↑	↑	↑	↑	↑
K	125	↓	↓	↓	↓	↓	0 1	↓	↓	↓	1 2	2 3	3 4	5 6	8 9	12 13	18 19	27 28	41 42	↑	↑	↑	↑	↑	↑	↑	↑
L	200	↓	↓	↓	↓	0 1	↓	↓	↓	1 2	2 3	3 4	5 6	8 9	12 13	18 19	27 28	41 42	↑	↑	↑	↑	↑	↑	↑	↑	↑
M	315	↓	↓	↓	0 1	↓	↓	↓	1 2	2 3	3 4	5 6	8 9	12 13	18 19	27 28	41 42	↑	↑	↑	↑	↑	↑	↑	↑	↑	↑
N	500	↓	↓	0 1	↓	↓	↓	1 2	2 3	3 4	5 6	8 9	12 13	18 19	27 28	41 42	↑	↑	↑	↑	↑	↑	↑	↑	↑	↑	↑
P	800	↓	0 1	↓	↓	↓	1 2	2 3	3 4	5 6	8 9	12 13	18 19	27 28	41 42	↑	↑	↑	↑	↑	↑	↑	↑	↑	↑	↑	↑
Q	1,250	0 1	↓	↓	↓	1 2	2 3	3 4	5 6	8 9	12 13	18 19	27 28	41 42	↑	↑	↑	↑	↑	↑	↑	↑	↑	↑	↑	↑	↑
R	2,000	↑	↑	↓	1 2	2 3	3 4	5 6	8 9	12 13	18 19	27 28	41 42	↑	↑	↑	↑	↑	↑	↑	↑	↑	↑	↑	↑	↑	↑
S	3,150	↑	↑	1 2	2 3	3 4	5 6	8 9	12 13	18 19	27 28	41 42	↑	↑	↑	↑	↑	↑	↑	↑	↑	↑	↑	↑	↑	↑	↑

↓ = use first sampling plan below arrow. If sample size equals or exceeds lot or batch size, do 100% inspection.
↑ = use first sampling plan above arrow.
Ac = acceptance number.
Re = rejection number.

Table 16 Master Table for Reduced Inspection (Single Sampling)—MIL–STD–105D

Acceptance quality levels (reduced inspection)†

Each cell shows the pair "Ac Re" (acceptance number, rejection number). ↓ = use first sampling plan below arrow; ↑ = use first sampling plan above arrow.

Sample size code letter	Sample size	0.010	0.015	0.025	0.040	0.065	0.10	0.15	0.25	0.40	0.65	1.0	1.5	2.5	4.0	6.5	10	15	25	40	65	100	150	250	400	650	1,000
A	2	↓	↓	↓	↓	↓	↓	↓	↓	↓	↓	↓	↓	↓	↓	0 1	↓	↓	1 2	2 3	3 4	5 6	7 8	10 11	14 15	21 22	30 31
B	2	↓	↓	↓	↓	↓	↓	↓	↓	↓	↓	↓	↓	↓	↓	↓	0 1	0 2	1 3	2 4	3 5	5 6	7 8	10 11	14 15	21 22	30 31
C	2	↓	↓	↓	↓	↓	↓	↓	↓	↓	↓	↓	↓	↓	↓	0 1	0 2	1 3	1 4	2 5	3 6	5 8	7 10	10 13	14 17	21 24	↑
D	3	↓	↓	↓	↓	↓	↓	↓	↓	↓	↓	↓	↓	↓	0 1	0 2	1 3	1 4	2 5	3 6	5 8	7 10	10 13	14 17	21 24	↑	↑
E	5	↓	↓	↓	↓	↓	↓	↓	↓	↓	↓	↓	↓	0 1	0 2	1 3	1 4	2 5	3 6	5 8	7 10	10 13	14 17	21 24	↑	↑	↑
F	8	↓	↓	↓	↓	↓	↓	↓	↓	↓	↓	↓	0 1	0 2	1 3	1 4	2 5	3 6	5 8	7 10	10 13	↑	↑	↑	↑	↑	↑
G	13	↓	↓	↓	↓	↓	↓	↓	↓	↓	↓	0 1	0 2	1 3	1 4	2 5	3 6	5 8	7 10	10 13	↑	↑	↑	↑	↑	↑	↑
H	20	↓	↓	↓	↓	↓	↓	↓	↓	↓	0 1	0 2	1 3	1 4	2 5	3 6	5 8	7 10	10 13	↑	↑	↑	↑	↑	↑	↑	↑
J	32	↓	↓	↓	↓	↓	↓	↓	↓	0 1	0 2	1 3	1 4	2 5	3 6	5 8	7 10	10 13	↑	↑	↑	↑	↑	↑	↑	↑	↑
K	50	↓	↓	↓	↓	↓	↓	↓	0 1	0 2	1 3	1 4	2 5	3 6	5 8	7 10	10 13	↑	↑	↑	↑	↑	↑	↑	↑	↑	↑
L	80	↓	↓	↓	↓	↓	↓	0 1	0 2	1 3	1 4	2 5	3 6	5 8	7 10	10 13	↑	↑	↑	↑	↑	↑	↑	↑	↑	↑	↑
M	125	↓	↓	↓	↓	↓	0 1	0 2	1 3	1 4	2 5	3 6	5 8	7 10	10 13	↑	↑	↑	↑	↑	↑	↑	↑	↑	↑	↑	↑
N	200	↓	↓	↓	↓	0 1	0 2	1 3	1 4	2 5	3 6	5 8	7 10	10 13	↑	↑	↑	↑	↑	↑	↑	↑	↑	↑	↑	↑	↑
P	315	↓	↓	↓	0 1	0 2	1 3	1 4	2 5	3 6	5 8	7 10	10 13	↑	↑	↑	↑	↑	↑	↑	↑	↑	↑	↑	↑	↑	↑
Q	500	↓	↓	0 1	0 2	1 3	1 4	2 5	3 6	5 8	7 10	10 13	↑	↑	↑	↑	↑	↑	↑	↑	↑	↑	↑	↑	↑	↑	↑
R	800	↓	0 1	0 2	1 3	1 4	2 5	3 6	5 8	7 10	10 13	↑	↑	↑	↑	↑	↑	↑	↑	↑	↑	↑	↑	↑	↑	↑	↑

↓ = use first sampling plan below arrow. If sample size equals or exceeds lot or batch size, do 100% inspection.

↑ = use first sampling plan above arrow.

Ac = acceptance number.

Re = rejection number.

† If the acceptance number has been exceeded but the rejection number has not been reached, accept the lot but reinstate normal inspection.

Table 17   MIL–STD–414

A
AQL Conversion Table

For specified AQL values falling within these ranges	Use this AQL value
to 0.049	0.04
0.050 to 0.069	0.065
0.070 to 0.109	0.10
0.110 to 0.164	0.15
0.165 to 0.279	0.25
0.280 to 0.439	0.40
0.440 to 0.699	0.65
0.700 to 1.09	1.0
1.10 to 1.64	1.5
1.65 to 2.79	2.5
2.80 to 4.39	4.0
4.40 to 6.99	6.5
7.00 to 10.9	10.0
11.00 to 16.4	15.0

B
Sample Size Code Letters[1]

Lot Size	Inspection Levels				
	I	II	III	IV	V
3 to 8	B	B	B	B	C
9 to 15	B	B	B	B	D
16 to 25	B	B	B	C	E
26 to 40	B	B	B	D	F
41 to 65	B	B	C	E	G
66 to 110	B	B	D	F	H
111 to 180	B	C	E	G	I
181 to 300	B	D	F	H	J
301 to 500	C	E	G	I	K
501 to 800	D	F	H	J	L
801 to 1,300	E	G	I	K	L
1,301 to 3,200	F	H	J	L	M
3,201 to 8,000	G	I	L	M	N
8,001 to 22,000	H	J	M	N	O
22,001 to 110,000	I	K	N	O	P
110,001 to 550,000	I	K	O	P	Q
550,001 and over	I	K	P	Q	Q

[1] Sample size code letters given in body of table are applicable when the indicated inspection levels are to be used.

Table 18 MIL–STD–414 (Standard Deviation Method) Master Table for Normal and Tightened Inspection for Plans Based on Variability Unknown (Single Specification Limit—Form 1)

Sample size code letter	Sample size	Acceptable Quality Levels (normal inspection)														
		15.00	10.00	6.50	4.00	2.50	1.50	1.00	0.65	0.40	0.25	0.15	0.10	0.065	0.04
		k	k	k	k	k	k	k	k	k	k	k	k	k	k
B	3	0.341	0.566	0.765	0.958	1.12	→	→	→	→	→	→	→	→	→
C	4	0.393	0.617	0.814	1.01	1.17	1.34	1.45	→	→	→	→	→	→	→
D	5	0.455	0.675	0.874	1.07	1.24	1.40	1.53	1.65	→	→	→	→	→	→
E	7	0.536	0.755	0.955	1.15	1.33	1.50	1.62	1.75	1.88	2.00	→	→	→	→
F	10	0.611	0.828	1.03	1.23	1.41	1.58	1.72	1.84	1.98	2.11	2.24	→	→	→
G	15	0.664	0.886	1.09	1.30	1.47	1.65	1.79	1.91	2.06	2.20	2.32	2.42	2.53	2.64
H	20	0.695	0.917	1.12	1.33	1.51	1.69	1.82	1.96	2.11	2.24	2.36	2.47	2.58	2.69
I	25	0.712	0.936	1.14	1.35	1.53	1.72	1.85	1.98	2.14	2.26	2.40	2.50	2.61	2.72
J	30	0.723	0.946	1.15	1.36	1.55	1.73	1.86	2.00	2.15	2.28	2.41	2.51	2.61	2.73
K	35	0.745	0.969	1.18	1.39	1.57	1.76	1.89	2.03	2.18	2.31	2.45	2.54	2.65	2.77
L	40	0.746	0.971	1.18	1.39	1.58	1.76	1.89	2.03	2.18	2.31	2.44	2.55	2.66	2.77
M	50	0.774	1.00	1.21	1.42	1.61	1.80	1.93	2.08	2.22	2.35	2.50	2.60	2.71	2.83
N	75	0.804	1.03	1.24	1.46	1.65	1.84	1.98	2.12	2.27	2.41	2.55	2.66	2.77	2.90
O	100	0.819	1.05	1.26	1.48	1.67	1.86	2.00	2.14	2.29	2.43	2.58	2.69	2.80	2.92
P	150	0.841	1.07	1.29	1.51	1.70	1.89	2.03	2.18	2.33	2.47	2.61	2.73	2.84	2.96
Q	200	0.845	1.07	1.29	1.51	1.70	1.89	2.04	2.18	2.33	2.47	2.62	2.73	2.85	2.97
			15.00	10.00	6.50	4.00	2.50	1.50	1.00	0.65	0.40	0.25	0.15	0.10	0.065
			Acceptable Quality Levels (tightened inspection)												

All AQL values are in percent defective.

→ Use first sampling plan below arrow, that is, both sample size as well as k value. When sample size equals or exceeds lot size, every item in the lot must be inspected.

References

Bowker, A. H. and G. J. Lieberman (1972). *Engineering Statistics,* 2nd ed., Prentice-Hall Inc., Englewood Cliffs, N.J.

Grant, E. L. and R. S. Leavenworth (1972). *Statistical Quality Control,* McGraw-Hill Book Co., New York.

Guttman, I., S. S. Wilks and J. S. Hunter (1971). *Introductory Engineering Statistics,* 2nd ed., John Wiley and Sons, New York.

Koopmans, L. H. (1981). *An Introduction to Contemporary Statistics,* Duxbury Press, Boston.

McClave, J. T. and F. H. Dietrich (1979). *Statistics,* Dellen Publishing Co., San Francisco.

Mendenhall, W., R. L. Scheaffer and D. D. Wackerly (1981). *Mathematical Statistics with Applications,* 2nd ed., Duxbury Press, Boston.

Miller, I. and J. E. Freund (1977). *Probability and Statistics for Engineers,* 2nd ed., Prentice-Hall, Inc., Englewood Cliffs, N.J.

Ott, L. (1977). *An Introduction to Statistical Methods and Data Analysis,* Duxbury Press, Boston.

Stephens, M. A. (1974). "EDF Statistics for Goodness of Fit and Some Comparisons." *Journal of Am. Stat. Assn.,* vol. 69, no. 347, pp. 730–737.

Tukey, J. W. (1977). *Exploratory Data Analysis,* Addison-Wesley Publishing Co.

Walpole, R. E., and R. H. Myers (1978). *Probability and Statistics for Engineers and Scientists,* 2nd ed., Macmillan Publishing Co., New York.

Answers to Odd-Numbered Exercises

Chapter 2

Sections 2.2 and 2.3, page 12

2.1 (a) L, R, S (b) $\frac{1}{3}$ (c) $\frac{2}{3}$ 2.3 (a) I I, I II, II I, II II
     (b) $\frac{1}{4}; \frac{1}{2}$ 2.5 $\frac{3}{10}$

Sections 2.4 and 2.5, page 20

2.7 $\frac{5}{8}$ 2.9 (b) 0.9 (c) 0.4 (d) 0.1 (e) 0.5 (f) 0.1 (g) 0.1   2.11 (a) 0.999
     (b) 0.90   2.13 $\frac{14}{17}$ 2.15 (a) $\frac{3}{5}$ (b) $\frac{2}{5}$ (c) yes   (d) yes

Section 2.6, page 29

2.19 (a) $k = 6$ (b) 0.648   (c) 0.393   (d) $6\left[\dfrac{b^2}{2} - \dfrac{b^3}{3}\right], \quad 0 \le b \le 1$

2.21 (a) $\frac{1}{2}$ (b) $\frac{1}{4}$

Section 2.7, page 40

2.23 (a) $\frac{3}{4}$ (b) $\frac{4}{5}$ (c) 1, $F(x) = x^2, \quad 0 \le x \le 1$
2.25 (a) $p(0,0) = p(0,2) = p(2,0) = \frac{1}{9}$ $p(0,1) = p(1,0) = p(1,1) = \frac{2}{9}$
     (b) $p(0) = p(1) = \frac{4}{9}, p(2) = \frac{1}{9}$ (c) $\frac{1}{2}$

2.27

X_1	X_2			
	0	1	2	3
0	0	$\frac{3}{84}$	$\frac{6}{84}$	$\frac{1}{84}$
1	$\frac{4}{84}$	$\frac{24}{84}$	$\frac{12}{84}$	0
2	$\frac{12}{84}$	$\frac{18}{84}$	0	0
3	$\frac{4}{84}$	0	0	0

2.29 (a) 1, $0 \leq x_1 \leq 1$ (b) 0.5 (c) yes 2.31 (a) $\frac{7}{8}$ (b) $\frac{1}{2}$
(c) $\frac{2}{3}$ 2.33 (a) $\frac{21}{64}$ (b) $\frac{1}{3}$ (c) no

2.35 (a) $\dfrac{2}{x_1}$, $0 \leq x_2 \leq \dfrac{x_1}{2} \leq 1$ (b) $\frac{1}{2}$ 2.37 $\frac{11}{32}$

Section 2.8, page 52

2.39 1 2.41 $\frac{5}{16}$ 2.43 \$60,000 2.45 (a) $\frac{5}{3}$ (b) $\frac{7}{18}$
2.47 (a) 66 (b) 96

Sections 2.9 and 2.10, page 55

2.49 $(-20.95, 167.61)$ 2.51 $(0, 105.42)$

Supplementary Exercises, page 56

2.53 (a) 0.57 (b) 0.18 (c) 0.9 (d) 0.32
2.55 $p(0) = 0.0144$, $p(1) = 0.1408$, $p(2) = 0.4352$, $p(3) = 0.4096$ 2.57 $(0.4)^{1/3}$
2.59 (a) $e^{-1} - 2e^{-2}$ (b) $\frac{1}{2}$ (c) e^{-1} (d) $f_1(y_1) = y_1 e^{-y_1}$, $y_1 \geq 0$;
$f_2(y_2) = e^{-y_2}$, $y_2 \geq 0$
2.61 (a) 1 (b) 1 (c) no 2.63 (a) $3e^{-10/3}$ (1 $- e^{-5/3}$)
(b) $1 - e^{-5}$ 2.65 $\frac{1}{2}$

Appendix 2.11, page 61

2.67 $\frac{1}{5}$ 2.69 168

Chapter 3

Sections 3.2 and 3.3, page 68

3.1 (a) 0.1536 (b) 0.1808 (c) 0.9728 (d) 0.8 (e) 0.64
3.3 (a) 0.537 (b) 0.098 3.5 (a) 16 (b) 3.2 3.7 2
3.9 (a) 400 thousand dollars (b) 474.34 thousand dollars
3.11 0.15625 3.13 $1 - e^{-25/3}$

Sections 3.4 and 3.5, page 75

3.15 (a) 0.9 (b) $(1 - p)^2$ 3.17 0.09 3.19 0.1 3.21 0.06
3.23 0.83692

Section 3.6, page 80

3.25 (a) 0.090   (b) 0.143   (c) 0.857   (d) 0.241   3.27 80, 800, no
3.29 (a) 0.982   (b) $1 - (0.018)^3$ 3.31 (a) 0.9997   (b) 2
3.33 47.5

Section 3.7, page 84

3.35 (a) $\frac{4}{7}$ (b) $\frac{6}{7}$ (c) $\frac{1}{3}$ (d) $\frac{4}{7}$ 3.37 100, 1666.67, (18.35, 181.65)

Section 3.8, page 86

3.41 (a) 0.148   (b) $\frac{1}{27}$ (c) 0.44   3.43 0.41

Section 3.9, page 88

3.45 $1 - p + pe^t$

Supplementary Exercises, page 90

3.51 0.0521   3.53 (a) $k/e^{-\lambda t}$ (b) 3.30
3.55 (a) 0.09   (b) 0.76   (c) 40, 24   3.57 0.04096

Chapter 4

Section 4.2, page 96

4.1 (a) $\dfrac{x - a}{b - a}$, $a \le x \le b$ (b) $\dfrac{b - c}{b - a}$ (c) $\dfrac{b - d}{b - c}$ 4.3 $\frac{1}{4}$ 4.5 $\frac{3}{8}$

Section 4.3, page 101

4.9 0.735   4.11 (a) $\frac{1}{2}, \frac{1}{4}$ (b) $1 - e^{-6}$

Section 4.4, page 105

4.15 (a) 22000, 1100000   (b) no   4.17 (a) 1, $\frac{1}{2}$, $4y_2 e^{-2y_2}$ for $y_2 > 0$
(b) $\frac{3}{2}, \frac{3}{4}, 4y_3^2 e^{-2y_3}$ for $y_3 > 0$

4.19 (a) 140, 280 $\dfrac{1}{\Gamma(70)(2)^{70}} y^{69} e^{-y/2}$ for $y > 0$ (b) 206.93

Section 4.5, page 110

4.21 (a) 0.3849   (b) 0.3159   (c) 0.3227   (d) 0.1586   (e) .366
4.23 0.0062   4.25 7.3%   4.27 (a) 0.9544   (b) 0.83
4.29 0.51   4.31 0.0228

Section 4.6, page 114

4.35 (a) 0.8208   (b) 4.7, 0.01

Section 4.7, page 118

4.37 $\dfrac{1}{16}\left(\dfrac{y-10}{2}\right)^{-1/2}$, $12 \le y \le 60$ 4.39 (a) $e^{-2.5}$ (b) 0.019

4.41 42.92

Supplementary Exercises, page 120

4.43 2×10^{-7} 4.45 (a) 105   (b) $\frac{3}{8}$, 0.026   4.47 0.98
4.49 (a) 2   (b) 8   4.51 $2e^{-1}$ 4.53 (a) $2\lambda\pi r e^{-\pi\lambda r^2}$
    (b) $\Gamma(\frac{3}{2})/\sqrt{\lambda\pi}$

Chapter 5

Sections 5.2 and 5.3, page 133

5.1 (b) 1.663, 0.228097   (c) (0.70481, 2.61519)
5.3 (b) -1.11, 39.1217   (d) $(-19.8741, 17.6541)$

Section 5.4, page 138

5.7 385   5.9 153   5.11 0.0013   5.13 0.9876   5.15 0.0062

Section 5.5, page 145

5.17 10.15   5.19 29   5.21 $a = 1.01, b = 3.01$
5.23 $g_1 - 1.895(s)/\sqrt{8}, g_2 = 1.895(s)/\sqrt{8}$ 5.25 $a = 0.15, b = 1.84$

Section 5.6, page 147

5.27 $\frac{1}{20}$, 0.0000006

Supplementary Exercises, page 148

5.29 0.0062   5.31 (a) $\mu_1 - \mu_2$ (b) $\dfrac{\sigma_1^2}{m} + \dfrac{\sigma_2^2}{n}$

5.35 $a = 1.725, b = -1.725$ 5.37 $v/(v - 2)$

Chapter 6

Section 6.2, page 155

6.1 (a) $\hat{\theta}_1, \hat{\theta}_2, \hat{\theta}_3,$ and $\hat{\theta}_4$ (b) $\hat{\theta}_4$ 6.3 (a) $\bar{X}$ (c) $\dfrac{1}{n} \sum_{i=1}^{n} X_i^2 + 3\bar{X}$

6.5   MSE $(\bar{X}) = \dfrac{1}{12n} + \dfrac{1}{4}$ 6.7 $\bar{X} - 1.645(s)\left(\dfrac{\Gamma((n-1)/2)\sqrt{n-1}}{\Gamma(n/2)\sqrt{2}}\right)$

Section 6.3, page 165

6.9 $(2\,05.81, 214.19)$ 6.11 $(17.98, 18.82)$ 6.13 139
6.15 $(0.0563, 0.1837)$ 6.17 $(0.2636, 0.5364)$ 6.19 $(0.658, 0.842)$
6.21 $(173.79, 186.21)$ 6.23 $(9.52, 10.08)$ 6.25 $(0.15, 0.53)$

Section 6.4, page 177

6.27 193   6.29 $(0.2521, 0.5879)$ 6.31 $(-0.1193, 0.3574)$
6.33 $(-1.52, 12.38)$ 6.35 (a) $(0.1416, 0.2384)$ (b) $(0.1767, 0.2043)$
6.37 $(0.4765, 7.0797)$ 6.39 $(28.72, 29.28)$

Section 6.5, page 188

6.41 (a) $\bar{X} \pm z_{\alpha/2}\sqrt{\lambda/n}$ (b) $(3.608, 4.392)$ 6.43 $\hat{\beta} = \dfrac{1}{n\alpha} \sum_{i=1}^{n} X_i$

6.45 $\hat{p} = 1/X$

Section 6.6, page 191

6.47 $(Y + 1)/2$

Section 6.7, page 193

6.49 $(-3.009, 21.009)$ 6.51 $(16.022, 20.778)$

Supplementary Exercises, page 194

6.53 $(2.05, 2.15)$ 6.55 $(0.57, 13.43)$

6.57 $n_1 = (-n\sigma_1^2 \pm n\sigma_1\sigma_2)/(\sigma_2^2 - \sigma_1^2)$

6.59 $(2\bar{X} + \bar{Y}) \pm t_{0.025}\sqrt{\hat{\sigma}^2\left(\dfrac{4}{n} + \dfrac{3}{m}\right)}$ 6.61 $Y/(n - Y)$

Chapter 7

Section 7.2, page 200

7.1 $z = -4.22$; reject   7.3 $z = -1.77$; do not reject

7.5 $z = -1.22$; no   7.7 $z = -0.53$; no   7.9 $t = -2.52$; no

7.11 $t = -7.47$; yes   7.13 $\chi^2 = 48.64$; yes

Section 7.3, page 204

7.15 $z = -4.21$; yes   7.17 $t = 2.97$; reject   7.19 $t = 1.11$; no

7.21 $t = -0.25$; no   7.23 $t = -0.35$; no   7.25 $F = 1.07$; no

Section 7.4, page 223

7.27 $\chi^2 = 1.23$; do not reject   7.29 $\chi^2 = 1.67$; do not reject

7.31 $\chi^2 = 0.54$; no   7.33 (a) $\chi^2 = 13.71$; no   (b) $z = -2.05$; yes

7.35 (a) $\chi^2 = 2.05$; do not reject   (b) $z = 0.49$; do not reject

Section 7.5, page 233

7.37 $\chi^2 = 133.5$; reject   7.39 (b) $x^2 = 4.99$; do not reject

7.41 (a) $D = 0.53$; reject   (b) $D = 0.52$; reject

Supplementary Exercises, page 236

7.43 $z = 2.11$; do not reject   7.45 $t = -0.54$; no

7.47 $\chi^2 = 21.875$; yes   7.49 $z = -4.66$; yes   7.51 $\chi^2 = 1.29$; no

7.53 $t = 4.52$; yes   7.55 $F = 3.07$; no

Chapter 8

Sections 8.2 and 8.3, page 247

8.1 (a) $\hat{\beta}_0 = 0$; $\hat{\beta}_1 = \frac{6}{7}$ 8.3 $\hat{y} = -0.06 + 2.78x$

8.5 $\hat{y} = 480.20 - 3.7511x$ 8.7 $\hat{y} = 10.208 + 1.925x$

Section 8.4, page 251

8.9 (a) 0.29   (b) 0.53   (c) 0.07   (d) 0.01   (e) 19.16
     (f) 0.03   (g) 24.18   (h) 11.02

Section 8.5, page 257

8.11 $t = 6.66$; yes   8.13 (2.25, 3.31)   8.15 $t = -17.93$; yes
8.17 (5.75, 13.50)   8.19 (a) $\hat{y} = 36.68 - 0.33327x$
     (b) SSE $= 1.3467$; $s^2 = 0.1683$ (c) $t = -7.38$; yes

Section 8.8, page 268

8.21 (a) 1.71 ± 0.81 (b) 1.71 ± 1.7 8.23 1.69 ± 0.35
8.25 198.87 ± 11.7 8.27 33.308 ± 3.192
8.29 $t = -0.17$; do not reject

Supplementary Exercises, page 269

8.31 (a) $r = 0.9155$ (b) $r^2 = 0.8381$ (c) $t = 5.08$; yes
8.33 $\hat{y} = -0.1935 + 1.2206x$; $r^2 = 0.5921$ 8.35 (a) $\hat{y} = 40.93 - 0.1343x$
     (b) $t = -4.21$; yes   (c) $(-0.19, -0.08)$ (d) $(30.31, 32.21)$
     (e) $(30.91, 35.37)$ 8.37 (a) $\hat{y} = 2.76 + 0.866x$
     (b) $r = 0.9853$; $r^2 = 0.9705$ (c) $(19.074, 21.086)$
8.39 (a) $z = 5.111$; reject $z = 9.406$; reject   (b) $z = -2.48$; reject

---

Chapter 9

Sections 9.2, 9.3, and 9.4, page 287

9.1 (b) $F = 38.84$; yes   9.3 $F = 1.06$; do not reject
9.5 $t = 3.04$; reject

Section 9.6, page 301

9.11 $F = 2.6$; do not reject

Supplementary Exercises, page 310

9.15 (a) $F = 84.96$; yes   (b) $t = -2.99$; yes   9.17 (b) $t = 40.54$; yes
     (c) 88.4875   9.19 (a) $H_0: \beta_4 = 0$ vs. $H_a: \beta_4 \neq 0$
     (b) $H_0: \beta_1 = \beta_2 = 0$ H_a: at least one of these β's is nonzero
9.21 (a) $E(Y) = \beta_0 + \beta_1 x_1 + \beta_2 x_2 + \beta_3 x_3$
     (b) $E(Y) = \beta_0 + \beta_1 x_1 + \beta_2 x_2 + \beta_3 x_3 + \beta_4 x_1 x_2 + \beta_5 x_1^2 + \beta_6 x_2^2$
        $+ \beta_7 x_1 x_3 + \beta_8 x_2 x_3 + \beta_9 x_1 x_2 x_3 + \beta_{10} x_1^2 x_3 + \beta_{11} x_2^2 x_3$

(c) $H_0: \beta_4 = \beta_5 = \beta_6 = \beta_7 = \beta_8 = \beta_9 = \beta_{10} = \beta_{11}$
    $H_a:$ At least one of these β's is nonzero
9.23 $t = -2.06$; no

Chapter 10

Section 10.2, page 322

10.1 (a)

Source	d.f.	SS	MS	F
Treatments	2	11.075	5.538	3.15
Error	7	12.301	1.757	
Total	9	23.376		

(b) $F = 3.15$; do not reject

10.3 $F = 8.63$; yes   10.5 $F = 6.63$; yes   10.7 $F = 3.53$; yes

10.9 $F = 0.24$; no

Section 10.4, page 330

10.15 (a) $t = -0.67$; no   (b) $(-1.39, 0.59)$ (c) $(3, 4.4)$

10.17 (a) $(-3.38, -0.82)$ (b) $\mu_1:(5.70, 7.74)$
                                      $\mu_2:(7.10, 9.14)$
                                      $\mu_3:(7.80, 9.84)$

Section 10.5, page 335

10.19 (a)

Source	d.f.	SS	MS	F
Treatment	2	23.167	11.5835	12.59
Block	3	14.25	4.75	5.16
Error	6	5.5	0.9167	
Total	11	42.917		

(b) $F = 12.59$; yes   (c) $F = 5.18$; yes   10.21 $F = 6.36$; yes

10.23 (a) $F = 39.46$; yes   (b) $F = 1.93$; no   10.25 (a) $F = 15.80$; yes

(b) $F = 14.69$; yes

Section 10.7, page 345

10.31 $(-1.414, 1.054)$ 10.33 (a) $(-2.128, -1.152)$

Section 10.8, page 356

10.35 (a) $A \times B: F = 32.4$; reject   (b) $\mu_1 - \mu_2: -4.5 \pm 4.51$
$\mu_1 - \mu_3: -2.5 \pm 4.51$
$\mu_1 - \mu_4: 2 \pm 4.51$
$\mu_2 - \mu_3: 2 \pm 4.51$
$\mu_2 - \mu_4: 6.5 \pm 4.51$
$\mu_3 - \mu_4: 4.5 \pm 4.51$

10.37 $A \times B: F = 1.43$; do not reject
$A: F = 5.92$; do not reject
$B: F = 15.67$; reject

10.39 (a) $A \times B: F = 4.47$; do not reject
$A: F = 29.66$; reject
$B: F = 9.04$; reject
(b) carbon at 0.5% and manganese at 1%

Supplementary Exercises, page 359

10.41 (a) randomized block design   (b) $F = 3.88$; yes   (c) 2.4 ± 33.48
10.43 (a) Completely randomized design

(b)
Source	d.f.	SS	MS	F
Treatment	2	57.6042	28.8021	0.36
Error	13	1109.3333	85.3333	
Total	15	1166.9375		

(c) no   (d) (73.68, 88.32)

10.45 (a)
Source	d.f.	SS	MS	F
Truckload	14	159.29	11.378	8.35
Extractor	5	84.71	16.942	12.44
Error	70	95.33	1.362	
Total	89	339.33		

(b) $F = 12.44$; yes
10.47 (a) completely randomized design   (b) $F = 7.79$; yes
(c) -5.65 ± 11.72

Chapter 11

Section 11.2, page 370

11.1 $T_B \geq 43$ 11.3 $T_B = 29$; no   11.5 $T_A = 27$; no
11.7 $T_A = 32$; no

Section 11.3, page 377

11.9 $T \le 4$ where T is the smaller of T_+ and T_- 11.11 (a) $T_- = 1$; yes
(b) no 11.13 $T_- = 11$; yes

Section 11.4, page 383

11.15 $H = 7.154$; yes 11.17 (a) $H = 6.66$; yes (b) $T_A = 71$; yes
11.19 (a) $F = 1.33$; do not reject (b) $H = 1.22$; do not reject

Section 11.5, page 389

11.21 $F_r = 7.85$; reject 11.23 $F_r = 1.75$; no

Section 11.6, page 398

11.25 $r_s > 0.646$ 11.27 $r_s = 0.657$; no 11.29 (a) $r_s = 0.423$
(b) no

Supplementary Exercises, page 400

11.31 (a) $T_{after} = 47$; yes 11.33 $T_+ = 19.5$; no
11.35 (a) $H = 14.61$; yes (b) $T_A = 38.5$; reject
11.37 $F_r = 1.33333$; no 11.39 (a) $F_r = 11.76667$; yes
(b) $T_+ = 2.5$; do not reject 11.41 $H = 9.207$; reject
11.43 $F_r = 7.714$; yes

Chapter 12

Section 12.2, page 412

12.1 (a) $(14.7722, 15.2844)$ (b) no, $(14.7591, 15.2618)$
12.5 (a) $(81.0934, 87.7866)$ (b) no

Section 12.3, page 415

12.7 $(0, 12.267)$, no

Section 12.4, page 417

12.9 (a) $(0, 0.1443)$ (b) no, $(0, 0.1377)$ 12.11 (a) $(0, 0.1906)$ (b) no

Section 12.5, page 420

12.13 $(0, 12.0014)$ 12.15 no

Sections 12.6 and 12.7, page 428

12.17 (a) sample size is 125, acceptance number is 10
      (b) sample size is 125, acceptance number is 8
      (c) sample size is 50, acceptance number is 5
12.19 accept

Supplementary Exercises, page 429

12.21 (a) (38.9155, 46.9345)   (b) no   12.23 (39.81, 46.04)
12.25 (0, 0.9448), yes

Index

473